OXFORD STUDIES IN ANAL

CW01044911

Series Editors
Michael C. Rea   Olive

The doctrine of the atonement is the distinctive doctrine of Christianity. Over the course of many centuries of reflection, highly diverse interpretations of the doctrine have been proposed. In the context of this history of interpretation, Eleonore Stump considers the doctrine afresh with philosophical care. Whatever exactly the atonement is, it is supposed to include a solution to the problems of the human condition, especially its guilt and shame. Stump canvasses the major interpretations of the doctrine that attempt to explain this solution and argues that all of them have serious shortcomings. In their place, she argues for an interpretation that is both novel and yet traditional and that has significant advantages over other interpretations, including Anselm's well-known account of the doctrine. In the process, she also discusses love, union, guilt, shame, forgiveness, retribution, punishment, shared attention, mind-reading, empathy, and various other issues in moral psychology and ethics.

Eleonore Stump is the Robert J. Henle Professor of Philosophy at Saint Louis University.

Cover Image: At the request of Fr. Christof Wolf, S.J. (Loyola Productions Munich), Dr. Piotr M.A. Cywiński, Director of the Auschwitz-Birkenau Memorial and Museum, asked Paweł Sawicki to photograph the image of Christ's crucifixion which was found after the war in Cell 21 in Block 11 at Auschwitz and which was made by Stefan Jasieński while he was dying in that cell. The cover concept is by Michael Gale.

Also published by
OXFORD UNIVERSITY PRESS

Wandering in Darkness
Narrative and the Problem of Suffering
Eleonore Stump
Also available in paperback

The Oxford Handbook of Aquinas
Edited by Brian Davies and Eleonore Stump
Also available in paperback

Reason, Metaphysics, and Mind
New Essays on the Philosophy of Alvin Plantinga
Edited by Kelly James Clark and Michael Rea

OXFORD STUDIES IN ANALYTIC THEOLOGY

Analytic Theology utilizes the tools and methods of contemporary analytic philosophy for the purposes of constructive theology, paying attention to religious traditions and the development of doctrine. This innovative series of studies showcases high quality, cutting edge research in this area, in monographs and symposia.

Atonement

ELEONORE STUMP

OXFORD

UNIVERSITY PRESS

OXFORD
UNIVERSITY PRESS

Great Clarendon Street, Oxford, OX2 6DP,
United Kingdom

Oxford University Press is a department of the University of Oxford.
It furthers the University's objective of excellence in research, scholarship,
and education by publishing worldwide. Oxford is a registered trade mark of
Oxford University Press in the UK and in certain other countries

First published 2018
First published in paperback 2020

Published in the United States of America by Oxford University Press
198 Madison Avenue, New York, NY 10016, United States of America

British Library Cataloguing in Publication Data
Data available

Library of Congress Cataloging in Publication Data
Data available

ISBN 978-0-19-881386-6 (Hbk.)
ISBN 978-0-19-886774-6 (Pbk.)

For John
ut ardeat cor meum
in amando Christum Deum
(Stabat Mater)

My life flows on in endless song
Above earth's lamentation.
I hear the real though far-off hymn
That hails a new creation.

Above the tumult and the strife,
I hear its music ringing.
It sounds an echo in my soul—
How can I keep from singing?

What though the tempest loudly roar,
I know the truth: it liveth.
What though the darkness 'round me close,
Songs in the night it giveth.

No storm can shake my inmost calm,
As to that rock I'm clinging.
While love is lord of heaven and earth,
How can I keep from singing?

When tyrants tremble sick with fear
To hear their death knells ringing,
When friends rejoice, both far and near,
How can I keep from singing?

In prison cell and dungeon vile,
Our hearts to them are winging.
When friends by shame are undefiled,
How can I keep from singing?

Foreword

To commend this new work on the atonement by Eleonore Stump, I think it is helpful to introduce a parable, the resolution of which sums up her extraordinary achievement.

In the story of *The Snow Queen* by Hans Christian Andersen a little boy called Kai has caught splinters in his eyes and in his heart. These splinters distort his perception and desires so that he admires only mathematical perfection and boasts of his rational knowledge. In this evil mood, the Snow Queen takes him to her palace. Here he is left alone on a frozen lake, trying to form the word 'eternity' from blocks of ice, without which he can never leave.

Whatever other interpretations may be found, the trap into which Kai falls in *The Snow Queen* serves as a warning about the care needed in applying analytic methods to reach eternal truths. The warning is that the clear and precise analyses of concepts that have been orphaned from the living realities from which they are drawn risk generating frozen representations, incapable of grasping those realities and chilling the mind and heart.

The danger to which *The Snow Queen* draws attention has been especially severe for the Christian understanding of the atonement, or what Stump calls in Chapter 1 the *at onement*—the 'making one' with God achieved through the passion and death of Christ. On the basis of other Christian claims about God, notably that God *is* love (1 John 4:8) and desires all persons to be saved (1 Tim. 2:4), the atonement is or ought to be an act of supreme love, with love as its means and its goal. Yet without great care the notion of the repayment of a debt, arguably the most influential metaphor of the atonement, freezes out love. On such a view, Christ, in his assumed human nature, endured the penalty or paid the price in suffering which would otherwise have had to be exacted from all sinful human beings to balance the scales of divine justice.

Some of the problems with this approach have long been recognized but Stump throws them into stark relief. In particular, she argues that this "Anselmian" interpretation, with its implicit mechanistic metaphor of balancing scales, does not in fact solve the problem of separation from God. Accounts based on such principles in fact make this problem worse from the point of view of the *at onement*. Instead of divine love, the dominant image of God also risks becoming that of an implacable, merciless, or even sadistic debt-collector. Like Kai in the story of *The Snow Queen*, the doctrine of the atonement then turns cold, the chilling effect of which has tended to permeate, for many people, through the reception of the entirety of Christian revelation.

As Stump explains, the main alternative strand of the Christian tradition has been to treat the chief obstacle to union with God as lying in something lacking in human beings that prevents them being united in friendship with God. This "Thomistic" interpretation has focused on the healing of human disorders through the infusion and cultivation of the virtues and gifts of the Holy Spirit in the life of grace. The implicit metaphor is organic rather than mechanistic and, in many ways, this approach is more promising than the Anselmian interpretation. But this solution does not wholly explain how these divine gifts heal all the impediments to the ruptured relationship with God. And if God can give the Holy Spirit to anyone, why was the Christ's passion and death necessary? The connection with the Holy Spirit is stated in Scripture (John 16:7), but without an explanation, Christ's passion and death can seem gratuitous.

Stump presents a radical alternative, the root metaphor of which is neither mechanistic nor organic but adopts the relationship of persons as its central theme. More precisely, the root metaphor is *second-person relationship*, the stance that 'I' take to 'you' and 'you' take to 'me' that is irreducible to an impersonal world of objects, or even isolated living and growing things. The fruition of second-person relationship is love, which Stump describes as two interconnected desires that are blocked by the consequences of sin: the desire for the good of the beloved, which is blocked by guilt; and the desire for union with the beloved, which is blocked by shame. Since the goal of the atonement is divine friendship with God that begins in this life and is glorified in eternity, any plausible account of this atonement therefore has to answer two key questions. How do we deal with human guilt? How do we deal with human shame?

The answers offered here draw insights from a rich diversity of sources informed by a lifetime of scholarship. No one can explain Stump's work better than Stump, but I risk sketching a few general themes of her arguments to encourage further reading.

The first crucial step focuses on the notion of the mutual indwelling of persons such that we receive life from Christ and he receives a kind of simulacrum of the deadly stain of sin in himself. The resultant inhibition of shared attention with God generated by this poison is manifested in the Cry of Dereliction from Calvary. Christ's suffering here makes union with sinful humanity possible and opens the door to salvation.

The second step is that we cease to resist second-person union with God, without which the work of reintegrating the human psyche in the life of grace cannot get started. But this quiescence is a delicate matter since the will cannot be violated or obliterated. Hence the drama of salvation can in some cases come down to one surrender (not submission) in a human person's will, like a huge pyramid balanced on the point of a pin. This surrender is facilitated for human beings by the suffering of Christ but also by their experience of suffering. This step thereby links theodicy (the subject of Stump's earlier book, *Wandering in Darkness*) and the atonement.

The third step is the vanquishing of shame and guilt. The shame of being a member of a fallen race is defeated by the honor that this shame has been shared with the Deity, especially in the passion and death of Christ. The defeat of the varieties of individual shame results from a person's allying his truest or deepest self with the God who joins himself on the cross to every post-Fall person. Guilt is vanquished by satisfaction, not in the sense of a crude book-balancing exercise, but by a generous self-giving that will also incline the sinner to make amends to victims of his wrongdoing. These amends are proper but insufficient relative to those whom a wrongdoer has treated unjustly or harmed. But here too Stump offers a way forward, namely that Christ does for the wrongdoer what the wrongdoer should do for the victims of his moral wrongdoing but is unable to do himself. Even the sting of the memory is removed in the end, not in the sense of rewriting the past but in the sense of weaving it into a story that increases glory.

This summary is presented here only to whet the appetite of the reader to study this book carefully. Those who invest the time to do so will not only be given a radical new perspective on the atonement but will benefit from insights into a rich tapestry of other major and interconnected themes of revelation. These themes include the Eucharist, the notion of an "office of love," a second-personal account of deification by degrees, the reason for the incarnation, the difference between surrender and submission, the quiescence of the will, justification, and sanctification, the temptations of Christ, the meaning of sacrifice, and the errors in Meister Eckhart's account of sanctification. Stump's treatment of these themes offers many new insights and often assists in breaking long-standing deadlocks. On some topics addressed in her previous writings, the reader will also benefit from a deeply mature account of these topics, now integrated with other matters and presented in an extremely readable way.

For those who set out to study this work carefully some advice may be helpful. As Stump explains in some detail at the beginning of the book, this is a work of philosophical theology. As such, she tests the coherence of doctrinal claims, attempts explanations, uncovers connections with other doctrinal propositions, and so on. Her goal does not require her to test or validate the theological premises themselves and the arguments do not require that these premises are true. Hence the content is or should be of interest to the broadest possible readership, including those who share little or none of the faith in the content of revelation that is the subject of the study. In addition, much of what is presented here in a theological context can be transposed to more secular frameworks. After all, atheists also have to find ways to deal with the problems of guilt, shame, and social fragmentation.

Those readers who are theologians may also notice that the book has had to omit many topics that are connected with the atonement. In part, this is a simple matter of practicalities: a full survey of the implications for moral and sacramental theology would require many volumes. Moreover, the various Christian churches and ecclesial groups will differ on the details. Stump has set herself in this book a more fundamental task: to identify, explain, and justify the first principles of the atonement. Once these principles are grasped, subsequent commentators will be able to explore the implications, just as Aristotle claims that anyone is capable of carrying on and articulating what has already been well outlined (*Nicomachean Ethics*, I.7.1098a22–23).

As regards the style, Stump argues systematically and carefully but this book is not an exercise in cold logic. On the contrary, the style is deeply humane and she interweaves concrete human experiences and dramas throughout her arguments. This regular recourse to metaphors and narrative vignettes, especially the permutations in the relationship of her Everypersons, Jerome and Paula, facilitates understanding and helps to ward off the risk of frozen abstractions.

The resolution of *The Snow Queen* serves in a similar way to sum up the meaning of Stump's achievement in this book. Hans Christian Andersen does not leave Kai alone in the palace to freeze to death manipulating blocks of ice. Fortunately for Kai, his childhood friend Gerda eventually finds him. Her tears wash the splinters out of his eyes and heart. He is able to recognize her, the blocks of ice arrange themselves into the word 'eternity', and they are able to walk out of the palace. That second-person relationship proves to be the key that unlocks the door of the Snow Queen's trap, just as Stump has applied the principle of second-person relationship so fruitfully in this present book to unlocking the mystery of atonement.

One final observation: many of the themes explored in this book have had parallels in the unusual manner of its composition. In particular, those of us who have accompanied Eleonore over the past three years have been acutely conscious of the implications of the medical diagnosis she mentions in her preface. My promise to her was to store her draft chapters and to see the book through publication in case she herself was not able to do so. I am very thankful that she has completed the manuscript herself and that I can celebrate its publication with her.

On behalf of all her readers and those who will be influenced by this work of deeply humane philosophy, I therefore also have the opportunity to thank her personally. I thank you, Eleonore, for rescuing us from our frozen and closed circles of thought on that aspect of Christian revelation, the atonement, that touches most deeply on our hopes for peace, for joy, and the fulfillment of the desires of our hearts.

Andrew Pinsent
Faculty of Theology and Religion

University of Oxford
Christmas 2017

Preface

It had been my intention to write one book that brought together both the problem of suffering and the doctrine of the atonement, and to consider the biblical narratives most pertinent to them, because it seemed to me that these two topics of philosophical theology are part of one larger tapestry of thought. But in the end it proved impossible to do so. The examination of the problem of suffering grew to be such a big book that it had to be published on its own, as *Wandering in Darkness: Narrative and the Problem of Suffering*; and the examination of the doctrine of the atonement had to be relegated to this separate book, *Atonement*. (And, unfortunately, in the end I found I could not fit detailed discussion of the biblical narratives about Christ's passion into this book either, so that task needs to be postponed to some other book.) The difficulty with presenting one large idea in two books is that in this book, *Atonement*, I need to presuppose many basic things from the earlier book, *Wandering in Darkness*. Like others in such circumstances, I have done my best to sail between Scylla and Charybdis. I have tried not to require readers to read the previous volume before they can pick up this new book; but I have also tried not to repeat the whole preceding book in this one. It is hard to find the right course in such a case, but I have done what I could. And even in those places that include the most summary of preceding work, there is considerable new material that advances the arguments of this book.

The difficulty affects even this preface. Things explained at length in the preface to the *Wandering* book apply also to this book, but I am shy about repeating them here. The one exception has to be my use of the names 'Paula' and 'Jerome' as my versions of 'Everyman.' Given the focus on personal relations in this book, I wanted to use not the faceless 'Smith' and 'Jones' common in philosophical prose, but rather the names of people for whom personal relationship was a most notable part of their lives. Paula was an accomplished, learned, highly admirable woman, who was a life-long companion of Jerome, that most erudite and productive Church Father, whose translation of the Bible into the Vulgate and much other work altered the course of the Western church. Jerome could be irascible, not to say venomous, but he loved and honored Paula as a companion in Christ; and she loved and humanized him. When she died, he fell to pieces; and he seems to have pulled himself together only when her daughter Eustochium began to fill her mother's place in his life. (And if it turns out that some skeptical historian finds part of this story non-veridical, then the mythology of Paula and Jerome is what counts for my purposes.) So the story of Paula and Jerome made their names seem like good ones to use in this book, instead of 'Smith' and 'Jones.' And, really, it is helpful to have some names like 'Everyman'; otherwise, the prose tends to become awkward and ugly.

The doctrine of the atonement is the central doctrine of Christianity, and it has been the subject of intense, highly intelligent, theologically sophisticated scrutiny for roughly two millennia. There is therefore some suspicion of hubris or heresy—or even lunacy—about an attempt to rethink the doctrine, in the face of so much fruitful theorizing about it by such excellent minds in the history of the Christian tradition. This suspicion has been for me something of a weight on the progress of this book. In the end, what lifted that weight was my being diagnosed with a potentially life-threatening illness. Samuel Johnson said that the prospect of hanging concentrates the mind wonderfully, and I can report from personal experience that such a diagnosis will do so too. With that diagnosis, I retired self-deprecating suspicion about the nature of the project and just worked at finishing the book. Still, I have done what I could to address the suspicion head-on, even if only briefly, in Chapter 1. Here, in the Preface, I would like to add, in my own defense, that Anselm also tried to rework the interpretation of the doctrine anew, in the face of a millennium of preceding intense reflection on it; and I note that he seems not to have been troubled by a similar suspicion. There is room, then, for innovation in philosophical theology that is neither unorthodox nor perverse. At any rate, as I explain in Chapter 1, both Thomas Aquinas and John Henry Newman thought so. Each of them argued that it is possible to have theological development that is both orthodox and sensible; and they are good authorities to have as support in an enterprise of this sort.

So, in the tradition of Anselm, and also Aquinas and Newman, in this book I have tried to think through the doctrine of the atonement afresh. Nevertheless, I am also sure that any human expertise is always vested in community. Consequently, although I have not adopted wholesale the interpretation of the doctrine given by any of the erudite and reflective thinkers in the history of the Christian tradition, I have tried to learn from their work as I could.

I have also tried to learn from my contemporaries. This manuscript has had the benefit of the comments of many others, who have worked through it carefully in part or in whole or who were lively audiences for presentations of a part of it.

Separate reading groups at Baylor University (led by Trent Dougherty), the University of St. Andrews (led by Alan Torrance and Andrew Torrance), and the University of York (led by David Worsley and David Efird) worked carefully through a preceding version of the manuscript over the course of months and sent me extensive comments on it. Trent Dougherty at Baylor and Alan Torrance and Andrew Torrance at St. Andrews also each organized one-day workshops on the manuscript, in which I had the benefit of extensive thoughtful presentations and incisive questions by numerous people as notable for their generosity as for their philosophical and theological ability. I am also grateful to Trent Dougherty, Michael Rea, and Brandon Warmke for their helpful and insightful papers on the manuscript given at an APA author-meets-critics session that was held in advance of the publication of the manuscript.

Reading drafts of some of the chapters were given as the Stanton Lectures at Cambridge (2018). I also presented papers based on individual chapters to audiences at various places, including Rutgers University, Austral University (Buenos Aires), University of St. Thomas (St. Paul), Purdue University, University of Notre Dame, Trinity College (Dublin), the Thomistic Institute (Harvard), Fuller University, Sewanee: The University of the South, Stanford University, Hong Kong Baptist University (Hong Kong), and the American Academy of Religion meeting (2016). I am grateful to the audiences in all these places for their helpful comments and questions.

In addition, colleagues and friends, both local and distant, worked patiently through earlier versions of some or all of the chapters and gave me helpful comments. I am particularly grateful to John Greco and Michael Rea, who, in spite of their own pressing and busy schedules, wrote extensive, probing comments on every chapter. I also owe a great debt to Jeffrie Murphy, who read and reread the material on love and forgiveness, and who gave me the benefit of his own long and serious reflections on these topics, not only by pointing me to the right works of his own and others to challenge my views but also by many thought-provoking comments in correspondence. Yehuda Gellman, Moshe Halbertal, Jon Levenson, and David Shatz generously looked over my comments on sacrifice and relevant stories in the Hebrew Bible. Still others, such as David Jeffrey, Paul Philibert (+2016), and Bas van Fraassen, read parts of the manuscript and gave advice and support *in ecclesia*, for which I am most grateful. My daughter Monica Green, who is a clinical psychologist, also gave me invaluable help with some of the psychology literature. (I suppose that it goes without saying that thanking one's highly accomplished adult daughter for help with professional literature has to be accompanied by a mixture of pride, love, and wonder that we have all lived so long!)

Finally, the manuscript was the subject of two of my graduate seminars, and my graduate students also provided insightful and challenging comments on every chapter.

I have listed the names of all the particular people who gave comments or were in these reading groups in the acknowledgements section below. I am very grateful to all of them, and to the audiences for the presentations, for their questions and comments.

My former research assistant Matthew Shea also provided great help with the endnotes and other research work on the manuscript. My current research assistant Katherine Sweet has picked up where Shea left off and has helped with the process of getting the manuscript ready for the press. My secretary Barbara Manning, the *sine qua non* of the office, was a great aid in keeping track of the myriad details of the project. I could not do what I do if she were not so superb at what she does. And I owe a special debt of thanks to Andrew Pinsent, who in spite of the many other demands made on his time graciously agreed to write the Foreword for this book and who gave me helpful comments on the manuscript, too. He also patiently helped me keep safe all the many drafts of the chapters as I revised them on the basis of the comments that friends and colleagues sent.

Then there is the issue of the cover image. Stefan Jasieński escaped from Poland and made his way to Great Britain during World War II; there he joined the Polish resistance in exile. In 1943, he and other Polish fighters were parachuted back into Poland to work with resistance groups. Eventually, in July 1944, he was assigned to work that was centered on Auschwitz; he served as a liaison between the underground resistance in Auschwitz and resistance groups elsewhere in Poland and beyond. His efforts were instrumental in averting a German proposal then being floated to liquidate the whole camp at once. But this work of his was short-lived. On August 28, 1944, he was seriously wounded and captured, and he was then himself imprisoned in Auschwitz. After a short stay in the prison hospital, he was transferred to cell 21 in the notorious death Block 11, where he eventually died, probably sometime in the first week of January 1945. During his months in that cell, suffering and dying slowly, he managed somehow, by some miraculous gift of psychic resources and material ingenuity, to leave a record of his life and his love in pictures etched with his fingernails into the cement of his cell wall.

What I know of Stefan Jasieński I first learned from this book, which I bought in the Auschwitz Museum store: *The Lost Art of Auschwitz*, Photography and Text by Joseph P. Czarnecki, Introduction by Chaim Potok (New York: Atheneum, 1989). But I bought the book because I had seen Jasieński's images for myself when I walked through Block 11 with the Auschwitz tour. The images, and the story of the man who produced them, are unforgettable. One of those images is a stunning depiction of the crucifixion of Christ, and the story of the production of the image is part of the power of the picture. I cannot conceive of anything that would serve better to convey iconically the thought of this book than Jasieński's depiction of Christ's crucifixion. And I am honored to honor Jasieński by using his image of Christ on the cross as the cover of this book.

But I would never have been able to do so if it had not been for the intervention of my friend Fr. Christof Wolf, SJ (Loyola Productions, Munich), who is an accomplished filmmaker networked around the world. Though there are photographs of this image of Jasieński's available in print and on the Internet, none of them are of sufficiently high quality to be used as a cover image. Wolf contacted the director of the Auschwitz Museum, Dr. Piotr

M.A. Cywiński, who was generous in his willingness to help. Dr. Cywiński arranged for Paweł Sawicki to take a high-resolution photograph of the image, and Sawicki's excellent photograph now provides the cover of this book. I could not be more grateful to Christof Wolf, Piotr Cywiński, and Paweł Sawicki for their help and efforts in providing that photograph and so making it possible for this image to be used to grace this book.

For the cover of *Wandering in Darkness*, I asked my friend Mike Gale for help in finding an image because I trust his artistic creativity and religious insight greatly.[1] With help from Dan Schutte,[2] Gale found and worked with the photograph that is now the image on that book. It is a beautiful image, and I am grateful to the two of them for their help in producing it. So when it came to the cover of this book, *Atonement*, I petitioned Gale again for help, but this time for help in crafting a sensitive way in which to display the picture on the cover, so that the honor due Jasieński's image would be enhanced and not diminished by the presentation of the picture and the necessary graphics. I know no one I would rather trust with this task than Gale, and I am grateful to him for his excellent work, which has resulted in this memorable cover for the book.

Finally, this preface would be incomplete without expressions of gratitude to my family and my community. I am blessed with a loving husband, dear and lovely children (the in-law ones as well as the ones born to me), and a growing group of smart and adorable grandchildren. Without all their love and support, I am certain that this book would not have been written. In addition, I am fortunate to share life and work with wonderful committed friends and colleagues; and I could not be more grateful for the Jesuit community, here and elsewhere, and for the far-flung Dominican community of which I am a professed member. The friendship of the local and distant faithful priests around me, including particularly Fr. Theodore Vitali, CP, has been a great support. I am especially grateful for my many years of companionship with Fr. John Foley, SJ, theologian, musician, and composer of liturgical music that is sung by Catholics and Protestants around the world. His music has mediated the power of the tenderness of Christ to me and sustained me in difficult times. And if there is anything melodic in *Wandering in Darkness* and *Atonement*, his companionship has been the cello voice for it. This book is dedicated to him. At the YouTube link *John Kavanaugh, How Can I Keep from Singing*, you can hear him sing the folk hymn that is part of the dedication, together with his old friend, Fr. John Kavanaugh, SJ, whose death was a sorrow to John Foley and to me. If you would like to hear him sing the song he wrote for the mass when I was received into the Catholic Church, you can go to this YouTube site: https://www.youtube.com/watch?v=6dIPzRX2qpQ&feature=youtu.be. (The video for this site was very ably produced by my current research assistant Katherine Sweet.)

Acknowledgments

I am grateful to the following members of reading groups.

The reading group at St. Andrews: Max Botner, Kimberley Kroll, Christa McKirland, David Moffitt, Ryan Mullins, Kevin Nordby, Stephanie Nordby, John Perry, Jeremy Rios, Sarah Lane Ritchie, Jonathan Rutledge, Taylor Telford, Alan Torrance, Andrew Torrance, Koert Verhagen, and N.T. Wright.

The reading group at York: Joshua Cockayne, David Efird, Spencer Johnston, and David Worsley.

And the reading group at Baylor: Alina Beary, Michael Beaty, Nik Breiner, Kevin Diller (Taylor University), Trent Dougherty, C. Stephen Evans, Sarah Gutierrez, Alex Hoffman, Derek McAllister, Burke Rea, and Brandon Rickabaugh.

I also appreciate very much the generous help of my colleagues and friends, who read some part of the manuscript, or all of it: Godehard Brüntrup, Donnie Bungum, Lindsay Cleveland, Scott Cleveland, Sarah Coakley, John Cottingham, Claire Crisp, Oliver Crisp, Ingolf Dalferth, Scott Davison, Evan Fales, Chad Flanders, John Foley, Yehuda Gellman, John Greco, Moshe Halbertal, Jonathan Jacobs, David Jeffrey, Jon Levenson, Nicholas Lombardo, Michael McKenna, Robert MacSwain, Peter Martens, David Meconi, Jeffrie Murphy, Timothy O'Connor, Faith Pawl, Timothy Pawl, Paul Philibert, Andrew Pinsent, Michael Rea, David Shatz, Matthew Shea, Richard Swinburne, Kevin Timpe, Bas van Fraassen, Theodore Vitali, and Brandon Warmke.

In addition, I am grateful to the participants in my seminars for their excellent help with the manuscript: Joel Archer, Peter Berger, Donald Bungum, Justin Claravall, Matthew Cortese, Thomas Croteau, Kevin Cutright, Vincent Davila, K.J. Drake, Laura Estes, Everett Fulmer, Audra Goodnight, Sean Hagerty, Luke Kallberg, Daniel Kennedy, David Kiblinger, James Kintz, Yvonne Angieri Klein, James Lee, Sarah Legett, Peter Martens, Patrick McCaffery, Colleen McCluskey, James McGuire, Michael Mohr, Dane Muckler, Jonathan Nebel, Justin Noia, Carl Joseph Paustian, Luís Pinto de Sá Alexandra Romanyshyn, James Dominic Rooney, Kathleen Schmitz, Matthew Shea, Hayden Stephan, Katherine Sweet, Luke Townsend, Becky Walker, Anna Williams, John-Paul Witt, Chong Yuan, Yiling Zhou, and Patrick Zoll.

Eleonore Stump
Honorary Professor, Wuhan University
Honorary Professor, Logos Institute, St. Andrews
Professorial Fellow, Australian Catholic University
Patron of the Aquinas Institute, Blackfriars Hall, Oxford
Robert J. Henle, SJ, Professor of Philosophy, Saint Louis University

Contents

Part I

What Is Wanted, What Is Needed to Get What Is Wanted, and What Will Not Work

1

Methodology, Problems, and Desiderata

INTRODUCTION

The doctrine that Christ has saved human beings from their sins, with all that that salvation entails, is the distinctive doctrine of Christianity. It is powerful in its ability to move people, with heart-melting love or with repudiation and rejection. Evaluating these differing attitudes, however, requires first understanding the doctrine; and understanding the doctrine is not an easy matter. Over the course of many centuries of reflection on the doctrine, highly diverse understandings have been proposed, many of which have also raised strong positive or negative emotions in those who have reflected on them. In this book, in the context of this history of interpretation, I want to consider this theological doctrine with philosophical care.

It is important to begin with a consideration of the nature of the project of this book. It is an exercise in philosophical theology.

Natural theology, which has a time-honored place in philosophy, is the attempt to understand the metaphysical foundation of reality by the use of reason alone, without the use as evidence of anything contained in texts considered to be divinely revealed or in the religious tradition of reflection on those texts.[1] Typically, natural theology consists in a philosophical examination of questions about the existence and nature of God or of questions about traditionally accepted divine attributes; and, like other areas of philosophical endeavor, natural theology makes use of distinctions, analysis, and arguments.

By contrast, philosophical theology is the attempt to use such philosophical tools to investigate theological claims made by a particular religion, especially those claims put forward by that religion as revealed by the deity. Philosophical theology shares the methods of natural theology broadly conceived; but it lifts natural theology's restriction on premises, accepting as assumptions those claims supposed to be revealed or those claims that are the result of reflection on putatively revealed claims. Such claims include propositions that are supposed to be at least initially inaccessible to unaided reason. Philosophical theology tests the coherence of such doctrinal claims, attempts explanations of them, uncovers their logical connections with other doctrinal propositions, and so on.

In this respect, philosophical theology is like philosophy of physics or philosophy of biology. Philosophy of physics and philosophy of biology take as their starting points the data given by a science, and they engage in philosophical examinations of such data. The aim of philosophy of biology, for example, is not to do biology but to philosophize about the claims that biology takes to be true. For philosophy of biology, it does not matter if the biological claims are in fact true, provided that they are taken to be true in biology. Analogously, it does not matter for philosophical theology if the data drawn from theology are true. What matters is whether they are orthodox, that is, whether they are in fact accepted as true and mandatory for belief within a particular religious community. In this respect, philosophy of biology differs from biology, which has a central stake in the truth of biological claims; and philosophical theology differs from theology, which definitely does want to ask whether theological claims taken to be orthodox are true. It is, of course, not always easy to specify with precision what to count as 'orthodox' in theology; but, for the project of philosophical theology, there has to be at least some rough characterization of the theologically orthodox. For my purposes in this book, I will take as orthodox, that is, as the data to be assumed for this enterprise in philosophical theology, the claims of the creeds and early ecumenical councils and also those theological claims generally accepted as true and central to the faith by the broad majority of authoritative thinkers in the history of the Christian tradition.[2]

Because this book is meant to be a work of philosophical theology, nothing about the project of this book requires that the theological claims accepted as orthodox, that is, as the starting points in this book, are true. (On the other hand, of course, nothing about this project rules out supposing that they are true either. A project in philosophy of biology does not require that the biological claims at issue be true, but it does not rule out their truth either.) By parity of reasoning, I do not intend to maintain that the claims in the interpretation of the doctrine of the atonement I argue for in this book are true. Whether or not they are true is a matter for theology and not for philosophical theology. The claims in this interpretation of the doctrine might be true (and in fact I myself think that they are true); but in this book I do not conclude that they are true, and nothing about my project requires maintaining such a conclusion. Because I am engaged in philosophical theology, I am proposing the interpretation developed in this book only as one way of understanding a doctrine that Christian theology takes to be orthodox and true, and I am arguing that this interpretation makes better sense of the doctrine than other interpretations do. In my view, both those who want to defend the doctrine of the atonement and those who want to attack it would do better to attend to the interpretation of the doctrine developed in this book than to other alternative interpretations.

On that understanding of the methodology of this project, one aim of philosophical theology is to see whether the theological claims which are considered revealed by a particular religion or which are implied by such putatively revealed claims are understandable and defensible on the religious worldview in question. In general, the enterprise of philosophical theology is the employment of the techniques and devices of philosophy in analyzing, clarifying, extending, and debating the propositions that are supposed by a particular religion to have been revealed as among theology's starting points or that are taken to be implied by putatively revealed claims. Not even the doctrines officially designated as mysteries in the Christian tradition are impervious to rational investigation of the sort undertaken by philosophical theology. Regarding the doctrine of the Trinity, for example, that paradigmatic practitioner of philosophical theology, Thomas Aquinas, says: "It is impossible to arrive at a cognition of the Trinity of the divine persons by means of natural reason."[3] But he says this in the twenty-second of a series of seventy-seven articles of his *Summa theologiae* (ST) devoted to analyzing and arguing about the details of the Trinity—in other words, in the midst of approaching this mystery with the methods of philosophical theology.

As Aquinas explains in the very article in which he rules out the possibility of discovering by unaided human reason that there are three divine persons who are one God,

> There are two ways in which reason is employed regarding any matter ... in one way to provide sufficient proof of something fundamental ... in the other way to show that consequent effects are suited to something fundamental that has already been posited.... It is in the first way, then, that reason can be employed to prove that God is one, and things of that sort. But it is in the second way that reason is employed in a clarification of Trinity. For once Trinity has been posited, reasonings of that sort are suitable, although not so as to provide a sufficient proof of the Trinity of persons by those reasonings.[4]

On this understanding of the methodology in question, this book is intended to be a work of philosophical theology; it is meant to examine theological claims by reason, taken roughly in Aquinas's second way of employing reason on religion's claims.

In this connection, I need to acknowledge that, even though this book is a project within philosophical theology, it nonetheless counts as innovative in theology. That is, in trying to understand the data given by Christian theology, I am arguing for a relatively novel interpretation of the doctrine of the atonement; taken as a whole, the interpretation I argue for is not one that has been in evidence much or at all within the domain of theology. And so the question arises whether philosophical theology can appropriately be used in this way or whether, on the contrary, innovation in theology through philosophical examination ought to be alarming, or at least rejected as inappropriate.

This is a question that has been addressed by others in the history of Christian thought already, and for good reason. Some major doctrines of Christianity were codified centuries after the death of Christ, so that it must be possible for there to be some innovative development in ortho-dox Christian theological doctrine in consequence of philosophical and theological reflection. For that matter, the same issue arises with regard to the teachings of Christ himself. So, for example, worried about this very issue, Eusebius argues that the teachings of Christ are both new and yet also continuous with the revelation God gave to the Jews and others earlier. Eusebius says,

> that no one may suppose [Christ's] teaching to be new ... let us discuss this point briefly.... [E]ven if we are clearly new and this truly recent name of Christians has lately been known among all nations, our life and manner of conduct in accordance with the very teachings of our religion have not been recently fashioned by us, but, as it were, from the first creation of man have been established by the natural concepts of the God-favored men of old.... [I]t is clear that the religion which was recently proclaimed to all the Gentiles through the teaching of Christ must be considered the first and most ancient of all....[5]

Aquinas himself maintains both that all theological knowledge was given to the apostles and also that there is some progression in the understanding of theological truths over the course of years.[6] On his way of conceiving the issue, all theological wisdom was given to the apostles, but at least some of that wisdom was in bud. The task of subsequent generations is to contribute to unfolding that bud.

Of course, even if this view of Aquinas's is right, there is still a question of the criteria by which one distinguishes the development of doctrine from the invention of heresy or something worse. John Henry Newman, who was concerned with this question, wrote a book attempting to spell out such criteria.[7] Newman's criteria have not been persuasive to many people;[8] but his general approach, which emphasizes continuity with creedal statements and consistency with other doctrines accepted as orthodox, seems to me intelligible and sensible. By those lights, what is innovative in the interpret-ation of the doctrine of the atonement that I argue for in this book meets Newman's tests. For these reasons, although my interpretation is innovative, it still counts as orthodox or as derived from claims that are uncontestedly orthodox. For this reason, the interpretation of the doctrine that I argue for and the method of arriving at that interpretation stay within the general enterprise of philosophical theology.

THE WORD 'ATONEMENT'

The focus of this book is the Christian doctrine of the *at onement*, that is, the doctrine that attributes *at onement*, somehow, to Christ. Here, and throughout this first chapter, I am using the awkward neologism '*at onement*' in order to avoid what sometimes seems to be invincible misconception regarding the meaning of the word 'atonement.'

In her own discussion of the word, Linda Radzik says,

> The *Oxford English Dictionary* defines 'atonement' as "The action of setting at one, or condition of being set at one, after discord or strife" [footnote omitted] .... The etymology of 'atonement' is 'at-one-ment' [footnote omitted]. However, when I first happened upon this fact, I did not believe it. For many speakers of English, the word has come to be strongly associated with images of suffering. To atone is to undergo some kind of pain or sacrifice for wrongful acts. A demand for atonement is usually perceived as threatening—a demand for punishment—rather than a call to the resumption of friendly relations.[9]

I share Radzik's view as regards the ordinary understanding of the word 'atonement.' To many people, this word indicates the project of placating an offended God by the gift of a bloody sacrifice.[10] I intend no such meaning for the word. And, in fact, different religious or scholarly communities, operating at different times and places, have understood the word 'atonement' in highly various ways. So, even though in the understanding of many contemporary people, the word 'atonement' is frequently taken narrowly to mean just making things right with God by means of Christ's crucifixion and death, I will use the word in this book in its etymological and more neutral sense. It is necessary to have some word to designate the nature and effects of Christ's passion and death (or, alternatively, Christ's life, passion, and death)[11] with regard to the salvation[12] of human beings; and, of the various terms available from the long history of the discussion of the doctrine, 'atonement' seems to me to be the least tendentious, carrying the least theological baggage.

Consequently, in the remainder of this book, I will describe the aim of this book as a consideration of the doctrine of the atonement of Christ. But I will write the word as '*at onement*' in this first chapter, in an effort to call attention to the broader meaning of the term. In the usage of the term that I intend, the word refers to the passion and death of Christ (or the life, passion, and death of Christ) in their nature and their effects with regard to human salvation, whatever their nature and effects might be. After this chapter, which I hope will alert the reader to the use of the term that I intend, I will simply write the word in the usual way, as 'atonement.' It is my hope that taking the term 'atonement' to mean *whatever* the nature and effects of Christ's passion and death are as regards human salvation will give the word 'atonement' a connotation neutral among theological controversies. Specifying what is left vague and indefinite by the 'whatever' in my adopted meaning of 'atonement' is one of the chief goals of this book.

THE SHAPE OF THE PROJECT

Someone might object that I should have written 'Jesus', rather than 'Christ', in the paragraphs above. On this objection, the *at onement* is to be connected with a historical person, the human being Jesus, whose life and actions are reported by the Gospel narratives and other New Testament texts, which are themselves historical documents that stem from certain historical communities. On this objection, to investigate the doctrine of the *at onement* is to excavate the historical record in order to discover the thought or the communal attitudes of the persons or groups who were writing and exercising influence in this early Christian period.

An enterprise of that sort no doubt has its points, but it is not my intention to engage in it here. My aim in this book is not history but philosophical theology. For that purpose, what is important is not the exploration of the developing thought of early Christian communities or even the excavation of the intentions of those whose historically situated experiences resulted in the New Testament texts. For the same reasons, I will not be concerned with the kinds of historical questions for which some theologians have worked hard to find answers, as, for example, these questions: Who was Jesus? What was his self-understanding; that is, how did he see his relation to God? What did he understand about his role in salvation history? What did he think about his suffering and death, before it or during it? Trying to find the answers to these questions has its points, too, but I do not mean to engage in this kind of historical investigation either.

Rather, what is at issue in this book is just the understanding and implications of a doctrine taken to be theologically orthodox and binding on all Christians, as that doctrine is understood in its most philosophically and theologically sophisticated form by those whose views are authoritative for at least very many Christians.

Of course, the figures who might reasonably be taken to be authoritative in this way typically did suppose that the doctrine of the *at onement* is explicitly or implicitly contained in New Testament texts, and they also typically supposed that the persons or communities whose experiences resulted in the production of New Testament texts accepted the doctrine in its theologically orthodox form. But my concern is not with such claims about the relation of the doctrine to the New Testament texts or to the early Church community. My concern is only with the doctrine itself. Since this is so, where my concern with the doctrine does lead naturally to consideration of New Testament texts,

I will simply take those texts to have the general meaning given them by those who are widely regarded as theologically authoritative figures.

I distinguish here between the meaning of a claim in a biblical text and the interpretation of that claim. So, for example, the first line of Psalm 22, uttered by Christ during his crucifixion, as reported in Gospel texts, is typically taken to be an expression of Christ's own experience at the time of his passion; and I will accept this as the meaning of the line, in accordance with its typical understanding in much of the history of Christian tradition. But the *interpretation* of that line so understood is highly controversial even among theologically authoritative figures. In my view, for the purposes of my project, my acceptance of their understanding of the meaning of the line does not commit me to accept any of their interpretations of the line.

In addition, and for similar reasons, I will accept for the purposes of my project the views regarding the people in the biblical stories and the authorship of the biblical books which are part of the traditional orthodox theology under investigation. That is, I will assume that the Gospel of John was written by the apostle John, who had the characteristics typically assigned to him in Christian tradition. It may be that the historical reality was otherwise; but my aim here is not to investigate early Christian history or the truth of claims made by authoritative Christian thinkers about early Christian history. My purpose is the philosophical examination of the theological doctrine of the *at onement*. For that purpose, it matters what the shape of the doctrine is, but it does not matter what the history was out of which the doctrine developed. Insofar as anything about the authorship of biblical books affects interpretation of the theological doctrines under consideration, I will take as part of the theological data being investigated in this book that attribution or authorship which traditional theologians have accepted.

Analogously, if the subject of this book were the philosophical investigation of the orthodox doctrine of the incarnation, it would not matter what Nestorius actually believed; it would matter only what the orthodox theologians who ruled out Nestorianism thought that Nestorius believed. The doctrine of the incarnation was shaped in such a way as to rule out Nestorianism, but only Nestorianism as the shapers of the doctrine supposed it to be. And so it is their understanding of Nestorius's beliefs, not Nestorius's actual beliefs, that are relevant to a philosophical consideration of the doctrine of the incarnation.

Similarly, then, for purposes of philosophical theology, interpretations of the doctrine of the *at onement* are constrained by their fit with biblical texts; but because what is at issue for philosophical investigation is the theological doctrine as it is part of Christian orthodoxy, the understanding of the biblical texts relevant for the project of this book is the understanding had by those who formulated the theological doctrine of the *at onement* in its orthodox version.

It is important to recognize that there is no necessity for the reader to accept these understandings as veridical for the sake of this project, any more than there is any necessity to accept theism in order to discuss either the argument from evil or a defense against it. Examining the nature and implications of a theological doctrine is a different project from showing the doctrine to be true. Nothing in what follows in this book requires the reader to accept the truth of any of the presuppositions I employ in consideration of the doctrine—though, as I explained above, by parity of reasoning, nothing prevents the reader from taking all of them to be true either.

So, because my focus in this book is the doctrine of the *at onement* and not its origin or historical development, my earlier phrasing was appropriate: the *at onement* as I am investigating it in this book is something attributed to Christ, not just to the man Jesus, and I will accept biblical texts about Jesus as texts about Christ.

THE CHALCEDONIAN FORMULA AND ITS IMPLICATIONS

For the same reasons, in this book, by 'Christ' I will mean what the Chalcedonian formula mandates as the appropriate referent for the term: one person—who is the second person of the Trinity and is thus God—with two natures, one fully divine and one fully human.

It is one of the implications of the Chalcedonian understanding of Christ that there are in Christ two minds, one human and one divine; and consequently, on the Chalcedonian formula, there are also two wills in Christ, one human and one divine. Some people might suppose that this description of Christ is incoherent and that philosophical reason can demonstrate that there could be nothing meeting this description. It is certainly true that the doctrine of the incarnation, like the doctrine of the Trinity, counts as a Christian mystery. But elsewhere, using the methods of philosophical theology, I have examined the doctrine of the incarnation and defended it against at least some of the major arguments attempting to show its incoherence.[13] Because this is not a book on the doctrine of the incarnation, I will just assume here the results of that earlier discussion; I will take for granted here the results of my own work and that of others, showing that the doctrine of the incarnation is intelligible and not demonstrably incoherent.[14] The point of this book is not to try to elucidate everything in Christian theology but only to examine the doctrine of the *at onement*, as that doctrine is expressed in orthodox Christian theology.

On the doctrine of the *at onement* as I am understanding it for my purposes here, with the Chalcedonian formula for Christ as ingredient in it, *at onement* is the work of God, since the person with whom the *at onement* is connected is a divine person. On the other hand, the *at onement* is connected with this divine person in his assumed human nature, that is, as this divine person is incarnate as the human being Jesus of Nazareth. When Christ suffers and dies, he suffers and dies as incarnate, in the human nature had by the incarnate Christ.

On this orthodox understanding of the doctrine of Christ's *at onement*, it is true to say that God suffers and that God dies. But God suffers and dies in the human nature God has assumed. In his divine nature, God neither suffers nor dies, since neither suffering nor dying is compatible with the divine nature. In fact, on this understanding of the doctrine, at least one major point of God's assuming a human nature was God's making it possible for God to suffer and die. Therefore, while it is true that God cannot suffer or die in his divine nature, on the Chalcedonian formula it is not true that God cannot suffer or die. God can do both, in the human nature God assumed; and it is part of the doctrine of the *at onement* that God suffers and dies in the crucifixion of Jesus.

AT ONEMENT AND OTHER PHILOSOPHICAL OR THEOLOGICAL ISSUES

On the understanding of God's nature common to philosophical theologians such as Augustine and Aquinas, God in his divine nature is eternal and so outside of time.[15] But if God is outside time, then God's having an assumed human nature is not something characteristic of God at some times but not at others. It is something characteristic of God always. On this view, God is never in the state of not having an assumed human nature. For this reason, as I will explain in more detail later, on the understanding of God as eternal, God is never unable to suffer or die. The capacity for suffering and dying is something characteristic of God always, in the human nature whose assumption is always with God.

For some philosophers and theologians, the divine attribute most important in any attempt at philosophical theology will be divine simplicity. As this divine attribute is understood by some contemporary thinkers, it invalidates anything that attributes to God the status of being an entity; and it rules out any discourse about God that seems anthropomorphic. But in my own view, this understanding of divine simplicity depends on a mistaken reading of the relevant Thomistic texts typically adduced to support it, as I have argued in detail elsewhere.[16] In the remainder of this book, I will therefore leave to one side worries of this sort that some thinkers suppose are raised by the doctrine that God is simple.

As this brief discussion should highlight, it is difficult to discuss the doctrine of the *at onement* in isolation from other philosophical and theological views. It makes a great difference whether God is to be understood as being eternal or being in time, for example. As will quickly become apparent in the subsequent chapters, philosophical views about the nature of goodness, love, justice, guilt, and shame are also crucial, as are theological views about the nature of goodness, love, and justice in God. And this is only a beginning of philosophical or theological views crucial to interpretations of the doctrine of the *at onement*. But every book has to start somewhere, and it would not be possible to make the doctrine of the *at onement* the focus of this book if every philosophical and theological view relevant to the doctrine had to be constructed and argued for *de novo*.

In other work, I have examined and defended many of the philosophical and theological views relevant to the doctrine, most notably in my work on the thought of Thomas Aquinas.[17] Since in that earlier work I have ready to hand, examined and argued for, many of the positions that make a difference to the doctrine of the *at onement*, in this book I am simply going to presuppose much of Aquinas's worldview as the background for this investigation of the doctrine of the *at onement*. In my view, the part of Aquinas's worldview that serves as background for this project is as close to what C.S. Lewis called 'mere Christianity' as one finds in a philosophically gifted theologian. And where it includes something not universally accepted in the Christian tradition, such as the doctrine that God is eternal rather than temporal, it serves to highlight the difference that controversy over this doctrine makes to interpretations of the doctrine of the *at onement*.

By saying that I am presupposing Aquinas's views here, then, I mean only that the background worldview—including, for example, the theory of goodness, the account of the nature of justice, the view of love and forgiveness, the understanding of the divine attributes, and other things of this sort which I will need to rely on in this book—is that of Aquinas. There is prudence in this approach. Since Aquinas's views are the ones I have done the most to elucidate and defend elsewhere, I can rely on that previous work as undergirding for this book, and so this book can focus on the doctrine of the *at onement*, rather than on all the ancillary concepts in the background. In addition, however, in my view, Aquinas is one of the best and most sophisticated philosophical minds in the West. His views are well worth wrestling with, whether or not one is convinced by him in the end; and they are frequently more persuasive than the competing alternatives. So there is this reason for presupposing his worldview also.

For those who reject certain parts of the relevant Thomistic worldview—those who think of God as temporal rather than eternal, for example, or those who hold a divine command theory of ethics—this book can nonetheless serve as a propaedeutic, helping to make clear what the implications are of the particular non-Thomistic elements in their own worldview, at least as regards assessment of the doctrine of the *at onement*.

Finally, although, in my view, this background worldview is also biblically based, the biblical texts relevant to the doctrine of the *at onement* figure significantly in the chapters that follow; and so they also serve as a check on the background worldview of Aquinas that are adopted as theological data in this book.

THE DOCTRINE OF THE *AT ONEMENT* AND THE THEOLOGICAL TRADITION

In saying that I am going to presuppose much of Aquinas's worldview, I do not mean that I am committing myself to Aquinas's interpretation of the doctrine of the *at onement*. The doctrine of the *at onement* differs from other major Christian doctrines, such as the doctrine of the incarnation, for example, in having no formula specifying its interpretation. With characteristic clarity and cogency, C.S. Lewis put the point this way:

Theories about Christ's death are not Christianity: they are explanations about how it works. . . . We believe that the death of Christ is just that point in history at which something absolutely unimaginable from outside shows through into our world. And if we cannot picture even the atoms of which our own world is built, of course we are not going to be able to picture this. Indeed, if we found that we could fully understand it, that very fact would show that it was not what it professes to be—the inconceivable, the uncreated, the thing from beyond nature, striking down into nature like lightning. You may ask what good will it be to us if we do not understand it. But that is easily answered. A man can eat his dinner without understanding exactly how food nourishes him. A man can accept what Christ has done without knowing how it works: indeed, he certainly would not know how it works until he has accepted it.

We are told that Christ was killed for us, that His death has washed out our sins, and that by dying He disabled death itself. That is the formula. That is Christianity. That is what has to be believed. Any theories we build up as to how Christ's death did all this are, in my view, quite secondary: mere plans or diagrams to be left alone if they do not help us, and, even if they do help us, not to be confused with the thing itself.[18]

Lewis seems to me entirely right in this view, which I share, and which I affirm with regard to my own interpretation of the doctrine also: if it does not help, it should be left alone; and even if it does help, it is not to be confused with the thing itself.

So, although creedal or conciliar statements rule out some interpretations as unorthodox, for the doctrine of the *at onement* there is no analogue to the Chalcedonian formula for the incarnation. For this reason, it is possible for there to be highly divergent interpretations, all of which count as orthodox. My own appropriation of what in Aquinas's interpretation of the doctrine seems to me intelligible and defensible underlies this book. But there are many good minds in the history of the Christian tradition from the Patristic period to now who have attempted to give helpful interpretations of the doctrine; and, whether or not those thinkers are cited in what follows, I have tried to learn from the most influential or intellectually powerful among them, and not just from Aquinas.

In the end, my own interpretation of the doctrine of the *at onement* highlights elements of the doctrine that are not the subject of much or any reflection in the work of Aquinas. In writing this book I have tried to learn from varying interpretations of the doctrine of the *at onement* which are found in different periods in the history of the Christian theological tradition, but I have not adopted wholesale any one of them, not even that of Aquinas. Although I rely heavily on Aquinas's thought, I am not either presupposing or defending Aquinas's interpretation of the doctrine of the *at onement* in this book.

THE NATURE OF THE PROBLEM

It is widely supposed, by both Christians and non-Christians alike, that the doctrine of the *at onement* is the most important doctrine of Christianity; and Christians often speak of the value of the *at onement* itself as infinite or at least so great as to be incommensurate with all other created goods. Alvin Plantinga, for example, thinks that the value of the *at onement*[19] is so great that it is more than sufficient as the basis of a theodicy. He says,

> consider the splendid and gracious marvel of incarnation and atonement. I believe that the great goodness of this state of affairs, like that of the divine existence itself, makes its value incommensurable with the value of states of affairs involving creaturely good and bad.... no matter how much evil, how much sin and suffering a world contains, the aggregated badness would be outweighed by the goodness of incarnation and atonement, outweighed in such a way that the world in question is very good....[20]

I am not concerned here with Plantinga's claim that the value of the *at onement* can be the basis of a successful solution to the problem of evil.[21] What is of interest for my purposes is the obvious presupposition of his position, shared largely or universally by Christians, namely, that there is a very great value in the *at onement*. But, on the Christian doctrine of the *at onement*, what is in fact so valuable about the *at onement*? Although the answer to this question might seem elementary, on reflection the question turns out to be remarkably difficult to deal with. Any attempt to answer it depends on finding an answer to another, even more difficult question: On Christian doctrine, what exactly is the *at onement*? That is, what is it that is accomplished by the passion and death of Christ (or the life, passion, and death, of Christ)?

Through the use of philosophical reason on theological doctrines, this book is an attempt to give an answer to these questions. It will concentrate on the question about the nature of the *at onement*, on Christian doctrine.[22] This is by far the harder of the questions. Because the value of the *at onement* is obviously a function of the nature of the *at onement*, the answer to the question about the value of the *at onement* will emerge fairly straight-forwardly once the nature of the *at onement* has been elucidated.

We can begin reflection on the question about the nature of the *at onement* by considering the purpose of the *at onement*. There is little if any controversy in theological discussion, now or in the history of Christian philosophy and theology, over the claim that the *at onement* is the solution to a problem. But what is that problem?

The word 'atonement' is a relative newcomer to the English language.[23] As my usage in this chapter suggests, the word was coined to indicate the nature of the solution to the problem, as Christian theologians understood it; and so the word itself gives us a direction in which to go to understand the character of the problem. 'Atonement' is a word that was devised to express the idea that the *at onement* is a making one of things that were previously not at one, namely, God and human beings. So if the *at onement* is the solution to a problem, then, it seems, the problem should be thought of as the absence of unity or oneness between God and human beings.[24]

In subsequent chapters, I will say a great deal more about the notion of unity or oneness between God and human beings, not only its nature but also the means by which it is achieved. Here I want to call attention only to the absence of such unity and the source of that absence, as the Christian tradition came to see the issue.

As Augustine and the tradition after him understand this absence of unity, it is a function of the human proneness to wrongdoing or sin,[25] where sin is understood as action which is morally wrong and contrary to a perfectly good God.[26] (Since this is an exercise in philosophical theology, which assumes Christian doctrine as data, I will use 'moral wrongdoing' and 'sin' as roughly interchangeable in what follows.) In Chapters 2 and 3, I will examine in more detail the nature of moral wrongdoing and such related topics as guilt, shame, justice, and love. For now, however, to understand the Christian tradition on this score it is enough to take sin as something that is contrary to the will (or to the will and the nature) of a perfectly good God[27] in virtue of being morally wrong—where by 'morally wrong' I mean something like undermining or destroying some goodness in the world without suitable justification for doing so, rather than something like the violation of a Kantian duty.[28]

Undoubtedly, human beings have a tendency to moral wrongdoing. The traditional Christian account of the *at onement* includes the view that there is an absence of unity or closeness between God and human beings because of this tendency on the part of post-Fall human beings.

Here it is necessary to say just one brief word about the qualification 'post-Fall.' It is part of orthodox Christian doctrine that the character of human beings which impedes closeness between God and human beings was not in human nature as God created it but instead has resulted from the events traditionally called 'the Fall', however those events are to be understood. Sorting out what the Fall is supposed to be and coming to grips with the claim that God is not responsible for post-Fall human nature is important for some projects;[29] but it is not important for my project in this book. Here these theological claims will just have to be added to the background worldview taken for granted, in the interest of concentrating on the subject of this book, which is the doctrine of the *at onement*.[30]

Whatever exactly unity or closeness between persons is, it will be at least in part a function of harmony between them. A person who does something that is contrary to the will or the will and the nature of a perfectly good God thereby undermines harmony between himself and God. Since doing something sinful is going contrary to God's will or God's will and nature, it is clear that sin introduces distance between human beings and a perfectly good God.

For Augustine and the orthodox Christian tradition after him, the source of sin lies in the will.[31] Without doubt, the impairment in the will that is sin is correlated also with impairments in intellect.[32] But, as Augustine and the subsequent tradition tend to see it, the foundational defect is nonetheless in the will. On views such as Augustine's, the proneness in the will to sin is the heart of the problem to which the *at onement* is the solution. All the other impairments that need remedy in a full solution to the problem of human sinfulness have their source in the will's proneness to wrongdoing, in the will's internal fragmentation and its intractability to itself. In what follows, I will assume that this view is standard for orthodox interpretations of the doctrine of the *at onement*, and I will take it for granted in subsequent chapters.

THE ELEMENTS OF THE PROBLEM

So understood, the problem to which the *at onement* is the solution has multiple components, and they need correspondingly different remedies in any solution to the problem that is to be successful.

In the first place, there is the very proneness to sin itself. While this defect in the will remains in a person, it includes present dispositions to sin. These themselves have something sinful about them,[33] and they also make a person liable to sinful acts in the future.

That this is so, and widely known to be so, undermines community and impedes closeness among human persons. Many laws, customs, and manners are designed to protect each person against the others, because each person knows that any of the others is capable of great evils, of betraying trust, of doing harm to the vulnerable, of engaging in injustice towards the powerless, even of things as terrible as abusing a child.

In fact, the defect in the will not only makes it difficult for a person to live with others, but it also makes it difficult for him to live with himself. One can distrust oneself as well as others, and such distrust is an additional obstacle to human closeness with other persons. One source of a person's insecurity in relationships with other persons is the fear on his part that if others really knew him, it would be reasonable for them to want to reject him.

If fear and insecurity get the upper hand in a psyche, they can have the added disadvantage of producing greater or lesser degrees of self-deception; a person can shield himself from things about himself he is unwilling or unable to face, with the result that he becomes seriously self-deceived about himself.[34] And, of course, suppressing parts of one's personality or hiding oneself from oneself in self-deception only increases distance from other persons. One is then alienated both from oneself and from others.

It is not hard then to understand why people in the post-Fall human condition would be prone to anxiety or depression.[35]

The post-Fall human condition is therefore a serious obstacle to flourishing, in one's own life and in one's relations to other persons. And, of course, for all these same reasons, the human proneness to moral wrongdoing is also a major source of distance from God. The post-Fall human condition that wards off closeness between human persons will ward off closeness between a human person and God, too.[36] I do not mean that a perfectly good God turns his back on human beings in consequence of their sinfulness. As I argue in Chapter 3, part of what it is for God to be perfectly good is for God always to desire union with human beings. But union is reciprocal, and it requires mutual closeness. Insofar as a human person wards off closeness with others, he also wards off union with God.

In addition to the human proneness to sin, there is also the fact that sinful human dispositions are invariably actualized, sooner or later; with the theological exception of the incarnate Christ (and Mary, for some in the history of the Catholic tradition[37]), the history of the world records no totally sinless adult human person. Every human person past the age of reason, whenever that might be, can look forward to a future in which he engages in moral wrongdoing, in one way or another, at one time or another.

These difficulties constitute the first component in the problem of the post-Fall human proneness to moral wrongdoing to which I want to call attention. We can think of it as the forward-looking component of the problem whose source is the defect in the human will. Its effects are felt in the present as destructive in the future of human flourishing and closeness with other persons, including God.[38]

Someone might object that this component of the problem of sin is not remedied by the *at onement* because, as the objector sees it, the *at onement* is a remedy only for past sin. But this objection cannot be right. No human being who has dispositions to sin can be completely united with a perfectly good God, because the will of such a human being, at least in its dispositions, is at odds with the will of God.[39] So until the disposition to sin is removed from a human person, that person is not saved from the living death of life apart from God. If the *at onement* does not provide this salvation, then something else must. And what would it be? Furthermore, even if that question had a ready answer, the answer would point to something that was a savior of human beings but was not Christ. And now we have a theological *reductio* of the objection. On the doctrine of the *at onement*, Christ is the Messiah, the one who saves human beings from sin and everlasting distance from God; and there is no other. So, whatever else it does, the *at onement* must also be the remedy for the forward-looking component of the problem of sin.

Of course, there is obviously also a component to the problem of human sinfulness that does have to do with the past. On Christian doctrine, with the exception of the incarnate Christ,[40] every human person who does not die before the age of reason is not only prone to moral wrongdoing but has also actually done morally wrong actions of some sort.[41] Every such person can look back to a past in which he has done things that go contrary to God's will and nature. The result is that every human person past the age of reason suffers from guilt with regard to at least some past actions. I do not mean that every person past the age of reason suffers from feelings of guilt. That is no doubt true, but it is not my point here. The point is that every person past the age of reason is in fact guilty, whether he feels it or not, because his life history includes his having done morally wrong actions of some sort.

Analogous things can be said about shame. No one doubts that guilt and shame are distinct, though the nature of the distinction can be difficult to spell out. In Chapter 2, I will have more to say about both shame and guilt. But for now it is enough to notice that they are both concomitants of past moral wrongdoing. And, in fact, shame is more intractable than guilt. We are accustomed to think of the antidote to guilt as repentance (or perhaps repentance and making amends) on the part of the guilty person, and forgiveness on the part of the relevant others.[42] Shame, however, is a different matter; and a remedy for it seems much harder to come by than a remedy for guilt.

Furthermore, unlike guilt, shame can have more sources than a person's own wrongdoing, as I will explain in more detail in Chapter 2. For example, shame can have its source in a person's being victimized by someone else's wrongdoing. But if the *at onement* is a full solution to the problem of human sinfulness, then it will need to address all the varieties of shame too.

So, as this discussion makes manifest, the problem of human wrongdoing is both forward-looking and backward-looking; and it includes three elements:

(1) occurrent dispositions to moral wrongdoing, with their liability to future morally wrong acts,

and past morally wrong acts with their consequent

(2) guilt, both in (a) its impairments in the psyche of the wrongdoer and (b) the ill-effects of the wrongdoing in the world,

and

(3) shame.

If the *at onement* is a solution to the problems brought about by moral wrongdoing which result in distance between God and human persons, then these are the elements of the problem that the *at onement* should somehow remedy if it is to be a successful solution.

KINDS OF INTERPRETATIONS OF THE DOCTRINE OF THE *AT ONEMENT*

The history of interpretation of the doctrine of the *at onement* is marked by various attempts to explain how the passion and death of Christ are a successful solution to the problem of the post-Fall human condition and its tendency to moral wrongdoing. These interpretations can be conveniently grouped into three main kinds, depending on their theories about the obstacles to a solution of the problem, that is, about what it is which makes the problem of human sinfulness hard to solve.[43]

One of these kinds, popular in the Patristic period but more neglected since then, locates the main obstacle to a solution of the problem in the power of Satan. For ease of reference, I will call this view of the doctrine of the *at onement* just 'the Patristic interpretation', although there is in fact considerable variation among Patristic authors as regards the formulation of this kind of interpretation of the doctrine, and not all Patristic authors adopt this view.[44] As the Patristic interpretation focused on Satan is generally understood, it sees Satan as having a hold over human beings because of the human proneness to sin. Before the passion and death of Christ, human sinfulness put human beings in the control of Satan, who held sway over them in some morally or quasi-legally appropriate way, that is, with some justice or some, as it were, legal rights. By trying to extend his control over human beings to Christ in his passion and death, Satan somehow lost whatever justice or quasi-legal rights he had with regard to his domination of human beings. In consequence, through the effects of Christ's passion and death on the reign of Satan, human beings were redeemed from slavery to Satan.[45] By this means, on the Patristic interpretation, the *at onement* was the solution to the problem of sin.

This kind of interpretation of the doctrine of the *at onement* has been the recipient of highly unfavorable comment, not only by contemporary theologians but also by Christian philosophers and theologians in the history of the tradition. But I myself do not think it is sensible just to consign it to the rubbish bin of history. It seems to me implausible that so many excellent minds in the Patristic period would have found acceptable a theory that seems, in the form presented above, so obviously defective. To me, it seems more likely that this widely accepted summary of the Patristic interpretation focused on Satan is inaccurate than that this interpretation is as hopelessly foolish as the summary above apparently shows it to be. In addition, this interpretation sees the *at onement* as a cosmic drama, involving not only the whole human race but all creation and all intelligent creatures in it. This focus on the *at onement* as central to the whole story of creation is not shared by other, later interpretations, which may have lost something of explanatory power in omitting it.[46]

Nonetheless, whatever the merits of this kind of interpretation may be, even at best it is hard to see it as a full or complete interpretation of the doctrine of the *at onement*, if the problem the *at onement* is meant to solve is the problem of human sinfulness. How could an interpretation of this Patristic kind focused on Satan explain the removal of either guilt or shame, for example? Furthermore, at least from the time of Anselm onwards,[47] two other kinds of interpretation have eclipsed this Patristic interpretation.[48] So, although some scholars are interested in reinvigorating it now,[49] nonetheless, historically considered, this Patristic kind of interpretation has not won wide support for a long time. For these reasons, then, I will set aside further consideration of the Patristic kind of interpretation that understands the *at onement* as a victory over Satan. It may be that the Patristic interpretation is deep and wise and helpful, but trying to discover the hermeneutical key that shows it in that light is much too big a task to be attempted in passing in this book.

From Anselm's time onwards, the two main kinds of interpretation of the doctrine discussed by philosophers and theologians are also conveniently characterized by what they see as the main obstacle to the solution for the human proneness to moral wrongdoing. The first of these kinds of interpretation locates this obstacle in something in God, and the second locates it in something in human beings. Someone might suppose, naturally enough, that these two differing kinds of interpretation are the Catholic and the Protestant kinds, respectively; but this would be a mistaken supposition. There are Catholic interpretations to be found in both the differing kinds. It is less easy to say whether Protestant interpretations come in both kinds as well;[50] but that is at least in part because it is not always easy to interpret the details of the major Protestant interpretations.[51]

Still, it is not hard to see the interpretations of the *at onement* given by Anselm, Luther, and Calvin as falling largely or entirely into the same kind of interpretation. Without doubt, their interpretations differ in ways that are philosophically and theologically significant; but they share certain basic features that ally them. For ease of reference, I will call this kind of interpretation 'the Anselmian kind.' On the theories of the Anselmian kind of interpretation, the chief obstacle to the remedy for human sin lies in something about God.[52] The other kind of interpretation can be suitably represented by the interpretation given by Aquinas.[53] This second kind of interpretation, which for ease of reference I will call 'the Thomistic kind', supposes that the main obstacle to the remedy for human sin lies in human beings themselves.

In this chapter, I will just sketch the lineaments of these two kinds of interpretations and the difficulties attending each of them. In Chapter 3, I will look in more detail at the Anselmian kind. The Thomistic kind will underlie the subsequent chapters.

THE ANSELMIAN KIND OF INTERPRETATION OF THE DOCTRINE OF THE *AT ONEMENT*

Interpretations of the doctrine of the *at onement* suitably grouped into the Anselmian kind locate the main obstacle to a solution to the problem of human sinfulness in God's justice or God's honor or some similar divine attribute. As the proponents of interpretations of the Anselmian kind see it, in consequence of their post-Fall sinfulness, human beings have violated God's righteous commands, or otherwise acted contrary to God's justice or God's honor, and so have offended God. This offense against God generates something like a moral debt or liability to penalty, and that debt or penalty is so enormous that human beings by themselves can never repay it or satisfy it. Although God has the power to cancel the debt or abrogate the penalty, in some sense of 'power', God is nonetheless unable to do so. That is because it would be a violation of God's justice to cancel a moral debt or abrogate a penalty, or it would be in some other way incompatible with God's goodness, or it would be a blot on God's honor, or God would not be taking human sin seriously enough if God simply canceled the debt,[54] or something else along these lines. Instead, God's justice or honor or some other divine attribute requires that the full debt owed or penalty incurred be paid. Therefore, God cannot simply forego imposing the requisite penalty or extracting the debt owed. Instead, because of the relevant divine attributes, God must require the payment of the debt or impose the just punishment for human sin in order to be able to forgive human beings and accept reconciliation with them.[55]

In his influential treatise on the doctrine of the *at onement, Cur Deus homo*, which gives us the classic source for this kind of interpretation, Anselm says,

> you must hold with the utmost certainty that without recompense—that is, without a spontaneous payment of the debt—God cannot leave sin unpunished and a sinner cannot attain happiness ... Someone who does not pay [the debt] owed says 'forgive' in vain ... [56]

Interpretations of the doctrine of the *at onement* of the Anselmian kind consequently tend to emphasize the passion and death of Christ as paying the penalty for human beings, or serving to repay the moral debt for human beings, or constituting a penance for human sin, or something else along these lines.[57] On interpretations of this kind, God is not only perfectly just but also infinitely merciful; and so he brings it about that he himself endures the human penalty, or pays the human debt in full, or makes the requisite penance, by assuming human nature as the incarnate Christ and in that nature enduring the penalty or paying the debt or providing the penance which would otherwise have had to be imposed on or exacted from human beings. And then, because the incarnate Christ has endured in full the penalty or paid in full the debt or provided in full the penance owed by human beings, God forgives or pardons human beings their sins and accepts reconciliation with them. By this means, through God's mercy exercised in Christ's passion and death, human beings are saved from their sins.

Anselm sums up this kind of view by saying,

> [human salvation] could not have been brought about unless man repaid what he owed to God. This debt was so large that, although no one but man owed it, only God was capable of repaying it, assuming that there should be a man identical with God.... [T]he life of this man is so sublime and so precious that it can suffice to repay the debt owed for the sins of the whole world, and infinitely more besides.[58]

THE THOMISTIC KIND OF INTERPRETATION OF THE DOCTRINE OF THE *AT ONEMENT*

By contrast, interpretations suitably grouped into the Thomistic kind typically locate the obstacle to a remedy for human sinfulness in human beings themselves. For Aquinas, the chief obstacle to human salvation is that a human will does not will the good or even want to will the good.[59] By the objective, non-relativized standards of God, every human being (except Christ) has a will infected with the radical human tendency toward moral wrong.[60] So human beings do not will what God wills, and the result is distance between human beings and God.

On the interpretation of the *at onement* that Aquinas inherits and develops,[61] the solution to the problem of human sinfulness, so understood, consists in the paired processes of justification and sanctification. On Aquinas's view, without violating human free will, God's operative grace produces in a human person a will for a will that wills the good; and God's cooperative grace works with that partially healed human will to increase in it the strength for willing the good.[62]

For Aquinas, Christ's passion and death produced many good effects for human beings. But the main one is that of providing the grace that heals the defect in the human will through the processes of justification and sanctification. By his passion and death, Christ provided this healing grace to human beings who are united to him in faith and love. So, for example, Aquinas says,

> grace was bestowed upon Christ, not only as an individual, but inasmuch as he is the head of the Church, so that it might overflow into his members; and therefore Christ's works are referred to himself and to his members...Consequently, Christ by his passion merited salvation, not only for himself, but likewise for all his members.[63]

On the kind of interpretation represented by Aquinas's account, then, the passion and death of Christ are a solution to the problem of human sinfulness because they are responsible for the grace that heals the human will.

PROBLEMS WITH INTERPRETATIONS OF THE ANSELMIAN KIND

In my view, interpretations of both the Anselmian and the Thomistic kind present perplexities and concerns; and, at best, they also seem incomplete as solutions to the problem of human sin.

Consider, to begin with, interpretations of the Anselmian kind. By now, there is a large literature raising objections against one or another variant of this kind of interpretation of the doctrine of the *at onement*. In the short summary that follows here, I am only sketching some of the most important of these objections. There is also a large literature attempting to address these objections, which I am not summarizing here. In this introductory chapter, I want only to gesture towards these widely known complaints against the Anselmian kind. In Chapter 3, I will focus in detail on what seems to me the fatal and unfixable flaw in all interpretations suitably grouped into the Anselmian kind.

So, first, there are problems internal to interpretations grouped into the Anselmian kind. To start with one of the obvious ones, contrary to what interpretations of this kind intend, they do not in fact seem to present God as foregoing anything owed him by human beings or omitting any of the punishment deserved by human beings.[64] On interpretations of the Anselmian kind, God exacts every bit of what is owed or visits the whole punishment deserved; he allows none of the debt to go unpaid or the guilt to be unpunished. It is true that what is owed or deserved is visited on the incarnate Deity; but what this element in the Anselmian kind of interpretation shows is only that God himself has arranged for the debt to be paid in full or the full penalty to be borne, not that God has agreed to overlook or forego any part of it. There may be something specially benevolent in God's paying to himself what is owed to him or bearing himself deserved human punishment, but it remains the case that no part of what is owed is left unpaid or unpunished.

Furthermore, although interpretations of the Anselmian kind mean to emphasize God's justice or goodness, the account they give of the way in which the penance due or the debt owed or the penalty deserved is paid seems actually to rest on a denial of justice. On the Anselmian kind of interpretation, it is a violation of God's goodness or justice or honor not to punish the sins of a human person guilty of those sins or not to exact the payment of a debt owed to God by sinful human beings or not to insist on the penance due God from human beings. But, according to interpretations of the Anselmian kind, what God does to act compatibly with his goodness or justice is in fact to fail to punish the guilty or to exact the payment of the debt or the penance from those who owe it since sinful human beings do not get the punishment they deserve or pay the debt or penance they owe. Worse yet, instead of punishing the guilty or exacting payment or penance from the sinful who owe it, God visits their merited punishment on the innocent or exacts the payment of their moral debt or penance from someone who does not owe it. It seems, in fact, that the most obvious divine attribute operative in the *at onement* on such interpretations of the doctrine is *not* God's goodness or justice. How is justice or goodness served by punishing a completely innocent person or exacting from him what he does not owe? And if God could after all forego punishing the guilty or forego getting the sinful to pay what they owe, contrary to what such interpretations in theory insist on, then why did God not simply do so? What justice or goodness is served by God's inflicting someone else's deserved suffering on an innocent person who does not deserve it or exacting payment of a moral debt from a person who does not owe it?[65]

The variation on the Anselmian interpretation which claims that Christ paid the full penalty for all human sins has an additional disadvantage in this regard. On orthodox theological doctrine, the penalty for sin is damnation, permanent absence of union with God. And yet it is not the case on any version of the Anselmian interpretation, even Calvin's,[66] that Christ suffered permanent absence of union with God, so that this variation on the Anselmian interpretation has to construct some equivalence to human damnation that Christ does undergo.

Then there is the problem of application. Even on the Anselmian kind of interpretation, a human being needs to do something to apply the benefits of the *at onement* to himself. He needs to have faith, or appropriate Christ's payment of the debt to himself in some other way. But why? On most (though not all) interpretations suitably grouped into the Anselmian kind, Christ has taken on the penalty or paid the moral debt or penance in full for all human beings.[67] But if Christ has completely taken on the penalty or completely paid the debt or penance for everyone, then it is not clear why anything more would be needed from anyone else. On the Anselmian kind of interpretation, it is something about God that is the obstacle to human salvation from sin; but God's justice or goodness or honor are satisfied completely by Christ's atoning work. If so, however, then no human beings owe anything further to satisfy God. Why then does any human person have to do anything more? And why are there any human beings who are not saved?

Secondly, in addition to these difficulties internal to such Anselmian interpretations, there are also external difficulties. That is because it is not clear how, on interpretations of the Anselmian kind, the passion and death of Christ could constitute a full remedy of the problem to which the *at onement* is meant to be the solution. Even if, contrary to the objections I have just raised, this kind of interpretation succeeds in explaining how God does actually forego the punishment or debt or penance incurred by human sin, how God's goodness or justice is preserved, and how the need for the application of Christ's work is to be explained, it seems that at least the forward-looking problem of human sin remains. On the Anselmian kind of interpretation, nothing about the passion and death of Christ alters the human proneness to sin. Even if, on this kind of interpretation, the *at onement* is efficacious to remove the penalty or debt a human being incurs in sinning, the human proclivity to sin is not removed just by paying the debt or penalty for past sin. The forward-looking problem of human sinfulness is consequently not solved—or, more accurately, not even addressed—by the Anselmian kind of interpretation.

As far as that goes, it seems that not even all the backward-looking problem is solved. In addition to other sources of shame, past sin leaves a human person with shame over what he now is, namely, a person who has done such things. But having an innocent person suffer the penalty or pay the debt incurred by one's own sin does not take away that shame. If anything, it seems to add to it. There is something painfully shaming about being responsible for the serious suffering of an innocent person, even if that suffering was voluntarily undertaken on one's behalf. In George Eliot's *Middlemarch*, when Fred Vincy is stricken with guilt and shame over his inability to pay the debts he incurred through profligate gambling, part of what makes the shame worse for him is that, at great cost to himself, his friend Caleb Garth pays part of that debt for him. So, on the Anselmian interpretation of *at onement*, shame seems to remain even after Christ's *at onement*.

In fact, it seems that even guilt remains. A person's guilt makes it the case that others would be warranted in desiring something from the wrongdoer, some punishment or some making amends in the form of satisfaction. But it seems that if Christ has given to God what is owed to God for all human sin, then Christ's doing so should be sufficient to remove a person's guilt. But it seems that even if Christ's *at onement* has paid the debt for human sin to God, others might still be warranted in requiring that the wrongdoer undergo punishment or make satisfaction. For example, imagine Franz Stangl, the commandant of Treblinka, in the period after the end of the war but before he was captured by the Allies and brought to trial. Suppose that during that period Stangl came or returned to Christianity and that he accepted Christ as his savior. On the Anselmian kind of interpretation of the doctrine of the *at onement*, Stangl's guilt is then removed and his debt to God has been paid by Christ. Nonetheless, is there anything about this supposed state of affairs that keeps others from a warranted belief that Stangl is guilty of crimes and a warranted desire that Stangl be punished? Even if Christ paid the penalty or the debt owed to God for Stangl's sin, as the Anselmian kind of interpretation maintains, it seems intuitively clear that the prison term Stangl was given was warranted as punishment. But if Stangl had no more guilt in consequence of the fact that Christ paid the penalty or debt for all human sin, then we are left with the counter-intuitive conclusion that Stangl's punishment was unwarranted[68] or that the penalty for Stangl's sins was paid twice.

In addition, there is also the issue of the suffering of the victims of human wrongdoing. Nothing in the Anselmian interpretation addresses this component of the problem of guilt either. Those who suffered as a result of Stangl's wrongdoing, for example, do not have their suffering addressed by Christ's paying to God the debt owed by Stangl or undergoing the penalty due to Stangl. How does Christ's *at onement* make amends to them for their suffering? And if Christ's *at onement* does not make amends to Stangl's victims for what Stangl did or does not defeat the evil Stangl committed, then even a converted and repentant Stangl could not suppose that Christ's taking on his punishment could wipe out his guilt. Nothing about God's imposing on Christ the punishment due for Stangl's wrongdoing takes away the suffering of Stangl's victims, does it? And insofar as the suffering of the victims remains, why would Stangl's guilt for that suffering not also remain? Even if Stangl believed that Christ endured the punishment deserved by Stangl, Stangl would still have to live with the knowledge of the horrors he had perpetrated. Or think about the point this way. How would Stangl's sense of responsibility for that suffering be compatible with his living blissfully in heaven?

It is hard to see, then, in what sense, on the Anselmian interpretation, the *at onement* is a complete solution even for guilt, to say nothing of shame. In later chapters, I will return to this problem to examine it in greater detail. For now, what is important to notice is that there are problems for the Anselmian kind of interpretation as regards even the backward-looking problem that it seems best suited to address.

PROBLEMS WITH INTERPRETATIONS
OF THE THOMISTIC KIND

The Thomistic kind of interpretation has the *comparative* advantage of providing some help with both the forward-looking and the backward-looking problems of human sin.[69] The most obvious difficulty for the Thomistic interpretation is to show any connection between its solution to the problem of sin, on the one hand, and the passion and death of Christ, on the other.

We can begin with the forward-looking problem of sin, on the Thomistic interpretation. The operative and cooperative grace of God received in the paired processes of justification and sanctification is the means by which the defect in the human will is remedied. In Chapter 7, I will describe Aquinas's understanding of these processes in detail. For purposes of this introduction, a very short summary will suffice.

On Aquinas's view, one kind of grace that God bestows on a human will is the grace God gives to strengthen a human person's will for added power to will some particular good in response to that person's higher-order desires that God do so. In Aquinas's terminology, this is cooperative grace, because in giving it God is cooperating with a person's own higher-order desires. Suppose, for example, that Paula wants to become a vegetarian but finds it very difficult to give up meat. She finds eating meat morally objectionable, and so she has a higher-order desire for a will that wills not to eat meat; she has corresponding first-order desires not to eat meat, too. But because she is habituated to eating meat, she also has first-order desires to eat meat; and those are the desires on which she often enough acts, to her own moral consternation. If in this condition Paula asks God for help, then, on Aquinas's view, God will cooperate with Paula's will[70] so that Paula has the strength of will to will the good she herself wants to will, namely, not eating meat.[71]

The process in which God cooperates with a human person's higher-order desires for a will that wills one or another particular good is the process of sanctification.[72] If only it is not interrupted but continues to its final conclusion, this process of moral improvement will eventually culminate in a state of complete moral goodness in a person.[73]

The process of sanctification not only involves a higher-order desire for a will that wills some particular good thing, but it also presupposes a more general higher-order desire as well. That is because a person in the process of sanctification must have a higher-order desire for a will that wills to will the good. So, in the process of sanctification, all the more localized higher-order desires of the person being sanctified are predicated on an all-encompassing or global second-order will for a will that wills the good.[74]

The generation of this global second-order act of will is the process of justification,[75] which is the technical theological term for moral and spiritual[76] regeneration.[77] On Aquinas's view, this second-order act of will is the volitional component of faith.[78] It is a free act of the will in which a person hates his own moral wrong and longs for God's goodness.[79] Grace brings about this act of will in a person also, but not in response to a higher-order act of will on his part.[80] The grace in question is therefore not cooperative grace but rather operative grace. Nonetheless, like cooperative grace, operative grace is responsive to states of a human person's will; and its operation on a human will is compatible with the libertarian freedom of that human will.[81]

The production by operative grace of the second-order act of will of faith in the process of justification is the beginning of the spiritual and moral change that is completed, at the end of the process of sanctification, by cooperative grace. By grace, through these processes, over time, the human propensity to moral wrong is remedied. And so there is a solution to the forward-looking problem of human sin.

As for the part of the backward-looking problem of sin involving guilt, Aquinas supposes that God's justice does not require that any debt or penalty owed to God be paid or any punishment be imposed. Aquinas says,

> if [God] had willed to free [human beings] from sin without any satisfaction, he would not have acted against justice.... [I]f God remits sin, which has the formality of fault in that it is committed against himself, he wrongs no one: just as anyone else who, without satisfaction, overlooks an offense against himself acts mercifully and not unjustly. And so David said when he sought mercy: *Against thee only have I sinned* (Ps. 1:6), as if to say: *[You can] remit [my sins] for me without injustice.*[82]

With this disclaimer on Aquinas's part, it seems that the bestowal of grace can constitute a full remedy for guilt. (It is important, however, to notice what is often missed in citations of this text, namely, that Aquinas is here making two different claims: first, that satisfaction is not necessary for God's forgiveness, and, second, that satisfaction is not necessary for saving human beings from sin. I will return to the distinction between these two claims later in this book.)

Insofar as a person has undergone the moral and spiritual regeneration of justification, he is not the person he used to be. There is a sense, then, in which he is now a new person.[83] The states of will and intellect in a justified person are different from those he had before. And so the reactive attitudes suitable towards him when he was his former self are not appropriate with regard to his regenerated self. At the Nuremberg trials, Goering was defiant, but Speer convinced many people that he was repentant;[84] and there was a corresponding difference in the reactive attitudes among the Allies to these two men in consequence. Speer was spared a great deal of the contempt and vituperation directed at Goering.[85]

Furthermore, a person in the process of sanctification is someone who has a global second-order will for a good will and whose first-order will is also growing in its willing of particular goods. A person in this condition who has done serious wrong will want himself to try to make it good. He will consequently not reject what would otherwise count as punishment for him. Rather, he will do what he can to rectify his wrong himself, and he will want to cooperate with others in the restoration of justice where his own past wrong is concerned. In his guise as a repentant Nazi, Speer was concerned to do what he could to make amends for his participation in the Nazi government. He cooperated with his captors and accepted willingly his incarceration; when it ended, he devoted a large part of his writing and lecturing to revealing the evils of the Nazi regime and his own acts in it.[86]

It seems then that, on the Thomistic kind of interpretation, both elements of the backward-looking problem of guilt have a solution.[87]

For similar reasons, the backward-looking problem of shame also seems to have a remedy. A person's shame attaches to the acts he did in his old self, as the person he used to be before he was healed by grace. And so, although he recognizes that he was the person who did those acts, it is also true that he no longer identifies with that person. To this extent, it seems that the shame of his past actions no longer attaches to him as the new self that he is.[88]

By grace, then, in the processes of justification and sanctification, both the backward-looking problem and the forward-looking problem of sin seem to have been remedied. (I have been careful to hedge this claim and the related ones above, however, because there are complications in this connection that will need to be addressed in later chapters.)

The Thomistic kind of interpretation therefore has this apparent advantage over the Anselmian kind, in that it seems to include a remedy for all the problems of sin. Its main disadvantage, which is considerable, is that, unlike the Anselmian kind of interpretation, it seems unable to connect this remedy with the passion and death of Christ. On the Thomistic interpretation, what is the connection between the giving of grace and Christ's passion and death supposed to be?

It is true that Aquinas thinks Christ merits grace for human beings. But, as the quotation from Aquinas cited above makes clear, Aquinas does not think that God's forgiveness of human persons or God's saving human beings from sin requires the passion and death of Christ or any kind of payment of the debt or penalty incurred by human sin. On the contrary, Aquinas says repeatedly that God could have saved human beings from sin without Christ's passion and death. So, for example, in addition to the text cited above, Aquinas says,

> simpliciter and absolutely, it was possible for God to deliver human beings otherwise than by the passion of Christ, because 'nothing is impossible with God' (Luke 1:37).[89]

But if God is able and willing to forgive human beings or deliver them from their sinfulness without the payment of any debt or penalty, and if the problem of human sinfulness is solved by God's giving of grace, then it is hard to see what relation there is between Christ's passion and death and the giving of grace. At any rate, it seems clear that, on the Thomistic account, Christ's atoning work is not necessary for the giving of grace since Aquinas explicitly claims that God could have saved human beings and remitted their sins without Christ's passion and death.

In fact, it is difficult to avoid the conclusion that, on the Thomistic kind of interpretation, Christ's passion and death are irrelevant to the remedy for the problem of human sinfulness. On the face of it, on Aquinas's account, God has the power to give the grace that heals the human proneness to sin. And it is hard to see any reason for supposing that God would not be willing to give this grace other than the sorts of considerations of God's goodness, justice, or honor given in interpretations of the Anselmian kind. But this kind of reason is rejected in interpretations of the Thomistic kind, as the quotations from Aquinas's text given above show. And so it seems as if, on the Thomistic kind of interpretation, Christ's passion and death are gratuitous to the giving of grace.

Furthermore, if Christ's passion and death are gratuitous, then it is unjust on God's part to require that Christ suffer and die, since it is unjust to require an innocent person to suffer for a good that could be gotten just as well without the suffering.

Worse yet, on the Thomistic kind of interpretation, Christ's passion and death seem not only gratuitous but in fact inefficacious. On the Thomistic kind of interpretation, not only could the good in question apparently be gotten without Christ's passion and death, but it seems that in fact it could not be gotten *with* Christ's passion and death. That is, Christ's passion and death seem to have no intrinsic role in the production of this good.

To see this point, let it be the case for the sake of argument that, on the Thomistic kind of interpretation, for some reason God cannot or will not give grace to human beings without Christ's passion and death. Still, what is there about Christ's passion and death themselves that are connected to God's giving of this grace? If Christ's passion and death are to be efficacious as the remedy for human sin, it seems that there ought to be something about the passion and death of Christ itself that is involved in the remedy; that is, Christ's passion and death ought to be directly or else somehow crucially instrumental to the giving of grace to human beings. But it is difficult to see what connection there could be, on the Thomistic kind of interpretation, between Christ's suffering and dying and God's giving grace. There is, of course, such a connection on the Anselmian kind of interpretation; but this is a connection that the Thomistic kind of interpretation rejects. For the Thomistic kind of interpretation, it is not the case that a perfectly good God is unable to give grace to human beings without the passion and death of Christ.

So whereas it appears that the Anselmian kind of interpretation gives a central role to Christ's passion and death but fails to connect this role in any full and satisfactory way to the solution for human sin, it appears that the Thomistic kind of interpretation highlights the solution for human sin but fails to connect it in any direct and satisfactory way to Christ's passion and death.

FURTHER PROBLEMS FOR INTERPRETATIONS OF BOTH KINDS

In addition to the problems peculiar to each kind of interpretation, both the Anselmian and the Thomistic kinds of interpretation share vulnerability to further difficulties.

In the first place, there is reason to expect that there would be some connection between the good brought about by the passion and death of Christ, on the one hand, and the good integral to God's reason for allowing the particular suffering of any particular human being, however that reason of God's is explained. That is, there ought to be some connection between the doctrine of the *at onement* and solutions to the problem of evil. Whatever the reason God has for allowing the particular sufferings of a particular person, it seems that her suffering somehow needs to conduce to her ultimate good.[90] But if there is salvation from sin leading to union with God, *that* does seem to be the ultimate good for all human beings. Since what is at issue in both cases is something that is the ultimate good for a human being, or for all human beings, then it seems that there should be some intrinsic connection between the benefits postulated by an interpretation of the doctrine of the *at onement* and the benefits highlighted by a theodicy or defense. The benefit provided for a particular sufferer by means of her suffering ought to have some connection to the good brought about by Christ's passion and death insofar as the benefit either is the ultimate good or something crucially conducive to the ultimate good for the sufferer.

On the Anselmian kind of interpretation, however, the primary good that comes to human beings from Christ's passion and death has to do simply with God's ability to forego punishing human beings for their sins or exacting the moral debt owed for their sins while at the same time preserving his justice (or honor or goodness or similar attribute). But, for this good, Christ's passion and death are sufficient, on the Anselmian kind of interpretations. Given the *at onement*, then, this good is available for every human being whether she suffers or not. Consequently, it is hard to see what connection there could be between the good for human beings provided by Christ's passion and death, on the Anselmian kind of interpretation, and the good (whatever it might be) that comes to a particular person from her suffering. The ultimate good for her, as for all other human beings, is provided completely and solely by the passion and death of Christ and its effects with respect to God.

I do not mean to say that the Anselmian kind of interpretation makes theodicy harder. If Plantinga is right,[91] a theodicy or defense can be constructed out of considerations based on the value of the *at onement* alone, since (as Plantinga argues) the value of the *at onement* is so great that it outweighs any disvalue of sin and suffering. My point here is only that on the Anselmian kind of interpretation, it is hard to see a natural connection between the good brought about by Christ's passion and death and any goods putatively justifying God in allowing the particular suffering of any particular human being.[92] But it seems that, in principle, there ought to be such a connection.

The same sort of difficulty afflicts the Thomistic kind of interpretation. On the Thomistic kind, Christ's passion and death are supposed to be somehow connected to the grace that God gives to human beings to remedy the defect of will in them. But if Christ's passion and death, or God's love and goodness in the giving of grace, or some combination of both, are sufficient to provide this grace for human beings, then it is not clear what connection there could be between the good of God's grace, on the one hand, and any goods that might defeat the particular suffering of any particular person. For the Thomistic kind of interpretation, as for the Anselmian, the ultimate good for all human beings is completely provided by Christ's passion and death.

For interpretations of both kinds, then, since Christ's passion and death are sufficient to provide the greatest good for human beings, however that good is understood and whatever the interpretation is of the means to that good which is provided by Christ's passion and death, it is not clear what role is left for human suffering. On each kind of interpretation, the connection, which ought to be apparent, between the *at onement*, on the one hand, and the good available for sufferers through their suffering, on the other, is hard to conceive.

Secondly, interpretations of both kinds were developed on the basis of reflection about the narrative of the passion and death of Christ given by each of the four Gospels and commented on elsewhere in the biblical texts. For that reason, one check on the adequacy of each kind of interpretation is its fit with those biblical texts, and especially the Gospel narratives. But consider just Christ's cry of dereliction from the cross, given in some of those narratives: "My God, my God, why have you forsaken me?"[93] Christian tradition has generally taken Christ's uttering this quotation from Psalm 22 to indicate his own experience of being forsaken by God. It is hard to see, however, that either the Anselmian or the Thomistic kind of interpretation has the resources to explain Christ's having such an experience. And there are analogous problems as regards other parts of the Gospel narratives, such as the narrative of Christ's anguish in the Garden of Gethsemane over his impending death. Neither kind of interpretation seems to have the resources to explain why so many Christian martyrs went to their dreadfully painful deaths with peace and serenity but Christ agonized over his.

With regard to the narrative about the cry of dereliction, interpretations of the Thomistic kind are the most disadvantaged. If the point of Christ's passion and death is God's providing grace that solves the problem of human sinfulness, then what about this process would drive any kind of wedge between Christ and God? In fact, it is part of Aquinas's own interpretation of the passion and death of Christ that even while Christ suffers in his human nature, he is also completely united to God in love even in his human nature.[94]

Interpretations of the Anselmian kind might be thought more promising in this connection, since they present the passion and death of Christ primarily as a propitiation of a perfectly good and just God, offended at human sin. Calvin goes so far as to suppose that, in the process of dying, as part of Christ's taking on the punishment merited by sinful human beings, Christ experiences hell and feels it as warranted for him.[95]

But even interpretations of the Anselmian kind seem hard pressed to explain the cry of dereliction, interpreted as an expression of Christ's abandonment by God, or just as an experience of apparent abandonment. That is because interpretations of the Anselmian kind emphasize both God's justice and Christ's perfect sinlessness. A sinless man might suffer physical pain for the sake of the guilty; he might even experience terrible physical torments of the sort some people assume there is in hell. But how could a sinless man be abandoned by a good and just God? What goodness or justice would there be in God's separating himself from a human person who is himself perfectly good and just? And what would the separation consist in? Separation from God is not a matter of physical distance; it is a matter of opposition in wills. But how could the will of a perfectly good and just God be in opposition to the will of a perfectly good and just human person? Furthermore, if it is not possible for a perfectly good and just God to be separated in will from a perfectly good and just human being, then is it any more possible for a perfectly good and just God to produce a false or illusory experience of such separation in a perfectly good and just human being? Is deception of the innocent possible for a perfectly good God?

So adequacy to the biblical narratives is yet another problem shared by interpretations of both the Anselmian and the Thomistic kinds.

Then there is an oddity about both kinds of interpretation that has to do with the Trinity. In addition to the doctrine of the *at onement*, the doctrine that God is triune is one of the foundational doctrines of Christianity, distinguishing Christianity from the other two Abrahamic religions. For doctrines other than the *at onement* that are also central to Christianity— that God is the creator of the world, for example—the Trinitarian understanding of God is to the fore. God the Father creates through the Word (which is God the Son) in love (which is God the Holy Spirit). But, on either the Anselmian or the Thomistic kind of interpretation of the doctrine of the *at onement*, there are no Trinitarian explanations of the *at onement*; and it is not easy to see how to add a Trinitarian element to either kind of interpretation. Although adherents of both kinds of interpretation typically have things to say about the actions of the Holy Spirit, these actions seem not to have any essential connection with Christ's passion and death on the cross. Although Christ himself claims that without his passion and death the Holy Spirit would not come (John 16:7), neither kind of interpretation has the resources to explain why this should be so. For each kind of interpretation, then, the explanation of *at onement* lacks a central role in Christ's *at onement* for the Holy Spirit; and so the interpretation does not make *at onement* an operation of the whole Trinity.

In addition, there is the problem that, on Christian doctrine and in traditional Christian theology, there are at least some human beings who are saved without their having any knowledge of Christ's passion and death or any conscious willingness to connect to it. Baptized infants are the most notable example of human beings in this class. But so are the so-called anonymous Christians, those people who have never heard of Christ or who take themselves to be adherents to religions other than Christianity but who are nonetheless somehow saved through Christ. Karl Rahner was responsible for making the idea of the anonymous Christian famous, but the idea itself can be found even in the work of Aquinas, who accepts it explicitly.[96] Neither the Anselmian nor the Thomistic kind of interpretation can explain both why the passion and death of Christ are necessary or crucially instrumental to human salvation and yet salvation is possible for people such as baptized infants or anonymous Christians.

Then there is the question of the life of Christ. Both the Thomistic and the Anselmian kinds of interpretation focus on the passion and death of Christ as salvific. But surely the details of the life of Christ have some role to play in salvation.[97] What role this might be is hard to see on either the Thomistic or Anselmian kinds of interpretation. If, for example, Christ had come into the world as an adult, as Adam did in the story of the Garden of Eden, and had immediately endured passion and death, what would be lost in the Anselmian kind of interpretation? *Mutatis mutandis*, analogous questions can be raised as regards the Thomistic kind of interpretation.

No doubt this list of problems could go on a long time, but I want to finish with two that are connected in one way or another to ritual. Biblical texts claim that Christ's passion and death constitute a sacrifice, where the practices of ritual sacrifice and the narratives of sacrifice in the Hebrew Bible constitute a context for the claim.[98] And, in the Gospel narratives, Christ makes a ritual connection between bread and wine, on the one hand, and his body and blood, on the other. (Differing groups of Christians have used different terms for the rite which Christ instituted by this means. For ease of reference, I will simply use the Thomistic term 'Eucharist.') A successful interpretation of the doctrine of the *at onement* ought to be able to illuminate an essential connection between *at onement* as a solution to the problem of human sin and the ritual of sacrifice and the rite of the Eucharist. But neither the Thomistic nor the Anselmian kind of interpretation seems able to provide such a connection either as regards sacrifice or as regards the Eucharist. It is not easy to see, on either kind of interpretation, what role in the remedy for human sin there could be for sacrifice or Eucharist if Christ's passion and death are by themselves sufficient for this remedy.

To begin with sacrifice, the Anselmian kind of interpretation sees Christ as giving for sinful human beings the penalty or the debt or penance that human beings owe God; but neither paying what is owed by another nor enduring the penalty of another is a sacrifice. On the contrary, the special character of sacrifice is not so much as addressed by the Anselmian kind of interpretation. By contrast, Aquinas himself does affirm and discuss Christ's passion and death as a sacrifice. But the Thomistic account gives no help in connecting sacrifice to the giving of grace that results in justification and sanctification.

As far as the Eucharist goes, Aquinas does assign a role to the Eucharist as regards grace; but, just as in the case of grace in general, it is not clear, on the Thomistic kind of interpretation, how the grace given through the Eucharist is related to the salvific effects produced by Christ's passion and death. Is the grace that is somehow connected to Christ's passion and death insufficient, so that it has to be supplemented through the grace produced by the Eucharist? Aquinas himself does not think so, as I will explain in Chapter 9; but then, on this view, it is hard to see what the connection is between the grace of the Eucharist and the grace to which the passion and death of Christ are instrumental.

The Anselmian kind of interpretation is even more disadvantaged here. Given the Anselmian understanding of the *at onement*, it is difficult to see how there could be an essential connection between the salvation of human beings from their sins and the Eucharist. On the contrary, on the Anselmian kind of interpretation, the Eucharist seems to be left adventitious to the story of salvation. The whole work of salvation is done by Christ's satisfying God's justice (or honor or goodness), and any benefits derived from the Eucharist are non-essential in this regard.

A ROADMAP

For these reasons, although there is a great deal to learn from both the Thomistic and the Anselmian kinds of interpretation of the doctrine of the *at onement*, it seems to me there is something missing, at best, or wrong-headed, at worst, about both these kinds of interpretation. In these circumstances, I propose to try rethinking the doctrine. With all respect due to those in the tradition who have thought deeply about the doctrine and with all care to learn from them, I want to try to understand the doctrine afresh. I want to see whether there is an interpretation of the doctrine of Christ's *at onement* that is coherent, morally acceptable, and consistent both with other theological doctrines and with biblical texts relevant to the *at onement*. I will argue that there is.

It is important to reiterate here what this is an argument for. It is not an argument for the truth of the doctrine of the *at onement*. As I hope goes without saying, an argument to that conclusion would be exceedingly difficult to come by. On the other hand, of course, the argument of this book, that the doctrine is coherent, morally acceptable, and consistent with relevant theological claims, is clearly also pertinent to considerations of the truth of the doctrine; and those who antecedently accept the doctrine as true can find help in understanding and defending the doctrine in the considerations of this book.

In the chapters that follow, I will begin my project by sketching the Thomistic moral psychology on which I will rely in the rest of the book. There are other theories of moral psychology that would work as well, but it is necessary to have some account of the moral concepts central to discussions of the doctrine of the *at onement*. And since Aquinas's account is the best I know, and also one that I have discussed and defended elsewhere, I will rely on it in this book. Chapter 2 therefore gives a brief overview of this moral psychology and so constitutes a toolkit for the rest of the book.

Next, I will turn to the idea, common to all Anselmian kinds of interpretation, that Christ's *at onement* is a necessary condition for God's forgiveness and acceptance of reconciliation with sinful human beings. In Chapter 3, I will argue that this idea is itself incompatible with the best account I know of God's love, that given by Aquinas. On Aquinas's account of love, Anselmian kinds of interpretation in fact imply that God is not loving. For that reason, I will argue, without a different and better account of God's love than the Thomistic one—and I do not believe that there is a better one—Anselmian kinds of interpretation should be rejected. Contrary to their advertised intention, they do not work because they are inconsistent with God's love and so also with God's goodness. For this reason, they are unsalvageable. Consequently, after Chapter 3, I will not consider the Anselmian kind of interpretation as a viable contender for an acceptable interpretation of the doctrine of the *at onement*. In my view, the Thomistic kind of interpretation is preferable, and an acceptance of the basic lineaments of the Thomistic kind underlies the rest of the book.

With Chapter 3, the introductory section of this book, Part I, is complete.

In Part II, I begin the constructive side of the project. I propose to approach the first part of the constructive project this way. One can think of Christ's *at onement* as a bridge that spans the gap between the condition in which sinful human beings find themselves, on the one hand, and the desired union with God that the *at onement* is meant to provide, on the other hand. What Christ's life, passion, and death do is to provide that bridge. Understanding the *at onement* therefore requires understanding the nature of the bridge.

To that end, it is important first to look in detail at the end to which the bridge is meant to lead. And so in Part II, I examine the nature of union and the obstacles to union between God and human beings; and I argue that this union consists in a kind of mutual in-ness. In Chapter 4, I consider the part of the union in which God is within the psyche of a human person. In Chapter 5, I turn to the story of Christ's cry of dereliction on the cross; and I argue that this story gives us a way of seeing human psyches as within the human mind God has when God is incarnated in Christ. These two chapters therefore delineate the union between God and human beings that Christ's *at onement* is meant to achieve.

To finish this picture of the end point to which the bridge of Christ's *at onement* leads, it remains to ask what it would be like for a human being in this life to be in such a union with God. In line with traditional terminology, I will call the condition of this-worldly union with God 'life in grace'; and I will call a person in such a condition 'a person in grace.' A person in grace wills what God wills, but it is important to recognize that willing what God wills admits of radically different interpretations. In Chapter 6, I show that one of these interpretations, influential in some parts of Christian tradition and frequently associated with Meister Eckhart, has to be ruled out as incompatible with other elements of the doctrine of the *at onement* and (equally importantly) with the doctrine that God is perfectly loving. In Chapter 7, I turn to Aquinas's alternative interpretation of a life in grace. On Aquinas's view, a person in grace is in intimate personal relationship with God and has God present to her in mutual love. On the Thomistic view, this condition is marked not only by the infused virtues but also by the gifts and fruits of the Holy Spirit and the indwelling Holy Spirit itself. The beginning of the process of acquiring all these virtues, gifts, and fruits is justification; and sanctification is its continuation. For Aquinas, the twinned processes of justification and sanctification are needed even for that union between God and a human person which is possible in this life, as well as for its completion in the afterlife in heaven.

This Thomistic account of a life in grace illuminates the obstacle in the human will to union with God. With the help of this understanding of the obstacle, I turn in Part III to a consideration of the bridge that overcomes the obstacle in the human will and leads to the desired life in grace. This is the *at onement* itself.

In Chapter 8, I consider in detail some of the stories of Christ in the Gospels in order to examine the way in which Christ's life, passion, and death help to remove this obstacle and to make a life in grace possible. In Chapter 9, I consider what is required to maintain a life in grace once it has been initiated. It is one thing for Christ's passion and death to initiate life in grace for a person and another thing for it to help a person to persevere in that life. In Chapter 9, I discuss both suffering and the Eucharist as aids to perseverance. I argue that, in harmony with the account given in Chapter 7, a person's suffering and her participation in the rite of the Eucharist can be understood as means for helping a person to persevere in the union that Christ's *at onement* provides. And so, with Chapter 9, Part III, the constructive side of the project, is complete.

In my view, the interpretation of the doctrine of Christ's *at onement* that emerges from the chapters of Part III satisfies the desiderata for a successful interpretation of the doctrine of the *at onement*, as I have described them in this introductory chapter. What remains, then, for Part IV, the final section of the book, is just to show that this is so. In Chapter 10, I consider the way in which the interpretation of the *at onement* that I have argued for solves the problems of human guilt and shame. And, in Chapter 11, the conclusion, I look briefly at the other desiderata given in this chapter to show that these are also met by the interpretation of *at onement* argued for in the earlier chapters.

As I hope will be clear in what follows, the interpretation of the doctrine of the *at onement* that I argue for in this book accommodates much of what is best in both the Anselmian and the Thomistic kinds of interpretation; but it can also explain what is challenging for them or incomplete and unexplained by them. In light of these conclusions, the value of the *at onement* is then also clear.

2

Guilt, Shame, and Satisfaction

INTRODUCTION

Because there is no explicit creedal formula spelling out the doctrine of the atonement, then, in addition to consistency with other theological doctrines, the main constraints on interpretations of the doctrine come from biblical texts, on the one hand, and moral psychology and ethics, on the other. In Chapter 1, I discussed some issues of methodology regarding the primary biblical texts relevant to the doctrine. In this chapter, I want to say something briefly about some of the relevant moral psychology and ethics.

It is not possible to examine the doctrine of the atonement without relying on some account of ethics and value theory. For the reasons I gave in Chapter 1, the ethics and value theory underlying this book is that of Aquinas.[1] It is an ethics that accepts an objective goodness which is tied ultimately to the nature of God and which is founded on a correlation of being and goodness. In its normative ethics, it is built around the virtues; but it is a decidedly non-Aristotelian virtue ethics, and it privileges relationship and the second-personal among the things it values most.[2] Its most central virtue is love, and all the rest of its normative ethical theory rests on this virtue.

In my view, there is nothing in this ethics and value theory that is incompatible with the particular theological claims separating one group of Christians from another. Clearly, the ethics and value theory brought into this discussion needs to be Christian, and Aquinas's ethics and value theory are as close to generically Christian as is reasonable to expect. It is true that this is a theologically based ethics; but those concerned about its theological basis need not reject it out of hand. It can be transformed largely or entirely into a secular ethics by transposing from second-personal relationship with God and other human beings to second-personal relationship solely with other human beings. For all these reasons, it is suitable to appropriate this part of Aquinas's philosophy in the project of this book.

Tied to this basic virtue ethics and value theory are certain elements of moral psychology that typically play a crucial role in discussions of the doctrine of the atonement.[3] Guilt and shame are key concepts. So is another thing which is even harder to characterize but which is also important in discussions of atonement. Aquinas's expression for this thing is 'a stain on the soul.' The idea of a stain—a kind of morally undesirable residue left by wrongdoing—is connected to still another notion that matters greatly in this context, namely, the notion of satisfaction for moral wrongdoing.

In this chapter, I will give a brief overview of these concepts as I will use them in this book, so that later chapters are not burdened with stray forays into explanations of moral psychology. And because one's moral psychology is at least in part a function of one's philosophical psychology, I include here also a discursus into a helpful part of Thomistic psychology, namely, his theory of agency, though I will keep this discursus to a minimum. In my view, although this theory of agency is helpful, it is not essential to my account. Other theories of agency that can do as well at explaining the relevant phenomena could be substituted for it.

This chapter is thus devoted to providing a small toolkit that will prove to be useful throughout the rest of the book.[4] Because the concepts examined here are crucial for interpretations of the doctrine of the atonement, their analysis also helps to circumscribe the area within which acceptable interpretations can be found.

LOVE

It will be helpful to begin with an account of love, because love is foundational for Aquinas's ethics and grounds the understanding of guilt and shame I adopt.[5] For Aquinas,[6] love requires two interconnected desires:[7]

(1)   the desire for the good of the beloved,[8]

and

(2)   the desire for union with the beloved.[9]

Aquinas recognizes different kinds and different degrees of love between persons.[10] For example, Aquinas thinks that it is possible to desire the good for humanity in general and also to desire some sort of union with all humanity— say, in the shared beatific vision of heaven;[11] and so a person can have an impartial love of all human beings. But Aquinas also supposes that some loves are and ought to be greater than others;[12] a person ought to love all human beings, but not equally. She should love some people more than others in virtue of having certain relationships with them that ought to make her love for them greater than her love for humanity in general. Some relationships make possible a deeper and more intimate union between the persons so related. I will call such relationships 'the offices of love.'[13] The most important office of love is that between a human person and God; and, because of the nature of that office, the love between a human person and God is the greatest of loves possible for a human person.

Certain things are also worth noting with regard to each of the desires of love.

To begin with the second desire, it is worth pointing out here that, whatever exactly the union is which is desired in love, the desire for it is not equivalent to the desire to be in the company of the beloved. Other philosophers have remarked that one can love a person without desiring to be in that person's company,[14] and being in someone's company is obviously not equivalent to being united to her. It is manifestly possible to be in the company of someone when one is alienated from her, rather than united to her. So desiring union with a person might not include a desire to be in that person's company, at least not now, as that person currently is.

With regard to the first desire, the goodness in question is not to be identified with moral goodness only. It is goodness in the broader sense that encompasses the beautiful, the useful, and the pleasant, as well as moral and metaphysical goodness. Furthermore, because Aquinas holds that there is an objective standard of goodness, the measure of value for the goodness at issue in love is also objective.[15] The good of the beloved has to be understood as that which truly is in the interest of the beloved and which truly does conduce to the beloved's flourishing.

What exactly this is depends, of course, on how one understands the objective standard of value.

Aquinas shares with other thinkers in the Christian tradition the conviction that personal relationship is the genus within which the greatest goods for human beings fall.[16] For Aquinas, God is characterized by one mind and will; and so God is a person, in our sense of the word 'person.'[17] A union of love with God is thus a personal relationship, too; and it is the greatest of personal relationships. The greatest good for a human being is to be in a relationship of love in union with God. Furthermore, this greatest good for a human being is also the best condition of a human being.[18] To be united with something is to be made one with it, to one degree or another, since union comes in degrees. To be made one with God, however, is deification,[19] at least in some analogous or extended sense.[20] It is hard to see what could be a greater state for a human person than being made like God. And so full or complete union with God is an intrinsic upper limit on human flourishing.

Furthermore, because the greater the good, the more shareable it is, the greatest of goods for human beings is consequently also the most shareable. On Aquinas's scale of value, then, the greatest good for a human being is more precisely described as the shared union of love among human beings and God. Heaven is this greatest good made permanent and unending. The worst thing for human beings is the permanent absence of such shared union with God.

As is clear from this description of the Thomistic scale of value, it is also part of Aquinas's worldview that a human being's life is divided into two unequal portions, one very little portion before death and another infinitely enduring portion after death. For reasons having to do not with his theology but with his philosophical psychology,[21] Aquinas maintains that the state of a person at the end of the little portion of his life in this world determines his state in the infinitely extended portion of his life after death. That is, on Aquinas's views, the state of a person after bodily death is *not* determined as a sum of merits or demerits in a life, contrary to what so many people imagine Christian doctrine mandates. It is determined more nearly in the way things go when one person proposes marriage to another: everything depends on the *current* condition, the *current* love, of the person to whom the proposal is made.[22] In what follows, I will also presuppose this part of Aquinas's worldview, since it is a standard part of the orthodox theology in which the doctrine of the atonement is embedded.[23]

It is important to see here also that, because of the strong connection Aquinas maintains between God and goodness,[24] anything that contributes to the objective good for a person also brings her closer to God. The beloved's closeness to God and her flourishing as the best person she can be will, therefore, be co-variant. So to desire the good of the beloved, on this standard of goodness, is to desire for the beloved those things that in fact contribute to the beloved's flourishing, and these will also increase the beloved's closeness to God.

On the other hand, although the lover must desire *as good for the beloved* what he wants for the beloved, nothing in this account of love requires that the lover understand that good as something that conduces to the beloved's flourishing or to the beloved's union with God. What the lover desires for the beloved must in fact do so; but the lover need not understand that it does so in order for the lover to desire these things as good for the beloved. A person's desires need not be transparent to him. Nonetheless, because the standard of value is objective, the things that the lover desires as the good of the beloved have to be those that actually do, directly or indirectly, contribute to the beloved's flourishing and nearness to God.

It is easy to become confused here, because there is an ambiguity in the notion of desiring something as someone's good.[25] There is a difference between intrinsic and derived desires. A mother who gives her child a harmful drug under the misimpression that the drug will heal the child has an intrinsic desire for the health of her child and a derived desire to give the child the drug in question, in the belief that the drug will produce health. The desires in question in Aquinas's account of love are intrinsic, not derived, desires. A lover can have the two desires of love with respect to a certain person and yet do harm to that person, provided that what does harm to the beloved is not something for which the lover has an intrinsic desire.

It is also important to see that the two desires of love are not independent of each other but rather interrelated in mutually governing ways. And when the two desires of love appear to conflict, the claim that the ultimate good for human beings is union with God gives a method for harmonizing them. Union with God is shareable, and persons united with God are also united with each other. *Ultimately*, then, the same thing—namely, union with God—constitutes both the final good[26] for each of the persons in a loving relationship and also their deepest union with each other.[27] For these reasons, love is, as it were, a systems-level feature, emerging from the interrelated desires for the good of the beloved and for union with the beloved.[28]

In addition, it should be noted here that the presence of a desire does not imply the absence of the thing desired. The fulfillment of a desire is compatible with the continuance of the desire. When both the desires of love are fulfilled, the lover finds joy in the beloved, but he does not cease desiring what he now has—namely, the good of the beloved and union with her.[29]

Finally, on this account, love is obligatory, in the sense that, for any person, the absence of love is morally blameworthy, and the presence of love is necessary for moral good or excellence.[30]

We can conclude this very brief presentation of Aquinas's account of love by considering the way in which it applies to the special case of God's love of human persons.

On traditional Christian doctrine, God is perfectly loving to all human beings. And so God desires the good of each human person and union with her.[31] But, for God, the two desires of love converge. That is because, as I explained above, the ultimate good of a human person, her ultimate flourishing, just is union with God. So in desiring the good for a human person and union with a human person, God is desiring the same thing, at least where the ultimate good is concerned.

In addition, there is this difference between the love of one human being for another and God's love for a human being. In the case of love between human beings, when one person Paula desires union with another person Jerome, Paula needs to be responsive to Jerome. Suppose, for example, that Jerome is incurably musically illiterate (because of a right-hemisphere stroke, for example), but that Paula is a composer. Then, if Paula understands Jerome's condition, it would be cruel of her, not loving, to insist on trying to share her musical creativity with him. But in God's case things are the other way around. When God loves Jerome, God's love is not responsive to goodness in Jerome. Instead, God's love is the source of whatever goodness or excellence there is in Jerome.

On Aquinas's view and on all resolutely anti-Pelagian views, any goodness whatsoever in creatures is derived from God directly or indirectly. Like many others in this tradition, Aquinas supposes that there is nothing good in any creature, including human persons, which is not in one way or another a gift of

God's, whereby God enables creatures to imitate something in God's nature.[32] On this view, in loving Jerome and desiring the good for Jerome, God is offering goodness to Jerome. If Jerome does not resist God's love, then God's love is productive of goodness in Jerome, not responsive to the goodness Jerome has already produced in himself by himself.

For these reasons, anything good in Jerome and any closeness to God on Jerome's part is brought about in Jerome entirely by God, but it is also true that Jerome is ultimately responsible for whether or not he is in union with God. Even on resolutely anti-Pelagian views, because Jerome can always resist the love of God, God's bringing about goodness in Jerome is responsive to *something* in Jerome. It is always open to Jerome to resist God's love and grace or to cease resisting it; and so, even on anti-Pelagian views, Jerome has alternative possibilities for willing with regard to God's giving him grace.

So, *mutatis mutandis*, Aquinas's account of love applies also to God's love for human beings. Although God's love for human beings is in some respects a special case, nonetheless Aquinas's account of love as consisting in two mutually governing desires, for the good of the beloved and for union with the beloved, holds with regard to God's love, too.

GUILT, SHAME, AND THE DESIRES OF LOVE

In consequence of past sin or moral wrongdoing[33] a person can both be and also feel guilty, but guilt is not the end of the problem as regards past sin. There is also shame,[34] which is also part of the backward-looking component of the problem engendered by human wrongdoing.[35] I do not mean that every person guilty of moral wrongdoing feels shame in consequence of what he has done. No doubt, like felt guilt, felt shame is ubiquitous; but I mean only that in consequence of past sin, a person in fact is shamed, somehow less lovely or less honorable than he might have been and might have hoped to be had he not engaged in wrongdoing.

Shame and guilt are objective; but of course they can also be felt in a subjective way, and the objective and subjective versions can be dissociated. So, for example, a person can be shamed without feeling shamed. Consider, for example, John Newton. When he was a young man, Newton was involved in the slave trade. On three different occasions, he was even the captain of a slave ship; and, on those three ships alone, he was responsible for transporting many Africans. The conditions on the ships were unspeakable. A large percentage of the Africans transported died during the voyage; the suffering of those who survived was heartbreaking. When he became a slave trader, Newton lost much of his honor and loveliness by comparison with decent people. He *was* then shamed, although he himself did not *feel* shamed over his slave-trading until much later in his life, after a religious conversion convicted him of the moral horror of the slave trade. Alternatively, a person can feel shamed when in fact he is not shamed. A person could feel shame over what he takes to be his low scores on a test important to him, when he actually got high scores but the testing company mistakenly sent him someone else's bad results. Analogously, a person can be guilty, even if he does not feel guilty, as Herman Goering was at Nuremberg; and, as everyone has experienced, a person can feel guilty without being guilty.

No one doubts that guilt and shame are distinct, but there is considerable controversy over the nature of the distinction. Elsewhere, I have argued that the difference between shame and guilt can be understood in terms of the two desires of love, on a Thomistic account of love.[36]

A person who *is* shamed and a person who *is* guilty are such that it would be appropriate for others to repudiate both the desires of love with regard to them. But the first desire of love, for the good of the beloved, is central in the case of guilt; and the second desire of love, for union with the beloved, is central in the case of shame. With regard to a person who is guilty, others would be warranted in being angry at him or wanting to punish him or extract satisfaction from him—in other words, to visit on him things that he himself would find not good in some sense or other. With regard to a person who is shamed, others would be warranted (on one scale of value or another) in rejecting not his good but *him*, that is, in putting distance between themselves and him.[37]

Similarly, a person who feels guilty and a person who feels shame each anticipate a warranted repudiation, on the part of real or imagined others, of both of the desires of love as regards himself. But a person in the grip of felt guilt will tend to be focused more on the first desire, and a person suffering from feelings of shame will tend to worry more about the second. A person who feels guilty will be anticipating warranted anger (or other negative reactive attitudes in the same family of emotions) on the part of real or imagined others;[38] and he will be anxious about things others may reasonably want to impose on him which are punishments, in their view, and which are not for his good, in his view.[39] His concern will therefore be that real or imagined others will have for him a desire opposite to the desire for the good for him, as he sees it. By contrast, a person who feels shame will be anticipating rejection and abandonment which is warranted on some standard of value on the part of real or imagined others; and consequently he will be more anxious about marginalization or isolation. His anxiety will be directed towards a distance, an absence of union, forced on him by others with whom he himself desires some kind of closeness.[40] His worry will therefore be that real or imagined others will reasonably repudiate the desire for union with him.[41]

It is important in this connection to see that there are also significant disanalogies between guilt and shame.

First, the standard of value by which a person is and feels guilty is a moral standard, and moral standards are generally considered to be ultimate. They are not trumped by other standards, whatever those other standards are.[42] But the standards by which a person is and feels shamed are highly variable, and they range from trivial to deep. A person can be shamed by one such standard and honored by another deeper standard which trumps the first one.

Secondly, a person who is guilty has intrinsic characteristics that are subpar on the moral standard, and having these defective intrinsic characteristics is a kind of suffering for the guilty person, since they keep him from full human flourishing.[43] Something similar *may* be true with regard to a shamed person. If the standard by which a person is shamed is connected in some crucial way to human flourishing, then he may suffer from those defects in himself that are impediments to human flourishing in one way or another. But shame need not be analogous to guilt in this way. That is because shame can also arise even when the standard by which a person is shamed is a light or trivial one, not connected in any deep way to human flourishing. In that kind of case, a person who is shamed may suffer only from the reactions of those real or imagined others shaming him. He may not in fact have any subpar intrinsic characteristics. If others did not see him as subpar, he would not suffer or be diminished in his human flourishing. So, for example, a person shamed by some trivial standard of fashion in a tiny community, such as a local high school, will suffer from the reactions of others to him; but the shamed person will not have any intrinsic defects that keep him from full human flourishing.

Finally, a person who is guilty but does not feel guilty is for this very reason in some sub-optimal condition; he is self-deceived or morally callous or something else along these lines. Something similar could be said in some cases about a person who is shamed but does not feel shamed; but it could also happen that a person who is shamed and does not feel shamed is for that very reason worthy of admiration. A case of this sort can arise when the standard by which a person is shamed is itself worthy of rejection and the shamed person's rejection of that standard evinces courage or nobility.[44]

(These differences between guilt and shame have implications for the remedy for guilt and shame, as Chapter 10 will make clear.)

Clearly, one can have and feel guilt or shame before God too. When it is God's anger or rejection that is at issue and is anticipated with anxiety, the problems of guilt and shame are correspondingly greater.

A THEORY OF AGENCY

With this much by way of a distinction between guilt and shame, we can turn to the problems facing a person suffering from each of them. To sketch these problems, however, it helps first to have a theory of agency. In my view, Aquinas's psychology and its account of agency are useful and defensible; but they are not necessary for my purposes in this chapter. As far as I can see, it is possible to make roughly the same points with other accounts of agency; but since I have explained and defended Aquinas's moral psychology in detail elsewhere,[45] I will use it here.

For Aquinas, any action, even a mental action, is the product of coordinated activity on the part of an agent's intellect and will.[46] Aquinas takes the will to be not a neutral faculty, but rather a certain bent or inclination for goodness.[47] (By 'goodness' in this connection Aquinas means goodness in general, not this or that specific good thing; and the goodness in question is the good broadly considered, as distinct from the moral good only.[48]) As Aquinas sees it, the intellect presents to the will as good certain things or actions under certain descriptions in particular circumstances, and the will wills them because it is an appetite for the good and these things or actions are presented to the will as good.[49]

On the other hand, the will in its turn also moves the intellect. In fact, for Aquinas, the will exercises some degree of efficient causality over the intellect. (By contrast, on Aquinas's views, nothing, not the intellect or anything else either, exercises efficient causality on the will.[50]) In some circumstances, the will can command the intellect directly to adopt or to reject a particular belief.[51] It can also move the intellect by directing the intellect to attend to some things and to neglect others,[52] or even to stop thinking about something altogether. Since the will wills something only in case the intellect presents it as some sort of good, the fact that the will can command the intellect to stop thinking about something means that the will can, indirectly, turn itself off, at least with regard to a particular action or issue. (This is only a limited ability on the part of the will, however, since the apprehensions of the intellect can occur without any preceding act of will and so in some cases may force an issue back on the agent's attention.[53])

On Aquinas's theory of action, then, any act of moral wrongdoing stems not only from a moral flaw in the will but also from a corresponding flaw in the intellect, which apprehends as an apparent good what is not a real good or which takes a lesser good as better than something that is in fact a greater good. In his slave-trading years, John Newton thought that slave-trading was acceptable, and he wanted to engage in it. And so he had morally deplorable states of intellect and will.

Repeated wrong acts can build up habits or dispositions which render a person more liable to the same or similar wrong acts in the future. These are vices, and there are virtues and vices of the intellect as well as of the will. So, for example, wisdom is an intellectual virtue which makes its possessor apt in moral discernment on matters of great weight. Enough moral wrongdoing, however, can build up in the intellect the opposite of wisdom, namely, the habit or disposition of folly, which is a kind of moral stupidity in serious cases.

Very serious cases illuminate this point. Consider in this connection Adolf Eichmann. While he was in Argentina after the war, in his reflections on his contributions to genocide, Eichmann expressed his great satisfaction at having succeeded in killing so many Jewish people; his one regret was that he did not kill them all. He showed no signs of any remorse; on the contrary, he hoped fervently for a resurgence of Nazism in Germany so that the killing could resume.[54] These reflections of his make clear that he had lost conscious contact with any decent moral standards. From Aquinas's point of view, Eichmann in Argentina is a paradigm of a fool. He has a severely impaired speculative intellect, unable to apprehend correctly the nature of moral goodness; and in consequence his practical intellect is also grossly deficient in its ability to make particular moral judgments. The result is that his intellect is radically self-deceived and his will is morally monstrous.

On Aquinas's theory of agency, over time Eichmann's morally wrong choices succeeded in radically misprogramming his intellect, which in turn made his moral choices worse, until he became an extreme case of human evil. The fact that his evil choices could have such an effect on the intellect is explained by the will's ability to exercise control over the intellect—in this case, indirect control. Eichmann wanted to be a great man in the Nazi hierarchy, and he was willing to do what it took to get himself noticed and promoted by Nazis in positions senior to him. But a wrong action can be willed by the will only in case the intellect has succeeded in finding some description under which it seems good.[55] And so in a case in which the will wants what in fact is not good, as a result of the command of the will the intellect directs its attention to just the evidence which supports the goodness of what the will wants and turns away from any countervailing evidence. The misprogrammed intellect then allows the will to want as good what it might have rejected before the misprogramming of the intellect; and the warped will, in turn, misprograms the intellect further. If the process continues long enough, a person can become evil enough to be guilty of crimes against humanity.

On Aquinas's account of agency, then, a person's will and intellect are in a dynamic interaction that allows each of them to corrupt the other, one step at a time. This account makes it easier to understand the well-documented fact that the descent into moral monstrosity tends to be gradual rather than precipitous; and it also shows, at least in part, how it is that a person's conscience can become horribly dulled. Furthermore, breaking into the cycle of the spiraling corruption of intellect and will clearly will be difficult. The outrage of virtually the whole civilized world was not enough to turn Eichmann from his conviction that he had never been responsible for any serious evil and that there was nothing for which he should feel any remorse. The shame of his internationally publicized trial and the deluge of shaming publications documenting his part in mass murder inspired him to no repentance or moral sorrow. A severely misprogrammed intellect with a correspondingly twisted will is hard to fix because all of the previous misprogramming has to be undone, one bit after another.[56] But this is an undoing for which the agent has no will or desire (or which his will is even set against) and which his intellect does not find good. Consequently, unless there is something from outside that can break the cycle, the corrupting interaction of will and intellect will simply continue.

THE PROBLEMS FOR THOSE SUFFERING FROM SHAME

With this brief description of Aquinas's theory of agency, we can turn to the problems posed by guilt and shame, beginning with shame. Shame can be connected to guilt, of course; and understanding shame in terms of the second desire of love helps to explain its connection to moral wrongdoing. A person might be as concerned about the alienation of others from him because of some morally wrong action on his part as he is worried about their desire to inflict something bad on him for that action. That is, the wrong a person has done may prompt in others a repudiation *of him* as well as a desire to punish him, and he may care more about the first possibility than the second. And so a person can have and feel shame for moral wrongdoing.

This understanding of shame also explains why a person who cares about some moral wrong he has done can be shamed just in his own eyes because of it. In consequence of what he has done, he himself can have the opposite of a desire for himself; he can find himself ugly and repulsive. And so a person who is unable to forgive himself for evil he has done can be characterized by self-loathing as well as self-laceration. Self-laceration is a person's attempt to punish himself; self-loathing, which is a response of shame, is a person's desire, as it were, to divorce himself.

In fact, this way of thinking about the connection between shame and moral wrongdoing helps explain why so many people are inclined to believe that shame is nothing more than an auxiliary to guilt and that it should melt away with the forgiveness or absolution of guilt. But, in fact, there are things peculiar to shame, too.

To begin with, shame can be stimulated by many things other than concern over one's own moral wrongdoing. There are different varieties of shame, because there are different sorts of reasons for rejecting the second desire of love with regard to a person. A shamed person can be thought seriously deficient by himself or others on the basis of highly varying scales of assessment, not just moral standards; and these can range from religious values to short-lived ideals of bodily beauty current in a particular community. Just think of the difference between a drunken priest who scrambles the most sacred words of a significant religious ritual and a sick priest who falls and spills the chalice of consecrated wine. Very different varieties of shame will afflict them.

Seeing these varying sources of shame helps to explain why a remedy for shame can seem more difficult to find than a remedy for guilt. The remedy for guilt seems to be repentance and satisfaction or making amends, which appear to remove the guilt. But a person's ugliness or inferiority on some scale of value he himself accepts is a matter of something in that person's life; and the history of a life, like everything else about the past, is fixed and unalterable. On the view of virtually all philosophers and theologians, even God cannot change the past. A person's life history remains what it was, and so do those things in that person's life that shame him.

Although the guilt and shame consequent on moral wrongdoing constitute the canonical problem to which the atonement is the solution, in my view these reflections show that there is a corollary problem of shame which springs from sources other than a person's own past sinful acts and which is also in need of remedy.

In the first place, a person can feel shamed or be shamed[57] in consequence of the depredations of other human beings. On June 2, 2012, the *New York Times* reported on an 18-year-old Afghani woman, Lal Bibi, who was gang-raped and beaten for days by men in a local militia as punishment for the actions of a cousin of hers who offended someone in the militia. Her relatives brought her, battered as she was, to a hospital and filed a complaint against her attackers; but the relatives explained that if the complaint was not acted on satisfactorily, they would have to kill her to remove the shame from the family. Lal Bibi herself said, "If the people in government fail to bring these people to justice, I am going to burn myself. I don't want to live with this stigma on my forehead."[58] Her heartbreaking words make vivid the anguish of this kind of feeling of shame.

Shame can also arise because of defects of nature, as when a person is shamed because of bodily deformity. Joseph Merrick, the so-called Elephant Man, is as good an example as any of someone afflicted with this kind of shame. In his youth, Merrick suffered horribly from the disease that afflicted and deformed him. Outcast from a society horrified at his condition, he was a half-feral, hunted, and hiding human being before he was finally found and helped by a compassionate doctor.

Thinking of shame in terms of the second desire of love illuminates these kinds of shame. For example, it helps to explain the connection between shame and ugliness. We are accustomed to think of what attracts us in another person as that person's beauty—not just external beauty but the beauty of the psyche or the beauty of the life of a person. A physically ugly but much beloved person will be praised as having inner beauty. The admiring biography of John Nash, the mathematician who became schizophrenic and was dysfunctional for much of his life, is entitled *A Beautiful Mind*.[59] When a person strikes us as admirable, as distinct from worthy of shame, we tend to find *him*, and not just some appearance or capacity of his, beautiful in some sense. On the other hand, a person who feels sure that others will find him ugly by some standard or scale of value will also expect those others to turn away from him.[60] Such turning-away is the opposite of that desire of love which is a desire for union.

Even if we think of shame in terms of weakness or powerlessness rather than ugliness, as some people do, the point remains fundamentally the same. We are attracted to power, and we tend to turn away from those without it. We refer to those who lack power or are fallen from it as the devalued, degraded, debased, defiled, despoiled. They are diminished somehow in social standing or cultural stature, and they lack attractiveness for us in consequence.

As these reflections make clear, even in cases where a person's shame has nothing to do with past sinful acts of his own, human evil nonetheless can have some direct or indirect role in the production of the shame. For example, a person can be or feel shamed in consequence of being victimized by sinful acts on the part of other people, as Lal Bibi was. Shame arising from defects of nature can have such a connection to human evil, too. The dreadful deformities of the Elephant Man would not have produced in him as painful a shame as he felt if the people in his community had not reacted to those deformities with the rejection and contempt they did. But even if we consider defects of nature that are kept private or secret forever, they can nonetheless be a source of shame for the person who suffers them, who imagines himself defective by comparison with others who have no such defect. Shame over the very defects of nature has a connection to human sin too. On traditional Christian doctrine, all defects in nature are a consequence of the Fall, which is itself a result of original sin. On the doctrine of the Fall, there was no natural evil, and consequently no shame over defects of nature, before the sin resulting in the Fall.

So there is a kind of shame that does not have its source in a person's own evil acts, but that is still a consequence of human evil, in one sense or another, because it stems directly or indirectly from the evil of people other than the shamed person.

This sort of shame, for which the shamed person bears no blame whatsoever, is also a route to a person's alienation from himself and others. A shamed person can adopt towards himself the attitude of the real or imagined others who turn away from him; at worst, he can see himself—rightly or wrongly—as radically inferior (on some standard of comparison) to others, who strike him as the normal or desirable people. In that case, he can appraise himself simultaneously both as a human person whose value as human is infinite but also as a social being worthy of rejection by others. That is, a shamed person will be divided into the self that is shamed and the good and fully human self that has internalized the standards giving rise to a feeling of shame. Since he is divided against himself in this way, he will also fail to be close to others, whose ability to be united with him is undermined because he is not united with himself.[61]

Consequently, shame can be a potent source of distance between the shamed person and others, and it can also introduce distance between a shamed person and God. A shamed person's repudiation of himself, as ugly or otherwise meriting rejection, is as effective as the inner dividedness generated by moral wrongdoing at preventing or undermining union between himself and God.

I recognize, of course, that the traditional account of the atonement understands the problem to which the atonement is the solution as a problem of sin, of the will's morally wrong division against itself; and I accept the traditional account. The reflections on shame here are not meant to suggest otherwise. They are intended only to call attention to the corollary problem of shame that can stem from a person's own wrongdoing or that of others. And that shame also needs a cure if a person suffering from it is not to be at a distance from others, including God. Insofar as the atonement is meant to promote union between God and human persons, then, it seems that it will need to be a remedy for all the kinds of shame. And if the atonement is meant to be the reversal of the ill effects introduced into earthly life by the Fall, then there is yet another reason for supposing that all the sorts of shame need to be overcome by the atonement. Even relevant biblical texts, which typically focus on atonement as a solution to the problem of sin, allude in various places also to a problem of shame. For example, in Psalm 25:2, the psalmist prays that God will save him from shame.[62] Isaiah prophesies not only that Israel will be established in righteousness but also that it will forget its earlier shame (Isa. 54:4; see also 61:7). Zephaniah prophesies that God will give Israel praise instead of shame (Zeph. 3:19). And so on.

It is worth noticing in this connection that neither the Anselmian nor the Thomistic kind of interpretation of the doctrine of the atonement includes any explicit remedy for shame, or at least for the kind of shame that is not a consequence of a person's own past sins. On both kinds of interpretation, something about Christ's atonement rectifies something about a person's guilt and by this means promotes union between God and that person. But it is not immediately clear why this remedy for guilt would also alleviate even just the shame of having done wrong. And if the source of a person's shame is something other than a person's own sin, then the distance between God and the shamed person introduced by shame will not be eliminated just by a remedy for the shamed person's guilt. Consequently, the problem of distance between a shamed person and others is not directly addressed by the atonement as either the Anselmian or Thomistic kind of interpretation understands it.

THE PROBLEMS FOR THOSE SUFFERING FROM GUILT

By contrast with a shamed person, a person who is guilty of something is confronted with two kinds of problems peculiar to guilt.

The first problem lies in himself, in his morally defective[63] states of intellect and will and the corrupt habits from which they stem or to which they contribute. These defective states are at the center of the psychic problem for a wrongdoer; but, as I will explain below, they are not the whole problem. There are also other defective psychic and relational states; but they are easier to see in connection with the notion of satisfaction, and so I am postponing discussion of them till later in this chapter.

The second problem for a guilty person lies in the world, in the effects of his wrongdoing on others. The suffering of the human beings Newton kidnapped and enslaved was horrible, and he was responsible for it. Just restoring Newton's intellect and will to the state and condition of a morally good person, through repentance, for example, leaves unaddressed the suffering he caused. And even if there are no particular victims for a person's wrongdoing, as when someone simply wastes inherited great wealth in trivial pursuits and fails to contribute to society as he might have done, there remains for him the problem that the world is worse than it might have been because of what he did or failed to do.

This second problem can itself be subdivided into two subsidiary or component problems. First, there is the actual harm that a wrongdoer did, by his action or his omission, so that in one sense or another the world is worse because of him. And then there is the injustice of his acting as he did. It is clear that harm and injustice can come apart. A person Jerome can do harm without doing an injustice to another person Paula,[64] but he can also do an injustice to Paula without doing her any harm.

Suppose, for example, that Jerome is a tourist in a poor and remote desert region of the world, and suppose that two inhabitants of that world, Paula and her young child, approach him and beg for a share of his water because they lack other means for getting water and are desperately thirsty. Suppose also that Jerome has sufficient water for himself and others as well. Then suppose that Jerome rejects Paula's plea for water. It is obvious that his rejection is a morally wrong action—most people would feel moral disapprobation at it; and it is an action that does Paula and her child harm. But it does not constitute an injustice against Paula, because she does not have a right to any of Jerome's property, including his water. Because rights and obligations are not correlative, it is possible for a person to violate his obligations towards others and harm them even when those others do not have rights against him.[65]

On the other hand, Jerome can do Paula an injustice without doing her any harm. Suppose that Jerome utters malicious gossip about Paula to her friend

Julia; and suppose that Julia is certain the gossip is false, so that by his action Jerome lowers himself, not Paula, in Julia's eyes. Then Jerome has done Paula an injustice, but he has not harmed her.

In most cases, of course, harm and injustice go together; but it is helpful to see that they can be disassociated, because seeing their separability helps illuminate the fact that, typically, a wrongdoer has two different problems as regards the effects of his wrongdoing on the world. There is the harm he has caused, but there is also the injustice he has done.

These (and a few more that will emerge below) are, then, the problems of guilt engendered by a seriously wrong action.

Clearly, for discussion of the doctrine of the atonement, it is important to consider what will remove guilt. It is perhaps not so hard to see what will remedy the defective states of the wrongdoer's intellect and will. A sufficiently deep and thorough repentance will fix these defective states in the psyche. But it is less easy to see what will remove guilt as regards the damage and injustice of the wrongdoer's act.

Satisfaction or making amends is generally thought to be able to handle this part of the problem of guilt, but whether it can in fact handle all of it is open to question. Just fixing the harm a wrongdoer has done is generally not enough to fix the injustice he has done to the person he has harmed. And, of course, often the harm done cannot be fixed either, so that the best that a wrongdoer can do is to offer compensation.

But if the wrong is serious enough, even compensation is unavailing as reparation for it. In Charles Dickens's *A Tale of Two Cities*, an arrogant wealthy aristocrat causes the death of a child of very poor parents by the aristocrat's reckless and disdainful disregard of the poor as he drives his carriage through their streets. When he sees that his carriage has killed the child, then, to make up for what he has done, the aristocrat throws a gold coin at the father of the child. Even if we assume that the gold is appropriate and sufficient compensation for the life of the child—an assumption which most people, me included, would reject but which I want to accept for the moment for the sake of the point here—this compensation is not sufficient by way of reparation for the wrong done. To compensate for the harm one has caused is not enough to remove the guilt of having done the harm. If it were, then the wealthy would be better placed than other people to ameliorate their wrongdoings. But this is clearly not the case. The gold coin cannot remove the guilt of the aristocrat. When in the story the father of the child throws the gold coin back at the aristocrat, the readers of the story are gratified. Even if one assumes that the gold is worth significantly more than the life of a poor child in that culture, the outweighing value of the gold does not make amends for the child's death.

What is needed for the removal of a wrongdoer's guilt is therefore a difficult matter.

SATISFACTION ON ANSELM'S ACCOUNT

The preceding considerations put us in a position to examine the notion of making amends or satisfaction, which is also crucial to interpretations of the doctrine of the atonement. Satisfaction is typically supposed to be the central element in the solution to the problem of guilt with regard to the ill effects on the world of wrongdoing. In this connection, it is important to see that there are two different notions of satisfaction that need to be disambiguated in this context.

The first notion of satisfaction is evident in Anselm's writings on Christ's atonement. Anselm says,

> Someone who does not render to God . . . [the] honour due to him is taking away from God what is his, and dishonouring God, and this is what it is to sin. As long as he does not repay what he has taken away, he remains in a state of guilt. And it is not sufficient merely to repay what has been taken away: rather, he ought to pay back more than he took, in proportion to the insult which he has inflicted. For just as, in the case of someone who injures the health of another, it is not sufficient for him to restore that person's health, if he does not pay some compensation for the painful injury which has been inflicted, similarly it is not sufficient for someone who violates someone else's honour, to restore that person's honour, if he does not, in consequence of the harmful act of dishonour, give, as restitution to the person whom he has dishonoured, something pleasing to that person. One should also observe that when someone repays what he has unlawfully stolen, what he is under an obligation to give is not the same as what it would be possible to demand from him, were it not that he had seized the other person's property. Therefore, everyone who sins is under an obligation to repay to God the honour which he has violently taken from him, and this is the satisfaction which every sinner is obliged to give to God.[66]

Anselm's claims presuppose the distinction between harm and injustice delineated above: no one can harm an omnipotent God, but it is still possible to treat God unjustly, that is, in some way that insults or dishonors God, as Anselm puts it. And, in general, as Anselm thinks, it is not enough to repair any harm a wrongdoer has done in the world. The wrongdoer has to add in something extra, some gift that is pleasing to the person dishonored (as Anselm puts it), to make up for the injustice of the wrong action. Reparation and this something extra, this gift that is extra compensation for injustice done, is satisfaction, in Anselm's sense of the term.

This Anselmian way of thinking about satisfaction given to God has implications for a theory of satisfaction where the wronged person is another human being, too. To remedy the problems for a person Jerome suffering from guilt with regard to wrong done against another human being, on the Anselmian attitude towards satisfaction, Jerome must do the following things:

(1) He must repent his former wrongdoing, so that with respect to the act in question Jerome comes to have the state of intellect and the state of will of a morally good person;

(2) If his action did harm, then Jerome must contribute as he can to undoing the harm his action did;

(3) If his action was unjust, then Jerome must contribute as he can to undoing the injustice, through the gift-giving part of the kind of satisfaction Anselm indicates.

On Anselm's approach to satisfaction, without these things, or some suitable substitute for them, it is not morally permissible for the wrongdoer to receive forgiveness or be reconciled with the person he has wronged. Anselm draws this conclusion explicitly where God's pardon is concerned. Anselm says,

> There is nothing more intolerable in the universal order than that a creature should take away honour from the creator and not repay what he takes away.... There is nothing...which it is more unjust to tolerate than the most intolerable thing in the universal order.... [No one will] say that God ought to tolerate something which it is the greatest injustice in the universe to tolerate, namely: that a creature should not give back to God what he takes away.... [I]f there is nothing greater and nothing better than God, then there is nothing, in the government of the universe, which the supreme justice, which is none other than God himself, preserves more justly than God's honour.... There is nothing, therefore, which God preserves more justly than the honour of his dignity.... It is a necessary consequence, therefore, that either the honour which has been taken away should be repaid, or punishment should follow. Otherwise, either God will not be just to himself, or he will be without the power to enforce either of the two options, and it is an abominable sin even to consider this possibility.[67]

Given the character of Anselm's interpretation of the doctrine of the atonement,[68] it is not surprising that, for Anselm, satisfaction made for the offense against God caused by a person's wrongdoing is a matter of that person's giving God a gift that will please God and so fulfill God's justice, thereby enabling God to pardon that person his sins and to accept reconciliation with him. On Anselm's approach to satisfaction, satisfaction made to God for human wrongdoing is a necessary precondition for God's forgiveness of wrongdoers. On Anselm's view, God's pardon of wrongdoers and God's forgiveness of them is dependent on God's receiving satisfaction for the wrong done. So, for Anselm, the point of satisfaction is to bring the offended party to a condition requisite for his acceptance of reconciliation with the wrongdoer.

SATISFACTION AND THE STAIN ON THE SOUL

As I explained in Chapter 1, Aquinas rejects the Anselmian interpretation of the atonement. We might expect, then, that in his own affirmation of satisfaction as part of the process of atonement Aquinas would have a notion of satisfaction different from that of Anselm, and this is in fact what we find.

On Aquinas's view, moral wrongdoing leaves the wrongdoer with defects or impairments beyond those in the wrongdoer's intellect and will. Aquinas calls these additional defects 'a stain on the soul'; and, for the sake of convenience, I will simply adopt his phrase. As Aquinas sees it, satisfaction has as one of its main points removing the stain on the soul.

When a person repents what he did, his intellect accepts that doing that act was in fact morally wrong, and his will rejects the doing of it. In consequence of his repentance, then, the flawed configuration of his intellect and will are removed and replaced by morally good configurations instead. This can happen in such a way as to leave relatively untouched any morally wrong dispositions or habits in the intellect and will. But if the repentance is deep enough and fervent enough, then it may also alter for the better any habits of the intellect and will which were building or already in place and which were inclining the agent to morally wrong acts.

Given Aquinas's account of agency, then, one might suppose that, for Aquinas, repentance of a sufficiently wholehearted sort would be enough to wipe out all the psychic defects, both occurrent and habitual, introduced into an agent by his own moral wrongdoing. On Aquinas's understanding of the nature of moral wrongdoing, it seems as if a repentant person should have the same moral status as he did before the wrongdoing in question. But this is not in fact Aquinas's view.

For Aquinas, serious moral wrongdoing can leave deleterious effects on the psychic and relational states of the wrongdoer beyond its influence on his intellect and will. According to Aquinas, even for a wholeheartedly repentant agent, there remains a stain on the soul. In trying to explain what this is, Aquinas says,

> The stain is neither something positive in the soul, nor does it signify a privation only: rather, it signifies a certain privation of the soul's brightness.... It is like a shadow, which is the privation of light because of the obstacle of some body, and which varies according to the diversity of the bodies which constitute the obstacle [to the light].[69]

To see what Aquinas has in mind here, in addition to states of intellect and will, we need to consider also other psychic states of an agent's, hard to characterize but significant for his life and relations.

To begin with, there are cognitive and conative faculties besides intellect and will, and wrongdoing can leave them in a morally worse condition, too.

For example, there is memory. The very memory of having engaged in a great evil that caused suffering to others diminishes something in the loveliness of the wrongdoer's psyche too. By staying in memory, the evil a person has done remains part of the wrongdoer's present. Consider, for example, Otto Moll. Moll was at the head of the work detail managing the exterminations at Auschwitz; he participated in the gassing and cremation of very many people, and he himself shot people too weak to be herded into the gas chambers. At his interrogation at Nuremberg, he evinced a strong desire to dissociate himself psychologically, to exculpate himself, from the horrors he had engaged in. But even if it had been the case that Moll was genuinely repentant (and there is no evidence that he was), there would have been something morally grieving about the state of his psyche just in consequence of his remembering having engaged in such acts in the past. The memory of that evil is not itself an evil act, but there is something morally distressing about the continued presence of the evil in memory nonetheless. That may be one reason why morally monstrous people, even when they are completely repentant, still find their memories an affliction.

Then there are the empathic capacities. Most people cannot simulate the mind of a person who commits the kind of morally monstrous acts Moll did; and we give expression to that incapacity by saying "I can't imagine how a person could do something like that!" But the perpetrator himself does understand what it feels like to do an evil of that sort and, what is worse, what it feels like to *want* to do an evil of that sort. One might say that, in addition to the defects (and the defective dispositions) in the intellect and will of such a wrongdoer, there is a kind of moral elasticity in the evildoer's psyche. The hard barrier—the "I can't!"—that ordinarily decent people have in their psyches against Moll's kind of grotesque evil is missing in Moll, and the consequent moral flabbiness in his psyche is repellent.[70] Because they are not moral defects in the will, such psychological leftovers of moral wrongdoing are not by themselves culpable or worthy of punishment; but there is something morally lamentable about them all the same.[71]

The moral leftovers of serious evil in the psyche of the wrongdoer, the stain on the soul, can cause others to react with revulsion to a person who has done serious evil even when no one anticipates any continued evil on his part. Repentance alone does not take away totally such repugnant features in the psyche. And so, by itself, repentance is not sufficient to restore a wrongdoer to the moral wholesomeness he had before his evil acts. Consequently, even if there is nothing worthy of blame (or blame and punishment) in a thoroughly repentant wrongdoer, the leftover stain on the parts of the psyche other than intellect and will may still leave him in a morally worse condition than he was before he did the evil in question, not because he is blameworthy for these psychic leftovers of evil, but because he is somehow more morally shabby, more morally malodorous, one might say, than other people.

In addition, as Aquinas himself supposes in the quotation above, there is a relational component to the stain on the soul. Included in the stain is an absence of some relational characteristic which a person would have had absent his morally wrong act and which in other circumstances would have contributed to his inner loveliness.[72] The relationship Aquinas himself focuses on is the wrongdoer's relationship to God, which is disrupted because, by his wrong action, the agent distances himself from God. But there are also other relationships, those just between human beings, to consider.

To see this point, we can begin by considering a wrongdoer's relationship to himself. A person can be alienated or estranged from himself, as well as from others.[73]

Aquinas's own views entail that there will be such internal alienation in cases of significant moral wrongdoing. That is because, according to Aquinas, in doing a morally wrong action a wrongdoer becomes divided within himself. For Aquinas, a human being cannot be wholly integrated in evil, but only in good.[74] On Aquinas's optimistic views of human nature, human beings are built in such a way that neither a human intellect nor a human will can fail entirely, on some deep or not fully conscious level, to be connected to the good. So, in order to will a wrong action, a person has to suppress something in his intellect, which thus becomes divided against itself; and some part of his will has to reject what some other part of his will desires.[75] For this reason, someone who fails to will the good also fails to be integrated within himself to one degree or another. To that extent, such a person is divided in will and also double-minded; and, to that extent, he is alienated from himself.

A person internally divided in this way cannot be close to others either.[76] He cannot reveal his mind to another person if he has hidden a good part of his mind from himself. And if he is internally divided in what he cares about,[77] then whichever part of his divided will another person is in harmony with, she will be separated from some other part. To that extent, she and he will not be united; he will want something she does not want (or vice versa), no matter what the state of her will is. For this reason, in serious moral wrongdoing, to one degree or another, a person isolates himself from others. And this point holds even if the other in question is God.

It may be that an agent's alienation from himself ceases when he repents the evil he did, because the repentance undoes the internal division in his intellect and will. And so, someone might suppose, repentance alone is sufficient to reduce the agent's alienation from others as well. With regard to the former morally wrong act, the intellect of the repentant person has ceased to be double-minded, and his will is wholehearted as well. But if his evil was great enough, his repentance by itself is not enough to end his alienation from others. The internal integration achieved through his repentance does not instantly, by itself alone, restore his relationships with others, who were put at some distance from him by his wrongdoing.

Consider, in this connection, Albert Speer. Speer was able to survive Spandau prison as well as he did and to write *Inside the Third Reich* while he was in prison because his friend Rudolf Wolters spent his time and his resources unstintingly to support Speer and Speer's family. When *Inside the Third Reich* appeared, Wolters was stunned to find that there was no mention of him or acknowledgement of his help anywhere in Speer's highly successful book. It seems clear, in hindsight, that, in his new role as repentant Nazi, Speer found it prudent to distance himself from Wolters, whose postwar devotion to Hitler was embarrassing to Speer.[78] But Wolters was devastated by what he took to be Speer's betrayal of Wolters's self-sacrificial friendship.[79] Even if Speer had eventually managed to repent that betrayal, Speer's repentance alone would not have been sufficient for restoring the disturbed relationship between them. A relationship has a life of its own; the internal healing of Speer's divided self is not the same thing as the healing of the broken relationship between Wolters and Speer.

Someone might suppose here that the relationship between friends, such as Speer and Wolters, *should* be healed as soon as the betrayer of the relationship is repentant. On this view, Wolters *should* have resumed his previous relationship with Speer if Speer had been repentant; and then, in that case, in consequence of Speer's repentance and Wolters's acceptance of Speer, the two of them would have been reconciled and their relationship restored to what it had been before.

But this supposition rests on the mistaken assumption that a relationship is not affected by the past states of the persons in it, that only their present condition is relevant to the relationship. As my remarks above about memory show, however, at least through memory the past lives on in the present. Wolters knew that Speer had not cared about him or honored his devotion, and both he and Speer remembered that Wolters had not mattered to Speer in anything like the way Speer had mattered to Wolters. For such reasons and others, a past state or set of events influences the present relationships of human beings. Even if Speer and Wolters had been reconciled, through repentance on Speer's part and acceptance of Speer on Wolters's part, Speer's past betrayal would have left altered in sad ways their present and future relationship.

Furthermore, even if Wolters had never learned of Speer's betrayal, if Speer had successfully hid that betrayal from Wolters, Speer's hiding would impact his relationship with Wolters detrimentally in another way. And this general conclusion remains even if, after having repented his betrayal of Wolters, Speer himself suffered amnesia about it. There was a point in time after which Speer was a person who had betrayed the trust of his friend; before that time, he was not. And that difference in Speer's history alters his relationship to his friend, in morally relevant ways, which repentance alone does not undo. If an amnesic Speer and a clueless Wolters wound up sitting next to each other at a dinner party, people at the party who knew the true history of both men would wince, wouldn't they? There would be something jarring in the thought that those two men, the betrayer and one of those betrayed by him, should be sharing a meal without either of them being aware of that contemptible betrayal in Speer's past. In my view, our sense that it would be jarring is a moral judgment on Speer even in his supposed repentant condition.

The case of Speer's betrayal of Wolters, which introduces distance into their previously close relationship, is still a relatively small-scale evil. By his complicity in the Nazi war crimes, Speer removed himself a distance of light-years from ordinary human beings. He became a person who contributed to the murder of millions of people, and any relationship he might have had to other people has to be affected by that past evil. Even deep, fervent repentance on his part would not alter that past fact about him, and so by itself it also would not alter the disturbed and distant relationship between him and other people either. When it comes to someone such as Speer, the wrongdoing is monstrous, political, on an international scale; but the scale of the evil complicates the case without fundamentally altering Aquinas's point about the stain on the soul.

So Aquinas's idea that we have to consider the stain on the soul when we think about the effect of moral wrongdoing on the perpetrator of the wrong is helpful; and it seems right even if we bracket his theology and consider only human relationships. Moral wrongdoing can leave a stain on the soul either in its effects on the wrongdoer's psyche or in the disruptions it makes in the wrongdoer's relationships or both. Either of these effects seems to lessen the inner comeliness that the wrongdoer might otherwise have had. The internal psychological effects certainly do. But so do the impaired relationships. Being separated to one degree or another from people to whom one would otherwise have been connected in close or caring ways takes away from the wrongdoer something that would have been lovely in him. Since it is through his own doing that the loveliness is diminished, there is something appropriate in the metaphor that represents the diminution as a stain.[80]

For Aquinas, one of the main points of satisfaction is the removal of the stain on the soul.

SATISFACTION ON AQUINAS'S ACCOUNT

Although Aquinas thinks that every act of serious moral wrongdoing leaves a stain on the soul, he also thinks that this stain is not permanent; and in various places he discusses the way in which it can be removed. So, for example, he says,

> although the act of sin, by which a human being distanced himself from the light of reason and the divine law, ceases, the person himself does not immediately return to the [state] in which he was [before he sinned]. Rather, there is necessary some motion of the will contrary to the previous motion [of the will in sinning].[81]

On Aquinas's views, this motion of the will includes the making of satisfaction. Contrary to Anselm's understanding of satisfaction, then, for Aquinas, the obstacle to union with God that satisfaction removes is not in God but rather in the wrongdoer.

Understood in this way, satisfaction[82] is a fruit of penance, as Aquinas explains penance.[83] The other parts of penance taken in this sense are confession and contrition. Contrition is to be understood as sorrow for previous acts of wrongdoing,[84] and confession is an acknowledgement of those actions as wrong. (Confession and contrition combined are what we generally mean by 'repentance.') Aquinas thinks that confession, contrition, *and* the satisfaction made by penance are a kind of medicine for sin;[85] they heal what has been damaged by moral wrongdoing.[86]

Here it is important to see that on Aquinas's approach to satisfaction, satisfaction must depend on God's forgiveness, not the other way around, as on Anselm's approach to satisfaction. God's forgiveness is God's love addressed to a wrongdoer Jerome. That is, God's forgiveness of Jerome is a matter of God's desiring the good for Jerome and union with Jerome even in the face of Jerome's wrongdoing.[87] And on Aquinas's anti-Pelagian views, God's desiring these things will produce good in Jerome if Jerome does not refuse that good; certainly, on the rejection of Pelagianism, any good in Jerome is itself a gift of God's grace.

This point applies to satisfaction itself. Even the will with which a wrongdoer accepts making satisfaction is a result of grace. Without God's grace operative on a person's will, on Aquinas's account, satisfaction would be impossible. So, for example, Aquinas says,

> We can speak of penance in two ways. The first way has to do with the disposition to penance. Taken in this way, penance is infused immediately by God, without our working directly... In the other way, we can speak about penance as regards the acts by which we cooperate in penance with God's working. The first source of these acts is the work of God converting the heart....[88]

But God's giving Jerome the grace he needs for contrition, confession, and satisfaction stems from God's desire for Jerome's good and for union with Jerome—and this is God's love and forgiveness of Jerome.[89]

So, for Aquinas, unlike Anselm, a wrongdoer's satisfaction does not enable God's forgiveness; rather God's forgiveness and love operating in the wrongdoer enable the wrongdoer's satisfaction.

The satisfaction that is a fruit of God's love and forgiveness bestowing grace is a matter of trying to repair what was hurt by the wrongdoing. It includes trying to remedy the harm done to others, but it also has a role to play in ameliorating the stain on the soul.[90] The stain develops in part because by his wrongdoing the wrongdoer damages his own psyche and also puts some distance between himself and others. In penance, the wrongdoer is attempting to restore himself as well as the things he damaged in the world, and he does what he can to re-traverse the distance he himself put between himself and those he injured.

So, on Aquinas's approach to satisfaction, its point is to make amends as one can to those who have suffered from the wrong done and to repair as one can what the wrong has injured in the world, including the stained soul of the wrongdoer and the relationships impaired by his wrongdoing.[91] The primary recipients of a wrongdoer's satisfaction are those who were wronged by him; but, by means of satisfaction, the wrongdoer also alters the stain on his own soul left by his wrongdoing. (Whether this is enough for the removal of guilt is another matter, and a complicated one. I will return to it in Chapter 10.)

THE PARABLE OF THE PRODIGAL SON

One way to highlight the difference between the Anselmian and the Thomistic understandings of satisfaction is to see how the parable of the prodigal son needs to be understood on their differing approaches.

In the parable, the son has harmed his father and done him an injustice: he has taken his father's money, abandoned the family, and gone away to live the life of a wastrel. At a certain point, his money runs out; and the son suffers the afflictions of real destitution. At that point, he sees the error of his ways; and he wants to go home. As he goes, he plans the words of repentance that he will say to his father when he gets to his father's house. (For my purposes here, I will simply stipulate that the son is genuinely repentant and can also be known to be repentant by his father just in virtue of the son's coming home. I will also stipulate that the father is a morally good man who does no wrong or unjust actions in the parable. These stipulations ward off red herrings in the consideration of the parable here.) The father sees his son when the son is on the road home but still some distance away; and the father runs out to meet him. When he gets to his son, the father falls on his son's neck and kisses him, before the son has a chance to say a word.

If we adopt the Anselmian approach to satisfaction, then this is how we will have to understand the parable. At this point in the story, when the father kisses his son but the son has not yet had a chance to say or do anything with respect to his father, the father has still not forgiven his son; or, at least, he *ought* not to have forgiven him yet. On the Anselmian approach to satisfaction, the father cannot with justice forgive his son or accept reconciliation with his son until his son has not only repented but also made satisfaction. Even if we assume that because the son's returning home expresses his repentance and therefore also counts as his apology to his father, nonetheless, on the Anselmian approach, the son must provide some kind of present pleasing to his father, some compensation, that counts as the son's satisfaction, before the father can in justice forgive his son and be reconciled with him.

On the Anselmian approach, then, satisfaction is *and ought to be* a requisite for forgiveness and reconciliation. Without satisfaction, something that ought to be there for the morally appropriate granting of forgiveness and reconciliation is missing. For Anselm, there is no obligation to forgive on the part of the father who has been harmed by his son or against whom his son has done an injustice; but the father *may* appropriately forgive his son once the son has made satisfaction in the form of some compensation, some pleasing present, to make up for his wrongdoing against his father.

By contrast, for Aquinas, it is not only morally permissible for the father to forgive his son before the son makes satisfaction, but it is even morally permissible for the father to forgive his son before the son repents. Forgiveness is a matter of having the two desires of love—for the good of the beloved and for union with the beloved—even when the person loved has done one an injury or an injustice (or both). Consequently, it is in fact not only morally permissible, but actually morally obligatory for the father to have both these desires with regard to his son always, even when the son is unrepentant, since love is obligatory on Aquinas's account. For the same reason, it is not only morally permissible but even obligatory for the father to have both the desires of love with regard to his son without his son's having made satisfaction.

In Chapter 3, I will examine the consequences of this account of love and forgiveness further. It has the implications, for example, that one can desire the good for the beloved even while one also desires and is warranted in desiring something bad for that person.[92] It also has the implication that forgiveness is compatible with a desire to punish the forgiven person.[93] These and other consequences of this account of love and forgiveness are a focus of Chapter 3. For now, the important thing to notice is just that, on this account, forgiveness is unilateral and unconditional; it requires no prerequisites of any kind on the part of the wrongdoer.

Nonetheless, there is still a point to satisfaction, on Aquinas's approach to satisfaction. If the returned prodigal son really is repentant, then he will be not only sorry for his own acts of injury and injustice against his father but also deeply grateful for his father's unconditional love and forgiveness. In this state, he will surely have a desire to do what he can to make amends to his family. This attitude, this desire and the acts to which it gives rise, are the heart of satisfaction, on Aquinas's approach to satisfaction.

For Aquinas, then, satisfaction depends on forgiveness; it is not a prerequisite for forgiveness. In making amends to his father, the prodigal son restores a relationship between himself and his father, not because he is somehow earning the forgiveness of his father but because, as already forgiven by his father, he is himself returning to his father, across the distance which *he*—not his father—put between himself and his father. By his satisfaction, the prodigal son has a chance of restoring the relationships he broke and removing the stain on the soul that he caused by his wrongdoing. And *this* is one of the main points of satisfaction, on the Thomistic approach.

VICARIOUS SATISFACTION

Because the kind of satisfaction important in interpretations of the doctrine of the atonement is vicarious satisfaction, it is important also to say something here about this notion. The basic idea is that when a person Jerome ought to make satisfaction (of one kind or another), at least in some circumstances it is possible for someone else Paula to make this satisfaction for him. Paula can be the *Stellvertreter* for Jerome. The German word '*Stellvertreter*' is an important term of art in much Protestant theorizing about atonement,[94] and there is no one really good English equivalent for it. So in what follows I will just help myself to the German word and say that Paula is the *Stellvertreter* for Jerome when Paula is acting to make vicarious satisfaction for Jerome, who ought to make satisfaction (in either the Thomistic or the Anselmian sense).

It is important to see that the differing Anselmian and Thomistic approaches to satisfaction yield differing understandings of vicarious satisfaction and differing conditions on the *Stellvertreter*.

To see this difference, think about the children of high-ranking Nazis, many of whom were still very young when the war ended. When they became adults, some of these children were seriously alienated from their Nazi family members but experienced a need to do something to make up for what their Nazi family members had done. They had a desire, a need, to act as *Stellvertreter* for their Nazi parent.

The child of an SS general who had operated with the *Einsatzgruppen* in the Soviet Union and who had been hung for crimes against humanity after the war said,

> I always wanted to punish, to hurt myself; if I had this father, I told myself...I must pay for it.[95]

The nephew of Reinhard Heydrich (Himmler's second in command) said,

> I began to feel this guilt when, only weeks after the war, I saw the photographs
> and read what had been done.... This feeling of responsibility only intensified
> over the next twenty years. I was...deputizing for all the others: my aunt
> [Reinhard Heydrich's widow], who felt proud of her husband; his three children,
> who...felt and feel nothing; my mother, who, having always instinctively disliked
> my uncle, was able to hide comfortably behind that early rejection.... *Somebody*
> had to feel guilt for the devilish things my uncle had done.[96]

Martin Bormann (the son of Hitler's villainous assistant, who was also named
Martin Bormann) devoted his life to compensating for the evil his father had
done. Gita Sereny says about the younger Martin Bormann,

> In May 1945 [when the war ended], then fifteen, he very nearly killed himself. But
> he decided to live, became a Catholic, a priest, a missionary in Africa, then,
> leaving priesthood, became a teacher and married.... German and Austrian
> schools and colleges are asking him to speak to their children....[97]

It was the younger Bormann's purpose in those speeches to children to help
them see what went wrong in the world his father helped to build so that they
themselves might never collaborate with evil. He told Sereny,

> Some fifty years ago...a few people created horror, but far too many, knowing
> about it, tolerated it...The obscenity...will only be stopped if we accept indi-
> vidual responsibility for never in a single instance allowing it to go unchallenged.
> That, I think, is our task—yes, as our parent's children.[98]

As those recorded bits of conversation indicate, these adult children of high-
ranking Nazis felt some impetus to try to make up, in one way or another, for
what their Nazi family members had done.

Martin Bormann gave himself first to the priesthood and work in Africa and
then concentrated on the education of children in Germany, acting in all of
this "as our parent's children," as he puts it—as *Stellvertreter* for his own
father, as I would say. At the time at which Martin the younger was reflecting
on the horrors his father perpetrated, Martin the elder was dead. (It is thought
that he died trying to escape Berlin while the Russians were overrunning the
city, although there has always been dispute over this claim.) Could Martin the
younger then be the *Stellvertreter* for his dead father? That is, could Martin
the younger make satisfaction for his father in the period after the war and
after the death of his father? I want to consider these questions apart from any
consideration of the thorny issues of communal guilt, that is, apart from any
examination of the question whether or not these adult children of Nazis were
right to want to make satisfaction. For my purposes here, what matters is not
whether these adult children ought to try to make satisfaction; the question is
rather *what* they were doing when they tried to compensate for the evil of their
family member.

It is important to see that this question has different answers depending on whether we adopt the Anselmian or the Thomistic approach to satisfaction.

For Anselm, satisfaction is one and only one part of what is necessary for a wrongdoer to get forgiveness. Insofar as Martin the elder is dead and so not in a position to contribute the other necessary conditions for forgiveness, there is no question of forgiveness for Martin the elder when his son acts as his *Stellvertreter*. Still, it is possible, on the Anselmian approach to satisfaction, for Martin the younger to make satisfaction for his dead father. Martin the elder was guilty of crimes against humanity, as the Nuremberg indictment of high-ranking Nazis termed it; and so those damaged by Martin the elder's wrongdoing were all humanity. Insofar as Martin the younger gave his life to help others, Martin the younger was giving (or trying to give) a present helpful and pleasing to humanity in compensation for the great damage done by his father. And this is something Martin the younger could do even when his father was no longer able to participate in the process in even the remotest way because his father was dead.

On the Anselmian approach to satisfaction, then, Martin the younger can be a *Stellvertreter* for his father without there being any conditions on his father at all, because what is at issue on the Anselmian approach is the giving of a gift of some sort to the offended or injured party. Anyone can give such a gift on behalf of a wrongdoer. One could do so even if the wrongdoer were living, unrepentant, and completely set against the giving of any compensation. (If it turned out that Martin the elder had not died in the collapse of Berlin but had survived in Argentina, like Eichmann, and had seen and hated his son's attempts at satisfaction, then Martin the elder would have been in such a condition.) Even for such a wrongdoer, however, it is still possible for someone to act as *Stellvertreter*. Of course, in such a case, the wrongdoer has not met the Anselmian conditions for obtaining forgiveness; but it remains the case that the *Stellvertreter* has made satisfaction to one degree or another for the wrongdoer.

On the Thomistic approach to satisfaction, things look very different. At first glance, it is not clear that, on Aquinas's approach, it is so much as possible for there to be a *Stellvertreter*. Whatever good is done by the efforts of Martin the younger, it seems that it can have no effect on the stain on the soul of Martin the elder. The efforts of the son do nothing to alter the grotesque damage in the psyche of the father or to restore the father to any acceptable place (to say nothing of an honorable place) in the human family. For these good effects of satisfaction, on the Thomistic approach, the wrongdoer himself must make satisfaction—or so it seems.

And yet consider this case. Suppose that Martin the elder lived after the end of the war but was in some highly restricted conditions—suppose, for example, that he was left paralyzed and aphasic by a bomb strike as he was fleeing Berlin and spent the next twenty years in a nursing facility in Berlin, able to communicate only by gesture, body language, and other such restricted means, but able to understand the language of others. And suppose that in this condition he came to know about his son's efforts at making satisfaction for him. Suppose that, by some miracle or other, he was repentant and welcomed what his son was doing on his behalf. That is, suppose that he loved his son very much, was deeply grateful for his son's efforts on his behalf, wished these efforts all possible success, and so on.

In this kind of case, it does seem possible for there to be a *Stellvertreter* even on the Thomistic approach to satisfaction. The condition that allows vicarious satisfaction on the Thomistic approach is that the wrongdoer identify with the *Stellvertreter*, at least in the sense that the wrongdoer loves the *Stellvertreter*'s efforts at satisfaction and identifies with the *Stellvertreter* by loving what the *Stellvertreter* is doing for him. To this extent, the wrongdoer wishes well to the *Stellvertreter* and desires to unite himself, to one extent or another, with the *Stellvertreter*. And since these are the desires of love, the condition for vicarious satisfaction, on the Thomistic approach to satisfaction, is that the wrongdoer love the *Stellvertreter* in his role as *Stellvertreter*. If the wrongdoer does so, then even though he himself is not doing any of the work of satisfaction, it is still possible that the *Stellvertreter*'s work of satisfaction can do something to remove the stain on the soul from the wrongdoer, to one extent or another.

Given Aquinas's approach to satisfaction, then, it makes sense that Aquinas emphasizes the need for the wrongdoer and the *Stellvertreter* to be united in love. So, for example, Aquinas says,

> [with regard to satisfaction], which one takes upon oneself voluntarily, one may bear another's punishment, insofar as they are in some way one.[99]

In general, he says,

> the penalty of satisfaction is in a certain sense voluntary. It can happen that those who differ with respect to guilt [worthy of] penalty are one with respect to the will in a union of love. For this reason, sometimes someone who has not sinned voluntarily bears the penalty for another person.[100]

And elsewhere, in connection with Christ's passion, Aquinas claims that one person can compensate for another's wrongdoing insofar as they are one in charity.[101]

On the Thomistic approach to satisfaction, it makes sense that the wrong-doer has to love the *Stellvertreter* at least with regard to the satisfaction that the *Stellvertreter* is making. The stain on the soul of the wrongdoer cannot be remitted by what the *Stellvertreter* does unless the wrongdoer identifies with what the *Stellvertreter* does by way of satisfaction, so that the wrongdoer has both the desires of love with regard to the *Stellvertreter* in those actions by which the *Stellvertreter* makes satisfaction for the wrongdoer. For Aquinas, the

Stellvertreter is completely successful if the stain on the soul of the wrongdoer is removed; and so the wrongdoer needs to be allied with the *Stellvertreter* in what the *Stellvertreter* does.

On the Anselmian approach to satisfaction, by contrast, it is not clear why a wrongdoer would need to be united in love to the *Stellvertreter*. On any traditional interpretation of the doctrine of the atonement, something is needed from a human person Jerome if Jerome is to receive the benefits of Christ's atonement. But, on Anselm's approach to vicarious satisfaction, it is not clear why this would be so. On the Anselmian approach, Christ's atonement makes amends to God for human sin by giving God a gift that is pleasing to God and that is sufficient to outweigh all human evil. But, then, this gift is what it is and gives God the valuable present regardless of whether human beings unite themselves to Christ in love. And so it is not clear why on the Anselmian approach to satisfaction, Jerome's uniting himself in love to Christ is necessary for Christ to be a *Stellvertreter* for Jerome. Nothing about Jerome's loving Christ adds anything of value to Christ's gift to God. On the contrary, on the Anselmian approach to satisfaction, the *Stellvertreter* is successful if the offended party is placated; and the *Stellvertreter* can accomplish this end even if the wrongdoer is dead and does not know that satisfaction has been made.

So, on both the Anselmian and the Thomistic approach to satisfaction, it is possible that there be vicarious satisfaction, that one person act as *Stellvertreter* for another. But, though the words are the same, the things referred to by the words vary greatly depending on which approach to satisfaction we take.

CONCLUSION: WHERE THINGS ARE

In this chapter, I have tried to elucidate some of the concepts that are key for discussion of interpretations of the doctrine of the atonement: love, guilt, shame, the stain on the soul, satisfaction, and vicarious satisfaction. In this brief overview, I cannot begin to do justice to the complexity of these concepts or to the large literature on them; but I hope to have done enough to make it easier to use them without too much further explanation in the chapters to follow.

The atonement is a solution to the problem of the human proneness to moral wrongdoing. As this chapter helps to elucidate, that problem is in large part a matter of guilt and shame (shame generated either by one's own sins or the sin of others), as well as the other leftovers of moral wrongdoing. The work of the atonement then is to remedy, somehow, all these things.

It is hard to see what would constitute a remedy for shame, since shame is a matter of relative standing in comparison with other human beings in consequence of something in one's past life and condition, but the past is fixed, and not even God can alter it.

As for guilt, as this chapter has illustrated, it is possible to understand the obstacles to a remedy for guilt in different ways. The nature of the remedy needed depends on which of these ways is accepted.

In Chapter 3, I will argue against the Anselmian approach to satisfaction and the whole Anselmian kind of interpretation of the doctrine of the atonement. With the conclusion of that chapter, I will have completed the introductory material laying out the methodology of this project, the problems to which the atonement is meant to be the solution, the things that cannot work as a solution to those problems, and the desiderata for an acceptable interpretation of the doctrine.

In the remainder of the book, I will present the solution as I understand it, beginning with a sketch of what life in the saved state would look like and proceeding to an examination of Christ's passion and death (or incarnation, life, passion, and death) as a means to that state. And, in the last part of the book, I will show that this solution can handle all the desiderata for an acceptable interpretation of the doctrine.

3

The Anselmian Interpretation
of the Atonement

Love, Goodness, Justice, and Forgiveness

INTRODUCTION

In all its varieties, the Anselmian kind of interpretation of the doctrine of the atonement supposes that God is somehow required by his honor or goodness or justice or some other element of his goodness to receive reparation, penance, satisfaction, or penalty to make up for human wrongdoing as a condition for forgiving sinful human beings and accepting reconciliation with them.[1] On the Anselmian kind of interpretation, God does forgive human beings and does accept reconciliation with them—but only because Christ makes amends to God for human sin. God's forgiveness and reconciliation with human beings are therefore dependent on God's receiving reparation for human wrongdoing. Without such reparation being made to God, God's honor or goodness or justice or some other divine attribute would preclude God's forgiveness and reconciliation. Just as some philosophers of law suppose that it can be morally impermissible for a victim to forgive someone who has wronged her without the wrongdoer's having made amends to her, so the Anselmian kind of interpretation supposes that it is incompatible with God's nature to forgive human beings unless amends have been made to God for human wrongdoing.

It may help in this connection to see Anselm's own way of putting the point in his *Cur Deus Homo*.[2] Anselm's text is in the form of a dialogue, but in the interest of brevity I have elided the interlocutor's responses, which are largely just affirming of Anselm's thought. (I have marked the omissions with ellipsis dots.) Trying to explain why God's forgiveness of wrongdoers is necessarily dependent (as Anselm supposes) on God's receiving reparation for human sin, Anselm says,

Let's go back and see whether it is fitting for God to forgive sin [*peccatum dimittere*] by mercy alone, without any repayment of the honor that has been taken from him.... Forgiving sin in this way is the same as not punishing it. But to order sin in the right way when no recompense is made *just is* to punish sin. So if sin is not punished, it is left unordered.... But it is not fitting for God to leave anything unordered in his kingdom.... So it is not fitting for God to leave sin unpunished in this way.... And there is something else that follows if sin is left unpunished in this way: someone who sins will have the same standing before God as someone who does not sin. And that does not befit God.... Pay attention to this as well. Everyone knows that the justice of human beings is subject to this law: what God gives as a reward is proportionate to the greatness of a person's justice.... But if sin is neither discharged nor punished, it is subject to no law ... Therefore if injustice is forgiven by mercy alone, it is freer than justice, which is utterly absurd.... [3]

For Anselm, therefore, a perfectly good God cannot forgive human wrong-doers without repayment of the debt owed to God by human wrongdoers. Forgiveness without such repayment would be a violation of the goodness and justice of God.

As Anselm explains the atonement of Christ, human wrongdoing has generated a kind of enormous debt. God has the power to cancel this debt, but God cannot in justice do so. A perfectly good God cannot simply forgive human moral wrongdoing or accept reconciliation with wrongdoers without some kind of repayment. As Anselm explains elsewhere in the *Cur Deus Homo*, the sin or debt is so great because it is against God, and human beings already owe God so much, because they derive their very being from God, that it is not possible for human beings to make reparation to God for their sin. In fact, only God has the ability to provide such repayment. But only humans owe it and ought to provide it. God is infinitely merciful, however, and so he brings it about that he himself in human guise provides the needed reparation. The second person of the Trinity becomes incarnate as a human being in order to combine the resources of the Deity with the obligations of humankind.[4] As incarnate, through his passion and death (or through his life, passion, and death), Christ satisfies the honor or justice or goodness of God. In conse-quence, the way is open for God to forgive human beings their wrongdoing; and once God has forgiven them, God can also be reconciled with them. And so, by God's mercy exercised through Christ's atonement, human beings are able to be saved and brought to heaven.

In contemporary times, Thomas Torrance explains a similar idea this way:

the cross is so terrible, because the guilt it deals with is so infinite and terrible. And guilt is terrible because at the back of it there is the full force of the divine resistance to sin, God's godly wrath. The chasm that separates man from God in the very existence of sinful man is the black abyss of hell.... It is because the godly majesty of God, the righteous law of God, the holy love of God, stands inexorably in the path between mankind and God that the gravity of the situation is infinite. It is such that God and only God himself can deal with it.... [5]

Explaining J. McLeod Campbell's rejection of the Anselmian kind of interpretation of the doctrine of the atonement, James Torrance helps elucidate this same Anselmian attitude. Defending Campbell's rejection of this Anselmian attitude, Torrance says,

> [on this kind of interpretation of the doctrine of the atonement], the justice of God *is* the essential attribute, and the love of God (or the mercy of God) is an arbitrary attribute.... The demands of justice must be met before God can be merciful and this he does by providing One in Jesus who satisfies the demands of justice on behalf of the elect, in virtue of which there is forgiveness and salvation for these in whose stead Christ died. This McLeod Campbell rejected. God is love as truly as he is just. [6]

Different versions of the Anselmian kind of interpretation draw conclusions that are variations on the same basic theme. Penal substitution versions suppose that, without some substitute's bearing the penalty, God must sentence all human beings to damnation as the punishment for their wrongdoing. [7] Versions closer to Anselm's own account concentrate on some sort of repayment that a good and just God must receive. And, in contemporary times, Richard Swinburne has put the point in terms of the penance that must be given to God before God can in any morally appropriate way forgive wrongdoers. [8] Swinburne's own account emphasizes Christ's atonement as a sacrifice made to God. [9] Trying to improve on Swinburne's version of the Anselmian interpretation by defending a penal substitution variant on it, Steven Porter puts the Anselmian kind of interpretation that he wants to defend this way:

> If moral sense can be made of the idea that the punishment of sinners is what God requires for forgiveness and that this punishment was provided for in the crucifixion of Christ, then, whatever else this conception of the atonement may have in its favor, it plainly establishes a lucid rationale for Christ's voluntary sacrifice. [10]

At least for those varieties of the Anselmian interpretation that accept the doctrine of God's eternity, God's forgiveness of human wrongdoers and God's acceptance of reconciliation with them is not later in time than Christ's atonement. Or, to put the same point the other way around, Christ's making amends to God is not *temporally* prior to God's acceptance of reconciliation with wrongdoers, because, on the doctrine of God's eternity, *nothing* in time is temporally prior to anything in the life of God. But, on all variants on the Anselmian kind of interpretation, Christ's making amends to God is *logically* prior to God's forgiveness of sinners and God's acceptance of reconciliation with them. Christ's atonement is requisite for both. It is true that, on the

Anselmian kind of interpretation, God arranges for Christ's incarnation and Christ's making amends to God. So, on the Anselmian interpretation, God is never *unwilling* to forgive wrongdoers. But God's *actual* forgiveness of sinners and *actual* acceptance of reconciliation with them is dependent on Christ's making amends. The fact that God arranges the condition for his forgiveness of human beings does not make that condition any less necessary for God's forgiveness and acceptance of reconciliation.

There are then two claims central to all the variants on the Anselmian kind of interpretation of the doctrine of the atonement. First, without Christ's making amends to God, God would not forgive human wrongdoers or accept being reconciled with them. And, second, the main (or only) point of Christ's atonement is to satisfy a condition needed for God's forgiveness and reconciliation. Oliver Crisp, who is in this tradition of interpretation, likens God's acceptance of reconciliation with human beings to the pardon of a monarch.[11] On the Anselmian kind of interpretation, it is a pardon that is won for human beings by the atonement of Christ and that would not be given without that atonement. God's forgiveness and reconciliation with human beings, God's granting the pardon, is conditional on God's receiving what human sin owes God in the atonement of Christ.

One notable but often unremarked feature of the Anselmian kind of interpretation is the affective reaction it inspires. All interpretations of the doctrine of the atonement emphasize joy as the reaction to Christ's atonement on the part of people who take themselves to be saved by it. But different kinds of interpretation of the doctrine emphasize different objects for that joy. Because they take the point of Christ's atonement to be winning God's forgiveness for human sin, proponents of the Anselmian kind of interpretation tend to suppose that a redeemed person will rejoice in being liberated from guilt. The metaphors used in this tradition of interpretation to describe a person's coming to faith highlight this object of joy. So, for example, in *Pilgrim's Progress*, John Bunyan describes his protagonist, whose name is 'Christian', this way:

> the high way up which Christian was to go, was fenced on either side with a Wall, and that Wall is called *Salvation*. Up this way therefore did burdened Christian run, but not without great difficulty, because of the load on his back. He ran thus till he came at a place somewhat ascending; and upon that place stood a Cross.... [J]ust as Christian came up with the Cross, his burden loosened from off his shoulders, and fell from off his back...Then was Christian glad and lightsome and said with a merry heart, *He has given me rest, by his sorrow; and life, by his death.*[12]

Commenting on this Anselmian approach to joy in her magisterial book, *The Crucifixion*, Fleming Rutledge uses the same metaphor; she says, "The joy...is that of being released from the burden of sin."[13]

It is significant that, for those in the Anselmian tradition, the object of the joy is oneself and one's condition. But this way of thinking about the joy brought about by belief in Christ's atonement seems to me yet another mark against the Anselmian kind of interpretation. To rejoice in one's pardon, in one's liberation from guilt, is a self-regarding emotion; and so it misses joy in the very thing wanted by means of the atonement. Joy is in fact one of the fruits of the indwelling Holy Spirit, but the object of that joy is supposed to be Christ himself.[14] And I think it is worth noting that in Bunyan's magnificent chronicle of his own spiritual journey, *Grace Abounding to the Chief of Sinners*, when Bunyan describes what he himself takes joy in, it is undoubtedly Christ and his own union with Christ. That work of Bunyan's is decidedly non-Anselmian in its attitude towards Christ and human salvation.

It should be added in this connection that not all versions of the Anselmian kind of interpretation take the point of Christ's passion and death to be a pardon. A pardon implies that the persons pardoned are guilty. Some versions of the Anselmian kind of interpretation suppose that what Christ's passion and death achieve on behalf of human beings is a forensic status of *not guilty* given by God through Christ to human persons who are in fact guilty and sinful and remain so even with this verdict. So, for example, N.T. Wright says,

Within... covenant theology, the God-given means for putting the whole world right, we discover the running metaphor of the *law court*.... [This] is the utterly appropriate metaphor...[15]

And he explains the metaphor this way:

How can God act in such a way, declaring Abraham and all believers 'in the right', 'acquitted', even though they are ungodly and sinners? The answer: Jesus.[16]

On this variation on the Anselmian kind of interpretation, the forensic status given human persons through Christ is a legal fiction, if not an actual moral falsehood. By analogy, if the court at Nuremberg had declared Goering *not guilty*, the verdict would have been wrong: Goering was guilty. That fact does not change even when the judge is God, as Wright himself acknowledges: those declared 'acquitted' and 'in the right' are, as he says, "ungodly and sinners" and therefore guilty.

Furthermore, even if we consider those who submit to the system of judgment yielding the verdict of *not guilty*—for example, because they are repentant—the point remains the same. At Nuremberg, Speer proclaimed his repentance, but he was still guilty, as his very repentance testifies. If the court had declared him *acquitted*, the court's judgment would have been wrong. Speer was guilty, and it would have continued to be true that he was guilty even if God had declared him *acquitted*. And even if we imagine that somehow God's verdict can make ethical reality contrary to fact, so that if God declares Speer acquitted, then it somehow becomes true that Speer is not guilty,

nothing about such a verdict changes Speer. He remains a person complicit in
the horrible suffering of millions of people, and his internally fragmented self
remains the same as well. He would not have been fit for union with a perfectly
good God even if he had worn his status *acquitted* as a badge on his chest.

Coming into the earthly Paradise, newly created by God, Milton's Satan
discovers the nature of this problem. He has escaped hell and come to the
beauty and goodness of Eden, but he cannot join it; he can set foot in it, but he
cannot be part of it. He says in torment, "Which way I fly is Hell; myself am
Hell."[17] Throughout much of the earlier part of the poem, Satan has been
declaring himself more righteous than God, but he finishes this speech by
saying, "Evil, be thou my good" (l.110), thereby vividly evincing the reason
why there is only hell for him wherever he flies. There is no rest or peace for a
spirit that wants both good and evil in the same way at the same time. And no
forensic verdict alone can alter this problem for any person. In this respect,
both pardon and forensic verdict are by themselves entirely inefficacious to
effect the reconciliation with God that they proclaim.

Of course, typically, the Anselmian kind of interpretation adds something
to the basic account of atonement to explain how some human beings are in
fact sanctified, so that some people are saved and others are not; and, often
enough, there is a role for the Holy Spirit in this story of sanctification.[18] So, on
some accounts, the Holy Spirit applies the work of Christ's atonement to
individual people who have faith. For example, Crisp says,

> God ordains the salvation of Redeemed Humanity in eternity and then brings
> about the reconciliation of Redeemed Humanity by Christ's atoning work, a work
> that is then effectually applied to the elect in time by the secret work of the
> Holy Spirit.[19]

But it is worth noticing that, on the Anselmian kind of interpretation, the work
of Christ's atonement itself is just the obtaining of a pardon from God for
human wrongdoers. The rest of the process resulting in the salvation of some
human beings is not itself part of Christ's atonement.[20] Consequently, on this
view, Christ alone is not sufficient for salvation. But this conclusion is a
reductio of this view, since, on traditional Christian teaching, there are indis-
putable biblical texts claiming or implying that in his person and work Christ
is the sole savior of humankind.

In my view, the most disadvantaged of the variants on the Anselmian
interpretation is the penal substitution theory of the atonement.[21] It should
be said here that virtually all interpretations of the doctrine of the atonement
suppose that Christ's atonement rescues human beings from punishment.
What makes the penal substitution theory distinctive is its explanation of
the way in which Christ's atonement does so. Aquinas, who is not an adherent
of the penal substitution theory, explains the rescue from punishment
this way:

We are waiting to be freed from punishment, which awaits the guilty. For we shall be freed by Christ from sin, [which is] the cause of punishment.[22]

The idea of the penal substitution theory, however, is that human beings are freed from punishment because Christ bears the punishment that would otherwise have been theirs.

There is by now a large literature critical of the penal substitution theory,[23] and the objections I raised earlier to all versions of the Anselmian interpretation apply to the penal substitution theory also.[24] As I pointed out in Chapter 1, the Anselmian kind of interpretation addresses only the backward-looking problem of the human proneness to moral wrong. By itself, it offers no solution to the forward-looking problem, which has to do with present dispositions to moral wrongdoing and the consequent liability to future wrong acts. And, in fact, there are reasons for questioning whether the Anselmian interpretation is successful even in its treatment of the backward-looking problem. It leaves the problem of shame untouched, and there is also some question whether the Anselmian interpretation is successful when it comes to guilt.[25]

But, in addition to these general problems shared by all variants of the Anselmian kind of interpretation, there are others more specific to the penal substitution theory. For example, it is generally supposed that the doctrine of the atonement shows God as specially merciful. Mercy, however, is a matter of foregoing at least some of what is owed;[26] and, contrary to what it intends, the penal substitution theory of the atonement does not, in fact, present God as foregoing what is owed him because of human sin. According to the penal substitution theory, God exacts the full extent of the punishment due for human sin; God allows none of it to go unpunished. It is true that, on this theory, it is God who fully endures the punishment which sinful human beings deserve. This part of the story is perplexing; but what it shows is only that God has borne the punishment, not that God has agreed to forego any part of the punishment.

The proponent of the penal substitution theory might respond that God's foregoing what is owed to God consists precisely in God's not requiring that human beings endure the punishment for their sins but instead enduring it himself in the person of Christ. But it remains the case that on the penal substitution theory no part of the punishment due is omitted.

In response, the proponent of the penal substitution theory might object that God's justice precludes God's overlooking sin and that therefore, when Christ endures the punishment due for sin, God has dealt with sin in the only way a perfectly just God can. And since Christ is one in being with God the Father, the one enduring the punishment is the one against whom the sin was committed. Therefore, God's actions in and through Christ's atonement constitute mercy even if they do not omit punishment for sin.

But, apart from the other perplexities raised by this rejoinder, it seems not to emphasize God's justice, as it means to do, but rather to rest on a denial of it. The proponent of the penal substitution theory claims that any human being's sins are so great that it is a violation of justice (or some other divine attribute) not to punish that person with damnation. According to the proponent of the penal substitution theory, however, what God does is to punish not the sinner but a perfectly innocent person instead (a person who, even on the doctrine of the Trinity, is distinguishable from God the Father, who does the punishing). But how is this punishment just?[27] How is justice (or goodness or honor) served by God's punishing a completely innocent person in the place of the guilty?[28] And if God could after all forego punishing the guilty, why does he not simply do so?

Furthermore, as regards punishment, most versions of the penal substitution theory seem inconsistent both with the theory itself and also with regard to another fundamental Christian doctrine.

As regards self-consistency, penal substitution theories claim that in his suffering and death on the cross Christ paid the full penalty for human sin; and yet, on traditional Christian doctrine (typically also accepted by penal substitution theories) the full penalty for sin is everlasting damnation. But no matter what sort of agony Christ experienced in his crucifixion, it certainly was not (and was not equivalent to) everlasting damnation, if for no other reason than that Christ's suffering came to an end.[29] In addition, it is part of the theory that Christ voluntarily bears the punishment due all humanity. But it is not possible for something to be both voluntary and also a punishment.[30] So, for example, quoting Kant, Herbert Fingarette says,

> It is the humbling of the will that is of the essence [of punishment]. It is in this sense, as Kant said, 'If what happens to someone is willed by him, it cannot be a punishment'.... It is impossible to will to be punished' [footnote omitted].[31]

As regards consistency with other Christian doctrines, many (but not all) versions of the penal substitution theory maintain that Christ paid the penalty for all sin so that human beings do not have to do so. But it is a fundamental Christian doctrine that God justly condemns some people to everlasting punishment in hell. If Christ has paid the penalty for all sin, how is God just in demanding that some people pay the penalty again? And, for the variant which supposes that Christ has paid the penalty for the sin of only some human beings, because God has arranged a pardon for only some human beings and not for all of them, then this variant is inconsistent with God's justice in another way, since justice requires giving equal treatment to equal cases.[32]

So there is reason for worrying specially about the penal substitution version of the Anselmian kind of interpretation.

No doubt, any particular version of the Anselmian kind of interpretation—including Anselm's own—differs in some respect or other from the short description I have given of it here. In the thought of the Reformers in particular, there are sophisticated details and nuances necessarily omitted here.[33] But the aim of this book is not the elucidation of particular historical interpretations of the doctrine of the atonement; it is rather a philosophical investigation of the theological claims comprised in the doctrine itself. And, for that purpose, the summary above suffices. In my view, the general outline of that summary is correct in its characterization of the heart of those interpretations of the doctrine of the atonement that are suitably classified as falling into the Anselmian kind, and the varying details and nuances do not alter the general characterization or evaluation of those variants on the Anselmian interpretation.

In what follows in this chapter, I will leave to one side all the particular problems with the penal substitution theory or any other individual version of the Anselmian interpretation. Instead I want to examine what I think is the central and irremediable problem with all variants on the Anselmian kind of interpretation. This problem has to do with the divine attribute of love.

Love is not the attribute the Anselmian kind of interpretation emphasizes, of course; it tends to highlight God's justice. But God's justice must be part of God's goodness, and God's goodness must find its ultimate or highest expression in love. Furthermore, the claim that God is love is itself part of the revelation (I John 4:8) that orthodox Christian theologians mean to accommodate.[34]

For reasons I gave in Chapter 1, in what follows in this book, I will simply avail myself of Aquinas's understanding of love and of the other standard divine attributes.[35] His understanding of the divine attributes is not innovative with him and represents well the Christian tradition from the Patristic period to his own time. In addition, his own analysis of the divine attributes is philosophically acute, and his account of love is the most insightful and defensible of any I know, medieval or contemporary. Those who want to reject the conclusions of this chapter on the grounds that they do not accept the Thomistic account of love will need to find an account of love that is at least as true to the phenomena as the Thomistic account is but that does not lead just as readily to the rejection of the Anselmian kind of interpretation of the doctrine of the atonement. For my part, I do not think that there is such an alternate account of love.

In Chapter 2, I presented and defended Aquinas's general account of love as consisting in two desires, for the good of the beloved and for union with the beloved, and I explained the alterations that need to be made to that general account in order to apply it to God. On traditional Christian doctrine, God is perfectly loving to all human beings. And so, on Aquinas's account of love, God desires the good of each human person and union with her.[36] But, for

God, the two desires of love converge. In desiring the good for a human person and union with a human person, God is desiring the same thing, at least where the ultimate good is concerned. In addition, God's love is the source of whatever goodness or excellence there is in a person; all goodness in creatures is derived from God directly or indirectly. So, in loving a person, God is offering goodness to that person. If she does not resist God's love, then God's love is productive of goodness in her, not responsive to the goodness she has already produced in herself by herself.[37] Aquinas's account of love therefore applies also to God's love for human beings. Although God's love for human beings is in some respects a special case, nonetheless, *mutatis mutandis*, Aquinas's account of love as consisting in two mutually governing desires, for the good of the beloved and for union with the beloved, holds with regard to God's love, too.

In this chapter, I will examine the implications of the divine attribute of love, construed Thomistically, for God's justice, goodness, and forgiveness; and I will show the difference that the Thomistic account of God's love makes to interpretations of the doctrine of the atonement. I will present the account of forgiveness implied by Aquinas's account of love, and I will defend it against a number of possible objections to it. The resulting Thomistic account of forgiveness is explanatorily powerful, in my view. It has the implication that, in some cases of serious evil, forgiveness is not sufficient to remove guilt or to make possible reconciliation between the wrongdoer and others.[38] What else is needed in such cases includes making amends or making satisfaction. This conclusion about the need for satisfaction can appear to be a result favoring the Anselmian kind of interpretation of the doctrine of the atonement. But, contrary to what one might at first suppose, the fact that there can be such a need for satisfaction is finally just one more consideration telling decisively against the Anselmian kind of interpretation.

On the Thomistic account of love and its resulting account of forgiveness, then, the Anselmian kind of interpretation of the doctrine of the atonement can be seen to be unworkable. So far from preserving the divine attributes of goodness, justice, and love, the Anselmian kind of interpretation is in fact incompatible with God's love—and so also with God's goodness and God's justice.[39]

FORGIVENESS: THE BASIC NOTION

There is by now a considerable body of literature on the nature of forgiveness, and a certain understanding of forgiveness has become common.[40] A representative common account holds that for a person Jerome to be morally justified in granting forgiveness to someone Paula who has wronged him, Paula must first repent and apologize and then must make amends to Jerome; and it also holds that Jerome's forgiveness is a matter of his forswearing resentment against Paula in consequence of her making amends.[41] Making amends is commonly construed as reparation of damage done and some additional compensation or penance for the injustice of the wrong. So, for example, Richard Swinburne, who defends such a common account of forgiveness, says,

> An agent's guilt is removed when his repentance, reparation, apology, and penance find their response in the victim's forgiveness.[42]

Finally, on the common account, morally appropriate forgiveness and reconciliation go together. A victim who forgives a wrongdoer in a morally appropriate way is thereby also appropriately reconciled with the wrongdoer. With Jerome's morally appropriate forgiveness of Paula, Paula's guilt is removed; and so there can and should be reconciliation between them.

As has been pointed out by others, however, there are many problems with this common account. To begin with, Jerome may feel reactive emotions other than resentment. He may instead feel contempt or alienation or fear with regard to Paula.[43] And the claim that the moral permissibility of forgiveness depends on the wrongdoer's having made amends has counter-intuitive consequences. It implies, for example, the counter-intuitive evaluation that the father in the parable of the prodigal son should have waited till his son had made amends before he forgave his son. It implies that no one should forgive the dead, who can no longer make amends. And it implies that a victim is hostage to the good will of the wrongdoer before he can reach the relative psychic stability of morally appropriate forgiveness.[44] Finally, insofar as forgiveness seems a response to something in the past and reconciliation is an attitude towards a relationship in the future, it seems clear that forgiveness and reconciliation can come apart. The victim might forgive the wrongdoer in morally appropriate ways but be too traumatized by her wrong against him for reconciliation with her to be morally appropriate for him, for example.[45]

In my own view, in the context of the current discussion of forgiveness, a much more promising account of forgiveness is implied by Aquinas's account of love. Whatever exactly is required for morally appropriate forgiveness,[46] it must involve some species of love for the person in need of forgiveness. A person who refuses to forgive someone who has hurt her or been unjust to her is not loving towards the offender, and a person who does forgive someone who has treated her badly also manifests love of one degree or another towards him. So whatever else forgiveness is,[47] it seems to include a kind of love of someone who has done one an injury or committed an injustice against one.

Since love emerges from the interaction of two desires, for the good of the beloved and for union with her, the absence of either desire is sufficient to undermine love. To the extent to which love is implicated in forgiveness, the absence of either desire undermines forgiveness, too.[48] So, for example, a resentful desire for revenge is incompatible with love of the person against whom the desire for vengeance is directed. A resentful or vengeful person does not love his enemy in virtue of the fact that he desires what is bad, rather than what is good, for his enemy. For the same reason, such a person does not forgive his enemy either. On Aquinas's account of love, however, this is not the only way to fail to forgive. For Jerome to forgive Paula when she has hurt him or treated him unjustly, it is not enough for Jerome to have only one of the desires of love, the desire for the good, for Paula. It is also necessary for him to have a desire for union with Paula—if nothing else, then at least the generic desire for union that is an element of the general love for humanity.[49] If Jerome desires the good for Paula but rejects totally any desire for union with her, he fails to love her, in virtue of lacking a desire for union with her. For that reason, he also fails to forgive her.

Since forgiveness, like love, includes a desire for union, it also includes a desire for reconciliation. On this account, then, forgiveness and the desire for reconciliation go together. But, like the desire for union itself, a desire for reconciliation need not be fulfilled. Whether or not the desires of love are fulfilled is not solely up to the person loving. It is possible for a person to love unrequitedly; and, analogously, it is possible for a person who forgives someone to fail to be reconciled with her. It might be the case, for example, that something in her wards off the fulfillment of his desire for reconciliation.

Finally, on Aquinas's account, love is obligatory,[50] in the sense that, for any person, the absence of love detracts from moral excellence,[51] and the presence of love is necessary for it.[52] Given the connection between love and forgiveness, it follows that forgiveness is also obligatory[53] in the same way and to the same extent.[54] It does *not* follow that any given wrongdoer has a right to forgiveness from any person whom he has hurt or against whom he has committed an injustice.[55] On Aquinas's view (as also on many contemporary accounts), rights and obligations are not correlative.[56] Jerome can have an obligation with regard to Paula even if Paula does not have a correlative right with regard to Jerome. So even though Paula has no right to Jerome's forgiveness, on Aquinas's views Jerome would be subject to appropriate moral censure if he refused to forgive Paula. In refusing to forgive her, Jerome would be unloving towards her; and in being unloving, Jerome would be worthy of moral disapprobation.

On this account, then, forgiveness is unilateral and unconditional. It does not depend on a wrongdoer's making amends or even being repentant, and it can be given to the dead, insofar as one can desire the good for a dead person and peace or accord with him rather than alienation from him. On this view of forgiveness, we also get the right reading of the parable of the prodigal son: the father does not need his son to make amends before he can forgive him and accept reconciliation with him in morally appropriate ways.

THE THOMISTIC ACCOUNT OF FORGIVENESS: A COMMONSENSICAL OBJECTION AND ITS RESOLUTION

Suppose that Jerome and Paula are partners and that Jerome is abusive towards Paula, who loves him. Someone might object that Aquinas's account of love and the concomitant account of forgiveness have the counter-intuitive implication that Paula ought to continue to endure Jerome's abuse in order to continue loving him since, on Aquinas's account, Paula is obligated to love Jerome and so also to forgive him. It seems to follow that she is also obligated to stay with Jerome and maintain her companionship with him in order to continue having towards him the two desires of love. Consequently, on this objection, Aquinas's account of love and forgiveness requires Paula to be an enabler of Jerome's abusiveness towards her. And, in general, the objection supposes, Aquinas's account seems to leave no room for righteous indignation or any other kind of combating of human wrongdoing. On the contrary, it seems to connive with every kind of injustice in the name of love and forgiveness.[57]

But this objection is mistaken. To see that this is so, consider that to desire the good for Jerome requires foregoing the bad for Jerome; but what the good and the bad for Jerome actually are will depend on Jerome. The desire for Jerome's good need not include the willingness to give Jerome what he wants. Desiring Jerome's good requires giving him what he wants if that would be for his good—or insisting on the opposite of what he wants if *that* would be for his good. What is best for Jerome is whatever it takes to bring Jerome to a more just or less harmful condition in mind and will. Paula's calling the police or hiring a lawyer might be the best for Jerome in some circumstances. So for Paula to love Jerome, she must desire the objective good for Jerome—but *what* that good is will be determined by Jerome's character and the current state of his mind and will.

For this same reason, Paula's desire for union with Jerome need not include a desire to remain in companionship with Jerome. If Jerome is entirely unrepentant, or if his repentance is genuine but not trustworthy and the chances are excellent that he will soon hurt Paula again, then Paula's desire for union with him need not—in fact, should not—involve a willingness to live with Jerome. At worst, by his actions, Jerome can destroy any significant office of love he held or might hold with Paula. In that worst case, Paula's desire for union with Jerome can appropriately come to no more than the sort of desire for union involved in the generic love of humanity provided for in Aquinas's account of love.

So, when Paula forms the two desires of love for Jerome, the nature of the appropriate fulfillment of those desires has to be a function of Jerome's state. Whether Paula should have any continued companionship with Jerome, and the character and extent of such company, depends on Jerome's state. If Jerome poses a serious threat to Paula's having what is good for her, then Paula's staying with Jerome or otherwise allowing Jerome to harm her enables Jerome to violate the desires of love for her. But his failure at loving her is not good for Jerome. Paula is not loving Jerome, then, in letting him harm her or treat her unjustly; rather, she is violating the desires of love with regard to Jerome in being an enabler of his wrongdoing against her.[58] Insofar as Paula's forgiveness of Jerome is a matter of loving Jerome when he has acted wrongly towards her, then the same points apply to forgiveness.

Consequently, it is possible for Paula to forgive Jerome unilaterally, without repentance on Jerome's part, because it is up to Paula alone whether she desires the good for Jerome and union with him. But *the way* in which the desires of love in forgiveness are fulfilled, or whether they are fulfilled at all, will depend crucially on the condition of the wrongdoer being forgiven. Paula's *desire* for the good for Jerome cannot be fulfilled if, in self-destructive impulses, Jerome refuses the good offered him. And Paula's *desire* for union with Jerome cannot by itself effect reconciliation with him as long as his state of character and current condition keep her from being close to him.

A person can forgive unilaterally, then, just as she can love unrequitedly. But the desires of love in forgiveness, like the desires of love generally, are inefficacious by themselves to bring about what they desire. A person who forgives, like a person who loves, has to be responsive to the person who is the object of her desires; and so she cannot have what she wants, in love or forgiveness, just by wanting it.

Since God is perfectly loving, these conclusions about forgiveness apply to God as well. Like human persons, God can forgive a wrongdoer unilaterally and unconditionally, in the sense that, even without any repentance on the wrong-doer's part, God can still desire the good for her and union with her. Since God is perfectly loving, God always does desire the good for a person, and this good is God's union with her. Because failure to forgive involves failure to desire the good for a wrongdoer or failure to desire union with her, failure to forgive is also a failure to love. Therefore, since God loves every person, God also actually forgives every wrongdoer, whether or not she accepts either God's love or God's forgiveness. Finally, in desiring union with every person, God is also accepting reconciliation with every wrongdoer, whether or not she (or anyone acting on her behalf) makes amends for her wrongdoing.

AGAINST THE IMPLICATIONS OF THE THOMISTIC
NOTION OF FORGIVENESS: HATRED AND ANGER

At this point, someone might object to these conclusions about God's love and forgiveness on the basis of biblical texts that seem to be about God's hatred. It is true that the book of Wisdom claims that God loves everything and hates nothing that God has made, and the first Epistle of John claims that God is love.[59] But there is a line in Malachi in which God says that he hated Esau.[60] Furthermore, there are Gospel texts in which Christ says that on Judgment Day, he will say to some people 'I never knew you. Depart from me, you who do evil' (Matt. 7:23; cf. Luke 13:27). Telling some people to go away does seem the opposite of desiring union with them. And so it seems as if Christ does not love the people he sends away but rather hates them. It can seem, then, that, contrary to what I claimed above, according to these and other biblical passages God does not love and forgive all wrongdoers, and God does not accept reconciliation with all of them either. Rather, God's love is replaced by hatred at least sometimes, with regard to some people, whom God therefore does not forgive.[61]

But here it is worth noticing that, on the Thomistic account of love, there are two different kinds of hatred,[62] one of which is the opposite of love and one of which is actually a species of love.[63] Hatred of both kinds will be the same in desiring not to be united (in some sense) with the hated person. The two kinds of hatred will differ, however, in their ultimate desires for the person who is the recipient of these attitudes.

To see this distinction in kinds of hatred, it helps to have in mind a particular case of very serious moral wrongdoing; so consider again the case of Otto Moll.[64] Someone contemporary with Moll who wanted to be united with Moll during Moll's time in power in Auschwitz, that is, someone who wanted to join Moll in his evil acts and ambitions, would have been wanting what is in effect not good for Moll. Moll would have been much better off being opposed than being joined, given that his actions and desires were so evil. Furthermore, real union is possible only among people who are themselves integrated around the moral good.[65] Consequently, however much one might ally oneself with a person such as Moll, it will not be possible to be united with him while he is committed to serious evil. The closest one can come to such a person while he is sunk in such evil is to stay at a distance from him and hope for a change of heart for him. So to want to stay at a distance from a person such as Moll can be to want what is objectively good for him, and the desire for union with him will in any case not be able to effect union while Moll remains in his evil condition.

For all these reasons, there is a kind of hatred that is a species of the desires of love. It is a matter of desiring not to be united with a wrongdoer now, when he is bad enough that the alienation of others is the best thing for him in the circumstances, *and* one wants this alienation from him *as the best* for him in the hope of ultimate union with him.[66]

On the other hand, there is also a kind of hatred that is the opposite of love. In the grip of this kind of hatred, one will desire to be at a distance from Moll; but one will desire this alienation from Moll *as what is ultimately bad* for Moll. That is, a person in the grip of this kind of hatred will be glad if Moll becomes worse, increasingly distant from his own flourishing and from shared union with God. This is hatred, too, but it is the kind of hatred that is incompatible with love.

In the grip of the kind of hatred that is a species of love, one will desire distance from Moll, but Moll's ultimate flourishing will also be something one wants. For these reasons, one will want Moll ultimately to have as much real good as he can, and one will desire union with Moll if and when Moll's condition allows it. This kind of hatred of Moll is a form of love for him. But one can have a hatred of Moll that makes one desire the very opposite of the ultimate good for Moll and ultimate union with Moll. A person hating Moll in this way would be disappointed or grieved if Moll repented and reformed his life. This kind of hatred is incompatible with love.

A similar sort of distinction can be made as regards anger.[67] Anger also comes in two kinds, one of which is a species of love and one of which is the opposite of love.[68] Sometimes the distinction is expressed by calling the first kind of anger 'righteous indignation' and the second kind 'wrath.'[69] In both kinds of anger, an angry person wants something that is in some sense not the good for the person with whom she is angry. But if she also has a desire that the wrongdoer will become someone with whom she can be appropriately *not* angry and for whom she can will the unconditional good, then her anger is a species of love.

Suppose, for the sake of example, that Moll had a morally decent mother who loved him. Then if Moll's mother desired that Moll lose his position at Auschwitz, she would have been desiring something which was in some sense bad for Moll. That is because it is bad for a person when he loses what he himself very much wants,[70] and Moll wanted very much not to lose his position at the camp. On the other hand, if what a person has his heart set on is itself very bad, then it is good, all things considered, that he suffer the bad of not getting what he wants. It would have been better *for Moll* if he had lost his position at Auschwitz; that is, it would have been better for Moll himself if he had died as someone other than the moral monster he was enabled to become in consequence of the position he held at Auschwitz. And so, in this sort of case, for Moll's mother to want what is in some sense bad for Moll is for her to want what is ultimately and objectively the good for Moll.

If, on the contrary, Moll's mother would have been glad if Moll had never changed for the better but had stayed the sort of person towards whom her anger was righteous, then her anger towards Moll would have been the opposite of love. It would have been wrath.

Some of the controversy over whether anger is a morally good reaction to wrongdoing or whether anger is always tainted by a 'payback wish'[71] can be resolved by seeing the distinction between these two kinds of anger. Wrath may well be vindictive and so not conducive to the good of either the wrongdoer or the victim; but righteous indignation is the reasonable and also the loving response to some kinds of wrongdoing. Furthermore, although forgiveness requires forswearing wrath, insofar as forgiveness is loving and wrath is not, forgiveness does not require giving up righteous indignation. A victim can have righteous indignation against someone who has wronged her even while she desires the good for him and union with him.

This account of forgiveness therefore has the consequence that a person can count as forgiving a wrongdoer even while she also is angry at him or hates him. Moll's mother might well have been angry at her son (or even hating of him) and yet also simultaneously forgiving him. This complex condition in her is a function of Moll's state. Forgiveness can be unilateral, but actual reconciliation cannot; it has to be mutual. Insofar as the putting away of anger or the putting away of hatred are part of a process of reconciliation,[72] such putting away has to be responsive to the wrongdoer's condition. Moll's mother might well yearn for the good for her son and union with him, even while she is bitterly angry with him because of his participation in moral monstrosity. If he were ever to repent and try to make amends, he might ask his mother for forgiveness. And then, if his mother had in fact all the while had for her son the two desires of love, she might well say to him, "You have always been forgiven. I have just been waiting for you to find your way back from the horror you were in."

Contrary to first impressions, then, it is not this consequence of the Thomistic account of forgiveness—that one can count as forgiving while remaining angry at the wrongdoer or even hating him—that is counter-intuitive. Rather, it is the rejection of this consequence that is counter-intuitive. If we rejected this consequence in the case of Moll and his mother, then we would have to suppose that being angry at her son or even having hatred towards her son is incompatible with the mother's loving him. On that supposition, while his mother is angry with Moll or hates Moll, she does not have for him either of the two desires of love. That is, she lacks a desire for Moll's repentance and reform, or she even has a desire that he not repent and reform so that she can continue hating him or being wrathful at him. This is the condition of a person who says to the wrongdoer with fervor and convic-tion, "I hope you rot in hell forever!" But surely it is counter-intuitive to suppose that, in virtue of being angry at her son or hating him for his evil, his mother has to be in so morally ugly a condition as to be glad if Moll never reformed. On the contrary, anger and hatred can be compatible with love, as these considerations show. For the same reasons, they can be compatible with forgiveness too.

Given these ways of characterizing the two differing species of hatred and anger, one might wonder what the difference between hatred and anger is in the case where each of them is a species of love. One way to make the distinction is to see them as having somewhat different emphases as regards the two desires of love.[73] When Paula is angry with Jerome, she will focus more on the desire for something that is not for his good in some sense. When she hates Jerome, she will be more intent on a desire not to be united with Jerome.[74] In the case of the anger that is a species of love, Paula is rejecting what is the good for Jerome now, while maintaining a desire for what is ultimately the true good for Jerome. In the case of the hatred that is a species of love, Paula is rejecting Jerome himself, while maintaining a desire to have ultimately what is true union with Jerome. Taking the distinction between hatred and anger in this way explains why hatred is a more serious breach in personal relations than anger, even when each of them is a species of love. When Paula is angry with Jerome, she is still mindful of Jerome and connected to him, although that connection might consist in her being mindful of what Jerome deserves for his wrongdoing. But when Paula hates Jerome, she will focus her desire on distance from him. She will turn her back on him, as we say.[75] To the extent to which personal relations require face-to-face interaction, turning one's back on someone makes a decisive break—at least for a while—in those relations, as anger need not do.

So forgiveness requires one's maintaining towards a wrongdoer the desire for his good and the desire for union with him, but both these desires of love have to be responsive to things in the wrongdoer. If he is intransigent in his wrongdoing, then the desires of love might be restricted to the desires that constitute a kind of anger or hatred, provided that they are encompassed within a desire for ultimate union with him. Encompassed in this way, the desires of this kind of anger or hatred are a species of love. Without such an encompassing desire, the anger or hatred in question is opposed to love.

The two biblical lines about God, that he loves everyone and that he hates Esau, are therefore compatible if the hatred at issue in the statement about Esau is understood as the kind that is a species of love. As for the Gospel text in which Christ expresses a desire that on Judgment Day some people go away, the reason he has for this desire is implied in his characterization of them: 'you who do evil.' Those who do evil are those who have persisted in rejecting the divine love that would have produced in them the good missing when they do evil. Because they reject God's love, the anger or hatred that is one of the species of love is the only kind of love with which God can love them while they are in that condition.[76] For all these reasons, the biblical texts claiming or implying that God hates some people are compatible with the claim that God is perfectly loving and therefore also always forgiving of every wrongdoer.

AGAINST THE THOMISTIC ACCOUNT OF FORGIVENESS: JUSTICE, RETRIBUTION, AND THE DESIRE FOR THE GOOD OF THE BELOVED

In this connection, it is necessary to say something briefly about retributive punishment. Justice is a virtue, and it is an element of the goodness of God, too. On the view of some people, retributive punishment is the configuration justice takes towards certain people in certain circumstances.

So, for example, Fingarette says,

> retributionists through the centuries have insisted that we must punish offenders for their offenses. On my view, in this insistence they...have been right.[77]

And he defends this position by grounding the moral necessity of retributive punishment in the very nature of law. He says,

> It is part of what it means for the law to exercise its power over us, to require things of us, that those who don't of their own will comply are normally punished.[78]

Cynthia Ozick raises a different sort of objection to accounts that seem to favor forgiveness over punishment. She says,

> [F]orgiveness is pitiless. It forgets the victim. It negates the right of the victim to his own life. It blurs over suffering and death. It drowns the past. It cultivates sensitiveness toward the murderer at the price of insensitiveness toward the victim.[79]

To people such as Fingarette and Ozick, who are in favor of retributive punishment in the interests of respect for law and justice, it may seem as if Aquinas's account privileges love over justice in a morally inappropriate way, because it mandates forgiveness.[80] On the view of such objectors, the wrong a person does might make it morally necessary to maintain towards that person the attitudes of anger or hatred that are not a species of love, because what the wrongdoer deserves, what is his due, is only retributive punishment and not forgiveness.

On this view, it is mistaken to suppose that forgiveness is always obligatory even if one also holds that the wrongdoer has no right to it. On the contrary, in certain circumstances, it can be obligatory to fail to forgive, in the interest of justice. For the putative objector, Aquinas's views of love and forgiveness do not take moral wrongdoing seriously enough.[81] If Jerome has committed a grave enough wrong against Paula, then Paula should neither forgive him nor love him. Instead, in the interest of justice, she should seek only retributive punishment for him. To do anything else is to make the world a worse place than it might otherwise be in virtue of condoning, by inappropriately forgiving, significant moral wrongs.[82]

To evaluate these claims as an objection to Aquinas's account of love and forgiveness, it is crucial to understand whether, in the view of the putative objector, warranted retributive punishment is a good for the person punished. That is because if the putative objector believes that retributive punishment is a good for the person punished, then he has no quarrel with Aquinas's views of love and forgiveness. On Aquinas's views, a person could count as loving and forgiving of someone even if he also desired some punishment for that person, provided that he has a warranted desire for the punishment as a good for the other.[83] To provide an objection to Aquinas's account of love and forgiveness, then, the putative objector must accept the supposition that retributive punishment is not a good for the person punished.

So we need to include this supposition in the objection if it is to have force against the Thomistic account of forgiveness. But then we also need to examine the supposition. For this purpose, it helps to return to the case of Moll. On the supposition the putative objector accepts, it would have been better *for Moll* if he had escaped retributive punishment; Moll would have been better off if he had not been judged and punished for the evil acts that he had done. On the objector's supposition, it would have been better for Moll if he had been allowed to live out the remainder of his life without retributive punishment.

But, in my view, this supposition is false. To see why, consider the period between the time of Moll's wrongdoing and the time at which punishment was imposed. There are three possibilities for Moll in this period: he could be repentant; or, if he were unrepentant, he could be capable of repentance or incapable of it. We can take these possibilities in turn and look at the objector's supposition in connection with each of them.[84]

If Moll were repentant during the period in question,[85] then presumably he himself would welcome some penalty assigned him as a way in which he could do something, no matter how limited, to make amends for his evil. Albert Speer presented himself as a repentant Nazi at the Nuremberg trials, and it was part of the repentance he expressed that he accepted as good and appropriate the sentence of imprisonment assigned him at his trial.[86] And, in general, it does seem true that a person genuinely and deeply repentant for serious moral wrongdoing will see the penalty assigned him as a good he himself wants.[87] He will be more pained over his wrongdoing and more tormented by his guilt if there is nothing he does to make up for it. And this attitude seems not only understandable but in fact reasonable and right. Speer was imprisoned and other high-ranking Nazis were not but rather escaped to continue to live free elsewhere. But, by comparison with, say, the unpunished Nazis who lived out their lives in a small community of unrepentant exiles in Argentina, Speer's life seems much better.[88]

Consequently, for cases of repentant wrongdoers, the putative objector's supposition that retributive punishment is not a good for the punished person is false. So, seeking punishment for a repentant Moll is compatible with the first desire of love and therefore with forgiveness as well.

Suppose then that, during the period in question, Moll were unrepentant but capable of repentance. As Moll's own testimony during his interrogations makes clear, engaging in morally horrific acts takes a terrible psychic toll on a person. As Moll portrayed himself, he suffered a nervous breakdown after his work at Auschwitz, and he continued to endure an afflicting mental illness afterwards. If there is any possibility of peace and psychic healing for a person such as Moll, it seems much more likely to come if Moll is repentant than if he is not. But it is also plausible that such a person is much more likely to find repentance if he is compelled through judgment and the imposition of punishment to accept the verdict of the rest of the world on him. The problem for Moll in his unrepentant state is that he is still in denial about the evil he did and still determined to validate his morally monstrous actions as morally acceptable. As the story of the Nuremberg trials show, being forced to go through that trial and face its verdict and punishment could bludgeon the denial of wrongdoing even on the part of some hardened perpetrators of evil. And so, understood in this way, the judgment and punishment of a wrongdoer such as Moll are a good for him, even if he lacks repentance, provided only that he is capable of it.

In this case too, then, the objector's supposition is false, and seeking punishment for an unrepentant Moll is compatible with love and forgiveness of him.

Consider, then, the third and final case. Suppose that Moll is unrepentant and, for the sake of this thought experiment, stipulate that Moll is incapable of repentance, for one reason or another. Even so, it remains the case that Moll can become morally worse. Increase in moral depravity is itself an evil for Moll, and it will take a further toll on Moll's psyche. Insofar as punishment restricts Moll and reins him in, it helps to prevent in him the additional moral evil attendant on his holding the view that he can do horrific acts with impunity. If Germany had not lost the war, if Moll had not been captured and brought to judgment, who does not suppose it likely that Moll would have sunk even deeper into evil and concomitant psychic pathology?

And so, even if judgment and punishment do not make Moll better, they can keep him from getting worse. In this case also, then, retributive punishment of Moll is a good for Moll and therefore also compatible with the desires of love and with forgiveness.

For these reasons, the supposition of the putative objector that warranted retributive punishment is not a good for a wrongdoer is mistaken.[89] But since this supposition is mistaken and such punishment can be a good for a perpetrator of evil such as Moll, then this objection to Aquinas's views of love and forgiveness is mistaken as well. It is possible to take justice very seriously, it is possible to hold that imposing warranted retributive punishment on a wrongdoer is at least sometimes obligatory, and still to maintain that love

and forgiveness are always obligatory, even love and forgiveness for wholly
unrepentant wrongdoers.[90]

AGAINST THE THOMISTIC ACCOUNT OF FORGIVENESS: GOD'S LOVE, GOD'S JUSTICE, AND GOD'S MERCY

The issue of justice can arise with regard to God's love, too. An objector might
suppose that whatever the case might be as regards human justice and
forgiveness, God's justice requires that God not love some people, the unrepentant evildoers such as Otto Moll, for example. On the putative objector's
view, however we might interpret biblical texts about God's love or hatred,
God's justice requires that God hate unrepentant evildoers with the hatred that
is the opposite of love.

The heart of the notion of justice in the Western tradition influenced by
Aristotle is the idea that justice consists in giving to each person what is his
due, that is, what is owed to him or what counts in some way as his own. But
here it has to be said that there is some question about how to understand
God's justice towards a human person. The acceptance of God's grace and of
God's love are good states for a human person. Consequently, these states also
result from an infusion of God's grace into that person. And because God is
perfectly loving, and love consists in desires for the good of the beloved and
union with the beloved, God will infuse the grace needed for these good states
into anyone who does not reject that grace.[91] The love and forgiveness of God
therefore precede any goodness on the part of a person Paula, including even
Paula's acceptance of grace.

For this reason, we can speak of human merit only in an extended sense, in
which those goods in a person that are produced by grace are graciously
attributed to that person, although in reality it is God's goodness that is
productive of all good and all real merit in human persons.[92] On any resolutely
anti-Pelagian view, even Paula's acceptance of grace is the product of grace,
which God gives every person who does not reject it. And God's *offer* of grace
extends always to every person, those who are still innocent and those who are
evildoers, even those who are unrepentant evildoers.

So if justice is a matter of giving every person his due but everything good in
a human person is already a product of grace given her by God, it is not easy to
understand what God's giving a human person her due might be. However we
are to understand God's justice, it cannot be a matter of God's weighing up the
greater or lesser amount of good in a person which that person has gotten or
failed to get for herself by herself.

Aquinas supposes that God's justice is a matter of something's being owed
to God. On Aquinas's view of God's justice, then, the objector's complaint can

be formulated this way: God owes it to himself not to love the unrepentant perpetrators of serious wrongdoing, but to hate them with the hatred that is the opposite of love.

In response to this objection, I would say that it *is* reasonable to suppose that the justice of God requires God to have what is owed to God. But what is owed to God is surely that God should have what his perfectly good will wants. What God wants is that God's goodness should be given to his creation to the maximal extent possible.[93] As I have been at pains to show above, God's perfectly good will is the will with which God loves everything that he has made, unrepentant wrongdoers included. Since love includes a desire for the good of the beloved, what is owed to God by God's justice is therefore that God should have as much good for each human person and as much union with each human person as is possible, which is as much as each human person will allow. And there is biblical warrant for this view; I Timothy 2:4 claims that God desires the salvation of every human person.

God's justice is therefore not a response to the merits in a human person that she has acquired for herself by herself. On all anti-Pelagian views, there are no such merits. On the contrary, God's justice is God's having what is owed to God; and that is God's having God's will, which is the will of love. And so God's justice is encompassed in God's love; it is not in any way opposed to it. God's justice is simply one aspect of God's goodness and love.[94]

Similar things can be said about God's mercy. Like God's justice, God's mercy is a matter of giving goodness to human persons. God's mercy differs from God's justice insofar as God's mercy perfects God's justice by expelling from a human person those defects which keep that person at a distance from God.[95] But, then, God's justice is not opposed to God's mercy. God's justice and mercy, like God's love generally, always seeks the ultimate good of every human person and produces it in her, if only she does not reject that grace of God's. And the ultimate and final good, which God seeks for each person, is union with God.

So God loves and forgives every person, even those persons who reject God's love wholly, with one species of love or another; and God's justice is fulfilled in God's doing so.

A FINAL OBJECTION AGAINST THE THOMISTIC ACCOUNT OF FORGIVENESS

The Nature of the Objection

In my view, these reflections lay to rest the concern that Aquinas's account of love privileges love over justice. But these same reflections can raise concerns on the other side of the issue. It might seem to an objector that the Thomistic account of love and forgiveness weighs considerations of justice more heavily than the forgiveness that a repentant person hopes for. And so it might seem to an objector that Aquinas's account is eviscerated of whatever is attractive and consoling about a theory mandating love and forgiveness, because it privileges justice over love.

To appreciate this objection to the Thomistic account, it is helpful to consider an extreme case.

Imagine, for example, a person kidnapped and transported on one of Newton's slave ships. Then Newton's victim, the enslaved person, might manage even in these circumstances to desire the good for Newton and union with Newton. That is, she might desire that Newton would repent and radically reform his life (in the way Newton actually did), so that Newton was fit to have equal moral standing with other morally decent human beings. In fact, Newton did repent and reform; his repenting was a great good for him, and his reform restored him to the human family from which his monstrous evil had distanced him. So, in this thought experiment, in desiring that Newton would repent and reform, his victim is in effect desiring what was actually the good for Newton and union with Newton.

But while Newton is still utterly unrepentant of his evil of slave-trading, his victim might also hope that some punishment for his evil might befall him, and she might also fervently desire not to be associated with him. In other words, she might have morally appropriate anger against Newton and hatred of him.[96] But the desires of anger and hatred would not be incompatible with her also desiring that Newton repent and reform.

In this thought experiment, then, on the Thomistic account of love and forgiveness Newton's victim counts as loving and forgiving Newton even while she has anger and hatred for him and hopes for punishment for him. And, by parity of reasoning, something analogous can be said about God and God's relations to human wrongdoers. The inscription Dante puts on the gate of Hell in *The Inferno* says that Hell is founded on God's love. On the Thomistic account, it could add 'and on God's forgiveness.'

And now the problem with the Thomistic account of forgiveness, as the putative objector sees it, should be clear. What a repentant person hopes for is pardon and reconciliation, and even the perpetrators of moral monstrosity can repent. In *The Sunflower: On the Possibility and Limits of Forgiveness*,[97] Simon Wiesenthal presents the case of a dying German soldier who is guilty of horrendous evil against Jewish men, women, and children, but who desperately wants forgiveness and reconciliation with at least one Jew before he dies. It will seem to such a repentant person a mockery of forgiveness to be told that he is forgiven and even loved but that he will nonetheless be punished and rejected. And so since the Thomistic account of love yields the conclusion that there are circumstances in which people (or even God) can love and forgive an evildoer even while they fail to grant him reconciliation, the putative objector will hold, the Thomistic account of love and forgiveness is harsh and counter-intuitive, at best, and self-inconsistent, at worst.[98]

In my view, however, this objection is mistaken. The mistake has its source in two false assumptions on the putative objector's part: (1) that the repentance of a wrongdoer such as the repentant solder in Wiesenthal's story is sufficient to undo the damage done *to the soldier* from his evil actions against his victims, and (2) that the effects on the world of past wrongdoing do not matter to the wrongdoer's actual reconciliation with others.

The Resolution of the Objection: The Limits of Repentance and the Psyche of the Wrongdoer

In general, when a person such as the German soldier in *The Sunflower* engages in a morally monstrous action against others, his will desires that action as a kind of good (pleasurable, prudential, moral, or some combination of these goods) in those circumstances at that time; and his intellect validates what his will desires.[99] If something in his intellect and will were not on the side of his acting in those evil ways, he would not engage in those actions. Repentance heals these flaws in the intellect and will of the evildoer; when he repents, his repentance undoes what went wrong in his intellect and will when he engaged in his evil acts. In genuine and deep repentance, his intellect accepts single-mindedly that he was wrong in those acts, and his will wholeheartedly rejects doing such acts. As a result of his repentance, then, the flawed configurations his intellect and will acquired when he engaged in his evil acts are removed and replaced by morally good configurations instead.[100]

The putative objector assumes that the flawed configurations in intellect and will are all the ill effects *in a perpetrator* from his morally evil acts and that, when these are removed, the perpetrator returns to the psychic condition he was in before he engaged in those acts. And so the objector supposes that in consequence of his repentance an evildoer such as Wiesenthal's German soldier should count as having the same moral condition of psyche as he did before he engaged in the atrocities he committed. For this reason, it can also seem to the putative objector that the repentant soldier should have the same moral standing, with respect to his victims or others grieved at his evil, that he had before his wrongdoing.

But if the repentant soldier is able to have the same moral condition and the same standing with respect to others that he had before his evil acts, then it seems that the reaction of others to that soldier ought to reflect this state in him. Aquinas's account of love implies that a lover has to be responsive to the condition of the beloved. Therefore, as the putative objector sees it, people who understand the state of the German soldier ought to respond to the repentant soldier just as they responded to him before his evil acts. Consequently, on the objector's view, if the soldier's repentance is genuine and deep, no one should reject him or desire anything bad for him. Rather, the soldier ought to be both forgiven and reconciled with others.

So, for the objector, people who fail to accept reconciliation with the soldier do not count as either loving or forgiving of the repentant soldier, contrary to the implications of Aquinas's account as I have presented it.

It is worth noting here, however, that many thoughtful people will find this attitude on the part of the putative objector highly counter-intuitive. For such people, there are some morally evil acts which ought to alter relations between the wrongdoer and others forever.[101] In *The Sunflower*, Wiesenthal asks numerous people who are notable moral authorities whether, under any conditions, they would find reconciliation with the repentant German soldier morally acceptable. Although some categorically favor doing so, a good number reject reconciliation with fervor.

In my view, the solution to the puzzle raised by such opposed responses to Wiesenthal's case and the resolution to this objection to the Thomistic account is to see that the putative objector's assumption about what repentance alone can accomplish is mistaken.

To see why, it is helpful first to remember what Aquinas calls 'a stain on the soul.'[102] Aquinas thinks that there are impairments in a person's psyche which are brought about by grave wrongdoing but which are not remedied by repentance alone. The soldier's repentance remedies what was disordered in his intellect and will when he did those morally monstrous acts.[103] But there are also other elements in his psyche that are still in need of repair even after his repentance; these are comprised in Aquinas's 'stain on the soul.' For example, there is something morally lamentable about being able to remember doing and wanting to do the kind of evil the repentant German soldier in *The Sunflower* had done. The psychic relics of past evil include relational characteristics, too. When others affected by that soldier's atrocity relate to him afterwards, they have to relate to him as a person who remembers what it was like to do such things, even if he is now repentant; and this fact alone will alter their relationship. For example, the soldier knows that these others know that he is a person who was capable of treating human beings as he did. Something that might have been innocent or trusting in his relationship with others has consequently been replaced by something sadder, if not actually by fear or trauma, on the part of those affected by his acts.

So the effects of grave wrongdoing on the part of a person such as the German soldier extend beyond his intellect and will, and his repentance alone does not heal all these effects. For this reason, it will also not be true that forgiveness of him by, for example, one of his victims, and a willingness on her part to be reconciled with him, is sufficient to effect her actual reconciliation with him even if he is repentant. On the Thomistic account, it is true that if she forgives him, then she also has a desire to be reconciled to him. But this desire on her part cannot be fulfilled when his wrongdoing has left him in a morally deplorable condition. On the contrary, because his evil is so great, it can destroy his possibility of ordinary human relationship with not only his victims but also all those affected even indirectly by his evil. His wrongdoing can damage things in him critical for the sort of relationship he once had or might have had with others to such an extent that the relationships can never be restored to what they were or might have been. And this condition *in the soldier* will not be healed simply by his repentance, however wholehearted and trustworthy that repentance might be.

The Resolution of the Objection: The Limits of Repentance and the Effects of Wrongdoing on the World

So far I have highlighted the damaging effects of serious moral wrongdoing on the psyche of the wrongdoer, but it is important not to let the focus on those effects obscure the plain fact that there can also be lasting damage of such wrongdoing on its victims. In addition to the physical harm the wrongdoing does, it can leave a victim with an array of psychic damage. She might have traumatic memories of the past that continue to affect her in the present in a variety of ways. And her trust—her very ability to trust—in other human beings might also be undermined. If the evil she suffered was bad enough, she may lose what Linda Radzik calls 'default trust', a kind of generalized and unreflective trust that the world is safe enough and human beings are good enough to make her participating in the world compatible with her sanity.[104] If a victim's trust is significantly undermined, then she may be *willing* to reconcile with the wrongdoer, but her willingness may not be sufficient to effect reconciliation between them. When the wrongdoing has been serious enough to do damage even to default trust in her, then, humanly speaking, any reconciliation between her and the wrongdoer may not be possible for her while she is in that condition.[105] In such a case, her condition may make it psychologically very difficult for her or even morally impermissible for her to act on her desire for reconciliation. And this can be so even if she also has a moral obligation to forgive the wrongdoer and to desire reconciliation with him.

Think about the point this way. Suppose that Jerome is Paula's priest, with whom Paula has had a deeply trusting and long-lasting relationship; and then suppose that Paula discovers that for some time Jerome has been molesting Paula's young daughter Julia. In these circumstances, even if we stipulate that Jerome becomes thoroughly repentant and Paula knows that he is, then it might nonetheless be morally bad if Paula were to readmit Jerome to company with her and Julia. (Paula might also need to seek punishment for Jerome, which seems like a contravention of the first desire of love; but for my purposes here I am concentrating on the second desire of love, for union with another person.) It might be the case that Paula should not readmit Jerome to the same companionship she had with him before his wrongdoing, not only for Julia's sake but also for her own. For the wellbeing of herself and her child, it might be better if she kept Jerome at a distance, even if he is totally trustworthy in his repentance and Paula knows that he is. The memory of what he did lives on for all of them, and just that memory alone can make connection with him a reliving or at least a reawakening of the memory of the evil he did. And, of course, memory is not the end of the problem. For the sake of Julia's healing and her own, Paula may need to regain a sense of control and dignity, to diminish her sense of helplessness and vulnerability, by keeping Jerome at a distance. It could nonetheless be the case that Paula has a desire for Jerome's good—his continued repentance and reform, for example—and that she also would be glad if there were some day when she and he might meet in any kind of companionship again, even if it is only in the beatific vision in heaven.

In this case, then, Paula would be forgiving Jerome and willing to be reconciled with Jerome, even while actual reconciliation with him is not morally permissible for her now. On the other hand, clearly, Paula could ward off reconciliation without forgiving Jerome. If Paula's reaction to learning of Jerome's evil were to want to see him damned in hell, if she were to be savagely glad if Jerome never succeeded in making any real reform, so that she could continue to be utterly alienated from him, then she would not be forgiving him. But then there would also be something morally wrong with Paula. She *ought* to desire the good for Jerome and union with Jerome, even if that good and that union require a considerable and lengthy process of reform on Jerome's part and healing on her part, even if the past requires that actual reconciliation with Jerome be postponed indefinitely.

So Paula can desire Jerome's reform and his return to equal moral standing in the human community, she can desire that she might one day have companionship with Jerome again, even while reconciliation with Jerome is not now morally permissible for her, and Paula recognizes that it is not.[106] And when, as in the case of the dying German soldier in *The Sunflower*, it seems as if there is no human power to overcome the lasting effects of the wrongdoing because the evil that was done is so overwhelming, then no amount of love and forgiveness on the part of the victims or others in community with the victims will be sufficient to enable the fulfilling of their desire for reconciliation with the evildoer. In such cases, desiring reconciliation with a repentant wrongdoer who also desires reconciliation is still not enough by itself to effect reconciliation.

The Resolution of the Objection: Forgiveness and Reconciliation Can Come Apart

For these reasons, if wrongdoing is grave enough, then a person can forgive and also be willing to reconcile with an evildoer such as *The Sunflower*'s German soldier without its being the case that, humanly speaking, the desired reconciliation is possible or morally permissible for her as matters stand.[107] The desired reconciliation may have to be postponed until amends are made; and if the wrongdoer could not make amends because the evil he did is beyond the scope of human power to amend, then it may not be humanly possible for there to be morally permissible reconciliation with him. But it does not follow that, even in such a case, one should not *desire* the evildoer's true good and his return to the human companionship even with his victims. If what a person really wanted for an evildoer such as the German soldier is that he be condemned to hell forever, then she would not be loving of him or forgiving of him; and, however understandable this failure on her part to love and forgive might be, it is morally unlovely in her all the same. She *should* forgive him and desire reconciliation with him, even if he himself has no power to make the *fulfillment* of that desire morally permissible.

Seeing that it might not be humanly possible to have morally permissible reconciliation with a wrongdoer, even when forgiveness of him is obligatory, helps to explain the highly divergent reactions of morally sensitive and reflective thinkers to the case of the dying soldier in *The Sunflower*. Asked to comment on this case, Theodore Hesburgh, CSC, the influential former president of Notre Dame, says,

> My whole instinct is to forgive.... [108]

And the Nobel Prize-winning Anglican archbishop Desmond Tutu says,

> Many claim to follow the Jewish rabbi who, when he was crucified, said, 'Father, forgive them for they know not what they do.'... It is clear that if we look only to retributive justice, then we could just as well close up shop.... Without forgiveness, there is no future.[109]

On the other hand, explaining why he himself would reject forgiveness of the soldier, the revered Jewish rabbi Abraham Joshua Heschel says that it is "preposterous to assume that anybody alive can extend forgiveness for the suffering of any one of the six million people who perished."[110] And, supporting Heschel's attitude towards forgiveness of the soldier, his daughter, Susannah Heschel, a noted scholar in her own right, adds,

> My father, Rabbi Abraham Joshua Heschel, wrote that 'the blood of the innocent cries forever.' Should that blood cease to cry, humanity would cease to be....

Rather than asking for forgiveness, the descendants of the Nazis should continue to hear the cries of Jewish blood, and thereby preserve their own humanity.[111]

In my view, the apparently opposed views of these thinkers to the case of the soldier in *The Sunflower* can all be justified. Those who argue in favor of forgiveness of the soldier are surely right. Forgiveness of him is obligatory, just as love is. But those who repudiate with fervor any forgiveness of him are also right, if we suppose that under the heading of 'forgiveness' they understand the removal of guilt, reconciliation, and restoration to equal moral standing in the human community.

Here, then, is the resolution of the putative objector's complaint. Although forgiveness, like love, is always obligatory, reconciliation does not immediately follow on forgiveness, even for repentant wrongdoers. It can be obligatory for a person to *desire* reconciliation with someone who has wronged her; but *reconciliation* itself is a matter of a mutual relationship between two people, and no one person can effect unilaterally, by herself alone, a mutual relationship. In this respect, forgiveness is like love itself. One can desire union with another person; but whether that desire can be fulfilled or not depends greatly on the other person. For perpetrators of grave evil, even their fervent repentance and the forgiveness of their victims may not be enough for morally permissible reconciliation, either because the psychic condition of the repentant wrongdoer stands in the way or because the effects of his wrongdoing constitute an obstacle or both. Nevertheless, one can continue to desire union even when one understands that, as matters stand, union is morally impermissible or otherwise not possible. The morally decent mother of the German soldier was apparently unaware of his evil actions; but if she had known of them, she could still continue to love her morally monstrous son even while she recognized with pain that he could not and should not return to his previous companionship with her in his current condition.[112]

So, the putative objector is right that on the Thomistic account of love and forgiveness, a person's repentance by itself might not be sufficient for his obtaining reconciliation with his victim, even if she forgives him and is willing to be reconciled with him. But the objector is mistaken in supposing that this implication undercuts the Thomistic account.[113] Grave moral evil can leave a wrongdoer in such a condition that without some remedy for a stain on his soul and some way of making sufficient amends, reconciliation with him is ruled out on moral grounds. That is why even if a person such as the German soldier in Wiesenthal's *Sunflower* were wholly repentant, someone could turn away from him or require punishment of him and nonetheless count as having both forgiveness and love for him. The Thomistic account is neither harsh nor counter-intuitive in its implication that a loving and forgiving person could still warrantedly refuse a repentant evildoer reconciliation. It is only realistic about the toll evil takes on those who engage in it.

ONE LAST CONSIDERATION IN SUPPORT OF THE ANSELMIAN KIND OF INTERPRETATION OF THE DOCTRINE OF THE ATONEMENT: THE NEED FOR SATISFACTION ON THE THOMISTIC ACCOUNT OF FORGIVENESS

With these objections resolved, the conclusion of the first part of this chapter stands: God's forgiveness, like God's love, is unilateral and unconditional. It does not depend on anything; rather, it is a function of God's nature, which is perfectly good and therefore also perfectly loving. God's love and forgiveness, and God's acceptance of reconciliation with human wrongdoers, are there for every human person, even those who are unrepentant wrongdoers. And so the Anselmian kind of interpretation of the doctrine of the atonement, in all its variants, is wrong.

Nonetheless, someone might suppose that there is still one hope for the Anselmian kind of interpretation just because, on the Thomistic account of forgiveness, forgiveness and reconciliation can come apart. In cases of serious wrongdoing, something in addition to forgiveness may be necessary for reconciliation. 'Making amends' is one customary name for the additional element that, added to repentance, can effect reconciliation; 'satisfaction' is another. It is evident that satisfaction plays a crucial role in the Anselmian interpretation of the atonement, and so someone might suppose that the implication regarding the need for satisfaction to effect reconciliation in cases of serious wrongdoing weighs strongly in favor of the Anselmian interpretation, against all competitors, even on the Thomistic account of forgiveness.

But here it is important to be clear about the two very different roles that satisfaction might be supposed to play as regards reconciliation, given the two differing approaches to satisfaction examined in Chapter 2. The Anselmian kind of interpretation of the doctrine of the atonement relies on one of these approaches, and the Thomistic kind of interpretation relies on the other one. The need for satisfaction to effect reconciliation would constitute some support for the Anselmian kind of interpretation only if the satisfaction needed were the satisfaction the Anselmian kind of interpretation claims that Christ's atonement is.

From the point of view of the Anselmian interpretation, something beyond the repentance of sinful human beings is needed if God is to forego rejecting and punishing them, and this something else is the satisfaction made to God by Christ's passion and death (or Christ's life, passion, and death). Christ pays the debt owed to God or bears the punishment God's justice must mete out to sinners or something else of this sort. Because Christ does this, the justice or goodness or honor of God is met. Consequently, God can forgive human beings and accept reconciliation with them consistently with God's maintaining his justice or goodness or honor. God's forgiveness of human beings and acceptance of reconciliation with them is thus dependent on Christ's making satisfaction to God.

On this Anselmian approach to satisfaction, Christ's atonement constitutes satisfaction because it gives God something due to him; and the point of Christ's satisfaction is to provide a perfectly good God with this needed condition for pardoning human beings. It is true that God arranges for the condition to be met. But the point remains that God's forgiveness and acceptance of reconciliation depends on Christ's making satisfaction to God.

By contrast, on the Thomistic approach to satisfaction, God always loves every human being; and, for this reason, God also always forgives every wrongdoer. Since forgiveness carries with it the desire for union, nothing else on the part of the wrongdoer is needed for God's forgiveness and acceptance of reconciliation with sinful human beings, including even with those who are unrepentant. On the Thomistic approach, the role of satisfaction has to do not with providing a condition needed for God's forgiveness or acceptance of reconciliation. Rather it has to do with helping to repair the wrongdoer's damage, the damage he has done in the world and the damage he has done to himself, in the stain on his soul. So understood, satisfaction has a role in effecting reconciliation, but it has this role because it alters something in and for the wrongdoer, not because it gives God a needed condition for God's forgiveness and acceptance of reconciliation.

Given the importance of these varying approaches to satisfaction and the difference they make to evaluation of the Anselmian and Thomistic interpretations, it is worth considering more carefully the relation of satisfaction to reconciliation on the Thomistic account of forgiveness.

THE THOMISTIC ACCOUNT OF FORGIVENESS: WHAT SATISFACTION CAN DO

Contrary to the views of some contributors to Wiesenthal's *The Sunflower*, on the Thomistic account of satisfaction there is no human wrongdoing so evil that the disturbed effects and the lamentable psychic relics of the wrongdoing committed cannot be remedied. For *any* moral evil, there is a remedy in satisfaction. As Wiesenthal's book shows, this is an optimistic conclusion that many contemporary thinkers are unwilling to accept.

The English term 'satisfaction' is a transliteration of the Latin, and it has come into common use; but this translation of the Latin is unfortunate, because the English word 'satisfaction' has infelicitous connotations in this context. We typically think of a person's being satisfied if he has *gotten* enough. But the sense of satisfaction at issue for Aquinas is a matter of *giving* enough.[114] We are tempted to suppose that one person has given enough just in case someone he has injured has gotten enough. For example, we say,

"I have apologized profusely, but nothing I do will satisfy him." But this is not the sense of doing *enough* at issue in satisfaction as Aquinas understands it.

As Aquinas explains a wrongdoer's own satisfaction, it is a matter of his doing voluntarily what would be punishment, simply considered, if it were imposed on him against his will.[115] The point of his satisfaction is also different from the point of punishment. On the Thomistic approach to satisfaction, the primary aim of the wrongdoer's satisfaction is the restoration of the wrongdoer to as much as is humanly possible of the psychic condition and relative standing with others that he had before his wrongdoing.[116]

Satisfaction presupposes contrition, since the desire to make amends stems from sorrow over what one has done. And contrition presupposes confession (at least in the form of acknowledgement to oneself) since it is not possible to sorrow over one's morally wrong acts if one has not acknowledged that those acts were morally wrong. According to Aquinas, confession, contrition, and satisfaction constitute a kind of medicine for sin,[117] because together they go some way to remedying the effects of the wrongdoing and removing the stain on the soul. The *enough* of satisfaction is the wrongdoer's having given enough because, in his repentance (that is, his contrition and confession) and his making amends, he has done all that he could do. Contrary to what the connotations of the English term 'satisfaction' might lead us to suppose, then, satisfaction on Aquinas's approach is not a matter of trying to satisfy an offended party. Rather, it is a matter of trying to do enough to undo the damage done to others and to oneself by wrongdoing.

On the Thomistic approach to satisfaction, the parable of the prodigal son would become morally ugly if it were re-written in such a way that the father waited to see whether his prodigal son was repentant or whether his son would make satisfaction to him before the father bestowed forgiveness on his son or accepted reconciliation with him.[118] If in the story the father demanded satisfaction from his son before forgiving him or welcoming him home, the parable would be morally unpalatable. But we can see the point of satisfaction on the Thomistic view if we take the parable as it stands, including the father's unilateral and unconditional forgiveness of his prodigal son and the father's acceptance of reconciliation with him, and then consider how the story in the parable might have been continued after the father's welcome of his son. Could the returned prodigal son simply have accepted his father's forgiveness and picked up at home where he had left off, maybe joking with his older brother about how fast he had wasted his share of his father's inheritance when he deserted the family in a fit of narcissistic rebellion? And if the returned son did comport himself in this way, does anyone seriously suppose that the rest of the family would be able to relate to him in the way it did before the son left home? On the contrary, if the returned prodigal son really is repentant, then he will be not only sorry for his injustice against his family but also grateful for his father's love and forgiveness. In this state, he will have a desire to do what he can to make amends to his family.

This desire and the acts to which it gives rise are what Aquinas has in mind with the notion of satisfaction. In making satisfaction, the prodigal son alters his relationship with his family, not because he is meriting their forgiveness and acceptance of reconciliation with him, but because by making amends when he has already been forgiven he is himself returning to his family, across the distance produced when *he* moved away from *them*. In discussing the full remission of sins, Aquinas maintains that sins are fully remitted when the soul of the *offender* is at peace with the one offended.[119]

In fact, Aquinas himself distinguishes satisfaction from retributive punishment on this score. About retributive punishment, he says that a judge decides how amends are to be made for the wrong done; but when amends are made through satisfaction, "the offence is atoned according to the will of the sinner...."[120] This emphasis is what we would expect from the previous explanation of the nature of the stain on the soul. The stain develops when the wrongdoer puts some distance between himself and others by his wrong acts, and so it will also be the wrongdoer who needs to re-traverse that distance. There is psychological sense in this view, too. The wrongdoer will be at peace with others when he has a sense of having done what he can to make amends.

THE THOMISTIC APPROACH TO SATISFACTION: THE CASE OF JOHN NEWTON

One of the implications of the Thomistic approach to satisfaction is that a wrongdoer's making satisfaction depends on his having received forgiveness from God, and not the other way around. To underline this point, it is helpful to focus in detail on a particular case. (The details of this case will also be useful in the review of guilt and shame in Chapter 10.) So, return to the case of John Newton and consider the way in which the satisfaction made by John Newton should be understood, on the Thomistic approach to satisfaction.

A protracted religious conversion changed Newton's life dramatically. First, he left off slave-trading and the life of a seaman; then he got a theological education; and eventually he was ordained as an Anglican priest. Gradually, he took on an increasing role in the cultural and religious life of England. Somewhere in the course of the religious reform of his life, he became horrified at what he had done in the slave trade, and he was stricken at the suffering he had helped to bring about.

In this condition, he wrote hymns, many of which are still sung today. As many people know, he is the composer of the famous hymn "Amazing Grace."

The opening lines of that hymn express not only his own confession and contrition, but also his understanding of the great unconditional, unilateral love and forgiveness of God and his own equally great gratitude for it: "Amazing grace—how sweet the sound—that saved a wretch like me! I once was lost but now am found, was blind but now I see."

In the grip of this gratitude for the unconditional love and forgiveness given by God to him, a person who had been a slave-trader, Newton worked hard to help bring about the abolition of the slave trade in England. He joined forces with the English abolitionist William Wilberforce and others to alter public opinion about the slave trade. His pamphlet *Thoughts Upon the Slave Trade* was influential and made a great difference to the debate in Parliament. In that pamphlet, Newton recounted in heart-wrenching detail the suffering he caused the Africans in his slave ships; and he said, "I hope it will always be a subject of humiliating reflection to me, that I was once an active instrument in a business at which my heart now shudders."[121] He lived long enough to see his efforts victorious. The Slave Trade Act, which abolished the slave trade in England, was passed in 1807; and Newton died shortly thereafter. Newton's efforts at bringing about the abolition of the slave trade were his satisfaction. And this satisfaction was his response to the amazing grace that he felt had already been given to him.

On Aquinas's account of God's love, it gives goodness to those who do not reject it. Newton's satisfaction and even his desire to make satisfaction are thus themselves the effects on Newton of the grace of God. When Newton did not resist the love and forgiveness God offered him, then God's grace brought about in Newton the good states of will that eventuated in Newton's willingness to make satisfaction and Newton's persistence in carrying that willingness through into action. So understood, a wrongdoer's satisfaction is dependent on God's love and forgiveness; in its nature, it is an expression of gratitude to God for God's love and forgiveness. On the Thomistic approach, then, Newton's satisfaction for his moral wrongdoing was a consequence of God's antecedent love and forgiveness, God's acceptance of reconciliation with him, working in Newton's psyche.

No doubt, Newton did well to shudder at what he had done in the slave trade. But what about others, to whom the slave trade was an abomination and to whom it had always been abhorrent? What about the transported slaves themselves? When Newton was first deeply, wholeheartedly repentant for his participation in the slave trade, but before Newton had done what he could to make amends, how would others have reacted to him? At that point in his life, he was a repentant slave trader. As he himself saw it, God had forgiven him and accepted reconciliation with him. But if others around Newton shrank from him at that time, who would have blamed them? Who would have wanted to be in companionship with Newton, even if he were repentant? One might pity him in his repentant state or have compassion on him, but who would have wanted to be friends with a repentant slave trader? Would any of the Africans who had been on his ships have been happy at the prospect of dinner with him, even if they had been persuaded of the depth of his repentance?

By the time Newton died, however, he was not only friends with abolitionists such as Wilberforce and others who hated the slave trade, he was held in honor by them. And it is not hard to see why. His passionate efforts on behalf of the abolition of the slave trade were his satisfaction; and that satisfaction was successful in making him a different man from the man he had been, even from the man he was when he first repented. For this reason, his satisfaction altered his relationships with others as well.[122] When Wilberforce was friends with Newton, Wilberforce was friends not just with a repentant slave trader; he was friends with a powerful enemy of the slave trade.

On the Thomistic approach to satisfaction, satisfaction alters the wrongdoer and his relationships because it changes what the wrongdoer is and helps to remedy the ill effects of his wrongdoing. It is true that satisfaction cannot undo the harm done in the original wrongdoing. Newton could not take away the sufferings of the Africans who had been transported on his ships or restore life to those who had died. But in confessing publicly the horrors of his acts as a slave trader, in expressing his heartbroken grief over those acts, and in giving himself to the cause of the abolition of the slave trade, Newton did what he could to make up for what he had done. The etymology of the Latin 'satisfacere'—'satis' (enough) plus 'facere' (to do)—captures this idea of doing what one can and by this means doing enough to regain moral standing in the human community.

When it comes to wrongdoing considered as sinning against God, Aquinas recognizes that no one can make any amends to God. But Aquinas takes the 'enough'—the 'satis'—in satisfaction to indicate that when a wrongdoer such as Newton does what he can, God, who does not demand the impossible of human persons, takes what Newton can do by way of making amends as *enough* on Newton's part.[123]

It is worth noting in this connection that, on Aquinas's optimistic view, it is possible for satisfaction not only to restore a wrongdoer's standing in the human community, but even to leave a person in a more admirable moral state than he would have been if he had not engaged in the moral wrongdoing in the first place. For a person such as Newton, whose moral wrongdoing left him shuddering at the memory of it, Aquinas says that satisfaction will not restore his innocence:

> this dignity the penitent cannot recover. Nevertheless, [the wrongdoer] recovers something greater sometimes....[124]

Satisfaction made by a repentant wrongdoer can leave the wrongdoer with "a greater grace than that which he had before...."[125] In Sierra Leone, there is a town named in honor of Newton.

So far I have focused on a wrongdoer's guilt, but it is worth noting that, on the Thomistic approach, satisfaction helps with a wrongdoer's shame too. A person who is and feels shamed anticipates on the part of real or imagined others a warranted rejection of him. Such a person is (or reasonably anticipates being) cast out from others with whom he wishes to have some kind of union. If a person's shame is spread through a large enough group, the shamed person has the status of an outcast with respect to that group. If the evil is great enough, a person can even become an outcast with regard to human society in general, as many people, understandably enough, felt that the repentant German soldier in *The Sunflower* ought to be. But, as Newton's case illustrates, satisfaction can restore a person who has or deserves the status of moral outcast not only to a welcome in human society but even to a position of honor in it. Newton's satisfaction not only altered his relative standing with others in his community or in the whole human family, but it also altered his relationship with God. It did not provide a condition for reconciliation with God; on the contrary, it presupposed God's forgiveness and acceptance of reconciliation with him. What it altered was Newton himself, the deplorable *relicta* in his psyche and the damaged state of the world for which he was responsible. And so it went some way to remedying Newton's shame also.

ADJUDICATING BETWEEN THE ANSELMIAN AND THE THOMISTIC APPROACHES TO SATISFACTION

Satisfaction comes into the evaluation of the Anselmian kind of interpretation of the doctrine of the atonement because it can seem as if the need for satisfaction in removing guilt weighs decisively in favor of the Anselmian kind. But this is a mistaken view of the matter. On the contrary, careful consideration of the relation between forgiveness and satisfaction weighs heavily against the Anselmian kind.

As reflection on wrongdoing shows, in cases of serious wrongdoing, something besides a wrongdoer's repentance and his victim's forgiveness may be needed in order to restore a wrongdoer to moral standing in the human community and to reconciliation with those affected by his wrongdoing. There may need to be some making amends, some satisfaction, for the wrong done. On the Anselmian approach to satisfaction, however, the satisfaction made by Christ is made to God. It does nothing to make amends to the human victims of wrongdoing; and it does nothing to remedy the stain on the soul of wrongdoers either. On the Anselmian approach to satisfaction, the point of Christ's satisfaction is to provide a condition for God to grant wrongdoers pardon, to forgive them and accept reconciliation with them. But nothing about the provision of this condition for God alters either the psychological state of a wrongdoer or the condition of those whom the wrongdoer harmed. Insofar as the damage to these things is part of the guilt of the wrongdoer, satisfaction on the Anselmian approach does not succeed in removing the guilt of the wrongdoer. In fact, satisfaction on the Anselmian approach is not so much as aimed at the removal of such guilt.

One can think of the issue this way. On orthodox Christian theology, the point of the atonement is to make it possible for a post-Fall human person such as Newton, guilty and shamed, to be united with God in everlasting joy. In heaven, Newton is united with God in a way that allows Newton to see, through his union with the omniscient, eternal mind of God, all that has transpired in time. But God can see all the heartbreaking, shaming cruelty of Newton's acts in the slave trade; and in heaven Newton sees it also. Not only that, but everyone else redeemed in heaven will be able to see it as well.[126] Satisfaction on the Thomistic approach can provide something to make that vision tolerable, because such satisfaction can make the life of the wrongdoer such as Newton honorable. But satisfaction on the Anselmian approach has no such effects. On the Anselmian approach, Christ's satisfaction gives God what God needs to grant human beings pardon, but it does not change a wrongdoer such as Newton himself. And since this is so, on the Anselmian approach to satisfaction, contrary to what is commonly supposed, satisfaction cannot alter Newton's guilt; and it does not even address Newton's shame.

Someone who espouses a kind of theological relativism[127] might suppose that guilt is removed entirely just in case God decides to pardon it or to declare the guilty acquitted. Such relativism is a minority position in the theological tradition, and for excellent reason, since it seems to undermine morality in a radical way.[128] But even a supporter of theological relativism will still have to contend with the issue of shame. The Thomistic approach to satisfaction can explain why, in heaven, Newton's shame over his past evil would be alleviated. The Anselmian approach cannot do so. And if there is no alleviation of Newton's shame for his past slave-trading, then it is hard to see how Newton's shame over what he had done would not undermine his joy in heaven. By comparison with others in heaven, whose lives have included no horror such as Newton's slave-trading, Newton looks ugly; and since the past is unchangeable, so apparently is Newton's ugliness.

So not only does the need for satisfaction to effect a wrongdoer's reconciliation with his victims and his restoration to the companionship of equal moral standing in the human family not tip the scales in favor of the Anselmian kind of interpretation, but in fact reflection on the need for satisfaction is one more decisive consideration against the Anselmian interpretation.

A LAST OBJECTION AND A PROMISSORY NOTE

In the preceding reflections, I have highlighted the Thomistic approach to satisfaction as satisfaction is made by human beings for wrongdoing. But, like the Anselmian kind of interpretation of the doctrine of the atonement, the Thomistic kind of interpretation also has a role for the vicarious satisfaction made by Christ; and someone might object that this chapter should have compared Anselm's account of Christ's making satisfaction with the Thomistic account of the same process. But the Thomistic account of Christ's satisfaction actually emerges from the role for satisfaction made to the human victims of wrongdoing that is detailed in this chapter, and that Thomistic understanding of Christ's satisfaction is part of the account of the doctrine of the atonement which subsequent chapters will illuminate. Consequently, consideration of it has to wait till that account has been sketched in Part III. As I will show in Chapter 10, consideration of Christ's satisfaction, on the Thomistic approach to satisfaction, only confirms the conclusions about satisfaction in this chapter. The Anselmian kind of interpretation is not helped by considerations of the Thomistic approach to Christ's satisfaction; it is only rendered more unacceptable by them.

CONCLUSION

On the Anselmian kind of interpretation of the doctrine of the atonement, God's justice or goodness or honor does not allow God to forgive human beings for their moral wrongdoing or to accept reconciliation with them without requiring repayment of their moral debt or imposing on them the penalty their wrongs deserve or receiving penance to make up for their wrongs. It is necessary that there be satisfaction made to God if wrongdoers are to receive God's forgiveness and acceptance of reconciliation.

In Chapter 1, I called attention to concerns about the ability of the Anselmian kind of interpretation to handle the backward-looking problem of shame and the future-looking problem of the human propensity to moral wrongdoing; but this chapter shows a much deeper problem with the Anselmian kind of interpretation. On Aquinas's explanatorily rich account of love, which yields a powerful account of forgiveness, the central claims of the Anselmian kind of interpretation are antithetical to God's love.

On biblically based Christian views, God's love embraces every human being; and so God desires the good for every human being. That good is union in love between human beings and God; and so God also desires union with every human being. Because love is necessary and sufficient for forgiveness, God also forgives each human being. A perfectly loving God can and does forgive unconditionally and unilaterally, just as he can and does love unrequitedly. It is true that, like human beings, God cannot have what he wants in love or forgiveness just by wanting it. In order for there to be union of love between God and a human person Paula, Paula has to have the two desires of love for God, too. But these are good things in Paula; and since they are good, then, on all anti-Pelagian views, they are the effects of God's grace working in Paula, a grace that God, in love, will give to every person who does not refuse it.

The rejection of Pelagianism does not imply that Paula is a puppet in God's hands. It is open to Paula to reject grace or to cease rejecting grace; and God's giving of grace to Paula is responsive to which of these states Paula is in. Since this is so, Paula is ultimately responsible for her state and condition even though God is responsible for all the good in Paula. By the same token, if there is little good in Paula, the person ultimately responsible for this state of Paula's is only Paula. The good state of will in Paula which would have brought Paula into union with God would have been produced in Paula by God if Paula had not rejected it. If there is to be union between God and a human person, then God's love, like human love, has to be responsive to something in the loved person, even though, unlike human love, God's love is responsible for all the good that there is in the beloved human person.

Like the Anselmian kind of interpretation, the Thomistic account of God's love gives a place to justice. But, for Aquinas, nothing in God's justice is opposed to God's loving and forgiving human persons unconditionally and unilaterally. That is because, although Aquinas accepts the idea, central also to the Anselmian interpretation, that God's justice is a matter of God's being true to himself, for Aquinas what God is true to is his own goodness; and God's goodness is never incompatible with God's love, which desires to bring every human person into union with God.

Commenting approvingly on the rejection of one version of the Anselmian kind of interpretation by J. McLeod Campbell, James Torrance says,

> Campbell saw that fundamental to the whole issue [of atonement] was the doctrine of God. Instead of thinking of God as the Father, who loves all humanity, and who in Christ gives us the gift of sonship and who freely forgives us through Jesus Christ, [the Calvinist adherents to the Anselmian kind of interpretation] thought of God as One whose love is conditioned by human repentance and faith, and whose forgiveness had to be purchased by the payment of the sufferings of Christ on behalf of the elect.[129]

Campbell and Torrance seem to me right in this assessment. As the arguments of this chapter show, contrary to the Anselmian kind of interpretation, God's love, God's forgiveness, and God's acceptance of reconciliation with wrongdoers are not dependent on satisfaction being made to God. They stem from the very nature of God.

There is a role for satisfaction in the removal of a wrongdoer's guilt and the reconciliation of others with him. In cases of serious wrongdoing, forgiveness can be insufficient to remove guilt and restore relationships; satisfaction can also be needed. But the considerations that show the need for satisfaction also make its role evident. The very argument that satisfaction is needed for the removal of guilt and the establishment of reconciliation makes clear that the role of satisfaction is not to provide the conditions necessary for God's forgiveness or God's acceptance of reconciliation with wrongdoers. Rather its role is to repair the damage the wrongdoer did to himself and others, so that the wrongdoer can be returned to a morally decent condition in himself and to equal moral standing with others. And, on anti-Pelagian views, the good of making satisfaction for moral wrongdoing is itself God's gift to a human wrongdoer. Satisfaction thus depends on God's love, forgiveness, and acceptance of reconciliation, and not the other way around, as the Anselmian kind of interpretation assumes.

To suppose that satisfaction is a prerequisite for God's forgiveness and acceptance of reconciliation, as the Anselmian kind of interpretation does, is to suppose that if a wrongdoer (or a suitable substitute for the wrongdoer) did not make satisfaction to God, God would not forgive the wrongdoer and would not accept reconciliation with him; that is, God would not accept union with the wrongdoer and so would not will the good for the wrongdoer. In that case, absent satisfaction, God would not love the wrongdoer. But, as the biblical text I John 4:8 claims, God is love. To suppose, then, that God would not forgive or accept reconciliation unless satisfaction had been made to God is to suppose that, without satisfaction, God is not God.[130]

Even when we consider anger, hatred, and retributive punishment, the Thomistic conclusion about God's love stands: without any conditions of any kind, but only because of God's own nature, God loves and forgives every person, even those persons who are unrepentant or who reject God's love wholly; and God accepts reconciliation with them, to whatever extent their own condition allows. When Christ prays to God the Father on behalf of those who crucify him, "Father, forgive them, because they don't know what they are doing," what is at issue is unconditional and unilateral forgiveness on God's part, since at the time of Christ's prayer there is not even repentance on the part of the wrongdoers.[131] A morally perfect God can forgive a wrongdoer unconditionally and unilaterally, in the sense that God can desire the good for the wrongdoer and union with him no matter what the state of the wrongdoer is. Even the anger and hatred God has towards some people are the kind of anger and hatred that are compatible with love. These reactive attitudes co-exist in God with an acceptance of reconciliation with those people for whom

God has anger or hatred, and they come with a continual offer of divine grace that would produce goodness and closeness to God in any wrongdoer who did not reject that grace. What God ultimately desires for every person, even those with whom he is angry or those whom he hates, is union with them.

It is even compatible with Aquinas's account of love that God will punish some perpetrators of moral wrongdoing and that some perpetrators are punished with the worst thing for human beings, endless exclusion from union with God. On traditional Christian views, there are some human persons whom God hates and sends away from God. But, on Aquinas's account of love, this hatred on God's part is a species of love and not opposed to it; and those hated and sent away are not those to whom God is unwilling to give grace. They are those to whom grace is continually offered by the infinite and unstoppable love of God, which never fails to embrace even those hated and rejected. Those who are hated and rejected are so not because they are not loved and forgiven, but because they themselves will not cease rejecting the love and forgiveness of God, which are always there for them. The only sin God does not forgive, Aquinas says, is final impenitence, that is, a refusal of love that never ends.[132]

So when in the Gospels Christ says that there are some people to whom he will say, "I never knew you. Depart from me, you who do evil,"[133] his rejection of them is a function only of their rejection of love; and even their rejection of God does not result in a loss of love or forgiveness on God's part. It results only in God's having a desire for union, an acceptance of reconciliation, that cannot be fulfilled.[134] If God tells such people to go away, it is an expression of God's recognition of the impossible. It is impossible even for God to unite himself in love to human persons who reject God. So the recognition that the fulfillment of God's desires of love for such human persons is impossible co-exists in God with the desire for union with those same persons. God loves and forgives even those whom he tells to go away. If they were to cease rejecting God's love, his love and forgiveness would bring them to union with him.[135]

For all these reasons, then, a careful consideration of God's love rules out the Anselmian kind of interpretation of the doctrine of the atonement. The Anselmian interpretation of the atonement is unworkable, and there is no way of salvaging it. It has inextricably woven into it a denial of the love of God.

For my part, in what follows, I will adopt Aquinas's account of love as foundational for reflection on the doctrine of the atonement.[136] Whatever Christ's life and death bring about, it is not the case that they are needed as a condition requisite for God's forgiveness or acceptance of reconciliation with any human being.

Part II

What Is Wanted: What It Is Not and What It Is

4

Union

God's Omnipresence and Indwelling

INTRODUCTION

In Chapter 3, I argued that the Anselmian kind of interpretation of the doctrine of the atonement is unworkable because it is incompatible with God's love. In my view, on the best account available of the notion of love, the God of the Anselmian interpretation is not a loving God. For this reason, interpretations of the doctrine of the atonement that locate the main obstacle to union between God and post-Fall human persons in something in God, in the way that all versions of the Anselmian interpretation do, are unsalvageable. The other possibility, the Thomistic kind of interpretation of the doctrine of the atonement which locates the obstacle to union in something in human beings, is therefore preferable.

The main problem for the Thomistic kind of interpretation is to show what Christ's passion and death have to do with uniting God and human beings.[1] On the Thomistic interpretation, which takes the obstacle to union to lie in human beings, it can appear that Christ's passion and death are not only gratuitous but even inefficacious for removing the obstacle and effecting that union.

In addition, the Thomistic kind of interpretation shares two serious problems with the Anselmian interpretation. The first problem has to do with the connection between the role assigned to Christ's atonement and the benefits attributed to suffering. In fact, the Thomistic kind of interpretation of the doctrine of the atonement seems in tension with the project of theodicy. That is because, once Christ's passion and death have done their work, there seems no good left to assign as the benefit that is supposed to defeat any individual person's suffering.[2] The second problem has to do with adequacy to the biblical stories, in particular the stories about Christ's passion and death. For example, if Christ's passion and death are designed only in order to remedy something in sinful human beings, it is difficult to know how to understand the texts which describe Christ as bearing human sin; and it is hard to see how to understand the text describing Christ's cry from the cross that God has abandoned him.

Nonetheless, the Thomistic kind of interpretation has the advantage of assigning the problem to which the atonement is the solution to the right place, namely, to something in human beings; and, from this point onwards, I will assume that the Thomistic kind of interpretation points us in the right direction for an adequate interpretation of the atonement.

To take the next step in the direction of such an adequate kind of interpretation, I want to consider in detail the nature of union between God and human beings, which is the goal that the atonement is supposed to achieve. Since the atonement is a means to union between God and human beings in the face of the obstacle to union constituted by sin and its consequences, it is helpful to have some more clear understanding of the nature of union, both between human persons and between human persons and God. Because Christ's atonement is the means to that end, understanding the end will shed light on the means that the atonement is meant to be.

It should be said at the outset of this discussion that the more one thinks about the nature of union, the oneness of things that are in themselves more than one, the harder union becomes to understand.[3] Nonetheless, for the purposes of this book, I will take union among persons to be a matter of their being somehow one without thereby ceasing to be more than one. This characterization sounds paradoxical, of course; and it is not easy to spell it out in such a way that the threatening incoherence is warded off. I have great sympathy with C.S. Lewis's characterization of the puzzle in his *Screwtape Letters*. He has a senior devil say to a junior devil whom he is mentoring,

> The whole philosophy of Hell rests on recognition of the axiom that one thing is not another thing, and, specially, that one self is not another self. My good is my good, and your good is yours. What one gains another loses. Even an inanimate object is what it is by excluding all other objects from the space it occupies; if it expands, it does so by thrusting other objects aside or by absorbing them. A self does the same. With beasts the absorption takes the form of eating; for us, it means the sucking of will and freedom out of a weaker self into a stronger... Now, the Enemy's philosophy is nothing more nor less than one continued attempt to evade this very obvious truth. He aims at a contradiction. Things are to be many, yet somehow also one. The good of one self is to be the good of another. This impossibility He calls *Love*...[4]

One way to get some intuition for how to resolve the puzzle is to think of union between persons roughly on the model of empathy. Whereas union between persons *simpliciter* is a mutual uniting of whole selves, empathy is a small-scale and limited unilateral analogue on the part of one person Paula with another person Jerome in consequence of Paula's sharing of Jerome's feelings. As I will explain in more detail later below, when Paula empathizes with Jerome in his pain, Paula has a painful feeling; and the painful feeling that she has is her feeling. On the other hand, that painful feeling is in Paula as Jerome's pain, not hers; and she feels and understands it as Jerome's feeling of pain. By rough analogy, in union *simpliciter* between Paula and Jerome, Paula has Jerome's psyche somehow accessible to her *within her own*; only she feels and understands that accessible psyche as Jerome's, not hers. And the same will be true, *mutatis mutandis*, of Jerome. This mutual *within-ness* of individual psyches or persons, however exactly it should be spelled out, is union.

It is important to reflect carefully on union between God and human persons because that union is often lamentably misconceived as a seat in a particularly good location (as heaven is popularly construed)—or, worse, as a ticket for such a seat, so that union with God is construed as a means to Paradise, not as an end in itself.

As I argued in earlier work,[5] neither physical proximity nor the personal contact attendant on mere proximity is necessary or sufficient for union; what is necessary are mutual closeness and mutual personal presence of the most significant kind.[6] In this chapter, I will consider what it is for God to be present to a human being and God's half of the mutual in-ness needed for union.[7] In Chapter 5, I will examine the other half of what is wanted for union between a human person and God. In that chapter, I will develop an issue only touched on in this one, namely, the way in which human psyches are also within the mind of God. In my view, the best insight into that other part of union between God and a human being is given by the narrative of Christ's cry of dereliction on the cross, which will therefore be the focus of Chapter 5.

Together Chapters 4 and 5 sketch the nature of union between God and human beings in this life. (The nature of union in an afterlife can safely be left to one side, for my purposes in this book.) For ease of reference, and for reasons that will become clear later, I will use old theological terminology and say that a human being who is in this sort of union with God in this life is a person in grace and her life is a life in grace.

In Chapters 6 and 7, I will consider what the life in grace is like, both what it is and what it is not, to round out the picture of the good that Christ's passion and death are meant to provide. With this much insight into union with God, we will be in a better position to reflect on the things that are obstacles to life in grace. When the end of the process and the obstacles to that end are illuminated, it will be much easier to think about the atonement as a means to that end and as a solution to the problem of the post-Fall human condition with its attendant guilt and shame.

In this chapter, then, I will explore the presence of God to human beings and the way in which that presence enables God to be within the psyche of a human person in grace, in some theologically and psychologically complicated way deeper than omniscient propositional knowledge alone would make possible. I will begin with a brief examination of God's presence at a time and at a place, by way of metaphysical background, because consideration of this part of God's presence to creation will turn out to be important in later chapters; and then I will turn to God's personal presence to individual human beings. As I hope this chapter and the next will make manifest, union with a triune God involves all three persons of the Trinity. And so this chapter will also include an examination of the role in union that is had by the third person of the Trinity, the Holy Spirit. As I will explain in this chapter, God's omnipresence[8]—God's presence at all times and places to all human persons at once—includes the indwelling of the Holy Spirit in all those human persons who are in grace.

The idea that the Spirit of God indwells in human beings who are in grace raises a number of questions in connection with the atonement. At the conclusion of this chapter, I will briefly raise three of them. First, there ought to be some connection between the passion and death of Christ and the indwelling of the Holy Spirit. In the Gospel of John (16:7), Christ explains to his disciples that without his passion and death the Holy Spirit will not come. But why not? Given the character of the indwelling of the Holy Spirit, why would Christ's passion and death be necessary for it? Second, the Hebrew Bible recounts many stories from the period before Christ when the spirit of God comes on a person or into a person. How are the cases in these stories different from the case postulated by Christian theology in which the Holy Spirit comes to dwell in a person in grace? Third, if the passion and death of Christ are required for the kind of union that involves the indwelling of the Holy Spirit, why should that indwelling be valued so highly that it is acceptable to have at the price of the passion and death of Christ? Or to put the question another way, what is the relation of the indwelling of the Holy Spirit to the remedy for the problem of the post-Fall human condition, which is what the passion and death of Christ are supposed to effect?

GOD'S PRESENCE WITH REGARD TO TIME

In later chapters, it will be useful to have available an account of God's presence to creation in all its modes. So I will begin the description of God's presence to human beings by saying something briefly about God's presence with regard to time and space;[9] and then I will focus on God's personal presence *to* and *with* human persons, first through what is now generally called 'mind-reading' and 'shared attention' and then through God's second-personal indwelling in those human persons who are in grace.

God's presence with respect to time is formulated in the doctrine of eternity.[10] Contrary to the way it is sometimes described, eternity is not just timelessness. Rather it is a mode of existence characterized both by the absence of succession and also by limitless duration. Because an eternal God cannot have succession in his life, neither of the series (the so-called 'A series' or 'B series') characteristic of time can apply to God's life or to God's relations with other things. That is, nothing in God's life can be past or future with respect to anything else, either in God's life or in time; and, similarly, nothing in God's life can be earlier or later than anything else either.

On the other hand, because eternity is also limitless duration, God's life consists in the duration of a present that is not limited by either future or past. Since the mode of existence of an eternal God is characterized by this kind of presentness, the relation between an eternal God and anything in time has to be one of simultaneity. Of course, the simultaneity associated with an eternal God cannot be temporal simultaneity. Taking the concept of eternity seriously involves recognizing that it introduces technical senses for several familiar words and phrases, including 'now' and 'simultaneous with', as well as for the present-tense forms of many verbs. The relations between eternity and time therefore require a special sense of 'simultaneity.' In earlier work, Norman Kretzmann and I called this special sort of simultaneity 'ET-simultaneity', for 'simultaneity between what is eternal and what is temporal.'[11]

The logic of the doctrine of eternity has the result that every moment of time, as that moment is *now* in time, is ET-simultaneous with the whole eternal life of God. Or, to put the same point the other way around, the whole of eternity is ET-simultaneous with each temporal event as that event is actually occurring in the temporal *now*.

It helps in this connection to consider the question: "Does an eternal God know what time it is now?" For the sake of discussion, suppose that, for things in time, there is an absolute temporal *now*, as distinct from a *now* that is merely relative to some particular temporal entity. Could an eternal God know what time the absolute temporal *now* is?

On the supposition that in time there is an absolute *now*, then in time there is a fact of the matter about how far history has unrolled. With regard to the inhabitants in time, at any given moment in time as that moment becomes the absolute *now*, history has unrolled *so* far and no further. This fact of the temporal matter is something an eternal God can know. Furthermore, because the whole of eternity is ET-simultaneous with each temporal event as it is actually occurring in the absolute temporal *now*, for every time an eternal God can know all the events actually occurring at that time as well as the location of that time with respect to other times; God can also know that that time is experienced as the absolute *now* by temporal entities at that time.

But after these things, there is nothing further for God to know about what time it is now. There is no time in the eternal *now*; and, in the eternal *now*, God is present to every temporal event, as it is occurring in the absolute temporal *now*. In the life of an eternal God, no *temporal* moment has any more claim than any other to be *for God* the absolute *now*.

One crude but helpful heuristic device for depicting the relation of eternity to time is to think of the time line as having an illuminated, yellow point indicating the absolute temporal *now*. Then, for things in time, only one point on the line is ever yellow, although what point is yellow is always different. For God in the eternal *now*, however, the entire time line is yellow.

An analogy may also help here. Edwin Abbott's story *Flatland* was written in order to illuminate the difficulties of thinking oneself *up* the ladder of being by inviting readers to think their way *down* the ladder of being. In Abbott's story, there is more than one mode of spatial existence for sentient beings, some of whom are two-dimensional in the Flatland world and some of whom are three-dimensional. So, there is both the two-dimensional Flatland mode of spatial existence, for the story's sentient squares, and the more ordinary three-dimensional mode of spatial existence, for more familiar three-dimensional sentient creatures. In Abbott's story, a sentient square in the Flatland world makes contact with a sentient three-dimensional sphere and struggles to understand what life in the three-dimensional world could possibly be.

For the sake of the analogy, suppose that the Flatland world is finite and linearly ordered with an absolute middle. Then there is an absolute Flatland *here*, which in the Flatland world can be occupied by only one Flatlander at a time. Nonetheless, if Flatland were small enough, then, with respect to a sentient observer in the three-dimensional world, all of Flatland could be *here* at once (where the *here* of Flatland and the *here* of the three-dimensional world are only analogous to one another, not identical). And yet it would not follow and it would not be true that all of the Flatland world would be *here* with respect to any sentient two-dimensional occupant of Flatland. So it could be true both that only one sentient square in Flatland could be *here* at once (with respect to the *here* of Flatland) and also that all of Flatland could be *here* at once (with respect to the *here* of the three-dimensional world). The reason for this apparently paradoxical claim is that the whole of the Flatland world can be encompassed within the metaphysically bigger *here* of the three-dimensional world.

An analogous point holds with regard to *now*, on the doctrine of eternity. The doctrine of eternity has the implication that, with respect to time, sentient temporal beings are in the position of Flatland's sentient square as they try to understand a metaphysically greater God, whose *now* is eternal—limitless duration without succession—rather than the more limited and more familiar temporal *now*. With respect to God in the eternal *now*, all of time is encompassed within the eternal *now*, in the sense that all of time is ET-simultaneous with the one eternal *now*.[12] Just as the whole Flatland world can be *here* for someone in three-dimensional space, so all of time can be *now* for God in the eternal *now*.

The result of God's eternity is that in respect of time God can be more present with regard to a human person Paula than any other contemporary human person Jerome could be. As regards Paula, her contemporary Jerome can be present only one time slice after another. When Paula is thirty years old, for example, neither her three-year-old self nor her sixty-year-old self are available to Jerome. But eternal God is present at once to every time of Paula's life; none of Paula's life is ever absent or unavailable for God.

GOD'S PRESENCE WITH REGARD TO SPACE

As for space, *mutatis mutandis*, analogous things can be said, because God is not material, any more than God is temporal.

Aristotle says that a place contains a material body only if the outermost edge of what is contained and the outermost edge of the place coincide.[13] If this is right, then since God is not a body and so has no outermost edges at all, God cannot be *in* a place, in the sense that the place contains him. (For similar reasons, nothing can be in God in this sense; in the Aristotelian sense of 'place', God cannot be a place for material things.) But although God cannot be present *in* a place as in a container, God can be present *at* a place.

Presence at a place is a complicated notion. In earlier work,[14] Norman Kretzmann and I tried to capture this relation in terms of God's having direct and unmediated causal contact with and cognitive access to things at a place.[15] I now think, however, that the attempt to capture presence at a place in terms of direct and unmediated cognitive and causal connection misses something.

Consider, for example, Homer's depiction of Zeus. Wherever in physical reality he is, Homer's Zeus has direct and unmediated causal contact with the Trojans at the place of the Trojan War and also direct and unmediated cognitive access to them. That is, Zeus knows directly and immediately what is happening to the Trojans in the fighting with the Greeks, say, and he can affect the way the fighting goes just by willing it. But Zeus can continue to have such cognitive and causal contact with the Trojans at the place of the Trojan War even when he is (as Homer sometimes says) having dinner with the Ethiopians. While Zeus is among the Ethiopians, however, he is absent from the place of the Trojan War, not present at it.

Elsewhere I have argued that what is missing for Zeus in this Homeric story can be explained in terms of shared attention.[16] It is hard to overemphasize the importance of shared attention for human life and development. It is currently the subject of much discussion among philosophers, psychologists, and neuroscientists,[17] but all attempts to give a clear and adequate account of it seem at best incomplete.[18] Still, it is a phenomenon everyone recognizes, and clear examples of it are easy to find. When a mother looks into the eyes of her baby and the baby looks back, they are sharing attention. As between adults, shared attention is partly a matter of mutual knowledge, of the sort that prompts philosophical worry about the possibility of unstoppable infinite regress: Paula is aware of Jerome's being aware of Paula's being aware of Jerome's being aware, and so on. The object of awareness for Paula is simultaneously Jerome and their mutual awareness—Jerome's awareness of her awareness of his awareness and so on—and the object of awareness for Jerome is simultaneously Paula and their mutual awareness. These lines are misleading in multiple ways and inadequate to capture the phenomenon of shared attention, but they help to give some idea of it.

Although as between human persons, shared attention is most often mediated by vision, it can be mediated by other senses as well. A congenitally blind child can share attention with its mother by sound or by touch, for example. In the case of an immaterial God, shared attention can occur without any mediation by the senses, provided that there is a certain kind of mutual awareness between God and a human person. The senses are typically the vehicle for establishing shared attention, but they are not essential to it.[19]

Between human persons, presence at a place includes not shared attention, but the mere *availability* for shared attention; and something similar can be said about Homer's human-like Greek gods. In the case of Zeus in the story, Zeus is not present at the place of the Trojan War when he is having dinner with the Ethiopians, because, even though he has direct and unmediated cognitive and causal contact with that place and the things in it, he is not available to share attention with the Trojans at that place. Zeus's power extends to the place of the Trojan War; but, one might say, his face does not. A Trojan might address a prayer to Zeus while Zeus is among the Ethiopians, in the assurance that Zeus would hear it and could immediately answer it by altering the course of the war. But it is possible for Greek gods to engage in face-to-face interaction; and Zeus is not available for that kind of interaction with anyone at the place of the Trojan War while he is away among the Ethiopians. For this reason, Zeus is not then present at the place of the Trojan War either.

So one ingredient in a person's presence at a place is that person's availability for sharing attention with other persons also present at that place. *Mutatis mutandis*, this point about the connection between shared attention and presence at a place applies also to God. God's having direct and unmediated cognitive and causal contact with everything at any place is still insufficient for God's being present at every place. In order for God to be present at every place, as God is on the doctrine of divine omnipresence, it also needs to be the case that, for any person at any place who is able and willing to share attention with God, God is available to share attention with that person.

On orthodox theological doctrine, then, the relation of omnipresent God to a human person located in space is analogous to the relation between the sentient three-dimensional observer and the sentient two-dimensional square in Abbott's *Flatland*. The space that is *here* for the sentient two-dimensional square is much more limited than the space that is *here* with regard to the three-dimensional observer, who is metaphysically greater than the sentient square. Analogously, although only a limited region of space is *here* with regard to a human person in a place, for God the entirety of space is *here*, even in the sense that God is available at once to share attention with any human person at any location in space.

In this respect, there is parity between God's relation to space and God's relation to time. In one and the same eternal present, omnipresent God is available to share attention with any person at any location in any time. Because of the way God is present at a place and in a time, for all persons, in whatever place and time they are, God is at once present, in power and knowledge and also in person.

CLOSENESS

In addition to presence at a place or in a time, there is yet another kind of presence possible as between persons, a significant personal presence. This is the kind of presence that is required for union between persons. We can understand significant personal presence in terms of a particular kind of rich shared attention and mutual closeness, and so something needs to be said at least briefly about each of these notions here.[20]

The relation *being close to*, which holds only among persons as I am employing it here, is irreflexive (a person cannot be close to himself[21]), asymmetric (a priest can be close to a family in crisis without its being the case that they are close to him), and intransitive (a mother can be close to her son and he can be close to his wife without its being the case that the mother-in-law is close to her daughter-in-law).

It is clear that closeness comes in degrees and that it is shaped by the offices of love.[22] An office of love is a relationship that configures what is appropriate to share in a union of love. So, for example, the office of love between a mother and her daughter is different from the office of love between a woman and her teacher. Different things are appropriate to share in the differing offices. And, of course, the character of the persons in the office also shapes the nature of the sharing appropriate as well as the degree of closeness possible. It is possible, for example, for a mother to be close to her daughter when her daughter is five years old and when her daughter is thirty years old. But the age of the daughter makes a difference to the things the mother can appropriately share with her daughter and the degree of closeness they can have. Mutual closeness requires some parity between the persons in the relationship as regards their willingness to be open to the other, but it does not require symmetry in the depth or degree of what is shared with the other. In what follows, I will give a general sketch of the nature of closeness, but this variability in it by office and by character of the persons in the office should be understood throughout.

So, to begin with, closeness requires some openness of mind of one person to another. For example, Paula is close to Jerome only if Jerome shares his thoughts and feelings with Paula. Furthermore, not just any thoughts and feelings will do here. For Paula to be close to Jerome, Jerome has to share with Paula those thoughts and feelings of his that he cares about and that are revelatory of him. Jerome would not be close to Paula if he shared with her a great many of his most trivial thoughts but nothing of what was important to him or revealing of him. The more Jerome can share with Paula of what matters most to him, the closer Paula will be to him.

There are also other necessary conditions involving desires and states of will. The most important of these has to do with the desire for a person. Just as it is possible to know a person with a knowledge which is not reducible to knowledge *that*, so it is possible to desire a person with a desire which is not reducible to desire *that*. It is also possible to desire something without that thing's being necessary for anything other than the fulfillment of the desire itself. For Paula to be close to Jerome, Jerome must have a desire of this sort for Paula. When Jerome desires Paula in this way, and when the desire is sufficiently great, then it is appropriate to say that Jerome needs Paula. Jerome's needing Paula in this sense is, then, a matter of Jerome's having a great desire for Paula and Paula's being necessary for Jerome's fulfilling his desire for Paula (as distinct from anything else that is lacking to Jerome).

Paula is close to Jerome only in case Jerome needs Paula in this sense, to one degree or another. If Jerome had no need at all for Paula, he would not care whether or not he had Paula in his life; it would be a matter of indifference to him one way or another. In that case, it would be counter-intuitive to suppose that Paula is close to him. Furthermore, insofar as the fulfillment of Jerome's need for Paula is at least in part in Paula's control rather than Jerome's, Jerome's having a need for Paula makes Jerome to some extent vulnerable to Paula.[23] And so Jerome's being vulnerable to Paula in some degree is also requisite for Paula's being close to Jerome.

In addition, closeness requires certain higher-order desires and acts of will. If Jerome wants to reveal his thoughts and feelings to Paula and if Jerome desires Paula in the sense just described, but if Jerome is alienated from his own desires as regards Paula—if he desires to have different desires from those he has regarding Paula because he thinks that his relationship to Paula is detrimental to his flourishing, for example—then to that extent Paula is not close to Jerome. For Paula not to be closed out from Jerome to some degree, it is therefore necessary that Jerome have psychic integration of desires, or wholeheartedness.[24]

In general, a person alienated from himself and self-deceived in consequence cannot have someone else fully close to him.[25] Jerome cannot reveal his mind to Paula if Jerome has hidden a good part of his mind from himself. And if Jerome desires not to have the desires he has with regard to Paula, then to that extent he does not desire closeness with Paula either. For that matter, if Jerome is divided within himself as regards any of his desires, Paula will be distant from some part of Jerome, no matter which of his conflicting desires she allies herself with.

So, for Paula to be fully close to Jerome, in the way needed for union, it is necessary that Jerome be integrated in himself. To the extent to which a person is divided against himself, to that extent he cannot be at one with others either. The lack of internal integration is therefore inimical to the union desired in love.

This conclusion is a strong claim that some people will be inclined to resist. To them, it will seem as if the condition requiring internal integration for union is too strenuous. On this objection, even a person seriously alienated from himself can have other people united to him with the requisite closeness. How else, the putative objector will argue, can we explain the way in which troubled people succeed in finding help from counselors or spiritual directors, for example? An internally conflicted person opens his mind and heart to the counselor who is helping him; and so his counselor becomes close to him. By this means, with the counselor's help, the troubled person begins to achieve a more harmonious inner state. How could psychic healing ever occur, the objector will ask, if a person alienated from himself could not have other people close to him?[26]

But, in my view, this objection confuses what we ordinarily accept as closeness with what closeness really is and what we all want closeness to be too. It is true that, if closeness is understood in an ordinary way, an internally fragmented person can have close friends; it is true that a counselor for an internally divided person can be close to her. That is, she can reveal things about her life and feelings to the counselor, and she can even have higher-order desires about the sort of person she wants to be which lead her to want to reveal herself to the counselor. And so on. But, insofar as she is alienated from herself, she will also have conflicting desires, desires to hide things from herself as well as from her counselor. That is why expertise and training are needed on the counselor's part. In order to help her, the counselor will need to deal skillfully with her resistance to what she also desires. The kind of closeness the counselor has to her is, therefore, compatible with his being closed out—*by her*—of a great deal of her inner life. And so the general point at issue here remains, even if it is acknowledged that, on some ordinary account of closeness, an internally fragmented person can have others close to her. Complete, satisfactory, thoroughgoing closeness to a person is closeness of a more strenuous kind. And that kind of closeness, which is what one wants in loving union with another, requires internal integration on the beloved person's part.

And here one other point needs to be made about internal integration.

Like many other philosophers, Aquinas thinks that there is an objective moral standard and that it can be known by the exercise of reason. In fact, he thinks that the objective moral standard, at least in its rudiments, is so accessible to ordinary reason that no human intellect is ever totally in ignorance of it. A human being Jerome who takes something objectively evil—say, beating his partner Paula—as a good morally acceptable for him to do will, therefore, always be double-minded.[27] With some part of his mind, Jerome will take beating Paula to be good; but with some other part of his mind, however far from full conscious awareness it may be and however vague and uncertain it may be, he will nonetheless understand that beating her is morally wrong. And if Jerome is double-minded about the goodness of beating Paula, Jerome will have some first-order desires for beating her but also some first- and second-order desires opposed to doing so.[28]

It follows from this optimistic view of human nature that no one can be wholehearted in evil.[29] Rather, complete internal integration is possible only for a person single-mindedly understanding and wholeheartedly desiring the good. To one extent or another, a person engaged in moral wrongdoing will be double-minded and also internally divided in will.

It is, therefore, a consequence of these views that the ability of one person Paula to be close to another person Jerome is a function of the degree of *Jerome's* own integration in goodness. A person who lacks one or another degree of integration in goodness will hide some part of his mind from himself. To this extent, he will not be able or willing to reveal his mind to someone else. He will also have first-order desires that conflict with some of his other first-order desires or with his second-order desires or both. Consequently, to this extent he will be alienated from some of his own desires, whichever desires are operative in him.[30] Insofar as Jerome is in such a condition, Paula will be closed out from him to one degree or another, no matter what she does. Rudolf Hess, the commandant of Auschwitz, said about his marriage, "Of course, I loved my wife, but a real spiritual union—that was lacking...My wife thought I wasn't satisfied with her, but I told her it was just my nature, and she had to be reconciled to it."[31] Paula's becoming fully close to Jerome requires that Jerome grow in single-mindedness and wholeheartedness; and this growth can occur only to the extent to which Jerome becomes integrated around the good. Without this sort of integration, the full closeness necessary for union in love is undermined or obviated.

Mutatis mutandis, all these points hold for God's being close to a human person, too. As I argued in Chapter 3, God himself has the attitudes and desires needed for God's closeness to any human being.[32] What is crucial, therefore, for God's actually being close to a person such as Jerome is Jerome's attitudes and desires with regard to God and Jerome's internal integration around the good.[33] I do not mean to say that anything about a human person could keep God from loving that person, since it is possible to love someone unilaterally. For the same reason, the internal fragmentation of a human person cannot keep God from exercising God's providential care to work that person's good and to shepherd that person towards union with God. The point here has to do only with that closeness necessary for union. On the account of closeness I have argued for here, even God cannot be close to a person and united with a person who is divided within himself.

Mutual closeness is necessary for the union desired in love, and so union between God and a human being Jerome requires not only that God be close to Jerome but also that Jerome be close to God. And someone might worry that the conditions for closeness given here cannot be applied to God; on this objection, given this account of closeness, it is not possible for Jerome to be close to God under any conditions. In my view, however, this objection is mistaken.

In the first place, on orthodox theological doctrine, God puts a revelation into history; and so God reveals his mind and will to human beings. In this respect, then, God meets one of the conditions for allowing human beings to be close to him. It is, of course, not the case that a limited human psyche can comprehend completely in all its complexity the infinite mind of God. But the openness of mind needed for closeness does not require that *everything* in the mind of one person be open to another. It requires only that some things important to that person be shared with the other. That is why even a five-year-old daughter can be close to her mother, although there will be very much in her mother's mind that is beyond the five-year-old's comprehension.

Secondly, since the sort of desire at issue in one person's needing another is not correlated with any defect or lack on the part of that person, nothing about the divine attributes rules out such desire, and so also such need, on God's part. In this sense, even the God of classical theism can need his creatures. Even a classical theist such as Aquinas can accept the view Job expresses when Job says to God, "You will call, and I will answer you. You will have a desire to the work of your hands" (Job 14:15). In fact, on Aquinas's account of love, which takes a desire for union with the beloved as one of the constituent desires of love, God has to have a desire of this sort for his creatures if he is to love them.[34]

But what about the condition having to do with vulnerability? On the conception of God as sovereign and ultimately self-sufficient, it certainly looks as if nothing that matters to God is dependent on anything human beings do; a fortiori, it appears as if it is not possible for God to be vulnerable to human beings. But these appearances are mistaken, too. There is a biblical text claiming that God wants all human beings to be saved (I Tim. 2:4); but, on traditional Christian doctrine, not all human beings are saved. Because God gave human beings free will, God allowed certain things that matter to God— the salvation of all human beings—to depend on wills other than God's own. In this sense, then, God makes himself vulnerable to human beings.[35] In addition, of course, there is also the incarnation. In becoming incarnate, God makes himself radically vulnerable to other human beings.[36]

And so it is not the case that classical theism rules out a human person's being close to God, on the analysis of closeness I have been arguing for here.

PERSONAL PRESENCE: SHARED ATTENTION, MIND-READING, AND EMPATHY

Mutual closeness is necessary for union; but two persons could be close to each other and still not united to each other because something separates them even while they remain close during the separation. Such a situation is a staple of romantic literature, for example. What is missing for the separated friends is the personal presence of one to the other, and so a particular kind of presence is also necessary for union.

It is clear that there are various kinds of presence for human beings as well as for God. For human beings, for example, Paula's being present with regard to Jerome could be nothing more than a matter of her being *here now* where and when Jerome is located. Analogously, as I explained above, even for immaterial God, there is a kind of presence that involves relations to both space and time. The relations involved in presence with regard to space and time are typically characterized as presence *in* or presence *at*. In addition, however, there is another kind of presence, a second-personal presence, that one person can have with regard to another; and it is the kind of presence crucial for union.

This personal presence is the kind we have in mind when we say, for example,

> "She read the paper all through dinner and was never present to any of the rest of us,"

or

> "He sat with me at the defendant's table, but he was never really present with me during the trial."

In these examples, there is presence at a time and in a place; but a significant personal presence, characterized by one or another kind of second-personal psychological connection, is missing. Typically, this kind of personal presence is characterized as presence *with* or presence *to* another person.

Personal presence comes in differing degrees and kinds. There is the minimal kind that can arise when one momentarily catches the eye of a stranger on a bus. At the other end of the scale, there is the kind of intense and intimate mutual personal presence that is possible between two persons who are close to each other and engaged in mutual gaze. It is a particularly significant personal presence,[37] and it requires shared attention. If Jerome were to say of Paula, "She was distracted all through dinner and was never really present to me," one of the things he would be complaining about would be Paula's failure to share her attention with him.[38]

It is hard to capture the notion of shared attention in a philosophically precise way, but it seems to require mind-reading and empathy, among other things.[39]

Because of recent work in neuroscience and developmental psychology, especially work on the impairments of development among autistic children, we have learned a great deal about the neurological systems that make empathy and mind-reading possible and the kind of cognition these systems produce. Whatever ties together the different clinical signs of all the degrees of autism spectrum disorder, the most salient feature of the disorder is an impairment in the cognitive capacities enabling mind-reading.[40] The knowledge which is impaired for an autistic child, however, cannot be taken as knowledge *that* something or other is the case. A non-autistic pre-linguistic infant is capable of mind-reading; she can know her mother, and to one extent or another she can also know some of her mother's mental states. But she is not capable of knowledge *that* a particular person is her mother. Conversely, an autistic child can know *that* his mother is sad—say, because she has told him so and she is a reliable authority on such matters for the child. But the impairment characteristic of autism can leave the child without the direct and immediate knowledge of the sadness of his mother.[41] What is impaired for the autistic child is just a non-propositional knowledge of persons and a direct intuitive awareness of their mental states. In typically functioning human beings, mind-reading yields just this kind of cognition, namely, a non-propositional, direct, and immediate intuitive awareness of persons and their mental states.[42]

Research in neuroscience has shown that the capacity for this kind of knowledge of persons is subserved at least in part by what is now called 'the mirror neuron system.'[43] The mirror neuron system makes it possible for one person to have knowledge of the mental states of another person when that knowledge shares something of the phenomenology of perception. Like the perception of color, for example, the knowledge of persons in mind-reading is direct, intuitive, and hard to translate without remainder into knowledge *that* (but very useful as a basis for knowledge *that* of one sort or another).

Neurons in the mirror neuron system contribute to making the knowledge of mind-reading possible because they fire both when one does some action oneself or has some emotion oneself *and also* when one sees that same action or emotion in someone else.

The point is easier to appreciate if we focus on empathy with another person's pain, which is currently also thought to be a result of the cognitive capacities subserved at least in part by the mirror neuron system.[44] When Paula sees Jerome cut himself with a knife, *she* feels *his* pain because Paula's mirror neuron system produces in Paula an affective state that has at least some of the characteristics of the pain Jerome is experiencing.[45] Paula does not actually suffer physical pain resulting from a laceration in her tissues; but, in her empathy with Jerome, she has some kind of feeling of pain. Only, in Paula, that feeling is taken off-line, as it were, because in her it is not connected to tissue damage, as it is in Jerome.[46] In addition, even though in empathy Paula feels pain that is her pain, in the sense that the pain is in her and she herself feels it, she nonetheless recognizes this pain as Jerome's pain, not hers. The final result of the neural interactions begun by the mirror neuron system is that Paula knows *that* Jerome is in pain; but she knows this because, in consequence of the mirror neuron system, she first knows Jerome's pain.[47]

In general, in mind-reading, one person somehow has within herself something of the mind of another. In mind-reading Jerome, to one extent or another Paula will know the action Jerome is doing, the intention which Jerome has in doing it, and the emotion Jerome has while doing it. And Paula will know these things in Jerome through having herself some simulacrum of the mental state in Jerome. Something of Jerome's mental state will be in Paula, but in a different way.

One researcher on mind-reading, Vittorio Gallese, tries to explain the relevant neural mechanisms involved in the knowledge of persons this way:

> [brain systems] map...multimodal representation across different spaces inhabited by different actors. These spaces are blended within a unified common intersubjective space, which paradoxically does not segregate any subject. This space is *"we" centric*...The shared intentional space underpinned by the mirror matching mechanism is not meant to distinguish the agent from the observer.[48]

And he goes on to explain empathy in this way:

> Self-other identity goes beyond the domain of action. It incorporates sensations, affect, and emotions.... The shared intersubjective space in which we live from birth continues long afterward to constitute a substantial part of our semantic space. When we observe other individuals acting, facing their full range of expressive power (the way they act, the emotions and feelings they display), a meaningful embodied link among individuals is automatically established.... [S]ensation and emotions displayed by others can also be empathized with, and therefore implicitly understood, through a mirror matching mechanism.[49]

In other words, in mind-reading between human beings, there is a sense in which one person has a kind of intuitive entrance to the thought, affect, and intention in the mind of another person. And so because of the intermingling of minds made possible at least in part by the mirror neuron system, one person can have a kind of direct access to the mind of that other. In such mind-reading, one human person can be present *with* another in a way more powerful than mere presence at a place or in a time. If Paula is riding the subway next to Jerome, then she is minimally present to Jerome in virtue of being at a time and at a place where Jerome is also, so that she is available for shared attention with him, if he should happen to look at her while she is looking at him, for example. But if he is a blank book to her, if he manages to close his mind to her, then to that extent she is not able to be present to him with any significant personal presence. In virtue of the fact that his mind is closed to her, she is distant from him even while standing next to him.

It would not alter this conclusion if it turned out that Paula had propositional knowledge of Jerome's mental states. If some authority reliable for Paula were to confide in her somehow what Jerome is feeling and thinking, Paula would know that Jerome has a certain set of feelings and intentions. But she would still be distant from Jerome, in consequence of his having closed her out from mind-reading him herself.

On the other hand, if Jerome's mind is open to Paula, then the kind of presence *to* a person made possible at least in part by the mirror neuron system is greatly strengthened. When Paula mind-reads Jerome, the relevant neural systems in Paula give Paula a direct, quasi-perceptual awareness of something in Jerome's thoughts, emotions, and intentions. This awareness arises in Paula because in mind-reading Jerome she is in effect herself experiencing something of Jerome's mental states. In this experience and awareness, she is also present *with* Jerome, with personal presence, in a way she could not be if his mind were closed to her.

There is a limited degree of this kind of personal presence when Paula winces as she sees Jerome slice his finger with his steak knife, even if Jerome is unaware that Paula is observing him. This is a kind of unilateral presence of one person with another. There is also a mutual personal presence of a limited kind that is possible even when the two people involved are strangers to each other or know and heartily dislike each other. For example, Paula can wince at Jerome's pain and he can be aware of her doing so even while she thinks that his suffering that pain serves him right, and they share awareness of her attitude towards him.

But there is a much greater degree of personal presence when two people who are mutually close to each other in a loving relationship share mind-reading of each other with empathy in intense shared attention. In mutual personal presence of this intimate kind, in the context of mutual closeness, there can be something stronger than the asymmetrical relation involved just in one person's mind-reading another. In mind-reading, one person somehow has within himself something of the mind of another. In mutual personal presence of this intimate kind, there can be a mutual "in-ness" between the persons who are close to each other and sharing awareness, in a way that yields a powerful personal presence of each to the other.

When this kind of mutual and shared second-personal presence occurs,[50] one way to describe the connection between the two people in question is to say that they are united in love. This kind of experience is a staple of romantic literature and poetry, but it is also common between human beings in non-romantic and non-erotic relationship as well, as, for example, between a mother and her child or between a sick person and her loving care-taker.

Mutatis mutandis, these points about personal presence and shared attention apply also to God. Given the reasons above for thinking that God can be in a relationship of mutual closeness with human beings, it is clear that God can have personal presence to or with human persons as well. In what follows, I will argue that, on Christian doctrine, the personal presence generated by mind-reading and empathy are also possible for God, and so is the shared attention needed for significant personal presence.[51] In fact, not only can God share attention with human persons, but something analogous to mutual "in-ness" is possible for God with respect to those who love him. But, for God, this "in-ness" has an ontological reality that is not available in the case of mutually loving human beings. For lack of a better word, I will use an old theological term and refer to this most intimate and powerful kind of second-personal presence and in-ness that God can have to a human person as God's 'indwelling' in that person.

On the doctrines of eternity and omnipresence, God is simultaneously present to every creature at every time and place. Given the reflections on presence in this chapter, the only thing that makes a difference to the kind of personal presence—significant personal presence or otherwise—that God has to a human person is the condition of the human person herself. In this respect, God's relation to a human person Paula is different from the relation of Jerome to Paula. If Paula wants Jerome to be personally present to her, she alone will not be able to bring about what she wants, because the relationship she wants is up to Jerome as much as it is up to her; and, for one reason or another, Jerome may fail to meet the conditions requisite for his being personally present to Paula. But, given the doctrines of eternity and omnipresence and these views about closeness and presence, things are different when it comes to God's being significantly present to a human person. If Paula wants God to be present to her, what is needed to bring about what she wants depends only on her, on her being able and willing to be open to God and to share attention with God. Because God is omnipresent, then if Paula is able and willing to do her part, omnipresent God will be present to her with significant personal presence.[52] If she is not, then God will have only minimal personal presence with respect to her.

GOD'S PRESENCE WITH HUMAN PERSONS: EMPATHY AND MIND-READING ON GOD'S PART

Since on orthodox theological doctrine God is omniscient, God knows all truths; and so God has propositional knowledge (or the divine equivalent of propositional knowledge[53]) as regards all the mental states of all human beings. God knows *that* Paula is sad or *that* Jerome intends to go out. But it seems that with respect to human persons, God cannot have empathy or the mind-reading kind of knowledge.[54] And so it seems that one kind of presence with a person, of the sort prized by human beings, is not possible for God to have with respect to human beings.[55]

When Paula has empathy with Jerome, she feels within herself what Jerome feels. But in virtue of having no body, God has no feelings either. This is the point of the scholastic doctrine that God is impassible. Strictly speaking, a *passio*, which is the thing an *impassible* God does not have, is a feeling; and a feeling at least includes bodily sensations. Nothing immaterial can have bodily sensations, and so immaterial God has no feelings either, in this sense of 'feeling.' (This claim is different from the claim with which it is often confused, namely, the theologically unacceptable claim that God has no emotions.[56])

Mind-reading extends to more than knowledge of the feelings of another person, but all mind-reading is like empathy in having a shared character and a qualitative feel. When Jerome mind-reads Paula, he shares something of Paula's mental state in virtue of somehow feeling that mental state in himself. A mental state that is Paula's is somehow also Jerome's and felt by Jerome (except that Jerome experiences it as Paula's, rather than as his own). Jerome knows Paula's intention to shake his hand, say, because his mirror neuron system forms the neural pattern it would form if *Jerome* were going to move his arm to shake her hand; and so, by feeling it within himself, he knows Paula's intention to shake his hand in the mind-reading mode of cognition. An immaterial God cannot form an intention to move his arm to shake her hand, however, because he has no arm to move. And so although God can know *that* Paula intends to shake Jerome's hand, it seems that he cannot mind-read Paula's intention in the direct and intuitive way Jerome can.

And the point generalizes. A human psyche is too small and God's mind is too great, one might say, for God to contain human mental states within himself in the shared way the mirror neuron system enables as between human beings. Of course, the greatness of God's mind allows God cognitive access superior to any kind of cognitive access had by a more limited mind. And yet there is something worth prizing that is lost if the kind of sharing and presence with a person that is enabled by mind-reading and empathy is ruled out for God. By way of analogy, the greatness of God's nature makes it impossible for God to suffer, but something worth prizing would be lost if it were not true to say that God suffers.

But, in this respect, Christianity has special resources because of the doctrine that God became incarnate in Christ. The Chalcedonian formula for the incarnate Christ stipulates that Christ is one person with two natures. The one person is the second person of the Trinity and is thus God, and the two natures are the divine and the human. It is one of the consequences of the Chalcedonian formula that there are in Christ two minds, one human and one divine, but only one person—a divine person—who is the possessor of these two minds.

As I explained in Chapter 1, the far-ranging and significant implications of the Chalcedonian formula can be seen by thinking about suffering and death. When Christ suffers and dies, he does so in the human nature of Jesus; but the person suffering and dying is God. So, while it is theologically correct to say that God cannot suffer or die in his divine nature, it is not theologically correct to say that God cannot suffer or die. On the Chalcedonian formula, accepted as orthodox theological doctrine, it is correct to say that God suffers and that God dies. God can do both, in the human nature God assumed in Christ.

And on the doctrine of eternity, God's having an assumed human nature is not something true of God at some times but not at others;[57] rather, it is something characteristic of God always in the limitless eternal *now*. God is therefore never in the state of not having an assumed human nature.[58] For this reason, the human capacity for suffering is something that is never not characteristic of God, in the human nature whose assumption is never absent from God.[59]

For the same reasons, God can have empathy with human persons and can also mind-read them, since God can use the human mind of the assumed human nature to know human persons in the knowledge of persons way.

In addition, although it is part of orthodox theological doctrine that in Christ the two natures do not mingle, nonetheless, in virtue of the fact that only one person has these natures, and that one person is divine, Christ can act in such a way as to use elements of both natures in his actions. That is, even while acting in his human nature, Christ can use powers that are beyond the merely human and that are available to him only through his divine nature. For example, acting in his capacity as a human being, Christ does miracles; but he is able to do these miracles because in his human actions he can harness the divine power over nature.

In the same sort of way, in his human nature, Christ can mind-read in ways not possible for mere human persons. When he does, it is the human nature employed in the mind-reading; but the person doing the mind-reading is divine and has access to divine power. It is therefore possible that Christ has the ability to mind-read human beings deeply, or even miraculously, in a way that mere human persons could not do. In fact, it seems in principle possible that, since God is present to every time and space, Christ can use his human mind and the power of his divine nature to mind-read at once the entire mind of every human being at every time and space.[60]

So, the Chalcedonian formula for the incarnate Christ gives a way of explaining and defending God's knowledge of persons through mind-reading and the presence with a human person that God's mind-reading enables God to have. And if the mind-reading of Christ can occur in miraculous ways, employing the power of God to extend greatly the ordinary human capacity for mind-reading, then in the incarnate Christ God can have at once, with respect to all human persons, the unilateral personal presence brought about in empathy and mind-reading.

SECOND-PERSONAL PRESENCE: UNION IN LOVE AND INDWELLING

The kind of presence mediated by the mind-reading that God can have with all human persons in consequence of the incarnation falls short of the second-personal presence obtaining between persons united in love, however. When Christ mind-reads others in ordinary ways or miraculously, he does so because of the power of his human capacity for mind-reading, divinely enhanced or not. But, miraculous or merely human, by itself this kind of mind-reading produces a unilateral, not a mutual, presence. And so there is an asymmetry about it that limits one person's presence with another.

It is part of orthodox theological doctrine, though, that when a person Paula comes to faith, she opens herself up to God in love. In an act of free will that is part of faith, Paula accepts God's grace and begins a relation of mutual love with God.[61] In entering into this relationship, Paula accepts not only God's grace but also God himself. (I will have much more to say about this process later, in Chapters 7 and 8.)

On orthodox theological doctrine, when Paula comes to faith in this way, the third person of the Trinity, the Holy Spirit, comes to dwell in her. However exactly it is to be understood, on the theological claims involving the Holy Spirit, the indwelling of the Holy Spirit puts the mind of God within Paula's psyche. On Trinitarian doctrine, there is only one mind and one will in God,[62] and this one mind and one will are common to all three persons of the Trinity. Therefore, in consequence of the intimate connection established by the Holy

Spirit's indwelling Paula, the relationship of love between God and Paula yields second-personal presence of God with Paula.[63]

But how are we to understand the theological claim about the Holy Spirit's indwelling? The indwelling Holy Spirit is a common topic of Christian theology,[64] but it is actually not easy to specify what this indwelling could be.

We can start by saying what it cannot be. God's indwelling in Paula is not merely a matter of God's having direct and immediate causal and cognitive access to Paula's mind. Since God is omnipotent and omniscient, God has this kind of access to the mind of every human being, with regard to propositional knowledge (or the divine analogue to propositional knowledge). Through the human mind of Christ, God also has access to every human mind with the non-propositional knowledge garnered by mind-reading. For every person, it is possible for God to know the mind of that person with direct and unmediated awareness of the mind-reading kind. (For similar reasons, it is also possible for God to communicate in a direct and unmediated way with the mind of every person.) These kinds of cognitive relations between God and human beings hold, then, for every human person. But the indwelling of the Holy Spirit is found only in those people who are in grace. And so these kinds of cognitive relations alone are insufficient as an explanation of the nature of the Holy Spirit's indwelling.

God's indwelling a person in grace is part of the union in love between her and God. So we might try understanding indwelling as an analogue to the psychic relation between human persons who are united in love. The psychic relation between mutually loving human beings is a particularly intimate kind of mutual awareness, with mutual mind-reading accompanied by shared attention, when the persons in that relationship are mutually close to each other. And so we might suppose that the indwelling of the Holy Spirit is the analogous set of relations between God and a human person. But this approach to explaining the indwelling of the Holy Spirit is not quite right either. The indwelling of the Holy Spirit is meant to be something ontologically greater than mutual closeness accompanied by intense shared attention. In the Holy Spirit's indwelling, God himself is supposed somehow to be within each person in grace. Although, as I explained above, immaterial God cannot be contained within a material container, the indwelling of the Holy Spirit does include God's being somehow within the psyches of those who are in grace.

At this point, it may help to return to Gallese's attempt to describe the kind of relations that are involved in mind-reading. According to Gallese, when Jerome mind-reads Paula's intention to shake his hand, for example, his mind goes into the configuration it would have if he were Paula and preparing to shake hands. But this configuration is in Jerome off-line, that is, it is not actually connected in an active way to Jerome's muscles. He has the motor configuration for shaking hands, but on his part no hand-shaking occurs. So, when Jerome mind-reads Paula's intention, the configuration of Paula's intention is in Jerome; and because it is, it is Jerome's; but it is in Jerome as Paula's intention, and not as his. This complicated state is what Gallese is trying to describe when he says that there is an intersubjective part of the human brain that enables a real sharing of mental states.

Gallese is talking about brain systems in order to make a point about mental states. Aquinas makes a very roughly analogous point about the mechanisms of cognition for perception, and it may help here to see that point too. For Aquinas, when a person Jerome sees an object, such as a coffee cup, the configuration or form inhering in the cup that makes the matter of the cup be a cup is transferred to Jerome's mind. The form that is in the cup is then also in Jerome's mind, only in an encoded state. Or, as we might say, the configuration of the cup is transferred through a certain pattern of firing by Jerome's retinal cells to Jerome's visual cortex. In theory, it would be possible for a competent neuroscientist who understands the neural coding involved to look at the configuration in Jerome's visual cortex and infer correctly that what is impacting his visual system is a cup. So, in some sense, the configuration of the cup is in both the cup and Jerome, only in differing ways. Analogously, we might say, when Jerome mind-reads Paula's intention, there is a form or configuration in Paula's brain that is found also in Jerome's. He mind-reads her because he shares this form or configuration with her. The same configuration is in each of them, only differently, insofar as it is off-line in Jerome.[65]

Furthermore, although the configuration of the cup is really in Jerome's mind when he sees the cup, that configuration is processed in Jerome in such a way that, without ceasing to be the form of the cup, it enables Jerome to have cognition of the cup. Analogously, when the configuration of Paula's intention is in Jerome's mind, that configuration is in his mind in such a way as to enable Jerome to have cognition of Paula's intention, not his. So, the configuration of Paula's mind is in Paula's mind and in Jerome's at once, but Paula feels it as hers and Jerome feels it as belonging to Paula. It is possible, then, for a person Jerome to have neurologically and psychologically within his brain and mind something that is his own and yet is also part of Paula's brain and mind.

Furthermore, it is also possible for Jerome to feel this dichotomy, so that it is subjectively accessible to him. That is, Jerome can consciously identify a mental state as within his own mind and yet somehow not his but Paula's. It is easiest to see this point in connection with empathy. If Jerome sees Paula impale her bare foot on a nail in the garden, he will wince with pain. So, something of Paula's pain is in Jerome; he winces because he feels it within himself. But even while he feels this pain in himself, he also is conscious that what he feels with pain is Paula's pain and not his own. He is sharing with Paula what is Paula's. What Jerome has is, you might say, Jerome's Paula's painful feeling.

As the quotation from Gallese above makes clear, there are neurological systems that are intersubjective, in which something shared is processed without being assigned to particular subjects. But neurological research also suggests that the brain has the opposite sort of capacity as well; it has multiple systems for identifying parts of oneself as one's own—body parts, thoughts, and the self in general.[66] If there are brain systems that enable shared mental states, there are also brain systems enabling the distinction between self and other.[67] Because of these systems in the human brain for recognizing some mental states as one's own, it is also possible for a person Jerome to be aware of a mental state within his own mind as not his own but someone else's.

Since this is so, it is possible for the sort of intersubjectivity of mental states that is enabled by the mirror neuron system and evident in mind-reading to be replaced by something greater. Instead of a mere psychological sharing of mental states, there could be a sharing of persons. It is possible, that is, that what is in Jerome's mind is not just another person's thought or affect, but in fact that other person himself. If such a thing is possible, then 'indwelling' is not a bad word for this kind of relationship of one mind to another.

Science fiction is replete with stories in which malevolent non-human beings indwell a human mind,[68] so that there are, as it were, two persons (with two different minds and two different wills) within the same human body, one of whom is a human being himself and one of whom is not. And folklore has sometimes tended to explain certain kinds of mental illness along the same lines, as a demonic person engaged in occupation of a human being's mind.[69] Such stories are frightening and revulsive because in the stories the indwelling person invades a vulnerable human person, against the human person's will or at least without his consent. Typically, in such cases, the invader has only hatred and contempt for its human victim.

On the other hand, when two people Paula and Jerome are psychically united to one another in love with the sharing of attention that union requires, the interweaving of their psyches occurs only with the willingness of each to each. Paula's psyche is open to Jerome's because Paula wants it to be, and the same is true of Jerome's psyche with respect to Paula. When they have the resulting shared openness wanted by each of them, it yields gladness and peace. Furthermore, insofar as they love each other, each of them wishes for the good of the other. And so the vulnerability of each of them to the other in the openness of love is acceptable to each of them, because of the trust each is rightly willing to place in the other. In the fullest expression of such uniting in love between Paula and Jerome, each of them is as second-personally present with the other as is possible between two human beings. Depictions of human persons united in love in a variety of relationships is a perennial theme in great literature, and hardly anyone is completely immune to its attractions.

But, on traditional Christian doctrine, an even more powerful second-personal presence of shared love is possible for God in the indwelling of the

Holy Spirit, where what is united is not just thoughts and feelings but persons themselves. As in the case of two human persons united in love, the indwelling of the Holy Spirit requires welcome on the part of a person Paula. When Paula comes to faith and accepts God's grace in love, then and only then the Holy Spirit itself comes to indwell in Paula. In coming to faith, Paula freely accepts God; and the consequent indwelling of Paula by God's Holy Spirit is characterized by shared love, freely given and freely accepted.

In a union of love between God and Paula, what is within Paula's psyche is not just the thoughts and intentions of God, but God himself, only in such a way that there is no mingling of natures. Nothing of Paula's own individual personhood is lost in the process. Paula's mind remains her own, and her awareness of her mind as her own also remains. Because God and Paula remain what they are even in this uniting, Paula does not have free range of the divine mind; she does not become omniscient, for example. Still, when the Holy Spirit indwells in her mind, Paula will be aware of the Spirit's mind within her own, and there will be shared mind-reading and empathy between them, so that there is a kind of intimacy between them that surpasses what would otherwise be available to Paula alone or in union with another human being.[70]

In consequence of the indwelling of the Holy Spirit, Paula will have as present as possible, not only with herself but even within herself, the God who is her beloved. That is why the list of the fruits of this union[71] begins with love, joy, and peace—love, because her beloved, who loves her, is present to her; joy, because of the dynamic interaction with her beloved, who is present to her in second-personal ways; and peace, because her heart already has what it most desires, her beloved, present to her.[72] On traditional Christian doctrine, there is no faith, no life of grace, without the indwelling Holy Spirit, with its concomitant love, joy, peace, and the other fruits of the Holy Spirit.[73]

And so in the indwelling of the Holy Spirit, God is present to a person in grace with as much second-personal presence as is possible in this life, surpassing even the presence possible between two human persons united in mutual love. It is a union that makes the two of them one without merging one into the other or in any other way depriving the human person of his own self, his own mind and will.

QUESTIONS

This account of the nature of God's presence to a person in grace in the indwelling of the Holy Spirit raises many questions. As I promised at the outset, here I will raise briefly just those few that are most pressing for my purposes.

First, God's indwelling a person in grace is meant to be the end point, or the summit, of what the atonement achieves for persons in this life; but the Hebrew Bible notes many occasions in the period before the time of Christ in which the spirit of God comes on[74] or into a person.[75] If the atonement of Christ is somehow necessary for the indwelling of the Holy Spirit, then those earlier cases either must also be somehow tied to Christ's atonement or else be somehow different from the indwelling of the Holy Spirit. But what makes the indwelling of the Holy Spirit different from the Holy Spirit's coming on a person in earlier cases, in the period before Christ?

Secondly, what is the relation of the Holy Spirit to the remedy for the post-Fall human condition which the atonement is supposed to be?

And, finally, why is the passion and death of Christ necessary for the indwelling Holy Spirit? As I explained at the outset, in the Gospel of John (16:7), Christ tells his disciples that without his passion and death the Holy Spirit will not come. But why not? Given the description of the character of and conditions for the indwelling of the Holy Spirit, why would Christ's passion and death be necessary for it?

It is not possible to examine even cursorily all the cases in the Hebrew Bible of God's spirit coming on a person or even to list all those cases. But here is a representative set of examples. Exodus (31:3 and 35:31) says that the spirit of God came upon the workmen God called to make special articles wanted for the ritual worship of God.[76] Numbers 11:25 says that God put his spirit into some of the elders of Israel so that they prophesied. (Num. 24:2 makes a similar claim about Balaam, who was not one of the Israelites but did prophesy by the spirit of God.) Judges 3:10 says that the spirit of God came on Othniel, one of the judges of the tribes of Israel, for purposes of judging. Judges 15:14 reports that the spirit of God came on Samson so that he was very strong and won battles. I Samuel 11:6 claims that the spirit of God came on Saul, and he became very angry and initiated war with the enemies of Israel. And Nehemiah (9:20 and 9:30) suggests that the point of God's sending the spirit of God on human persons was for the sake of their teaching God's word to God's people.

In some of the cases in the Hebrew Bible, the spirit of God comes on or into a few selected human persons for the purpose of giving them some more than merely human ability, in workmanship, as in the case in Exodus, in physical strength, as in the case of Samson, or in passion for the defense of God's people, as in the case of Saul. In such cases, the spirit of God comes on people for only a limited time. The most common purpose for the spirit's coming on a person in this way seems to involve prophecy, as in the case in Numbers. These cases are in evident contrast with the case of the indwelling Holy Spirit. The indwelling of the Holy Spirit comes to all persons in grace; it is not limited just to a few people. It is not given for a particular purpose. It is not given for a limited time; it remains as long as a person remains in grace. And it is not designed to enable a person to do some particular task that is somehow more than human.

In this connection, it is also worth noting that when the spirit of God comes on a person for a particular purpose in these earlier cases, the presence of the spirit of God somehow overshadows the human mind of the person in question. Balaam, for example, describes himself as in a trance but with his eyes open when he prophesies under the influence of God's spirit (Num. 24:15). In such a case, the human mind of the person under the influence of God's spirit functions differently from its normal functioning, if in fact it functions at all in its own right in such cases and is not simply overtaken by the spirit of God. In some sense, in such cases, it is not quite right to say that there are two minds operating simultaneously in the human person, insofar as the human mind is operating through the influence of God's spirit.

On the other hand, I Samuel 16:13 says that the spirit of the Lord came on David when Samuel anointed him, and it stayed with him thereafter. In the case of David, it is hard to see any difference between the spirit's coming and remaining on David and the indwelling of the Holy Spirit. But here it is also important to note that although there is an explicit Gospel claim that the indwelling of the Holy Spirit is tied to Christ's passion and death, this claim does not imply that the Holy Spirit indwells only people coming after the passion and death of Christ. Given the eternal nature of God, the effects of Christ's passion and death can be felt at any point in time.[77] (It is for this same reason that Christ can bear the sins of all human beings.) Furthermore, it is also part of Christian doctrine that, through God's revelation, human beings before the time of Christ had faith in the coming of the Messiah, so that they also were saved by faith in the Messiah, whatever exactly they may have known about the Messiah.

So because, through the eternity of Christ's divine nature, the effects of Christ's atonement can range over any time, and because God can reveal the Messiah beforehand to his people, it is possible to maintain both that the Holy Spirit was given because of Christ's passion and death and that David had the indwelling Holy Spirit. But whatever the right description of David's relation to the Holy Spirit may be, what sets the indwelling of the Holy Spirit apart from other cases in which the spirit of God only comes on a person has to do with the purpose of the indwelling. The Holy Spirit's indwelling in a person unites God and that person to one degree or another. The union is a shared second-personal relationship in which God and a human person are attuned to one another and resonate to one another in shared attention.[78]

The purpose for the indwelling Holy Spirit is also highlighted by the list of the gifts and fruits of the Holy Spirit that accompany the Spirit's indwelling. The gifts contribute to a person's sanctification and so to the deepening of union between God and a human person, and the fruits are the states resulting from the union: love, joy, peace, and the rest. Consequently, in this union between God and a human person, the selfhood of the human person is kept entirely intact or actually enhanced. For a person in this state, God is Emmanuel, "God with us," not only psychologically but also literally, that is, ontologically and spiritually.

Of course, to characterize the indwelling of the Holy Spirit in this way falls short of explaining how the indwelling Holy Spirit has these effects. In Chapter 7, I will discuss in detail the processes of sanctification and justification, the role of grace and free will in this process, and the connection of these processes to the indwelling Holy Spirit. For now, it will have to be enough to explain that there is this connection and that it is the basis for the value of the indwelling.

By far the hardest question is still left, however: What is the connection of the indwelling Holy Spirit to the passion and death of Christ? That there is one is supported by the Gospel text quoted above and mandated by the logic of the theological doctrines at issue here. If the indwelling Holy Spirit constitutes union and conduces to its fullest degree, then since union is what atonement is designed to effect, the passion and death of Christ must be the means to the indwelling. In Chapter 8, I finally turn to this difficult question.

CONCLUSION

If we think about the notion of presence in all its richness, we can see that a simple consideration of God's relation to space alone is insufficient to elucidate God's omnipresence. God's omnipresence is a matter of God's relations to space certainly but to all space at all times at once, because omnipresence is an attribute of an eternal God. More importantly, because God has a mind and a will, it is possible for God to be not just present at a space but also present with and to an embodied human person occupying that space. The assumption of a human nature ensures that an eternal God is never without the ability to empathize with human persons and to be present with them in the way that empathy and mind-reading enable. And, in the indwelling of the Holy Spirit, God can be more powerfully present in love and more united with a human person in grace than any human person could be. On God's side, in the indwelling of the Holy Spirit, God's union with a human person is a matter of God's being present with a human person in grace as much as eternal divine power permits and mutual love allows. The implementation of this union to the fullest degree possible in this life (and the next) is the end to which the atonement is the means.[79]

5

Mutual Indwelling and the Cry
of Dereliction from the Cross

INTRODUCTION

In Chapter 4, I explained that union in love between two human persons requires mutual closeness and rich shared attention; and I argued that union in love between a human person and God is marked by the addition of something ontologically greater than is possible between two human persons. Union in love where one of those united is God includes the actual indwelling of the human person by the Holy Spirit. On the doctrine of the Trinity, there are three divine persons who are only one God, with only one will and only one mind, and who are nonetheless still three. On orthodox Christian doctrine, when a human person Paula comes to faith, the third person of the Trinity, the Holy Spirit, who is God, comes to indwell in her. As I tried to show in Chapter 4, this indwelling makes union between God and a human person something more ontologically robust qua union than the more metaphysically limited union possible between two human persons.

When it is part of personal presence between two human persons who are mutually close to each other, shared attention helps to configure or organize the two of them into something that is somehow one and greater than the sum of its parts. That is, whatever exactly union between persons is, it is a matter of there being two persons who are somehow one even while staying disparate from one another.[1] When there is mutual closeness between two people, then their sharing attention with one another is one mode for configuring the two of them into one composite system. It leaves the disparate persons in the organized whole the same individuals they are outside that whole, and yet it melds them into something unified, with causal power vested in the composite configured whole. The organized system constituted by their union has emergent powers for cognition and volition not found in the disparate persons when they are alone.[2]

In union where those who are united are both human, the oneness of such an organized whole is limited and fragile. It is merely episodic, not least because shared attention, the main glue of the union, is hard to sustain for long; and it is fragile, because both mutual closeness and shared attention are readily disrupted. As between God and a human person, however, the dynamic whole has a different ontological character because God can be present to a human person in a metaphysically greater way than another human person could be. In union between human persons, something of Paula's psyche is within Jerome's, and similarly something of Jerome's psyche is within Paula's. But in the mode of union operative in God's indwelling Jerome, the Holy Spirit itself is within Jerome. In this condition, Jerome has internal access to the mind of God to some (no doubt very limited) degree, and God is available to Jerome for shared attention of an intense and loving kind because the Holy Spirit is within Jerome.[3]

It is worth noticing that, so described, the indwelling of the Holy Spirit conforms Jerome to the nature of the incarnate Christ in some analogous and limited way. The incarnate Christ has two natures, one fully human and one fully divine. In consequence, there are two minds and two wills in Christ, one human and one divine. Analogously, but in a metaphysically much smaller way, with a much more limited degree of unity, when the Holy Spirit comes to indwell Jerome, Jerome comes to have within himself two minds with two wills, one his own human mind and the other the mind of God. Unlike the incarnate Christ, of course, Jerome cannot claim the divine mind as his own; and the divine mind is not incarnate in Jerome. And yet it is nonetheless true that Jerome has intimate access to the mind of God because the Holy Spirit is within him.

It might seem that with the indwelling of the Holy Spirit in Jerome, he is united with God maximally, as regards the mode of union if not as regards the degree of that union. But in fact this impression is mistaken. It is a maximal mode of union if we are thinking in terms of the more metaphysically limited kind of union possible between human persons. But by the measure of the mode of union possible with God, the indwelling of the Holy Spirit is only part of the story of union between God and a human being.

In praying to God the Father for his apostles before his crucifixion, Christ asks that the apostles may have a kind of union of the sort that exists between Christ and God. He says, "As you, Father, are in me and I in you, so may they also be one in us" (John 17:21); and he goes on to say, "I in them and you in me, that they may be made perfect in one" (John 17:23). Here the model for union between God and human beings is the union between Christ and the Father, and this union consists in *mutual* in-ness: Christ is in the Father and the Father is in Christ.[4]

On this model, in order to be complete, the metaphysically greater mode of union possible for God and human beings requires an indwelling that is mutual. Just as in shared attention between human beings, something of the mind of Jerome is in the mind of Paula and something of the mind of Paula is in the mind of Jerome, so there can be a much greater mutual in-ness higher up on the ladder of being. Within the deity itself, there can be mutual in-ness of the whole person, when one person of the Trinity is united to another. It is not the thoughts and feelings of the Father that are in the Son, or the thoughts and feelings of the Son that are in the Father. Rather, as Christ says, the Father is in the Son, and the Son is in the Father. What Christ asks for with regard to his followers is an analogous kind of union. In *that* union, Christ himself is in persons in grace. And so is the Father, since the Father is in the Son. But there is mutuality here too. In the union Christ is praying for, Christ's followers are also "in us"—in the Father and the Son. And so even for human beings, when it comes to union with God, a kind of mutuality of indwelling persons is part of union.

Therefore, the subject of Chapter 4, the Holy Spirit's indwelling in each person in grace, is only part of the story of union between God and human persons. There is also the indwelling of each person in grace within God, on a limited analogy with the union among the Father, the Son, and the Holy Spirit. Like the indwelling of the Holy Spirit in persons who are in grace, the indwelling of human persons in God will be a one–many relation: one divine person in many persons in grace, and many persons in grace in one God.

But how are human persons supposed to indwell in God? What could this notion even mean? And how would it be accomplished?

In this chapter, I want to address this issue by looking with patience-trying care at one very small biblical story, which describes what is usually called 'the cry of dereliction from the cross.' I will begin by focusing just on the cry itself, to try to understand the condition of Christ that it expresses. Then I will show what the cry of dereliction can teach us about the indwelling of human persons in God.

At that point, I will have completed my examination of the union in this life between God and a human person in grace. In Chapters 6 and 7, I will examine what it is like for a human person to live in grace, that is, in a condition to which a person can be brought because of the atonement of Christ. When we see more clearly what the end point of the process of atonement is supposed to be, we will be greatly aided in our attempt to understand what the atonement is and the means by which it can bring a person to a life in grace.

THE PUZZLE FOR INTERPRETATION OF THE CRY OF DERELICTION

Any interpretation of the doctrine of the atonement has to take account of those biblical texts traditionally taken to be foundational narratives for the doctrine. Among these texts, one of the narratives that has been most difficult to interpret is the story describing Christ's cry of dereliction from the cross. According to the Gospels of both Mathew and Mark, among the things Christ says on the cross is "My God, my God, why have you forsaken me?"[5]

There are so many things puzzling about this line attributed to Christ that it is hard to know how to begin to spell them out.

First, in numerous Gospel narratives, in the time before his passion, Christ shows that he himself is intimate with God and that God is present with him. His connection of mind and will with God is powerful. The cry of dereliction, however, apparently implies that, at least at the time of the cry, this connection is broken, although the longing for it remains in Christ.

The problem is that, on the face of it, there is nothing in the narrative apart from the suffering of Christ that could account for this breaking of connection. But it seems that suffering alone cannot account for it either. In fact, there are many stories of suffering in the Bible in which believers endure suffering without any sign of wavering in their connection with God. Furthermore, it seems that Christ ought to be exemplary of faith in suffering. But how is such a view of him compatible with his cry of dereliction? Calvin puts this point bluntly:

> let the pious reader consider how far it is honourable to Christ to make him more effeminate and timid than the generality of men. Robbers and other malefactors contumaciously hasten to death, many men magnanimously despise it, others meet it calmly. If the Son of God was amazed and terror-struck at the prospect of it, where was his firmness or magnanimity?[6]

Furthermore, on orthodox Christian theology, Christ came into the world in order to save human beings; and the means God chose for Christ to do so includes his suffering and dying on the cross. As the stories of Christ in the Garden of Gethsemane highlight, Christ himself has a strong desire not to suffer in this way; but in the end his desire to will what God wants him to will triumphs in him. Consequently, in advance of his crucifixion he accepts his suffering and death in obedience to God's will. Furthermore, he understands that his suffering and death in obedience to God's will for the sake of the salvation of human beings constitutes the fulfillment of his mission as savior. So, since his suffering is something he undertakes voluntarily in obedience to God for the pre-ordained divine purpose, what sense is there in his cry of dereliction as an expression of that suffering? How could he cry out that he is forsaken by God when he knows that he is doing God's will by suffering and understands that he came into the world in order to suffer in this way?

Worse yet, there is the problem of distance itself. The cry of dereliction implies that, at the time of the cry, either there was in fact distance between Christ and God or else Christ had an illusory experience of a distance that was not actually there. But both these options are hard to understand. On orthodox Christian doctrine, God is perfectly good and loving, and Christ is sinless. How is one to understand distance between one perfectly good person and another? What would such distance consist in? Or, if we suppose that Christ had an experience of distance when there was none, how are we to understand a perfectly good God's allowing so painful an illusion to afflict Christ, who was already undergoing physical suffering that was so terrible?

Then there are also serious complications introduced by the Chalcedonian formula of the incarnation: the incarnate Christ is one divine person (the second person of the Trinity) with two natures, one fully human and one fully divine. The person who is Christ is human in virtue of having a human nature, but he is also God in virtue of having a divine nature. The cry of dereliction is even more puzzling when one adds these theological claims into the story. The distance between Christ and God implied by the cry of dereliction will also be an internal fragmentation within Christ on these claims, since the person who expresses that cry is also the God to whom the cry is addressed. How is such an experience to be explained? For that matter, how is it even to be made intelligible?

Finally, on the Chalcedonian formula, anyone in the state attributed to Christ during the cry will be seriously fragmented in psyche. But how could there be internal divisions and self-alienation in the psyche of a sinless person? Internal fragmentation, alienation from some part of oneself, seems a function of some psychic state that is not morally perfect (even if it were entirely non-culpable).[7]

So, how is Christ's cry of dereliction to be understood? I will argue that finding the answer to this question carries with it one possible explanation of human persons indwelling in God.

THE CRY OF DERELICTION IN ITS CONTEXT

The history of interpretation of the Gospels includes many attempts to explain the cry of dereliction.[8] Some of these amount to an attempt to explain it away. For example, it was recognized early on that the cry is the opening line of Psalm 22. That Psalm has traditionally been interpreted by Christians as prophesying the suffering of the Messiah, including many of the details in the passion of Christ. The ending of this Psalm is characterized by a peace and quiet trust that seem lacking in the cry which is the Psalm's opening line. And so some people take the cry of dereliction to be shorthand for the whole Psalm, and especially for its trusting, reassuring ending. So, for example, Thomas McCall points out that the ending of the Psalm is reflected in Christ's calm and confident words during the crucifixion in the period after the cry. McCall says,

Luke appears to tell us *what* Jesus cried just before 'he breathed his last': "Jesus called out with a loud voice, 'Father, into your hands I commit my spirit'" (Luke 23:46). This is no statement of despair. This is no cry of utter and total abandonment. There is no hint here of a severed or even strained relationship. There is no sense here of a Father who has rejected his Son or who has turned his back on him ... [Rather, these] are words of complete trust.... [9]

And McCall sums his position up this way: "We should take Jesus' quotation of the first lines of this psalm as a signpost to the whole psalm."[10]

On this sort of interpretation of the cry, then, Christ is making use of a Jewish convention that cites the first line of a Psalm to express the whole of the Psalm. The cry therefore is not to be understood as an expression by Christ of an experience of desolation.

But this is an implausible interpretation of the cry, in my view.[11] After all, nothing about the convention that lets the first line of a Psalm serve as a reference for the Psalm as a whole prevents a person from uttering any particular lines of the Psalm, as the citation of lines from the Psalms in the New Testament makes clear. So it was possible for Christ to give utterance to the lines at the end of the Psalm, as well as to the cry that expresses the Psalm's opening line; and doing so would obviously have been a much wiser thing to do in the circumstances. Since the rebukes of the bystanders include the derisory innuendo that God has in fact abandoned Christ, it is at least highly misleading, not to say damaging to the faith of his followers, for Christ to cite this Psalm by its first line if its last lines are what he intended to express.

As far as that goes, the first line itself is not *cited* by Christ but rather *uttered* as a cry by Christ on the cross as he is dying. In that context, it is strongly evocative of desolation. The context in which the line is uttered colors its meaning. "My God, my God, why have you forsaken me?" has one sort of resonance when it is expressed as a liturgical line in a context of ritual prayer, for example. It has another sort of resonance entirely when it is expressed as a cry by a lone man who is being tortured to death by political and religious authorities hostile to him.

In this chapter, I will therefore take the cry of dereliction to mean what it appears to mean, and I will reflect on ways in which it might be interpreted so understood.

It is also worth noting that the cry of dereliction is set within the larger context of Christ's own preparations for death, including the Passover meal he shares with his disciples and his prayer in the Garden of Gethsemane.[12] As that larger story is told, the cry of dereliction is the expression of an experience which is the culmination of a process that begins much earlier.

To take just one example of the many notable details of this larger narrative, three of the Gospels (Luke, Mark, and Matthew) describe Christ as psychically pained and conflicted in the Garden of Gethsemane. Matthew and Mark (the

Gospels that include the cry of dereliction) describe Christ in the Garden as distressed. Matthew says Christ was "sorrowful" (26:37), and Mark says he was "amazed" (14:33). Luke says that, as Christ prayed in Gethsemane, an angel strengthened him; and, after that strengthening, Christ was in an agony (22:43–4). But I note these details, however tempting, only to leave them to one side for now, in the interest of focusing just on the cry of dereliction, which is a large enough subject by itself. (I will return to the story of Christ in Gethsemane in Chapter 8.)

In addition, in the interest of brevity I will omit explicit examination of most commentary on the cry of dereliction found in the history of interpretation of the Gospels, although I have read and learned from much of it. My purpose here is not an examination of the history of interpretation of this story but rather a philosophical inquiry of the experience expressed in the cry. If the experience expressed by the cry of dereliction is to be interpreted within the constraints of orthodox Christian theology, which takes both God and Christ to be without any evil or sin, how is it possible to make sense of that experience?

In my view, concentrating on this question will shed light on the larger issue of the nature of the union between God and human beings. Ultimately, in my view, because the cry of dereliction is one of the most puzzling parts of the narratives of the suffering and death of Christ, philosophical investigation of it provides insight into the nature of the atonement itself.

DISTANCE BETWEEN PERSONS: CLOSENESS AND SHARED ATTENTION

We can begin thinking about the cry of dereliction by considering distance between persons. Distance is the opposite of closeness between persons; and union is the intrinsic limit of closeness when it is mutual and crowned with shared attention. So to examine the cry of dereliction, with its expression of an experience of great distance from God, it is helpful to have the nature of closeness and union between persons clearly in mind. As I explained in Chapter 4, closeness between two persons requires an ability and a willingness on the part of each person to share himself, his thoughts and feelings, with the other. But this ability and willingness to share oneself in turn requires psychic integration. Internal division in the psyche arises because a person is divided against himself in will, or is double-minded and self-deceived, or both. Someone who is internally divided against himself in these ways is not united with himself and therefore cannot be fully united with anyone else either. He will be unable or unwilling to share at least certain parts of himself with anyone else, either because he does not really know himself or because he does not want to want what he wants or both. In that last chapter, I also explained that, on an optimistic view of human beings, it is not possible for a person to be internally integrated in moral evil. No one is so evil that there is not some part of his mind and will that retains some hold on the good. Since this is so, it follows that all moral wrongdoing fragments a psyche. And because fragmentation in psyche diminishes a person's ability to share himself, it also is an impediment to closeness and union. Closeness and union therefore require integration around the good. Where distance between persons is not a function of something in their external environment, then internal fragmentation, the failure to be integrated around the good, will be responsible for it.

On Christian views, the ultimate good for any human person is union with God. That is why, for God, the two desires of love collapse into one; for God, they come to a desire for union with the beloved. Since God is perfectly loving and loves every person that he has made, it follows that God also always has a desire for union with every person. For these reasons, if there is an obstacle to union between God and any human person, the reason for it has to lie in something about human beings. One obstacle to union between a human person and God stems from internal fragmentation in the human person. A person's moral wrongdoing can leave him divided against himself, in a state that wards off closeness with others, including God. Such inner fragmentation is therefore sufficient to undermine or obviate union between God and a human person.

But since for union shared attention is required as well as mutual closeness, a lack of shared attention can also be a source of distance between persons. Where shared attention is missing, union is precluded too.[13] Even between persons who are mutually close, distance can be introduced and union can be warded off by a lack of shared attention.

Many different things can disrupt or prevent shared attention. Obviously, simple physical distance between mutually close persons can have this result. To take a small and homely example, when a loving father sends his misbehaved two-year-old to her room, she and he are in this condition. There is mutual closeness between them, but, momentarily anyway, there is no shared attention and therefore no union just then either. Distraction can have the same effect. If the father and daughter were together but the father's attention was only on his work and not on his daughter, shared attention would be precluded then too; and so there would be distance between them.

In fact, anything that diminishes or takes away one person's ability or willingness to meet another person face-to-face will hinder shared attention. Shame, for example, will do so. A shamed person typically finds it difficult to meet the gaze of others, even if the shamed person is in no way culpable for her shamed state; and so shared attention can fail to occur in such cases too.

Great pain, physical or psychological, can have the same effect. A person in great pain might be unable to meet another person face-to-face, with shared attention, because it is difficult for her to focus on anything besides her pain. Instructions to labor coaches helping women during the pain of childbirth emphasize that if a laboring woman is in great pain, shared attention between her and her coach may be interrupted unless there is insistent intervention on the part of the coach.[14] As these instructions imply, a person in pain may find it difficult to attend to another, even with the help of that other, and even if she had antecedently planned on attending to that other. In cases such as this, there can be mutual closeness between two persons, but the normal manifestation of this closeness in significant personal presence through shared attention is blocked because shared attention is disrupted by something external, such as pain, which gets in the way.

The absence either of mutual closeness or shared attention is sufficient, then, for distance between persons; and the absence of shared attention alone can introduce distance between two people even when those persons are internally integrated around the good and otherwise mutually close. So, in addition to shame and guilt, which can fragment a person, things that disrupt shared attention introduce distance, too, at least for the time during which the obstacle blocks shared attention.

DISTANCE BETWEEN PERSONS AND THE CRY OF DERELICTION

On the view I am accepting here, the cry of dereliction is an expression of Christ's experience of distance between himself and God. Given these reflections on distance between persons, there are fundamentally three possibilities, each of which would be sufficient to account for Christ's experience of distance from God. (Of course, the presence of one of them does not preclude the presence of any of the others as well.)

First, it could be that

(1)   something about God prevents closeness between God and Christ.

The natural reading of the cry suggests this possibility, because the formulation of the cry seems to assign responsibility for the experienced distance to God: why have *you* forsaken me? On this possibility, the distance between God and Christ has its source in God. God fails to be close to Christ, at least at the time of the cry; and it is God's doing that he is not close to Christ.

But if the source of the distance between God and Christ lies in God, then it must stem from something in God's will, since nothing external to God could constrain God's will. At the time of the cry, then, God is not close to Christ because God does not want to be.

Since closeness is necessary for union, however, if God does not want to be close to Christ, then (at least for that time) he also does not want union with Christ. But a desire for union is one of the desires of love. Consequently, on this possibility, at least for the time of the cry, God lacks one of the desires of love for Christ.

Second, it could be that

(2)   something about Christ prevents closeness between God and Christ.

On this possibility, the distance between God and Christ has its source in Christ. Although God has the desires of love for Christ, Christ fails to be close to God, at least at the time of the cry; and it is Christ's doing that he is not close to God. Since, on this possibility, God is willing to be close to Christ, nothing external to Christ prevents closeness between Christ and God.[15] Therefore, the distance between God and Christ is a function of Christ's will. On this possibility, then, at the time of the cry, Christ is not close to God because Christ does not want to be.

Consequently, on this possibility, by reasoning analogous to that described in connection with the first possibility, Christ lacks one of the desires of love for God. Union between God and Christ is precluded at that time because at that time Christ does not want it.

Someone might suppose that this is not a possibility worth taking seriously. The cry of dereliction not only suggests a history of intimate relations between Christ and God, but also a longing on Christ's part to have that intimacy immediately then: "*My* God, *my* God, ..." And so, the putative objector may conclude, it could not be possible that while uttering that cry, Christ also does not want to be close to God.

But this would be an invalidly inferred conclusion, in my view. Divisions in the will are a hallmark of the human condition. Catullus's conflicted desires for his love Lesbia have given us our most famous exemplar of this sort of internally divided mental state. Catullus says of the woman with whom he was obsessed, "Odio et amo"—"I love her, and I hate her." So it is certainly possible to long for a person and also to want not to be close to that person.

Third, it could be that

(3)   shared attention between God and Christ is hindered.

On this possibility, there is distance between God and Christ because one or the other of them lacks the occurrent condition of sharing attention with the other. In principle, this absence of shared attention is possible even if, at that time, God and Christ each are close to the other. Even if there is such closeness, it could still be the case that Christ experiences God as absent, because something is preventing the shared attention of second-person experience between God and Christ.

As the examples above regarding shared attention make clear, this third possibility itself admits of further sub-division, because the responsibility for the lack of shared attention can be assigned to either (or both) of the persons in the relationship. In the case of God and Christ, either

(3a)   something about God hinders shared attention between him and Christ

or

(3b)   something about Christ hinders shared attention between him and God.

As in the case of (2), someone might object that (3b) is not a real possibility, because on that possibility Christ turns his face away from God, as it were. But no one who turned his face away from someone else, the putative objector will claim, could experience that other as having forsaken him.

But this too is a mistaken conclusion on the objector's part, in my view. A person in great psychological or physical pain can experience as absent even those gathered around him in love to care for him. J.R.R. Tolkien's classic Christian trilogy *The Lord of the Rings* illustrates brilliantly many complicated psychological states presupposed in Christian doctrine, and it is helpful in this regard also. In particular, Tolkien's description of Frodo's state after he is wounded by the Black Riders and his mind wanders in Mordor makes the point at issue here in a sensitive manner. In the torment brought about by that wound, Frodo feels utterly lost and alone; when he finally comes to himself again, he is surprised to find that his friends are around him and have been the whole time. It was Frodo who in his anguish lost the ability to share attention with them, but he experienced them as disappeared from him. Or consider the scene in *The Lord of the Rings* in which Pippin looks in the palantir. The palantir connects Pippin's mind in a mind-reading way with the mind of the dark lord of Mordor, Sauron. That mind-melding is intensely distressing for Pippin, and he cries out in overwhelming anguish. At the moment of his cry, he is surrounded by those he loves—Merry, Gandalf, and others as well. They respond with instant alarm and energetic action, trying to make contact with Pippin and separate him from the palantir. But Pippin cannot hear them or see them, because his mind is overcome with the revulsive shock of the mind of Sauron. Anyone who has tried to soothe someone who has gone inward in great suffering by saying, "It's all right! I'm here! I'm here!" understands the insightful correctness of Tolkien's story in these scenes with Frodo and Pippin.

Furthermore, although nothing external to God can be an obstacle to God's ability or willingness to share attention with another person, for a human person shared attention can be prevented or undermined by things external to his own agency as well as by things attributable to his own doing. So (3b) itself admits of a yet further division, because it is clear that the obstacle in Christ to the sharing of attention with God could be either (3b1) a function of states of intellect and will in Christ or (3b2) a result of something in Christ other than beliefs and desires of his.

These, then, seem to be the possibilities for explaining distance between God and Christ at the time of the cry of dereliction.

Someone might object that these possibilities do not exhaust all the possibilities there are because Christ could have an illusory or non-veridical experience of God's absence from him. On the kind of case the putative objector is envisaging, Christ's experience of distance between himself and God is real; but it is a real, painful experience of something that is itself not real. Although Christ does actually have such an experience, there is in fact no actual distance between him and God. On the view of the putative objector, Christ's experience is therefore like the experience of a person who is in the grip of a hallucination or a delusion; the experience and the suffering it brings are real, but the person having the experience is out of touch with reality. Reality contains nothing corresponding to that experience.

In my view, this possibility is included within possibility (3). That is because, even if it were true that Christ's experience of distance from God were delusory, it would still be true that, at least for the time of that experience, there would be no shared attention between Christ and God. Obviously, if there were shared attention, then Christ would not experience God as absent in a delusory way or in any other way. So the putative objector's case in fact falls within the purview of possibility (3).

It therefore remains the case that these are the possibilities for explaining the (real or apparent) distance between God and Christ that underlies the experience Christ expresses in the cry of dereliction from the cross.

Although it could be the case that all the obstacles to union described in these possibilities are simultaneously manifested in that experience, for the sake of clarity, I will consider each of the possibilities separately.

THE POSSIBILITIES

POSSIBILITY (1). On this possibility, at least at the time of the cry of dereliction, God lacks a desire of love for Christ and does not want to be united with Christ, at least not at this time. In this case, Christ experiences God as distant from him because God really rejects Christ and is unwilling to be close to Christ, however much Christ might be willing to be close to God.

Put this way, however, this possibility is clearly ruled out by the doctrine that God is perfectly loving. On this doctrine, God always has the desires of love for every person; but one of these desires is the desire for union with the beloved. It is incompatible with God's nature that God lack the desires of love for any person. Consequently, God may fail to be united with a human person; but if he is, it will not be because God does not *want* to be united to that person.[16] And so, as an explanation for Christ's experience of distance between him and God, the first possibility is excluded by the doctrine that God is perfectly loving.[17]

POSSIBILITY (2). On this possibility, at least at the time of the cry of dereliction, closeness between God and Christ is lacking because of something attributable to Christ. At that time, Christ does not want closeness with God. Consequently, on this possibility, at that time Christ lacks one of the desires of love for God. Therefore, to this extent, in however double-minded a way it might be, Christ rejects God, even if, with some other part of his mind, he also longs for God.

In the ordinary case of relationship between human persons, there are many reasons why one person might reject another, however double-mindedly. The rejected person might be morally disreputable or dishonorable or have some other kind of defect. (In the case of Lesbia, she was destructive to Catullus even while she attracted him and solicited his attentions.) But such reasons obviously cannot apply when the rejected person is God, whose goodness, power, beauty, and other desire-attracting attributes are unsurpassable. Someone who does not want to be united with a person who is perfect in goodness and beauty thereby reveals a serious defect not in the person he rejects but rather in himself. Insofar as he rejects what is perfectly good and lovely, he himself lacks goodness in some respect. He does not desire the goodness that God is or the good that God desires. When God complains to his people, "you have forsaken me" (Jeremiah 15:6), the complaint is an accusation of moral wrongdoings on the part of God's people.

Manifestly, then, being distant from God for this reason is itself a morally defective state. But it is part of orthodox Christian doctrine that Christ is without sin of any kind; Christ is never in a morally defective state. Consequently, Christ never lacks the desires of love for God. It is not possible therefore to attribute to Christ a lack of the desire for union with God.

And so the second possibility can be excluded as well.

POSSIBILITY (3). On this possibility, at least for the time of the cry of dereliction, distance between God and Christ is introduced by a lack of shared attention between them. Because shared attention is missing, one of them is not present to the other at that time, even if there is mutual closeness between them in general.

If God is responsible for this lack of shared attention, as (3a) has it, then it can only be because God has decided for some reason to prevent his sharing attention with Christ, since nothing external to God can block God's making himself available to share attention with anyone. On this possibility, God does desire union with Christ; but, for some reason compatible with that desire, God is momentarily hiding his face from Christ.

A possibility such as (3a) seems to underlie Calvin's explanation of the cry of dereliction. Calvin says,

> Nothing had been done if Christ had only endured corporeal death. In order to interpose between us and God's anger, and satisfy ... [God's] righteous judgment, it was necessary that ... [Christ] should feel the weight of divine vengeance. Whence also it was necessary that he should engage, as it were, at close quarters with the powers of hell and the horrors of eternal death.... [N]o abyss can be imagined more dreadful than to feel that you are abandoned and forsaken of God, and not heard when you invoke him, just as if he had conspired your destruction. To such a degree was Christ dejected, that in the depth of his agony he was forced to exclaim, 'My God, my God, why hast thou forsaken me?' ... Hence Hilary argues, that to this descent [of Christ's into an experience of hell] we owe our exemption from death.[18]

Calvin thinks that the human penalty for sin is not only suffering and death but also condemnation to hell. On Calvin's view, since Christ bears the penalty for human sin, Christ has to suffer all the things that go into that penalty, including the experience of being condemned by God to hell. For Calvin, then, as part of the process of making satisfaction for human sins, Christ experiences God's rejection of him, including some of the torment of hell.[19] The cry of dereliction is Christ's giving voice to this most terrible experience of God's rejection.

Nonetheless, Calvin says,

> We do not, however, insinuate that God was ever hostile to him or angry with him. How could he be angry with the beloved Son, with whom his soul was well pleased? ... But this we say, ... [that] he experienced all the signs of an angry and avenging God.[20]

So Calvin is supposing that God did something to block the loving shared attention previously customary between God and Christ in order to inflict on Christ an experience of God's rejection and the consequent pains of hell. Calvin's explanation of the cry of dereliction is therefore an instance of possibility (3), in its (3a) version. Because Calvin supposes that God acts in this way without being in any way hostile to Christ, on Calvin's view even at the time of the cry of dereliction there is actually mutual closeness between God and Christ. But, Calvin thinks, God brings it about that for that time Christ in effect loses shared attention with God. As Calvin sees it, Christ feels that lack of shared attention as a manifestation of God's hostility towards him, although in fact God is well pleased with Christ and not at all angry with him.

The way Calvin puts flesh on the bones of possibility (3a) is ingenious, because it assigns an intelligible goal for God's putting distance between himself and Christ. In my view, Calvin's approach to (3a) is the best on offer. On that approach, Christ has an experience of distance from God because that distance is part of the punishment an angry God imposes on sinners in hell; and so Christ has this experience as part of his taking on the penalty for human sins. For Calvin, then, God's bringing about Christ's having this experience is part of the means by which God brings about human salvation.

The problems with possibility (3a), however, are also well shown by Calvin's account. On Calvin's explanation, God brings it about that Christ experiences as real what is in fact not real. God does not hate Christ; God is not willing that Christ be eternally separated from God; God has not actually judged Christ as sinful and worthy of damnation. On this view, then, God causes Christ to have an illusory experience; and to this degree God deceives Christ. Now it may be compatible with goodness to deceive a morally bad person, as when one lies to the Gestapo to protect the Jewish children in the house. But it is hard to see how it could be compatible with God's goodness to deceive a perfectly good person. It is worse if the deception is about very important matters, or matters very important to the deceived person, as it is in this case. Furthermore, it is difficult to see how to square Calvin's view with God's character as loving and as having the desires of love for Christ. How could God be willing the good for Christ if he is deceiving him? And how could God be willing to be united with Christ if he is causing Christ to have an illusory experience of God as distant from Christ in wrath at him?

It is, of course, compatible with God's love of Christ that God bring about suffering for Christ when Christ voluntarily takes on that suffering. There is a great difference in goodness between someone who imposes suffering on an innocent person, and someone who accepts an innocent person's volunteering for suffering. But the kind of experience Calvin attributes to Christ is incompatible with Christ's volunteering for it. If Christ volunteered to experience distance from God, Christ would thereby understand that the absence was not something imposed on him by an angry God.

It is true that Calvin supposes God has a good goal for bringing about this experience for Christ, namely, that the suffering the experience entails is instrumental to the salvation Christ achieves for human beings. But a perfectly good God would not choose means incompatible with his love and goodness to bring about a good goal. If Calvin himself did not accept this very claim, his explanation of the need for Christ's suffering in hell would itself fail. If one did not accept this claim, one could have no reason for accepting Anselmian intuitions about the need for making satisfaction to God. One could instead simply suppose, as Aquinas does, that God can bring about the salvation of human beings without any satisfaction being made to God for human sin.

And so Calvin's explanation of possibility (3a) fails. It is itself incompatible with God's love and goodness. And since there is no better explanation for possibility (3a), that possibility can be excluded as well.

We are now apparently left with the two versions of possibility (3b), namely, that (3b1) some state of Christ's intellect and will or else (3b2) something in

Christ other than his beliefs and desires is responsible for the lack of shared attention between God and Christ.

In my view, we can quickly rule out (3b1), for just the reasons canvassed above in connection with possibility (2). If there were nothing external to his own agency constraining him to do so, a perfectly good person would not think it was good or appropriate to turn his face away from a perfectly good God with whom he has mutual closeness, and he would not want to do so either. In no way would such a person's beliefs or desires be responsible for his turning his face from God's.

And so, of all the possibilities, only (3b2) remains: something in Christ other than his beliefs and desires is responsible for blocking in Christ his sharing attention with God, with the result that significant personal presence between Christ and God is lost, and Christ experiences the loss as God's forsaking him.

We could try making sense of this possibility by adducing the great pain caused by crucifixion. But here, as shown in the passage I quoted at the outset of this chapter, Calvin seems to me right. There is an a fortiori argument against the interpretation that great physical pain is responsible for Christ's loss of shared attention with God. Since so many others in Christian history have experienced pain at least as great as crucifixion without losing their ability to stay connected to God, it seems implausible to suppose that physical pain alone would have such an effect on Christ.

And so it seems that possibility (3b2) is ruled out as well.

At this point, it may seem as if we have excluded all the possibilities for explaining the cry of dereliction. Nothing attributable to God can be responsible for Christ's experience of distance from God. And we seem also to have ruled out all the possibilities that point to something in Christ which explains it. Christ's will is without the moral evil that could explain a distance between him and a perfectly good God, so his psyche is at one with God's. And it is implausible to suppose that the great physical pain of crucifixion is sufficient to explain Christ's distance from God either.

If nothing attributable to God and nothing in Christ's mind or body accounts for Christ's experience of forsakenness, then what is left to point to as the source of Christ's experience of distance from God?

MIND-READING AND MORAL EVIL

In my view, there is in fact one thing left which is worth exploring in this connection. To see this one thing, we need to consider mind-reading again. As I explained in Chapter 4, in mind-reading, one person knows intuitively what another person is doing and thinking, as well as something of the motive and emotion with which that person is acting. Currently, this kind of knowledge of persons is thought to be subserved at least in part by a neurologically distinct system, namely, the mirror neuron system. Recent research makes plain that it is possible for one person to have knowledge of the mental states of another person when that knowledge shares something of the phenomenology of perception. Like the perception of color, for example, the knowledge of mind-reading is direct, intuitive, and hard to translate without remainder into knowledge *that*, but very useful as a basis for knowledge *that* of one sort or another. John knows *that* Mary is going to give him a flower because he first knows Mary, her action, her emotion, and her intention—but these are things which he knows by, as it were, seeing them, and not by cognizing them in the knowledge *that* way.

Empathy is also currently thought to be subserved by the mirror neuron system. In empathy, one person Paula *sees* an emotion in another person Jerome because the mirror neuron system produces in her an emotional state like the emotion Jerome is experiencing, but taken off-line, as it were. In empathy with Jerome's suffering physical pain, for example, Paula will feel something of Jerome's pain, but she will feel it as Jerome's pain, not as hers. And, in general, in mind-reading Jerome, Paula will know what it feels like to do the action Jerome is doing, what it feels like to have the intention Jerome has in doing this action, and what it feels like to have the emotion Jerome has while doing this action. In all these cases, Paula will know these things through having herself some simulacrum of the mental state in Jerome. Something of Jerome's mental state will be in Paula, but off-line.

It may help here to notice that in one respect mind-reading is like dreaming. If Paula dreams that she is running, her brain will fire those motor programs it would fire if she were in fact running, but it fires them off-line, so that there is no muscle movement in Paula's legs even while her brain is running the motor programs usually used to produce that muscle movement in the legs. In the same way, through the mirror neuron system, Paula can have a mental state that is the same as or similar to Jerome's mental state, but without the brain's actually producing all the states it would have produced had Paula herself been in the condition Jerome is in.

In such a case, the mental state in Paula really is Paula's. But, unlike the mental state of Jerome's that Paula is sharing, Paula's mental state is not accompanied by the states of will and intellect this mental state has in Jerome. For example, in empathy with Jerome when he has impaled his bare foot on a nail, Paula may mind-read Jerome's feeling of pain. In that case, Paula will feel pain too, and the pain will really be Paula's, even if it is only empathic pain. But Paula will not believe that it is her foot that is hurt, and she will not want medical attention for her foot. So she will not have the states of intellect or will that she would have if she really were in the state that Jerome is in.

In the case of dreamed motion, when the brain's motor programs for running are firing, they are disconnected from the muscles in the legs and so do not produce actual running. In the case of mind-reading, the brain's mirror neuron system runs the programs it would run if Paula were doing what Jerome is doing, but it runs them disconnected from those states of will and intellect Paula would have if in fact she were doing those acts. In this way, Paula shares in Jerome's mental states but without having them as Jerome has them; instead, she has her own states of intellect and will, not Jerome's, even while she feels what she would feel if she were doing or suffering what Jerome is.

It is worth seeing that mind-reading and empathy between two people Paula and Jerome can occur when Jerome is engaged in doing an action that is evil or morally repulsive. That this is so helps explain why watching such actions, in real life or in videos, is so distressing to most people. Graphic videos of violence or abuse are disturbing because the dreadful scenes in those videos prompt mind-reading and empathy in the viewer too. The mirror neuron system gives the viewer some no doubt limited sense of what it feels like to do such things and to want to do them, even though it gives this sense in a way disconnected from the viewer's own intellect and will. Sensing what it feels like to do and to want to do such things can be very troubling if the things in question are deeply revulsive to one's moral sensibilities, to one's own beliefs and desires.

To see better why empathy and mind-reading of morally evil actions is and ought to be distressing, it is helpful to return to Aquinas's notion of the stain on the soul and to remember that serious moral wrongdoing leaves its effects on parts of the wrongdoer's psyche other than just his intellect and will. There are cognitive capacities besides intellect and will, and wrongdoing can leave them in a morally worse condition, too. For example, left to their own devices most people cannot simulate the mind of a person who does monstrously cruel things to another human being. But the evildoer himself does understand what it feels like to do an evil of that sort and what it feels like to *want* to do it. Such a condition is not by itself culpable or worthy of punishment; it does not count as a sin in its own right, since sin requires an act of will. But there is something morally deplorable about such a condition all the same. That a person is morally the worse for knowing what such things feel like is clear.

An extreme case of the stain on the soul can be found in the psychic state of Rudolf Hess. The psychiatrists who examined him at Nuremberg testified both to his self-serving cunning and to his "great instability."[21] The American Major Sheppard said of Hess, "I believe by the nature of his make-up, which reflects cruelty, bestiality, deceit, conceit, arrogance, and a yellow streak, that he has lost his soul and has willingly permitted himself to become plastic in the hands of a more powerful and compelling personality."[22] Something that was lovely in Hess before he participated in the Nazi horrors was lost by his evil actions, and repentance by itself would not have been sufficient to restore him to the moral wholesomeness he had before his evil acts.

That this is so helps to explain why even if Hess had been completely repentant after the war, people would still have wanted to stand at some distance from him. The moral plasticity in Hess's psyche, to which Sheppard called attention, was itself morally repellent to those around Hess. In complete repentance, Hess would have had the states of will and intellect that a morally good person has. But he still would have had the leftover stain on the soul, as Aquinas puts it.

Many things go into that stain, but one central element of it is certainly the knowledge of what it is like to do the evil things the wrongdoer did. An analogous kind of knowledge can be had, however, even without doing oneself the evil acts in question. When a viewer watches seriously evil acts in real life or on videos, the consequent mind-reading and empathy can introduce into the viewer some analogue of what it feels like to do the evil acts being seen and to want to do them. It can thus give the viewer not an actual stain on the soul but a simulacrum of the stain on the soul. That is why mind-reading the mental states of someone engaged in cruel abuse can produce feelings that are horrible to ordinarily decent people.

To clarify this notion of a simulacrum of the stain, it is helpful to consider empathic pain again. The empathic pain Paula has when she sees Jerome impale his bare foot on a nail will not be connected to tissue damage in her foot, or to the beliefs and desires she would have if it had been her own foot that is hurt. So although she feels a pain that is in some sense Jerome's pain, she does not incur the damage Jerome does from the event that causes this pain in Jerome. In the same way, when Paula sees Jerome doing something morally monstrous and mind-reads him as he is doing it, then the resulting empathic state in Paula is not connected to the rest of her psyche in the way those same states are connected to the rest of Jerome's psyche. Paula's will rejects doing the kind of acts Jerome is engaged in, for example, while Jerome actually wills to do them; and she is distressed by the empathic feeling she gets from Jerome, instead of accepting or welcoming it as Jerome does.

Consequently, such mind-reading of Jerome by Paula does not produce a real stain on the soul in Paula. She is not blameworthy or otherwise morally less than she might have been because of the feelings her mind-reading produces in her. In having such feelings, Paula is not engaged in any evil acts of intellect or will, any more than a person who dreams she is running is actually running. But the mind-reading will be disturbing to Paula anyway because she feels at the same time Jerome's evil mental states and her own distress at those mental states. And this is the sense in which the mind-reader of another person's moral evil gains something like a simulacrum of the stain on the soul of the evildoer even while she lacks those states that constitute the actual stain of the evildoer.

So the as-it-were stain on the soul of the mind-reader is not itself something morally lamentable in the mind-reader, because the mind-reader lacks the relevant psychic states of will and intellect of the evildoer and the leftover states in the other cognitive capacities. Because the mirror neuron system enables the mind-reader to have the mental states of an evildoer off-line, the mind-reader does not contract the actual stain of the person with whom she is connected in the mind-reading way. What the mind-reader gains is only a likeness of the stain of the evil person. She has in herself a representation of the evildoer's psychic states, but not the real thing in virtue of being alienated herself from the evil in question.

On the other hand, as in empathy in general, the feeling that the mind-reader has in such cases is real, and it is her own. For a morally decent person, a mind-reading connection with a person engaged in serious evil will produce psychological pain ranging from distress to the catastrophically traumatic. When Tolkien's Frodo is connected in a telepathic way with the minds of Mordor's Black Riders, the horror is so traumatic for him that he never recovers from the experience. The rest of his life is marked by a periodic recurrence of that experience of horror in memory and its consequent suffering.

Human beings are a highly social species, and the relevant neural systems, including the mirror neuron system, are part of what enables human beings to function as the social animals they are. Mind-reading and empathy connect people into smaller or larger social groups which can function as one because the exercise of the mind-reading and empathic capacities connects them psychically to one extent or another. The great good of this system is highlighted by what happens when it is impaired, as it is in autistic children. But the other side of the coin is that the same system also enables an empathic, mind-reading connection between the psyche of a morally decent person and the psyche of an evil person, and a psychic connection of that sort will be an affliction for the morally decent person.

MIND-READING, SHARED ATTENTION, AND CHRIST'S DISTANCE FROM GOD

This briefly sketched description of the effects of a morally decent person's mind-reading of someone engaged in evil acts gives us an additional option for understanding the distance between Christ and God at the time of the cry of dereliction on the cross.

Just as great physical pain on Jerome's part can hinder or block his ability to share attention with Paula, even if he and Paula love each other and are mutually close, so serious psychological pain can have the same effect. If it is sufficiently great, Jerome's psychological pain attendant on mind-reading the evil acts of some person Julia can have the same result. Jerome's mind-reading of Julia while she is engaged in evil acts can leave Jerome unable to share attention with Paula even though Paula is right there for Jerome, present to Jerome in every respect except for Jerome's inability to find her in his pain. When Frodo is in the grip of his mind-reading connection with the Black Riders, or when Pippin is mind-melded through the palantir with the mind of Sauron, the good and caring world around each of them becomes shadowy and hard for Frodo and Pippin to access. Their loving friends, deeply concerned for them and present with them, fade for them. In the grip of the telepathic connection to the Black Riders or Sauron, everything else, even the ordinary surrounding inanimate environment, is dimmed for each of them. The horror of the minds of the Black Riders fills Frodo's whole conscious mind and blocks out everything else, until finally he faints from pain. In Pippin's case, it takes the powers of the wizard Gandalf to enable Pippin to return to the daylight world and to make contact with his friends again.

In my earlier canvass of possibilities for sources of the distance between Christ and God, the love and goodness of God, on the one hand, and the love and goodness of Christ, on the other, seemed to rule out all the possibilities there are, except (3b). That possibility assigns responsibility for interrupted shared attention between God and Christ to something attributable to Christ. This last possibility did not seem promising either, because it was hard to see how anything attributable to Christ could be responsible for hindering shared attention between Christ and God, given the mutual love and closeness between them. Morally bad states of intellect and will are ruled out for Christ because he is sinless, and physical pain is insufficient to explain Christ's experience of abandonment too.

But the mind-reading capacities of human beings show us that, with regard to (3b), there is yet another option. Christ can be the source of the blocking of shared attention between Christ and God because of (3b2) something in Christ other than beliefs and desires of his, but this something need not be physical pain or fear over physical pain. Consideration of the empathic, mind-reading system suggests yet another way in which to understand Christ's experience of distance between him and God. Something relational between Christ and other human beings can hinder shared attention between Christ and God, too.

There is plausibility as well as sensitivity in Tolkien's portrayal of Pippin and Frodo when they are mind-melded with other minds of overwhelming evil. Overwhelmed by that telepathic connection, Frodo cannot find his friends, even though they are right there by him, filled with love and care for him. Their mutual love and closeness is not diminished, but Frodo cannot access it, because he loses his ability to share attention with his friends while he is suffering the horror of that telepathic connection with the Black Riders. And the same things are true of Tolkien's Pippin when his mind is connected to the mind of Sauron. If Tolkien's stories seem plausible as regards Frodo and Pippin, then it does not seem implausible to suppose that an analogous story, *mutatis mutandis*, could be told about Christ and his psychic openness to human evil.

Although it is part of orthodox theological doctrine that in Christ the two natures, the divine and the human, do not mingle, nonetheless, in virtue of the fact that only one person has these natures, and that one person is divine, Christ can act in such a way as to use elements of both natures in his actions. That is, even while acting in his human nature, Christ can use powers that are beyond the merely human and that are available to him only through his divine nature. For example, acting in his capacity as a human being, Christ does miracles; but he is able to do them because in his human actions he can harness the divine power over nature. In the same sort of way, nothing rules out supposing that, in his human nature, Christ can mind-read in ways not possible for mere human persons.

When Christ does so, the mind-reading occurs in Christ's human mind. But the person doing the mind-reading is divine and has access to divine power, and so Christ can have the ability to mind-read human beings in a way that mere human persons could not do.[23] In fact, since immaterial eternal God is present to every time and space, Christ can use his human mind and the power of his divine nature to mind-read at once the entire mind of every human being existing at every time and space. The power of the divine person in the incarnate Christ can give the human mind of Christ the power of having within himself in the mind-reading way the minds of all human persons at one and the same time.[24]

To suppose that there is such mind-reading in Christ is one way of interpreting the theological claim that on the cross Christ bore the sins of all human beings at all times, including times before the birth of Christ and after his death. On this supposition, through the power of his divine nature, the human psyche of the person of Christ is opened on the cross to the psyches of all human beings. At one and the same time, Christ mind-reads the mental states found in all the evil human acts human beings have ever committed. Every vile, shocking, disgusting, revulsive psychic state accompanying every human evil act will be at once, miraculously, in the human psyche of Christ, only off-line, without yielding an evil configuration in either Christ's intellect or will. In this condition, Christ will have in his psyche a simulacrum of the stains of all the evil ever thought or done, without having any evil acts of his own and without incurring any true stain on the soul.

The suffering of such a psychic connection all at once with the evil mental states of every human evildoer would greatly eclipse all other human psychological suffering. It would dwarf an experience of suffering such as that brought about by the telepathic connection to the minds of Mordor, no matter how evil those minds are and no matter how traumatic a telepathic connection with such minds would be.

Flooded with such a horror, Christ might well lose entirely his ability to find the mind of God the Father. For him in that condition then, God would be even more inaccessible than Frodo's friends were to him when the Black Riders occupied his mind. Furthermore, because in his psychic connection with the evil in every human being, Christ would also have the simulacrum of the stains on the soul accompanying all that evil, and he would feel the moral ugliness of that evil in himself. In that condition, why would he not feel abandoned by God? The ugliness of those stains is a world away from the beauty of God's goodness, and even the simulacrum of them would be very troubling.

In addition, there is undoubtedly shame for Christ in his mode of death. In front of his mother, in front of his friends who love him and his enemies who hate him, his mode of death leaves him naked, powerless, humiliated, crushed by physical pain, dying of torture. A noble soul might find a way to rise above such shame. In such cases, a great-souled person might still see himself as lovely by a higher standard, which measures moral and spiritual worth, as distinct from ordinary worldly goods. But this move is not readily available to Christ when he is mired in the painful simulacrum of the stains accompanying all human moral evil. The shame of his mode of death must be dwarfed by the feeling of that inward experience of human moral vileness.

So this interpretation of possibility (3b2) gives us what we were looking for: an explanation for a real distance between Christ and God that assigns no culpability for the distance and no lack of love to either Christ or God.

THE IMPORT OF THIS INTERPRETATION OF THE CRY

This interpretation of the cry supposes that there is a causal power in the incarnate Christ that is not had either by Christ in his divine nature alone or by any mere human being. This should not be a surprising claim since the same claim is implied by the traditional theological claim that Christ was able to use his divine power to do miracles in his human nature or that the second person of the Trinity was able to experience death in his human nature.

In his human nature alone, Christ could not mind-read all human persons completely or at once. And in his divine nature alone Christ cannot mind-read at all; at any rate, certainly sinful human psyches could not be received into the mind of God. So although a perfectly good God can indwell in the mind of even a sinful human being, the opposite is not true: a sinful human psyche cannot indwell in a perfectly good God, for the very reasons I gave to show that Christ suffers in receiving such psyches within his own mind. So neither in his human nature alone nor in his divine nature alone can Christ mind-read all at once all human beings.

But the configuration of the incarnate Christ is composite, and that configuration of the incarnate Christ confers on the whole a causal power that nothing else has. Because Christ is one person with both a human and a divine nature, he can use the human nature to mind-read, and he can use the power of the divine nature to enable a kind of miraculously great mind-reading which opens his mind up to the entire psyche of every human being. In consequence, human beings even in their post-Fall condition can indwell God because they are within Christ in his human mind, and Christ is God in the one divine person that has that human mind.

This openness on Christ's part to all human psyches is therefore Christ's contribution to mutual indwelling between God and human persons. On the cross, in the experience expressed in the cry of dereliction, Christ establishes at one and the same time an indwelling in God of all human beings even in their sinfulness. Then, when at any other time a human person Paula surrenders to God in faith and is open to God, the circuit for mutual indwelling between God and Paula is completed, because then the Holy Spirit comes to indwell in Paula. At that point, there is mutual indwelling between God and Paula. In that mutual indwelling, love flows and produces union in some incipient degree between her and God.

Putting the point in this way drastically understates it, because what the completed circuit actually allows is not just the sharing of intrinsic characteristics between the mind of God and the mind of a human person. Rather, because God is one of the relata, what is shared in the mutual indwelling of God and a human person in grace are the persons themselves, and not just their characteristics.[25] What is within each of them, one might say, is both of them.

This union is ontologically greater than any union possible between two human persons. In the Gospel of John, Christ prays for his disciples "that they all may be one, as you, Father, are in me and I in you, that they also might be one in us...I in them, and you in me" (John 17:21, 23). In the mutual indwelling of God and a person in grace, the human person is within God, in virtue of her psyche's being within the human mind of Christ, who is the second person of the Trinity; and God is within her, in virtue of the Holy Spirit's being within her psyche. And so, on this account, the triune God is within a human person and a human person is within the triune God. The union between God and a human person in grace is therefore analogous to the mutual indwelling of the Father and the Son in the divine union of love, as Christ in the Gospel of John prayed that it would be.

A position often attributed to Abelard and commonly considered heretical is the view that the point of Christ's passion and death is to teach by example what real love is.[26] If this supposedly Abelardian position marks one end of the spectrum for interpretations of the doctrine of the atonement, the account I am delineating here marks the other end of the spectrum. On the Abelardian view, the point of Christ's passion is to set an example for human beings. On the account argued for here, the point of Christ's passion is to provide for human beings a metaphysical analogue of the union of the persons of the Trinity, in which each person is within the other.

Some theologians, especially those within the Orthodox Christian tradition, emphasize the deification of a human person as the point of the atonement. The implicit understanding of deity in discussions of deification sometimes highlights standard divine attributes, which can characterize one individual taken in isolation from others: power, knowledge, and so on. But what this account of mutual indwelling implies is that there is a different understanding of deification provided by the Christian doctrine that the deity is triune. On this theologically complicated understanding of deity, deity is an irreducible plurality of persons and mutual in-ness of persons. To be made like God, then, requires not a particular set of unusually excellent intrinsic attributes on the part of an individual. Rather, it requires a particularly powerful metaphysical mutuality of indwelling among persons. Deification is irreducibly interpersonal on this account. Neither deification nor deity is anything that an individual person could have in isolation, not even a divine person, since there is more than one divine person in God.[27]

Thinking of deification as providing mutual indwelling of persons in union of love also helps to explain why deification can come in degrees. That is because mutual indwelling admits of degrees. There is, of course, one all-or-nothing characteristic of union: either union in any degree has been established or not; either there is some mutual indwelling of persons or there is not. But once mutual indwelling has been established, it then becomes a matter of degree how much indwelling or how much union there is.[28] Just as two human persons can be united in love in greater or lesser degree, so there can be a greater or smaller degree of mutual indwelling between God and a human person in grace. The greatest degree of such union is reserved to the afterlife, where a human person in grace is finally as fully integrated in goodness and love of God as she can be. And yet even in heaven there can be varying degrees of union. Even complete union admits of degrees. Each person in heaven will be as fully united with God as possible, but some human beings in heaven can have a deeper love of God and so a deeper union with God than others. Heaven is not egalitarian on orthodox Christian theological doctrine. Every person in heaven is completely filled with God's love; but, one might say, some persons can hold more love than others.[29]

A POSSIBLE MISCONCEPTION

At this point, someone might suppose that the aim of this book has been achieved: the nature of Christ's atonement has been explained. It provides a necessary condition for a metaphysically great kind of union, and only the incarnate Christ's passion can provide this condition. Therefore, by means of this interpretation of the cry of dereliction, the point and the process of atonement are sufficiently explained.

But this supposition is mistaken. This interpretation of the cry of dereliction gives only one necessary condition for mutual indwelling between God and a human person in this life. The other condition is that God be indwelling in that human person; and this is where the main problem for atonement lies. Some people are lonely because age, illness, war, or other external circumstances have left them bereft of company. But, beneath ordinary, externally imposed loneliness, there is a deeper, willed loneliness shared by all human beings, because the lack of internal integration in the human will excludes closeness, love, and union in their full or complete modes.

This willed loneliness shuts out even God. Whether one person Paula is close to another person Jerome, whether she is united to him in love, is not within Paula's sole control. It requires also certain states of mind and will in Jerome, including most notably Jerome's being integrated in himself. *Mutatis mutandis*, these claims about Paula apply also to God. Nothing about human beings can separate them from the powerful, providential, ever-present love of God. But what is *desired* in love is union. And even omnipotent God cannot unilaterally fulfill this desire of love. Even God cannot be united to Jerome if Jerome is alienated from himself. Insofar as Jerome is resistant to internal integration, he is in effect also resistant to union with God.

So although this interpretation of the cry of dereliction gives one powerful part of the account of atonement sought in this book, it does not yet provide the most difficult and significant part of that account.

ADVANTAGES AND IMPLICATIONS

Nonetheless, the interpretation of the cry of dereliction I have given here has some advantages and some notable implications as regards an understanding of the atonement.

For example, it is Christian doctrine that on the cross Christ bears the sins of all human beings. There are, of course, many explanations of this claim. Virtually all of them suppose that in taking on human sin during his crucifixion, nothing about Christ's intellect and will become truly, intrinsically, morally evil. On the other hand, most such explanations also suppose that there is some sense in which the evil of human beings becomes somehow transferred into or on to Christ. But it is not at all clear how both these claims could be true. So, for example, McCall says,

> One may nuance the claim that Jesus was the 'greatest sinner' by adding that this was the case despite the fact that 'he never committed a sinful action,' but this is hard even to understand. How is someone *really* a sinner if that person neither has a sinful nature nor commits sinful actions?[30]

As I have it explained it here, however, the mind-reading system has the resources to provide a promising solution to McCall's conundrum. When Christ is in mind-reading connection with all human beings, Christ has in his psyche a simulacrum of the stains of all the evil ever thought or done. In this way, he has the sins of human beings within himself. But he has this evil in his psyche off-line, as it were, that is, without the ordinarily associated evil states of intellect and will. Through mind-reading, then, Christ can have all human sin within himself on the cross without himself being sinful, that is, without having any morally evil beliefs or states of will of his own.

Furthermore, this interpretation of the cry shows one way to reconcile the experience expressed by the cry with the Chalcedonian formula for the incarnate Christ. On the Chalcedonian formula, the person who utters the cry of dereliction is also the God to whom the cry is addressed. So the distance between God and Christ during the cry must also constitute an internal fragmentation in Christ. But the experience of the one person of the incarnate Christ in this condition is in fact intelligible; and it does not stem from any sinfulness on his part, as the self-alienation of human beings typically does. If the human mind of Christ is opened to all the evil of every human psyche, then it is understandable that the experience would introduce separation into the composite that is the incarnate Christ. In that condition, the human mind of Christ may be so overwhelmed that, momentarily at least, it cannot access the mind of God in the divine nature that the incarnate Christ also has. Nonetheless, this radical internal fragmentation in the composite whole that the incarnate Christ is does not stem from any moral fault in Christ. It stems from the effects on Christ's human psyche of being entered by post-Fall human psyches with all their evil. And so we have an account of self-alienation in the composite incarnate Christ that does not stem from any culpability of Christ's.

Finally, someone might wonder why the confluence of human psyches into the human psyche of Christ took place in the process of Christ's dying and why it occurs in the context of great physical suffering. Why could it not have occurred as soon as Christ reached adulthood, and without Christ's enduring any physical pain? And, of course, these questions only highlight another question: Why did Christ have to die at all? What is it about the process leading to the union of God and human persons that makes the death of Christ unavoidable or efficacious to that end?

Here it is worth noting that numerous biblical texts attest to the need for Christ's suffering and death. So it is possible simply to take as one more theological datum for reflection the claim that Christ needed to suffer and die in order to bear all human sin and so provide salvation for human beings. Nonetheless, in the context of the interpretation of the cry of dereliction given in this chapter, it is possible at least to gesture in the direction of some explanation of this biblically based claim.

In this connection, it is helpful to see that, on the cross, the severe internal division between the natures of Christ in the period when Christ bears human sin and experiences God as absent is quickly matched by another extreme division within Christ. That is, because very shortly after uttering the cry of dereliction, Christ dies in his human nature; that is, Christ's human soul separates from Christ's human body. Nonetheless, the person of Christ remains united to each of these separated human parts.

During this period of his human death, Christ's body remains in the tomb; but Christ's soul is elsewhere. On traditional doctrine, in this period, Christ's soul descends into hell. Calvin says about the doctrine that Christ's soul went down into hell,

> we must not omit the descent to hell, which was of no little importance to the accomplishment of redemption. For although it is apparent from the writings of the ancient Fathers, that the clause which now stands in the Creed was not formerly so much used in the churches, still, in giving a summary of doctrine, a place must be assigned to it, as containing a matter of great importance which ought not by any means to be disregarded.... This much is uncontroverted, that it was in accordance with the general sentiment of all believers, since there is none of the Fathers who does not mention Christ's descent into hell, though they have various modes of explaining it.[31]

However the doctrine of Christ's descent into hell is to be understood, it is traditional Christian doctrine that, in the days between his death and resurrection, the person of Christ, with his divine nature, is also united to each of two things, namely, the human soul and the human body of Christ,[32] that are not united to each other.[33]

It is clear that there are degrees of unity. As Aquinas (following Aristotle) holds, there is less unity in a heap of grains of sand than there is in two pieces of wood glued together, and there is less unity in those glued wood pieces than there is in a water molecule or in any other whole that is one substance united by a configuration that gives the composite its emergent powers.[34] By parity of reasoning, a composite that is united into one by some means of union can begin to be fragmented in various ways without having the union actually completely dissolved.

On traditional Christian doctrine about the death of Christ, in Christ's suffering and dying, the unity of the composite Christ loosens, because Christ's soul and body separate from each other. This division takes place within the human nature of Christ. By comparison, on the interpretation of the cry of dereliction argued for here, during this same period, the unity of the composite Christ loosens, because Christ's human mind comes to be at a distance from the divine mind of Christ. So in this one period, the internal division in the composite Christ between Christ's human and divine natures is matched by the internal division in the human nature of Christ, between Christ's soul and body.

Seen in this light, the death of Christ at this time makes sense. Once the unity in the incarnate Christ begins to loosen through Christ's bearing human sin, then it is not surprising that the unity of the composite Christ should continue to unravel into the separation of Christ's human soul and body in death. On the Chalcedonian formula, there are three components in Christ: the person, the divine nature, and the human nature. The loosening of the unity of these three components that is begun when Christ's human nature bears the sin of all humanity, so that the divine nature begins to have some distance from the human nature, has its culmination in death, when the composite is as far dissolved as it can be and still count as the incarnate Christ. And Christ's suffering physical pain concomitantly with bearing human sin has a kind of logic about it, too. On the interpretation of the cry argued for here, the physical pain of crucifixion is an outward correlate of the inward anguish of the experience expressed by the cry. I am not wedded to this explanation of the connection between the experience underlying the cry, on the one hand, and the physical suffering and death of Christ, on the other; and it is not necessary for my interpretation of the cry of dereliction or my interpretation of the doctrine of the atonement. But that this interpretation of the cry yields this explanation of Christ's death seems to me one more benefit of it.

TWO WORRIES AND THEIR RESOLUTION

There was a medieval dispute between Franciscans and Dominicans over the reason for the incarnation.[35] The Dominicans in the dispute maintained that the incarnation would not have happened if human beings had not fallen from their sinless state, and the Franciscans argued that the incarnation would have had a point and would have happened even if there had been no Fall.[36] It may seem that in my discussion of mutual indwelling between God and a human person I have sided with the Franciscans and given them added ammunition. On my explanation of union in love between God and a human person, mutual indwelling is part of union; and, as I have explained mutual indwelling here, it requires that God have a human mind. For those not inclined to cheer the Franciscan position, this apparent implication of my position will be worrisome. On the other hand, for those who do side with the Franciscans, there is the mirror image worry. Now it seems as if only human beings and not angels also can be united to God in love. God does not also have an angelic nature. So if it takes sharing a nature with a created species in order to have mutual indwelling with the creatures of that species, then it seems as if only human beings and not also angels can have real union with God in love.

But this worry in both its guises is mistaken, in my view. Consider the angels, for example. What is there that rules out God's opening his mind, his divine mind, to the minds of the angels? Nothing at all, as far as I can see. Mutual indwelling between God and the good angels is both possible and actual, on traditional Christian doctrine. And, in fact, the same thing would be true as regards human psyches, except for the fact that they are sinful. The divine nature itself cannot be made sin for human beings. God's goodness is God's nature, on the doctrine of simplicity; and that goodness cannot be intimately joined with what is sinful. That is why human sinfulness is an obstacle to union with God in heaven in the first place. There would be no need for salvation for human beings if human beings could be united to God while they were still sinful. So what requires that God assume a human nature in order to have mutual indwelling between God and human beings is the sinfulness of human psyches. Through the mind-reading system, the human nature of Christ can receive that sinfulness and can do so without culpability, as this chapter has been at pains to show. That is why it is the post-Fall nature of human beings that calls for Christ's incarnation and atonement.

And so my description of mutual indwelling actually supports the Dominican position in the medieval debate, not the Franciscan one.

Someone might suppose, however, that the explanation I have given of my position here makes the position self-inconsistent, because it both maintains and also denies that sinful human beings can be united with God. It denies that sinful human beings can be united with a perfectly good God, but it maintains that sinful human beings are united with Christ, who is God. But this objection overlooks the cry of dereliction that has been central in this chapter. When sinful human beings indwell the human mind of Christ, the anguish their presence in his psyche causes Christ finds voice in the cry of dereliction. Anguish is no more compatible with God in his divine nature than sin is, and heaven with anguish is not heaven. God needs to assume a human nature if God is to undergo what the indwelling of post-Fall human psyches bring him. But the union of human beings with God in heaven requires uniting with God in his divine nature, and for that union human beings need to be made perfectly good too, through the process of sanctification.[37]

This stance towards the Franciscan and Dominican dispute itself raises another worry, however. Someone might object that, on this interpretation of the cry of dereliction, union between God and human beings relies on a permanent state of inner fragmentation and anguish for Christ, at least in his human mind, since the indwelling of human psyches into the mind of Christ is permanent, insofar as union between Christ and human persons is permanent. What happens to Christ in the process of crucifixion endures without end, in one sense, because Christ as the second person of the Trinity is eternal and so always is simultaneous with every moment of time, including the time of the crucifixion.[38]

There is one sense in which this worry is right, but it is an attenuated sense that cannot be avoided by any interpretation of the cry of dereliction which accepts the standard divine attribute of eternity. On the doctrine of eternity, there never is a *when* in the life of God in which God does not have a human nature and does not suffer in that human nature. To assume otherwise is to introduce succession into the life of God and so to make God temporal. And so, given the doctrine of eternity, the anguish of the cry of dereliction is permanent for God, on anyone's interpretation of the cry.

On the other hand, however, nothing in this claim or in the interpretation of the cry which I have argued for has the implication that the union between God and human beings is marked only by an indwelling of human minds that is anguishing for Christ. On the contrary, once Christ's psyche is open to the indwelling of human psyches, that indwelling will include not only a human psyche in its unredeemed state but also the psyches of the redeemed in their final sanctified state. Just as God has present to him at once the whole life of a human person, from infancy onwards, in the same way the mind of Christ is open to the psyche of a human person in the whole life of that person. The life of a person in grace includes in its first, unredeemed period things that are painful for Christ to bear. But, for a person in grace, the life which has such a dismaying early period eventuates in unending internally integrated goodness. The indwelling of a human psyche in that condition yields union of love.[39]

And so, on this interpretation of the cry of dereliction, the experience for Christ that begins in anguish eventuates in joy in the mutual indwelling of love between Christ and the redeemed.

CONCLUSION

Sustained philosophical examination of experiences that could explain the cry of dereliction from the cross therefore pushes towards an interpretation of the cry according to which the psyches of all human beings pour into the human mind of Christ, which is open to them in his suffering and dying. This openness on Christ's part during his crucifixion to all human psyches is his contribution to what is needed for mutual indwelling between God and human persons. Insofar as Christ is in the Father, then insofar as human persons are in Christ, they are also in the Father with the Son. And since the Holy Spirit is in every person in grace, in a person in grace there is the fulfillment of the prayer of Christ that there might be mutual indwelling between God and Christ's disciples as there is between Christ and the Father through the Holy Spirit.

In this complicated way, then, there is an account of union in love between God and human persons that is Trinitarian in character. And it is fitting that it should be. Since unity in God is Trinitarian, it makes sense that there should also be a Trinitarian character to union between a human person and God.

In my view, the interpretation of the cry of dereliction that I have argued for here is the only one that can explain the cry without attributing lack of love or other fault to either Christ or God. And it has the substantial added benefit of being able to explain the biblical texts describing the sinless Christ as bearing human sin and being made sin on the cross. But its main advantage for my purposes is its implications for a Trinitarian account of union between God and human persons, and it is this result that will make the most difference in the chapters that follow.

From this point on, I will take this mutual indwelling of God and a human person to be a life in grace, and I will call a person in such a life 'a person in grace.' Since life in grace is the best condition for a human being, a person's being in grace is both necessary and sufficient for her entrance into everlasting life in heaven and the fuller, deeper union with God made possible there. But bringing a human person to union with God is the purpose of the atonement. So, in the chapters that follow, I will also take it that the passion and death of Christ are designed both to bring a person to a life of grace and to keep her there throughout the course of her earthly life.

It is important to recognize that these are two different goals, as one can readily see if one thinks of marriage. If Jerome wants to be married to Paula, she will need to want the same thing if they are to be married. But once she is married, it will still be an open question whether she will stay married to him. Paula's original consent to be married is not sufficient for the marriage to endure. Analogously, when a person surrenders in faith and love to God and the Holy Spirit comes to indwell in her, there is at that point no guarantee that she will remain in the same frame of mind. She can turn away from God, just as she could turn away from a spouse; and if she does, she will break the union between her and God.

It is because there are two different goals at issue for the salvation of human beings that Augustine thought two different kinds of grace of God were necessary: one to establish the initial state of grace and the other to keep it in continuance. He called the grace necessary for continuance '*donum perseverantiae'*—the gift of perseverance. Unlike Augustine, I do not think that perseverance in its nature is the sort of thing that can be achieved with one gift of grace. But the process that leads to these twinned goals and the role of the passion and death of Christ in the process will emerge in the chapters that follow.

As a preliminary for a consideration of that process, I want first to eliminate one idea of the life of grace that seems to me unworkable. It has to do with the internal configuration of the psyche of a person in grace. There are alternate ways of conceiving of this configuration, and they are well represented by the differing views of Meister Eckhart and Aquinas on willing what God wills. In Chapter 6, I will consider these differing views, and I will argue that Eckhart's view is a dead end. With Eckhart's approach put to the side, I will then examine in detail the Thomistic notion of a life in grace. At that point, the end result effected by the atonement of Christ will have been sketched out. At that point, we will finally be ready to move forward to consider the process that leads both to the beginning of a life in grace and perseverance in it. That is the atonement itself, which will be the subject of Part III.

6

Willing What God Wills

Eckhart and Aquinas

INTRODUCTION

In Chapters 4 and 5, I worked at explaining what union is as between God and a human person in this life; and I tried to show that, on orthodox Christian claims interpreted in light of biblical texts, such union consists in mutual indwelling, even in this life. I examined the biblical story of the cry of dereliction, and I argued that one could make theological sense of that story by supposing that during the crucifixion Christ's human mind was open to all human psyches. The result of this openness is that human persons indwell in the human mind of the incarnate Christ, who is the second person of the Trinity and so is God. The other part of the mutual indwelling between God and human persons occurs when a human person comes to faith and the Holy Spirit comes to indwell in her in consequence.

With the indwelling of the Holy Spirit in her, the circuit of union initiated by Christ on the cross is complete; and the mutual in-ness of human and divine persons[1] enables the flow of united love. In this metaphysically great union, what is shared is not just the thoughts and feelings of the persons in the union but the persons themselves, with God and a human person each indwelling the other. This mutual indwelling is something analogous to the mutual indwelling of the persons of the Trinity, but metaphysically more limited since a human person cannot be within God in so thoroughly united a way as one person of the Trinity can be within another. Nonetheless, when Christ prays to God the Father regarding Christ's disciples, "As you, Father, are in me and I in you, so may they also be one in us" (John 17:21), this prayer is answered by the mutual indwelling between human persons and God enabled by human openness to God and Christ's openness to human psyches on the cross.[2]

It is important to be clear that, on this account of mutual indwelling, even so great a metaphysical union between God and a human person is available in this life. What is being characterized in this account is not something reserved for an afterlife in the beatific vision in heaven. Rather, it is the condition of every saved person in this life. No doubt, transposition to conditions in heaven alters this union in significant ways that increase dramatically both its degree of union and its joy. But, for my purposes, it is not necessary to try to tease out of orthodox theological doctrine the details of the character of this union as it exists in heaven. It would not be wise to try to do so either. Neither biblical texts nor Christian philosophical theology provide much detail about the nature of a person's life and character in heaven. Even Dante, who devotes one third of his *Divine Comedy* to trying to fill in such detail, stipulates that his descriptions are only speculative constructions made for pedagogical purposes. So trying to shed light on the effects of the atonement by describing a person's union with God in heaven is not a promising way to proceed. It is enough to consider the state of that union in this life.

In the previous chapters, I called a life in such union 'a life in grace', and I called a person in such union 'a person in grace.' On the account being developed here, then, the goal of the atonement of Christ is to bring human beings to a life in grace. In trying to understand what exactly the atonement is and how it accomplishes its goal, therefore, it helps to understand what a life in grace is. In examining the nature of mutual indwelling, I have tried to characterize the union that is at the heart of a life in grace; but I have left largely unexamined the psychic condition of a human person in grace, her internal states of mind and will.

In the Christian tradition, there is considerable discussion of the psychic or spiritual condition of a person in grace; and it will be the main focus of Chapter 7. But first, in this chapter, I want to consider two radically different understandings of the life in grace, one by Meister Eckhart and one by Aquinas. Although in his own day some of Eckhart's teachings were considered heretical, in contemporary times many scholars have disputed that medieval assessment and have taken Eckhart's views to be squarely within the Dominican tradition and even Thomist, at least in broad outline. Without commenting on this dispute over the general assessment of Eckhart's thought, in this chapter I want to highlight the clear divergence in their thought about a life in grace. Although Eckhart's understanding of life in grace represents one strand of thought among those who are inclined towards a non-Anselmian kind of interpretation of the doctrine of the atonement, it is nonetheless a strand of thought that ought to be rejected, as I will argue in this chapter. It will illuminate the nature of a life in grace if the disparate understandings of Eckhart and Aquinas are disambiguated, and it will help articulate the correct understanding of the life in grace if Eckhart's understanding of it is first set to one side.

There is no dispute between Eckhart and Aquinas (or among others in the Christian tradition) over the claim that, to be united with God, a human person has to will what God wills; and the claim that willing what God wills is willing the good is also not controversial. The difference between Eckhart and Aquinas has to do rather with what in the psychic state of a human person in this life counts as willing what God wills. Eckhart and Aquinas each understand being united with God as at least in part a matter of willing what God wills, and they each maintain that willing what God wills is necessary for a life in grace. But they differ widely as regards their understanding of willing what God wills and so also of the psychic state of a person in grace.

In what follows, I will argue that Eckhart's account of willing what God wills is not acceptable, even on Eckhart's terms, in virtue of the fact that the response to suffering it exhorts is inimical to the union at which it aims, and that therefore it is destructive of the very goal aimed at in the atonement of Christ. Whatever the means is by which the atonement brings a person to the state of mutual indwelling with God, it is not because the atonement enables a human person to be in the state Eckhart thinks constitutes willing what God wills. Eckhart's notion of a human person's willing what God wills cannot constitute a will in harmony with God's will; on the contrary, the state of will Eckhart recommends is spiritually pernicious because it is incompatible with union with God.

In Chapter 7, when I turn to examine the Thomistic account of life in grace, it will be helpful already to have examined Eckhart's kind of view. With Eckhart's notion of willing what God wills set aside, I will try to show in Chapter 7 what the psychic condition of a person in grace is, on Aquinas's understanding of grace. With that psychic condition sketched, it will then also be easier to reflect on the role of Christ's atonement in bringing a person to such a condition.

THE POST-FALL HUMAN CONDITION

Although it has significant implications, the difference between Eckhart and Aquinas on the subject of willing what God wills is subtle and nuanced. For the sake of highlighting the difference, it helps first to take a step back to sketch the post-Fall human condition, as it is understood in Christian doctrine. The difference between Eckhart and Aquinas is illuminated against this background.[3]

On the orthodox Christian doctrine accepted by both Eckhart and Aquinas, all post-Fall human beings are infected by a spiritual disorder that inclines them to privilege their own power and pleasure over greater goods. The greatest good for any human being is to be united in love with God. The worst thing for any human being is to be ultimately separated from God. If the spiritual illness of post-Fall human beings is not healed, the post-Fall human tendency to prefer one's own power and pleasure over greater goods will lead eventually to this worst thing for human beings, namely, permanent absence of union with God.

Although there is disorder in the intellect in this post-Fall human tendency, the foundational defect is in the will. One hallmark of this defect is the will's proneness to moral wrong even against its own desires for the good. Human beings will what they take to be good, but they can also simultaneously will against it. Furthermore, although human beings can have a second-order will to will the good, that higher-order will is frequently rendered ineffective by contrary first-order willing of what is in fact only an apparent good.[4] In such a case, a person wills the morally wrong thing he himself desires not to will. Commenting on his own failures to will what he himself takes to be the good and what he wants to will as the good, Augustine says,

> the mind commands the body, and is presently obeyed: the mind commands itself, and is resisted.... it commands that itself would will a thing;... [and it] never would give the command, unless it willed it; yet it does not [will]...[what it] has commanded.... it commands,... [because] it wills: and...the thing [is not] done which...[it] commanded,... [because] it wills it not.... But it does not command fully, therefore is not the thing done, which it commanded. For were the willing full, it never would command it to be, because it would already be.[5]

Worse yet, human beings can be in so lamentable a moral condition that even their second-order wills are corrupted; they not only will what is not good, but they also fail to will to will what is good, or they actually will to will what is not good.

On Aquinas's moral psychology,[6] no one ever gets so evil that there is nothing in her intellect or will that holds back from the evil she is immersed in, that disapproves of that evil and desires something better. Consequently, a human being who takes to be good something that is objectively evil will always be double-minded, in some complicated way that need not be accessible to the agent's own consciousness,[7] and the doubleness in her reason will be mirrored by a corresponding doubleness in her will. For these reasons, moral wrongdoing inevitably fragments a person, and this fragmentation will ward off or undermine closeness with other persons, including even God.[8]

The fragmentation in the will, the will's division against itself and its own resistance to the good it also wills, is the heart of the spiritual illness of the post-Fall human condition. The problem is that a person in such an internally divided condition is someone who is in some sense at war with himself, but a person alienated from himself cannot have someone else close to him. Union between persons requires that each of them be internally integrated. This point holds also where a human person's union with God is concerned. A perfectly loving God is always present to every human person, and internally fragmented human beings are no exception to this claim. But, in the case of an internally divided human person, this divine presence is without the mutual closeness required for union. While God has the power to produce unilaterally some kind of personal presence, for union even God's power is not unilaterally sufficient. Union between God and a person requires mutual closeness, and what is mutual cannot be produced unilaterally. A person in the post-Fall human condition, alienated from himself and fragmented in will, cannot be fully[9] united with anyone else, not even God.[10]

Forgiveness alone is of no avail as a cure for this post-Fall human condition.

God can forgive Jerome unilaterally, in the sense that he can desire the good for Jerome and union with Jerome, no matter what Jerome's internal condition is, even if Jerome is an unrepentant wrongdoer, even if Jerome is a person in hell. But God's love and forgiveness will have to be responsive[11] to Jerome's own state.[12] To the extent to which Jerome is alienated from himself, the desires of love and forgiveness, even on God's part, will be inefficacious. God can forgive Jerome unilaterally, just as God can love Jerome unrequitedly; but God cannot unilaterally have what he desires in love or forgiveness. Even through forgiveness God cannot unilaterally bring it about that he is united to Jerome in love. A person's internal fragmentation closes out even a forgiving God.

It is important to remember in this connection that God wills only what is good and that union with God, which is the best state for human beings, requires willing what God wills. But this very state is what seems to be missing in the post-Fall human condition in which the will is internally fragmented and wills against the good it also wants. The cure for the post-Fall human illness therefore requires that a post-Fall human person be brought somehow into the condition of committing herself to willing what God wills.

SUFFERING AS MEDICINAL

It should be clear that if internal fragmentation and the failure to will what God wills is the problem that keeps a person from union with God, then the atonement must be instrumental in the cure for this problem. Something about Christ's passion and death[13] must provide what is needed for a person's willingness to be internally integrated and to will what God wills. The true medicine for the human condition must lie in Christ's atonement.

Nonetheless, from the Patristic period onwards, the Christian tradition also thought of suffering as healing for this post-Fall human disorder.[14] Aquinas often speaks of suffering as God's medicine for the spiritual disease of post-Fall human beings. For example, Aquinas says,

Since pains are a sort of medicine, we should apparently judge correction and medicine the same way. Now medicine in the taking of it is bitter and loathsome, but its end is desirable and intensely sweet. So discipline is also. It is hard to bear, but it blossoms into the best outcome.[15]

The same general point appears recurrently in Aquinas's commentary on Job. Arguing that temporal goods such as those Job lost are given and taken away according to God's will, Aquinas says,

someone's suffering adversity would not be pleasing to God except for the sake of some good coming from the adversity. And so although adversity is in itself bitter and gives rise to sadness, it should nonetheless be...[acceptable to us] when we consider its usefulness, on account of which it is pleasing to God.... For in his reason a person rejoices over the taking of bitter medicine because of the hope of health, even though in his senses he is troubled.[16]

In Chapter 9, I will look in detail at the relation between the atonement and suffering considered as remedies for the post-Fall human condition. There I will argue that the medicinal character of suffering is in fact ancillary to Christ's atonement, which provides the main remedy for the post-Fall human condition. But, in this chapter, for the sake of differentiating the views of Eckhart and Aquinas, I want to focus just on what the Christian tradition saw as the medicinal character of suffering. If the disease consists in failing to will what God wills and if suffering is a medicine for the disease, then something about suffering should contribute to bringing a person to the state of willing what God wills, and so also to the internal integration in goodness necessary for willing what God wills.

But why should suffering be thought of as medicinal for the will in this way? To understand the healing role the Christian tradition has ascribed to suffering, one needs first to recognize that suffering itself is a function of the will.

SUFFERING AND WHAT WE CARE ABOUT

Although it is tempting to think of suffering just as pain, a little reflection shows that this characterization of suffering is mistaken. There are things that human beings suffer which carry no physical or psychological pain with them.[17] A better way of thinking about suffering is to see it as a function of what we care about. Considered in this way, suffering has two sides, an objective side and a subjective side.

Because every human person has some care about what kind of person she is and about her wellbeing as that kind of person, part of what it is for her to suffer is for her to be kept, to one degree or another, from wellbeing. This is an objective side of suffering, since there is an objective fact of the matter about what will make a human person have wellbeing.

On the other hand, however, what we care about has a subjective side too. This is something to which a person is committed but which is not identical with his wellbeing and which may not even be compatible with it.[18] What is at issue in this subjective side of suffering can be thought of as the desires of the heart.[19] When the Psalmist says, "Delight yourself in the Lord, and he will give you the desires of your heart" (Ps. 37:4), we all have some idea of what the Psalmist is promising. We are clear, for example, that some abstract theological good which a person does not care much about does not count as one of the desires of that person's heart. Suffering also arises when a human being fails to get a desire of her heart or has and then loses a desire of her heart.

We care, then, about two kinds of things, our own objective wellbeing and also those things that are the subjective desires of our hearts. Suffering arises when something impedes or removes either of these kinds of things that we care about. Another way to put the same point is that we suffer because we lose or do not get what we want. Consequently, as many thinkers in different cultures and times have pointed out, human suffering arises because of human desire.

For this reason, there are two different ways in which human suffering can be avoided or alleviated. Either a human person can bring it about that she gets what she wants, or else she can want what she gets (or at least fail to will against what she gets).

It is rarely the case that a sufferer can reduce her suffering by bringing it about that she gets what she wants, however. And so it can seem that a person ought to give up desiring what she herself wants and take whatever happens as acceptable to her. To avoid or alleviate suffering, it seems that a person should just want what she gets. By bringing her desires into line with what actually happens, she can avoid the suffering that occurs when reality does not accord with her desires.

Being in this condition—not willing against what actually happens—can seem (and has seemed to some people) to be willing what God wills. It is part of orthodox Christian doctrine that whatever happens in the world happens in accordance with God's will, in one sense or another. It seems to follow therefore that when a person wills to accept whatever happens, she is willing what God wills. (I keep repeating 'seems' here because I will argue against this position in what follows.)

It is helpful to see one important implication of this position. Consider a person who is suffering because something has undermined or obviated her wellbeing but who frames her will to accept that suffering. If in this condition she is willing what God wills, then, in a paradoxical way she is after all bringing about her wellbeing. That is because willing what God wills is necessary for being internally integrated around the good, which is itself necessary for union with God, which is a person's ultimate good. So, if a person is willing what God wills by accepting her suffering, then by accepting her suffering she is actually contributing to her own ultimate wellbeing, even if something about her suffering detracts from her (earthly) wellbeing. So, if she is willing what God wills when she accepts her suffering, when her suffering frustrates her desire for her own wellbeing, the sufferer actually brings it about that she gets what she desires, although not in the form in which she originally desired it.

Suppose, for example, that a person Paula is undergoing tests for cancer and that she has very strong desires for health and life. And suppose that the test results come back with only bad news: not only does she have cancer, but it has metastasized to the liver, and she has only six months to live. In this situation, there is obviously one way in which Paula's desire for her own wellbeing is frustrated. But it can seem that, if in this situation she gives up her desire for life and health and instead wills in accordance with the lab tests, accepting that she will die, then she brings it about that she *does* have wellbeing, although in a spiritual sense rather than a biological one. If in accepting her suffering and death she is willing what God wills,[20] then, in giving up her own desire for health and life, she is growing in union with God, which is her ultimate good.

It is important to see, however, that, no matter how we understand willing what God wills, a similar move cannot be made as regards the desires of the heart. Suppose that Paula had her heart set on negative test results because she has a young daughter Julia, and she cannot bear the thought that Julia should have to grow up without her mother. Nothing about accepting her own imminent death will in any way give her her heart's desire as regards her daughter, and so it cannot undermine her suffering at the thought that her daughter will be motherless. It might be right that Paula's attempting to will what God wills by giving up her desires for her own (earthly) wellbeing leads to her (ultimate) wellbeing; but, clearly, giving up her heart's desire that her daughter not be a motherless child will not by itself bring it about that her daughter grows up with her mother. Consequently, when it comes to heart's desires, it looks as if the only way to avoid the suffering that arises from the loss of what one desires is just to give up those desires.

For these reasons, it can seem that the attempt to avoid suffering and the attempt to will what God wills converge on this point: one should give up the desires of the heart when their frustration causes suffering. It can seem, in other words, that Paula should simply accept that Julia's being motherless is God's will and should give up her heart's desire to be there for her daughter.

THE STERN-MINDED ATTITUDE

As this conclusion would have it, then, people should focus their care on their wellbeing, their ultimate, spiritual wellbeing, and *only* on it. In order to have some name by which to refer to it, elsewhere I called this stance 'the stern-minded attitude.'[21] It has power and an established position in the history of Christian thought. Many scholars attribute it to Eckhart; and, as far as I myself can see, it is actually Eckhart's position. It is not Aquinas's view, however. In fact, Aquinas rejects it, and I will argue in what follows that he is right to reject it.[22]

The stern-minded attitude is well represented in the Christian tradition from the Patristic period onwards until now. A particularly helpful example of it can be found in some writings (but not all of them) by Teresa of Avila. Writing to her sister nuns, Teresa says,

> Oh, how desirable is...[the] union with God's will! Happy the soul that has reached it. Such a soul will live tranquilly in this life, and in the next as well. Nothing in earthly events afflicts it unless it finds itself in some danger of losing God...neither sickness, nor poverty, nor death...For this soul sees well that the Lord knows what He is doing better than...[the soul] knows what it is desiring ...But alas for us, how few there must be who reach [union with God's will!]... I tell you I am writing this with much pain upon seeing myself so far away [from such union]—and all through my own fault.... Don't think the matter lies in my being so conformed to the will of God that if my father or brother dies I don't feel it, or that if there are trials or sicknesses I suffer them happily.[23]

Not feeling it when one's father dies, not weeping with grief over his death, is, in Teresa's view, a good spiritual condition that she is not yet willing to attribute to herself. Teresa is here echoing a tradition that finds its prime Patristic exemplar in Augustine's *Confessions*. Augustine says that, at the death of his mother, by a powerful command of his will, he kept himself from weeping at her funeral, only to disgrace himself in his own eyes later by weeping copiously in private.[24]

In effect, the stern-minded attitude is unwilling to assign a positive value to anything that is not equivalent to or essential to a person's willing what God wills and so being in union with God. For stern-minded thinkers, that good for human beings is the only *real* good there is. Consequently, the stern-minded attitude is, at best, unwilling to accord any value to the desires of the heart and, at worst, eager to extirpate the desires themselves.

So, for example, speaking to a nun of his acquaintance, Anselm says,

> This world is nothing to you, nothing but dung, if you wish to be a nun and spouse of God...Do not visit your relatives, they do not need your advice, nor you theirs...Let all your desire be for God.[25]

Of course, there are other texts and authors in the Christian tradition one could cite that are in opposition to the stern-minded attitude. For example, commenting on his grief at the death of his brother, Bernard of Clairvaux says to his religious community: "You, my sons, know how deep my sorrow is, how galling a wound it leaves."[26] And, addressing himself, he says: "Flow on, flow on, my tears...Let my tears gush forth like fountains."[27]

Reflecting on his own unwillingness to repudiate his great sorrow over his brother's death—his failure, that is, to follow Augustine's model—Bernard says,

> It is but human and necessary that we respond to our friends with feeling, that we be happy in their company, disappointed in their absence. Social intercourse, especially between friends, cannot be purposeless: the reluctance to part and the yearning for each other when separated indicate how meaningful their mutual love must be when they are together.[28]

And when he is addressing *his* relatives coming to visit him, rather than talking to a nun about her going to visit *her* relatives, Anselm himself says,

> In coming...you have lit a spark; you have blown it into flame; and in this flame you have fused my soul with yours. If you now leave me, our joint soul will be torn apart, it can never again become two...If you stay with [my soul], we will be more than blood-relations; we will be spiritual partners.[29]

So, when it comes to the stern-minded attitude, the Christian tradition is of two minds. Not all its influential figures accept it; and, even among those who do, many, such as Anselm, are double-minded about it.

Eckhart, however, can be counted among the stern-minded. So, for example, he says,

> If you want to be free of all affliction and suffering, hold fast to God, and turn wholly to him, and to no one else. Indeed, all your suffering comes from this, that you do not turn in God and to God and to no one else.[30]

And a bit later in the same work, he says,

> Seneca, a pagan philosopher, asks: 'What is the best consolation in sorrow and in misfortune?' And he says: 'It is for a man to accept everything as if he had wished for it and had asked for it'; for you would have wished for it, if you had known that everything happens by God's will, with his will and in his will.... [In] that alone, that it is God's will that it should happen so, a good man's will ought to be so wholly one and united with God's will that he and God have only one will, though that should be for the man's harm or even his damnation.... [A]ll his blessedness consists in...willing and wanting to know nothing but God's will.[31]

And there are many other such places that one could cite. Elsewhere, for example, Eckhart says,

> [T]hrow all anxiety out of your heart, so that in your heart there be nothing but constant joy.... [E]ven if I had to see with my own eyes my father and all my friends killed, my heart would not be moved by it.... I have rightful joy only when neither sufferings nor torments can ravish it from me. Then I am translated into the divine being where no suffering has a place.... If you reach a state where

you feel neither suffering nor vexation from whatever may happen, so that
suffering is not suffering for you and that all things are sheer joy for you, then
the child is truly born [that is, you have achieved spiritual regeneration].[32]

Or, to take one last example, which makes the point in a more radical way,
Eckhart says,

> it is not sufficient for us to have a detached attitude of mind at a specific point in
> time when we wish to bind God to ourselves, but rather we should have a
> practiced detachment...We must learn to free ourselves of ourselves..., not
> holding on to what is our own or seeking anything, either profit, pleasure,
> inwardness, sweetness, reward, heaven or our own will. God never gives himself,
> or ever has given himself, to a will that is alien to himself, but only to his own
> will... [T]he more we cease to be in our own will, the more truly we begin to be in
> God's will.... We must train ourselves in self-abandonment until we retain
> nothing of our own.... We should establish ourselves...in the best and most
> precious will of God through a pure ceasing-to-be of our will and desire.[33]

These passages and many others seem to me to make clear that Eckhart holds
the stern-minded attitude in a fairly radical way.

Aquinas, on the other hand, is not to be included among the stern-minded.
In one place after another, he demonstrates that his attitude differs sharply
from the stern-minded attitude. To take just one example, in explaining why
Christ told his disciples that he was going to God the Father in order to
comfort the disciples when they were sad at the prospect of being separated
from Christ, Aquinas says,

> It is common among friends to be less sad over the absence of a friend when the
> friend is going to something which exalts him. That is why the Lord gives them
> this reason [for his leaving] in order to console them.[34]

Unlike Teresa, who repudiates grief at the prospect of losing her father, in his
general reflection here (as in many other places) Aquinas is accepting the
appropriateness of a person's grief at the loss of a loved person and validating
the need for consolation for such grief. So Aquinas is not to be included with
the members of the stern-minded group, any more than Bernard is.[35] On
Aquinas's view, then, having desires of the heart is not something to be
stamped out; consequently, suffering is a right reaction to losing or failing to
get the desires of one's heart.

A SIMPLISTIC VIEW OF WILLING WHAT GOD WILLS

At this point, it is important to address one possible confusion. Since it is part
of orthodox Christian doctrine that everything that happens happens in

accordance with God's will, someone might object that the stern-minded attitude must be adopted by all Christians. In what sense could Teresa be united with God in will if she grieved over her father's death? How could she be united with God, as she explains she wants to be, if her will is frustrated in what is in accord with God's will?

But this objection is presupposing too simple an understanding of God's will and too simple an understanding of being in harmony with God's will.

To see why, assume that at death Teresa's father is united with God in heaven. Then the death of Teresa's father has opposite effects for Teresa and for God: it unites Teresa's father permanently with God, but it keeps Teresa from union with her father, at least for the remainder of Teresa's earthly life. For this reason, love's desire for union with the beloved cannot be fulfilled in the same way for a human person as for God. If Teresa's will is united with God's will in desiring union with her father, then Teresa's will must also be frustrated at the very event, her father's dying, which fulfills God's will with respect to this desire.

Something analogous can be said about the desire for the good of the beloved, which is also a desire of love. If Teresa desires the good of her father, she can only desire what her own mind sees as that good;[36] but, unlike God's mind, her mind's ability to see the good is obviously limited. To the extent to which Teresa's will is united with God's will in desiring the good of the beloved, then Teresa will also desire for the beloved person things different from those desired by God, in virtue of Teresa's differing ability to see the good for the beloved person.[37]

If Teresa were tranquil over any affliction that happened to her father, it would be because she thought that by this tranquility her will would be united to God's will in willing the good for her father. In this thought of hers, 'the good' would be used attributively, to designate *whatever* God thinks is good. But this cannot be the way 'the good' is used in any thought of God's, without relativizing the good entirely to God's will. If we eschew such relativism, then it is not the case that anything God desires is good just because God desires it. And so it is also not true that God desires as the good of a beloved person *whatever* it is that God desires for him. When God desires the good for someone, then, God desires it by desiring particular things as good for that person. Consequently, to say that God desires the good for a person is to use 'the good' referentially.

For this reason, when, in an effort to will what God wills, Teresa desires *whatever* happens to her father as the good for her father,[38] she thereby actually *fails* to will what God wills. The object of God's desire is not *whatever* God wills. It is rather a specific good for Teresa's father, which is known to God in his provident wisdom. Teresa's being united with God in willing the good for her father therefore requires Teresa's willing for her father particular things that are in fact the good for him, as far as she can recognize that good.

This position can lead to an apparently paradoxical condition. So, for example, in his great lament over the death of his brother, Bernard of Clairvaux is willing to affirm both his passionate grief over the loss of his brother and his acceptance of God's allowing that death. Bernard says:

> Shall I find fault with [God's] judgment because I wince from the pain?;[39] I have no wish to repudiate the decrees of God, nor do I question that judgment by which each of us has received his due...[40]

Bernard therefore grieves over this particular death as a bad thing, even while he accepts that God's allowing this bad thing is a good thing.

The apparent paradox here can be resolved by the distinction between God's antecedent and consequent will.[41] On this distinction, whatever happens in the world happens only because it is in accordance with God's will, but that will is God's *consequent* will. God's consequent will, however, is to be distinguished from his antecedent will; and many of the things that happen in the world are not in accordance with God's *antecedent* will. To try to be in accord with God's will by taking as acceptable, as unworthy of sorrow, everything that happens is to confuse the consequent will of God with the antecedent will. It is to accept as intrinsically good even those things that God wills as good only *secundum quid*—that is, as the best available in the circumstances. But God himself does not will as intrinsically good everything he wills; some things might be only instrumental goods. What God wills in his consequent will, what is the best available in the circumstances, might be only what is instrumentally good, not what is intrinsically good.[42]

And so to accept as good whatever happens on the grounds that it is God's will is the wrong way to try to be united with God. One can desire as intrinsically good what one's own mind takes to be intrinsically good in the circumstances, or one can desire[43] as intrinsically good whatever happens, on the grounds that it is God's will. But only the desire for what one's own mind takes to be intrinsically good can be in accordance with God's will. For the same reasons, only a desire of this sort is conducive to being in harmony with God's will.

Consequently, the stern-minded attitude is mistaken in supposing that willing what God wills requires willing just those very things that God wills. Although it appears paradoxical, the closest a human person may be able to come, in this life, to being in harmony with God's will may include her willing things (say, that a beloved person not die) that are opposed to God's (consequent) will.

AQUINAS ON WILLING WHAT GOD WILLS

This is the interpretation of willing what God wills that Aquinas, unlike Eckhart, holds and defends. Like Eckhart, Aquinas maintains that the goodness of the human will depends on its conformity to the divine will.[44] But, unlike Eckhart's, Aquinas's understanding of this conformity is very different from that of the stern-minded attitude.

As Aquinas considers the issue, one objection to the view that a person is morally bound to will what God wills is that a human person does not always know what God wills.[45] In response to this objection, Aquinas says,

> we know that whatever God wills, he wills it under the character of the good. Consequently, whoever wills a thing under any character of the good has a will conformed to the divine will, when it comes to the reason of the thing willed. But we do not know what God wills in particular: and in this respect we are not bound to conform our will to the divine will.[46]

In explaining this view as a response to the objection, Aquinas says,

> the will tends to its object according as it is proposed by reason . . . And therefore if a human being's will wills that a thing be, according as that thing appears [to that person] to be good, his will is good. . . . Now a thing may happen to be good under a particular character, and yet not good under a universal character . . . ; and therefore it can happen that a [person's] will is good in willing something with regard to a particular reason, even though that thing is something that God does not will considered with regard to a universal reason . . . [47]

Aquinas thinks that this distinction—between a thing willed with regard to a particular good and a thing willed with regard to the good all things considered, or universally considered—contains the answer to yet another objection to the thesis that a human will is good only if it is in conformity with God's will. That objection is based on the very sort of case at issue for Teresa of Avila in the example I gave above. Aquinas puts the objection this way:

> if a human being were to will what God wills, this would sometimes be contrary to filial piety: for instance, when God wills the death of a father. If his son were to will it also, it would be against filial piety.[48]

From Aquinas's point of view, the objection is right in supposing that it would be a violation of filial piety and so of moral goodness if a person were to will the death of her father. But, for Aquinas, the objection is confused in supposing that in order for a person to conform her will to God's will, she needs to will the death of her father if this is what God wills. On Aquinas's view, a person's will can be conformed to God's will even when her will and God's will are in opposition as regards the death of her father. To be in conformity with God's will, Aquinas holds, it is enough for a human person to will what she wills under the character of the particular good available to her intellect. To will something in this way is to will it as God wills, namely, out of love of the good, that is, out of charity.[49] And, for Aquinas, this *is* to will what God wills.[50]

For Aquinas, then, a person can will (under a particular character) the opposite of what God wills (under the universal character)—say, that her father not die—and still be in conformity with God's will, provided only that her will is informed by love of goodness, which is in fact love of God.

DENYING ONESELF

Someone in the grip of the stern-minded attitude might object, however, that there is a biblical injunction to take up one's cross daily, to be willing to deny oneself—in fact, to be willing to crucify oneself.[51] To the putative objector, willing what God wills requires denying oneself; and denying oneself requires giving up the desires of one's heart.

Such an objector thinks that denying oneself consists, in effect, in a person's refusing to let his own mind and his own will exercise their characteristic functions. That is because a person who attempts to see as good whatever happens, on the grounds that whatever happens is willed by God, is trying to suppress, or trying to fail to acquire, his own understanding of the good. And a person who attempts to will as good whatever happens, on the same grounds, is trying to suppress the desires his own will forms, or trying not to acquire the desires his will would have formed if he were not in the grip of the stern-minded attitude.

On this objection, Aquinas's view of willing what God wills has to be rejected in favor of Eckhart's.

Eckhart himself supports this interpretation of denying oneself, and he modulates it in a drastic way. He thinks that even the desire for willing what God wills has to be stamped out. He says,

> So long as a man has this particular wish to fulfill the ever beloved will of God...then this man still has a will with which he wants to satisfy God's will ...[A]s long as you have the will to fulfill God's will,...you are not poor [in spirit]; for he alone is a poor man who wills nothing and desires nothing.[52]

As these lines from Eckhart illustrate, to attempt to deny the self in the most severe stern-minded way is to try not to have a self at all.[53] In fact, this seems to be the end Eckhart is striving for. He says,

> You might ask 'When is the will a right will?' The will is perfect and right when it has no selfhood and when it has gone out of itself, having been taken up and transformed into the will of God.[54]

There is, however, a different interpretation of denying oneself. On this interpretation, it is possible to let one's own faculties of intellect and will have their normal functioning and still deny oneself. For Aquinas, the model for denying oneself, and in fact the model for all post-Fall reactions to suffering,[55] is given by Christ's prayer in the Garden of Gethsemane.

In that prayer, Christ prays that God would let the cup pass from him. It is evident that, in this part of his prayer, Christ is giving voice to his desire not to endure the crucifixion.[56] The intellect and will of Christ are opposed to his coming crucifixion as a bad thing. On the other hand, Christ finishes that prayer by saying to God "not my will but yours be done." In commenting on Christ's words, Aquinas holds that in this prayer Christ willed something different from what God willed, because Christ willed not to endure the coming suffering and death when God was willing that Christ do so. Nonetheless, Aquinas thinks, in willing not to be crucified, Christ's will was still in conformity with God's will because Christ also willed that God's will take precedence over his own: "not my will but yours be done."[57]

We can see Aquinas's point here by understanding Christ's will during his prayer in terms of the hierarchical structure of the will. On this understanding, Christ had a first-order desire not to die, but he also had a second-order desire for a will that willed what God willed as regards his crucifixion. His first-order desire was in opposition to God's (consequent) will. But his will was nonetheless in harmony with God's will, insofar as Christ had a second-order desire to will the good that God willed.

If, contrary to the story in the Gospels, Christ had let his first-order desire override his second-order desire, then his will would not have been in conformity with God's will. In that case, Christ's first-order desire not to die would have been the will on which he acted; and his second-order desire, that God's will take precedence over his own, would have remained ineffectual. While he would have desired to have a will that willed what God wills, the will that was effectual in him and on which he acted would have been his first-order desire, which was in opposition to what God wills.

In the case in the story as it actually is in the Gospels, however, Christ let his will be governed by his second-order desire that God's will be done. In the course of his praying, in the story it became clear to Christ that God's will then was that Christ be crucified. Given this recognition and the second-order desire for a will to will what God wills, Christ formed a first-order desire for the crucifixion. When Christ finished his prayer, he acted on that first-order desire; and so Christ acted in accordance with God's will. In the struggle with his first-order desire not to be crucified, Christ's second-order desire governed his will; and, for this reason, Christ's will was in conformity with God's will. This is so even though Christ continued to have a first-order desire not to be crucified. That first-order desire was present but ineffective to govern Christ's subsequent actions. Although Christ continued to want not to be crucified, that desire was not the one on which Christ acted.

As Aquinas sees it then, Christ finds not being crucified desirable, but he also sees doing what God wants as desirable, in fact as more desirable than doing what he himself wants. Christ's intellect and will are thus committed to the desirability of letting God's desires take precedence over Christ's own. In this rank-ordering of desires, Christ does not give up his desire not to be crucified; he just acts counter to it when he understands that his being crucified is God's will. He desires to desire something contrary to his desire not to be crucified since doing so is God's will.[58]

To act as Christ does, on Aquinas's interpretation of Christ's prayer, is to deny the self by first having a self to deny. Unlike the no-self position of Eckhart, this position is compatible with sorrow, and tears, for the things lost in the desires denied. Aquinas says that, in his prayer in the Garden of Gethsemane, Christ taught people both that they should will what God wills *and* that they can count as willing what God wills even when they desire something that God does not will.[59] On Aquinas's view, Christ's will is integrated around the good in his prayer in Gethsemane, even if he continues to have a desire not to be crucified, because Christ's second-order will, for a will that wills the good which God wills, governs his first-order desires. The will Christ acts on is the will he himself wants to have.

In fact, a little reflection shows that, contrary to first appearances, the no-self position is actually incompatible with the Christian injunction of self-denial. That is because one cannot crucify a self one does not have. To crucify one's self is to have desires and to be willing to act counter to them. C.S. Lewis, who is arguing for a similar position, puts the point this way:

> it would not be possible to live from moment to moment willing nothing but submission to God as such. What would be the material for the submission? It would seem self-contradictory to say 'What I will is to subject what I will to God's will,' for the second *what* has no content.[60]

A person Jerome in the grip of the stern-minded attitude cannot deny his self because he has constructed his desires in such a way that, *whatever* he wills, he does not will counter to his own desires. Even if Jerome has a second-order desire for whatever it may be that is God's will (that is, even if, *contra* Eckhart, Jerome is not trying to eradicate this very will to be in harmony with God's will), Jerome will nonetheless attempt to stamp out of himself any first-order desires which are in conflict with that second-order desire. He does not want to let God's desires take precedence over his own; he wants to have no desires in conflict with God's desires, whatever God's desires may be.

That is why (unlike the real Teresa, who was full of very human emotions) a person Jerome in the grip of Eckhart's stern-minded attitude would not weep if his father died. When Jerome is in the stern-minded attitude, *whatever* happens[61] is in accordance with Jerome's first-order desires and is therefore not a source of sorrow to him. In virtue of the fact that he has tried to extirpate from himself all desires except the one desire for whatever it may be that is God's will, Jerome has no desires that are frustrated by anything that happens;

he remains committed to willing whatever God wills, or even to having no will of his own of any sort, not even the will to will what God wills.

By contrast, a self-crucifying denier of the self, such as Christ in the story of the Gethsemane prayer, has first-order desires for things his own intellect finds good, so that he is vulnerable to grief in the frustration of those desires. But he prefers his grief and frustration to willing what is opposed to God's will. In this sense, he wills what God wills. When Christ says, "not my will but yours be done," he is not expressing the no-self position, because he is in effect admitting that there is in him "*my* will"; that is, he is admitting that he has desires in conflict with God's desires.[62] On the other hand, in virtue of willing to prefer his suffering to the violation of God's will, he is also willing that God's desires take precedence over his. This is the sense in which he is willing that God's will be done; and this is the sense in which his will is in harmony with God's.

To deny oneself in the Thomistic sense is therefore a matter of having first-order desires and being willing to act contrary to them. Or, put another way, it is a matter of being willing to suffer the contravening of one's will. A person in this state of will can appropriately be said to be denying himself or taking up his cross. Furthermore, on the Thomistic view of willing what God wills, a person can be integrated in will even when he has some divisions at the first-order level of the will, provided only that his second-order will for a will that wills what God wills determines which of his divided first-order desires he acts on. On this view of willing what God wills, a person can be integrated in will even with fragmentation in his first-order desires, provided that his second-order and first-order wills are in harmony.

By contrast, the stern-minded attitude seeks to eradicate all desires other than the desire for God's will (if it does not actually forbid even this desire). Consequently, it in effect refuses to have a self to deny. And so it is more aptly characterized as an extreme attempt to avoid suffering rather than as self-denial. It takes willing what God wills and being integrated in will to consist in having no will of one's own, in one sense or another.

THE IMPLICATIONS OF ECKHART'S POSITION

It is worth pausing to reflect further on the fact that Aquinas's view of willing what God wills yields an understanding different from Eckhart's with regard to the will's being integrated around the good.

For Eckhart, a person Jerome who wills what God wills has a second-order desire for a will that wills what God wills, but he has no first-order desires for any particular thing.[63] His whole will is animated and governed only by that second-order will of his. It forms his first-order will into an acceptance of anything that happens, after it happens. But antecedently Jerome has no first-order desires for anything concrete and individual.

In fact, as the quotations from Eckhart given above indicate, there are some texts of Eckhart's which suggest that even this summary is not quite right. In some places, it seems that, for Eckhart, Jerome will not even have a second-order will for a will that wills what God wills. If these texts represent Eckhart's view accurately, then we would have to say that for Eckhart a person who wills what God wills simply has no will at all, not at the first-order or the second-order level.

A person in this condition will certainly diminish his suffering. Suffering results from the loss of what we care about, either as regards our heart's desires or as regards our wellbeing. Consequently, a person who cares about nothing will not suffer. But, by the same token, she will not work either to diminish whatever suffering comes to her, or to use the suffering as a means to greater wellbeing than she might have had without the suffering. She will simply continue to try to will nothing with her own will in favor of trying to have (in one way or another) what she thinks of as the will of God.

But, on the theologically traditional claims accepted by both Eckhart and Aquinas, the good of suffering lies in its medicinal character. On this view, suffering is supposed to help heal the defect in the will that keeps a person from union with God or else to promote a greater union with God than the sufferer would otherwise have had.[64] A person whose will is not integrated around the good cannot have other persons close to him with the mutual closeness needed for union, and so he cannot be united with God either. If suffering can heal the will's inner fragmentation, then the benefit is worth the suffering, on this view.

The problem for Eckhart, however, is that the response which he advocates to the suffering that is meant to help cure the disease of the self is in fact destructive of the self. For that reason, it is also destructive of the very possibility for union with God. Union between persons requires that there be two wills to unite. This fact is precisely the reason why an internally fragmented post-Fall will needs healing. There cannot be union between God's will and a post-Fall human will when the internal divisions in the post-Fall will keep it from being *one* will. The post-Fall will needs to be integrated within itself in order to make union with God's will possible. But, for these very reasons, an attempt on the part of a human person to have no will at all, which is the state of psyche that Eckhart seems to be recommending in some texts, is a striving after a state that wards off union between God and human beings.

And even if, on Eckhart's views, there is in a person of grace a second-order will to will what God wills, the general point remains the same. In willing *nothing* other than a will to will what God wills, a person does not have a will in harmony with God's. God wills particular good things as good; God does not will simply that God's will be done. So in trying to have no will of his own even just at the first-order level, a person fails to will the good and so fails to will what God wills.

Finally, it is worth noting that if a person can be in the condition Eckhart recommends only by wanting to be in it, then the position becomes incoherent. In order to be in the condition of having no will of his own at either the first-order or the second-order level, a person would need a third-order desire for this state of his will—but, then, he is still having a will of his own.[65]

And so in virtue of attempting to stamp out all will, or at least all first-order will, in a human person, Eckhart's recommended position for a human will in the face of suffering makes the response to the medicine more deadly than the original disease that the medicine was meant to heal.

CONCLUSION

In Chapter 3, I argued that the Anselmian kind of interpretation of the doctrine of the atonement is unacceptable and unsalvageable. It rests in effect on a denial of God's nature as loving, on the best available account of divine and human love. Consequently, it also has a radically mistaken idea of the problem that the atonement is trying to solve. On the Anselmian interpretation, the role of the atonement is not to bring a person to a life in grace but rather to provide for God the preconditions necessary if God is to forgive any human person her sins and to accept reconciliation with her. But the purpose of the atonement is union in love between God and a human person; and that union consists in mutual indwelling between them, which is a life in grace for a human person. It is that condition for a human person that the atonement provides. And insofar as a life in grace is sufficient for union with God in heaven, then a person in grace is someone for whom the problem of the post-Fall human proneness to moral wrongdoing has been solved.

In this chapter, I have therefore taken as my starting point the Thomistic interpretation of the doctrine of the atonement, on which the role of the atonement is to bring a human person into a life in grace; and I have argued against one interpretation—Eckhart's or else an Eckhart-like interpretation—of what a life in grace is. Understanding the internal psychic state of a person in grace is a help to understanding the atonement, but in this chapter I have argued that the psychic state Eckhart recommends for life in grace is actually pernicious to the traditionally understood purpose of both suffering and atonement. Whatever the internal configuration is of a human person in a condition of mutual indwelling with God, it is not the self-destructive absence of desire urged by Eckhart. Aquinas's view that Christ's prayer in the Garden of Gethsemane is the model for such a state is much more promising.

With both these interpretative roads, that of Anselm and that of Eckhart, clearly marked as dead ends, I will now turn in Chapter 7 to explore in detail Aquinas's understanding of the psychic configuration of a person in grace. Once we see this psychic configuration, it will be easier to discern places in the process of coming to a life in grace where there is a role and a need for the atonement of Christ.

7

Life in Grace

INTRODUCTION

In Chapter 6, I presented two alternative interpretations of willing what God wills, Eckhart's and Aquinas's, and thus also two alternative approaches to a life in grace. A life in grace is the goal of the atonement, and so insight into the nature of the goal illuminates the means to that goal which is provided by the atonement. Eckhart and Aquinas have radically different understandings of this goal, however, and I argued that Eckhart's understanding should be rejected as inimical to the goal it seeks to implement. By way of contrast, I briefly presented Aquinas's own understanding of that goal and argued that it is preferable to Eckhart's. In this chapter, I want to elaborate on the conclusions of the last chapter by examining in detail Aquinas's account of a life in grace.

Here, as elsewhere in this work, I rely on the thought of Aquinas in sketching out the Christian position in question (in this case, the nature of a life in grace) because Aquinas's thought is the part of the Christian tradition that I consider the best (and know the best), and because Aquinas's account falls within the genus of interpretations of the atonement that I have argued for in Part I of this book. So, in this chapter, I will not discuss the history of interpretation about grace and life in grace; rather, I will just present Aquinas's account of it. This book is not meant to survey the history of theology; it is meant as an exercise in philosophical theology, and so it aims to engage in philosophical reflection on the doctrine rather than to illuminate the development and history of the doctrine.[1]

Not only will I omit a historical survey of the views of those thinkers influential in the history of Christian philosophical theology, but I will not argue for my interpretations of Aquinas either. For many (but not all) of the elements of Aquinas's thought at issue in this chapter, I have presented the evidence and argued the case for my interpretations of Aquinas's views elsewhere.[2] My intention to do philosophical theology, not history of philosophy or history of theology, extends also to the thought of Aquinas. In this chapter, I will use his work as he used the work of Aristotle: to learn from it and employ it where it seems to me helpful. I am, however, including some Thomistic metaphysics of a mildly complicated sort because, in my view, it illuminates brilliantly part of the process of justification and sanctification that is otherwise hard to see. The significant implications of that metaphysics will come into this chapter and more fully into Chapter 10. I am not wedded to this metaphysics, and in my view its implications for life in grace could remain true even if the metaphysics were rejected. But, in my view, even with its complexity, this Thomistic metaphysics is still the best way to show those implications; and the implications matter for interpretations of the doctrine of the atonement. So I am including them here.

In the preceding chapters, I have sketched the way in which moral wrongdoing leaves a person alienated from himself; and I have argued that such divisions in the self undermine or prevent closeness and union between persons, including union between a human person and God.[3] Because the human propensity to self-alienation has its source in a disposition to moral wrongdoing, Aquinas (in line with the Christian tradition before him) understands this propensity primarily as a defect in the will;[4] and he takes this defect to be part of the universal post-Fall human condition.[5] On Aquinas's view, all human beings have a sort of latent disease in the will. In the right circumstances, it blows up into moral monstrosity; in all circumstances, it eventuates sooner or later in moral wrongdoing of one sort or another.[6] The pure and innocent among human beings are no exception to this rule. If we think of this tendency in the will as an analogue to the HIV virus in the body, then the innocent are those in whom the virus has so far remained latent; they are not healthy so much as asymptomatic.

Generally and unreflectively, we judge ourselves and our species in a self-flattering light. Discussions of the problem of evil often focus on the many evils of the world—warfare, terrorism, oppression, poverty, racism, sexism, cruelty to beasts, destruction of the earth, and on and on in an interminable, depressing list of depredations against whatever is vulnerable—in order to raise questions about the existence of a perfectly good, omniscient, omnipotent God. But another thing to wonder at is the moral evil of human beings, who in all cultures and all ages can be so vicious to one another and so destructive of the good of the rest of creation. One daily news story after another holds a mirror up to us. The worst moral horrors of the most morally revulsive people among us show us what the sickness of post-Fall human beings is. Human beings are capable of self-sacrifice and moral heroism, such as that exemplified by Sojourner Truth or Harriet Tubman, for example. But human beings are also capable of the sickening cruelty and the callous rapacity that destroys other persons and devastates the earth and breaks our hearts to read about in any morning's news. The sickness in the will that all human beings suffer can be seen in those we excoriate as the monsters among us. It is a serious and deadly sickness, and its horror and power are not diminished by the fact that it does not reach its full-blown symptomatic state in everyone.

In fact, people not only will what is morally wrong; they cling tenaciously to the moral wrong they will. They not only fail to will the good; they also fail to will to will it. They lack—or, what is more nearly true, they reject—a will for integration around the morally good. It is a trusting theological optimism on Aquinas's part to maintain that it is not possible for any human being to be totally integrated around what is evil.[7] His view that human evil only fragments a human psyche and leaves it alienated from its self, its best self, honors human beings. On his account, unlike that of some contemporary philosophers,[8] there is a limit to how evil human beings can be, even if that limit includes within its boundaries a very great deal.

If, as Aquinas thinks, this is a right description of the human condition,[9] then the problem the atonement is meant to solve is highlighted. All human beings in the post-Fall condition lack internal integration to some degree. They lack it not in the way in which a person lacks a limb, by some accident external to the will, but in the way in which a miserable person lacks a reform in his self-destructive habits, by a resistance to such integration on the part of a person's own internally divided will.

Alleviating such psychic fragmentation stemming from the post-Fall human propensity to moral evil is necessary for real love and union.[10] But it is not sufficient because shame also fragments a person, and shame is not the same as guilt. Nonetheless, since the issues surrounding shame are complicated and require extensive treatment, I will reserve further discussion of the problem of shame to Chapter 10. In this chapter, I will confine myself to presenting Aquinas's account of sanctification and justification, which he takes to be the remedy for the psychic fragmentation whose source is the human propensity to evil. The remedy for this part of the problem caused by the human inclination to moral evil is a remedy for guilt.[11] With guilt (and shame) remedied, the ever-present powerful love of God can find its fruition in union with a human person.

In this chapter, the union at issue is the incipient union between God and human beings in this life. On Christian theology, whatever exactly it is, complete and full union between God and human beings is found only in heaven. But a beginning degree of that union is not only possible in this life; it is required for a life in grace.[12]

What is needed to establish this nascent union is frustratingly complicated to describe. On the face of it, the remedy for post-Fall fragmentation seems simple because it is a problem in the will: nothing more is required than a person's willing in a certain way. Repairing a problem in one's will, unlike fixing a problem in one's leg or one's liver, requires only an act of will. What could be easier than a remedy that one has as soon as one wills to have it?

But, in fact, the truth is just the other way around. When the problem is in the will, the problem is, in one sense, insuperable. If a person has a bodily part that fails to function optimally, she can choose to do certain things about it. She can choose to take medicine or to have surgery, for example. Alternatively, if she is not able to make such choices, say because she is unconscious, then someone competent, a doctor, for example, can simply choose these things for her, on her behalf. When the problem is in the will, however, neither of these approaches will be successful.

If a person could effectively choose of her own accord to be integrated in will, she would already be integrated around some good, or on her way to that state. That is precisely why she could choose the good of integration effectively. But her lack of internal integration is just her unwillingness to unify herself in will. She is not internally integrated in will because she does not *want* to be. So if the remedy consists in her willing wholeheartedly to be integrated around the good, the remedy is available to her only when the defect it is meant to remove is already gone. The defect in the will is such that it could be fixed by the person who has it only if she did not have the defect.

On the other hand, no one else can fix her will for her either, not even God. To the extent to which God fixes her will, he wills for her a certain state of her will. But, then, to that extent, what is in her is God's will, not her own. If the lack of internal integration in her will is an obstacle to God's being close to her, God's determination of her will is an even greater obstacle. As I argued in Chapter 6 in rejecting Eckhart's position regarding life in grace, mutual closeness of the sort required for union depends on a harmony between two different wills. But if God determines a person's will, then the only will that operates in her is God's will. In that case, there will not be two wills to bring into union with each other. There will be only one will, God's will, which is in her as well as in God. Union between her will and God's will is not established by such means; it is obviated or destroyed.

How, then, is the problem in the will to be remedied? On the standard Christian answer to this question, which Aquinas inherits and develops,[13] the solution to the internal alienation resulting from the human propensity to moral wrongdoing[14] depends on the paired processes of justification and sanctification.[15]

SANCTIFICATION

It will be helpful to examine these processes in the reverse of the order in which Aquinas supposed them to occur. So consider that part of the life in grace that is sanctification.

As Aquinas sees it, God is always willing to aid the will of any person Paula who wants God to strengthen her in her willing of the good. Even if Paula's will is not strong enough to bring her first-order desires under the control of her good second-order desires, her will is strong enough to enable her to form the first-order volition to ask God to strengthen her will; and if she does so, God will give her the strength of will she wants and needs. This grace[16] that God bestows on the will of a person Paula in response to Paula's higher-order desire that God do so is *cooperative* grace,[17] because in giving it God is cooperating with Paula's own higher-order desires.

Suppose, for example, that Paula wants to become a vegetarian but finds it very difficult to give up meat. She finds eating meat morally objectionable, and so she has a higher-order desire for a will that wills not to eat meat; she has a corresponding first-order desire not to eat meat, too. But because she is habituated to eating meat, she also has a first-order desire to eat meat; and that is the desire on which she often enough acts, to her own moral consternation. Her will commands itself to will some good to which she is committed; but her will nonetheless does not will the thing it has commanded. On the theological view Aquinas accepts, if in this condition Paula asks God for help, then God will aid Paula's will so that Paula has the strength of will to will what she herself wants to will, namely, not eating meat.

If God were simply to produce a first-order volition[18] in Paula without responding to anything in Paula in doing so, then God would be violating Paula's free will, since (as Aquinas thinks) if a person's volition is produced only as a direct result of the exercise of efficient causality on the part of something external to the will, the volition caused in this way is not free.[19] But if God brings about a volition in Paula in response to Paula's second-order desire that God do so, then in helping Paula to integrate her first-order and second-order desires God does not undermine Paula's free will. Instead, he enhances or evokes it.[20] That is because it is ultimately Paula's own will which brings it about that she has the first-order volition she does, not in the sense that it is the strength or even the agency of Paula's will that produces the desired first-order volition in her, but rather in the sense that unless Paula had desired that God do so, God would not have acted on her will in this way. If Paula's second-order will had been different, her first-order volition would have been different also. When God gives Paula cooperative grace, then, God works on Paula's will to enable Paula to have the will she herself wants to have.

Furthermore, if God simply altered Paula's volitions without being responsive to Paula's own state of will, then the resulting volition in Paula would be God's and not Paula's. God's acting on Paula's will in that way would replace her will with God's will. On Aquinas's view, that is something which God, who does not undermine the nature of his creatures, would not do.[21] But if God strengthens in Paula the will Paula wants to have, then the ultimate source of the condition of Paula's will is not God, but Paula. In aiding Paula's will in this cooperative way in the process of sanctification, God is therefore not taking her will away from her. Rather, he is making her will more her own; he is providing its freedom,[22] in virtue of enabling Paula successfully to will what she herself wants to will.

For these reasons, if Paula petitions God for help in her struggle with her divided self, God can help to effect the changes Paula wants in her will, so that she is enabled to bring her first-order desires into accord with her own second-order desires. By this means, Paula will make progress in integrating her will around the good. If only it is not interrupted but continued to its final conclusion, this process of sanctification will eventually culminate in a state of complete moral goodness in Paula.

Someone might suppose that if this Thomistic account of sanctification were right, then, with one act of higher-order will, a human person could achieve, all at once, a full integration of her will around moral goodness. She would just need to desire that God unify her will in this way. But this supposition fails to take account of the reality of human psychology. Sanctification is generally a lengthy process just because, typically, a human person's will for the good is limited and intermittent, as everyone who has ever tried to reform a bad habit is aware. In such circumstances, if God were to give her a will wholly integrated around the good, he would be violating her will, because he would be giving her a will that she does not want, at least not at that time in that respect. Although sudden wholesale changes in the organizational structure of a person's will are in principle possible,[23] they are rare and subject to back-sliding. And so, ordinarily, the path to full internal integration is slow.

Typically, a person's higher-order volition for some particular good first-order volition and her desire for God's aid in strengthening her in that first-order volition will result in some integration in her will. As her higher-order desires become effective in their command of her first-order desires, as her will becomes more unified, she will be in a position to form further higher-order desires that continue her will's integration around the good. In consequence, God can also give her more aid to strengthen her will still more in willing the good that she increasingly wants to will; and this strengthening of her will in turn enables her to desire yet more cooperative giving of grace, and so on.[24] Those people we admire greatly for their wholeheartedness and moral excellence grew into the characters for which they are admired. They were not born with them, and they did not get them all at once.[25]

Sanctification therefore generally takes time. On the traditional theological doctrine that Aquinas accepts, if the process of sanctification is brought to completion at all, that completion occurs only in the afterlife.

JUSTIFICATION

Sanctification not only involves a higher-order desire for a will that wills some particular good thing, but it also presupposes a general higher-order desire as well.[26] That is because a person in the process of sanctification must have a higher-order desire for a will that wills the good. Paula's second-order desire for a first-order desire not to eat meat, for example, is predicated not only on her desires as regards her own contribution to the ethical treatment of animals but also on her general higher-order volition to be an ethical person. She cares about the sort of person she is. She does not just live in a helpless state of disapproving of herself. Rather, her care about what kind of person she is sometimes at least is translated into action. She wills that her will and character be such that she herself can approve them as good, and at least sometimes her will obeys its own higher-order command. So, in the process of sanctification, all the more localized higher-order desires of the person being sanctified are predicated on an enduring global second-order volition for a will that wills the good. But where does this global higher-order volition come from?

The answer to this question is contained in the complicated doctrine of justification, which is the technical theological term for moral and spiritual regeneration.[27] Although such regeneration is a theological matter for Aquinas, the phenomenon itself is common and commonly recognized, as our familiarity with the practices of Alcoholics Anonymous, for example, testifies. Talking about the recovery from alcoholism as AA understands it, which is a particular kind of moral and spiritual regeneration, Norman Care says,

> There are cases in which a person has apparently altered his or her character and other cases in which, despite strenuous effort, change was not realized... so that whether one can change remains unsettled. I do not mean to suggest that parts of character are determined in any sense that is interesting for philosophy. I mean rather, and simply, that there are aspects of character that are so salient in one's makeup, so fixed as a matter of practical fact, that the prospect of changing them (at any rate, to the person involved) is tantamount to the prospect of changing one's identity at the deepest level.[28]

This change at the deepest level is a kind of rebirth, as Care's terminology about changing one's identity expresses.

Speaking of the pain afflicting those who have not experienced such regeneration, Care says,

> when my past is seen to be flawed (it contains wrongdoing by me) and amends are not feasible (in some cases not even possible), peace of mind is pushed out of reach.... It may be that some people are able to meet the conditions of the backward-looking index of peace of mind... [But] when the [backward-looking] index is misused, people may be left without peace of mind insofar as their lives

come to be flawed via contingencies grounded in factors over which their control [as the kind of persons they are] was nil or controversial. In certain cases a person may suffer a deep loss of peace of mind involving the pain not only of bad feeling over particular actions but also of distress over the kind of person he or she apparently is. In such cases the problems of recovery, of going on with one's life, can be formidable.[29]

In a description that could, in my view, fit any human life, Care says about people who are alcoholics and in such an unregenerate condition,

the lives of many of us simply turn out ... to have in them very problematic parts whose survey we are unable to bear; and then, insofar as our lives contain these problematic parts, we are left with the worry and suspicion that we do not fit the conceptions of ourselves by which we mean to govern ourselves .... [T]he human condition is such that many of us are or will be condemned by our pasts to be without peace of mind.[30]

The change of practical or psychological identity[31] which alters the elements of character that a person had previously felt helpless to reform or had not cared to reform is the regeneration that justification initiates, on Aquinas's account of justification.

We can begin unraveling the complications of the theological understanding of regeneration in justification by considering briefly the nature of faith and its role in justification. On Aquinas's views, a person's moral and spiritual regeneration begins with faith on her part. Faith is the means to the rescue of a person from her own propensity to moral wrong and from the inner loneliness to which it gives rise. And a person is justified by faith alone,[32] in the sense that the whole process of sanctification will reach its ultimate conclusion in heaven provided only that she has faith and continues in faith.[33] Faith is therefore the necessary and sufficient condition for salvation from sin and for the attainment of shared union with God.

The crucial element of faith for Aquinas is a state of will in which a person in the kind of condition Care describes, sick of his own evil and pained by it, longs for goodness and ceases resisting God's help to get it. For Aquinas, when, through God's grace, faith is formed in a person who has surrendered resistance to God, that faith includes an act of will in which he hates the evil in himself, yearns for the goodness that is God's, and accepts God's grace.[34] This is an act of will that consists in a higher-order desire for a will that does not will evil but wills the good instead. In the desire for the goodness that is God's, it also includes a willingness to accept God's help, to one degree or another, in making that sort of goodness one's own. For these reasons, this act of will depends on a person's recognition of his propensity to wrongdoing and his past wrong actions and on his acceptance of God's love and forgiveness even so.[35]

The will of faith is therefore the global second-order will to have, through God's help, a will that wills the good, universally understood. The formation of this will of faith in a person is his justification. This act of will and perseverance in it are necessary and sufficient for a life in grace.

Because of Aquinas's commitment to a tight interconnection between the faculties of intellect and will,[36] on his account a person's act of will in faith is necessarily accompanied by certain states of intellect, which may, for example, include a person's belief (however tacit and unacknowledged it may be) that God will give her help if she does not refuse it. In faith, a person has the belief (in whatever particular terms she frames it) that God will instill into her psyche what is needed for goodness if only she does not resist God's doing so. But I mention the matter of the state of the intellect only to set it to one side. For my purposes in this chapter, the salient thing is the condition of the will in justification.[37]

Finally, it is important to add here that the global second-order will of faith that justifies a person is compatible with any amount of first-order willing and even second-order willing of particular evils, provided that that willing does not destroy the second-order desire of faith. It is possible, in other words, for Paula to have a second-order desire for a will that wills the good and also for Paula to reject a particular reform that she sees as morally needed but that she finds herself unable to accept at a particular time. So, for example, she might have the will of faith and she might believe that becoming vegetarian is morally obligatory for being a good person; but she might also have a second-order will for a will to eat meat, on the grounds that the reform would be too strenuous for her at this time, given the current stress in her life—and so on, with depressing familiarity. This condition is, of course, one way of being divided against oneself.

By itself, then, justification only begins the process of integration around the good; it does not complete it. Paula's forming the justifying global second-order desire for a will that wills the good starts the process of moral and spiritual regeneration for Paula, but sanctification is the process that completes it. In sanctification, God works together with Paula's enduring global second-order will of faith in a cooperative enterprise that gradually integrates Paula in goodness. And so Aquinas thinks that a person's justification is inevitably followed by her sanctification if only she perseveres in the global second-order will of the act of faith. That is because Aquinas believes that God loves all human persons; and so, on Aquinas's account of love, God desires the good for every human person and desires to draw every person to union with God. As long as Paula does not resist God's help or reject God's grace, God's desires of love for Paula will be efficacious and will produce increasing goodness in Paula. For this reason, as long as Paula has a second-order will for a will that wills the good, through sanctification she will eventually have what she herself wants, namely, a will entirely integrated in goodness.[38]

For justification as for sanctification, the higher-order desire of the will of a person in the process is a desire for a desire for what is good—and so it is also a desire for God.[39] Because Aquinas sees goodness as God's nature under a certain description, on Aquinas's views a person who longs for God's goodness is a person who longs for God.[40] Like the higher-order will in sanctification, the second-order will of justification is thus one of the desires of love of God, namely, the second desire of love that seeks union with the beloved,[41] and so this second desire of love is included in the act of will essential to faith. It is a desire for a person, where the person is God. Justification can therefore also be thought of as the beginning of love of God. That is why in his commentary on Romans 4:3,[42] Aquinas wholeheartedly endorses Paul's reading of the line about Abraham in Genesis (15:5): Abraham believed God, and God counted it to him as righteousness.[43] The love of God and God's goodness expressed in Abraham's believing God is an incipient union with God and therefore also an incipient righteousness in Abraham.

Since God is perfectly loving and always present[44] to every human person, the only thing missing for mutual closeness between God and a human person is on the side of the human person. Sanctification and justification are the two parts of the process that provide what is missing, namely, a person's coming to love God and then growing in love for God. For this reason, justification and sanctification not only integrate a person around the good and thereby unite her with herself, they also unite her, in ever-increasing degree, with God in love.

GRACE AND FREE WILL

Given this necessarily brief exposition of the theological doctrines of justification and sanctification, we can profitably return to the question I raised above: Where does justification's higher-order desire for a will that wills the good come from? How does it originate?

We might suppose that it originates, like any other desire, in the will of the person who forms that desire. But from Augustine's time onward, for philosophical and theological reasons, the tradition of thought Aquinas inherited rejected this answer. It is not possible to review that history in passing here, but the basic idea behind it is not hard to understand. If what needs to be explained is the ultimate origin of a moral and spiritual rebirth, then it is hard to see how it could be explained as a function of the will of the person whose moral and spiritual regeneration it is. As I explained above, any will that wants to will the good is already in the process of such regeneration.

The impetus for regeneration therefore has to come from without. But, for the same reason, there can be no question of *cooperative* grace in justification. God can cooperate with a human person's will in the process of sanctification because God's grace can work together with the good higher-order desire that is already present in the will of the human person being sanctified. The very beginning of moral regeneration, however, is the point at which the will first forms the global higher-order desire for a will that wills the good. The formation of that higher-order desire in the will cannot be the result of cooperation between God and a higher-order desire in the human will, because the thing whose origin needs to be explained is precisely *that* higher-order desire in the human will.

It is Aquinas's position, which he inherits from Christian tradition long established by his time, that a human person's global second-order desire for a will that wills the good is both free and also produced in her by God's action on her will. The grace that produces the will of faith is *operative*, on his views, not cooperative; and yet the will of faith is also a free act of will on the human person's part.[45] To understand why Aquinas thinks that the will of faith can be free and yet also produced in a person by God, it helps to look very briefly in more detail at Aquinas's account of the will.

As Aquinas sees it, before the beginning of the regeneration that is justification, a person Paula has a resistance to forming the second-order desire in which she repudiates her own evil and desires God and God's goodness, although the providence of God works in ways intended to shepherd her towards giving up that resistance. If, in consequence of that shepherding, Paula gives up her resistance and her will becomes quiescent, then at that point God puts operating grace into her will. Because of that divinely given grace, Paula's will forms the global higher-order desire that is the will of faith.

According to Aquinas, then, before the beginning of Paula's moral and spiritual regeneration, abstractly considered there are three possibilities for her will as regards the justifying act of will of faith.

(1) The will can detest its past wrongdoing and love God's goodness. (Call this 'an acceptance of grace.')

(2) The will can cleave to its past wrongdoing and reject God's goodness. (Call this 'a refusal of grace.')

(3) The will can simply be turned off as regards its past wrongdoing and God's goodness. (Call this 'the quiescence of the will as regards grace.')[46]

On Aquinas's account of the will, then, the will can accept God's grace or reject it, but the will can also just be inactive or turned off.[47] On this third possibility, when the will is quiescent, it does not refuse grace, but it does not accept it either.

Furthermore, in theory, the will can move directly from any one of these positions to the other.[48] That is, the will can move from rejecting to quiescence, from quiescence to assenting, from assenting to rejecting, and so on. The will's motion is thus analogous to bodily motion. Paula can walk east, or Paula can walk west; but Paula can also simply cease walking east. Paula's ceasing to walk east is not by itself an instance of her walking west. Further-more, Paula can move from walking east to ceasing to walk east without having to walk west in order to do so. Finally, Paula's ceasing to walk east is not a special kind of walking; it is simply the absence of walking, an inactivity or quiescence in those particular bodily parts that function to produce walk-ing. The will's ability to be quiescent is like this, and the notion that the will can be quiescent in this way is an important part of Aquinas's account of justification.

As Aquinas understands justification by faith, an adult human person Jerome who is fully functional mentally but lacks faith has a will that refuses grace, however tacitly or subconsciously,[49] until at some moment, in surrender to God, that refusal gives way to a state of quiescence in the will as regards God's grace.[50] When and only when Jerome's will is quiescent in this way, God infuses grace into Jerome's will.[51] With this infusion of grace into the will, Jerome forms the global higher-order state of will that detests his own past wrongdoing and desires the goodness of God. In effect, this is a desire for a will that wills the goodness of God, and so it is also a desire for God. Consequently, it is the beginning of Jerome's love of God.

On Aquinas's views, this higher-order desire is necessary and sufficient for salvation.[52] That is, this desire and the correlative intellective states count as justifying faith; and, as long as that faith continues in a person, it is followed by his sanctification, whose ultimate end is his complete internal integration in the good and his complete union with God.

Aquinas does not discuss the subjective phenomenology of the psyche of a person who comes to a state of quiescence in the will with regard to grace. But it is not hard to find an analogy to illustrate the idea. Suppose, for example, that Jerome is suffering a dangerous allergic reaction to a bee sting and rightly fears death because of that reaction, but suppose also that Jerome nonetheless vigorously refuses his doctor's attempt to inject him with the urgently needed antidote because he has an almost ungovernable fear of needles. Jerome might not be able to bring himself to will that the doctor give him the much-needed injection. That is, if the doctor were to ask Jerome whether he is willing to accept the injection, Jerome might not be able to bring himself to say 'yes.' But Jerome might nonetheless be able to stop actively refusing the injection, knowing that if he ceases to refuse it, the doctor will press it on him. If Jerome stops actively refusing the injection, then his will becomes quiescent with regard to the injection, neither accepting it nor refusing it, but simply being turned off in relation to the injection.

A person Paula whose will is quiescent with respect to grace is in an analogous condition, on Aquinas's account. When God gives Paula the grace of justifying faith while her will is quiescent, God is infusing that grace into Paula's will when it has ceased to reject grace but has not yet accepted it either. In this condition, Paula's will is just inactive. But the inactivity is a surrender, not a mere calm or indifference, because in moving into that quiescence Paula feels her quiescence as a letting go of resistance to God and God's grace, just as the bee-sting victim understands his quiescence as a letting go of resistance to the injection he fears.

On this interpretation of Aquinas's explanation of justification, the will of faith is brought about in Paula by God; but Paula is still ultimately in control of her will, because it is up to Paula either to refuse grace or to fail to refuse grace, and God's giving of grace depends on the state of Paula's will.[53] Because ultimate control over the state of Paula's will is thus vested in Paula, Aquinas's explanation can give an answer to a question Augustine wrestled with unsuccessfully, namely, why God does not cause the justifying act of will in everyone.[54] For Aquinas, whether or not God causes the justifying act of will in Paula is dependent on whether or not Paula's will has ceased to reject grace, and that is something for which Paula is ultimately responsible. Furthermore, since Paula not only is ultimately responsible for her state of will but also has alternative possibilities with regard to willing,[55] it does seem right to hold, as Aquinas does, that the justifying act of will is a free act, even in a libertarian sense of 'free', although it is in fact produced in Paula by God.

Although Paula is in control of her will and responsible for it in this way, it is worth noticing that Paula manifests this control not by activity of one sort or another but rather by the abandonment of activity. Surrender of resistance and quiescence of the will are the start of the moral and spiritual regeneration required for internal integration, and for all the things for which internal integration is necessary, including especially love.

In this connection, it is important to see that surrender is not the same as submission. For Jerome to submit to another person Paula is for Jerome to desire that something be done or that something be the case just because Jerome believes that Paula desires that Jerome desire *this*, even when Jerome himself would not desire *this* or would even desire the opposite of *this* if it were not for Jerome's fear of what Paula would do if Jerome did not desire what Paula wants him to desire. It is certainly possible for Jerome to submit to Paula in this way while Jerome helplessly hates Paula. By contrast, in the sense of surrender at issue here, for Jerome to surrender to Paula is for Jerome to let go of resistance to loving *Paula*. And when he does, his surrender eventuates in his desiring her and desiring union with her.[56]

On this way of thinking about the difference between submission and surrender, one can submit to someone without surrendering to her, and one can surrender to someone without submitting to her. In consequence of his surrender to Paula, Jerome could desire Paula and union with Paula without thereby desiring *that* something-or-other be the case or be done just because he knows that Paula desires that he desire this. Jerome might in fact desire what Paula desires, but only because he himself desires it as good, and not for the reason that Paula desires that he desire this. On the other hand, Jerome might desire Paula but actually not desire what Paula desires; he might instead desire that Paula change *her* desires to bring them into harmony with what *he* desires.[57]

So, surrender is not to be confused with submission.[58] In fact, Aquinas takes submission as I have understood it here as a kind of servility, and he sees servility as incompatible with love of any kind, including love of God. He says,

> Servitude is the opposite of freedom. A free human being acts of his own accord [*cause sui est*] ..., but a slave is a human being who is moved by another in doing what he does, rather than acting of his own accord. But anyone who does something out of love for it acts of his own accord, as it were, because he is moved to act by an inclination which is his own. And so it is incompatible with the notion of servility that anyone acts out of love.[59]

The surrender at issue in spiritual and moral regeneration is therefore not submission; and, as I have explained it here, surrender is not only compatible with freedom, it in fact requires it.

ARISTOTELIANISM, PELAGIANISM, AND A SIDE-NOTE ON ALCOHOLICS ANONYMOUS

Justification is the necessary and sufficient condition for salvation and so also for a life in grace, on Aquinas's account; and it is followed by sanctification in all people who live past the first moments of justification, so that the process of sanctification is also part of life in grace. A life in grace is a morally excellent life, and so a discussion of a life in grace presupposes a certain ethics. As I explained in Chapter 1, for my purposes in this book I will rely on Aquinas's philosophical theology as background; and so I will also take Aquinas's theologically based ethics as the context here.

It has become a commonplace among scholars to see Aquinas as Aristotelian in his ethics,[60] and there is some reason for it. Aquinas's ethics is a virtue ethics, centered around a list of the virtues that includes virtues that, at least on the surface, appear to be identical to those on Aristotle's list: wisdom, justice, courage, and temperance. On the Aristotelian ethics that many scholars suppose Aquinas accepts, a moral virtue is a habit which is acquired through practice and which disposes the will to act in accordance with reason in varying circumstances. But the description of Aquinas's account of justification and sanctification given above makes clear that the interpretation of Aquinas as Aristotelian in his ethics cannot be right.

In fact, although Aquinas recognizes the Aristotelian virtues, he thinks that they are not real virtues. He himself affirms Augustine's definition of a virtue:

A virtue is a good quality of the mind by which one lives righteously, of which no one can make bad use, and which God works in us without us.[61]

This is manifestly an un-Aristotelian definition, not least because it is impossible to acquire for oneself by practice a disposition that God works in a person without that person. Commenting on the Augustinian definition of virtue, which takes a virtue to be infused into a person by God, Aquinas says,

This definition comprises perfectly the whole formula of virtue.[62]

Aquinas recognizes that the Aristotelian virtues, acquired through practice of the acts correlated with a virtue, do not fit this definition because of its last clause: "which God works in us without us." He says,

acquired virtue, to which these words do not apply, is not of the same species as infused virtue.[63]

And so acquired virtues are not habits that contain, as Aquinas says, the whole formula of virtue, as the infused virtues do. In addition, Aquinas accepts a unity of the virtues thesis, but only for the real virtues, the ones infused by God, and not for the Aristotelian or acquired virtues.[64]

Aquinas is therefore not an Aristotelian in ethics. He is not a Pelagian either.[65] Roughly construed, Pelagianism is the thesis that there can be some good in a human will that is not provided directly or indirectly by God's grace. The rejection of Pelagianism therefore includes the view that God's help, God's grace infused into a person (though without in any way precluding the freedom of that person's will), is necessary for a person's moral goodness. She cannot produce it in herself by herself.

Because the scholastic prose in which the anti-Pelagianism of Aquinas's account is described is bloodless, it may help in understanding this part of Aquinas's account to look at an analogous anti-Pelagianism provided through the lens of Alcoholics Anonymous (AA). Defending AA's as-it-were anti-Pelagianism, Norman Care argues that there are fixed elements of character which a person cannot alter in herself without undergoing a change in her deep identity. He puts the anti-Pelagian point this way:

some elements of personality or character may be fixed...People may thus be stuck with elements of character that they cannot budge (even despite strenuous effort).... [P]eople may be powerless over themselves in certain respects.... [O]ur psyches are fragile in ways that show up in our failings to meet the sometimes interestingly different and sometimes conflicting terms of how persons are given by the variety of conceptions associated with the practices (including moral practices), institutions, ideologies, and general theories that structure our common life; and...these failings are sometimes traceable to fixed elements in personality or character, that is, elements over which our control is nil or controversial.[66]

As Care sees it, on this secular analogue to anti-Pelagianism,

> Some, perhaps many, of us suffer constitution-affecting luck that places us outside the mainstream model of the in-control agent to some degree or other, for one period of time or other ... What is meant here by saying that inclination, capacity, and temperament are matters of luck is .... that these elements of the self ... are the 'built-ins' of my nature. [footnote omitted] As such, they are ... considered to be logically prior to the power of my will as expressed in my choices. These luck factors ... form, in a phrase I borrow from Harry G. Frankfurt, 'necessities of the will.'[67]

On Care's analogue to anti-Pelagianism, the elements of character bequeathed a person by constitutional luck are "not present to one's will as an item to be challenged and overcome; ... [they are] instead in one's will and ... structure one's moral-emotional psychology ab initio."[68]

For Care, for Aquinas, and for all resolutely anti-Pelagian views, then, the principle that *ought* implies *can* is false. A human person ought to will only good, but an unaided post-Fall human will is unable to form even the first volition of moral regeneration, the will for a will that wills the good, not because something external to the will forbids it, but because the will itself resists it.

On Aquinas's optimistic view of human life, however, there is a principle which is similar to the false principle that *ought* implies *can* and which is not false but true: *ought* implies *can-with-help*. This principle is not a self-help principle, or a semi-Pelagian principle that attributes to a post-Fall person the ability to will the beginning of her own moral regeneration. Rather, the help in question on Aquinas's view is God's aid to the will enabling it to accept God's love and grace. All that is required of a human person to enable that aid to flow to her is that she cease resisting it, in a move that is not an act of will at all but only a surrender, a ceasing of an act of will of resistance.

It may help here to notice that the famous Twelve Steps, and Twelve Promises, of AA have a similar view. Care's moving and painfully honest description of his own experiences with alcoholism and AA makes the point. Care describes an alcoholic life this way:

> The characterization of its phenomenology requires not the terminology of disease or genetics, but ... such heavy moral-psychological words as isolation, despair, worthlessness, and the classic triad anger, resentment, and fear, as well as the negative staples of guilt, shame, regret, and remorse. This is the condition ... [the alcoholic] is in and from which the AA program proposes the possibility of relief.[69]

And Care comments,

> AA recognizes what friends, family, and well-wishers may not be able to recognize, that recovery in such a case is not simple, quick, or easy ...[70]

The first two of the Twelve Steps are generally well-known. As Care quotes them, they are these:

> (1) We admitted we were powerless over alcohol—that our lives had become unmanageable.
> (2) Came to believe that a Power greater than ourselves could restore us to sanity.[71]

Commenting on the beginning of the process of regeneration promised by AA, Care says,

> No one gains the sobriety-cum-serenity... [an alcoholic] seeks just by learning and knowing the Twelve Steps.... Step 1 is in effect a surrender of sorts.[72]

The Twelve Promises of AA are less well-known, but they are worth mentioning in this connection too. In the interest of brevity here, I list only three of them, the first and the fourth and the last, as Care quotes them:

> (1) We are going to know a new freedom and a new happiness....
> (4) We will know peace....
> (12) We will suddenly realize that God is doing for us what we could not do for ourselves.[73]

In this connection, it is helpful to consider the description given by the founder of AA, Bill Wilson, of life before the surrender that begins the process of recovery. (I take it as quoted by Care.) In my view, Wilson's words give a kind of insight into the whole human condition. Although Wilson's description of the life before surrender is meant to single out the life of an alcoholic as specially painful, something like this pain and this moral bankruptcy afflicts all human beings in the post-Fall human condition, on the views shared by Aquinas with the rest of the Christian tradition. And the hope promised not to a person who is a cured alcoholic but rather to a person who will live his whole life as a recovering alcoholic is relevantly similar to the hope promised to a person who will live his whole life in grace as both faithful and repentant.

Wilson says about the alcoholic before the surrender that begins recovery,

> No other kind of bankruptcy is like this one. Alcohol, now become the rapacious creditor, bleeds us of all self-sufficiency and all will to resist its demands. Once this stark fact is accepted, our bankruptcy as going human concerns is complete.[74]

And this is what Wilson says about the alcoholic in recovery, in his comment on the last of the Twelve Steps, which says that "God is doing for us what we could not do for ourselves":

> Our Twelfth Step... says that as a result of practicing all the Steps, we have each found something called a spiritual awakening. To new A.A.'s, this often seems like a very dubious and improbable state of affairs. 'What do you mean when you talk

about a "spiritual awakening"?' they ask. Maybe there are as many definitions of spiritual awakening as there are people who have had them. But certainly each genuine one has something in common with all the others. And these things which they have in common are not too hard to understand. When a man or a woman has a spiritual awakening, the most important meaning of it is that he has now become able to do, feel, and believe that which he could not do before on his unaided strength and resources alone. He has been granted a gift which amounts to a new state of consciousness and being. He has been set on a path which tells him he is really going somewhere, that life is not a dead end, not something to be endured or mastered. In a very real sense he has been transformed, because he has laid hold of a source of strength which, in one way or another, he had hitherto denied himself. He finds himself in possession of a degree of honesty, tolerance, unselfishness, peace of mind, and love of which he had thought himself quite incapable. What he has received is a free gift, and yet usually, at least in some small part, he has made himself ready to receive it.[75]

The process and hope offered by AA, as sketched in Wilson's words, are analogous to the process and hope offered by the theological doctrines of justification and sanctification, with this one caveat, that the active-sounding last phrase in Wilson's description—"he has made himself ready for it"—would be better put in passive terms. Aquinas would say that such a person has surrendered to God's love.

On Aquinas's anti-Pelagian views, surrender on the part of a person Paula enables her justification, which will be followed immediately by the beginning of her sanctification. In sanctification, Paula wants to will a particular good thing; and she does not despair of being successful in this higher-order desire of hers. But she does abandon her efforts to be successful on her own. She abandons the attempt to use her own strength of will to make her will be what she wants her will to be. Instead, she recognizes her need for help. Rather than struggling for what she wants to be, she lets go of the struggle and surrenders to God's love and grace. The result is a strengthening of her will and a concomitant increase in her integration around the good. These good things in her will therefore stem from God's action on her will; they do not stem from her own efforts, although it is her own will that is ultimately responsible for the strengthened state of her will.

In an un-Aristotelian spirit which is decidedly anti-Pelagian, then, Aquinas is committed to the traditional Christian claim that there is no good in a human person that is not the result of God's grace.

AQUINAS'S ETHICS

To understand the ethics Aquinas builds on this claim and his concomitant understanding of a life in grace, it helps to begin with the central place in ethics

Aquinas assigns to love. In discussing the virtues, Aquinas asks whether it is possible to have the infused virtue of love without also having the moral virtues; and, in response, he says,

> All the moral virtues are infused simultaneously together with love.[76]

In fact, he is emphatic that there can be no moral virtue at all without the infused virtue of love. He says,

> It is written: 'He who does not love abides in death' (I John 3:14). Now the spiritual life is perfected[77] by the virtues, since it is by them that we live rightly, as Augustine states (*De libero arbitrio* ii). Therefore, the virtues cannot be without love.[78]

Because he accepts a unity of the virtues thesis and thinks that all the virtues are infused, it seems to follow that for Aquinas all the virtues are infused at once, in an instant. And this is in fact what he does think. On his view, a person begins the process of sanctification through justification in coming to faith; and the transition to faith occurs in a datable, discernible instant. So, for example, Aquinas says,

> the endpoints of justification are grace and the privation of grace. Between these there is no mean...and therefore the transition from one to the other is in an instant,...And so the whole justification of an impious person occurs in an instant....[79]

In this same instant, it is also the case that all the virtues are simultaneously infused. Actually, Aquinas supposes that in the one datable instant at which a person Jerome comes to faith, not only are all the virtues infused into Jerome, but the Holy Spirit is also given to Jerome. The indwelling of the Holy Spirit begins in this instant.[80] In the instant of a human person's acquiring faith, the indwelling Holy Spirit unites that person with God to some nascent degree; and in so doing, it makes God available to her to know, to love, and to enjoy.

When Aquinas describes the Holy Spirit, he says that the name of the person of the Holy Spirit is 'Gift.' In saying this, he is validating a claim of Augustine's: "the gift of the Holy Spirit is nothing but the Holy Spirit."[81] To explain this claim, Aquinas says,

> We are said to possess what we can freely use or enjoy as we please.... A rational creature does sometimes attain to this,...so as freely to know God truly and to love God rightly. Hence a rational creature alone can possess the divine person. [But] this must be given to a rational creature from God, for that is said to be given to us which we have from another source. And so a divine person can be given and can be a gift.[82]

This is a position Aquinas maintains and develops in many places. So, for example, in commenting on Paul's wish for the Ephesians, "that you may be able to comprehend, with all the saints, what is the breadth and length and height and depth [of the love of God]," (Eph. 3:18) Aquinas says,

> It is evident from John 14:21 that God reveals himself to one who loves...and that he shows himself to one who believes.... Now it should be noted that sometimes to comprehend means 'to enclose', and then it is necessary that the one comprehending totally contains within himself what is comprehended. But sometimes it means 'to apprehend', and then it affirms a remoteness or a distance and yet implies proximity. No created intellect can comprehend God in the first manner. But the second kind [of comprehension] is one of the gifts [of the Holy Spirit], and this is what the Apostle means when he says [to the Ephesians] 'that you may comprehend'—namely, that you may enjoy the presence of God and know him intimately.[83]

In Romans 5:5, Paul says "the love of God is poured forth in our hearts by the Holy Spirit who is given to us." In one of the many places in which Aquinas comments on this line, he says,

> The love of God can be taken in two ways. In one way, for the love by which God loves us; in another, for the love by which we love God. Both these loves of God are poured into our hearts by the Holy Spirit, who has been given to us. For the Holy Spirit...to be given to us is our being brought to participate in the love who is the Holy Spirit.[84]

In his commentary on the Gospel of John, Aquinas characterizes the relation of the Holy Spirit to the person in whom the Spirit dwells this way:

> The Father...will give the Holy Spirit, who is the Consoler, since he is the Spirit of love. It is love that causes spiritual consolation and joy....[85]

And in commenting on a line in Ephesians, where Paul says that the Ephesians have the promise of the Holy Spirit (Eph. 1:13), Aquinas says,

> The Holy Spirit is given with a certain promise, since by the very fact that he is given to us we become the children of God. For through the Holy Spirit we are made one with Christ.[86]

According to Aquinas, then, in the first instant of faith, every person of faith comes to have the Holy Spirit itself indwelling in her in an incipient union of love. And this is not the end of the story. The Holy Spirit's coming brings with it, in that one and the same datable instant, not only all the infused virtues but also all the gifts and fruits of the Holy Spirit.[87]

The gifts of the Holy Spirit are infused dispositions in the will that render a person attentive to God and apt to follow the inner promptings of God. Speaking of these gifts, Aquinas says,

> These perfections are called 'gifts', not only because they are infused by God, but also because by them a person is disposed to become amenable to the divine inspiration....[88]

And a little later he says,

> the gifts are perfections of a human being, whereby he is disposed so as to be amenable to the promptings of God.[89]

There are seven such gifts: piety, fortitude, fear of the Lord, wisdom, understanding, counsel, and knowledge. And there are twelve fruits of the Holy Spirit: love, joy, peace, patience, long-suffering, goodness, benevolence, mildness, fidelity, modesty, continence, and chastity.[90] About these, Aquinas says,

> Among the fruits of the Holy Spirit, we count love, since the Holy Spirit himself is love. And that is why it is written (Rom. 5:5): 'The love of God is poured forth in our hearts by the Holy Spirit who is given to us.' The necessary result of [this] love ... is joy, because every lover rejoices at being united to the beloved. Now love has always the actual presence of God whom it loves ... and that is why the consequence of love is joy. And the perfection of joy is peace ....[91]

On Aquinas's views, then, in the first instant of coming to faith, a person Jerome will have present not only with himself but even within himself the God who is his beloved. That is why the list of the fruits of this union begins with love, joy, and peace—love, because his beloved, who loves him, is present to him; joy, because of the dynamic interaction with his beloved, who is present to him in second-personal ways; and peace, because his heart already has what it most desires, his beloved, present to him.[92] And so once Jerome surrenders to God's love, not only does God's Spirit come to indwell in Jerome, but in fact the circuit is finally completed, and there is mutual indwelling—Jerome in Christ, and the Holy Spirit, which is the Spirit of Christ, in Jerome.

As Aquinas explains it, there is no life in grace without the indwelling Holy Spirit, with its concomitant love, joy, peace, and the other fruits of this union, as well as all the gifts of the Holy Spirit and all the infused virtues. But without the surrender that is necessary for the initial infusion of grace, the Holy Spirit will not come to indwell a human person; and there will be no infused virtues, no gifts and fruits of the Holy Spirit, no justification or sanctification, and no union with God.

TWO PROBLEMS AND A SOLUTION

Here it is important to pause and take stock, because, manifestly, there are two problems with the preceding account of justification and the thesis that all the virtues are infused at once with grace when a person comes to faith. The first problem is that this thesis about the virtues seems highly counter-intuitive or just plain false. It seems that no one gains all the virtues at once, but that, on the contrary, there are people who have only some virtues and not others. And the second problem is that this account seems to be contradicted by the description of sanctification as occurring gradually over the course of a lifetime. If all the virtues and the gifts and fruits of the Holy Spirit are infused at once, how could it also be true that sanctification is gradual?

To see the solution to the first problem, it is important to recognize what the preceding passages make abundantly evident, namely, that, on Thomistic ethics, the essence of moral excellence is second-personal.[93] An Aristotelian virtue is an intrinsic characteristic, a property that can be gotten and preserved by an individual acting by himself as an individual agent. But the Thomistic understanding of moral excellence requires a much different characterization. As is clear from Aquinas's emphasis on love as the foundational virtue, the virtue without which no other virtue is possible, a human person's moral excellence is a function of her relation to God and other persons.

The quotations above demonstrate that, for Aquinas, it is open to every human person to have a second-personal connection of love with God, and every person who is in grace has such a connection. In relationship with God, a human person can know God's presence and something of God's mind in a direct and intuitive way that is in some respects like the mind-reading between human persons. On Aquinas's views,

> There is one general way by which God is in all things by essence, power, and presence, [namely,] as a cause in the effects participating in his goodness. But in addition to this way there is a special way [in which God is in a thing by essence, power, and presence] which is appropriate for a rational creature, in whom God is said to be as the thing known is in the knower and the beloved is in the lover . . . . In this special way, God is not only said to be in a rational creature but even to dwell in that creature . . . .[94]

The gifts of the Holy Spirit are a manifestation and an outgrowth of a second-personal relationship of love with God on the part of a person Paula. Every gift of the Holy Spirit has its source in God's indwelling in Paula; and, in addition to its other functions, as Aquinas says, the indwelling of the Holy Spirit renders Paula attentive to God and apt to follow the inner promptings of God. In fact, for Aquinas, the Holy Spirit so fills a person with a sense of the love of God and God's nearness that joy is one of the principal effects of the Holy Spirit.[95] Aquinas says,

> the ultimate perfection, by which a person is made perfect inwardly, is joy, which stems from the presence of what is loved. Whoever has the love of God, however, already has what he loves, as is said in 1 John 4:16: 'whoever abides in the love of God abides in God, and God abides in him.'[96] And joy wells up from this.[97]
>
> When [Paul] says 'the Lord is near,' he points out the cause of joy, because a person rejoices at the nearness of his friend.[98]

And, in *Summa contra Gentiles* (SCG), expanding on the idea that a person of faith is friends with God, Aquinas says:

> In the first place, it is proper to friendship to converse with one's friend.... It is also a property of friendship that one take delight in a friend's presence, that one rejoice in his words and deeds ... and it is especially in our sorrows that we hasten to our friends for consolation. Since then the Holy Spirit constitutes us God's friends and makes God dwell in us and us dwell in God,[99] it follows that through the Holy Spirit we have joy in God.[100]

On Aquinas's view, a second-personal connection of love between two human persons enables them to have what Aquinas calls 'connaturality' with each other.[101] For Aquinas, as the passages above make clear, it is possible for a human person also to have connaturality with God.[102] Because of Aquinas's commitment to the unity of the virtues thesis, which for him encompasses also the gifts and fruits of the Holy Spirit, this second-personal connection and the resulting connaturality with God is one or another degree of the optimal ethical condition for a human person. In this condition, a person in grace will not need to try to reason things out as regards ethics or struggle on her own to acquire good moral habits. She will be disposed to think and act in morally appropriate ways because of her second-personal interaction with God.

And so there is a solution to the first problem for Aquinas's view. If we think of a virtue as an acquired moral excellence, then it is abundantly clear that no one gains all the virtues at once. But if we think of virtue as Aquinas does, as one or another manifestation of a union (in some incipient degree) with God, then it is clear that a person can gain the moral excellences all at once in a datable instant, the instant in which one comes to faith and receives the indwelling Holy Spirit.

In this instant, the work done by Christ on the cross is complemented. On the interpretation of the cry of dereliction argued for in Chapter 5, when Christ utters the cry of dereliction, he is opening his human psyche to receive the inrushing and indwelling psyches of all human beings. For a human person who surrenders in love to God, the indwelling of the Holy Spirit in her completes Christ's work. At that instant, as between her and God, there is some degree of union of a metaphysically great sort because there is mutual indwelling between her and God. When in the Gospel of John Christ prays that his disciples may all be one as he and the Father are one, he finishes that part of his prayer with the line addressed to God the Father: "I in them and you in me" (John 17:23). The union between Christ and the Father is a maximally unified, metaphysically great mutual indwelling, one might say; and in a much more limited way, the union between Christ and a person in grace when the Holy Spirit comes into that person is also a mutual indwelling.

The counter-intuitive character of Aquinas's unity of the virtues thesis is further reduced by seeing that, on Aquinas's view, the virtues can co-exist with contrary dispositions in a person.[103] The possibility of fragmentation in a human psyche—more accurately, the proneness to this fragmentation in a post-Fall human psyche—means that the mere presence of morally excellent dispositions is not enough by itself to render a person internally integrated around the good. So, for example, Aquinas says,

> sometimes the habits of moral virtue experience difficulty in their works by reason of certain contrary dispositions remaining from previous acts.[104]

One of the objections to his unity of the virtues thesis that Aquinas quotes is a claim made by Bede to the effect that the saints are made humble by contemplating their lack of certain virtues. On the view of the putative objector, then, it seems that even a saint can have only some virtues and not others. In response, Aquinas says,

> Certain saints are said not to have certain virtues insofar as they experience difficulty in the acts of those virtues ... even though they have the habits of all the virtues.[105]

Here Aquinas is validating the obvious truth that even a person in a morally excellent condition has some morally good acts that are difficult for him to do. As Aquinas sees it, this fact is compatible with the claim that every person in grace has all the moral virtues because, in fact, for post-Fall human beings, having a disposition to a morally good act is not enough to be able to do easily the act associated with that disposition.[106] The presence of a contrary disposition may make acting on the virtuous disposition difficult. As Aquinas sees it, then, although a person cannot acquire *morally excellent* dispositions by his own actions, through repeated acts of a *morally wrong* sort he can by himself acquire dispositions inclining him to the opposite of virtue. And in infusing all the moral virtues, God does not thereby remove the contrary dispositions at the same time.

With this last clarification, the counter-intuitive appearance of Aquinas's unity of the virtues thesis is shown to be mistaken. And this resolution of the first problem with Aquinas's ethics provides the solution to the second problem as well.

Although all the virtues and the gifts and fruits of the Holy Spirit are infused at the same time in the first instant of the Holy Spirit's indwelling a person of faith, nonetheless the old acquired sinful dispositions remain; and they can make it difficult—*not* impossible, but difficult—to act in moral ways. And that is why sanctification, which is a cooperative process between God and a person in grace, takes such a long time and goes so gradually, even though all the virtues, gifts, and fruits are infused at once in the first moment of faith.

These considerations also show why the state of will characterizing a person in grace is well-represented by Christ's prayer in the Garden of Gethsemane, as I described it in Chapter 6. A person in grace wills what God wills in virtue of willing to will the good. But this condition is compatible with ongoing division in the first-order will, or even in the second-order will, which both wants and does not want some particular good. Even when the will is integrated around the good to the extent that a first-order desire against some particular good loses in the inner battle, that first-order desire may well not be totally extinguished. And, of course, sometimes the first-order desire against the good wins in the battle too. Nonetheless, as long as the higher-order will to will what God wills remains in a person, she remains in the process of sanctification. That is why the Christian life is a life of repentance.

GOD'S ACTION ON THE WILL

This solution to these two problems with Aquinas's account of ethics[107] raises another problem, however: if God can infuse moral virtues into the will of a person Jerome, then why does God not also simultaneously remove all contrary, morally wrong dispositions from Jerome's will?

The first thing to see in this connection is Aquinas's insistence that *nothing* operates on a human will with efficient causation. For example, Aquinas canvasses the necessity involved in the operation of each of the four Aristotelian causes, including the efficient or agent cause (as he sometimes calls it); and he argues that there can be no agent or efficient causation on the will, because any such causation is, in his view, coercive. As he puts it,

> the necessity of coercion is entirely repugnant to the will.... it is impossible for something to be coerced or violent *simpliciter* and [also] voluntary.[108]

Elsewhere he says,

> if the will is moved by any external principle, the motion will be violent. By being moved by an external principle, I mean a principle that moves in the manner of an agent and not in the manner of an end. But the violent is altogether repugnant to the voluntary. It is therefore impossible that the will be moved by an external principle as an agent cause. Rather every motion of the will must proceed from an interior principle.[109]

Aquinas does not waver from this conviction even when it comes to divinely infused grace. So, for example, he says,

> God moves everything in accordance with its own manner.... And so he also moves human beings to justice in accordance with the condition of human nature. But in accordance with his own nature a human being has free choice. And so in a human being who has the use of free choice, there is no motion from God to justice without a motion of free choice.[110]

In SCG, Aquinas says,

> Now it might seem to someone that a human being is compelled to some good action by the divine aid [of grace] .... But it is plainly shown that this is not true. For divine providence provides for all things in accordance with their own manner ... But it is characteristic of a human being (and every rational nature) that he acts voluntarily and is master of his own acts..., and compulsion is contrary to this. Therefore, God does not compel a human being to good action by his aid [of grace].[111]

In another place, in *Quaestiones disputatae de veritate* (QDV), Aquinas sums up his position by saying,

> God can change the will with necessity, but he cannot compel it.[112]

But here we need to pause. What does it mean to say that God can change the will with necessity but cannot compel it? If omnipotent God changes something with necessity, how could it possibly be true that God does not also compel it?

Aquinas himself answers this question in some detail, and it is worth quoting his answer at length. He says,

> to will something is to be inclined to it. But compulsion or violence is contrary to the inclination of the thing compelled. Therefore, when God moves the will, he brings it about that an inclination succeeds a previous inclination in such a way that the first is removed and the second remains. And so that to which God leads the will is not contrary to an inclination now existent but rather to an inclination previously inhering [in the will]. And so there is no violence or compulsion.
>
> Similarly, there is in a stone an inclination to a downward place, because of its heaviness; and while this inclination remains, if the stone is thrown upward there will be violence. If, however, God removed from the stone the inclination of heaviness and gave it an inclination of lightness, then its upward motion would not be violent for it. In this way, a change of motion can be without violence. [And] this is the way in which we should understand that God changes the will without its being the case that God compels the will ....
>
> God changes the will in two ways. In one way, by moving it only, as when he moves the will to will something, without impressing any form on the will, as when he brings it about, without the addition of any disposition, that a human being wills something that he previously did not will.[113] In another way, [God changes the will] by impressing some form on the will itself. For just as from the very nature which God gave to the will the will is inclined to will something ... so too from something added on to it, as grace or virtue is, the soul is further inclined to will something to which it was not previously determined by a natural inclination.
>
> This added-on inclination is sometimes complete and sometimes incomplete. When it is complete, it brings about a necessary inclination for that which it determines in such a way that the will is inclined by nature to desire the end of necessity, as happens among the blessed .... But sometimes the added-on form is not complete in every way, as is the case with wayfarers.[114] And then the will is inclined because of the added-on form, but not of necessity.[115]

Aquinas is here calling attention to what he takes to be an important difference in the ways in which God can change the will. But just what is this difference, and why does it matter?

The example Aquinas gives having to do with the motion of a stone is helpful in this regard. On Aquinas's view, a stone is configured in such a way that it is inclined to fall downward. If the stone is thrown upward while it still has this configuration, then some violence or compulsion is exercised on the stone, because the stone is moved contrary to its own inclination or configuration. But it is possible to change the configuration of the stone. The configuration that makes the stone inclined to fall downward could be removed by God, and the stone could instead be given a new configuration, an inclination to move upward. In that case, the stone would presumably be like fire; it would be naturally disposed to move upward. If God were to alter the configuration of the stone in this way, then he would change the stone in such a way as to make the stone move upward. But now the upward motion would not occur as a result of any compulsion or violence on God's part.

In the same way, Aquinas emphasizes in one place after another that God's giving of grace is not simply God's willing that a human will actually will something or other. Rather, it is God's infusing of a form, the form of grace, after a previous form in the human will has been lost. And because a human being is capable of voluntary action, as a stone is not, the previous form is not something taken away by God, but rather something abandoned by a human person himself in consequence of surrendering to God.

Because grace justifies the person who receives it, Aquinas supposes that the previous form, which is lost before the introduction of grace, is the form of culpability or guilt. This is the configuration of the will before it detests its own evil and longs for the goodness of God. A person's surrender to God, her ceasing to resist God's love and grace, deletes this configuration in her will and leaves her will quiescent. After her ceasing to resist, then God introduces into her will the grace which enables her to long for God's goodness and accept the help of God's grace. In QDV, Aquinas puts the point this way:

> grace...expels guilt—not that guilt which is but that guilt which previously was and [now] is not. For grace does not expel guilt in the manner of an efficient cause; for if it did, then it would have to be the case that grace acted on existing guilt to expel it...Rather, grace expels guilt in the manner of a formal cause (*formaliter*). For from the very fact that grace inheres in its subject as a form, it follows that guilt is not in the subject.[116]

And in another place in QDV, Aquinas says,

> God brings about graced spiritual being in us without the intervention of any agent [cause], but still with the intervention of a created form—and this is grace.[117]

And so, on his view,

> grace does not expel guilt in the manner of an efficient cause (*effective*) but in the
> manner of a formal cause (*formaliter*).[118]

Aquinas goes to great lengths to explain what the manner of a formal cause is
in cases such as this. For example, in explaining why justification occurs in an
instant, he says,

> when some mean must be recognized between the endpoints of a change, the
> transition from one endpoint to another must be successive, because that which is
> moved continuously must first be changed to the mean before it is changed to the
> final endpoint.... But when there cannot be a mean between the two endpoints
> of a change or motion..., then the transition from one endpoint to the other does
> not occur in [a period of] time but rather in an instant. And this happens when
> the two endpoints of a motion or change are... privation and form.[119]

For Aquinas, then, before a person Jerome comes to accept God's love and
grace in the act of will of justifying faith, Jerome's will is characterized by a
configuration which is culpable. God could simply will that Jerome detest his
own sin and love God's goodness. But if God did so while that culpable
configuration remains in Jerome's will, then God would compel Jerome's
will and exercise violence on it. In his goodness, however, God deals with all
things in accordance with their nature; and so, according to Aquinas, God
does not deal violently with the human will, which is a power for voluntary
acts. Instead of compelling it to will something, God instead gives Jerome's will
a new configuration after the old configuration in Jerome's will has ceased to
be there. As Aquinas says, the end points of the change that constitute God's
infusion of grace are *not* two opposite forms, but rather a privation of a form
and a form.

But the quiescence of the will in the surrender to God's grace *is* a privation
of a form. When Jerome moves from rejecting grace to quiescence with respect
to grace, the result is a privation of form in his will as regards grace. Once
Jerome's will is quiescent in this way and has a privation of the form it
previously had, *then* God acts to produce in Jerome's will an acceptance of
grace. And when God acts in this way, God's action counts as formal causation, rather than efficient causation, because in giving grace to Jerome's will,
God does not first expel from Jerome's will the configuration of resistance.
That configuration is lost as a result of Jerome's ceasing to maintain it when he
surrenders to God's love and grace.

The great importance of the distinction between the exercise of efficient
causation versus the exercise of formal causation on a human will can readily
be seen by recognizing its implications as regards the freedom of the will. If
God were to act on Jerome's will with efficient causation, then it would be
entirely up to God which configuration there is in Jerome's will. But because,

on Aquinas's view, God acts on the human will only with formal causation in the giving of grace, then, in fact, what configuration there is in Jerome's will is ultimately up to Jerome even though the configuration Jerome has in grace is given to Jerome's will by God. If Jerome were not to cease resisting God's grace, then the gift of grace would not be given to Jerome. God might offer Jerome grace continually, but God will not in fact put this grace in Jerome's will while Jerome is resisting it. Furthermore, even though God acts directly on Jerome's will in the giving of grace, Jerome nonetheless has alternative possibilities with regard to grace. That is because it is up to Jerome alone whether he resists grace or ceases resisting grace. Consequently, although the configuration in Jerome's will when he accepts grace and comes to faith is a form given to the will by God, so that Pelagianism is ruled out, it is still true that Jerome has free will, even in the libertarian sense of 'free', with regard to grace. Ultimately, the one responsible for whether or not Jerome has grace is Jerome.

And so, on Aquinas's view, in the process of justification, first through the surrender to God's love and grace on the part of a person Jerome, the culpable configuration of Jerome's will is lost, leaving his will with a privation—an absence of a configuration as regards God's love and grace. Then in turn this privation is taken away from Jerome's will by the form of grace that God adds to Jerome's will. The grace divinely infused in this way gives Jerome's will a new configuration with regard to grace, not by restructuring some configuration present in Jerome's will but by adding a configuration to Jerome's will when his will lacks a configuration with regard to God's grace. It is for this reason that Aquinas says that divinely infused grace operates on the will in the manner of a formal cause and not in the manner of an efficient cause.

And now it should be clear why, on Aquinas's views, sanctification is a gradual process, even though all the virtues and the gifts and fruits of the Holy Spirit are infused into a person simultaneously in the first moment of faith when the person receives the indwelling Holy Spirit. The grace that is given in the infusion of the virtues and the gifts adds a configuration to the will where the will is open to receive it. But the grace given in justification does not by itself expel any other already existing morally wrong dispositions built up in Jerome by his past bad actions. If grace did expel those morally wrong dispositions, then God's infusion of grace would constitute efficient causation on Jerome's will, expelling a configuration already present in Jerome and substituting a new one. Instead, however, God's infusion of grace exercises only formal causation on Jerome's will. It adds a configuration only to the part of Jerome's will that lacks a configuration; it adds a form where there is a privation of a form, and not where there is a form still present.

For every post-Fall human being past the age of reason who comes to a life in grace, by the time of justification and its infusion of grace, he will have acquired morally bad configurations in the will. But because in the infusion of grace God operates on a human will only with formal causation and not with efficient causation, the infusion of grace leaves such morally bad habits in place even while it adds the virtues and the gifts. Sanctification takes place as the person of faith gradually overcomes those bad habits, not by his own power, but by asking God for help in overcoming them and receiving co-operative grace in consequence.

It is useful in this connection to highlight the hierarchical character of the will. When a person Jerome has the infused virtue of justice, say, then he has a will that wills to will what is just. This is a second-order desire for justice, and it will generate in Jerome a desire to do what is just, which is a first-order desire for justice. But if Jerome has ingrained habits of racism, for example, then his desires for justice will co-exist in Jerome with first-order desires for things that are racist and therefore unjust. On Aquinas's views, Jerome cannot conquer the unjust habits on his own; but he can ask God for help in conquering them. When Jerome does so, to the extent to which he really means what he says in asking for God's help, then to that extent Jerome is surrendering his will to the help he has asked for. In these circumstances, to one degree or another, he lets go of his resistance to being wholeheartedly just where issues of race are concerned.

Consequently, in such a case, when Jerome asks for God's help with his persistent racism, there is in Jerome's will a privation of form with regard to the willing of justice as regards issues of race. To the extent to which Jerome is wholehearted in asking God for help with his racism, God can infuse the grace which strengthens Jerome's will to will the just things he himself wants to will. In infusing this grace, then, God is helping Jerome's will to be what Jerome wants it to be. To this same extent, God is also helping Jerome to gain in integration around the good. The process of sanctification is slow because a person typically is willing to surrender only a little at a time with regard to the morally bad habits in his will.

It is worth noticing, then, that in one sense the acquisition of the infused virtues and gifts initially adds to Jerome's internal fragmentation, because the infused dispositions will be at war with any bad dispositions already in Jerome's will. For Eckhart, a life in grace is an attempt to will what God wills by having no first-order (and maybe even no second-order) desires of one's own. But, on Aquinas's account of the processes of justification and sanctification, a life in grace is marked by continued or even exacerbated fragmentation in the will. For a person in grace, there is a global second-order will for a will to will the good, specific second-order desires for a will that wills particular goods, and nonetheless contrary first-order desires opposed to at least some of these more particular second-order desires. The introduction of the new second-order desires for a good will (of either the global or the specific sort) thus divides the will against the remaining first-order desires for what is not good. Contrary to Eckhart, then, and in accord with Aquinas's account of Christ's prayer in the Garden of Gethsemane, the optimal state of grace for a person in this life, the state of willing what God wills, includes significant internal fragmentation.

On the other hand, as I have argued elsewhere in support of Harry Frankfurt's account of the identification of a person,[120] a person's true self is to be identified with his higher-order volitions. So, insofar as justification brings about in Jerome a global second-order will for a will that wills the good, Jerome himself is identified with this will of faith, the state of will in which Jerome repudiates his own moral evil and longs for God and God's goodness. Through justification, then, in his true self, Jerome is allied with God against the evil in himself. In this sense, in spite of the divisions remaining in his will, justification brings Jerome to will what God wills and so produces a kind of internal integration in Jerome, insofar as the civil war within Jerome is governed by a will that is allied with God's will. That is why it makes sense that, although in discussing just such divisions in the will Paul says, "The good that I would do, I do not do; but the evil that I would not do, I do" (Rom. 7:19), he nonetheless finishes in this way: "And so it is not I who do [the evil that I would not do], but the sin that is in me" (Rom. 7:20). Insofar as Paul identifies with his global second-order will of faith, for a will that wills the good, his true self is the self that wills what God wills. And that is the sense in which it is true for him to say, "it is not I who do [the evil that I would not do]." Even in his internally fragmented state, he himself, the true self, is willing what God wills.

CONCLUSION

A life in grace thus begins with a surrender to God and God's love on the part of a person Jerome as Jerome is coming to faith, where a certain state of Jerome's will is central to faith. That surrender includes a change in Jerome's will from the state of resisting God's love and grace (however tacitly or covertly) to quiescence, the cessation of resistance. Once Jerome's will is in this quiescent state, the whole process of justification and sanctification can get started.

In justification, when Jerome's will has ceased resisting grace, God infuses operative grace into Jerome's will. This grace moves Jerome's will to the will of faith, to repudiating his own evil and longing for God and God's goodness; and so it instills into Jerome's will a global second-order will for a will that wills the good.

With that global second-order will in place, Jerome can begin the process of sanctification. In sanctification, God cooperates with this overarching second-order willing of Jerome's and other more specific second-order willings on Jerome's part to bring Jerome's will into ever-increasing integration around the good. If it is not impeded, if Jerome does not slide back into resisting grace, this process culminates in Jerome's full integration around the good and full union with God.

For Aquinas, the passivity of surrender, which is not the same as submission but rather significantly distinct from it, is thus the necessary beginning of the regeneration on which love and union with God and with other human persons depend. For every human being, the consequent internal integration around the good is gained with difficulty, against resistance to it—or, what is equivalent, from Aquinas's point of view, against resistance to God.[121]

Justification and sanctification are thus not possible without the surrender to God that is the beginning of moral and spiritual regeneration. In sanctification, a person lets go of the effort to bring her will through her own activity into the state she wants it to have. Instead, she seeks God's aid for her will, to strengthen her will in the good she herself wants to will. But, in the process of justification, a person lets go in a more radical way. In justification, she surrenders to God by letting go of activity in the will entirely where grace is concerned. She abandons her resistance to God by moving into quiescence in the will, so that God can regenerate her will without compelling it or breaking it as a will.

Both justification and sanctification are therefore essentially relational, and so is their goal. The point of justification and sanctification is not the growth of intrinsic, morally desirable properties in a human person, even if such intrinsic increase in goodness is a much-desired outcome of these processes. The point of the processes is rather the establishment and deepening of a relationship of love between a human person and God, a relationship that is undermined or obviated by the absence of psychic integration in that person. And the ultimate end of these processes is a relationship of union between that person and God. A union of love between God and a human person is what justification and sanctification aim at and effect.

In his passion Christ does what he can do unilaterally to achieve union with human beings; he opens himself up at once to the psyches of all post-Fall human beings, so that their psyches come to indwell in Christ in the human mind that Christ assumed as his own. But this unilateral opening of Christ's human mind to all human persons would be of no avail, would accomplish no union between God and human beings, unless the circuit were completed by something correlative in human beings, which is the indwelling of God's Holy Spirit in human beings.

This indwelling of the Holy Spirit has to be something for which human beings are ultimately responsible, however. It is not something that God can do unilaterally for human persons. If God unilaterally entered a human psyche while that psyche was resisting God, the result would not be the union of the human person with God through mutual indwelling. Rather, the result would be something more nearly like the overthrow of the human psyche under the violent incursion of an overwhelming external force. That sort of entering of the psyche of another person is in effect an alien invasion, the kind of thing that is a staple of science fiction, in which the alien invasion of a human psyche is greeted by the invaded human person with loathing and dread, not love. For love and the union of mutual love, God cannot unilaterally bring about the indwelling of the Holy Spirit. That indwelling requires an initiating surrender on the part of a human person.

It should be clear, then, that the most difficult, delicate, and challenging part of this whole process of the salvation of human beings from their own evil is the initial surrender to God. This surrender is also the most necessary, the most crucial part of the process of bringing a human person to flourishing in union with God. Without this surrender, that process cannot so much as get started. Even the omnipotent power of God is not able to produce union or sanctification in a person's will without this surrender on her part. And yet God alone cannot bring about this surrender. It depends ultimately on her. But, sadly, for this one needful thing, for this surrender to God, any person in a post-Fall condition will also have a powerful resistance to it, however tacit or hidden that resistance may be, however much it may be worthy of compassion more than judgment or punishment.

All human salvation is therefore like a huge pyramid balanced not on the head of a pin exactly, but more nearly on its point. Without this one surrender in a human person's will, without this one small movement from a person's resistance to his quiescence in the will with respect to God's love and grace, a movement which God cannot bring about and which a post-Fall human person does not want to bring about—without this, no human being can come into union with God or even into real union with any other human being. The self-alienation of post-Fall human beings fends off real love and closeness with other human persons as well as with God. Without this crucial surrender, then, a person's psyche will slide into more and more of an irrevocable loneliness whose source lies not in illness, poverty, or age but only in the will itself. And so this surrender is as important as it is apparently out of reach for any post-Fall person.

Part III

What Is Needed to Get What Is Wanted and the Atonement of Christ

8

The Temptations of Christ and Other Stories

INTRODUCTION

In Chapter 7, I showed the way in which the entire complicated pyramid of interwoven grace and free will that leads to union with God balances upside down on the delicate and difficult point of surrender to God's love on the part of a post-Fall person. Everything that God can do unilaterally to achieve union with human beings is done by Christ on the cross, but God cannot unilaterally bring about surrender to God on the part of a human person Paula. That surrender remains ultimately within Paula's control. But the problem for Paula is that this one thing which is essential to her flourishing and which is crucial to her having her deepest heart's desires[1] is something that her internally fragmented will both wants and rejects. God would preclude the necessary state of surrender in Paula if he tried to produce it unilaterally; and, when all is said and done, Paula does not want to produce it herself, at least not enough to will it effectually.

God's part of the mutual indwelling between God and a human person is accomplished by Christ on the cross, but the work of Christ is actually most needed in eliciting that person's surrender to God's love and grace. And yet, after all, how is there anything the incarnate Christ can do? Salvation balances on this fragile point of surrender, which even omnipotence cannot bring about. As God, Christ cannot help. As human, what can he do?

In this chapter, I will try to answer this question. As I will try to show, Christ's passion and death (Christ's life, passion, and death) enable a powerful metaphysical union of mutual indwelling between Christ and every person in grace, not just by Christ's allowing human psyches to indwell in him, but equally or more importantly by Christ's providing the best means for facilitating human surrender to God. The result of these reflections is a non-Anselmian (and non-Abelardian[2]) interpretation of the atonement, in the family of Thomistic kinds of interpretation. Those accustomed to see the atonement as some kind of payment of a debt or substitutionary punishment for sin will not find that view in this chapter. But, for those who worry that this non-Anselmian interpretation is soft on sin, in Chapter 10 I turn to the issue of the seriousness of moral wrongdoing. There I argue that in fact it is the Anselmian kind of interpretation of the doctrine of the atonement that does not take sin seriously enough.

As I explained at the outset of this book, for the doctrine of the atonement, there is no analogue to the Chalcedonian formula for the incarnation. That is, there is no creedal formula that specifies the way in which the doctrine is to be interpreted. As a result, there are various interpretations of the doctrine that are compatible with orthodox Christian theology. There are nonetheless constraints on any interpretation of the doctrine that is to be counted as orthodox. It must be consistent with acceptable ethical theory, and it must not violate acceptable interpretations of biblical passages relevant to the doctrine. The ethics and the biblical passages constitute a constraint not only on interpretations of the doctrine of the atonement, but also on elements presupposed by such interpretations. In preceding chapters, I have used Aquinas's account of love and goodness to set boundaries for acceptable interpretations as far as ethics goes, and I have argued that interpretations in the Anselmian camp violate those boundaries. In this chapter, I want to say more about some of the relevant biblical passages.

Many of these biblical passages are in the form of narratives. In other work, I showed that there is a kind of knowledge that is not propositional but that nonetheless really is knowledge; and I argued both that such knowledge can be acquired in second-person experience of other persons and that it can be transmitted through stories.[3] On my view, there is a kind of knowledge provided by narratives that is not available otherwise, or at least not as completely or perfectly available. This narratively derived knowledge can be significant for philosophical reflection; comprehension of narratives can also make a contribution to philosophy. In my view, this point holds especially for philosophy of religion and philosophical theology, where the knowledge of persons is sometimes central to the philosophical discussion. And so the biblical stories can be significant for philosophical reflection on theological claims.

It is important to point out, however, that the converse is also true. Depending on what one is trying to understand, it may be that philosophical reflection needs to be in service of the interpretation of narratives, for the sake of knowledge of the world and the place of human beings in it that philosophy seeks to find.[4] In my view, this point is particularly salient for philosophical theology. Because the end point for philosophical theology is reflection on one concrete particular with a mind and a will (however else God is also to be described), the goal for philosophical theology includes centrally the knowledge of persons. That is why it makes sense that stories constitute constraints on some theories of philosophical theology. The propositional knowledge of philosophy is useful to philosophical theology, but only as part of the means for the knowledge sought by theology. For some of the knowledge at issue, philosophical reflection will be most useful as an aid to reflection on the narratives, rather than the other way around. For interpretations of the doctrine of the atonement, the stories of Christ in the Gospels are one of the main sources of constraining the examination of the doctrine of the atonement in philosophical theology.[5] Any interpretation of the doctrine that could be shown to be incompatible with those biblical texts would thereby also be shown to be unacceptable. For these reasons, in this chapter, I will examine at length certain Gospel stories.

I will devote most of my attention to the story of the temptations of Christ, which is found in varying form in two of the Gospels, Matthew and Luke. (I rely on the details in both the Gospel of Matthew and the Gospel of Luke but adopt the ordering of the temptations given in the Gospel of Luke because it is most illuminating for my purposes.[6]) Any story as rich as biblical stories typically are will be susceptible of multiple acceptable interpretations, all of which may have something useful to teach. In the case of the temptations of Christ, the story has been the focus of intense scrutiny by excellent minds over centuries; and so there are many good interpretations, all of which are worth serious consideration. My own favorite among all of them is that given by the poet John Milton in his great work *Paradise Regained*, which I will draw on below.[7] Nonetheless, in this chapter, I want to look at the story in my own way, as it is helpful for my purposes in this book; but by putting forward the interpretation of the story that I offer here, I do not mean to rule out other interpretations that may be helpful for other purposes. Nothing about the way in which I want to look at the story implies that all other ways of looking at it are ruled out. As far as that goes, my own interpretation of the story is informed by what I have learned from others; and it constitutes a focus on only one particular part of the story, because that part is useful for considerations of the doctrine of the atonement.

With the help of this reflection on the story of the temptations of Christ, I will then look very briefly at other narratives in the Gospels that, in my view, confirm and develop the same conclusion as the story of the temptations. What all these stories show is something that is at least difficult to explain well without the help of the stories, namely, the relationship between the passion and death of Christ and the processes of justification and sanctification. There are, of course, other biblical texts that are also important for interpretations of the doctrine of the atonement; I will turn to some of them in the final chapter.

THE TEMPTATIONS OF CHRIST: A ROUGH SUMMARY

Since not everyone has the biblical story of the temptations of Christ clearly in mind, it will be helpful to begin with a brief summary of it. Of course, any summary will be tendentious, because it is not possible to summarize in any reasonable way without interpreting to some degree the story one is summarizing. My summary inevitably includes some interpretation, though I have tried to be careful to keep it to a minimum. With that *apologia*, here is a rough summary of the story.

At his own insistence, at the start of his public ministry, Christ is baptized by John the Baptist, who bears public witness that Christ is the long-awaited Messiah. During Christ's baptism by John, there is a miraculous and perceptible presence of the Holy Spirit and a divine voice from heaven which proclaims that Christ is the Son of God. Immediately after this public, powerful event, the Holy Spirit brings Christ into the wilderness, where Christ remains, fasting and praying, for forty days. At the end of this period, Satan comes to him in the desert to tempt him.[8]

In the story, Satan does not come in disguise but is recognizable to Christ as the fallen, rebel angel that he is. Christ is also recognizable to Satan as the prophesied Messiah and the Son of God. (As Milton reads the story, Satan knows what happened when Christ was baptized. So if there is no other evidence available to Satan than the baptismal events, they are enough to provide Satan with the knowledge that Christ is the Son of God who is meant to save post-Fall human persons.) At any rate, it is clear in the story that Christ and Satan each recognize the other for what he is. There are no scenes in which one of them is amazed to learn the identity of the other. Even so, Christ is apparently willing to engage with Satan's temptations, as distinct from, for example, giving Satan the silent treatment.

In the story, Satan makes three suggestions to Christ, which are his three temptations of Christ.

The three suggestions of Satan are odd, and Christ's answers are even odder, so that reflection on the details is required to make sense of them; and I will turn to the details below. Here I want to sketch just the basic elements of the story. Later in this chapter, I will look in painstaking detail at one especially remarkable feature of Satan's suggestions, namely, their point—or their point as it is useful to understand for my purposes in this book. (No doubt, for other purposes, other motives in Satan's suggestions would be salient and could also be found in the narrative.[9])

Satan's first temptation is to suggest that Christ use his divine power to satisfy his hunger by turning the stones around him into bread. Satan says to Christ, "If you are the Son of God, speak to this stone that it be made bread" (Luke 4:3). It is worth noting in this connection that Satan proposes Christ's doing a miracle by addressing the stone directly, with second-person address.[10]

Christ responds to this suggestion of Satan's by saying, "It is written, 'Man does not live by bread alone, but by every word of God's'" (Luke 4:4).[11]

The response is puzzling, of course. If one were to suggest to a dinner guest that she might like some salmon, it would be puzzling to hear her decline the salmon by saying that human beings do not live by salmon alone. That claim is certainly true, but it is hard to see what it has to do with an offer of a bit of salmon.

But Christ's line is a quotation, and the quoted passage provides context for Christ's answer. Christ is quoting a line that Moses says to the Israelite people when Moses is reminding them that, against all hope and expectation, beyond need and desire, God hand-fed his people in the wilderness with bread given from heaven. Even that bread, Moses tells the people, is not sufficient to keep them in life. What is most urgently needed in order for them to live is the word of God.[12]

In the second temptation, Satan takes Christ up to the top of a mountain and somehow, from there, lets Christ see a panorama of human power and greatness. In this vision that Satan gives Christ, Christ can see all the kingdoms of the world at once. Satan offers Christ all this human power and glory, with the explanation that human power and glory are in Satan's domain and available to Satan to bestow as he likes. The only condition for getting this human power from Satan is that Christ must worship Satan.

What is most puzzling about this temptation is its apparent stupidity. Christ clearly recognizes Satan, and Satan's status as outcast from God or rebel against God is also apparent to Christ. To worship Satan is therefore to abandon God and join his enemies. Satan cannot expect that, for the sake of a bribe or for any reason at all, Christ would be willing to abandon God and join Satan, given that Christ is God's Son and also full of the Holy Spirit in his experience in the wilderness. And so the point of this temptation is perplexing.

By contrast, Christ's answer to Satan includes the predictable line that one ought to worship God alone. The only noteworthy thing about this answer is that Christ gives his answer as a quotation from Deuteronomy in this case also (Deut. 6:13 and 10:20): "It is written, 'You shall worship God alone, and you shall serve only him.'" And Christ prefaces this quotation with a strong expression of rejection of Satan: "Go away, Satan"—or, "Get thee behind me, Satan," as the King James so evocatively (and literally) translates it (Matt. 4:10).[13]

Finally, in the third temptation, the story says that Satan sets Christ on a pinnacle of the temple in Jerusalem and suggests to him that he should fall from there, because the angels will save him from any harm if he is the Son of God. What Satan wants in this temptation is for Christ to fall but not be injured or hurt in any way. It is noteworthy that in this temptation Satan himself quotes a biblical text (Ps. 91:11–12).[14] The verses quoted affirm that God will send angels to care for the person God loves in order to save that person from all harm; God's beloved will not so much as injure his foot by bumping it against a rock.

In this third case, to refuse Satan's temptation requires not only an act of will, or an act of will and a verbal response, but also a bodily action, the action of standing on the pinnacle where Satan has placed Christ. Christ replies to this temptation of Satan's with still another quotation from Deuteronomy (Deut. 6:16): "It is said, 'You shall not tempt the Lord your God'" (Luke 4:12). And he does stand where Satan has put him.

The story in Luke ends with this quotation of Christ's and his rejection of Satan's last temptation. It says nothing about how Christ got down from the pinnacle of the temple. In the story in Matthew, however, it says that angels came and ministered to Christ. Milton imagines that these angels got Christ down from the pinnacle of the temple and provided him with food.[15]

In rough summary, then, this is the story of the temptations of Christ, as it is found in the Gospels of Luke and Matthew.

THE TEMPTATIONS OF CHRIST: WHAT SATAN WANTS

Without wanting to discount any of the excellent interpretations of this story, including especially Milton's, from which I have learned a great deal, for the purposes of this book I will look at the story of the temptations of Christ through an unfamiliar lens. To this end, it is helpful to begin by considering what the stakes are in this high-stakes game between Christ and Satan. That is, in the story, what could Satan gain if Satan defeated Christ in the process of the temptations? What could Christ lose?

It is sometimes unreflectively supposed that the point of Satan's temptations is to get Christ to sin, so that Christ falls from grace and is no longer the Messiah. But this is an unlikely explanation of what Satan stands to gain. On orthodox Christian views of Christ as the Son of God, Christ is not only sinless but in fact unable to sin.[16] On this view of Christ, if Satan were trying to tempt Christ to sin, then, in the story, Satan would be ignorant or stupid in virtue of not understanding what is implied by Christ's being the Son of God. Furthermore, it is hard to see what Satan would gain even if it were possible for him to wreck Christ as Messiah by causing him to sin. Certainly, history is full of human beings acclaimed as Messiah (or some other global savior) and subsequently found to be failures. If one proclaimed candidate for being the Messiah fails, nothing about that history precludes there being a real and successful Messiah at some other time.

Furthermore, even if this unlikely explanation about Satan's aim were right, that is, if Satan's aim were to get Christ to sin, this explanation of Satan's aim would be incomplete, because it would still not explain what it is that Satan wants to accomplish. If in the temptations Satan were to defeat Christ so that

Christ could no longer be the Messiah, what end that Satan wants does Satan win through this defeat of Christ?

In the story, Satan tells Christ that all earthly power is given into Satan's hands, so that military might, administrative success, and in general all political power, with its concomitant wealth and honor, are in Satan's control. And, Satan tells Christ, he shares power, wealth, and honor with human beings provided only that they worship him, where the worship in question no doubt is often enough tacit or unaware, on the story's presentation of Satan's world.

This part of the story therefore gives the story's audience one insight into Satan's motivation. Satan cares to control worldly goods and to get human beings to worship him. But by itself this detail of the story does not make clear what the order of motivation is for Satan. That is, does the story's Satan want human beings to worship him so that he can use them to control worldly goods, or does Satan want the control of worldly goods so that he can get human beings to worship him? And why would Satan want either one of these things?

In the story, Satan is presented as an adversary of Christ's because Satan is an enemy of God's. What God wins, Satan loses, and vice versa: what Satan loses, God gains. Milton's Satan says to the other fallen angels,

> To do aught good never will be our task,
> But ever to do ill our sole delight,
> As being the contrary to his high will
> Whom we resist. If then his providence
> Out of our evil seek to bring forth good,
> Our labour must be to pervert that end,
> And out of good still to find means of evil;
> Which oft-times may succeed, so as perhaps
> Shall grieve him...[17]

Once Satan is seen in this light, it is not hard to suppose that human beings are of interest to Satan largely, or maybe even only, insofar as they are the means to deprive God of something that otherwise might be God's or something that God in his goodness desires. In the New Testament (and, of course, on orthodox Christian doctrine) God desires that human beings be saved from their post-Fall human condition in order that they might be united with God. So, one might say, insofar as Satan is focused on enmity with God, every human being who is not brought to union with God is a win for Satan.

Contemplating what can be done to thwart and frustrate God, Milton's Satan proposes to his cohort of fallen angels that they corrupt mankind and wreck God's new creation in Eden on earth. Beelzebub, Satan's spokesman, explains Satan's strategy regarding Eden this way:

> ...though heaven be shut,
> And heaven's high arbitrator sit secure
> In his own strength, this place may lay exposed...

> ... here perhaps
> Some advantageous act may be achieved
> By sudden onset, either with hellfire
> To waste his whole creation, or possess
> All as our own, and drive as we were driven,
> The puny habitants, or if not drive,
> Seduce them to our party...
> ... This would surpass
> Common revenge, and interrupt his joy
> In our confusion, and our joy upraise
> In his disturbance...[18]

Thought of this way, what Satan wants is that human beings are in his camp, on his side, by worshipping him or by any more complicated means, because every human being who is not united with God is a loss for God of something God desires. What Satan wants is anything that can keep God from having something God desires, not in an attempt to achieve a final victory over God, which Milton's Satan recognizes he cannot achieve, but just for the spite of the thing, for the pleasure of revenge.

It might seem to someone that this interpretation is ruled out on orthodox Christian doctrine, because it is impossible for an omnipotent God to lack anything God desires. But this objection is mistaken, and there is biblical warrant for taking it to be mistaken. For example, there is the New Testament text that says, "God wants all human beings to be saved" (I Tim. 2:4).[19] But, on orthodox Christian doctrine, not all human beings are saved. And so it is possible even for an omnipotent God to fail to have something that God desires.

On this way of understanding Satan in the story, then, Satan wants control over human political power, wealth, and worldly honor only because these things provide a means by which Satan can detach human beings from union with God and therefore frustrate his enemy God to one extent or another.

This interpretation of what Satan cares about therefore provides an explanation of Satan's aim in the temptations of Christ. On this interpretation, what is at stake between Satan and Christ is not Christ's status as Messiah, but rather the spiritual condition of human beings, who might be saved by Christ or, alternatively, might be kept on Satan's side and remain unavailable for union with God. On this reading of Satan's aim, if Christ succumbs to Satan's temptations, fewer or no human beings will be saved by Christ; and then Satan will have defeated this plan of God's for saving human beings through Christ.[20]

This reading has the added advantage that it makes Satan's temptations of Christ something more complicated than such simple and obvious moral temptations as a temptation to gluttony or a temptation to prefer fame and honor to greater goods. It is difficult to take them seriously as temptations of that sort. The story is clearly dense, rich, and incredibly skillful. But consider just the temptation regarding worldly power. Is it really plausible to interpret that part of the story as suggesting that Christ might be tempted to abandon God and worship Satan in order to get worldly power for himself? Supposing that the story wants its audience to accept a picture of Christ as really susceptible to a temptation to worship Satan for the sake of power is not credible, in my view. But if we suppose that in the story Christ and Satan are wrestling over something that makes a difference to the number of human beings saved by Christ, then this temptation becomes much more complicated. Given the difficulty of the question about the means most suitable for the salvation of human beings, it is not hard to suppose that even a very smart and good person could make a mistake in finding an answer to the question.

Furthermore, it is compatible with Christ's having a divine nature that Christ make an epistemological mistake, a mistake in reason, in his human nature.[21] In this connection, it is important to keep in mind that on all orthodox theological understandings of Christ, Christ has a fully human nature. In consequence of having such a nature, Christ can grow in knowledge. There is controversy in the history of the Christian tradition about what Christ knew at any given time in his life, but there is no controversy over the claim that in the course of his earthly life Christ could gain knowledge he did not have before. As far as that goes, there is a biblical text warranting this claim. The Gospel of Luke says about the twelve-year-old Christ that he grew in wisdom and in stature (Luke 2:52). And, in addition, it is possible for Christ in his human nature to make an error—a non-culpable error—in reason or judgment. In fact, in the Gospel of Luke, by the time of the story of the temptations Christ has already made such an error. When the twelve-year-old Christ says to his mother, "Didn't you know that I had to be occupied with my father's matters?" (Luke 2:49), his question indicates that he attributed to his parents more knowledge and insight than they in fact possessed. At any rate, it is clear that he is surprised by their concern over his whereabouts; and so his earlier estimation of their epistemic state was evidently mistaken. An error of this sort is endearing, rather than culpable; but it is still an error. In fact, his parents did not know what the twelve-year-old Christ thought they knew, and that is why they had to look for him for three days before they found him.

On this way of reading the temptations, then, it makes sense that Satan would try tempting Christ, because on this reading Christ's making an error is conceivable. Since this is so, then Satan can reasonably hope to defeat God by a battle of wits with Christ, as Satan could not reasonably hope to defeat God by a seduction of Christ with an overt temptation to an obvious sin.

On the other hand, of course, as every academic believes with regard to at least some of his colleagues, errors in belief frequently are connected to states of will that are culpable or at least lamentable even if not culpable. Biased judgment rooted in sexism is an obvious example, but there are more subtle and complicated examples as well involving a non-culpable influence of will on belief. So, for example, speaking of his own resistance to religious belief,

Thomas Nagel says of the fear of religion that it "has large and often pernicious consequences for modern intellectual life."[22] So Satan's temptations can
be characterized as a battle of wits without implying that they are not real
temptations, that they do not serve as temptations to Christ's will, or that they
do not put a strain on the character of Christ.

And here another worry can arise. There has been considerable discussion
among theologians and philosophers of religion concerning an apparent
contradiction between the biblical claim that Christ was really tempted
(cf., e.g., Heb. 4:15) and the orthodox theological claim that Christ is impec-
cable, that is, unable to sin. It is not possible to review and comment on this
discussion in passing here, but there is a sense in which I do not need to do so.
As I explained in Chapter 1, my project is an attempt to examine by the use of
philosophical methods the theological doctrine of the atonement as it has been
framed in orthodox Christianity. Just as it is part of orthodox Christianity that
Christ has two natures, one fully divine and one fully human, so it is part of
orthodox Christianity both that Christ was really tempted and that Christ was
unable to sin. This part of Christian doctrine is therefore also part of the data
with which my project is working, and it is not part of my project either to
explain or defend it.

On the other hand, however, elsewhere I have argued that it is possible for
an agent to act with free will, in a libertarian sense of 'free', even if the agent
has only one option open to her.[23] Having alternative possibilities for action is,
in my view, an associated accident of free will but not part of its essence; that
is, a person who acts with free will, even in a libertarian sense of 'free',
generally does have alternative possibilities for action open to her, but she
need not. On this way of thinking about free will, Christ could freely refuse
Satan's temptations even if it is not true that he could accept them.

Someone might suppose that if Christ could not accept Satan's temptations,
then there is no real temptation. But this seems to me a mistaken view also.
The doctrine of Christ's impeccability specifies an end result, but it does not
specify the means by which that result is achieved. In case it helps in this
connection, consider the Greek myth of Atlas. According to Greek mythology,
Zeus punished the Titan Atlas for his attempted rebellion against the gods by
condemning Atlas to hold up the celestial spheres on his shoulders. It must
have been part of Zeus's punishment that Atlas had sufficient strength for the
job. Consequently, Zeus in effect guarantees that Atlas cannot fail to hold up
the celestial spheres. Nonetheless, Atlas is typically portrayed as straining
every muscle to do so. The doctrine of Christ's impeccability does not by itself
rule out an interpretation roughly analogous to this. The doctrine says only
that it cannot be the case that Christ sins. It does not rule out Christ's
struggling or suffering in order to avoid sinning.

So, for one reason or another, with regard to the temptations of Christ, we
can put aside worries about the issue of Christ's inability to sin.

As Milton reads the story of the temptations of Christ, at the time of the temptations Christ knew that his mission was to save human beings and bring them to union with God, but he did not know how he was to achieve this mission. In my view, this is a reasonable interpretation of the narratives. Given the fact that over many centuries the best philosophical minds have wrestled with the question of the means by which Christ's atonement can provide salvation for human beings, it is not unreasonable to suppose that a single human mind, even the human mind of the incarnate Christ, might also puzzle over this question. According to Milton, when the story of the temptations says that the Holy Spirit led Christ into the wilderness, where the temptations subsequently took place, the point of Christ's retreat into the wilderness is to give him space to reflect on the means for fulfilling his mission.

The high-stakes battle of wits between Satan and Christ can be understood as being exactly on this issue, then. And the stakes are the post-Fall human beings whose union or lack of union with God will result from whatever means of human salvation Christ chooses.

So, on this way of reading the story, what Satan is striving for in tempting Christ is that Christ should make a mistake about the best way to save post-Fall human beings and as a result save far fewer than he might otherwise have done. The question that animates this book is thus also central to the story of the temptations of Christ, on my reading of the story (and on Milton's): how is the salvation of human beings to be accomplished by what Christ does? Or, as I would put the question in light of the discussion in Chapter 7, by what means does Christ's passion and death—or Christ's life, passion, and death—help to bring about the twinned processes of justification and sanctification? In Chapter 1, I argued that Aquinas's theory of the atonement had the distinct advantage of explaining the process of psychic healing that salvation requires, but that it had the very significant disadvantage of not providing an explanatory connection between that healing and Christ's passion and death. In Milton's view, and in mine, something about the story of the temptations of Christ helps to provide one especially significant part of that missing connection. (The other part is set out in the explanation of Christ's cry of dereliction.)

With all these preliminaries and with this lens placed over the story, I want now to turn to the three temptations themselves.

It should be said that in what follows I am going to approach the details of the story with a kind of laser-like focus, because the story is dense. It is also set in a rich context that gives it resonances and depth; but, with great regret, for the sake of brevity, I will largely ignore that context in what follows. To take just one example of what I am omitting, Christ is in the wilderness for forty days, fasting the whole while; but Moses was also fasting in the wilderness for forty days before he received the law and the covenant of the law from God on Mount Sinai. And so there is a suggestion that in his forty-day fast Christ, as a new Moses, is initiating a period of a new covenant and a new law. Moses's fasting comes during the period when God fed the people of Moses with manna in the desert. Christ's fasting is also connected to a divine feeding with bread, but now with the bread that is the flesh of Christ in the Eucharist, as Christ himself explains in a different story (John 7:32–58). Or, to take just one more example, Elijah also fasts in the wilderness for forty days before beginning a powerful ministry combatting idolatry, and in that ministry he is persecuted by the political power of his day. But, of course, something similar can also be said about Christ. And so on and on. It is not possible to do everything in one chapter; and so, sadly, I will leave most of these rich and powerful resonances with earlier stories unexplored, in the interest of concentrating on just one feature of the story specially useful for my purposes.

THE FIRST TEMPTATION

As the story tells it, at the time of the first temptation Christ has not eaten for forty days, and he is hungry. His hunger gives urgency to the problem of his need for food, but the problem would be serious even if he had no hunger. Food is necessary for human life, and Christ has gone long enough without food that his need for food is great.

Satan suggests that Christ solve this problem by using the power of his divine nature in order to turn stones into bread: "If you are the Son of God, speak to this stone that it be made bread." It is hard not to suppose that Satan has the right of things here. In fact, one might see the implicit challenge in Satan's suggestion as a detail drawn from a deeper debate based on the problem of evil. If there is an urgent need on some human being's part, why would a good God not use his omnipotent power to satisfy it? Why allow suffering that one can prevent? If this first temptation is thought of as having the problem of evil hidden within it, then it is easier to understand that the exchanges between Christ and Satan are a battle of wits between two worthy adversaries. The question of why God does not use his power to fulfill human need is excellent and very hard to answer, as we ourselves know.[24]

It is true that Satan's suggestion is preceded by an unpleasant caveat: "if you are the Son of God." (That same tricky caveat precedes the suggestion of the third temptation too.) But it is hard to suppose that Satan intends this temptation as a fishing expedition to give Satan information about whether or not Christ is the Son of God. The story of the temptations is preceded by the story of Christ's baptism, during which a voice from heaven publicly proclaims Christ to be the Son of God; and there is no reason for thinking that this event and the heavenly voice are unknown to Satan. Furthermore, Satan's coming to tempt Christ in these ways in the wilderness presupposes an identification of Christ as very different from the ordinary run of human beings; and, of course, the nature of the temptations is such that only someone who could wield the power of God could be tempted by them. So it is not plausible, in my view, to take the caveat "if you are the Son of God" as an indication that Satan is trying to determine Christ's nature or is otherwise looking for information about Christ that Satan then does not have.

How then are we to understand the caveat? If it is not an attempt to elicit information, then what is it? One way to understand it is as having the character of a dare. In fact, dares are regularly presented in this way: "if you're so brave,...," "if you're so smart,...." In such cases, the caveat does not mean to elicit information either. Instead, it tempts the person being dared by suggesting that a failure to take the dare will render the person different from the person he wants to be, or inferior in status to the status that he might have had if he had taken the dare or to the status he had before the dare was made.

This feature of a dare is partly what makes dares hard to resist. The very making of the dare introduces a kind of fork in the road of life for the person being dared. The dare makes it seem that, if the youngster who was dared is unwilling to go into the reputedly haunted house, then it will be because in the moment of the dare he has become a coward. And even if the dared youngster knows for certain in himself that his failure to go into the house is not an act of cowardice, because he has some brave and noble reason for refusing to do so, nonetheless what he also knows is that his social standing will be altered significantly for the worse by his failure to go into the house, because he will bear the stigma of being a coward in his community even if he is not in fact a coward. Insofar as relational characteristics are also constitutive of him, then he is changed for the worse even if it is only his relational characteristics that have altered.

Understood in this way, Satan's caveat can be seen not just as a goad to push Christ in the direction Satan wants him to go, but as an additional attempt to muddy Christ's thought. The caveat suggests that if Christ does not turn the stones into bread, the only reason can be because Christ is not the Son of God. Since, on the view of both Satan and Christ, Christ *is* the Son of God, then there is no reason not to turn the stones into bread. If we think of this temptation in connection with the problem of evil again, the caveat in effect implies that the perfect goodness of God would unquestionably alleviate suffering if it could; and so if it does not do so, it can only be because of a lack of power on God's part—and, then, of course, God would not be God.

If it were understood in this way alone, the first temptation would be a real challenge. The problem of evil has been the focus for endless debate among the best minds in many cultures and periods. But, in these circumstances, the first temptation is much tougher, because it also has powerful implications for the means of atonement that Christ will choose to enact.

To see why, consider the nature of human suffering. As I argued in Chapter 6, suffering is a function of what we care about; and it also presupposes a standard of value for human life. On the standard of value central to Christianity,[25] second-person relationship is the genus within which the best thing for human life is found. Union with God is the greatest of these relationships, and it also constitutes the greatest human flourishing. So in effect the worst suffering for human beings is the absence of this union. Nothing in this line should be taken as making little of the ordinary instances of human suffering. The earth is soaked with the tears of the suffering, and the spectacle of the suffering of earth's sentient creatures, human and beast, is (and ought to be) heart-wrenching. Nonetheless, clearly, some sufferings are worse than others. And, on the standard of value central to Christianity, the worst suffering is the absence of second-personal relationship with a perfectly loving God.

On this view, then, hunger comes in various kinds. As Augustine puts it, addressing God, "You have made us for yourself, and our hearts are restless till they rest in you." So when Satan is recommending that Christ command the stones to turn into bread, to assuage hunger, his line will carry with it a great sweep of implications and resonances for those (including, of course, Christ) who are versed in the worldview presupposed by the story. There is suffering generated by having stones when bread is what is needed. But there is also suffering generated by a person's having a stony heart, which will not melt and surrender to God's love, so that the process of justification and sanctification can begin. In Ezekiel 36:26, God promises the people that he will take away their hearts of stone and give them living hearts that will enable them to be in union with a perfectly good God.[26] There is a sense in which Satan's suggestion in effect asks Christ to make good on this promise too. Why does Christ not take away not just his own hunger, not just all human hunger, but in effect all human suffering by the use of divine power on human stony hearts?

The Christian tradition has generally seen human suffering as God's medicine for post-Fall human beings, where those who are healthiest and closest to God get the worst suffering but even the worst and sickest among human beings get some. Discussing an analogous attitude in Judaism, Jon Levenson says,

> There is an interpretation of suffering that enables sufferers to overcome their hardened dispositions, to cut away the thickening around their heart – its foreskin, to revert to that biblical idiom – that impedes obedience and places ego where faithfulness should be.... [S]uffering has a powerful capacity to turn the sufferers away from the illusions of self-sufficiency and invulnerability, both of which appeal very readily to the successful but both of which, in the traditional Jewish view, powerfully inhibit the love of God and the strength and healing that it brings.[27]

If Christ were to use divine power to fix unilaterally and completely the problem of the stony human heart, then, presumably all other suffering could also be taken away, since the medicine of suffering would not be needed if human hearts were perfectly healthy.

In short, then, the first temptation requires Christ to solve the problem of evil if he is not to accede to the temptation; and if Christ does accede to the temptation, he will have determined on the unilateral use of divine power to heal the ailment of the post-Fall human condition, both the stony human hearts that are the source of human alienation from God and the whole panoply of sorrowful suffering that is on display in discussions of the problem of evil.

It is important to see in this connection that the action to which Satan is urging Christ is a matter of altering radically the nature of a created thing, a stone. Satan is urging Christ to act on the stone to remove the nature of the stone as a stone and to replace that nature with a different nature, the nature of bread. This kind of alteration is the kind that Aquinas says God will not exercise on a human will, namely, the alteration effected by efficient causation, where a new form is produced in something only after the preceding form is forcibly removed.[28] As Aquinas sees it, God's acting on the will with efficient causation in this way would not alter the will so much as destroy it as a will. If God by divine power removes the configuration of Paula's will and substitutes for it a configuration that God wills Paula to have, then the will that comes to be in Paula is God's will, not Paula's. Paula's own will was removed by God's power. And so the use of unilateral divine power to alter a human will is a Pyrrhic approach to the problem of human evil and the problem of human suffering that comes with it. By having its way, this exercise of divine power loses the very thing it is trying to gain.

It is also worth noticing that Satan urges Christ to speak to the stone in order to turn it into bread. Satan is recommending a second-personal relation to the stone, but it is a second-personal relation whose purpose is to do away with the stone. The stone being spoken to ceases to be a stone in consequence of this speaking. It is destroyed and replaced by bread. And so the imperious evil of Satan's first temptation can be seen in the very form of the act Satan wants Christ to do.

In the case of human beings, the consequence of acting on Satan's temptation would be even worse. That is because what will alleviate human suffering ultimately is union with God, and union between God and human beings is the goal of Christ's mission. But union between God and a human person Jerome requires mutual indwelling—the psyche of Jerome in Christ, and God's Holy Spirit in Jerome.[29] In Ezekiel, the passage in which God promises to take away the stony hearts of his people is followed by a passage in which God promises to put his Spirit into the people (Ezek. 36:27). But if God puts his Spirit into Jerome's psyche when Jerome has not voluntarily opened his psyche to God in a surrender of love, then God is not uniting with Jerome in coming into Jerome's psyche; God is just taking it over, in the manner of an alien invasion, of the kind that science fiction stories love to recount to produce shock and revulsion in their audience. In other Gospel stories, Satan is said to possess human psyches in just this sort of way, leaving the possessed human being in a horror of suffering.

This way of thinking about the first temptation, then, illumines the character of what Satan is urging Christ to do as a nightmare of evil.

This interpretation of the first temptation also makes it easier to understand Christ's response, whose perplexing character I noted above. Christ says, "Man does not live by bread alone but by every word of God."

This first part of Christ's response—"not by bread alone"—acknowledges the human need for bread and implicitly also all the other this-worldly things represented by bread, whose absence produces dreadful human suffering. But the line "not by bread *alone*" should also call attention to the fact that even the very rich and powerful suffer—from all the evils that psychic fragmentation and inner alienation produce, as well as the evils produced by the malice and envy of others. Abundant resources of all kinds is not sufficient to ward off suffering. It is possible to be in Edenic circumstances and be alienated from God, and that alienation is the worst suffering. So, for real life, for the real absence of suffering, bread and other such resources are insufficient. When Milton's Satan suggests to Christ that Christ save himself and others by turning stones into bread, the first response of Milton's Christ is to laugh. He says to Satan, "Thinkst thou such force in *bread*?"[30] Bread can assuage some hunger, but not the deepest hunger; and so there is no salvation in bread from the deepest suffering of human beings.

In the context of Satan's temptation, it is noteworthy what Christ goes on to pick out as both necessary and sufficient for human life: "Man does not live by bread alone but by every word that proceeds from God." What Satan had suggested to Christ is that Christ *speak* to the stones; and, insofar as Christ is the Son of God, as in the story he and Satan suppose that Christ is, then a word from Christ is a word of God's. So in suggesting to Christ that Christ speak to the stones, Satan is asking Christ to use a word of God's to produce bread out of stones and life for human beings out of their stony hearts. How then does this line of Christ's that a word from God is enough for life constitute a rejection of Satan's temptation?

It helps here to see that this line of Christ's is a quotation and to recognize, as Christ and Satan will do in the story, what the context of the quotation is. The line is from Deuteronomy 8:3, where Moses is explaining to the Israelite people that they must remember what God did for them when they were in the wilderness. In that passage, Moses is reminding the people that God fed them with manna, bread from heaven, when they were hungry. And Moses adds that God's point in letting them be hungry first, before God fed them, is so that the people would understand that they live not by bread alone but by every word of God's.

In the allusion of Christ's line to this context for the same line in the speech of Moses to the people, there is not only a reason for Christ's rejecting Satan's temptation but also the kernel of a solution to the problem of suffering. The ultimate point of the Israelites' suffering from hunger is their deepened relationship with God and their understanding of that relationship as central to their lives. God allows the Israelites in the desert to hunger before he feeds them miraculously because he cannot by himself alone effect union with them. He would not need the long slow wandering in the wilderness—with its changing cycle of human needs and suffering followed by miraculous divine helps in meeting those needs—if the relationship elicited by those experiences could be produced by God's power acting miraculously on human wills. The idea behind the story of the Israelites in the wilderness, then, is that without the wilderness formation, for which suffering plays a crucial role, the Israelites would not have developed the relationship to God that they did or to value that relationship as they subsequently do. And the implication of the story of Moses's speech to the Israelites is the apparently paradoxical claim that if God used his divine power to ward off *all* of this-worldly sorrow and affliction, he would not end suffering but rather enable it or even enhance it.[31]

Furthermore, Moses's line put in Christ's mouth has a different and added resonance. In another Gospel story, Christ explains that he himself is the true bread from heaven, and that true life consists in coming to him (John 6:30–51). In that story, Christ's association of himself with the manna from heaven in Moses's time is the prelude to Christ's urging people to come to him to alleviate spiritual hunger: "he that comes to me shall never hunger" (John 6:35), and *that* line has a connection, powerful in Christian theology, to the ritual of the Eucharist, which is itself intimately tied to Christ's passion and death. In the same Gospel, Christ is also identified as the Word of God.[32] Both in this association between Christ and the word of God and in Christ's identification of himself as the true bread from heaven, with its allusion to Moses's line about the purpose of manna, there is the same basic and deep thought: God cannot unilaterally produce the relationship with human beings that God wants. It takes a human person's coming to God. Even the Word of God cannot produce the desired union single-handedly.

If the Word of God could do so, God could have spoken to the Israelites in the wilderness, as Satan is suggesting Christ speak to the stones; and, with his word spoken then, God could have turned the Israelites all at once, by the exercise of his divine power, into people in union with him. But the word of God cannot do so. And therefore even omnipotent God uses such things as hunger and bread from heaven to elicit from people a surrender, made on their terms, to the love of God. It is up to them to let go of their death-grip on their stony hearts, so that God can give them a living heart and his Holy Spirit without their losing their personhood, their nature as persons. Losing its nature as a stone is what the stone would suffer if Christ acceded to Satan's first temptation.

With all this context understood, context which is available to all those (including Christ and Satan in the story[33]) who have in mind Moses's speech to the Israelites, we can see how it is that Christ's line to Satan rejects Satan's temptation. When Christ says, "Man does not live by bread alone but by every word of God's," he is calling attention to the *word* of God, and not the *power* of God, as the means of life. A word does not coerce, as Satan thinks it should. It opens up the mind of the hearer and invites the hearer to see the world in a certain way, so that, of his own accord and not coerced, the hearer comes to what he himself sees as good. Insofar as Christ is the word of God, Christ's means of atonement also requires foregoing coercion exercised through divine power. It also depends on an invitation to come to Christ. The good that Christ seeks through the process of atonement is lost, not gotten, through the coercive exercise of God's power.

So in refusing to use divine power to end human suffering and change stony human hearts, Christ is both narrowing his options for the process of atonement and also rejecting Satan's suggestion to turn stones into bread. Satan's first temptation is therefore a failure.

THE SECOND TEMPTATION

Milton's Satan introduces the second temptation in this way. Speaking to Christ, Satan says,

> ... all thy heart is set on high designs,
> High actions; but wherewith to be achiev'd?
> Great acts require great means of enterprise,
> Thou art unknown, unfriended, low of birth,
> A Carpenter thy Father known, thy self
> Bred up in poverty and streights at home;
> Lost in a Desert here and hunger-bit:
> Which way or from what hope dost thou aspire
> To greatness? whence Authority deriv'st,
> What Followers, what Retinue canst thou gain,
> Or at thy heels the dizzy Multitude,
> Longer then thou canst feed them on thy cost?
> . . .
>
> Riches are mine, Fortune is in my hand;
> They whom I favour thrive in wealth amain,
> While Virtue, Valor, Wisdom, sit in want.[34]

And Milton's Satan goes on to say,

> Thy actions to thy words accord, thy words
> To thy large heart give utterance due, thy heart
> Contains of good, wise, just, the perfect shape.
>   . . .
>
> These God-like Vertues wherefore dost thou hide?
> Affecting private life, or more obscure
> In savage Wilderness, . . .
> *Thy years* are ripe, and over-ripe. The Son
> Of *Macedonian Philip* had e're these
> *Won Asia* and the Throne of *Cyrus* held
> At his dispose . . . .
> Great *Julius*, whom now all the world admires,
> The more he grew in years, the more inflam'd
> With glory, wept that he had liv'd so long
> Inglorious: but thou yet art not too late.[35]

Finally, Milton's Satan finishes this way:

> to a Kingdom thou art born, ordain'd
> To sit upon thy Father *David's* Throne;
> *By Mother's side* thy Father, though thy right
> Be now in powerful hands, that will not part
> Easily from possession won with arms;
> *Judæa* now and all the promis'd land
> Reduc't a Province under *Roman* yoke,
> *Obeys Tiberius*; nor is always rul'd
> With temperate sway; oft have they violated
> *The Temple*, oft the Law with foul affronts,
> Abominations rather, as did once
> *Antiochus*: and think'st thou to regain
> Thy right by sitting still or thus retiring?
>   . . .
>
> If Kingdom move thee not, let move thee Zeal,
> And Duty; Zeal and Duty are not slow;
> But on *Occasions forelock* watchful wait.
> They themselves rather are occasion best,
> *Zeal* of thy Fathers house, Duty to free
> Thy Country from her Heathen servitude;
> So shalt thou best fullfil, best verifie
> The Prophets old, who sung thy endless raign,
> The happier raign the sooner it begins,
> Raign then; what canst thou better do the while?[36]

Satan's points here are easy to understand for anyone who has ever been seriously distressed over the oppression and obscene injustice that rule the world in one place or another. In order to bring down the tyrant, in order to protect the poor and oppressed, in order to save the women and the children from their cruel and rapacious overlords, it seems that it is necessary to build some kind of political base. Quietism in effect appeases and so collaborates with evil. Benazir Bhutto, Dietrich Bonhoeffer, Martin Luther King, Jr., Indira Gandhi, Andrei Sakharov, Desmond Tutu—to pick just a few moral heroes from recent times—are famous for thinking so. The use of political power to overturn evil is a moral imperative; and, if we except those champions of non-violent resistance, such as King, for example, our moral heroes take even the use of force to be sometimes obligatory in the cause of a just war.

Furthermore, it is hard to see how to preserve peace and justice in human affairs without some force to back it up. No one seriously proposes dismantling a state's police force entirely, because the ensuing chaos would cause incalculable harm to the most vulnerable in the society. Justice that is not supported by political power quickly evaporates into a memory or never progresses beyond a dream, as Martin Luther King, Jr.'s famous line implies.

And even if evil is momentarily so cowed that a society can count on living in peace, as in the Roman peace of Augustus, still that peace requires a considerable administrative apparatus to preserve and administer it, so that chaos and its concomitant evils do not return. But political power is needed for such extensive administration. It requires not just a police force but also an extensive system of tax collectors, lawyers, provincial governors, and all the rest, with which we ourselves are quite familiar.

Finally, even if Christ were to consider that his mission had to do with the spiritual good rather than the political good of human beings, Satan's temptation would still make sense. Noted philosophers and politicians through the ages have supposed that it is difficult to raise a good child in a bad state. Plato thought that state power should control culture in order to help virtue to flourish in the state, and Mao actually tried to use state power for that purpose. Even in the U.S., which seems willing to tolerate to a disfiguring extreme the vile, the violent, and the cruel in its public media, there are rules enforced by state power that set limits to the evil of the culture. Without all the machinery and apparatus of political power to enforce some boundaries, how is a good child to be raised in a culture? One can appeal to the heart of individuals for moral reform, certainly. But once that appeal is heard, is Satan not right that some kind of state with its administrative and police power is needed to set the conditions in which that reform can continue and flourish?

So Milton's characterization of Satan's second temptation is insightful. If the purpose of Christ's atonement is to bring human beings out of their post-Fall human condition and into a condition in which they can be united to God, why would a huge and powerful international political system headed by Christ not be exactly what is wanted and needed? In fact, why would it not be obligatory, as so many political reformers and dissidents have claimed?

Consider Sojourner Truth, who campaigned so effectively for the rights of black people and of women. What would she have said to someone who thought the moral life could be lived in quiet privacy?

And now it is also easier to understand what was previously the most perplexing part of the story of the second temptation, namely, Satan's explaining to Christ that Christ would have to worship Satan to accept his offer of political power. Of the three temptations, this is the only one that has any condition attached to it, let alone this condition, which seems designed to ensure that Christ reject the temptation.

There are two things worthy of notice about Satan's condition.

The first is that Satan's insistence on the condition seems entirely right, as everyone can readily see. It is not possible to engage seriously in politics without being prepared to accept compromise with one's opponents, even those opponents who seem to one to be in the devil's camp. Israeli politicians negotiate with Palestinians, and some Muslim leaders are willing to negotiate with Israel. The U.S. is willing to negotiate with Iran, which in its turn is willing to negotiate with the U.S. labor union leaders who work together with corporate business people; institutions committed to Catholic positions on abortion and contraception work together with the government on health care; and so on. Even those extremists committed to rejecting Western education entirely drive cars and use cell phones, which they themselves would have to admit are at least in part products of Western education.

And the second thing to notice is that Satan claims both that all political power, as well as the worldly goods of wealth and other such things, are under his control *and* that this control has been given to him. He does not happen to mention by whom he has been given it. But, presumably, the giver has more power than Satan does, and that is why the giver has the ability to give such power to Satan. And so the clear implication is that God himself has given Satan power over worldly affairs. Satan did not just seize this power over worldly goods and political power as a rebel against God. Satan holds it by right, one might say, as given to him by the highest governing power there is.

Seen in this light, the condition that the person getting political power should worship Satan while this person holds the Satanically-given worldly power is not an obviously foolish demand for idolatry or a blindly stupid request that Satan be given what is due only to God. It is a condition built into what is on offer, namely, political power. Accepting what has been given by God to Satan does require accepting Satan as one's superior, to whom some honor is due by right—by God-given right. That honor and the need for compromise inevitable in politics could reasonably enough be thought of as a kind of worshipping of Satan—a non-culpable honoring of what has to be accepted as overlord in such cases.

In the case of this temptation, as in the case of each of the others, Christ's response includes (or just is) a quotation from Moses's speech to the Israelites in Deuteronomy. Traditionally, scholars have supposed that there are two candidates for the source of Christ's quotation in the second temptation (Deut. 6:13 and Deut. 10:20); but my own favorite is the latter passage. Here is that passage in the 1917 JPS Tanakh translation:

> And now, Israel, what doth the LORD thy God require of thee, but to fear the LORD thy God, to walk in all His ways, and to love Him, and to serve the LORD thy God with all thy heart and with all thy soul; to keep for thy good the commandments of the LORD, and His statutes, which I command thee this day? Behold, unto the LORD thy God belongeth the heaven, and the heaven of heavens, the earth, with all that therein is. Only the LORD had a delight in thy fathers to love them, and He chose their seed after them, even you, above all peoples, as it is this day. Circumcise therefore the foreskin of your heart, and be no more stiffnecked. For the LORD your God, He is God of gods, and Lord of lords, the great God, the mighty, and the awful, who regardeth not persons, nor taketh reward. He doth execute justice for the fatherless and widow, and loveth the stranger, in giving him food and raiment. Love ye therefore the stranger; for ye were strangers in the land of Egypt. Thou shalt fear the LORD thy God; Him shalt thou serve; and to Him shalt thou cleave, and by His name shalt thou swear. He is thy glory, and He is thy God.... (Deut. 10:12–21)

The first part of this quoted passage rejects any implication that political activity is an ethical requirement for every person. It might be for some persons, but the only universal requirement is to serve God with all one's heart and mind and soul. Whether that requirement carries with it an obligation of political activity will vary from case to case. And the very next part of the passage rejects the idea that political activity, and the collaboration with evil implied in it, is necessary: everything belongs to God, not just the earth, but also the heavens and the heaven of heavens—that is, everything whatever that might be regarded as the realm of the fallen angels, such as Satan, however one imagines their proper or current sphere of rule. For this reason, whatever Satan might have been able to bestow on those who collaborate with him, God is able to bestow that very thing without any help or activity of Satan's. It may be, as Satan implies, that all worldly goods and power are given him by God to hand out to others as he chooses. But, in giving it to Satan to govern, God does not himself relinquish his own governance of anything, including Satan. And therefore God can in fact empower a human being with great influence over human affairs without its being the case that she has either political power or collaboration with evil.

Those who doubt this claim (in its theological form or its secular analogue) might think of Socrates or, closer to us, Sophie Scholl, to see the point. Sophie Scholl was executed by the Nazis when she was only 22 years old and had achieved virtually nothing worthy of note of any kind. But it is hard to overestimate her influence on contemporary imagination and therefore also by implication over human affairs.[37]

So in rejecting Satan's second temptation, Christ is rejecting not only the temptation but Satan himself. For his mission, he does not need the worldly power that Satan can give, and so he does not need or want Satan either. That is why Christ begins his response by saying to Satan, "Go away!"

And if we now think about the temptations in terms of Christ's mission to bring post-Fall human beings to union with God, we can begin to see the progression of the temptations. In rejecting Satan's first temptation, Christ is rejecting the unilateral use of divine power to change human psyches from their post-Fall condition to a state of inner integration around the good. And in rejecting Satan's second temptation, Christ is repudiating the use of human power—given by God to Satan to give to human beings—as a means of achieving the same end. Neither divine nor human power is able to move a human psyche into a condition in which it surrenders to the love of God, to begin the processes of justification and sanctification.

It should be said here that, as the speech of Milton's Satan in the second temptation implies, this repudiation of Satan on Christ's part does keep Christ private and obscure, as Milton evocatively puts it, in a backwater province of the Roman Empire, with a ragtag band of the uneducated and unaccomplished as his followers. And yet, of course, in the end, this very obscurity and that motley band of disciples also gave Christ the world-class empire of the Christian church, with some of the greatest minds of the Western world as his followers and defenders. The Church—the one catholic and apostolic church, however and wherever it is to be identified—is a mighty organization, with an enormous influence over the lives and psyches of human beings. It is not necessary to worship Satan to acquire influence over human affairs. Or, to put the same point the other way around, it is important to recognize the lamentable history of the medieval Roman Catholic Church, which shows what happens when one attempts to support and promote this institution of the one catholic and apostolic church through the use of worldly power, with its concomitant need to honor evil or at least to temporize with it. Combining a love of God and God's goodness with a bowing down to power, which is what Satan wants from Christ in this temptation, leads to the dominion of power, not to the love and fear of God.

THE THIRD TEMPTATION

Its Odd Character

Although, as I have tried to show, the first two temptations of Satan are skillful and smart, it is worth wondering whether they are of any interest to Satan, or whether Satan offers them only as a means to leave Christ less able to battle the third temptation. That is, it is worth asking whether, in the story, Satan has any real expectation that either of the first two temptations might be successful with Christ or whether his motive behind those first two temptations has largely to do with the third temptation.

A devout Catholic friend of a desperately sick, lapsed Catholic might say to the sick man, "Can I get you anything? A little soup? Something to read? A priest to hear your confession?"; and then one would know that only that third item on the list was of any real interest to the person making the suggestions. It is worth wondering whether Satan's temptations have an analogous character. I do not mean to suggest that Satan does not make the first two temptations in earnest or would not rejoice if they were successful. On the other hand, it seems to me that the story also invites one to wonder whether Satan does not present those first two temptations in the expectation that they will fail but in the hope that they might enable him to succeed with the third one. In chess, the Queen Sacrifice is a much-admired sophisticated ploy in which a player offers his opponent the opportunity to take his queen; but if the opponent does so, he sets in motion a sequence of plays that leads rapidly to the checkmate of the opponent.

The reason for this question about Satan's strategy has to do with the peculiar nature of the third temptation.

According to the story, in the third temptation Satan somehow puts Christ on a *pterugion* of the Temple—the Greek word translated 'pinnacle' in my summary of the story above. Both the Greek word and the English word 'pinnacle' designate a high pointed area of any kind on a building. (In fact, both the Greek word and the English 'pinnacle' are etymologically connected to a word signifying the wing of a bird, which does generally end in a pointed part of the wing.) Even the top of a gable is a pinnacle, in the sense of both the Greek and the English word. Nothing in contemporary understanding of the architecture of the Temple at the time of Christ rules out its having at least one pinnacle, in some sense of either the Greek or the English word. But the real question with regard to the architecture is whether the story means us to understand that the pinnacle on which Satan put Christ was such that in the nature of things a human being could not stand on it, or at least could not stand on it long or could not get down from it by any natural means. In short, the question is whether it takes a miracle for Christ not to fall from that pinnacle once Satan has put Christ there. Milton supposes that it does and reads the story of the third temptation on that assumption.

If Milton's reading is right, then the only escape route from the third temptation appears to have been blocked by Christ's rejection of the first temptation, where Christ repudiates using divine power to meet a natural human need of his own. The first temptation and Christ's manner of rejecting it therefore sets Christ up, it would seem, for failure in the third temptation. On this way of thinking about the third temptation, the density and complexity of the second temptation has a role in obscuring the connection between the first and the third temptations, and so it also adds to the likelihood that Christ will fail in the third temptation.

I point out this feature of the story because, if Milton's reading is right, then the third temptation is the one that is of real interest to Satan in the story. It is certainly the temptation that is of most interest for my purposes in this book.

Milton's reading has the advantage of rendering intelligible what Satan says to Christ in the third temptation: "If you are the Son of God, throw yourself down from here" (Luke 4:8). This line makes sense if the only alternative to falling is to stand or come down by miracle. If Christ could just stand for as long as he liked and then climb down, this line of Satan's becomes dumber, one might say. Why throw yourself down from a height if you can readily get down by ordinary clambering? Furthermore, without Milton's reading, this temptation becomes a somewhat stupid repetition of the first temptation. It would be a temptation inviting Christ to use his divine power to do what could be done by other means, and he has already rejected the use of divine power to aid himself in such circumstances.

It is true that Satan begins this temptation with the same caveat as he used in the first temptation: "if you are the Son of God," so that someone might suppose this third temptation is just a return to the tactic of the first temptation. But it seems to me better to see the story's Satan as very smart, as the cleverness of the first and second temptations suggest he is, rather than taking him to be so dumb as to return in short order to trying a tactic that has just failed for him.

So I will read this part of the story as Milton does. On this reading, Satan uses his own power over nature to put Christ on a high place which is configured in such a way that, in the ordinary nature of things, a human being cannot stand on it. To stand on it requires a miracle.

Satan's Line

Of course, in this third temptation Satan does invite Christ to do a miracle, only not the miracle of standing. The miracle to which Satan tempts Christ now has to do with Christ's falling.

This is an odd miracle to understand; but, in thinking about it, it helps to see all the temptations as having to do with power, either its use or its repudiation. The first temptation was about Christ's use of divine power; and the second was about Christ's use, with Satan's help, of human power. In his rejection of the first two temptations, Christ has repudiated the use of power to achieve his aim. The third temptation, however, seems to be about

Christ's powerlessness. Satan puts Christ on a high place and tempts him to fall helplessly from that height.

On the other hand, in the first two temptations Satan was only inviting or suggesting; Satan did not himself use the power at his own disposal to push his temptations on Christ. But in the third temptation Satan's power is very much in evidence. And the power that Satan uses to put Christ on the pinnacle of the Temple does shove Christ in the direction Satan wants him to go. Falling, as Satan wants Christ to do, is very hard for Christ not to do, given where Satan has put Christ. On Milton's reading, which seems right to me, it takes a miracle for Christ *not* to fall.

Furthermore, in this third temptation Satan wants Christ *not* to do the sort of thing he apparently *did* want Christ to do in the first temptation, namely, use Christ's own access to divine power to produce by himself some good for himself. On the contrary, in this third temptation, Satan is counting on Christ not to do the miracle required for Christ to stand on the pinnacle; and Satan seems right to count on it, given that his first temptation of Christ got Christ to reject that very kind of use of Christ's own divine power. The miracle that Satan in the third temptation *does* want Christ to do involves falling from the height of the pinnacle but being entirely uninjured by the fall. As Satan puts it to Christ, if Christ is the Son of God, then Christ can rely not on his own divine power but rather on the power of angels, sent by Christ's Father in heaven, to save him from the ordinary effects of such a fall.

Later in the Gospel of Luke, Christ says to his disciples, "I saw Satan fall like lightning from heaven" (Luke 10:18). That is also a fall from a great height, and Satan is ruined by it, but not killed or injured. Rather, Satan's fall is his transformation from someone intimate with God to someone who is hostile to God and allied with evil in consequence. This may be the sort of fall Satan has in mind for Christ when he sets him on the pinnacle of the Temple: no real suffering but a ruining of Christ's mission so that most human beings or many more human beings are left in Satan's domain.

Furthermore, in this third temptation, for the first time, Satan also quotes a biblical text. The source of his quotation is the Psalms, a biblical book noted for its expressions of closeness with God and trust in God. Satan cites this line from Psalm 91:11–12: "God has commanded his angels to take care of you. They will bear you up with their hands so that you do not hurt your foot against a stone." So Satan wants Christ to fall in the expectation that angels will save him from any harm. And since Satan begins this temptation by saying (again) "if you are the Son of God," then in this temptation he is also suggesting that if Christ is unwilling to fall, it can only be because he is not close to God or does not trust sufficiently in God. Since, in the story, in Satan's view and in Christ's view, too, Christ *is* close to God and *does* trust God, then it seems that Christ ought to do as Satan suggests.

The Psalm that Satan quotes in fact begins with expressions of trust in God:

> O you who dwell in the covert of the Most High,
> And abide in the shadow of the Almighty;
> I will say of the Lord, who is my refuge and my fortress,
> My God, in whom I trust,
> That he will deliver you from the snare of the fowler,
> And from the terrible pestilence.[38]

And the line in the Psalm immediately before the line Satan quotes sums up Satan's point: "No evil will befall you" (Ps. 81:10).

These are lines worth puzzling over, of course, given the heartbreaking evils that befall all human beings, including those who trust in God. But in this context Satan's use of this Psalm to frame the suggestion of his temptation can be understood as adding to the power of the temptation. The Psalms are part of God's revelation and so have God's authority behind them. If God warrants that no evil will come to those who trust in him, then on what basis could Christ not trust in God? How could he not evince that trust by falling from the height on which Satan has put him? And why would acceding to Satan's exhortation to fall constitute succumbing to a devilish temptation? So Satan's supporting his suggestion by quoting from the Psalm adds to the effectiveness of Satan's temptation.

If we read Satan's initial caveat "if you are the Son of God" as if it were in the manner of a dare, as I suggested we should in the case of the same line in the first temptation, then the dare in this case is a dare not about whether Christ really has any power over nature. Rather, it is a dare about whether Christ really has a relationship with God that is specially close, specially important—or, in short, a relationship closer to God than Satan's relationship is, that is, close in the manner of the Psalm. So understood, Satan's initial caveat is snidely insinuating that if Christ is special to God, Christ can undergo even things that would kill an ordinary human being and still emerge un-scathed. And if Christ is not willing to test this hypothesis, to accept the dare, it can only be because his standing with God is not—in Christ's own eyes—able to endure the test.

It is part of the impressive cleverness of this third temptation that, on Milton's reading, the only way for Christ not to fall into this temptation is, apparently, for him to fall into the first temptation and use divine power to serve his own needs. It is this feature of the third temptation that causes me to wonder whether in the three temptations taken together Satan is playing an analogue to the Queen Sacrifice in chess. He loses something that is of great value to him in Christ's rejecting the first two temptations, but it is precisely this loss that sets Satan up to win in the third temptation.

What Christ Rejects in the Third Temptation and What
Christ Accepts Later in the Gospel Stories

It is helpful in thinking about the third temptation to consider what Christ actually does and endures later in the Gospel stories. In the Gospel stories of Christ's life subsequent to Satan's temptations, Christ is betrayed by one of his most trusted inner circle, Judas. He is arrested by his countrymen and severely mistreated by those into whose power he falls. He is detained in frightening ways, isolated, mocked, beaten and flogged, and finally tortured to death naked in front of his mother and others who love him.

It is difficult to see all of this as no evil befalling him, on the understanding of the line in the Psalm that Satan quotes. No angels rescue Christ in any of those afflictions. In fact, when Christ stops his disciples from trying to protect him from the mob that comes to capture him, Christ points out to his disciples that he could call on angels to protect him but that he is not doing so. "Don't you know," Christ tells his apostles, "that I could call on my Father, and he would even now send me more than twelve legions of angels?" (Matt. 26:53). But, of course, as he is telling his disciples, he wills not to ask his Father for angels. So, no angels come, and Christ is crucified.

On the other hand, in the Gospel stories, the power of God does eventually operate on Christ's behalf to keep him from ultimate harm. After his crucifixion, Christ is resurrected by the power of God, so that the suffering he really endured is overturned in the end in resurrection. Then angels *are* part of that story, that is, the whole story. When the women come to the tomb to find that Christ is not in it, the ones who announce his resurrection to those women are the angels who are already there. The power of God is clearly in evidence then, at least as much as or more so than it would have been in the scenario Satan tempted Christ to, where the angels were to prevent Christ from any real suffering if he fell from the pinnacle.

It should be clear that the difference between what in the third temptation Satan wants Christ to do and what later in his life in the story Christ actually chooses lies precisely in suffering. The difference is not in the reliance on divine power to save him from death. Both in the scenario to which Satan tempts Christ and in the story of Christ's later life, there is a reliance on God's power to save Christ from death. The difference, which should be highlighted through reflection on the third temptation, lies only in the real suffering that precedes the divine rescue in the actual story as it unfolds in the Gospels.

On the scenario Satan hopes Christ will choose, Christ would appear to be enduring suffering as he falls. But, on that scenario, the appearance would be deceiving. The angels would have caught Christ right before he hit the ground. Anyone who saw only the initial fall would be deceived into thinking that Christ was suffering. And any initiate who knew the truth—for example, anyone who watched the whole fall and perceived that it had an angelic rescue at the end which prevented any real suffering—would take himself to be watching a display of power masquerading as weakness. By contrast, in the Gospel stories, what Christ chooses is suffering, real suffering, painful and hateful, and death.

So here is what Satan wants and is aiming at in the third temptation. He wants Christ to choose to fall from the height on which Satan has put him, and he wants there to be an appearance of suffering on Christ's part. But he also wants it to be the case that, actually, the angels come to save Christ miraculously just before he smashes on the ground. Consequently, Christ's suffering would be just an appearance. It would not be real suffering. On Satan's scenario in the third temptation, then, there would be no real affliction; there would be no real death. For this reason, there would also certainly be no sharing of the suffering and affliction of other human beings. Rather, Christ would be secure from all suffering within his special relationship with God, and he would only deceive the unsophisticated into thinking that he suffered as they do. Those not so deceived would know that, in the end, real power can evade suffering; and they themselves would no doubt hope to do so also through their own special alliance with power.

'Docetism' is the name generally given to the heresy[39] which claims that Christ's suffering was only an illusion, either because Christ himself was on the cross but only seemed to suffer, or for some other reason.[40] By contrast, the Nicene Creed specifies that Christ suffered and died.[41] In rejecting Satan's temptation, then, Christ is rejecting the path that the Docetists claim he took. In refusing Satan's third temptation, Christ rejects the use of divine power to evade real suffering while providing the illusion of it.

Why Satan Cares About this Temptation

Here it is worth pausing to wonder why Satan cares about this temptation. What does Satan gain if Christ succumbs to this temptation? And why is this a temptation for Christ? Why should Christ not simply do as Satan suggests? What is wrong with asking or presupposing or even demanding that God send his angels or use his power to prevent the suffering of his beloved son—or of all his beloved children, so that there is no suffering on the earth? What is the solution to the problem of evil? And, most importantly for my purposes, why would it matter to Christ's understanding of the means of atonement if Christ did as Satan urges?

To begin to see an answer to these questions, it is important to remember the conclusions of Chapter 7. The one thing needful in order for the process of justification and sanctification to begin is that a post-Fall human person cease resisting grace and surrender to the love of God. This one crucial thing cannot be given to her unilaterally by God. If God did try to produce it in her on his own, then God would be invading her and taking her over, instead of coming to indwell in her, with her personhood and individuality preserved. On the other hand, her condition leaves her unable to get by herself for herself this one thing needful for her flourishing and union with God. The nature of her problem is that she wants, and also does not want, to want the good. She wants and does not want love and closeness with others, most notably with God. Because her will is divided in this way, she herself cannot integrate her will by herself. In order to do so, she would have to want to do so effectually, overcoming not wanting to do so; but then she would already have the integration of will that is what she lacks and needs.

Nonetheless, what she *can* bring about on her own and by herself, not by action but by quiescence of action, is simply to cease resisting God. That surrender to God's love is not yet her will's acceptance of grace. But, as I was at pains to show in Chapter 7, her ceasing to resist allows God to act on her will—with formal but not with efficient causation—to bring her to a state of wholeheartedly willing to will the good. And all the rest of the process of her moral and spiritual regeneration can proceed from there.

If we focus on this crucial, fragile, difficult necessary condition for human salvation, that is, a person's ceasing to resist the grace of God and surrendering to God's love, then we can begin to see the reason for Christ's choosing real suffering.

Why does anyone resist love, even if he also seeks it and longs for it? The answer is surely that he expects something intolerable from love, even if he also expects something deeply desirable from it.

In fact, it seems to me that only a naive or unreflective person would wonder what there is about love that could strike a person as intolerable. There are so many things! In the first place, there is the vulnerability that love carries with it. For Jerome to love Paula is for Jerome to risk being hurt or humiliated or finally just rejected by Paula, who might not love him in return. And even if Jerome is loved by Paula, he can be betrayed or abandoned by her if she ceases to love him. Furthermore, in being loved by Paula, Jerome will be known by her. And then those things in Jerome that he himself finds unacceptable or shameful or loathsome will be brought to light. He will come to see himself in Paula's eyes, and that sight might be more than Jerome is willing to endure. In addition, Jerome's loving Paula and being loved by her will unite him to Paula to one degree or another. But to the extent to which he is united with Paula, some of what he does, some of the way in which he organizes his days, some of the roads open to him in his life will be shaped by Paula, and not simply by him alone. And this loss of his ability to determine things for himself by himself—or, as we might put it if we were unkind about it, this diminishment of Jerome's self-regarding and self-absorbed internal isolation—may well appear to Jerome as a loss of his autonomy and therefore as threatening.

Breaking out of self-willed loneliness is hard even for people whose lives have been comparatively easy. For those who have struggled with the depredations of other people or suffered from the mess they themselves have made of their lives, the painfulness of their inner condition and the difficulty of its remedy are much worse, as Norman Care's moving description of alcoholism, discussed in Chapter 7, makes clear. A specially poignant portrayal of a heartbreaking example can be found in Rachel Moran's fiercely honest and admirable memoir of the seven years of her life in prostitution, which began when she was 15. She says,

> Sexual coercion is very easily employed, especially upon those who have been pre-schooled by previous experiences of abuse. It causes a crack in the structure of the self...and the psychic fragmentation and disconnection so common to the findings of prostitution research. Over time it becomes second-nature, this process of fragmentation.... One of the ways I protected myself in prostitution was to...literally split myself into two characters; the authentic me, and the imaginary version.... If a client asked me what my favorite fruit was...I would answer with any fruit I could think of, but I would never admit to my true preference.... It is a cruel and confusing conundrum for prostitutes, who must come to understand that the maintenance and protection of their own identity is supported by the lies they tell their clients, while the dignity of that same identity is defiled and diminished by the truths uncovered by those who are intimately familiar with it. She is left struggling to keep hold of whatever aspects of herself she believes worth holding onto, and whatever they may be, their validity is under constant attack.[42]

Moran summarizes her view of this severe self-alienation in a line that to me, at any rate, is reminiscent of Christ's line in the Gospel of Luke (9:25)—'what does it profit a person to gain the whole world and lose himself?' Moran says,

> There is no currency that can ever re-forge the broken link between a woman [who has lost herself in the destitution of prostitution] and her private essential self.[43]

As Moran describes her own difficult struggle for self-integration, the process of recovery required an immense effort of work with a therapist; and so it required trust, at least a minimal degree of trust, in another human being, even one whose healing aid is part of his profession. The remedy needed for self-willed loneliness requires at least the smallest amount of ceasing to resist the care of someone else.

The problem of self-willed loneliness is exacerbated when the prospect of loving and being loved has to do with God. Even if Jerome believes of himself truly—*really truly*—that he is sincerely seeking God or genuinely struggling for the truth about God, Jerome can also resist finding God because of his fear of God or his resistance towards God or even just his anxious self-protective inner seclusion, common to all post-Fall human beings.

So it is not hard to see why someone would resist God—consciously or just tacitly and subconsciously—even if he also longs for God, with or without explicit awareness of that longing. Jerome can suspect, even tacitly or subconsciously, that his own smallness or shame or sin or any other unloveliness will all be magnified in his own eyes if they are seen in the light of God's overwhelming goodness.

And then, in addition to God's goodness, there is also the problem of God's power. For Jerome to open himself to God's sight may seem alarming, but to open himself to God's power can seem frightening enough to be well worth resisting. God's power and God's ability to get his own way in things, God's moral authority, God's status as judge of all that a person does or thinks or desires, God's omnipotent power—all these things can prompt a person to avoid God, however tacitly or subconsciously, as something to be dreaded. Thomas Nagel is unusual in his conscious awareness of his own attitudes on this score. Speaking of the fear of religion, he says,

> I speak from experience, being strongly subject to this fear myself: I want atheism to be true and am made uneasy by the fact that some of the most intelligent and well-informed people I know are religious believers. It isn't just that I don't believe in God and, naturally, hope that I'm right in my belief. It's that I hope there is no God! I don't want there to be a God; I don't want the universe to be like that.[44]

In addition to such conscious or subconscious dread of God, Jerome might picture himself, however tacitly, as a rebel against God's power; and Jerome might find himself attractive in that picture. Arguing about the problem of evil, John Stuart Mill proudly says, "I will call no being good who is not what I mean when I apply that epithet to my fellow creatures; and if such a creature [*sic*] can sentence me to hell for not so calling him, to hell I will go."[45] Milton's Satan famously says of himself, with manifest pride in the picture of himself that he describes to himself, "Better to reign in hell than serve in heaven."[46]

The general problem for post-Fall human beings as regards the love of God is evocatively sketched by C.S. Lewis in his work *Pilgrim's Regress*, modeled on Bunyan's *Pilgrim's Progress*. Lewis imagines that his analogue to Bunyan's *Everyman*, a character named 'John', has been taken captive by a personified version of the Freudian idea that belief in God (called 'the Landlord' in the story) is a belief which fulfills a wish found in the human subconscious. Personified Reason rescues John from his captivity to this personified Freudian idea by calling the idea into question with regard to some of the anti-religious characters—Victoriana, Glugly, Gus Halfways, and others in the land of Eschropolis—whom John has met on his journey. The story says that in response to Reason's skeptical question whether Victoriana or Glugly or Gus had a subconscious wish that the Landlord actually exist, John got a picture in his mind of Victoriana and Glugly and Gus Halfways and how they would look if a rumor reached them that there was a Landlord and he was coming to Eschropolis.[47]

Then John stood still on the road to think. And first he gave a shake of his shoulders, and then he put his hands to his sides, and then he began to laugh till he was almost shaken to pieces.[48]

There are times when the idea that there is power behind goodness is deeply consoling. But there are other times and circumstances when it can seem only like a nightmare, so that the Freudian idea that belief in God's existence is a wish-fulfillment belief is funny.

It is important to me to make clear that I am not ascribing any culpability or blame to any person merely in consequence of his being in such an internally fragmented state of resistance to God's love. There is no sense in which I mean to say that every failure to surrender to love on the part of a person, Jerome (who is one of my two *Everypersons*), is blameable or in any other way reprovable. A human being *can* be culpable for resisting love, but then it may well be for something more than the mere resistance alone. When in Jane Austen's *Pride and Prejudice*, Mr. Darcy persuades his friend Mr. Bingley to resist Bingley's love for Jane Bennet and Bingley initially does so, what is motivating both men is not the post-Fall human condition but ordinary class-consciousness and pride of family. Of course, there *is* the kind of culpable resistance that results from repeated acts of monstrous wrongdoing, as exemplified by Adolf Eichmann, for example. But for any person who resists love, especially God's love, it is also entirely possible that he is only in the grip of the brokenness and willed loneliness that is the post-Fall human ailment. And, in that case, such a person merits no derogatory judgment or disapproval of any kind, but rather only more love for the suffering he endures in this condition. And the point generalizes. Asked what she would say to other self-alienated women in prostitution, Moran answers,

> what I'd say I would say gently. There are no lectures to desperate women that I feel entitled to give. I know what destitution feels like, and I know from the lessons of my own life that the fear of its imminence is outweighed only by the agony of its arrival.[49]

I honor her for these lines.

So, to me, the question at issue here needs to be this: What will help a person in this state? What can a loving God do to aid such a person? And now we can see the point of the third temptation.

How vulnerable could Jerome feel to a person being crucified? How much power could Jerome fear from a person being betrayed by his friends, beaten by soldiers, and put to death by the ruling powers of his land? How threatening to Jerome could the moral superiority seem of a person mocked, shamed, and humiliated in front of others? How powerful would Jerome seem in his own eyes to rebel against such a beaten person? How attractive in his own eyes would Jerome feel to reject such a person proudly? If there is any aid to quell the resistance of a broken and lonely human heart, isn't real suffering and humiliation on the part of God himself a very good way to do so?[50]

It is also important to remember empathy in this connection. Human beings are naturally built to experience empathy when they perceive the pain of another person. Furthermore, one does not have to be in the presence of a suffering person to feel empathy for him. Narratives can also access the cognitive capacities engaged in empathy.[51] A person Paula can experience empathy with Jerome's pain even if Paula is only seeing a movie of Jerome's suffering or reading a story describing Jerome and his pain. If in actual second-person experience or only through narrative Paula empathically feels in herself the pain Christ is experiencing, how afraid will she be of the power of God? How threatened will she feel by Christ's superiority while she feels something of the pain Christ is suffering and the humiliation he is enduring? On the contrary, the story of Christ's suffering will incline Paula towards him at least as far as empathy will take her.

And then suppose it is also part of the story Paula accepts that Christ has voluntarily taken on the suffering he is enduring out of love for Paula. This element will also make a difference. If Paula empathically quails at Christ's sufferings *and also* believes that Christ suffers voluntarily out of love for her, in order to heal her own suffering and brokenness, then isn't Christ's real suffering and death a most promising way to melt her heart and soften her resistance to God's love?

And so in the Gospel stories of the passion and death of Christ, what is presented to the stories' audience is not the only remedy but the most suitable remedy, the one most likely to work, for a heart that needs to melt: God incarnate enduring real suffering and real death, in love, and so also in forgiveness, for those in need of that love.

In Psalm 130:4, the Psalmist says to God, "There is forgiveness with you; therefore, you are to be feared." It is an odd sequence: first, forgiveness, *then* fear. But these reflections show that the sequence makes sense. The forgiveness of God gentles a person into a surrender to God's love, which enables that person to overcome shame and guilt enough to turn towards God with the kind of fear that love engenders, a fear not of being punished but rather a fear of turning away from the beloved ever again.[52]

By contrast, consider Docetism, the heresy that holds that Christ only appeared to suffer. If the naive believed that Christ suffered when he did not, then they would have the same remedy for resistance to grace, but only as long as they stayed naive. Once their naiveté was breached, as naiveté generally is, their resistance to grace would return with added cynicism and black-spirited anger over having been so stupid as to believe the deceptive story. As for the sophisticated, those who never believed the story but instead supposed that Christ only appeared to suffer, they would understand that deception and power rule the world. And then they would be in the kind of state attributed to Satan in the story of Christ's temptations, a state that is inimical to love and attracted to power instead.

Christ's Rejection of the Third Temptation

And now we are in a position to answer the question I posed above: Why does Satan care about this temptation? It is evident why this third temptation matters more to Satan than the first two; and it is apparent why in the story Satan might use the first two temptations largely as a means to prepare for the third one. If Christ were to succumb to this third temptation, Satan would have set Christ on a course inclining him to a Docetist approach to his atoning work; and that approach would have been decidedly inefficacious. Consequently, if Satan were to succeed with the third temptation, Satan would have won the main thing at hazard between him and Christ in this battle of wits. He would have succeeded in keeping a much greater number of human beings in Satan's rebel alliance, and he would have achieved a much greater frustration of God's desires for union with human beings.

This is also the reason why Christ should reject this third temptation; and, in the story, Christ does reject it. He resists Satan by working a miracle to stand in order not to work a miracle in which he falls from a great height but is miraculously uninjured.

Someone might suppose that if the story of the third temptation is read as I am arguing it should be, then the third temptation puts no strain on Christ. But this view is mistaken. In rejecting Satan's third temptation, Christ is accepting not only his own suffering as a means of atonement but also the general principle that God may need to suppress the use of his power to prevent suffering in order to ward off greater harm to the people God loves.

By allowing his beloved Son to suffer when God could prevent it by sending angels (as Satan suggests) or by any other means, God is warding off a greater harm for human beings for whom Christ's real suffering can melt away a stony resistance. But what could be harder for a loving person to accept than the suffering of his beloved when he could prevent it? What is more agonizing for a parent of a sick child in the hospital than allowing her child to suffer at the hands of the doctors when she could prevent that suffering by taking her child home? And the analogous point holds as regards Christ. Christ's rejection of Satan's third temptation commits Christ to accepting great suffering for the sake of human flourishing. There is a defensible theodicy based on the love of God for human beings; but nothing about that theodicy or about God's love diminishes the lamentable character of suffering and the heartbreak that it causes.

The greater Christ's love for human persons, the greater the strain of accepting this course will be for him. In other work,[53] I argued that Christ's weeping after Lazarus dies does not have its source in sorrow over the death of his friend Lazarus, whom Christ knows he will resurrect momentarily; rather it stems from Christ's having put his companions Mary and Martha to great pain as part of his plan for their flourishing. In rejecting the third temptation, then, out of love for human beings Christ chooses his own real suffering over the sham suffering Satan offers. And that rejection of Satan's offer carries with it Christ's acceptance not only of Christ's own suffering but also of the suffering of others that is permitted by the love of God.

This reading of the story of the third temptation can thus explain both why Christ would turn down the third temptation and also why it is hard for him to do so. It has the additional advantage of explaining why Christ turns it down with the line he chooses: "You shall not tempt the Lord your God."

This line of Christ's rejecting Satan's temptation is even harder to understand than it otherwise might be, because the line seems to rule out requiring a miracle of God. What else would it mean to reject tempting the Lord? The idea seems to be that if a human person puts herself in a position where God has to choose either between working a miracle for her or allowing her to come to harm, then she has tempted the Lord, because she has forced God to choose between alternatives neither of which is desirable to God.

And yet it does take a miracle for Christ to stand on the pinnacle of the temple. What is there about acceding to Satan's temptation that constitutes tempting God when standing by miracle does not?

It helps in this connection to see that in the line with which Christ rejects Satan's third temptation, Christ is quoting again from Moses's speech to the Israelites in Deuteronomy. The way in which the line finishes in Moses's speech is especially noteworthy for my purposes here. Moses says to the people, "You shall not tempt the Lord your God, *as you did at Massah*" (Deut. 6:16, emphasis mine).

The line about Massah is a reference to an episode in Exodus 17.[54] In the story in Exodus, the Israelite people are journeying in the wilderness, and there is no water for them at Massah. They become not only thirsty but desperate, and they demand that Moses give them water. And, in fact, God does provide water for them in a spectacular miracle. In response to the people's angry and distressed demands, God tells Moses to strike a large rock with his staff, and enough water gushes from the rock to provide water for the whole large community.

This story about Massah has some perplexing features of its own. For instance, why does God wait to do this miracle until the people are so thirsty? If God is willing to get them all water from a rock by miracle, why does God not do so before the people become so distressed over the lack of water? And since God is in fact willing to provide a miracle for the people, what counts as their tempting God when they demand that God give them water by miracle? Why, in his speech to the people later, would Moses tell them that they must not tempt God as they did at Massah?

The answer to these questions lies in the end of the story of this episode in Exodus 17. The story finishes this way: "And Moses called the name of that place 'Massah' and 'Meribah', because the Israelites contended with God and tempted God, saying, 'Is God among us or not?'" (Exod. 17:7).[55]

In the story of the exodus of the Israelites from Egypt, God is engaged in forming them into a people who are related to God with special closeness and intimacy. The point of the miracle at Massah and the many other miracles that occur along the journey is to form in the people a deep trust of God and love for God. Consider the difference between their desperation over water and the line in the Psalm "though I walk through the valley of the shadow of death, I will fear no evil" (Ps. 23:4). There are myriad such lines in the Psalms. Here is another one: "you, O Lord, are a shield for me.... I am not afraid of ten thousands of people who have set themselves against me" (Ps. 3:3–6). The ultimate expression of such trust in God occurs in a line in the biblical book of Job. In the story in that biblical book, this line is said by Job in the midst of his own appalling suffering: "though God slay me, yet will I trust in him" (Job 13:15). On the lines from the Psalms, God can be trusted to protect a person from all evil—all real or ultimate evil, one might say. For Job, even death does not count as such an evil if God is with him.

What counts as tempting God at Massah, then, is not the request for a miracle to end suffering. It is the angry or cynical or black-spirited attitude behind the demand for the miracle: "Is God among us or not?" It is acceptable to want a miracle when one is suffering; it is joyous to receive a miracle that ends suffering. But it is not acceptable to suppose that God is not with the sufferer when the sufferer does not get the hoped for miraculous end to suffering. Refusing to trust God until there is an end to suffering through the use of God's power is what counts as tempting God. Since God's aim is drawing human beings closer to himself and since on traditional theological Christian and Jewish doctrine suffering is one way to do so, then to refuse to trust God in suffering forces God to choose between the loss of the good of that healing medicine of suffering or the loss of the good of human trust in God. And this forced choice is not a good thing—that is, not a good thing *for human beings*, who lose something desirable for them whichever way God chooses.

So Christ rejects Satan's suggestion that he fall from the pinnacle of the Temple and expect angels to catch him by reminding Satan of the episode at Massah. In alluding to the story at Massah, Christ is simultaneously affirming his refusal to do a miracle to turn stones into bread in the first temptation and providing the basis for his repudiation of the miracle Satan wants him to do in the third temptation. (In I Cor. 10, Paul connects the story of God's gift of water from a rock at Massah to Christ by saying that the rock which gave the water then was Christ, who now in the Eucharist, which commemorates Christ's suffering, continues to give bread and drink to all those in need. This is yet another way of tying the rejection of the third temptation to the rejection of the first.)

For these reasons, in the miracle of standing on the pinnacle, Christ is not tempting God. Christ stands because God is always trustworthy and always with him, even in real suffering. Even though God slay him, Christ will trust in God.

On the Psalmist's lines that Satan quotes, God's people can trust God for everything, even, for example, for water in the wilderness. But the whole story of God's love is deeper. On Job's line, even if God does not give water or whatever else is necessary for life, God is nonetheless worthy of trust—not because human beings can live without water or because dying of thirst is not a terrible suffering, to be avoided if at all possible, but because the ultimate good for human beings is union in love with God and what leads to it can defeat even the otherwise appalling afflictions of human beings. On the view of the Psalmist and of Job, God can be trusted to use deplorable, lamentable human suffering to ward off the very worst thing for human beings and to incline them toward the best thing—and so God can be trusted in everything, even the most abhorrent human suffering, even death.

The rejection of Satan's third temptation therefore sets Christ on the path to real suffering and death as the most promising means of eliciting the melting of a stony human heart. And in rejecting Satan's temptations, Christ affirms the trustworthiness of God to use suffering as part of the remedy for human willed loneliness and self-alienation.

THE END OF THE TEMPTATIONS

When Christ rejects the third temptation by standing on the pinnacle of the Temple, the temptations are over. The ending of the story is given variously in the Gospels of Matthew, Mark, and Luke.

Mark says only that angels tended Christ in the wilderness (Mark 1:13). Luke says that when Christ withstood the third temptation, the devil left Christ until another time (Luke 4:13). And Matthew says that when Satan left, the angels came and ministered to Christ (Matt. 4:11). What exactly the angels did is left vague there, but Milton supposes that the angels got Christ down from the Temple and fed him as well. In short, Milton supposes that the angels, whom Christ refused to summon to save him from falling, came when Christ stood instead of falling.

One might say that there is an analogous ending to the later story of Christ's real suffering. There too Christ refuses to summon angels to save him. What follows that refusal is not a miracle but rather Christ's suffering—his being humiliated and beaten, his suffering hours of agony in crucifixion, and his final death. But that suffering is followed by Christ's resurrection. Resurrection is undoubtedly a miraculous overturn of Christ's suffering, a miracle provided not by angels but by God himself.

In Moses's speech to the people in Deuteronomy, quoted three times by Christ during the temptations, Moses says to the people, "it is the Lord your God who goes with you; he will not fail you or forsake you" (Deut. 31:6). In the Gospel of John, Christ explains his relation to God the Father this way: "the one who sent me is with me; he has not left me alone" (John 8:29). Between this line of Christ's in the Gospel of John and Christ's resurrection at the end of the Gospel stories is the story of the cry of dereliction from the cross, when Christ cries, "My God, my God, why have you forsaken me?" In this cry Christ is isolated in his human nature, so that he experiences God as receding from him when in fact it is he who is collapsing into himself under the press of human evil.[56] But nothing about the fearful suffering expressed in the cry counts as God's leaving or forsaking Christ, however dreadful Christ's feeling of forsakenness is for him.

Suffering in any of its appalling varieties is not the end of Christ's story, and it is not meant to be the end of any human person's story either. Suffering is meant to be defeated in joy. There are some theologians who suppose that suffering lies within the divine nature itself or is somehow an intrinsic part of the life of the Trinity.[57] But in the Gospel stories, and in orthodox Christianity, the life of the Trinity is characterized by joy, not suffering; and human beings are invited into that life to share that joy. Joy, not suffering, is meant to be the end of the story; and suffering is tolerable and tolerated by a loving God only as a means to the good of the sufferer, not as any kind of intrinsic good.

So it is an appropriate end to the story of the temptations that the angels come to minister to Christ, as it is a most appropriate end to the story of the suffering and death of Christ that he is resurrected to return to love and joy with those who love him.[58] If Christ had not been resurrected, then his story might have given aid and support to those who suppose that suffering in all its grimness is somehow intrinsically worthy of choice. This is a stern-minded attitude that leads in the end to Eckhart's kind of position, where one refuses desire and the fulfillment of desire in joy out of the mistaken idea that God requires such a self-destructive attitude. But such an attitude does not lead to harmony with God. It actually consists in a refusal of love, the final state that characterizes Satan in the story of the temptations. It constitutes the very opposite of a union in love with God. So Christ's resurrection in joy and his reunion of love with those he loves is an end of the story of Christ's suffering which is necessary to make sense of the story, just as it is the end of the story of earthly suffering for all those who do not stay in the company of those who refuse joy and love.

There is one other noteworthy thing about the end of the story of the temptations. In the line with which the Gospel of Luke ends the story of the temptations, "the devil left him until another time," the word translated 'another time' is actually '*kairos*' (Luke 4:13). The Greek word '*kairos*' is translated variously, but at root it seems to mean 'a good time' or 'an opportune time' or 'a right time', as in 'He was waiting for the right time to tell her that he wouldn't be there for her birthday.' The right time, in this sense, is a time that is most favorable to the thing one is aiming at. The line with which the Gospel of Luke ends the story of the temptations implies that Satan returns to tempt Christ again at a time which is most opportune, that is, most opportune from Satan's point of view. On the interpretation of the story I have argued for here, that time is one which is more likely than other times to let Satan be successful in getting Christ to withdraw from his commitment to endure real suffering out of love for human beings in their post-Fall plight.

Some people contemplating this biblical line have supposed that this *kairos* is the time when Christ is on the cross, or even when Christ is uttering the cry of dereliction. But, in my view, this supposition has to be rejected. In the first place, it cannot account for Satan's action as a temptation of Christ. Once Christ is already suffering in crucifixion, he cannot be tempted to avoid suffering as a means of salvation for human beings. One might suppose that even when Christ is on the cross, Satan could tempt Christ to despair. But this supposition is not plausible either. Satan understands that Christ is the Son of God, as the story of the temptations makes clear; and if the Son of God can despair, the despair he endures will do him no real harm. It will not damn him, for example, since the Son of God cannot be ultimately separated from God.

One might suppose that Satan's motive changes when Christ is on the cross, so that Satan is then motivated only by malice, and not by any desire to win out over Christ in any significant contest. On this supposition, in his final temptation of Christ Satan is interested only in the pleasure of causing his enemy the pain of despair, or some other pain. But this is also not a plausible supposition. In effect, it reads Satan as both small and stupid—stupid, because he supposes that there is a benefit for him just in the pain of Christ, and small, because he is willing to trade the pleasure he gets from malice for any real advantage to himself. But in the story of the temptations, Satan is neither stupid nor small. And so it is better to look for an interpretation of the last line of the story of the temptations as Luke tells it which continues to read Satan in the same way he is portrayed in the story of his tempting Christ.

To me, it seems that a better candidate for the *kairos* in question occurs in the story of Christ's praying in the Garden of Gethsemane. That story is the only one in the Gospels, other than the story of the temptations (and maybe also the stories of Christ's resurrection), in which there is a mention of Christ's being aided and cared for by angels.

THE GARDEN OF GETHSEMANE

In the story, just before his crucifixion, Christ goes to the Garden of Gethsemane, a place familiar to him, to pray that if possible, he might be spared what is coming. In Matthew's version of the story, Christ makes this prayer three times. The first time it has this form: "My Father, if it be possible, let this cup pass from me: nevertheless not as I will, but as you will" (Matt. 26:39). The second time, it has this form: "My Father, if this cup may not pass away from me unless I drink it, your will be done" (Matt. 26:42). And the third time, Matthew says, Christ prayed the prayer again, with the same words. Mark reports that Christ prayed twice and that the words in the second prayer were the same as in the first prayer (Mark 14:39). Luke also reports two versions of the prayer; but Luke adds that between the first and the second prayer an angel came to Christ to strengthen him.

In Luke's version of the story, *after* the angel strengthens Christ, Christ is in an agony, and he sweats enough in his anguish that the sweat falls to the ground as if Christ were bleeding instead of sweating (Luke 22:44). In fact, all three versions of the story include some description of Christ as suffering greatly as he prays. The story in Matthew says that, as Christ was beginning the first prayer, he was grieved and astonished; Mark says that Christ was astonished and amazed. In both stories, Christ tells those with him, "My soul is very sorrowful, even to the point of death" (Matt. 26:38; Mark 14:34).

What impels Christ into this anguish? And why would the angel's strengthening Christ be followed by agony? Why would it not yield peace instead?

It is common to suppose that in the Garden of Gethsemane Christ is so anguished because he quails at the prospect of the coming physical pain. Calvin is eloquent in his rejection of this interpretation; and, although I quoted his remarks in an earlier chapter, it is worth calling them to mind again here. Calvin says,

> let the pious reader consider how far it is honourable to Christ to make him more...timid than the generality of men. Robbers and other malefactors contumaciously hasten to death, many men magnanimously despise it, others meet it calmly. If the Son of God was amazed and terror-struck at the prospect of it, where was his firmness or magnanimity?[59]

By contrast with interpreters who suppose Christ is shrinking from the prospect of *physical* pain, John Henry Newman attributes Christ's anguish in Gethsemane to some present experience of the *psychical* pain that Christ will endure during his crucifixion.[60] Newman begins his commentary on this part of the story of Christ's prayer in Gethsemane by making the general point that, "as His atoning passion was undergone in the body, so it was undergone in the soul also."[61] In fact, Newman argues that in his crucifixion Christ refused the medicinal drinks offered him in order to leave his mind unclouded, so that Christ could have the mental control needed to open his psyche as much as possible to this sort of suffering.[62]

It should be added, on Calvin's side, and Newman's too, that in the actual events of Christ's passion, while he is on the cross and before he dies, Christ does show just the calm Calvin admires even in robbers. Christ endures with self-possession and without quailing (or any kind of undue fearfulness) the betrayal, mockery, flogging, and humiliation that precede his crucifixion. There is no sign of flailing distress in any of the stories about his suffering those things. Furthermore, there is no sign of extreme emotion even in the very worst physical pain of the crucifixion. When Christ is being nailed to the cross, he prays to God to forgive those who are hurting him. In addition, as various commentators have pointed out, while Christ is suffering slow death on the cross, he declares, with authority and without any evidence of anguish, to one of the robbers being crucified with him, 'Today you will be with me in Paradise.'[63] Finally, on the cross, Christ has a care for his mother and uses his last hours to make sure she will be looked after by his disciple John. There is no sign of his falling apart under physical pain in any of these parts of the story, where one would expect it if Christ's anguish in the Garden of Gethsemane stems from a fear of physical pain and death. One might suppose that the stories about Christ during his crucifixion simply omit any sign of such falling apart because the story-tellers were in the grip of a hagiographical fervor incompatible with making Christ look, as Calvin says, weak and timid. But this supposition cannot be right either, since it is the same stories that describe Christ as in anguish in the Garden of Gethsemane.

So it seems to me better to connect Christ's distress in the Garden of Gethsemane with the only part of the crucifixion in which Christ also seems to be in anguish, namely, with the cry of dereliction. Newman certainly takes this approach. He thinks that the agony of Christ's suffering in soul which was manifested during the cry of dereliction actually began in the Garden of Gethsemane.[64]

One way to understand the cry of dereliction is to suppose that in the experience that gives rise to the cry Christ is opening his human psyche to the psyches of all other human beings, so that their psyches come to be in God through entering the human mind of Christ. In that experience, all the vile, cruel, abhorrent human evil anyone has ever done or wanted to do is available for Christ to experience within himself, in the way that human cognitive capacities for empathy and mind-reading enable, but to a much greater degree, as is possible only for the incarnate Son of God.

With this interpretation of the cry of dereliction, we are in a better position to review the details of the story about Christ's prayer in Gethsemane. In that story, the words used to describe Christ's distress as he goes to pray carry with them an implication of surprise and shock: he was astonished and very amazed, the stories say. But what would be shocking or surprising to Christ about what is coming? Not the facts of crucifixion, which have been known to him at least in outline for some time, as one story after another in the Gospels indicates. It is certainly even possible that Christ had also already had some idea that he would experience human evil within himself in the process of crucifixion. He does after all know the texts about the Messiah in the Hebrew Bible, and they make clear that the Messiah will bear the sin of human beings. But what might, even so, be a surprise to Christ, and a great shock, is what that evil feels like when it is within him. It is one thing to know *that* there is sadistic cruelty, for example; it is another thing entirely to have some non-propositional, as-it-were mind-melding knowledge of it, some feeling shared with the psyche of a human person who is addicted to such cruelty.

And so it may be that in the Garden of Gethsemane, as Christ goes to pray before his crucifixion, Satan finds that very time the *kairos* Satan was waiting for and uses it to try one last time to persuade Christ to abandon the path of his own real suffering as a means of salvation for human beings.

Newman reads the story of Christ in Gethsemane this way, and his words are vivid and evocative. I am not endorsing here Newman's whole interpretation of this story (and no doubt he would have had hesitations about mine if he had known it). But it is nonetheless worth quoting Newman's words at length, because they use vivid imagery that adds intuitive insight to what would otherwise be too abstract a description of Christ's suffering during his prayer in Gethsemane. This is how Newman describes Christ's anguish at that time:

> what was it [Christ] had to bear, when He thus opened upon His soul the torrent of this predestinated pain? Alas! He had to bear what is well known to us, what is familiar to us, but what to Him was woe unutterable.... He had to bear the sins of the whole world.... Sin could not touch His Divine Majesty; but it could assail Him in that way in which He allowed Himself to be assailed, that is, through the medium of His humanity.
>
> There, then, in that most awful hour, knelt the Saviour of the world, putting off the defences of His divinity, dismissing His reluctant Angels,... and opening His arms,... to the assault of His foe,—of a foe whose breath was a pestilence, and whose embrace was an agony. There He knelt,... while the vile and horrible fiend clad His spirit in a robe steeped in all that is hateful and heinous in human crime, which clung close round His heart, and filled His conscience, and found its way into every sense and pore of His mind, and spread over Him a moral leprosy....
>
> Oh, the horror, when He looked, and did not know Himself, and felt as a foul and loathsome sinner, from His vivid perception of that mass of corruption which poured over His head and ran down even to the skirts of His garments! Oh, the distraction, when He found His eyes, and hands, and feet, and lips, and heart, as if the members of the Evil One, and not of God! Are these the hands of the Immaculate Lamb of God, once innocent, but now red with ten thousand barbarous deeds of blood? are these His lips, not uttering prayer, and praise, and holy blessings, but as if defiled with oaths, and blasphemies, and doctrines of

devils? or His eyes, profaned as they are by all the evil visions and idolatrous fascinations for which men have abandoned their adorable Creator? And His ears, they ring with sounds of revelry and of strife; and His heart is frozen with avarice, and cruelty, and unbelief; and His very memory is laden with every sin which has been committed since the fall, in all regions of the earth, with the pride of the old giants, and the lusts of the five cities, and the obduracy of Egypt, and the ambition of Babel, and the unthankfulness and scorn of Israel.

Oh, who does not know the misery of a haunting thought which comes again and again, in spite of rejection, to annoy, if it cannot seduce? or of some odious and sickening imagination, in no sense one's own, but forced upon the mind from without? or of evil knowledge, gained with or without a man's fault, but which he would give a great price to be rid of at once and for ever? And adversaries such as these gather around Thee, Blessed Lord, in millions now; they come in troops more numerous than the locust or the palmer-worm, or the plagues of hail, and flies, and frogs, which were sent against Pharaoh. Of the living and of the dead and of the as yet unborn, of the lost and of the saved, of Thy people and of strangers, of sinners and of saints, all sins are there. Thy dearest are there, Thy saints and Thy chosen are upon Thee; Thy three Apostles, Peter, James, and John; but not as comforters, but as accusers, like the friends of Job, "sprinkling dust towards heaven," and heaping curses on Thy head....

It is the long history of a world, and God alone can bear the load of it. Hopes blighted, vows broken, lights quenched, warnings scorned, opportunities lost; the innocent betrayed, the young hardened, the penitent relapsing, the just overcome, the aged failing; the sophistry of misbelief, the wilfulness of passion, the obduracy of pride, the tyranny of habit, the canker of remorse, the wasting fever of care, the anguish of shame, the pining of disappointment, the sickness of despair; such cruel, such pitiable spectacles, such heartrending, revolting, detestable, maddening scenes; nay, the haggard faces, the convulsed lips, the flushed cheek, the dark brow of the willing slaves of evil, they are all before Him now; they are upon Him and in Him. They are with Him instead of that ineffable peace which has inhabited His soul since the moment of His conception. They are upon Him, they are all but His own....[65]

Newman's florid language provides a more melodramatic description of Christ's experience than I myself am comfortable with or find intuitive given the presentation of Christ in other Gospel stories; but Newman's vivid rhetoric does bring home the basic point. If in the Garden of Gethsemane Satan gives Christ a foretaste of the horrifying experience of the sort that Newman is trying to bring to life for his readers and that prompts the cry of dereliction on the cross, then in Gethsemane Christ might well be astonished and amazed.

And, of course, although Satan could give Christ this foretaste of bearing human sin in any number of ways, as the lines from Newman's sermon suggest, one easy way for Satan to do so at that last moment in the Garden, when Christ might still turn back from suffering, is for Satan to try to invade the psyche of Christ himself, to let Christ feel Satan's own malice and evil. The Gospel stories accept that Satan can occupy a human mind and cause it great distress. There is nothing, then, to rule out an interpretation of the story of Christ in Gethsemane on which Satan himself tries, at least momentarily, to enter Christ's human mind against Christ's will, to give Christ a foretaste of what is coming during the crucifixion, to give Christ just enough foretaste of the crucifixion for Christ to be shocked and in anguish at the experience of bearing human sin on the cross. But I am not wedded to this particular version of the kind of interpretation Newman presents. What I want to suggest is only that, in Christ's anguish in the Garden, Satan is using his most opportune moment for suggesting to Christ, in one way or another, that the real and not illusory suffering Christ means to undergo is in fact unendurable, that Christ has to let this cup pass whether or not it is God's will that Christ drink it.

This suggested interpretation of the story about Christ in Gethsemane has the added advantage of being able to explain why Christ is in agony *after* an angel comes to strengthen him. On this interpretation, the point of the angel's strengthening is for Christ not to yield to the temptation to give up on real suffering but rather to stand under Satan's horrible foretaste of the experience behind the cry of dereliction that Christ has on the cross. And if in fact the story implies that Satan himself made a no-doubt unsuccessful effort to enter the mind of Christ in Gethsemane, then a role for the angel is even easier to understand. On this way of thinking about the angel's role, if it was a strain for Christ to withstand Satan from without during the temptations in the desert, it is an agonizing struggle to reject him from within during this last temptation in Gethsemane and to accept the anguishing suffering that Christ will express in the cry of dereliction. It might well take the help of the ministering angel to stand and not yield under this suffering.

Someone might suppose that the angel's mission was a failure if Christ still had to struggle after the angel's strengthening of him. But to think so is in fact to have succumbed, as it were, to Satan's first temptation and to suppose that divine power should simply be used unilaterally to alter the state of human wills. In Gethsemane, the angel gives Christ's human will enough strength so that Satan's superior psychic power does not leave Christ helpless. But, in the end, it needs to be Christ's will that rejects Satan. If it is a will that is not Christ's but put into Christ by the angel, then it is the angel that has resisted Satan's assault, not Christ.

Furthermore, just as even heartbreaking human suffering can be defeated by its effects in a human life, so it may be that without this agonizing recognition of the experience which is coming during the crucifixion and some first practice at standing under it, Christ would have collapsed inwardly on the cross in a way that would have left him unable to finish his part of the process of mutual indwelling.

In addition, in the Gospels of Matthew and Mark, besides the story of the temptations, there is one other story in which Christ addresses Satan directly

(Matt. 16:21–3; Mark 8:31–3). In that story, Christ has been teaching his disciples that he must suffer and be killed; but Peter objects. Mark says only that Peter objected. As Matthew tells this story, what Peter actually says in response to Christ's revelation that he will suffer and be killed is this: "Far be it from you, Lord! May this never happen to you!" Christ rebukes Peter for this speech using words of second-personal address—but second-personal address to *Satan*; and the words Christ uses then are the same words Christ uses in rejecting Satan's second temptation in Luke: "Get thee behind me, Satan!" The rest of Christ's rebuke to Peter does seem entirely addressed to Peter. But the first line of the rebuke, with the association it draws between Peter's objection to Christ's real suffering and Satan's third temptation, is also some confirmation of the interpretation of Christ's temptations that I have argued for here.[66]

Finally, it is important to see that Christ's suffering on the cross accomplishes two different things, one of which is psychological and one of which is metaphysical, but both of which are crucial for human union with God. In rejecting Satan's third temptation, Christ chooses his own suffering as a most promising way to melt human hearts hardened into disappointment, bitterness, sorrow, and loneliness. This is the first thing that Christ does to help human beings achieve union with God. It mediates the human part of mutual indwelling between God and human beings, in which human beings open to receive the indwelling Holy Spirit. The second thing Christ does is something metaphysically great, which requires the power of Christ's divine nature to accomplish; and that is Christ's allowing the incursion of human psyches into his human psyche. This is God's part of the mutual indwelling between God and human persons, in which human beings indwell in God. So, through his passion and death, in one way and another, Christ provides for the mutual indwelling between God and human persons, so that they can be one with God, as Christ is one with the Father: Christ in the Father and the Father in Christ.

THE LIFE OF CHRIST

In this connection, it is worth touching just lightly on stories about Christ's life apart from the temptations and the crucifixion. Consider, for example, the birth narratives. Angels play a notable role in various episodes of the birth narratives in both the Gospel of Matthew and the Gospel of Luke. Here I want to call attention to just one of these episodes.[67] In the birth narratives, Mary, a pregnant woman of relatively modest means and status, is away from home because of government-enforced migrations of people. She begins to go into labor in the small town to which she and her husband have been compelled to go, and the best housing they can find for her labor and delivery is a stable with animals around. In the cold of the night in the stable, she gives birth to a baby boy; and then, for lack of anything better by way of a cradle to keep him safe from being stepped on by the beasts, she wraps the baby up and puts him in a feeding trough that the animals use.

The stable is close enough to the edge of the little town where they are that it is not far from fields where the local sheep and their shepherds are huddled up for the night. In the midst of this entirely lower-class setting, an angel in brightly shining light appears not to the kings or rulers of this world, but to the poor shepherds, to announce the birth of the Messiah. When the local king wants to know where the Messiah is born, he has to ask the assistance of biblically learned scholars and wandering Magi from the East. But the uneducated shepherds know right where the baby is because an angel tells them. In fact, not only are the shepherds visited by one messenger angel who gives them this news, but actually a whole synaxis of angels (well, a whole host of angels) fills the sky to sing a song of praise to God in a blaze of glory, for the benefit of the shepherds—and, of course, for the benefit of all those who hear the story that those lowly but highly honored shepherds tell.

The notable honor of the angel's announcement to the shepherds and the magnificence of the angels' song for the shepherds cast into sharp relief the meanness of the shepherds and also that of the little family sheltering with the animals in the stable. They are nobody, and they have nothing. The baby is newborn and helpless, and his family is vulnerable in their resources and social class too. All the details about the baby's birth in the cold of night and his first bed in the feeding trough only add to the impression of vulnerability or helplessness.

What is the point of having the birth narratives take this form? Why would God choose to have the Messiah make his entrance into human history in this mean and impoverished way, in this helpless and vulnerable state? It is easy to answer these questions once we imagine the difference it would make to the story if we altered any of these details. Suppose that Christ's parents had been wealthy or members of a royal household. That would make a significant change in the affect the story induces, wouldn't it? Or suppose that instead of coming into the world as a newborn baby, Christ had come into human history first as an adult, as one might suppose Adam did in the story in Genesis, for example. Take even the time and place of the Gospel birth narratives. Suppose that Christ had been born at mid-day in May, in a well-appointed accommodation. All these changes in the story would clearly make a significant difference to the story's ability to touch the heart.

In effect, the story of Christ's life begins as it ends on the cross, in powerlessness. The glaring difference between the glory of the angels and the circumstances of the baby and his family throws the weakness of the baby into sharp relief. A newborn at night in a cold stable among beasts is no threat to anyone. And neither is a man being mocked by his countrymen as he dies from the torture of crucifixion. The details of the birth narrative in the Gospel of Luke therefore provide some confirmation for the interpretation of the third temptation given in this chapter. What this interpretation and the details in the birth story underscore is that Christ's real and not illusory suffering is powerful enough to heal the most intractable part of the human ailment, the unwillingness to yield to the love one longs for.

In this connection, it is worth noticing that this same view of Christ's mission can explain one other notably odd feature of the Gospel narratives. In the Gospel of Mark, for example, the story introduces Christ's ministry by explaining that he preached throughout Galilee (Mark 1:14, 1:39) and that he taught with authority in the synagogues (Mark 1:21–2). But the story does not say *what* Christ preached or taught. The closest it comes to revealing any teaching of Christ's is the claim that he preached the Gospel. But if his teaching is important, if the Gospel he preached is central to salvation, then one would suppose that the story would feature Christ's teaching in some central way. But where one would expect this teaching to be, there is only nothing.

In Matthew and in Luke, the narrative does report details of Christ's preaching, most notably in the Sermon on the Mount. But the Sermon on the Mount is also odd, considered as preaching or teaching of any kind. Think, for example, of the beatitudes, with which the Sermon begins. The first one is "Blessed are the poor in spirit, for theirs is the kingdom of heaven" (Matt. 5:3; cf. Luke 6:20). Is this moral teaching? Does it give a rule for conduct? What would that rule be? This beatitude seems to be singling out a state of mind or heart or character for special approbation. But can one voluntarily choose such a state? And if one cannot, then in what sense is this beatitude a teaching about how one is to live?

At a certain point in the Gospel of John (6:28), people ask Christ with some vexation what they should do to work the works of God, and one can sympathize with their question and the spirit in which it is asked. What exactly is Christ's message? What is the content of his preaching? And, in particular, what *are* human beings supposed to do to be in a condition approvable by God?

But the desire to have from Christ a teaching that includes rules or a set of instructions for human conduct misses the mark entirely. If rules or instructions could produce internal integration around the good in the psyche of a human person, she would already wholeheartedly want to want the good—and that is precisely what a post-Fall human person does not want wholeheartedly. The idea that the content of a sermon or an instruction manual for human conduct could provide the solution to the post-Fall human illness would make sense only if one presupposed that the hearer for the sermon or the reader of the manual were already cured of the illness. To put the precepts of the teaching into play, the audience for those precepts would have to want to do so wholeheartedly enough to translate desire into action. But, of course, the desire to do so is what is lacking in the post-Fall human condition. Or, to put the thought another way, Pelagianism—the theory that there is some good that a human being can do on her own without grace—fails to take account of the depth of the human problem. Given the willed loneliness and brokenness characteristic of a post-Fall human will, it is not possible to bring a person to internal integration and wholeheartedness by sermons or instruction manuals for conduct.

That is no doubt why, in response to the people's demand to know what God expects them to do, Christ tells them to believe in him (John 6:29). Later in the Gospel of John, Christ cries to the crowd, "If anyone thirsts, let him come to me and drink" (John 7:37). Elsewhere in that same Gospel, Christ also urges those hearing him to come to him, and he adds this claim, "no one who comes to me will I ever throw out" (John 6:37). In another story in the Gospel of Matthew, Christ says, "Come to me, all you who are heavy-laden, and I will give you rest" (Matt. 11:28). And the point about rest is not hard to understand in this context either. A double-minded person wants and does not want the same thing, so that whatever he gets is not what he wants. There is no peace for a person in such a condition.

If the remedy for the post-Fall human condition is to surrender to the love of God, which is most manifest in the vulnerability and suffering of Christ, then it makes sense that Christ's teaching is in effect an urgent call to come to him. Such instruction as there is in Christ's teaching can be understood as a help to ward off self-deception in the process of coming to him rather than as a set of rules for salvation. Jerome might suppose of himself that he has given over resistance to God's love and grace; but if he finds that he hates others (cf., e.g., Luke 6:27), then he needs to consider whether he has not in fact just stayed or returned to his original state of resisting grace. The solution for him when he hates is not to make a greater effort to be a better person, but rather to come to Christ or come to Christ again.

This view of Christ's mission also gives insight into Christ's attempt to explain that mission by analogy with the bronze serpent of the story in Numbers 21.

In the story in Numbers, the Israelites express distrust of God and engage in rebellion against God; in consequence, God afflicts them with snake bites. (Rabbinic interpretation points out that the snake was the first in the biblical stories to slander God, and so it is fitting that when the Israelites slander God with their rebellious murmurings against God, they should be punished with the bites of snakes.) In response to the affliction of the snake bites, the Israelites come to Moses in repentance and ask for help. When Moses asks God for help, God tells Moses to make a bronze serpent and put it up high on a pole. Everyone who is bitten by a snake and comes to look at that serpent high on the pole is cured of the snake bite.

In John 3:14–5, Christ refers to this story as a way of explaining his crucifixion and its effects. Christ says that he himself must be lifted up as the serpent was lifted up in the wilderness, so that everyone who believes in Christ might have eternal life. The cure for snake bite required just coming to the serpent on the pole and looking at it. And Christ's line about his crucifixion implies that contemplating Christ on the cross and believing in him is sufficient for eternal life. To contemplate Christ on the cross is to see him as broken and suffering in love for broken human beings. And, on the interpretation I have argued for here, that view of Christ is the most promising way to melt the resistance that keeps a person hardened against love. With the ceasing of that resistance, all the other parts of spiritual regeneration can then begin and proceed.

THE PROBLEM OF EXCLUSIVISM

In John 14:6, Christ says to his disciples, "I am the way, the truth, and the life; no one comes to the Father except by me." On the interpretation of the doctrine of the atonement I have argued for in this and the preceding chapters, this claim is true.

The first thing to notice about this claim is that it is the expression of a kind of exclusivism. In fact, any worldview excludes others. If Maoist economics is the right way to prosperity or the good life for the citizens of a country, then unrestrained capitalism is not. If Kantianism is the right approach to ethics, then Confucianism is not. And so on. Adopting a worldview can seem disrespectful to those who reject it, because those others are judged as wrong or confused or in some other way deficient. There is thus a problem of exclusivism for any worldview, but the problem is exacerbated when it comes to religion. A religious worldview is a grand unified theory of everything, and the apparent deficiency in those who reject it is correspondingly great. For Christianity, the exclusivism has to do with salvation. As implied by Christ's claim in the Gospel of John, Christ is the way to the Father—the *only* way to the Father. Consequently, it seems that all those who do not hold the Christian worldview are apparently excluded from salvation.

And that is surely a lot of people. There are non-Christian people in other cultures who have never had much or any contact with Christian views. There are those who have considered Christianity and rejected it. There are small children who die before the age of reason and who lack Christian beliefs for that reason.[68] And then there is the problem of Judaism. On traditional Christian views, the patriarchs and other heroes of the Hebrew Bible had some theological beliefs about the importance of a Messiah in Israel's history. But it is hard to suppose that these beliefs included beliefs about the incarnation, passion, and death of Christ. Nonetheless, on biblically based orthodox Christian doctrine, the patriarchs and other notable people of faith in the Hebrew Bible found their way to the love of God, and they are among the saved in heaven. But either they found their way to God without Christ, in which case Christ's claim in John 14:6 seems to be false; or, if Christ's claim has to be accepted as true, then, contrary to Christian claims about the people of faith in the Hebrew Bible, they also seem excluded from salvation.

A good part of what makes these apparent implications of exclusivism hateful is that they seem—and in my view are—incompatible with the love of God. How could a loving God exclude people from himself for not sharing views that they may not ever have heard or that they heard and in good conscience rejected? How could a loving God exclude those who by misfortune die[69] before the age of reason? How could a loving God exclude those who trusted in him throughout Israel's history in the pre-Christian period?

To begin to resolve the problem generated by Christian exclusivism, it helps to see that what Christ identifies as necessary for salvation is actually not knowledge of a set of propositions that need to be believed. Instead, it is knowledge of a person. Christ says, "*I am the way, the truth, and the life.*"

But, clearly, it is possible to know a person and know that that person exists but to know that person under only one description and not under other relevant descriptions. One might know the pauper, for example, and not realize that he is the prince in disguise. For that matter, it is possible to be in relation to a person without much propositional knowledge about that person. The princess knows the frog, but she knows nothing about the prince who has been bewitched to be in the form of that frog. She knows that the frog exists, but she does not know that the prince exists; and so, a fortiori, she does not have true propositional beliefs making mention of the prince. In fact, it is even possible to be aware of a person without any conscious belief in the existence of that person. So, for example, in Tolkien's *Lord of the Rings*, Frodo is rescued from Black Riders by an Elf Lord who carries him off on his horse while Frodo is delirious with fever. Frodo is conscious enough to know the Elf; but in his delirious state he supposes that his rescue is only a dream. He has some knowledge of the Elf, even in his delirious condition; but he nonetheless does not believe that the Elf exists because he supposes that he is dreaming.

What these examples drawn from folklore and narratives show is something familiar to human beings about relations between persons, and the point translates also to the theological realm. One can have a loving connection to the person who is Christ, even while one rejects the theology about Christ. Karl Rahner thought that there are anonymous Christians, that is, people who are not self-acknowledged Christians but who are even so within the community of the saved in virtue of having a relationship of love with Christ. Aquinas himself thought that some pagans before the time of Christ might have had implicit faith in Christ in virtue of trusting God to be a rewarder of those who seek him.[70] And then there are these lines of Yehuda Halevi's:

> With all my heart, in truth, and with all my might,
> I have loved You, outwardly and inwardly.
> Your name is before me: How could I walk alone?
> He is my beloved: How could I sit solitary?
> He is my lamp: How could my light go out?
> How could I slip? He is a staff in my hand.
> They have held me in contempt, who do not understand
> That the same I endure for the glory of Your name is my glory.
> Fountain of life to me, I shall bless You while I love.
> My song, I shall sing to You as long as I exist.[71]

There is no reason for supposing that Halevi had any developed theological beliefs about Christ, but it would take an ideologically hardened person to deny that these lines manifest a knowledge and love of God.

What the line in the Gospel of John mandates as the one thing necessary for salvation is Christ, as Christ's many calls to come to him also testify. It is Christ that is essential, and not belief in theological propositions about Christ.[72] Furthermore, as the second person of the Trinity, Christ is God; and so love of what really is God is also love of Christ. It can therefore be true both that no one comes to the Father but by Christ and that some people who lack propositional beliefs mentioning Christ nonetheless come to the Father by Christ.

In my view, these reflections ward off the apparently hateful implications of exclusivism, but they do so apparently at the expense of the arguments in this chapter about the effects of Christ's passion and death on post-Fall human beings. If these reflections on the problem of exclusivism are right, what becomes of the role of Christ's life and suffering in the surrender that leads to the beginning of justification?

In the Gospel of John, explaining his passion and death, Christ says, "No one has greater love than to lay down his life for his friends" (John 15:13). I John 3:16 says, "We know by this what love is, because Christ laid down his life for us." And the widely known line near the start of the Gospel of John says, "God so loved the world that he gave his only-begotten Son" (John 3:16). One can grant the line that there is no greater love than that shown by God in Christ's passion and death and still hold that in many other ways, explicitly or subtly and beneath the level of consciousness, God makes a person feel God's love enough to help a person yield to it. The many stories of God's care for Israel in the Hebrew Bible are one such way, as the lines from Halevi testify. But even beauty in art or nature can count as such a means. Beauty is a kind of stealth bomber. It flies in under the radar of the reason to have its effect on desire, without a preemptive strike on the part of reason to stop it. By prompting longing of an ill-defined sort, beauty can start the motion whose end point of rest is love of God. And the general point applies to human persons below the age of reason too. Just as a mother can make her presence and her love known to a newborn who lacks all propositional knowledge and nonetheless resonates to her and is comforted by her, so God can be present as well.

On the interpretation of the temptations of Christ that I have argued for in this chapter, awareness of the passion and death of Christ (through narrative or by some other means) is a most promising way for God to help a human person towards the surrender to God that only she herself can give. Stories about Christ, together with Christian theology about Christ, are powerful in their aid to this same end; and, as I hope this book shows, there is in general much advantage in philosophical theology about Christian doctrine. But even those who lack or reject Christian theology may yet have great love of God because of God's presence to them in other ways. So although the passion and death of Christ is a most promising way of manifesting the love and forgiveness of God to those who need to come to Christ, a most promising way is still not a necessary way, not even for a perfectly good God (contra Anselm).[73] A person can come to Christ without accepting specifically Christian theological claims, and yet it could still be true that no one comes to the Father except by Christ.

But this is nonetheless not yet the end of the difficulties generated by the problem of exclusivism. If a person can come to God without explicit belief in Christian theological claims, it seems that there is no way of privileging one religion above another. If exclusion is the Scylla here, then relativism is the Charybdis. On the argument given in the preceding paragraphs, a person might suppose that, at least as regards salvation, other competing worldviews are apparently as good or as acceptable as Christianity. But then it seems that salvation can be achieved just as well by means that do not involve Christ's passion and death. In that case, however, it seems that there is no point in Christ's suffering. And if there is no point in Christ's incarnation, passion, and death, then they are apparently incompatible with the goodness of God. A perfectly good God would not will Christ's suffering if there were no good reason for it.

But here it is important to remember the arguments in the earlier chapters to the effect that union with God is metaphysically greater than union as between human persons only. When one of the relata in the union of love is God, the union is one constituted by the *mutual* indwelling of God and a human person. What is interwoven in that union are not just parts of persons, their thoughts and affections, but rather the persons themselves.

The passion and death of Christ enable this mutual indwelling in two different ways.

In this chapter, I have been at pains to explain the way in which Christ's life, passion, and death help a human person Paula towards the surrender in love without which the Holy Spirit of God will not come into her psyche.

But, for union between God and Paula, it is also necessary that Paula is somehow within God. On the interpretation of the cry of dereliction in Chapter 5, in his passion Christ opens himself up to the influx of all human psyches, so that on the cross Christ does God's part of the mutual indwelling for all human beings. By opening the human mind of Christ to the incursion of all human psyches, God allows all human beings to indwell in himself. Even those people who die as infants or those people who in this life hold no Christian theological beliefs or, finally, even those people who never surrender to receive the indwelling Holy Spirit, are all nonetheless in Christ at the time of his cry of dereliction. And so, given that God has chosen the atonement of Christ as the means of salvation, the passion and death of Christ are in fact necessary (that is, conditionally necessary) for salvation for all people. Christ's passion and death are what make possible the *mutual* indwelling that constitutes union with God for those persons who surrender to God's love.[74]

Furthermore, there is biblical warrant for supposing that the Holy Spirit can indwell in a person who lacks Christian theological beliefs in virtue of living before the time of Christ's life, passion, and death. David seems to have been such a person. I Samuel 16:13 says that when Samuel anointed David, the spirit of the Lord came on David from that day forward. In fact, this biblical text is compatible with the claim in the Gospel of John (16:7) that the Holy Spirit would not come without Christ's death. The Chalcedonian formula and the doctrine of the eternity of God together imply that the effects of Christ's passion and death can occur at any time. On the Chalcedonian formula for the incarnation, Christ is fully divine as well as fully human. Christ suffers and dies in his human nature; but, as divine and so eternal, Christ is not bound by human limitations of time and place. In the metaphysical unity of the Trinity, there is mutual indwelling of the Father and the Son through the Holy Spirit who is the bond of love between them. That love of God can be shared through the indwelling of the Holy Spirit with any human person at any time and place, and it will be a mutual indwelling through Christ's passion and death.

For all these reasons, it can be true that Christ is *the* way, as Christ's claim in the Gospel maintains, so that no one comes to the Father but by Christ; and exclusivism does follow from that claim. But it is possible to reject the hateful implications usually supposed to follow from such exclusivism without espousing a relativism that makes Christ's incarnation, passion, and death gratuitous. Rightly interpreted, Christ's claim that no one comes to the Father but by Christ does not imply that all those who lack or reject Christian theological beliefs are excluded from salvation. And yet it does not follow that there are any people for whom Christ's passion and death do not have an essential role in their union with God. Even if one accepts that there are people who find their way to the love of God without explicit or even tacit awareness of Christ's passion and death, it can still be true that Christ is the way to union with God.

REVIEW AND CONCLUSION

In the preceding chapters, I showed that the union which a perfectly loving God wants with human beings consists in a mutual indwelling. On the basis of a detailed consideration of Christ's cry of dereliction, I argued that in Christ's passion on the cross, through the power of his divinity, Christ's human psyche is opened at once to the psyches of all human beings, with all their evil, brokenness, and internal fragmentation. In opening his psyche in this way, Christ is unilaterally providing God's part in the union that God desires with human beings: through Christ's willingness to let them into him, human beings come to indwell in God. What else is needed for union between God and a human person is that God's Holy Spirit come to indwell her.

But for this purpose she has to surrender to God's love and become integrated around the good at least to the minimal extent of accepting grace and wanting to want the good. On Aquinas's views, as long as a person does not return to resisting grace, this integration will be carried out from its minimal beginning in justification to completion by means of the process of sanctification. A person who is in the process of sanctification is living a life in grace, and bringing a human person to this life in grace is what the atonement of Christ is meant to achieve.

There are differing understandings of what a life in grace is, however. In Chapter 6, I argued against an Eckhartian account of it and for a Thomistic account. On the Thomistic account, when a person is in grace, she has a will that wills to will the good; but that higher-order will in her may co-exist with contrary desires and volitions. As long as she retains the will to will the good, however, God's grace can work in her to increase her internal integration so that eventually she has fewer and fewer desires that are in conflict with God's goodness and with her own will to will the good. This process may be difficult for her; but, as long as she does not lose the higher-order will gained by God's grace in her surrender to God's love, this process will ultimately result in her complete wholeheartedness in willing the good in union with God.

This is Aquinas's account of the life in grace; but, as I explained in Chapter 1, the main problem with Aquinas's account is that it seems disconnected from the passion and death of Christ (or the life, passion, and death of Christ). We are now in a position, however, to sketch such a connection.

God's giving of operative grace in a person's justification is compatible with her having free will in a libertarian sense, because, even on the rejection of every form of Pelagianism, it is open to her will either to resist grace or to cease resisting grace, where ceasing resisting is not an act of will (let alone a good act of will) but only the cessation of her will's action. Consequently, although all the work and all the credit for her being in a state of grace is God's, it is ultimately up to her alone whether or not she lives a life in grace. The problem of her post-Fall condition is that God cannot unilaterally produce in her this acceptance of God's love, and in her post-Fall state she does not will it wholeheartedly either, or even wholeheartedly will to will it. And so the whole complicated structure of justification and sanctification, with the inter-weaving of grace and free will, has to rest on this one crucial point, her surrender to God's love so that God can give her the operative grace of justification without violating her will.

Detailed reflection on the Gospel stories shows that Christ's passion and death are a most promising way for God to help a human person to this surrender. The obstacle to salvation that even God cannot remove and that a human person is herself helpless to overcome can be melted away by Christ's suffering and death—and, actually, by all Christ's vulnerability, from Christ's entrance into the world as a defenseless infant to his leaving life through crucifixion. The stories of the temptations of Christ show forcefully the way in which Christ's suffering and death are connected to the processes of justifica-tion and sanctification that yield full union with God in the end. A person's ceasing to resist the grace of God and surrendering to God's love is the pinnacle on which, unsteadily, her salvation has to stand. If we focus on this crucial and difficult necessary condition for salvation, then we can begin to see the reason for Christ's choosing real suffering. What can be gained by weak-ness that could not be gotten through power is the melting of a heart accustomed to willed loneliness and hardened against the hope of joy.

In arguing earlier against the Anselmian kind of interpretation of the doctrine of the atonement, I showed that a perfectly loving God is also always forgiving, in the sense that God always desires the good of all human persons and also always seeks union with them. What needs to be provided by Christ's atonement is not something that dislodges for God an obstacle to God's forgiving human beings and accepting reconciliation with them. What is needed is rather something that gently disarms a human person's resistance to love, so that she is willing to accept the forgiveness that is always there for her in God's love.

Nothing about the claim that God loves and forgives every person is inconsistent with the biblical texts typically cited to inspire fear of God. For example, there is a biblical text which says that it is a fearful thing to fall into the hands of the living God (Heb. 10:31). That line is compatible with the claim that God loves and forgives every human person. The fire of God's love can be experienced as wild and exhilarating or harsh and hateful, depending on the love or lack of love on the part of a human person experiencing it. And something similar can be said about biblical claims describing God's anger and hatred. For those who never cease resisting God's love, God's love can still encompass them, but it will encompass them in the only way in which their rejection of love allows. As is well-known, the inscription Dante puts over the gate of hell in his *Inferno* declares that hell is founded on God's love.

One might suppose that nothing could be easier for a person than happily to accept being forgiven for sins, all sins, even those as yet uncommitted. But, of course, accepting God's forgiveness for a sin is not compatible with continuing to commit it, and so accepting forgiveness requires some kind of commitment to healing from one's internally fragmented state. In Dante's *Inferno*, a soul being carried off to hell complains to Satan that he had a papal dispensation for his sin before he committed it—to which the devil replies with a laugh that the soul must not have known that Satan is a logician.[75] One cannot simultaneously commit a wrong and accept forgiveness for that wrong. So, to accept God's forgiveness, a person has at least to will to will to be healed—and in this requirement she will find the basis for a knotty, tangled resistance to the very love and forgiveness she longs for. The love of God expressed in the suffering and death of Christ, with all the vulnerability shown by the stories of Christ's birth and life, is God's giving of himself in human life to help allay a human person's resistance to him.

The one thing needful for salvation, then, is not an acceptance of Christian theological doctrines or a commitment to a set of Christian beliefs, but rather coming to Christ. As various Patristic authors pointed out, the stretched out arms of Christ on the cross are an image of Christ's openness to human beings, in all their evil, and of Christ's welcome for those who come to him.

With this chapter, then, my project is in a sense finished, because I have shown the way in which Christ's passion and death yield union with God. But there is yet one major problem worth considering, and that has to do with perseverance. Because it is ultimately up to a human person Paula whether or not she surrenders to God's love, and because surrender is not submission, surrender remains in Paula's control; it does not deprive her of her free will and self-determination, as submission might well do. For this very reason, however, Paula can at any time close herself up again in resistance to love; she can always withdraw her surrender to love and return to self-willed loneliness.

Consequently, the difficulty of perseverance in the original surrender to God's love also poses an obstacle to union with God. It should be said that this difficulty is not of the same order of magnitude as the original surrender to love. Coming to union is harder than staying in it once its goods have been experienced. But nonetheless, because the will of a human person in that union continues to be free, perseverance remains a challenge. In Chapter 9, I will consider that challenge and the role of Christ's passion and death in helping to meet it.

After that, what is still important to consider is the way in which this particular interpretation of the doctrine of the atonement meets the desiderata for acceptable interpretations of the doctrine which I canvassed in Chapter 1. I will turn to that issue in the final section of this book, Part IV, which will consider the connection between the atonement of Christ, on the one hand, and, on the other, the defeat of guilt and shame and the other desiderata for an acceptable interpretation of the doctrine of the atonement.

9

Perseverance

Eucharist and Suffering

INTRODUCTION

In Chapter 8, I showed the way in which the atonement of Christ is the most promising way to help a human person Paula to the surrender to God's love that is the difficult necessary and sufficient condition[1] for her salvation from her own inner broken state. Once Paula has surrendered, she receives at once the infused virtues and the indwelling Holy Spirit together with all the gifts and fruits of the Holy Spirit. In this condition, Paula is a person in grace living a life in grace; she is in the process of sanctification, which will culminate eventually in complete union with God if it is continued to its end. But, as I explained at the end of that chapter, Paula can leave the life in grace at any time. Nothing about entering it cements her into it. She retains alternative possibilities with regard to it: she can remain in grace, or she can return to closing it out.[2]

In this respect, surrender is radically unlike submission. If Jerome submits himself to Paula, he wants what Paula wants him to want only because he desires to obey her will in order to avoid the penalties for not doing so (or to reap the rewards for himself of doing so). If what Paula wants is that Jerome bind himself in permanent slavery to her, then Jerome's submission could be irrevocable. But surrender to love is different. In consequence of his surrender to Paula in love, Jerome wants what Paula wants; but he does so because he wants and loves Paula.[3] Wanting and loving Paula remains in Jerome's control. If he ceases wanting and loving her, then he will also cease to want what she wants. And so surrender is never irrevocable.

For that reason, this surrender is also fragile. A version of the original difficulty in getting a person to surrender to God's love persists throughout every moment of the life of a person in grace.

Furthermore, the process of sanctification, of growing in integration around the good, is slow.[4] That is because even God does not act on the will of a person Paula with efficient causation; in giving Paula grace, God acts on her will only with formal causation. As a result, although God puts into Paula's will the grace that strengthens Paula's will in its willing of the good, God does not remove the configurations in Paula's will that she herself put there through her self-destructive habits of moral wrongdoing or her willed isolation in guilt and shame.

Aquinas is right, then, that in this life the model for the structure of the will of a person in grace is Christ's prayer in Gethsemane.[5] In that prayer, Christ evinces a first-order desire to escape his coming ordeal, but also a second-order desire to will what God wills because God wills it. When Christ recognizes that God's will is for Christ to suffer and die, then Christ gains or strengthens a first-order desire for this suffering and death. But this first-order desire is in conflict with the first-order desire to avoid suffering and death. Consequently, by the time of the last of his three prayers in the Garden of Gethsemane, there is this structure in Christ's will: a conflict between first-order desires, a second-order desire that takes sides in this conflict (because Christ wills to will what God wills), *and* a harmony in Christ's will because the first-order desire on which Christ acts is the desire that he himself in his second-order will wants to have. On Aquinas's interpretation of willing what God wills, as on Eckhart's, willing what God wills requires harmony in the will; but, on Aquinas's interpretation, unlike Eckhart's, harmony in the will does not require the complete absence of tension or conflict in the will. It is enough if a person acts on the will he himself wants to have when he wants to will what God wills.

And so because God's grace does not expel all previous self-destructive habits in the will, sanctification works slowly to integrate the will of a person in grace; and it does so in accordance with that person's desire that God help him. As is abundantly clear to everyone who has ever attempted any self-reform, the second-order will to will some particular good is often inefficacious. And this claim remains true even if the second-order will is a desire to have someone else help alter the first-order will. Counseling is typically a long process just because the person who comes to the counselor to be healed, however desperate his desire for healing may be, also has simultaneously a powerful investment in remaining unhealed.

The triangular structure represented by Christ's prayer in Gethsemane will be in a person Jerome while he remains in grace, but the relative strengths of the different parts of Jerome's divided will can be such that his will is *not* in harmony. Jerome's first-order desire for what is in opposition to his own second-order will for a good will may win out over that second-order will. In that case, Jerome's first-order will, the will on which he acts, is against what God wills, and Jerome acts against the good when he acts on that first-order will. In that condition, Jerome might repent and so remain in grace; but he might also just return to the condition he had before he ceased resisting grace.

In addition, the most fundamental problem in the will, the post-Fall hunger for one's own power and pleasure over greater goods, smolders underneath all willing throughout the life even of a person in grace. This is not any particular act of will but rather only an underlying bent in the will. It is called '*fomes*' in Latin philosophical theology; and this is a good word for it, because the root meaning of '*fomes*' is tinder, that is, something that can start a fire or keep it going when it starts to die down. It would be foolish to attempt any precise characterization of the *fomes*, but it is easy to recognize it in oneself and others. It is that part of the self that is ready to react with affront, of one kind and degree or another, at any crossing of one's own will, whether that crossing stems from the will of another person or just from involuntary suffering. Tolkien captures the phenomenon narratively in his story of the ring of power, which virtually no one is able to resist. The longing for the ring, the intense gratification that the ring gives when others are subject to the power of the possessor of the ring, and the violence of the possessor's reaction to any attempt to take the ring from him—these represent nicely the *fomes* of post-Fall human beings.

It is part of Christian doctrine that the *fomes* does not die out entirely in this life even in the very best of human beings. It is gone entirely only after death. Some wit has said acerbically that the doctrine of original sin is the only theological doctrine overwhelmingly confirmed by empirical evidence; but I would say that there are at least two such doctrines. The doctrine that the *fomes* does not die out in this life is the other one.

Because this is so, throughout this-worldly life even a person in grace Jerome will continue to generate new bad desires, leading to new bad actions, that in turn form new bad habits in the will. Nonetheless, while Jerome is forming these new bad habits, if he does not return to resisting grace totally, it will also be true, on Aquinas's account of the unity of the virtues, that Jerome will have all the infused virtues, the gifts and fruits of the Holy Spirit, and the indwelling Holy Spirit itself. In other words, to the extent to which Jerome forms any bad volition or does any bad act, Jerome adds to his own inner fragmentation. The process of sanctification, in which Jerome is integrated around the good, is therefore highly unlikely to be one of steady progress. It will be less like a walk up a mountain and more nearly like a roller-coaster ride, with plenty of movement down and backwards as well as movement up and forwards.

So there are multiple reasons why, even after an original experience of the love, joy, and peace of the incipient union with God in the indwelling Holy Spirit, Jerome might yet turn his back on sanctification and on God. In sanctification, Jerome has to battle against the bad habits he already had by the time he became a person of grace, and he will sometimes lose this battle. Sometimes these bad habits and sometimes just the tendency to prefer his own power and pleasure over greater goods will lead him into actual moral wrongdoing. And such wrongdoing will generate new bad habits in Jerome if he continues in its practice. In this condition, he might continually repent and stay in grace; but he might also just get sick of the struggle and give up on the process entirely.

In addition, sometimes the experience of suffering that comes to all human beings may lead a person to impatience or even to despair. As the Christian tradition affirms, and as I will explain in more detail below, suffering can be a powerful help for someone in the process of sanctification. But a person who suffers can also lose patience with the suffering; and, if the impatience is great enough, the sufferer can throw overboard in anger or grief the whole process of sanctification and his trust in God with it.

Furthermore, some people who are not prompted to abandon God because of the suffering they endure from outside themselves may nonetheless be strongly tempted to give up because of the suffering with which their own condition afflicts them. They may find not the depredations of others but rather the defects of their own post-Fall selves too hard to endure. A person's struggle with himself might also exasperate him into impatience or despair.

People impatient or despairing because of their own defects tend to fall into two sorts, depending on what it is about their condition that weighs on them. For some people, the issue is guilt. Their sins are so present before their own eyes that they lose their ability to trust God's unceasing forgiveness, and they fall into anxiety or depression over the wrath of God that they imagine they should anticipate. As Bunyan describes this condition in himself, in his moving and insightful memoir *Grace Abounding to the Chief of Sinners*, he continually rejected God's love and forgiveness, which were always there for him and were manifested to him in many ways, because of his conviction that he had forfeited God's forgiveness and love by his sinfulness. A person in this confused and miserable condition fears God's wrath or God's engulfment of him in condemnation.

For other people, however, the issue is not the kind of undigested guilt Bunyan experienced but rather shame. A person despairing in shame may have no trouble believing in God's forgiveness not just in general for all humanity but even for her in particular; and yet she may still be overwhelmed by her own sense of her spiritual unloveliness. In that condition, she may abandon the project of sanctification as hopeless *for her*, because, as she sees it, *her* inner ugliness (unlike that of other people, as she sees it) is insuperable. In this kind of despair, she will reject the love of God which she herself believes is there even for her, because in a kind of self-willed fit of Pelagian confusion she wants to be spiritually lovely before she accepts God's love.

There is a poignant example of this sort of despair in one of the characters in C.S. Lewis's *The Great Divorce*. In Lewis's story, a woman in a spiritual condition analogous to that of an animated decaying corpse refuses to engage in conversation with a spirit from heaven sent to help her because she feels she is not sufficiently well dressed to participate in that conversation. She refuses to accept the love being offered her because of her shame at her condition; she feels that she needs to be spiritually beautiful before she can accept the love and grace that are in fact the only things that can make her what she herself wants to be. In response to her proud and stubborn refusal of the love she wants, the spirit sent to help her tries to coax her forward just a step by saying to her,

> Don't you remember...things too hot to touch with your finger...[that] you could drink...all right? Shame is like that. If you will...drink the cup to the bottom—you will find it very nourishing: but try to do anything else with it and it scalds.[6]

In a maddeningly irrational way, a person in the condition of C.S. Lewis's shamed character hangs back from the love of God being offered her. She fears facing her own unloveliness, and she projects her view of herself on to God, whose love and forgiveness even for her she does nonetheless believe in and want, however half-heartedly. Consequently, in her double-minded attitude towards God's love prompted by her proud shame at what she takes herself to be, she fears the abandonment and rejection of the God whose love and forgiveness she nonetheless believes are there for her just as she is.

And, finally, there are people who vacillate between the fear of engulfment and the fear of abandonment. In brokenness, Jerome can fear that if he draws near to God, God will take him over in condemnation or wrath. In that fear of divine engulfment, Jerome can move away from God so that God becomes distant to him. But then Jerome will feel the distance he has put between himself and God and experience it as God's abandonment of him.[7] And so fear of engulfment can be one side of a pendulum swing that winds up on the other side in a sense of abandonment. The misery of wavering between fear of engulfment and fear of abandonment is another route to despair.

When a person falls into moral wrongdoing or despair, it is possible for him to repent and continue the process of sanctification. By its very nature, as I have sketched it here, the life of grace is a life of repentance, where the ongoing process of repentance is compatible with joy. But it is also possible for a person to deceive himself about his own condition and therefore to fail to move forward in sanctification but to fall back instead into his original broken condition of resisting God's love or something even worse.

To appreciate this point, it helps to remember the relations between the will and the intellect sketched in Chapter 2. On Aquinas's moral psychology, the will is a hunger for the good, so that the will desires what it does under the aspect of the good (where the good includes not only the moral good but also the pleasant and the useful). The will does not make identifications of the good; but it responds to the reports of the intellect, which thus acts on the will with final causation. On the other hand, the will *can* act on the intellect with efficient causation, so that what the intellect reports as the good is in part a consequence of what the will wants the intellect to report. The result is that every morally wrong act of will misprograms the intellect, which in turn leads the will into further moral wrongdoing.

If this interactive downward spiral goes far enough, it leads to folly, which in Aquinas's parlance is a kind of moral stupidity and self-deception.[8] In such a condition, a person loses touch with himself and moral reality. Adolf Eichmann refused an opportunity for a last confession before his execution, on the grounds that he had never done anything wrong and so did not need to make a confession. Sinking into self-deception and folly is another way to lose entirely the surrender to love a person might once have had. In the worst cases, moral monstrosity such as Eichmann's can result.

It is no surprise, then, that the list of the fruits of the indwelling Holy Spirit, which begins with love, joy, and peace, continues with patience and long-suffering. If a post-Fall person who is in the process of sanctification perseveres in his surrender to the love of a God who is omnipotent but still allows Jerome's suffering, then that person has *patience*. And if, when guilt or shame at his own unloveliness is the main challenge for him, he perseveres in willing to be loved by a God who has the beauty of holiness, then he has *long-suffering*.

But that these two, patience and long-suffering, are on the list of the fruits of the Holy Spirit also shows the riskiness of the process of sanctification. It is easy for a person to find either his suffering or his own ongoing brokenness unbearable. And in that impatience of suffering or intolerance of himself, he may return at any time to his original condition of resisting God's love entirely.

It is helpful to see in this connection that, in line with traditional orthodox Christian theology, Aquinas distinguishes moral wrongdoing into mortal sin and venial sin. Mortal sin is wrongdoing that will exclude a person from union with God and everlasting life with God unless it is corrected through repentance. It is called 'mortal'—that is, deadly—because it destroys the spiritual life of the wrongdoer's psyche. Venial sin is all other moral wrongdoing. Venial sin needs correction, sooner or later; but it is not toxic to the psyche in the way mortal sin is. The concept of mortal sin implies that in this life it is possible to leave the life of grace and never return to it.

At least from the time of John Cassian onwards, the Patristic and medieval Christian world held fixed a particular list of mortal sins—the seven deadly sins, as they came to be called—and their derivative sins. Nonetheless, it is important to see that on Aquinas's second-personal account of the ethical life, the nature of a mortal sin will be relational in character, rather than specified by a set of intrinsic characteristics of an action. Because moral excellence in human life is a matter of love, especially love for God, then whether a particular action constitutes a mortal sin or not depends, for Aquinas, on whether it breaks charity with God. As long as a person Paula retains the second-order will for a will that wills what God wills, that is, as long as Paula does not go back to resisting God's love and grace, then even Paula's wrongdoing or other self-willed defects can in their turn become material on which the process of sanctification acts, to produce more internal integration around the good in Paula.

Without doubt, it does seem as if some morally wrong acts in their very nature are such that it is hard to imagine that one could do them and not break charity with God. But, even so, the main element distinguishing mortal from venial sin is still love or charity. Those acts that are moral wrongdoings but that do not fracture the whole relationship of love with God are venial sins. What is essential to sanctification and so to ultimate and complete union with God is a second-order will for a will that loves God, that loves God's goodness, that wants God's grace, because while this second-order will remains in a person Jerome, God can work cooperatively with Jerome to integrate Jerome's will around the good without violating his will. But if this second-order volition is lost, God can no longer do so. That is why, at that point, Jerome's moral wrongdoing is deadly to him. So, even while losing ground in the struggle in the process of sanctification, Jerome can remain in a life in grace as long as he does not withdraw from the original surrender that opened him to the indwelling Holy Spirit and thus lose the global second-order will for a will that wills the good.

The upshot of all these considerations is that, while he is in this life, Jerome always retains the possibility of returning to resistance to God; and, for one reason or another, Jerome will be continually tempted to do so.[9] Speaking of the maintenance program of Alcoholics Anonymous, Norman Care says,

> As anyone with inside or outside experience of alcoholism knows, relapse is a standing threat.... [A]lcoholism for the real alcoholic can be a life-or-death matter and ... relapse can be fatal.[10]

Mutatis mutandis, a similar point holds as regards the whole process of moral and spiritual regeneration. And so perseverance in grace is also part of the story of Christ's atoning work. In this chapter, I want to consider perseverance in grace and those things that are an aid to perseverance.

PERSEVERANCE

There are then actually *three* parts to the process that brings a person Jerome to complete and permanent union with God. There is justification, which is the beginning, when Jerome ceases rejecting God. There is sanctification, which is the process designed to culminate eventually in Jerome's complete internal integration around the good and his full union with God. And there is also perseverance.

Perseverance is the persisting that keeps a person in sanctification from returning to the original resistance to God. The rejection of Pelagianism implies that there cannot be any good in a person that is not put there by God. But nothing in any Christian doctrine implies that there cannot be evil in a human person put there by that person. Whatever else a human person may be capable of, on orthodox Christian views a person is always capable of willing what is not good. And so the process of bringing Jerome to union with God requires Jerome's original surrender to God, his sanctification, *and* his perseverance in the process.[11]

Where perseverance is concerned, the process of a person's coming to union with God is like marriage in the contemporary Western version of marriage. In that version of marriage, there is a falling in love, followed by a mutual consent to marriage. But the union begun at the wedding has to continue; the consent vowed in marriage has to go on day after day. And on any given day, that original consent can be retracted. For the marriage to last, it is not enough that there was an original falling in love followed by a commitment to marriage.[12] There has to be continuing in that commitment, too. Perseverance is as crucial to the process of salvation as it is to marriage; but, as the reflections above illustrate, perseverance in sanctification is also almost as delicate and difficult as the original surrender to God is.

Augustine sometimes writes as if God could give a lifetime of perseverance in one single gift of grace given at a particular time to a particular person.[13] So, for example, Augustine says,

> There remains among these benefits [produced by grace] final perseverance, which will be requested in vain every day from the Lord, unless the Lord brings it about through his grace in him whose prayers he has heard.[14]

And a little later in the same treatise, Augustine says,

> these gifts of God ... are given to the elect who are called according to ... [God's] purpose, among which gifts are both to begin to believe and to persevere in faith to the end of life.[15]

And Augustine summarizes his position by reiterating,

> I defend, in accordance with the Scriptures, ... the position that both the beginning of faith and perseverance in it to the end are gifts of God.[16]

But if Augustine really means what he seems to say in these lines, namely, that God can give one gift of grace that yields perseverance in faith throughout life, then he seems to me mistaken in this way of thinking about God's part in a person's perseverance.

In describing the beginning of the process that brings a person Paula to union with God, I argued that God could not by himself alone produce the necessary state of will in Paula without destroying the possibility of the union which God wants with Paula. That is because two wills are needed for union; but if God puts a state of will in Paula, that state of will is God's and not Paula's. Consequently, there is only one will, God's will, that is in God and in Paula. But then there also are not two wills to unite. And that is why the beginning of the process which unites God and Paula is as tricky as it is. It has to depend on Paula, who (on anti-Pelagian views) is in no condition to will anything good of herself.

It is important to see that similar considerations apply with respect to perseverance, too. If God were to give Paula in one fell swoop the gift of a lifetime's perseverance, as it sometimes seems that Augustine supposes God could do, what God would be giving Paula is the inability ever to return to her original condition of resisting God. But then God would have taken away from Paula the alternative possibilities of a will that is truly her own, even on the rejection of Pelagianism, namely, the possibilities of either resisting God or ceasing resisting him. And so if God gave Paula one gift of grace that cemented her in a lifetime's perseverance, in this case, too, there would be just one will, God's will, which is in God and brought about by God in Paula.

Consequently, if Augustine meant what he seems to be saying in the lines quoted above, then he was wrong to think that God could give a person perpetual perseverance as one single gift of grace. The problem of perseverance is as difficult as the problem of Paula's original justification is. Day by day, hour by hour, Paula has to persevere in sanctification; and, at any moment in that time, Paula can return to her original state of rejecting God. For these reasons and in this respect, Paula's perseverance is like the beginning of the process of her coming to God: whether or not it continues through any given time has to depend ultimately on Paula.

And so the process of sanctification is risky, from God's point of view. Even if through Christ's passion and death, Paula is brought to surrender to God's love, Paula's will remains able to do evil after that point; and so Paula can at any time reject God's grace and return to her unwillingness to surrender to God's love. Paula's perseverance in sanctification in this life will therefore also be a challenging problem for a provident God, just as Paula's original surrender to love was.

Nonetheless, there are things God can do to help Paula not only to remain in the process of sanctification but also to grow into greater union with God through it. In this chapter, I will consider two things that the Christian tradition has generally taken to be divine aids to perseverance in sanctification, namely, the Eucharist and suffering; and I will ask what each of them has to do with the atonement of Christ. As stories of greatly admired Christians make clear, these are not the only helps given to people in the process of sanctification through God's providence. There are very many others as well. Sudden experiences of beauty in nature or art can prompt awe or joy or melting into a release of tears of sorrow that had been stuck or frozen before.[17] The community of others (in church and elsewhere) who can be companions in sanctification is another such help. And so on. My purpose in this chapter is not to explore all the helps to perseverance possible or available, but instead to focus on only two, traditionally recognized as weighty, namely, the Eucharist and suffering. I will try to show the role that each of these plays in perseverance and also the connection that each of these has to the suffering of Christ in atonement.

EUCHARIST: SOME PRELIMINARY POINTS

We can begin with the Eucharist and its role in perseverance. (I recognize, of course, that the names for this rite vary among Christians; but it is necessary to have some name by which to refer to it, and so for purposes of this chapter I will call the rite 'the Eucharist.' Nothing hangs on this name; and those who are uncomfortable with it should feel free to substitute the name they prefer.) In the Gospel stories, shortly before his passion and death, Christ gave his apostles bread and wine, which he identified as his body and blood; and he urged them to eat and drink them in remembrance of him. His doing so is commonly understood to be the establishment of the rite of the Eucharist. The general consensus among Christians is that Christ instituted the rite of the Eucharist, that the rite involves eating bread and drinking wine,[18] that the rite is connected to the passion and death of Christ in some way, and that there is some kind of significant relation between the bread and wine, on the one hand, and the body and blood of Christ, on the other hand. After these basic points, there is not much agreement among Christians about the rite.

Given the great diversity of Christian theological views about the Eucharist, I will begin by trying to sidestep the major points of controversy that divide Christians. Even with all the divergent views about the rite, the general Christian consensus includes the conviction that something about this rite makes a powerful connection between those participating in the rite and the passion and death of Christ. On any traditional Christian views, the Eucharist, whatever exactly it is, is connected to the atoning work of Christ.

Aquinas puts the general Christian attitude towards the Eucharist this way.[19] He says,

> it is manifest ... that Christ has freed us from our sins especially by his passion
> .... And so it is manifest that the sacraments of the Church have their power
> particularly from the passion of Christ, and this power is applied to us by the
> reception of the sacraments.[20]

As the complicated doctrine of transubstantiation manifests, Christian views about the Eucharist raise many philosophical and theological questions, some of them highly metaphysical;[21] but in this chapter I will leave most such questions to one side. My aim is just to explore the connection between the Eucharist and Christ's passion and death.

I will begin by trying to elucidate this connection using no more than the claims that are common across the divisions among Christians. As I will argue, even on such a sparse account of the Eucharist, one such connection has to do with a role that the Eucharist has in a person's perseverance in the life of grace.

On the sparse account of the Eucharist, common to the varying Christian views, the rite at least reminds those persons in grace[22] who participate in the Eucharist of the passion and death of Christ. And, at least, as the participants in the rite eat the bread, they are made mindful of the body of Christ, which they believe was broken for them; as they drink the wine in the rite,[23] they are made mindful of the blood of Christ, which they believe was shed for them. In my view, what is true as regards the Eucharist's role in aiding perseverance on this sparse account of the rite is compatible with all metaphysically richer interpretations of the rite. That is, the role of the Eucharist in perseverance on the sparse account is compatible with, for example, a Catholic belief in transubstantiation and the real presence of Christ in the consecrated bread and wine. But it is also compatible with the significantly different accounts of the Eucharist found among other Christian groups too.

So beginning with the sparse account of the Eucharist that is shared across Christian differences, I will examine this role for the Eucharist. But once I have done so, I will turn to Aquinas's metaphysically richer account of the Eucharist to sketch briefly what the rich account adds to the sparse account.

UNION AND STORIES

We can begin with a review of union between two human friends. Such union requires mutual closeness together with maximal shared attention. A person Paula has second-person experience of another person Jerome only if Paula is aware of Jerome as a person; her awareness is direct, intuitive, and unmediated; and Jerome is conscious. When there is also shared attention, then *mutual* second-person experience yields some degree of interpersonal connection. When that connection arises in a context of mutual closeness, the result is one or another degree of union between human persons.

For human beings, shared attention is at least partly a matter of mutual awareness, of the sort that prompts philosophical worry about the possibility of an unstoppable infinite regress: Paula is aware of Jerome's being aware of Paula's being aware of Jerome's being aware, and so on, and similarly Jerome is aware of Paula's being aware of Jerome's being aware...(continued *ad libi-tum*).[24] But in a union of love between God and a person in grace, the union requires more than just shared attention in a context of mutual closeness. It also requires mutual indwelling of God and that human person.[25] This union, metaphysically greater than that possible between human beings, is analogous to the union of love among the persons of the Trinity.[26]

Even the limited degree of union between two human persons yields a special kind of connection between one human mind and another. As far as that goes, even unilateral second-person experience of a person Jerome on the part of a person Paula gives Paula some degree of a non-propositional knowledge of persons where Jerome is concerned. Knowledge of persons is different from ordinary knowledge *that* something or other is the case. And one of the noteworthy things about such knowledge of persons is that it can be transmitted by means of stories.[27] While a person cannot express the distinct-ive knowledge of her second-personal experience as a matter of knowing *that*, she can do something to re-present the experience itself in such a way that she can share the second-person experience to some degree with someone else who was not part of it, so that at least some of the knowledge of persons garnered from the second-personal experience is also available to him.[28] And this is generally what we do when we tell a story.[29]

A story takes a real or imagined set of second-person experiences of one sort or another and makes it available to a wider audience to share. So a story can be thought of as a communication of a set of real or imagined second-person experiences that does not lose (at least does not lose entirely) the distinctively second-person character of the experiences. A story does so by making it possible, to one degree or another, for a person to experience some of what she would have experienced if she had been an onlooker in the second-person experience represented in the story. That is, a story gives a person some of what she would have had if she had had unmediated personal interaction with the characters in the story while they were conscious and interacting with each other, without actually making her part of the action in the story itself.[30]

What is noteworthy here, then, is that, to one degree or another, a story about a person Jerome can connect another person Paula, who appropriates the story, with the Jerome of the story in such a way that, although Paula is not face-to-face with Jerome, she nonetheless gains a kind of knowledge of Jerome. (How much knowledge she has will be a function of how well the story is told and of how competent at the comprehension of stories Paula is.)

If, after having appropriated the story, Paula actually meets Jerome and Jerome is open to Paula, then some mutual closeness, some shared attention, some union is possible between them. But, in this case, any union that occurs will have had its beginning in Paula's appropriation of the story about Jerome and the knowledge of Jerome that the story gave her; and the movement towards such union as then occurs between her and Jerome will be achieved faster or will become more quickly deep because the story has given the process a head start.

I have highlighted this point about stories because it matters for my purposes here. It is important to see that, with the exception of those few people who were present during Christ's crucifixion,[31] everyone who becomes aware of Christ's passion and death[32] and surrenders resistance to the love of God in consequence has to do so because of a story. Christ is a particular person, and his passion and death are historical particulars. Information about a particular person and about particular historical events in the life of that person cannot be given in the form of abstract universal generalizations. If such information is to be given in any explicit way, it has to be given in the form of a story (even if only a thin story in an academic history book) for everyone who was not actually present to that person during those events. And so, for every person Paula who was not present to Christ during Christ's passion and death but for whom awareness of Christ's passion and death is instrumental in her surrender to grace, she ceases resisting and surrenders to God's love because of a story[33] through which she has come to know Christ with the kind of knowledge of persons that stories can provide.[34]

And here is the second important thing to see in this connection. On orthodox Christian theology, when the knowledge of Christ mediated to Paula through the story elicits in her a ceasing of resistance to God, then, on Christian doctrine, Paula immediately meets God in the person of the Holy Spirit, who not only comes to her but stays with her as indwelling. What was just an individual, unilateral experience provided by the story becomes an actual mutual second-personal experience for her in consequence of the Holy Spirit's coming to her.

Consequently, on traditional Christian views of the way God has chosen to work in human history, the *story* of Christ's passion and death has an important role to play in bringing people to the mutual indwelling of union with God. For those people whose awareness of Christ is not mediated by historical presence with Christ during Christ's life, surrender to God's grace has one source in the story of Christ's passion and death. The knowledge of persons with regard to Christ that a person Paula gleans from a story is the beginning of the process that eventually leads Paula to union with Christ.

EUCHARIST AND CHRIST'S PASSION AND DEATH

With this much understanding of the role that the story of Christ's passion and death can play in the process of spiritual regeneration, we can now turn to the part in the process played by the rite of the Eucharist.[35] Among the major Christian theologians, Aquinas is the one whose views on the relation of the Eucharist to the process of salvation I know best. Since it is helpful to have some statement about that relation, I will begin with some representative texts from the works of Aquinas; but, in my view, those Christians whose theology of the Eucharist is based on a sparser metaphysical understanding of the rite than that of Aquinas should find these minimal statements about the Eucharist acceptable. Those who find something in his statements unacceptable (such as the word 'sacrament', for example) should feel free to translate Aquinas's language into their preferred terminology, because nothing in the contentious theology of the Eucharist makes a difference at this point in this chapter.

Although the passion and death of Christ are a sufficient remedy for the broken post-Fall human condition, on the traditional Christian view this remedy is efficacious only for persons who have faith, that is, for persons in grace.[36] So, Aquinas says,

> the power of Christ is applied to us by means of faith. But the power of remitting sins belongs to Christ's passion in a special way. And therefore in a special way by means of faith in his passion human beings are freed from sins.... And therefore the power of the sacraments... is principally from faith in the passion of Christ.[37]

When it comes to explaining the Eucharist and its relation to Christ's passion and death, Aquinas says,

> Neither the sacraments nor any created thing can give grace in the manner of a cause acting per se [that is, as an efficient cause]... but the sacraments function as an instrument of grace.... [T]he humanity of Christ is an instrumental cause of [our] justification, and this cause is applied to us spiritually by faith and corporeally by the sacraments....[38]

As Aquinas sees it, partaking of the Eucharist is not necessary to salvation; faith is efficacious for salvation even without the Eucharist.[39] Nonetheless, the Eucharist is an aid to perseverance in the process of sanctification that enables a person to grow in union with God. Aquinas says,

> the Eucharist is the sacrament of the passion of Christ insofar as a human being is perfected [by means of it] in union to Christ in his passion.[40]

So, as Aquinas presents the views that were already traditional by his time, Christ's passion and death work their effect of saving human beings from their proclivity to sin and of uniting them to God through faith, but the means by which this process is aided and strengthened *can* (and, on traditional Christian views, ideally should) include the Eucharist.[41]

EUCHARIST AND LOVE

The kind of faith needed for sanctification to begin and continue is not possible without a human person's love of God.[42] In one of the many passages in which he stresses this point, Aquinas claims that human beings are freed from their sinful nature by the passion of Christ in three ways, the first of which is

> by means of stimulating us to love, because, as the Apostle says in Romans 5, 'God commends his love to us since when we were enemies, Christ died for us.'[43]

As this passage indicates, although love of God can be elicited by other examples, it is stirred especially by reflection on the love shown in Christ's passion and death.[44]

Probably the most famous New Testament line about God's love occurs in the Gospel of John: "God so loved the world that he gave his only begotten son that whoever believes in him should not perish but have everlasting life" (John 3:16).[45] According to the same Gospel, the truth of that line is most manifest in Christ's passion and death: "there is no greater love than to lay down one's life for one's friends" (John 15:13). Christ's passion and death show God in the form of a human being, dying by prolonged torture in the sight of his mother, his friends, and his hostile, mocking enemies, all for the sake of saving sinful humanity from self-destruction. Clearly, Christ's passion manifests the love of God poignantly. In the powerlessness of Christ's passion and death, there is a power that can elicit the melting of heart, the giving up of resistance to God's love, which is the essential first step in the process of coming to union with God.[46]

There is a derivative power to the same effect in the *story* of Christ's passion and death. That derivative power is only intensified by biblical texts about the Eucharist and their explanation of the connection between the rite and Christ's passion and death.

In this regard, the first thing to notice about the rite of the Eucharist is the fact that the bread and wine of the rite are eaten by the participants;[47] but in the Gospel stories the words by which Christ instituted this rite identify the bread as his body and the wine as his blood.[48] Even for those Christians who take these words of Christ to be only symbolic, there is a kind of shocking intensity about the words and so also about the rite. For a person who participates in the rite, some things that are symbolically (or somehow, liturgically, really) the body and blood of the incarnate Deity are brought entirely inside that participant by being eaten. Clearly, the symbolism (or the symbolism and the reality of the presence of Christ in the bread and wine) invite a participant to a union that is radical in its energy and intimacy.

But it is an intimacy with Christ in Christ's suffering, as the explanation of the rite and the story of its initiation make clear. Those who participate in the rite will know not only the story of the rite's initiation but also the story of Christ's passion and death. Because it is possible to come to know a person through a story, even a story can serve to produce a direct and immediate intuitive knowledge of persons of the kind characteristic of second-person experience. It is noteworthy that on every occasion on which a person in grace Paula participates in the Eucharist, with the intensity that the Eucharist makes available to its participants, then in a forceful way she is brought back into connection with that same story about God's love in the passion and death of Christ. That is, as Paula participates in the Eucharist, she will remember the story of the passion and death of Christ that Christ endured out of love for her, as well as others, to save her from the self-destruction that would otherwise engulf her. Consequently, she will have in mind her own need for help because of things in herself that she herself finds hateful. But she will also have it brought home to her that, however alienated she may be from herself, God is not alienated from her. God, who is perfectly good and who knows Paula better than she knows herself, does not hate her for what she is, but rather loves her so intensely that he took on humanity and endured shame and agony for her, to unite her to himself in love.

The knowledge of persons with respect to Christ mediated by the story of Christ's passion and death will therefore be forcefully available to Paula again on every occasion in which she participates appropriately in the Eucharist. Insofar as Paula eats the bread and drinks the wine in faith, then in doing so Paula is both re-connecting with Christ's passion and death and also re-enacting her original surrender and acceptance of God's love.

Finally, between one participation in the Eucharist and the next, Paula will have lived life as a post-Fall person; that is, Paula will have new things in her self or her life that grieve or trouble her so that she is tempted to give up instead of persevering. But every time Paula participates in the rite, she will find that, however inclined she is to give up on herself or on God, God is still there, still loving her, still wanting her to come into union with himself. The result will be to elicit ever more love of God in Paula, and also joy and peace. And so, with every participation in the Eucharist, Paula will be strengthened for perseverance, in virtue of growing in love of God through her experience of God's continued love for her and presence with her.

A METAPHYSICALLY RICHER ACCOUNT

As is well-known, some Christian communities of faith suppose that the elements of the Eucharist are in some real sense Christ's body and blood. That is, when at the institution of this rite Christ says to his apostles about the bread, "This is my body" and about the wine, "This is my blood," some Christian communities take his words to mean what he says in some way more literal than symbolic.[49] On their view, in one sense or another, in the rite of the Eucharist, after the consecration of the bread and wine, the bread *is* the body of Christ; and, similarly, in some sense, the wine *is* his blood. As is also well-known, in his account of transubstantiation, Aquinas attempted to explain philosophically how it could be that something that has all the appearances of bread and wine could actually be the body and blood of Christ. Aquinas's account of transubstantiation has been the subject of considerable objection, not to say mockery, on the part of some scholars in the past. I myself think that his account is a small philosophical masterpiece and that it goes further to elucidate the metaphysics of this interpretation of the Eucharist than any other analogous account is able to do.[50] But for my purposes here, the truth or falsity of the Thomistic metaphysics of the Eucharist is not germane. What is of interest to me here is only the difference the Thomistic kind of interpretation of the Eucharist makes to the role of the Eucharist in the perseverance of a participant in the rite—that is, the difference it makes to her if the theological doctrine of the Eucharist is interpreted to mean that the bread and wine really are the body and blood of Christ and she believes that this is what they are.

First, it obviously makes a difference to a participant if she believes that, in the bread and wine of the Eucharist, Christ himself is really present to her in his body and his blood. In that case, in participating in the Eucharist, she herself is willing to come so close to Christ that she ingests within herself the bread and wine which, in her view, are somehow Christ's body and blood. The participation in the rite consequently makes for Paula an episodic but recurring experience of intense connection to Christ himself, who in the rite is then and there united with her in his body and blood through the bread and wine.

On the Thomistic view of the rite, although the bread and wine are within Paula when she ingests them, the spiritual order of 'in-ness' brought about by the rite is the reverse of the physical: in having the bread and wine that are the body and blood of Christ within her, Paula herself becomes part of the body and blood of Christ. Why this should be so is part of the metaphysically rich account Aquinas accepts and develops, which I am leaving to one side here. But that it is so is not only part of Aquinas's account and part of what a participant in the rite holds if she accepts this kind of account, but, on Christian doctrine, it makes sense that it would be. The metaphysically greater nature of the body and blood of the human nature assumed by God could not be contained within Paula, but it could encompass her when she is intensely open to God in love. The one–many relation that participation in the rite yields is between one God and many human beings who are incorporated into God in the incarnate Christ through participating in the rite.

Finally, it is worth noticing what difference the doctrine of God's omnipresence makes to the Thomistic interpretation of the Eucharist, on the understanding of the doctrine of omnipresence that takes it to include God's eternity.

On this understanding of the doctrine of omnipresence, God's eternity allows God to be simultaneously present to every time.[51] That is, for each moment of time, as that moment of time is actually temporally present, the whole of the life of eternal God is also co-present (where, of course, 'present' has to be understood analogically as between the temporal and the eternal present). Since this is so, the relevant simultaneity relation—ET-simultaneity (that is, Eternal–Temporal simultaneity)—between what is temporal and what is eternal is symmetric but not reflexive or transitive. A moment of time t_1 can be ET-simultaneous with the whole of eternity, which is itself ET-simultaneous with another moment of time t_2; and yet it will not follow that t_1 is simultaneous with t_2, on any sense of simultaneity.

On the Chalcedonian formula for the incarnate Christ, the person who is Christ is God the Son, and God the Son is God. Since God is eternal, so is God the Son; and since God the Son is the only person in the incarnate Christ, then the person of the incarnate Christ is also eternal. The doctrine of eternity implies that, in the life of eternal God, there never is a *when*[52] at which God is not incarnate. By the same token, there never is a *when* at which God is not suffering on the cross while incarnate in time. That is because the time of Christ's passion is also ET-simultaneous with the whole of God's eternal life; and the one person who is suffering in this passion is God, who is eternal. (It is helpful here to remember that although it is heretical to claim that God the Father suffers or that God can suffer in the divine nature, it is equally heretical to deny that God suffers.) And since there is no succession in God's life, there also never is a *when* at which God is not suffering, in the human nature that is also always with God in God's eternity.

When these complicated claims are coupled with the doctrine that the bread and wine really are the body and blood of Christ, the implications for interpretations of the Eucharist are significant. On these claims, in participating in the Eucharist, a person Paula is uniting herself to Christ through her eating the bread and wine that are the body and blood of Christ. But the Christ with whom Paula is uniting herself by this means is the very person who is presently in his passion on the cross. That is, the time of Christ's passion is ET-simultaneous with the whole present life of eternal God, which is itself ET-simultaneous with every moment of time, including the present at which Paula participates in the Eucharist. Consequently, since the person of Christ is God, then the Christ with whom Paula is uniting herself in the Eucharist is the God with whom Christ's passion is present.

By this means, through union with Christ in the Eucharist, Paula also has present to her what is present to the God with whom she is being united in the rite, and that includes Christ's passion. (The alternative to these claims is to accept succession in the life of eternal God or to deny that God suffers in Christ's passion—and both these claims are ruled out by the orthodox theology presupposed here.) In participating in the Eucharist, then, Paula is not just remembering Christ's passion. She is not just symbolically re-enacting it. Rather, through the connection between times that connection to an eternal

God can make for a temporal human being, Paula is present with Christ in his passion, and Christ in his passion is present to Paula then, as she participates in the rite.[53]

So on any theological account which accepts both the doctrine that Christ is really present in the elements of the Eucharist and the doctrine that God is eternal, it will turn out to be true that in participating in the Eucharist a person Paula is uniting with Christ in his passion on the cross. On these doctrines, when a person participates in the Eucharist, not only is Christ present to her, then, there, but so also is Christ's passion—not just a representation of it,[54] but the thing itself. And if she believes that this is so, even in some theologically inchoate way, then the experience of the Eucharist will be only more intense for her. In one of the few lyrical passages in his scholastic prose, Aquinas says that in the sacrament of the Eucharist a believer's soul is inebriated by the sweetness of the divine goodness.[55]

For all these reasons, then, although some incipient union with Christ in love is needed to participate in the Eucharist appropriately,[56] increased union through increased love is the effect of this rite, in one way or another, depending on the theology of the Eucharist adopted.

EUCHARIST AND PERSEVERANCE

Aquinas thinks that the Eucharist is to the spiritual life what food is to the biological life: it strengthens and nourishes, and it gives pleasure too.[57] But through the Eucharist the thing that provides the nourishment in the case of the spiritual life is not physical food; rather it is joy, which nourishes the spirit. In medieval times, it was common to call the Eucharist 'the bread of angels.' On medieval angelology, angels cannot eat bread or drink wine; but there is a sense in which they can also participate in the Eucharist, insofar as they are fed with joy in union with Christ. For human beings, who can feed on bread and wine, ingesting the Eucharistic bread and wine are a means to joy too.[58] And joy will be nourishing for the spiritual life of all those persons in grace who participate in the rite, whether or not they accept the metaphysically richer account of the Eucharist.

Describing this state in a human person, Aquinas says,

> the ultimate perfection, by which a person is made perfect inwardly, is joy, which stems from the presence of what is loved. Whoever has the love of God, however, already has what he loves, as is said in 1 John 4:16: 'whoever abides in the love of God abides in God, and God abides in him.' And joy wells up from this.[59]

So, without acting with efficient causation on the will of a person Paula, by means of the Eucharist God nonetheless provides a powerful aid to Paula's perseverance in grace. Without violating Paula's will, in the rite of the Eucharist God strengthens Paula's will for perseverance in two ways.

First, in her participation in the Eucharist, Paula is reminded of the story of Christ's crucifixion. And through the story—or through the story and the real presence of Christ in the bread and wine—she is connected to Christ's passion and death.[60] Because of this connection, in partaking of the Eucharist Paula relives her original surrender to God's love—except that because she is doing so *again*, with all that her history and experience bring to this repeated reliving, Paula grows in her openness to Christ as she participates in the rite. The result is not only increased commitment on her part, but increased joy.

Despair over her own sufferings or her own sinfulness might wear her down and incline her to give up. But joy in union with Christ will shield her to some extent against all these kinds of despair. Nothing about the rite takes any of her suffering away or alters its character as suffering. And yet even while she is suffering in one way or another, through the Eucharist Paula will also have her beloved God with her—her beloved God who also suffered and suffered out of love for her; and that presence will make a difference to her ability to bear up under her own suffering.

And, second, in the way described in Chapter 7, when through joy Paula increases in her openness to God, then God can also act on Paula's will with formal causation, adding strength to her will through grace. It is part of the process of sanctification, as I described it in Chapter 7, that every additional openness to God's love on the part of a person in grace is met with more grace given her by God. In the preceding paragraph, I have focused on the effects of the Eucharist on a person in grace, aiding her to persevere in openness to God; but this emphasis should not obscure the implications of the account of grace given earlier. Increased openness to God will be met by God with increased grace. And so the effects of the Eucharist are a cooperative second-personal interaction between a participant in the rite and God.

In these two ways, then, through the Eucharist Paula is strengthened in perseverance. By joining herself to Christ, by sharing her own suffering with a suffering Christ, Paula not only grows closer to Christ, but she herself grows like Christ. The *ultimate* end of the process is her joy in full union with God, who loves her.

SUFFERING

With this much elucidation of the role in perseverance played by the religious rite of the Eucharist, I want to turn now to the role of suffering in perseverance.[61] The role of suffering is much harder to see and understand than that of the Eucharist, not least because we are accustomed to think of suffering as antithetical in every way to human flourishing and as destructive of human joy. Even when we praise a person who suffers for not sinking under his suffering, we suppose that the sufferer is to be ranked more among life's losers than among life's winners. We sometimes think of a person who stands under suffering as heroic, and we tend to think of whatever is good in his life as happening in spite of the suffering. We are inclined to find perverse anything that values the suffering itself. Anything that obviates or undermines physical or mental thriving strikes us as lamentable.

The current disability rights movement is an exception to this general attitude. Like the gay pride movement, the disability rights movement wants to celebrate what others have generally pitied—or disrespected—as the suffering of misfortune. It wants others to see that those with disabilities are not among life's losers, or even among life's heroic overcomers of the tragic. On the contrary, the disability rights movement holds disability pride parades. Here is an excerpt from a text by Sarah Triano, the founder of the Chicago Disability Pride parade, as cited in Elizabeth Barnes's *The Minority Body*:

> The sad sack, the brave overcomer, and the incapable are worn-out stereotypes the parade refutes by giving us a time and space to celebrate ourselves as we are. First, we want to show the world the incredible joy that exists in our lives. We are part of the richness and diversity of this country and the world. The Parade is an international celebration of our continued and continuing survival. We also, by marching in this parade, are giving the world a chance to express pride in us, too![62]

From the Patristic period onward, the Christian tradition has held a roughly analogous position not as regards disability but rather as regards suffering. It has supposed that those who endure serious suffering are not the pitiable losers of life or even the heroic overcomers of tragedy but rather are those specially loved by God. That is because, on this view, suffering is not only medicinal for the human condition but is also a gift of God's to those who are nearer to God. So, for example, Gregory the Great says that the ways of Providence are often hard to understand, but that they are

> still more mysterious when things go well with good people here, and ill with bad people....[63]

He means that if apparently good people do *not* have suffering in their life, there is some reason for wondering whether they really are good people, that is, whether they really are among those who are close to God—or, in our terms, not Gregory's, whether these non-sufferers are really among life's winners, rather than life's losers.

John Chrysostom, who is in the same medieval tradition of thought as Gregory, shows the natural extension of this attitude. If suffering is a hallmark of being close to God and growing even closer, then suffering is itself something to be celebrated, something to be proud of. Chrysostom says of people who are scandalized at the sight of human suffering,

> They do not know that to have these sufferings is the privilege of those especially dear to God.[64]

And there is biblical basis for this attitude, too. In the New Testament book of Acts, when some of the apostles are sent to jail and then beaten for bearing witness to the events of Christ's life and death, the text says that they came away from this suffering rejoicing, with a sense of having been honored in being allowed to endure the suffering. In their view, too, their suffering was something to celebrate (Acts 5:41).

Clearly, there is something right about the contemporary unreflective rejection of suffering as bad. Someone who valued suffering as an intrinsic good would be perverse at best and mentally disturbed or evil at worst. But the traditional Christian attitude as represented, for example, by the story in Acts, is not supposing that suffering is a good in its own right. In the story in Acts, the apostles take suffering as something to celebrate because they suppose themselves to be honored in being allowed to have it and because they see it as a means of drawing closer to Christ. In their view, suffering is something to celebrate not as a good in its own right but as a hallmark or instrument of something else that is an intrinsic good.

In what follows, I want to look closely at the relevant Christian doctrines to see what can be said to explain and defend this attitude towards suffering, and then I will examine the connections among suffering so understood, perseverance in grace, and the atonement of Christ.

THE CONNECTION OF SUFFERING AND PERSEVERANCE: CONSOLATION, SANCTIFICATION LEADING TO GLORY, AND CHRIST'S ATONEMENT

In earlier work, I considered the traditional Christian attitude towards suffering as it figures in theodicy, and in what follows I will rely on some of that work. Here, however, I want to focus not on the role of suffering in theodicy but rather on the role the Christian tradition assigns to suffering in a person's spiritual and moral flourishing. The resultant idea is powerful, in my view, but complicated and challenging to elucidate. In the end, it does turn out to have a deep connection to theodicy as well. There is a biblical text in 2 Corinthians that expresses this idea in a paradigmatic way, and it will be helpful to approach the examination of suffering through the claims in that text.

In 2 Corinthians 1:5, Paul, generally taken to be the writer of the Epistle, makes this claim:

> as the sufferings of Christ abound in us, so also our consolations abound through Christ.

This is not a claim about what justifies God's allowing the suffering of a person in grace or what defeats that suffering for her. It is a claim just about a connection between suffering and consolation. According to this claim of Paul's, for a suffering person in grace in this life, her suffering is somehow correlated with the consolation she has in or with Christ. The comfort and help a sufferer has from Christ can intensify as her suffering increases.[65]

Later in the same Epistle, Paul concludes a complicated analogy between the Israelites at the time of the giving of the Law, on the one hand, and people in the process of sanctification, on the other, by saying of people in sanctification,

> ... beholding as in a mirror the glory of the Lord, we are all changed into the same image from glory into glory through the Spirit, the Lord.   (2 Cor. 3:18)

The details of Paul's analogy are elaborate, and this concluding claim is also intricate; but the basic idea is that a person in grace comes to have (even in this life) the glory of the loveliness of God (to some no doubt small degree) in virtue of being united with God (to one degree or another).

And Paul goes on to connect the glory of that union with suffering, in this way:

> our light afflictions, which last only for the moment, bring about for us a far greater eternal weight of glory.   (2 Cor. 4:17)

In other words, according to Paul in this Epistle, the suffering endured by a person in grace is one source of that person's glory or spiritual loveliness.

Finally, Paul explains that the role of suffering in bringing about glory has an intrinsic connection to the atonement of Christ. He concludes his exposition of that idea this way:

> for us, God made Christ, who knew no sin, [to be] sin, so that in Christ we might be made the righteousness of God.   (2 Cor. 5:21)

The thought of all these lines of Paul's in 2 Corinthians then is roughly this. A person in grace Paula will experience suffering of one kind and degree or another in this life. But that suffering will help to bring about for Paula, eventually, the greater good of glory, where glory is a matter of a union between God and Paula in which Paula has in herself something of the righteousness, and something of the beauty, of God. And through the suffering which Paula endures and which results in her growing in her own beauty of holiness in union with God, she will also have consolation that grows as her suffering intensifies. In a paradoxical way, then, according to the Epistle, her suffering conduces to her joy. And all of this will be somehow tied to the atoning work of Christ in which Christ bears—in fact, becomes—human sin so that human beings can become the righteousness of God.

So understood, the thought of 2 Corinthians will certainly raise some immediate objections.

Some people will point out that suffering sometimes leads to the opposite effects from those the Epistle cites—not to a person's increased closeness to God but rather to his distance from God in psychic dysfunction of one sort or another. Elsewhere I have argued that, though this claim may be true, it does not undermine the thought in the Epistle. Since human beings have free will, nothing can guarantee that anything which might be healing or helpful for the post-Fall human condition will actually have that effect.

Others will object to this response because it seems to them to blame those people whose suffering leads them away from God.[66] But this objection also seems to me mistaken. To say that a person is the source of his rejection of some good that might have been made possible through his suffering does not imply that the sufferer is culpable for this rejection. As many ethicists have pointed out, it is possible to attribute even a morally lamentable action or attitude to a person without supposing that that person is in any way culpable or blameworthy for it.[67] It may be that a person who moves further from God as a result of affliction is not to be blamed for doing so but only loved the more for the suffering that he endures in this rejection itself.

Finally, someone will object that there are afflictions, such as depression, which cut sufferers off from any religious consolation no matter what their suffering, so that the claim in 2 Corinthians that consolation increases with affliction is false.[68] But here it is worth pointing out that the Epistle does not claim that suffering and consolation always co-vary simultaneously. The increase in consolation may not occur at the very time of the increase in suffering; it may come only later, even much later. In his commentary on the passage in Romans where Paul claims that all things work together for good for those who love God (Rom. 8:28), Aquinas asks if '*all things*' includes a person's sins. And, contrary to what one might expect, Aquinas answers in the affirmative.[69] But clearly the spiritual consolation that stems from the suffering of being a sinful person[70] will not come at the very time that a person is engaged in sinful actions.

So this objection does not tell against the complex thought of 2 Corinthians. All things that in their immediate character are an affliction for a person and that can move a person further from God—all things, even sin—can serve as a means of moving a person closer to God, if only that person will not return to rejecting entirely the love and grace of God. And if God can use even sin to move a person closer to God, then, a fortiori, God can also use depression, which is not sinful, in a similar way. An excellent example of the way in which this process can work in the case of depression, and the praiseworthy endurance of the sufferer afflicted by depression, can be found in John Bunyan's *Grace Abounding to the Chief of Sinners.* The consolation that came after the depression lifted for Bunyan is also vividly shown in that work.

In what follows, then, I will leave these objections to one side and concentrate on unpacking the complex thought of the Epistle.

To begin to understand Paul's thought about suffering, glory, consolation, and the atoning work of Christ, it is necessary to work slowly through its elements, beginning with the nature and effects of suffering. When it is properly unpacked, what Paul's thought in the Epistle shows is the way in which the suffering of a person in grace is connected to the suffering of Christ and contributes to her perseverance in the process of sanctification, to help her complete the process instead of abandoning it. Furthermore, in completing the process of sanctification, a person in grace does not stay in the same state she was in when she began the process. Rather, on Paul's thought, a person who perseveres in sanctification through suffering continues to grow in closeness to God until she has as much joy and union with God, and as much loveliness in that union, as she is willing to have.

A BRIEF EXCURSUS ON SUFFERING AND THEODICY

In Chapter 6, I argued that suffering is a function of what a person cares about. And the things that people care about can be divided into two kinds, an objective kind that is the same for human beings across the various divisions among peoples, and a subjective kind that is peculiar to each individual. The subjective kind is a function of the desires of the heart:[71] there are things that have great value for a person just because she has set her heart on them, and she will suffer if she loses or fails to acquire them.[72] The objective kind has to do with human wellbeing. Every person has a care for her wellbeing, and at least in broad outline human wellbeing is an objective matter.[73] Those things that diminish human wellbeing will also be a source of suffering for the person undergoing the diminishment. So suffering stems from the loss of either the subjective or the objective kind of thing that human beings care about.

It is a common contemporary view that suffering of either kind diminishes flourishing. On the other hand, in the history of the Christian tradition, suffering has been considered medicinal for the post-Fall human condition; and so, in an apparently paradoxical way, suffering has been thought actually to lead to human flourishing. On this Christian view, although suffering diminishes flourishing in one sense, it can contribute to it in another deeper or more meaningful sense.[74]

In earlier work,[75] I examined this Christian view with respect to the involuntary suffering of an unwilling, innocent, mentally fully functional adult human person, and I discussed the justification given in Aquinas's theodicy for God's allowing the suffering of such a person. In his version of the traditional Christian theodicy, Aquinas maintains that God is justified in allowing[76] such suffering by one or the other of two possible benefits:[77] either the warding off of a greater harm (namely, the permanent absence of union with God) or the providing of a greater good (namely, the increased degree of everlasting shared union with God).[78]

Which of the two possible benefits goes to a particular sufferer on any given occasion is a function of the nature of his involuntary suffering; it depends on whether the suffering is involuntary *simpliciter* or only involuntary *secundum quid*.[79] If a person Jerome who does not have even implicit faith has involuntary suffering, it will be suffering that is involuntary *simpliciter*. God is justified in allowing suffering of this nature when it contributes to moving Jerome in the direction of the surrender to love and grace that is the necessary precondition for justification. Jerome's suffering is defeated for Jerome and God is justified in allowing it because the suffering contributes[80] to warding off a greater harm for Jerome. On this view, suffering can lead to Jerome's wellbeing in virtue of warding off this harm.

Norman Care describes the first step in moral and spiritual regeneration for alcoholics as a kind of surrender, and he asks what is needed to get a person to such surrender. He says,

> All...[an alcoholic] needs to join AA is 'a desire to stop drinking' [footnote omitted], but AA will not tell...[the alcoholic] that he has that desire or somehow force it on him. How...[the alcoholic] comes to have that desire, if he ever does, may have to do with his personal suffering or with the social, relational, or emotional byproducts of his suffering, such as family troubles, legal hassles, or the pain of remorse, guilt, or shame....[81]

This is a view about alcoholics, but it is a view that in one respect generalizes to all human beings in a post-Fall condition. For Aquinas and the Christian tradition before him, suffering has a healing role in helping to bring a person to the surrender that begins the process of regeneration.

On the other hand, for a person Paula who has already begun this process and is living a life in grace, involuntary suffering is involuntary only *secundum quid*. In virtue of being a person in grace, Paula has committed herself to the process that leads to union with God. Consequently, she has in some sense given a general consent to sanctification, which includes at least the suffering attendant on overcoming her tendencies to the wrongdoing that is self-destructive for her. She is in this respect like someone who has signed up for the cross-country team. She may complain bitterly about some things the coach asks of her; but she did join the team, and she knew when she joined what being on a cross-country team tends to entail. Her suffering is therefore involuntary only *secundum quid*; it is not involuntary *simpliciter*, as it would be if she had not signed on to the system (or the team) at all. For this reason, it is justifiable for God to allow Paula's suffering for the sake of a greater good for Paula. And so, on Aquinas's theodicy, for Paula, involuntary suffering is defeated in virtue of its contributing to providing for her the greater good which sanctification is designed to produce.[82] Suffering leads to Paula's well-being in virtue of contributing to this greater good.

It should be noted in this connection that the reason justifying God in allowing such suffering has to do primarily with the state of the sufferer that comes *after* the time of his suffering. What justifies God in allowing Job's involuntary suffering, for example, is not anything Job did before he suffered, contrary to what the mistaken Comforters in the story suppose. Rather, the explanation for Job's suffering has primarily to do with what Job is enabled to become in consequence of his suffering.[83] In this respect, on this theodicy, there is an additional analogy between suffering and medicine. Doctors who put a cancer patient through painful surgery and strenuous chemotherapy bring about suffering for the patient that is involuntary in at least some respects, too. The reason justifying their causing that suffering lies primarily in the future, rather than in the past. The medical treatments are justified by what they are meant to enable the patient to be—namely, a thriving or at least a living person.[84]

Finally, in earlier work, I argued that this Thomistic theodicy is at best incomplete, because it addresses only suffering connected to wellbeing. There is also the suffering stemming from the loss of the desires of the heart.[85] I tried to show that the Thomistic theodicy can be developed in a way that addresses this sort of suffering as well. A desire of the heart can be refolded, as it were, so that it is different in some of its features without losing the character distinctive of it. On traditional Christian views, whether the desire is felt and recognized for what it is or not, the deepest desire of any person's heart is a desire for God. As Augustine says to God in his well-known lines, "You have made us for yourself, and our hearts are restless till they rest in you." Part of the refolding of a particular heart's desire can include interweaving that desire with a desire for God. If a heart's desire is refolded in this way, then it is arguable that suffering can enable a person to have both her heart's desire and also her wellbeing, which is closeness to God. Consequently, however paradoxical it may sound, it is possible for God to give a person who is suffering from heartbreak the desires of her heart in virtue of that heartbreak.

And so, for complicated reasons that take a large book to explain and defend, I argued that a suitably augmented Thomistic theodicy could constitute a defense, in which a person's suffering of either heartbreak or loss of wellbeing could in fact contribute to her having the things she most cares about. On this defense, in an apparently paradoxical way, it is possible for suffering to conduce to the flourishing of the sufferer.

But I raise these issues only so that they do not constitute a distraction in what follows. In that earlier work, I tried to explain and defend a possible morally sufficient reason for God to allow human suffering. What is at issue here, however, is not the reason why a perfectly good God could be justified in allowing suffering. Here the issue is the connection between the suffering allowed and the benefit to the sufferer. What the next sections of this chapter examine is the way in which suffering is supposed to help bring about the flourishing of a person in grace, on traditional Christian views. Focusing on the justification for allowing suffering highlights suffering as something lamentable whose enduring or overcoming leads to a good end. But, on traditional Christian views, there is also something about suffering to celebrate, as the thought of 2 Corinthians illustrates. (To say this is not to say that it is permissible for any human person to allow suffering he could readily remedy or to cause suffering for the sake of the good worth celebrating. The goodness of a state of affairs is not sufficient to justify someone's bringing it about. That is why the focus of theodicy or defense is different from the focus on suffering in this chapter. As I argued in the earlier work on the problem of suffering, there is no easy inference from the good that suffering is meant to further to the permissibility of a human being's causing that suffering or failing to remedy that suffering if he can do so readily.[86])

In the rest of this chapter, I will concentrate on the role that suffering is meant to play in the flourishing of a person who is already in grace, namely, sustaining and developing her, with consolation and joy, through sanctification into deeper union with God. Looking at suffering in this way helps explain the sense of Chrysostom's line, quoted above, which implies that suffering is a gift and an honor.

THE MODES OF HUMAN FLOURISHING

The complicated thought of 2 Corinthians gives suffering a place in flourishing. On Paul's thought in that Epistle, something about suffering, which seems to deprive a person of flourishing, actually enables or enhances the flourishing of the sufferer.

Although discussions of human flourishing are by now something of a cottage industry, for my purposes here a person's flourishing can be thought of as his thriving.[87] So understood, the opposite of thriving is not being sick but rather something like being dysfunctional or deteriorating. The failure to thrive is a broad category that encompasses any kind of impairment or impediment[88] to the proper functioning of some part of a person or even of the whole person himself.[89] It may be that this usage is not the everyday meaning of the term 'thriving', but it is one sense of the term; and it is helpful to have some term by which to refer to the phenomenon in question. At any rate, a flourishing human life is a life that is an excellent one for a human being, and 'thriving' is a reasonable way to refer to the excellent condition of something living.

It is worth noting in this connection that even an impediment to the proper functioning of a human body and a consequent loss of some kind of physical thriving is not a disability. Striving for a workable account just of physical disability, Elizabeth Barnes says affirmingly,

> The disability rights movement tends to count a physical condition as a disability (and therefore as something they're working to promote justice for) if it has some sufficient number of features such as: being subject to social stigma and prejudice; being viewed as unusual or atypical; making ordinary daily tasks difficult or complicated; causing chronic pain; causing barriers to access of public spaces; causing barriers to employment; causing shame; requiring use of mobility aids or assistive technology; requiring medical care; and so on. As with most cluster concepts, there will no doubt be vagueness and borderline cases.[90]

Barnes seems to me right in this characterization. By itself, then, an impediment to thriving does not count as a disability, whatever the nature and severity of the impediment, if for no other reason than that a disability is at least in part a function of the society in which a person who has the impediment lives. What is at issue in what follows is therefore not disability, but the lower-level notion of an impairment or impediment[91] and the correlated contrary, thriving.

It is evident that thriving comes in different modes. To begin with, we can distinguish the thriving a person has when he suffers no impediments as regards his body from the thriving he has when he suffers no impediments as regards his mind. We can think of thriving, that is, either as bodily thriving or as thriving of the mind;[92] and it is possible to have one of these modes of thriving without the other. So, for example, there are people who are in excellent bodily condition but who suffer from mental illness or some other impediment of mind. Buzz Aldrin was in peak athletic condition when he flew to the moon in 1969, but he later acknowledged that he also suffered from serious depression.

An obstacle to thriving in mind can come not only from some disease of the mind or some damage to the brain; it can come also from heartbreak. A heartbroken person also lacks thriving in mind, in the sense of 'thriving' at issue here. Thriving in mind seems to require energy, confidence, groundedness in oneself, an ability to concern oneself with others, and things of this sort. Heartbreak is like being hit by a truck in one's psyche; it focuses a person intensely on himself. It may produce the energy of rage, but no one would mistake that energy for the constructive energy of thriving in mind.

It is also worth noticing that heartbreak can come from the suffering of another person too. A mother's heart's desire can be that her child thrives; and if that child struggles with a chronic and irremediable sickness, the mother may suffer heartbreak over her child's suffering.[93] That heartbreak will be an impediment to her own thriving in mind too.

Alternatively, it is possible to have great bodily impediments but to be thriving in mind. In her *New York Times Magazine* article chronicling her extended arguments with Peter Singer, Harriet McBryde Johnson, who was a disability rights lawyer, describes herself this way:

> I'm Karen Carpenter thin, flesh mostly vanished, a jumble of bones in a floppy bag of skin.... [M]y right side is two deep canyons. To keep myself upright, I lean forward, rest my rib cage on my lap, plant my elbows beside my knees ... I am the first generation to survive to such decrepitude.[94]

By her own description, Johnson suffers from significant impediments as regards bodily thriving. On the other hand, however, her meaningful work and her excellence at it, her very ability to handle exchanges with such opponents of the disability rights movement as Peter Singer with intelligence and courtesy and wit, all testify to her thriving in mind.

Impediments to either bodily thriving or thriving in mind are generally a suffering for the person who has them, on the understanding of suffering I gave above. Something on either the objective or the subjective scale of value (or both) is diminished for a person who has such impediments. But there is a general consensus that, other things being equal, thriving in mind outranks bodily thriving. For comparable impediments, however roughly such comparison might have to be made, an incapacity in mind is a greater obstacle to human flourishing than a bodily incapacity. Few people would be willing to trade diminished bodily thriving for comparable diminishments of thriving in mind.[95] And, on the scale of values at issue in the Christian tradition, this common attitude is right. On that scale of value, the best thing for human beings is a matter of relationships; and if they are serious enough, impediments with regard to thriving in mind are more of a barrier to relationships than roughly comparable impediments to bodily thriving, *ceteris paribus*.[96]

Commenting on the claim of some disability theorists that disability is mere difference from the typical human condition, not bad difference, Kevin Timpe says,

> Approximately 1/3 of cases of cognitive disability involve severe or profound disability; but even with a lesser degree of impairment, individuals are often not able to engage in abstract thought or apply abstract principles (including moral principles) across situations ... [reference omitted]. Even mild cognitive disability can impact agency and social interaction insofar as individuals with such a disability often are not capable of sufficiently understanding the consequences of their actions.... Furthermore, when one considers the social isolation and disruptions individuals experience as a result of the interconnections between

cognitive disability and emotional and developmental disabilities, it is plausible that there is bad-difference here.[97]

Timpe is surely right in his characterization of the obstacles to human well-being that cognitive impairments can cause. And yet even for human beings in such a condition, meaningful and fulfilling relationships of love are possible. Jean Vanier's work with human beings who have severe cognitive impairments has illuminated the capacity of such people for loving interaction and meaningful human engagement.[98] Eva Kittay makes this point in a moving way, worth quoting at length. She says,

> I grant that rationality and the capacity to determine one's own good are, at the very least, useful to being a part of a moral community. But I am not sure if either of them are necessary to have, and still less certain why lacking them disqualifies one from moral parity. Philosophers have made much of the importance of rational capacities for the exercise of moral judgments and moral actions, but many...have seriously understated the critical role other capacities play in our moral life..., such as giving care and responding appropriately to care, empathy and fellow feeling, a sense of what is harmonious and loving, and a willingness to reciprocate giving and receiving kindness and love...[Consider in this connection] a young woman, whose rational capacities are difficult to determine because she lacks speech among other skills, but her capacity to enjoy life, to share joy through smiles and laughter, to embrace those who love and care for her, and to bring joy to all whose lives she touches—an individual who, through her warmth, her serene and harmonious spirit, and her infectious love of life enriches the lives of others.... Whether or not she would know what it means to determine her own good may be in doubt, but the good she brings into the world is not.[99]

The social isolation of the cognitively disabled that Timpe rightly calls attention to is therefore not a result solely of the cognitive impairment on the part of the disabled, but rather a function of the cognitive impairment together with other facts about common human social organization.[100] L'Arche, Vanier's commune in which the severely cognitively impaired and their non-impaired caretakers live together in community, has shown the way in which loving and fulfilling social connection is possible even for those with severe cognitive disabilities.

And something analogous can be said about infants, whose capacities for typical adult cognitive functioning are not yet developed. The literature in developmental psychology has made abundantly clear that infants have capacities for intense second-personal connection from birth, when they are still far from anything that might be thought of as typical adult cognitive functioning.[101]

Furthermore, on the traditional Christian scale of value, the greatest human relationship is with God, and so the greatest thriving for a human person is in that relationship. And even serious impediments to thriving in mind are not a bar to a human person's relationship with God. Consider, for example, this report of religious experience on the part of someone suffering from significant mental illness:

> At one time, I reached utter despair and wept and prayed to God for mercy instinctively and without faith in reply. That night I stood with other patients in the grounds waiting to be let in to our ward.... Suddenly someone stood beside me...and a voice said, 'Mad or sane, you are one of My sheep'. I never spoke to anyone of this but ever since, twenty years, it has been the pivot of my life.[102]

Even among those with both bodily thriving and thriving in mind, few people have such powerful religious experiences. The religious experience this patient reports was so great as to center his life for a long time, on his telling of the story, and to bring him consolation throughout that whole period; the closeness to God of the original experience and the ongoing relationship with God it provoked were great enough to endure through many years of the patient's life.

One can see, then, that although, other things being equal, serious impediments to thriving in mind are more likely to undermine a person's flourishing than comparable impediments to bodily thriving are, flourishing of the sort most prized on the Christian scale of value—life in loving personal relationship—is nonetheless possible even with significant impediments to thriving in mind.[103] Furthermore, as the example of the patient's religious experience illustrates, when God is one of the relata in the relationship, then even those things that might obstruct relationship between two human beings, such as major mental illness, are not a bar to relationship. Manifestly, an omnipotent, omnipresent God could make relational contact with a human person challenged by a serious impediment to thriving in mind if only that person did not resist God's love and grace.

What such considerations should help us recognize is that bodily thriving and thriving in mind do not exhaust the modes of thriving for human beings. A human person can have impediments to thriving of both body and mind—because, for example, of the ill-treatment of others and the lasting bodily and psychological damage of that ill-treatment—and yet that person can have thriving as a human person.[104] There is thus a third mode of thriving.

THE THIRD MODE OF THRIVING

Harriet Tubman seems to me a good example of this third mode of thriving. She was born a slave, and from early childhood she was recurrently separated from her family. When she was 6 or 7, for example, she was farmed out to a different household as a house slave and nanny. In that job, child though she was, she endured severe beatings; and she was often deprived of sufficient food and adequate clothing. Later in life, as a result of the abuse of one slave master, she suffered a serious head wound, which left her with lasting neurological problems. Throughout the rest of her life, she seems to have suffered from narcolepsy and other manifestations of brain damage as a result of that injury.[105] It is difficult to believe that, in addition to the neurological problems she suffered, she did not also have lasting psychological damage from the trauma of the abuse she endured as a child. And this is only the beginning. The story of the suffering of her life is too great to be summarized adequately in short space here, and it is hard to read even in abbreviated form because the cruelty inflicted on her is heartbreaking.

When she was a young woman, Tubman succeeded in escaping from slavery; and she spent all the rest of her long life rescuing other slaves and working for the abolition of slavery, often in perilous circumstances. When a biography of her was being prepared during her lifetime, she asked Frederick Douglas to write a recommendation for the cover of the book; and this is what he, so worthy of honor himself, wrote to her:

> You ask for what you do not need when you call upon me for a word of commendation. I need such words from you far more than you can need them from me, especially where your superior labors and devotion to the cause of the lately enslaved of our land are known as I know them. The difference between us is very marked. Most that I have done and suffered in the service of our cause has been in public, and I have received much encouragement at every step of the way. You, on the other hand, have labored in a private way. I have wrought in the day—you in the night. ... The midnight sky and the silent stars have been the witnesses of your devotion to freedom and of your heroism. Excepting John Brown—of sacred memory—I know of no one who has willingly encountered more perils and hardships to serve our enslaved people than you have.[106]

The great honor in which Harriet Tubman was and is so rightly held by so many people, me included, bears witness to her thriving as a human being. She is not a bent or broken or otherwise failing specimen of the human species. On the contrary, she is a shining example of humanity. And we do not honor her out of compassion, as someone who heroically overcame the tragic circumstances of her life. Rather, anyone with integrity has to acknowledge that she sets a standard for human greatness and so also for thriving as a human being. But she had that thriving with serious impediments to thriving of body and of mind.

Or, to take a very different case in which the impediments to thriving of body and of mind originate not from human evil but from some circumstance in nature, consider Williams Syndrome. The Williams Syndrome Association describes Williams Syndrome this way:

> Williams syndrome (WS) is a genetic condition...characterized by medical problems, including cardiovascular disease, developmental delays, and learning

disabilities. ... Children with WS need costly and ongoing medical care and early interventions ... [T]hey struggle with things like spatial relations, numbers, and abstract reasoning, which can make daily tasks a challenge. As adults, most people with Williams syndrome will need supportive housing to live to their fullest potential.[107]

People with Williams Syndrome have significant impediments to thriving of body and mind; but they can also be remarkable for their thriving as human beings. One singer with Williams Syndrome, Meghan Finn, introduced herself this way to the audience who had come to hear her sing:

I have Williams Syndrome! ... Williams Syndrome has given me challenges and a lot of gifts, more gifts than I can ever imagine in my whole life. I can't stand loud noises, but I like to sing. I have flat feet, but I like to be with people. I have a definite explosive personality. Just remember us by our talents. We don't have stupidity. We just have love.[108]

One gifted singer with Williams Syndrome, Gloria Lenhoff, impressed those who knew her not just with her musicianship but especially with her way of bringing joy to others. Her father said about her,

Gloria has taught us what true love is. To be compassionate to those who are less fortunate than ourselves. But most of all she has taught us to recognize that everyone has something different to offer society.... Thank you, Gloria.[109]

The well-known neurologist Oliver Sacks was so moved by Gloria Lenhoff and the other people with Williams Syndrome whom he got to know through her and her family that he did a documentary about them and about the gifts of music and of empathy that many people with Williams Syndrome seem to have. In the conclusion of his documentary, he says this about Gloria Lenhoff and the other people with Williams Syndrome whom he met because of her:

there is no simple neurological basis for the appreciation of music and musical capacity. Many different systems of the brain are involved.... As far as I can see, all of these systems seem to be heightened with Williams syndrome ... It's as if the brain has been stimulated to grow in some ways, and prevented from growing in others. A strange, lop-sided brain, which sort of makes it impossible to use simple terms like 'able' and 'disabled'.[110]

By these words, Sacks means to convey his admiration for Gloria Lenhoff and her peers in the Williams Syndrome community and his strong belief that she and they are thriving human beings. He also wants to call attention to the fact that a distinction between *abled people* and *disabled people* fails to categorize correctly the reality of human lives. People such as Harriet Tubman and Gloria Lenhoff have great thriving as human persons, but they have this thriving together with serious impediments to thriving of body and mind. Their condition is thus a third mode of thriving.

The post-Fall human condition is itself a kind of brokenness of a person considered as a whole, insofar as the post-Fall defect in the will ripples out into every part of a person's psyche and life. And so it makes sense that a person could have both thriving of body and of mind, and yet the person considered as a whole could fail to thrive. Think just of people such as John Newton in his slave-trading years, when he was strong, smart, and successful enough to be made the master of a slave-trading ship. In that period, he used his thriving of body and mind to oppress others cruelly, so that, while he was a slave trader, however physically healthy and mentally able he was, however much he had what he then wanted, even so, considered as a person Newton was a bent and twisted specimen of a human being, not a thriving one. Who would want to be like him, as he was then? By the same token, then, a person such as Harriet Tubman can have impediments to thriving in both body and mind and yet be a paradigmatically thriving human person.

It is hard to know exactly what to call this third mode of thriving; but because it seems somehow to be the thriving of the whole person, rather than the thriving of a part of a person, as thriving of body or of mind is, I will call it 'personal thriving', for lack of a better term.

PERSONAL THRIVING AND FLOURISHING

On orthodox Christian theology, the best state for a human person requires willing what God wills; and the sanctification of a person Paula has as its ultimate aim the complete integration of Paula's will around the good, so that Paula wills always and only what God wills.[111] But, on Aquinas's view of a person in grace and on his interpretation of willing what God wills, Paula could be significantly fragmented in will and still count as willing what God wills, provided that Paula has and retains a second-order willing for a will that wills what God wills.[112] According to Aquinas, when Christ desired not to die, Christ had a will for something that God did not will; and, nonetheless, Christ was willing what God wills in virtue of having a second-order will to have a will that wills what God wills. On Aquinas's view, then, in this life a person Paula can count as being in grace, even as being Christ-like, when there is still significant fragmentation and brokenness in her will.[113] But if, on this view, a person can count as being in the best state for human beings in this life even with significant brokenness in the will, then it should not be surprising that, on this same view, someone's having impediments in other parts of a human person are also compatible with her personal thriving.

So thriving of body and thriving of mind are neither individually necessary nor jointly sufficient for personal thriving, as the cases canvassed here illustrate. And because it is the thriving of the whole person, personal thriving outranks thriving of either of the other two modes of thriving or both of them combined (*ceteris paribus*).[114] So, for example, a person who has significant impediments as regards the body might have greater personal thriving than someone who lacks those impediments (*ceteris paribus*). In my view, Harriet McBryde Johnson illustrates this point. She is greatly admirable for the thriving of her life, even with serious impediments to thriving of body. Similarly, a person can have personal thriving even with serious impediments to thriving of mind as well as body. Gloria Lenhoff, whose impediments extend to both body and mind, is a good example. As Oliver Sacks's reactions to her show, her personal thriving has drawn great admiration from those who have come to know her.

And then there is Harriet Tubman. I need to underscore the fact that, by coupling the names of Harriet McBryde Johnson and Gloria Lenhoff with that of Harriet Tubman, I am not implying any equality in their suffering or in the stories of their lives. In differing ways, Harriet McBryde Johnson, Gloria Lenhoff, and Harriet Tubman are good examples of the personal thriving to which I am trying to draw attention; but Harriet Tubman's suffering is in a league of its own, and so is the luminosity of her life. The story of Tubman's life shines through the many years since her death as an example of the power and beauty of the human spirit. Her great-heartedness, the indomitable power of her will, the generosity of her work, the accomplishments of her life, are magnificent. Even with the impediments as regards mind and body from which she suffered, the personal thriving exemplified in her life sets a standard for others.

But what about flourishing? Is personal thriving equivalent to flourishing? The question arises because of the desires of the heart. As I described it above, human flourishing is a matter of wellbeing *and* the desires of the heart. Thriving of body and thriving of mind are parts of human wellbeing, which is measured on an objective scale of value for human beings. But there is also a subjective scale of value, which measures what has value for a human being just because he cares about it. A person who loses what he cares about as measured on this scale of value loses heart, as we say. In this condition, a person is marked by sadness, sorrow, grief, or something else opposed to joy. A person who has lost his heart's desires does not seem to be flourishing. In the examples of personal thriving above, it is reasonable to suppose that each of the thriving persons lost something she had her heart set on at some time in her life. Does the loss of a heart's desire mean that a person can have personal thriving but still lack flourishing?

Here it is important to recognize that there are layers of depth as regards human desire. Some desires are deeper than others and give meaning to those others. For that reason, it is possible to lose one's heart's desire at one level, and yet, in virtue of that very loss, to gain it at a deeper and more meaningful level. A person who gains his heart's desire at a deeper level by losing it at a more superficial level may always show the evidence of his loss, but he will also be marked by the energy characteristic of joy.[115] What is notable about Harriet McBryde Johnson, Gloria Lenhoff, and Harriet Tubman is precisely their exuberance. Something about the deep desires of the heart does seem to have been fulfilled for each of them. They do not look like people whom life has defeated. On the contrary, they look as if they are living the lives they want. No doubt, each of them suffered the loss of her heart's desires at some time in her life, and yet there is something exultant about the life of each of them also.

Insofar as personal thriving includes those things characteristic of a life marked not by defeat but by joy, then personal thriving, the thriving of the whole person, seems clearly also to be the flourishing of that person. Human flourishing, then, is not just a matter of thriving in body or in mind or both. It is a matter of thriving as a whole person, and this thriving can occur even when a person suffers from significant impediments as regards both mind and body and even when she has experienced the loss of her heart's desires. The depredations of other human beings, the consequences of severe poverty, the misfortunes of nature, and other similar afflictions cannot take away from a sufferer the possibility of flourishing. For even resplendent human flourishing, it is not necessary that the impediments to thriving of mind or body be prevented or removed or that there never be any loss of the heart's desires.

I recognize, of course, the troublesome appearance of this claim and the dreadful misuses to which it can be put. But think of the matter this way. If this claim were not true, then human flourishing would be another monopoly of the wealthy Western industrialized countries, or at least the upper classes in them. Wealth can go a long way towards the prevention and amelioration of impediments to the thriving of mind and body through the nutrition, medical care, and education that wealth makes possible. But wealth is neither necessary nor sufficient for human flourishing, and consequently neither is the thriving of body or thriving of mind that wealth helps to produce. I want to add hastily that this claim should be no consolation for those people who cause suffering to others, or whose indifference contributes to it, or who fail to remedy it when they can readily do so. That flourishing is compatible with suffering does not imply that such people are not execrable in their conduct.[116]

THE FURTHER CLAIM: SUFFERING AND FLOURISHING

It is hard not to notice that, as the Patristic thinkers regarded suffering, some diminishments in thriving of body or mind can in fact be woven into personal thriving. That is, the bodily or mental diminishments in thriving, the obstacles to what a person cares about on both the objective and the subjective scales of value, can in fact contribute to personal thriving not because they constitute challenges that a person surmounts, but because those very diminishments are themselves ingredients in that person's thriving. The diminishments are integral to the personal thriving, in the sense that their removal would constitute the removal (or at least the lessening) of the personal thriving.[117]

For example, it is hard not to suppose that Harriet McBryde Johnson is as superlatively courteous and generous to her enemies as she is because of her life with impairments of body. In the same way, Gloria Lenhoff's Williams Syndrome seems to be one source of the care for others that her father finds so moving in her. And Harriet Tubman's suffering from the depredations of the slave society around her and her consequent impairments in both mind and body seem to be part of the fabric of her character, marked by her charismatic leadership in her society and her self-sacrificial care for others.

Or think of the same point the other way around. How many people who live an upper-class life without much serious suffering, without much of any impairment in mind or body, count as having great personal thriving? How many people in a life of ease, with little tribulation in it, seem to be an example of human flourishing that others would love to be like? On the contrary, greatness of personal thriving seems to be found largely if not exclusively among those who suffer greatly too.[118] It is difficult to think of anyone who lacks such suffering and yet excites powerful admiration for the personal thriving of his life.

That suffering can lead to great personal thriving seems to me overwhelmingly confirmed by evidence of all kinds, including historical reflection, psychological studies, and plausible fictional narratives.[119] But *why* it should be so is harder to see. And here it has to be acknowledged that, even in a big book, careful examination of every issue significantly related to the main theme is ruled out by considerations of space. Nonetheless, even so, I want to gesture at some explanation of the evident role of suffering in flourishing.

On the scale of value for flourishing which is maintained in orthodox Christian theology, and which is widely held even by those who do not accept that theology, human flourishing has relationships of love at its heart. On the Christian scale of value, the most significant relationship is with God, though relationships of love with other human beings are central as well. But the post-Fall human condition is characterized by a tendency to turn away from such relationships into willed loneliness and isolation;[120] and so the post-Fall human condition inclines a person in a direction that undermines flourishing, when flourishing is understood most properly as a matter of relationships of love.

Suffering can make a difference to this condition in varying ways.

In the first place, because suffering is generally aversive, it can drive a person to seek amelioration from the suffering.[121] For those who do not try to protect themselves from suffering by becoming as isolated as a non-self can be, in the way Eckhart seems to recommend, the amelioration of suffering will have to be sought at least in part in the remedies other people can provide. Or, if all remedies fail, then suffering can incline a person to seek just the consolation that other people can give by their presence and compassion. Even when suffering cannot be taken away or diminished, it can somehow be made more bearable by the consolation of the presence of loving others. That is one reason why women in labor find it good to have a caring labor coach with them. The presence of the labor coach cannot diminish the physical pain of childbirth. How could it? But nonetheless the presence of a kind person personally engaged and responsive to a woman in labor will make the pains of the labor more tolerable if the woman in labor will accept the care and compassion which that person offers. In this same way, suffering can also incline a person to seek the presence of God.

Secondly, it has to be said that, for those who suffer involuntarily[122] and whose wills are therefore set against the suffering, suffering can be an affront to the ego. In saying this, I do not mean to imply that this reaction is blameworthy. On the contrary, there can be something pathological about passivity in the face of suffering.[123] When, to the great scandal of the Comforters in the story, Job unleashes his furious protests to God for God's allowing his suffering, God himself says at the end of the story that only Job—not the pious Comforters but Job—has said what was right.[124] So I do not mean to imply any negative assessment by saying that the mere fact of suffering can be an affront to the ego of the sufferer. I mean only to call attention to the fact that, when a person cannot ward off from himself what his will is set against, he is driven to acknowledge that he is not sufficient for himself. In this spirit, he will also be more likely to be willing to seek help, human help or God's help.

For one reason or another, then, suffering can break in on a person's inwardness and isolation.[125] The aversiveness of suffering can fuel a person's willingness to seek connection with others. A suffering person may turn to other human beings, but it is also widely recognized that in suffering a person is likely to turn to God, even if this turning comes with anger or remonstrance, as it does in Job's case.[126] It is common to find religious belief and religious experience among those in deep distress. It is less common to find true religiosity among those at ease.

So, for example, Frederick Douglas rightly excoriates the lack of any real Christian faith among the slave-holders. He says about the religion of those who accept slavery,

> between the Christianity of this land, and the Christianity of Christ, I recognize the widest possible difference ... I love the pure, peaceable, and impartial Christianity of Christ; I therefore hate the corrupt, slaveholding, women-whipping, cradle-plundering, partial and hypocritical Christianity of this land. Indeed, I can see no reason, but the most deceitful one, for calling the religion of this land Christianity .... I am filled with unutterable loathing when I contemplate the

religious pomp and show, together with the horrible inconsistencies, which everywhere surround me.[127]

By contrast, like many of the slaves, Tubman had a great personal commitment to Christ; and, even by the standards of the faith-filled community around her, she was notable for religious experience. For Tubman, God was always present to her and engaged with her. One of her biographers describes an experience that was typical for her; it occurred at the time in her life when she was first contemplating returning to slave territory to rescue other slaves:

> She had great fears about her future course, and confided, 'The Lord told me to do this. I said, "Oh Lord, I can't—don't ask me—take somebody else."' But Tubman also reported that God spoke directly to her: 'It's you I want, Harriet Tubman.'[128]

Tubman may have begun her many successful raids to rescue slaves with fearfulness, but years later she was notable for her daring. Stories illustrating her courage abound. For example, she was visiting in New York when she discovered that a fugitive slave, Charles Nalle, had been captured by bounty-hunters, who intended to return him to his slave master in the South. She went to the place where Nalle was being held, and this is what a contemporary, Martin Townsend, reported about what she did then:

> Harriet ... rushed amongst the foremost to Nalle, and running one of her arms around his manacled arm, held on to him without ever loosening her hold ... In the melee she was repeatedly beaten over the head with policemen's clubs, but she never for a moment released her hold, but cheered Nalle ... with her voice, and struggled with the officers until they were literally worn out with their exertions, and Nalle was separated from them. True, she had strong and earnest helpers in her struggle.... But she exposed herself to the fury of the sympathizers with slavery without fear, and suffered their blows without flinching ... Harriet and a number of other colored women ... brought Nalle out [from the crowd of police and bounty-hunters], and putting him in the first wagon passing, started him for the West.[129]

As these anecdotes from Tubman's life illustrate, suffering is part of an ongoing process in a person's life in which flourishing can develop and increase. The correlation between suffering and flourishing depends on second-personal relationships of love; and such relationships are dynamic, not static, even where God is concerned. It is part of traditional Christian theology that God will give grace to anyone who does not refuse it;[130] but, clearly, a process of this sort will expand rapidly if it is continued. As I explained above in the discussion of the Eucharist, that is because the grace given enables a person to ameliorate her own inner fragmentation and so to be more willing to be open to love and goodness—and this increased openness on her part will be met with more grace that grows her in goodness, thereby resulting in more grace given, and so on. Seeing the relationship between God and a person in grace in this way explains the line in the Gospels (see, e.g., Matt. 25:29) that to him who has, more will be given. This is an odd distribution principle if one is thinking of goods that diminish when they are distributed, such as money or human honor; but it makes sense if one is thinking of grace and love. Love grows in consequence of being accepted and shared. Insofar as suffering opens a person to love and deepens her in closeness to God and others, it is an element in this growth.

By her own account, when Tubman began her incursions into slave terri- tory to rescue slaves, she was fearful. But she was eventually as honored for her courage as for her care and compassion for others. She made her way at night in winter into slave territory, where she herself was hunted, to bring other slaves out. She was a spy for the Union during the Civil War, at great peril to herself. She nursed Union soldiers wounded or sick with highly infectious diseases contracted in the unsanitary conditions of field hospitals. And the list could go on. What makes her exemplary for us increased in her throughout her life.[131]

In all the difficult and dangerous work she undertook, she was tough in her resistance of evil, but she was also a model of kindness and care for others who were suffering. And her watchword in every crisis was "The Lord will provide." That expression of trust had its source in her continual experience of God as present to her and loving of her. Through that ongoing relation- ship, there was for her increased closeness to God, and increased flourishing as well.

I have no wish to write anything that would seem in any way to make light of Tubman's suffering. The suffering inflicted on her by the people promoting and maintaining slavery highlights the terribleness of the human post-Fall disorder, for which no words seem negative enough. Nonetheless, with diffi- dence, I want to suggest that Tubman's life also illustrates well the complicated thought in 2 Corinthians set out above.

On the complex thought in the Epistle, in virtue of suffering, a person in grace can grow in flourishing, even with irremediable and significant impedi- ments to thriving of body or mind, until there is in her life such flourishing that it is right to think of it as glory. And—to take the next part of the Epistle's thought—the affliction that a person suffers in this process will have a correlated consolation in the presence of God with her.

Tubman's flourishing came to her in virtue of her suffering, and that flourishing was great enough to make her like Christ in her willingness to suffer for others. The result is that her life is an example of the best a human life can be: the connection that the Epistle makes between suffering and glory is illustrated in her life. And so is the Epistle's claim that for a person in grace consolation increases with affliction. That Harriet Tubman is as exceptional in her ongoing religious experience as in her great-heartedness and her suffering is evident not only from her own testimony but also that of others who knew her. Her contemporary biographer summed the matter up this way:

> [Harriet] spoke of 'consulting with God,' and trusted that He would keep her safe. Thomas Garrett once said of her, 'I never met with any person of any color who had more confidence in the voice of God, as spoken direct to her soul.'[132]

Thomas Garrett's evaluation of Harriet Tubman's religious life is surely right. At any rate, it is highly doubtful whether any of those in the relatively well-to-do slave-holding communities around her lived in the kind of ongoing powerful religious experience she had. And so the Epistle's correlation of glory and of consolation with suffering seems well illustrated in her life.

And here it is important to me to reiterate caveats I made just above.

I am not claiming that the good of human flourishing justifies any human being in causing or permitting or failing to remedy suffering of the sort Tubman endured. To say that a person flourishes as she does at least in part in virtue of her suffering does not imply that it would be acceptable for another human being to permit it, or to cause it, or to refuse to remedy it if he could readily do so. It is one thing to claim that some suffering can lead to the flourishing of the sufferer and another thing entirely to claim that a person is justified in causing or allowing such suffering on the part of another for the sake of that flourishing.[133]

Furthermore, nothing about suffering guarantees that a sufferer will grow in closeness to God; human free will rules out such guarantees.

In addition, the consolation that increases with affliction, as the Epistle describes it, may not come at the same time as the affliction; it may come only later. Even those who seem to lack all consolation because they are burdened by depression or something else that leaves them destitute of ordinary human peace may yet find that their suffering enables them to flourish later with greater peace and greater joy than others who have not experienced such desolation.

Finally, someone may suppose that for every one person such as Harriet McBryde Johnson, Gloria Lenhoff, or Harriet Tubman, there are countless others who do not flourish in their suffering. But such a claim about the relative proportion of people who suffer without ever flourishing in consequence seems to me unsupported by any good evidence. Suffering is not always transparent even to the sufferer, let alone to those around the sufferer;[134] and flourishing is similarly not transparent either. In this respect, consider Sophie Scholl, who was executed by the Nazis after a speedy show trial and buried in an outcast's grave at what was then the edge of Munich. Hardly anyone around the world then knew who she was, or cared to know either. But now she is honored the world over for the flourishing of her life, and her grave is never without fresh flowers. So it is possible for a person both to suffer and to flourish in ways invisible to others, at least for a time, at least in this life. Consequently, the claim that most sufferers find no flourishing in their suffering is not only unsupported but in fact is such that empirical support for it is in principle hard to come by.

With these caveats underlined, then it seems to me right to acknowledge that there is a connection between the flourishing of Tubman's life and the suffering she endured. It seems to me true to say, with the thought of the Epistle, that she flourished in virtue of her suffering. If there is something heartbreakingly shaming about the human species in consequence of its part in such horrors as the slavery of the antebellum South, then the gloriousness of Tubman's life is highlighted by contrast. With all the impediments as regards mind and body which were a suffering for her, who would not grant that the flourishing of her life greatly outranked that of the slave-holders whose lives had vastly less suffering than hers or even that of the Northerners who lived at ease and were content not to mingle themselves into the troubles of others? Who would pick one of those Southern slave-holders or those indifferent Northerners as exemplary of human flourishing? By contrast with the life of Harriet Tubman, their lives look sad or shaming for our species. And if, like the slave-holding Southerners or the uninterested Northerners, Tubman had just lived a life of relative wealth and comfort, it seems unlikely that she would have become the woman we now are honored to honor.

PERSEVERANCE AND CHRIST'S SUFFERING

With so much of the thought in 2 Corinthians elucidated, we are in a position to consider the last part of its complicated thought, namely, the connection the Epistle makes between Christ's suffering and the perseverance through suffering of a person in grace.

Whatever the connection between flourishing and suffering, it remains the case that living through suffering can be an ordeal and an anguish. Nothing about the flourishing of a person enduring such suffering takes away from suffering its character as suffering. And so even a person flourishing in suffering may falter in the face of that suffering, as the stories about Tubman's troubles also testify. Nonetheless, on the thought of the Epistle, consolation increases with affliction for every person in grace who suffers.

One way to think about this claim is that suffering can make a person more open to God, in the way I sketched above: God gives his grace in ever-increasing degree to those who are increasingly open to it. If in suffering a person increases in willingness to be open to God, God responds to that openness with increased grace, which also brings increased consolation with it. In addition, however, it is part of the story of Christ's atonement that, in the person of the incarnate Christ, God chose to suffer out of love for human beings. It will make a great difference to a sufferer if she believes that the God who is with her is a God whose own suffering was also great and was endured for her sake. This story will make a difference to a person in grace both as regards her ability to bear suffering and her willingness to persevere through it.

Here I need to underline again what I am *not* saying. The experience of consolation does not alter the fact of suffering; it does not make it not be real suffering. Having a beloved person as company in suffering does not take away the suffering. And the claim that Christ endured suffering for love of human beings to bring them to God does not either explain or justify God's allowing the particular suffering of any particular human person.[135] What is at issue here is only the difference it makes to a sufferer that, on the Christian story, Christ suffers with human sufferers and for them. People have varying tolerances for suffering, and a person may find the same suffering more or less hard to bear depending on the circumstances surrounding it. What Christian theology, including the doctrine of the atonement, implies is not just that God is always present to any suffering human person in virtue of God's being omnipresent, but also that the God who is present to her suffered for her in ways more dreadful than hers, whatever her suffering is.

So although the consolation that increases with affliction (on the thought of the Epistle) cannot make suffering not be suffering, it can alter the experience of suffering by adding the consolation of being accompanied in suffering by the love of the suffering Christ.

Furthermore, even incipient union between persons is mutual; and when the union is between a human person and God, then the union is one of mutual indwelling. The Holy Spirit of Christ is within a person when she is in grace; but she is also within Christ. Her spirit is within his too. Through this union, what is in her is also within Christ, and what is in Christ is also within her psyche. Insofar as this union is furthered through suffering on her part, her suffering connects her more deeply to Christ, who also suffers for her. Through her suffering, then, a person is joined to Christ in his suffering for her. She is with Christ in his suffering, as he is with her in hers. Or, what is more nearly true, because there is mutual indwelling, then in the union between Christ and a human person the sufferings of each are at least in an empathic way the sufferings of the other (at least in some analogous or extended sense).

Thinking about the union between Christ and a person in grace in this way helps to explain what is an otherwise startling claim in Colossians 1:24, where the writer claims that his own sufferings fill up what is still lacking in the sufferings of Christ. The writer can take his own sufferings to count somehow as among Christ's sufferings insofar as he is united with Christ. And this is not yet the end of this complicated claim in Colossians. Insofar as a person in grace is joined to Christ, she is also in solidarity or communion with other human beings who also are joined to Christ in their sufferings. Since the mutual indwelling of Christ and a human person is a one–many relation—one

God and many people—then the whole group of people in grace is one with each other in being within Christ and having Christ within them. The biblical line[136] that the church is the body of Christ is one way of expressing this thought.[137] The sufferings of Christ are therefore, in some extended sense, the sufferings of all those united to Christ in love; and they are united in Christ and with each other in their sufferings.

And here we are brought back to the thought of 2 Corinthians. On that thought, the suffering of people in grace that is matched by their consolation is in some sense also the suffering of Christ. With emphasis added, the line in the Epistle reads this way:

> as the sufferings *of Christ* abound *in us*, so also our consolations abound through Christ.

Insofar as mutual indwelling is a metaphysically great union of persons, it also melds suffering as between Christ and all suffering persons in grace; and that melding in community of suffering can yield consolation, too.

On this way of thinking about suffering, then, suffering can make a special intimacy with Christ. Not only is there great consolation in this intimacy and the thought of it, but 2 Corinthians also implies that those who have more suffering are more flourishing. They are more glorious in themselves, in the glory reflected from the glory of Christ, to whom they are united, than those whose suffering is less. For all these reasons, what might have been a counter-intuitive attitude towards suffering makes sense in the context of the story of Christ's atonement. On that story, out of love Christ is willing to endure great suffering for human beings. When a person in grace suffers, she suffers with Christ and is honored by Christ in her suffering in virtue of the fact that her suffering unites her more intimately with Christ.

Finally, Christ's suffering is not only the physical suffering of death by torture but it is also the suffering of having within himself the psyches of post-Fall human beings. At any rate, this is one way of understanding the cry of dereliction from the cross; and it is also one way of understanding the difficult line in 2 Corinthians that God made Christ, who knew no sin, to be sin for human beings. In consequence of Christ's accepting this suffering, he does his part for union with human beings, so that when a human person surrenders to God's love and receives the indwelling Holy Spirit, the indwelling is mutual between God and her. Through this mutual indwelling she moves into the process of sanctification that gives her all the infused virtues and the gifts and fruits of the Holy Spirit and that unites her with God. And so, with this elucidation, we have the last part of the thought of the lines in 2 Corinthians. The righteousness of a person in grace comes from the suffering of Christ, so that her sin becomes Christ's and his righteousness becomes hers, in mutual indwelling and union.

All of this is part of the story that a person in grace brings to her suffering; and while it cannot make suffering not be suffering, it can encompass the suffering in a context that greatly aids her in bearing it. Consequently, her suffering, conjoined with Christ's suffering, does not have just instrumental value for her. Rather, for the sufferer, this very suffering is part of her flourishing, because in her uniting to Christ in his suffering she has both consolation and glory—that is, she has what she cares about, both as regards her wellbeing and as regards what her heart is set on.

Consequently, on these theological views, through the suffering Christ endured in order to bring human persons to the surrender to love which starts spiritual regeneration and union with God, there is also a great aid to perseverance in the process of sanctification, in the suffering which is also part of a person's flourishing—and which is therefore worth not just honoring but even celebrating.

CONCLUSION

The reflections in this chapter make manifest that the process of salvation has three parts. There is the difficult and delicate beginning of the process that depends ultimately on the human person in the process; once a person surrenders in love, then God infuses into her will the operative grace that brings her to justification. Then there is sanctification, the extended part of the process in which a person cooperates with God to bring about her increased closeness with God through integration in goodness. And then there is perseverance in sanctification.

In no part of this tripartite process can God get what God wants by the unilateral use of power, without any contribution to the process on the part of a human person. Union would be lost, not achieved, if God did so. But the passion and death of Christ are a powerful means to elicit from a person Paula the surrender that is the prerequisite to her justification. By means of the story of Christ's passion and death, Paula can come to know Christ with the knowledge of persons. And when she does and surrenders to God's love because she does, then God himself comes to her in the indwelling Holy Spirit. At that point, in a way provided for by Christ's opening himself to human psyches in his passion and death, Paula comes to have the union of mutual indwelling with God. As long as she remains in this union, God can cooperate with her will to integrate her as a person and to bring her to flourishing as a person in full union with God.

Perseverance is as essential to the process of salvation as the original surrender to God is, and it is almost as difficult to maintain as the original surrender was difficult to elicit. On Christian theology, both the rite of the Eucharist and the experience of suffering have the power to support perseverance throughout the life of a person in grace. In differing ways, the result of the participation in the Eucharist and the experience of suffering on the part of a person in grace is that she is strengthened in connection to Christ, in her own suffering shared with Christ and in the presence to her in the Eucharist of the suffering Christ. And so, in both ways, she is aided in perseverance, through the love and joy and peace that are the first fruits of the indwelling Holy Spirit, even in the suffering, the sorrows and the sins of her life.

In Chapter 1, I pointed out that there ought to be some connection between the good brought about by the passion and death of Christ and the good justifying God in allowing suffering. That is, there ought to be some intrinsic connection between an acceptable interpretation of the doctrine of the atonement and an acceptable theodicy. But, on first glance, it seemed hard to find such a connection. The reason for God's allowing suffering has to be something that brings the sufferer closer to God, but this is also the benefit brought about by the atonement of Christ. And if one of these brings about the good in question, then it is hard to see why the other is needed.

But the reflections in this chapter about the role of suffering in perseverance show that the connection between theodicy and the doctrine of the atonement is in fact as intelligible as it is powerful. There is suffering that works together with Christ's atonement to aid in bringing a person to the initial surrender to God's love. And then there is suffering that aids in bringing a person into greater closeness with Christ and the suffering of Christ, with consequent consolation and flourishing, This suffering is an aid to perseverance for those in the process of sanctification. On the interpretation of the doctrine of the atonement argued for in this book, then, the good postulated as explaining God's reason for allowing suffering and the good proposed as explaining Christ's atonement converge; and the two theological explanations for suffering converge as well, as they ought to do.[138]

With this chapter, I have completed the exposition and defense of my interpretation of the doctrine of the atonement. What remains to be done is to show that this interpretation meets the desiderata for an acceptable interpretation that I set out in Chapter 1. That task is the subject of the next and final part of this book.

Part IV

The Desiderata for an Interpretation of the Doctrine of the Atonement

10

The Atonement and the Solution to the Problems of Guilt and Shame

INTRODUCTION

In the previous chapters, I explained what is wanted from atonement, namely, union between God and human persons; and I argued that this union consists in mutual indwelling between God and a human person in grace. Then I showed that Christ's passion brings about God's part in this indwelling and also serves to enable a human person's part. What is left to do now is to check whether the interpretation of the doctrine of Christ's atonement that I elucidated in these chapters in fact fits the desiderata for any acceptable interpretation of the doctrine. The most important desiderata have to do with the removal of guilt and shame, but there are also other desiderata, as I explained in Chapter 1.

Because the previous chapters contain a wealth of detail outlining the interpretation of the doctrine argued for in this book, in what follows I will begin with a very brief review of the main elements of that interpretation. (Readers who are confident that they need no such review should feel free to skip the next section of this chapter.)

With this review sketched out, I will then devote the rest of the chapter to the twin issues of guilt and shame; and I will argue that this book's interpretation of the doctrine of the atonement gives a good and morally acceptable explanation of the removal of guilt and shame by Christ's passion and death.[1] In the next and concluding chapter, I will turn to the remaining desiderata and show briefly the way in which they too are met by this interpretation of the doctrine.

A REVIEW

Part I

In Part I of this book, I discussed what is wanted in an acceptable interpretation of the Christian doctrine of the atonement. In the Christian tradition, the atonement is conceived of as the solution to a problem, namely, the absence of union between God and human beings; and the ultimate source of the distance between God and human beings is taken to be the human proneness to moral wrongdoing. Consequently, the problem for which the atonement of Christ is intended to be the solution includes three elements:

(1)   occurrent dispositions to moral wrongdoing, with their liability to future wrong or sinful acts,

and past wrong acts with their consequent

(2)   guilt, both in (a) its impairments in psyche of the wrongdoer and (b) its ill-effects in the world,

and

(3)   shame, where shame arises from sources that are tied directly or indirectly to human wrongdoing.

An acceptable interpretation of the atonement needs to show that these elements of the problem are solved by the atonement, as the atonement is conceived on that interpretation.

Guilt and shame can be explained in terms of the two desires of love, on Aquinas's account of love, namely, the desire for the good of the beloved and the desire for union with the beloved. A person who is and feels guilty reasonably anticipates that some real or imagined others will have a warranted desire for what she takes to be not her good; and a person who is and feels shamed reasonably anticipates that some real or imagined others will have a warranted desire to reject him.

Given this distinction between guilt and shame, there are different kinds of problems facing those suffering from guilt or from shame.

A person who is and feels guilty of something has two problems, one that lies in himself and another that lies in the world and that stems from the damage or injustice which he has done.

On Aquinas's theory of agency (on which I am relying in this book), any act of moral wrongdoing stems not only from a moral flaw in the will of the wrongdoer but also from a corresponding flaw in his intellect, which apprehends as an apparent good something that is not a real good or which takes a lesser good as better than something that is in fact a greater good. Repeated wrong acts can build up dispositions that render the wrongdoer more liable to the same or similar wrong acts in the future, and these habits or vices are also part of the problem of guilt. In addition, there is the problem of the stain on the soul, as Aquinas calls it. Wrongdoing not only distorts the wrongdoer's intellect and will, but it also has other morally lamentable effects; for example, it has deleterious effects on memory and on the cognitive capacities underlying mind-reading and empathy. Furthermore, wrongdoing leaves relational characteristics altered for the worse. Something sad can remain for the wrongdoer in his relations with those hurt by him, even if he is repentant, even if he is forgiven by his victims.

Besides the defective or diminished state of the psyche of the wrongdoer and his relationships, the wrongdoer has the additional problem of the damage done by his wrongdoing. This problem itself can be divided into two, because harm and injustice are not the same. In virtue of his wrongdoing, a guilty person will have done some kind of harm to something good in the world (even if only himself, in virtue of impairing himself through wrongdoing), and he will have acted unjustly towards someone or something (even if only himself and not also other human beings or beasts) by doing so.

Besides these problems stemming from guilt, there are also problems stemming from shame. A person who is and feels shamed may be shamed in consequence of his own moral wrongdoing. He may suppose that what he has done warrants in real or imagined others (or in himself) a repudiation *of him* rather than a rejection of what he takes to be his good through punishment of him.

Furthermore, a person's shame and the self-loathing it may cause him can be prompted by many things other than his own moral wrongdoing. There are different varieties of shame, because there are different sorts of reasons for someone's rejecting a shamed person. There is the shame arising from a person's suffering the sinful depredations of other human beings. There is the shame attending on the limitations or defects of nature. And there is also the shame attaching to a person just in virtue of his belonging to some group that is shamed in his culture or society.

So although the guilt and shame consequent on moral wrongdoing constitute the central problem to which the atonement is the solution, there are other sources of shame as well; and they are also tied, in one way or another, to human wrongdoing. Even shame over the defects of nature has a connection to human wrongdoing since, on traditional Christian doctrine, there was no natural evil, and consequently no shame over defects of nature, before the sin resulting in the Fall.

Shame stemming from any of its sources can be as powerful a source of distance between the shamed person and others as guilt is, and it can also introduce distance between a shamed person and God. A shamed person's repudiation of himself, as ugly or otherwise rejected for reason, is as effective as the inner dividedness generated by moral wrongdoing at preventing or undermining union between himself and God.

For my purposes in this book, I accept unreservedly the traditional Christian account according to which the canonical problem solved by Christ's atonement is human sinfulness. But since the atonement is meant to be the reversal of the distance between God and human beings introduced not only by personal sin but also, ultimately, by the Fall, then shame, including shame from any of its sources, needs a remedy in the atonement, too. At any rate, there are certainly biblical texts promising that the messianic age will take away shame as well as guilt. Isaiah 54:4, for example, claims that in that time Israel will forget the shame of her youth.[2]

Although it has been widely accepted for a long time, the Anselmian kind of interpretation of the atonement, in any of its forms, is in fact unsalvageable. It is incompatible with the doctrine that God is loving, and this incompatibility is irremediable. Consequently, the atonement needs to be understood as bringing about union between God and post-Fall human beings not by altering conditions that keep God from forgiving human wrongdoers and accepting reconciliation with them, as the Anselmian interpretation has it, but rather by altering something about human beings.

An analogous point holds as regards satisfaction. The vicarious satisfaction of Christ's atonement should not be understood as making up to God for the debt or offense of human beings, as the Anselmian approach to satisfaction maintains. Looked at in detail, the Anselmian approach to satisfaction is also unsalvageable. There *is* a role for Christ's vicarious satisfaction; but it serves to remedy something in human beings that is damaged or destroyed by the evil of human wrongdoers. It does not serve to enable God's pardon or forgiveness of human beings. The point of Christ's passion and death is not to win from God clemency for sinful human beings.

Part II

In Part II, I discussed in detail the nature of the union that the atonement is meant to help bring about. That union consists in a mutual indwelling between God and a human person in grace, in which the Holy Spirit of Christ is within a person in grace and her psyche is within Christ. To achieve this mutual indwelling, Christ needs to open himself to receive the psyches of all human beings, as he does when he bears all human sin on the cross. But a human being also needs to open to receive the Holy Spirit, who indwells every person in grace.

As I hope will be abundantly clear, this is a decidedly non-Abelardian interpretation of atonement. On the interpretation of the doctrine of the atonement often attributed to Abelard,[3] Christ saves post-Fall human beings from their sin by modeling for them what a truly good human person is like. His life, passion, and death serve to teach human beings how they should live. On this Abelardian interpretation, Christ counts as nothing more than a teacher; and the purpose of his life, passion, and death are only to provide the basis for persuading a human person to new states of intellect. But, on the interpretation of the doctrine I am arguing for, the main problem for post-Fall human beings lies in the will, not in the intellect. And in his passion and death,

Christ brings about a metaphysical alteration in himself and in every person of grace that enables a metaphysical condition of mutual indwelling between God and human persons.

The very things that leave a human person alienated from himself leave him divided against himself with regard to the love of others as well, including the love of God. It takes God's grace to integrate a person enough even to form a will to will the good. But God cannot unilaterally bring it about that there is such a will in a post-Fall person without losing the very thing that is wanted in union. What is required from a post-Fall person, then, is just a cessation of resistance to God's love. Even on anti-Pelagian views, it is open to a human person to resist or to cease resisting God's love. And so a post-Fall person's surrender of resistance to God's love is free, because that person has alternative possibilities open to his will, though one of them, surrender, is an absence of willing and not an act of will in its own right.

Once a person Paula has surrendered and ceased resisting God's love, then God gives her the operative grace needed for a will that wills to will the good; and, at this point, the union between her and God begins. In this condition, Paula has justification, which is the start of her spiritual regeneration. Because Paula has ceased resisting God, God can infuse grace into her will without violating it. Through this infusion of grace, Paula comes to the will of faith: she longs for God's goodness and repudiates her own evil. At this point, she also receives the Holy Spirit, which comes to indwell in her, and which brings with it all the infused virtues and the gifts and fruits of the Holy Spirit. With the indwelling Holy Spirit and the dispositions that come to Paula in consequence of receiving the Holy Spirit, Paula is a person in grace.

The advent of the Holy Spirit with the infusion of virtue does not remove the old dispositions that Paula acquired for herself through morally wrong acts. But it does introduce virtues over them, and it counteracts the old morally wrong dispositions with the newly infused virtues and gifts of the Holy Spirit. Paula is not integrated wholly around the good insofar as she still acts on some first-order desires for what is contrary to the good as she sees it; but she is in second-person relationship with God, and together she and God can then cooperate to make progress at integration for Paula. The hallmark of being a person in grace are the fruits of the Holy Spirit: love, joy, peace, patience, long-suffering, and the rest. As long as a human person does not return to her original resistance to God's love and grace, the process begun in this way will continue to work with her own will to strengthen her in willing the good. This part of the process is her sanctification; and if she herself does not abrogate it, it will culminate ultimately in her complete integration around the good and her full union with God.

All the complex metaphysical interweaving of God and human beings in mutual indwelling and all the human growth in internal integration around the good depend therefore on this one difficult and delicate thing, a human person's surrendering to God's love, which God cannot unilaterally bring about and which a human person in the post-Fall condition resists.

With this much explanation of the ethics, moral psychology, and theology that are the background and data for this project, I then turned in Part III to the atonement itself.

Part III

In Part III, I used the biblical narratives of the temptations of Christ to illuminate the way in which the passion and death of Christ are a means for bringing a human person to the one crucial thing, the one thing which even omnipotent God cannot do unilaterally but which is necessary for a human person's ultimate flourishing in union with God, namely, her surrender of resistance to God. The powerlessness, vulnerability, and suffering of Christ on the cross are arguably the most promising means for quieting a person's fear of God's love or for dissolving the willed loneliness in her brought about by guilt or shame in any of their varieties or by the brokenness stemming from the depredations of others.

Once the atonement is seen in the light shed on it by the story of the temptations of Christ, other parts of the story of Christ's life, including, for example, his birth as an infant to poor parents, also make sense as part of the atonement.

A person's surrender to God's love in response to Christ's atonement is met immediately by the indwelling Holy Spirit, with all the infused virtues and the gifts and fruits of the Holy Spirit; but the process that is meant to culminate in full and complete union of mutual indwelling is slow. It is implemented in part through suffering, which deepens a person in openness to God's love by strengthening her union with Christ. And because Christ suffers for her, she shares her suffering in second-person relationship with Christ through the indwelling Holy Spirit, which is also the spirit of Christ, on Trinitarian lore. For this reason, her consolation increases in virtue of her suffering and aids her in perseverance. In addition, in her suffering, she is also supported by the rite of the Eucharist, which is another, intense way of connecting her with the suffering of Christ.

In these ways, the atonement of Christ that enables a nascent union of mutual indwelling between God and a human person also strengthens her for perseverance and for growth in that union.

With these considerations presented in Part III, then, the interpretation of the doctrine of the atonement at issue in this book is complete. What remains for this section, Part IV of this book, is therefore an evaluation of this interpretation. Does this interpretation meet the desiderata for any acceptable interpretation of the doctrine, as I presented those desiderata in Chapter 1?

I will begin to answer that question in this chapter and finish doing so in the next and final chapter of the book.

THE PROBLEM OF SHAME: THE KINDS OF SHAME

Since the main desiderata for an acceptable interpretation of the doctrine of the atonement have to do with the removal of guilt and shame, in this chapter I will begin the evaluation of the interpretation given in the preceding chapters with a consideration of these desiderata. I will argue that, on this interpretation, the atonement of Christ constitutes a full solution to the problem of shame, in all its varieties, and to the problem of guilt, with all its parts.

We can begin with the problem of shame. It will be helpful to have in mind here the main kinds of shame.[4]

First, there is a kind of shame that attaches to a person in consequence of his own wrongdoing. So, for example, Newton had shame as well as guilt over his past slave-trading actions. Even when he was fervently repentant for his evil acts, he could reasonably anticipate that real or imagined others would have a warranted desire to turn away from him for what he had done, even if he had repented for it.

A different kind of shame can afflict a person in consequence of the wrongdoing of others. Consider, for example, Malala Yousufzai. When the Taliban began to close schools for girls and to intimidate girls persistent in attending those few schools that were still open to them, Malala[5] was outspoken in her defense of education for girls. And so there was a day when a Taliban gunman stopped her school bus, asked which of the girls was Malala, and shot her in the head. After multiple surgeries, she recovered; but she was left with a metal plate in her skull and an implanted device to help her hear. There is shame in the powerlessness of having been victimized in this way. Or think of Sophie Scholl. She was arrested by the Nazis for her participation in a small student protest against the Nazi government. Shaming her publicly was part of the Nazi proceedings against her. She was made an example of at a show trial, flamboyantly judged guilty, sentenced to death with maximum pompous show intended to shame her, and buried privately in an undistinguished grave on the outskirts of her city.

This is a kind of shame that does not have its source in a person's own evil acts but is still a consequence of human evil because it stems directly or indirectly from the wrongdoing of people other than the shamed person. There is a kind of diminution some people suffer that stems from the injustice inflicted on them by others. That injustice somehow alters their relative standing with respect to other people for the worse. If the examples of Malala and Scholl are not sufficient to make this point, then think of the adult survivors of childhood sexual abuse. For such people, who are the innocent victims of adult evil, shame can be crippling.

Some people in favor of retributive punishment might suppose that retributive punishment is sufficient as a remedy for this kind of shame, at least insofar as it seems to restore the right relative standing between the victim and the wrongdoer.[6] But although retributive punishment meted out to Malala's assailants or Scholl's attackers might do something to restore justice in their societies and might even restore some of what is owed to Malala or Scholl,[7] it still cannot take away their shame over having been rendered helpless and victimized in front of others; and it cannot heal their memories of that shame either. The ugliness of the shaming remains part of their life stories, no matter how their persecutors might be punished. So retributive punishment of the wrongdoer does not seem to hold out much hope as a full remedy for the problem of shame for those suffering from the evil of other human beings.

In addition to the two kinds of shame closely tied to human wrongdoing, there is also the shame whose source is the limitations or the defects of nature.[8] Joseph Merrick, the so-called Elephant Man, is as good an example as any of someone afflicted with this kind of shame. The dreadful distortions of his frame caused by his disease left him looking revulsive and fearful to others, who generally turned away from him. The cruelty of others was a source of shame for him, but the disfiguring disease alone was as well. On traditional Christian doctrine, the defects of nature are a consequence, even if an indirect one, of human sinfulness. On this view, there was no natural evil, and consequently no shame over the defects of nature, before the sin resulting in the Fall. So, insofar as defects in nature are somehow thought to be a function of the post-Fall condition of the world, which is itself a function of human sin, then this third kind of shame is also a consequence of human sin, not of course on the part of sufferers such as Merrick, but on the part of the human species in its origins.

Lastly, just as there is a pride in belonging to a certain family or people or nation, so there is shame that attaches to a person because of the social group to which he belongs.[9] Some children of high-ranking Nazis, for example, felt shame in being members of their families because of the actions committed by one of their parents, although the children themselves bore no guilt for their parents' actions.[10] Analogously, as many thinkers have noted, there can be a kind of shame attaching to being a member of the human species, too.[11] There are the moral horrors that the human species has committed against vulnerable people, the unspeakable suffering it has inflicted on the beasts, and the suicidal destruction it is perpetrating on the planet. Insofar as the shaming record of humanity is part of the story of the post-Fall human condition, it seems that this kind of shame also needs a remedy by anything that is to count as a full solution to the problem of human sinfulness.

So it is possible to classify shame into four major kinds:[12] (1) shame resulting from one's own wrongdoing; (2) shame stemming from being wronged by others; (3) shame following on some defect of nature; and (4) shame attaching to being a member of the human species. Of these four, the first three are personal, and the fourth is communal. For each of the first three, a person is and feels shamed because he himself is and feels personally deficient or less than he himself wants to be by some standard of value which he accepts and which he expects real or imagined others to accept as well. For the fourth, a person is and feels shamed because his group—in this case, the human species—is deficient or inferior by a standard of value that all people should and generally do accept.

Not only is the problem of shame a problem that the atonement could reasonably be expected to remedy but, in fact, the inefficacy of satisfaction made to God considered as a remedy for shame highlights yet another inadequacy of the Anselmian kind of interpretation of the doctrine of the atonement. Where the problem of shame is concerned, the debt Christ pays to God does not take away the shame of the victims of human evil, such as Malala or Scholl, and it does not remedy the relative standing of the victim and those who wronged her. A fortiori, it does not take away the shame attendant on the wrongdoing of a person such as Newton or the shame any person might feel over being a member of the human species. On the contrary, the very fact that the sins of a person such as Newton are loaded on to Christ on the cross ought to add to his shame, not ameliorate it, even if Christ's passion and death pay his debt to God. Having a perfectly good person suffer terribly to pay a debt Newton owes is not only likely to make Newton feel more shamed by his sins, but it seems clear that it ought to do so. On the scale of value which privileges human relationships, the negative value attaching to Newton's having a share of responsibility for Christ's suffering and death seems to fall into the same category as homicide—at least in its form of involuntary manslaughter. The fact that Christ voluntarily suffers and dies for Newton does not alter Newton's share of responsibility for Christ's suffering and death. Why should the luminous character of his love for Newton diminish Newton's shame at being responsible for the evil endured by so lovely a person?

Finally, although I began explaining the problem of shame by pointing to particular powerful examples of shame, it should be clear that the problem of shame affects every human being who lives to the age of reason. It does so obviously with regard to the fourth kind of shame. But it does so equally with regard to the other three. Every human being who lives to the age of reason, whenever that is, has one degree of shame or another stemming from his own moral wrongdoing, his suffering at the hands of others, and his afflictions from the defects of nature. Undoubtedly, some instances of shame are much harder to endure than others; but there is no human being past the age of reason who does not labor under all these kinds of shame at some time in his life. Although the problem of human proneness to moral wrongdoing, with its consequent guilt and liability to moral evil, is theologically more central to the doctrine of the atonement as traditionally interpreted, all shame is something that the atonement might reasonably be supposed to remedy as well if it is to be a complete solution to the post-Fall human condition and the problems generated by the human proneness to wrongdoing.

SHAME AND COMPENSATION IN HEAVEN

At this point, someone might object that, on Christian doctrine, the remedy for every kind of shame lies in the afterlife. In heaven, the putative objector will argue, all shame is compensated for, because everyone in heaven will rejoice at being in some exemplary and excellent condition. And so the atonement is not needed as a remedy for shame.

But this objection is confused.

Even if, on Christian doctrine, a person's condition in heaven were so great that it vastly outweighed any negative value stemming from shame,[13] we do not generally suppose that an outweighing compensation is sufficient as a remedy for the affliction being compensated. In the case of shame, in particular, shame will remain even after outweighing compensation for it, because the compensation is not intrinsically or essentially related to the shame.[14] Paying a person with good in heaven for the suffering of shame may do the shamed person some good, but that good will not include removing the shame. By itself, being in a glorious condition in heaven cannot take away from Newton the shaming stigma of having been a slave trader. The shame of a person stems from that person's deficiencies on some scale of values in consequence of something in the history of his life; and that history, like everything else about the past, is fixed and unalterable. Unless something can be done to alter the shame of that past, then even in heaven Newton will suffer from the shame of his past slave-trading, which will not go away or alter its character by Newton's being in heaven.

And, *mutatis mutandis*, a similar point can be made about Malala, Scholl, or Merrick. The past in which Malala was a spectacle for pitiless violence on a school bus, Scholl was a spectacle for murderous malice, and Merrick was a spectacle for horrified revulsion—that past remains no matter what might happen to any of them subsequently in heaven. Consequently, even if, on Christian doctrine, in the afterlife in heaven a person such as Newton is in an excellent condition that vastly outweighs the shame he endured in earthly life because of his slave-trading, the good of that heavenly condition alone is not a full remedy for the shame of Newton, or for such shame as that endured by Malala, Scholl, and Merrick either.

For these reasons, the problem of shame remains, even if the afterlife is a very great compensatory good for those who are in heaven. It remains the case, then, that if the atonement is the solution to the problems generated by the human post-Fall condition, it is reasonable to suppose that it should also be the full remedy for the problem of shame, in all its main varieties.

So, is there something about the atonement that can defeat the shame arising from the depredations of other persons, the defects of nature, and the post-Fall history of the human race, as well as the shame arising from a person's own wrongdoing?

THE REMEDY FOR SHAME

To find the answer to this question, it is helpful to consider the kind of thing that *could* constitute a full remedy for shame. The natural remedy for shame, understood as reasonable anticipation of warranted rejection by real or imagined others, is admiration or honor (where by 'honor' I mean something correlated with a real and admirable quality in the person honored, and not something extrinsic to that person, such as fame[15]). A person who is rightly honored or admired is so in virtue of having something attractive about him, and those who are attracted to him have some desire for him. To the extent that others have a warranted desire for him, they have the second desire of love for him, namely, the desire for union of one sort or another. And if others are warranted in being drawn to him and in desiring union with him, then the shamed person's shame is lifted.

Because a shamed person can be thought deficient by others on the basis of varying scales of value, it is possible for a person to be shamed on one set of standards and honored on another. Merrick is a good example here. Merrick suffered from the disease that deformed him and the shame that accrued to him from its disfigurement. By the end of his life, however, even Queen Alexandra was among those who publicly honored him. Frederick Treves, the doctor who rescued and befriended Merrick, plainly admired him. At Merrick's death, Treves said of Merrick:

> As a specimen of humanity, Merrick was ignoble and repulsive; but the spirit of Merrick, if it could be seen in the form of the living, would assume the figure of an upstanding and heroic man, smooth-browed and clean of limb, and with eyes that flashed undaunted courage.[16]

So, for the first three kinds of shame, personal shame, a full remedy for shame will consist in two things. First, the shamed person will have something beautiful, something admirable or honorable, about him on a standard of value more important than the standard by which he is shamed. And, second, this admirable or beautiful element in the shamed person's life will defeat the shame. That is, it will be greater and more worth having than what is lost through the shame, *and* the defects that are the source of the shame will be somehow inextricably interwoven into that greater good.

For the fourth kind of shame, the communal shame of the species, it would be enough if the species as a whole had something in its history that made the species lovely or admirable by some standard of significantly great value and that defeated the shame. Small-scale examples of this method for adding honor to something otherwise without it are commonplace. A not particularly noteworthy restaurant may carry a plaque proclaiming that many years earlier a world-renowned artist regularly ate there. A family currently low-ranking in its community may boast that some centuries ago one of its members was part of the royal family then governing the nation. A country not generally able to hold its own on the world stage may announce in its public advertising that it has had among its people the team that won the World Cup. And so on. Because the restaurant or family or country can count as its own something or someone very highly honored, the whole group gains in honor.[17] And it makes sense that it should be so. If the whole business, family, or nation can be shamed by what some parts of the whole do or do not do, then the whole can also be honored by the participation in it of some particularly admirable or lovely person or thing. And if somehow the shame has some intrinsic or essential relationship to the honor, then the honor not only outweighs the shame, it defeats it. By means of this sort, it is possible for there to be a full remedy for the fourth kind of shame also.

If something about the atonement is the full remedy for shame, then the atonement ought somehow to provide a good that defeats the shame, whatever kind of shame accrues to a person. And there would be such a remedy in the atonement if, on some deep or weighty standard of value, something about the atonement left a shamed person with honor or loveliness which is greater than his shame and with which his shame is somehow inextricably bound up.

PERSONAL THRIVING

Merrick's honoring by the society around him at the end of his life might lead someone to suppose that, by means of the sort of personal thriving exemplified by Merrick's life, a shamed person could himself provide the remedy that defeats shame, at least for the personal kinds of shame. Analogously, although it is not possible for a person such as Newton to return to innocence after such serious moral wrongdoing as engaging in the slave trade, it seems that it is possible for him to defeat the shame of his past by means of the personal thriving he manifested in his later life, in his work to abolish the slave trade.

Newton's passionate efforts on behalf of the abolition of the slave trade were successful in making him a different and more honorable man from the man he had been not only when he was a slave trader but even when he was first repentant.

A similar point applies to the other kinds of shame as well. Malala, for example, did not let the violent attack on her life quell her. In a way that caught the attention of the whole world, she continued to speak out on behalf of education for girls, even in the face of the threat of continued attack against her and with the challenges of her own ongoing medical problems. In consequence, she became a symbol of courage under oppression, and she has been honored for it internationally. In 2014, she became the youngest person ever to receive the Nobel Peace Prize.

Why not suppose then that such personal thriving manifested by a person shamed on one standard of value but greatly honored on another, deeper standard is sufficient as a full remedy for shame? Shame can be thought of as arising from a diminishment in thriving of body or of mind. But then it seems that it can also be overcome by the personal thriving manifested in Newton's intense efforts on behalf of abolition or Malala's superlative courage on behalf of other young women. Why would personal thriving such as theirs not count as a full remedy for shame? Why not suppose in fact that whatever defects such people suffer from, the defects are worth celebrating in consequence of being woven into great personal thriving, as the Patristic attitude towards suffering maintains?

The answer is that even the personal thriving Newton and Malala manifested in their exemplary acts does not *defeat* shame. The shame they suffered was not inextricably connected to their personal thriving. In Newton's case, his morally deplorable actions as a slave trader were not essential to his working for the abolitionist cause. Like William Wilberforce, he might have done so even without that shaming wrongdoing. And, *mutatis mutandis*, a similar point applies to Malala. She might have been a great advocate for education for girls in her country without having endured a murderous attack.

Analogous things can be said about the other kinds of cases mentioned above.[18] Personal thriving that brings widespread admiration is possible for anyone, even without his being first subjected to shame; and, generally speaking, even the character of that personal thriving can remain largely intact without shame. Scholl might have engaged in covert activities against the Nazis for which she was never caught, but for which she became greatly honored later. It is arguable that great personal thriving has a source in suffering;[19] but what is at issue in this chapter is the particular suffering of shame, and not suffering in general. No doubt, Scholl would have endured suffering if she had engaged in covert activities against the Nazis but had never been caught. That suffering then would have had its role in her personal thriving. But, in this counterfactual example, Scholl would nonetheless have escaped the humiliating shame of her show trial. So her shame is not in any sense necessary for her thriving, and for this reason her thriving does not *defeat* the shame she in fact endured. Although her personal thriving triumphs over the shame, if this is all that can be said about her history, then it seems as if she is something like a heroic overcomer of tragic and shaming circumstances, which remain as parts of her history that she might reasonably prefer to keep invisible from everyone's gaze.

Merrick's story is obviously the hardest kind of case here, but the point at issue applies even to such cases. Suppose that Merrick had never suffered a disfiguring disease, but that he nonetheless volunteered to minister to a community of people who did (lepers in one of the leper colonies extant in his day, for example). Then he would have been greatly admirable for his courage and compassion, even if he himself was not shamed by having such a disease. Consequently, his shame is not defeated by the admirable character of his life.

Unless shame is somehow ingredient in the personal thriving open to the shamed to have in virtue of suffering, the shame they endure is not defeated by their personal thriving, even if the shame is instrumental in bringing that thriving about. Harriet Tubman might not have had the particular, highly admirable personal thriving her life manifests without the shaming she endured from those supporting slavery, but then she might have had some other great personal thriving that stemmed from suffering without shame. Or think of the point this way. Even in her best times, why would we not suppose that Tubman remembered with pain the past shame to which human evil subjected her? And so the instrumental role of shame in personal thriving is not sufficient for a full remedy of shame. Consequently, the problem of shame remains.

Is there, then, any way in which the atonement serves to *defeat* shame?

THE ATONEMENT AND THE FOURTH KIND OF SHAME

The doctrine of the atonement holds that the atonement is the work of Christ; and the Chalcedonian formula specifies the orthodox understanding of Christ: one divine person, the second person of the Trinity, with one fully human nature and one fully divine nature. On this understanding of the doctrine of the atonement, it is true to say that God suffers and that God dies; but God suffers and dies in the human nature God has assumed.

Understood in this way, the very incarnation—God's assuming human nature in addition to God's divine nature—does seem to exalt human nature. For this reason, some philosophers and theologians have thought that the incarnation alone is sufficient as a remedy for the fourth kind of shame, the shame of humanity.[20] There is certainly some appeal in this thought; but, in my view, reflection on the nature of shame shows that this thought cannot be right.

The mere fact of God's adding human nature to himself does elevate human nature in some way, but having human nature distinguished in this way is compatible with its remaining shamed. Consider in this connection the visit of Pope Francis to some people serving prison terms for serious crimes. The Pope's visit elevates the prisoners in that prison above other prisoners in other prisons, but being singled out in such a manner is not enough by itself to remedy shame for those prisoners the Pope visited. Rather, it makes a difference what the Pope does when he visits the prison. If he simply visits, in his clean white papal clothes, and passes through, separated from the prisoners by his office, his power, and his innocence, then his visit serves largely to mark the difference between his status and theirs. While they are elevated as regards other prisoners in being singled out by the Pope for a visit, their shameful status as prisoners is left largely intact. That is because although the Pope visits them, he does not in any sense join them.

The Golden Adler in Innsbruck has a plaque on its wall letting all passersby know that Mozart ate there. But if Mozart ate there only because there was no other place to eat as he was traveling through Innsbruck, so that the restaurant was necessary to him but hated by him, then his eating there does not bring any honor to the restaurant. The restaurant is honored only if Mozart chose to eat there because something about the restaurant attracted Mozart, so that in some sense it became *his* restaurant. The affinity between Mozart and the restaurant is what gives the restaurant any claim to honor by Mozart.

The fact that joining is needed for honoring is no doubt why Pope Francis knelt before the prisoners in the prison he visited and washed their feet. In stooping to them in this way, he joins his humanity to theirs and thereby elevates their status. By being willing to touch their feet, and even to wash them, the Pope indicates his own identity with the humanity in the prisoners and his reverence for it. The Pope's joining the prisoners in this way is what honors them. In uniting his humanity with theirs in the washing of their feet, he undermines the standard of value on which the prisoners are shamed and highlights the deeper standard of value on which each prisoner is a beloved child of the Creator of all there is.

So not every kind of affiliation remedies shame or brings honor. The hallmark of shame is the distance of unshamed others from the shamed person and the warranted anxiety and depression which that distance provokes in the person shamed. What is required for the alleviation of shame is a uniting in the very conditions that would otherwise have lacked honor or been shameful.[21]

When, voluntarily, out of love for humankind, Christ died by torture naked on the cross, in the view of his helpless family, friends, and disciples, he himself participated in the shame of humanity. By this means, he made the shame of humanity something shared with the Deity, and that sharing is a great honor for the human race. It is one thing to be a member of the species that perpetrated the moral horrors of the twentieth century. It is another thing to be a member of the species to which, out of love, God joined himself in nature *and* in shame.

As I explained above, it is an additional objection to the Anselmian kind of interpretation of the atonement that having an innocent person pay the debt owed by a person such as Newton or bear the penalty incurred by Newton's wrongdoing does not take away Newton's shame at having acted wrongly. If anything, it adds to his shame, because there is something shaming in his being responsible for the serious suffering of an innocent person, even if that suffering was voluntarily undertaken on Newton's behalf. But, on the interpretation of the atonement argued for here, there is no question of Christ's paying a debt or bearing a penalty for Newton. Rather, Christ's suffering is a way of seeking Newton and inviting him to union with Christ. And there is only honor for Newton in being loved so much.

Someone might object that in being loved by Christ when one does not merit that love, one is not honored either; love given without being merited is no true honor.[22] But, in my view, this objection is based on a mistaken way of thinking about love. Jerome's love of Paula is not a response on Jerome's part to value he recognizes in Paula. On the contrary, Paula has the value she has for Jerome because he loves her. The same point applies where the love of God is concerned. In virtue of being loved enough by Christ for Christ to endure shame for the sake of union with humankind, Christ confers great value as well as great honor on humanity.

It is not just Christ's incarnation that heals the shame in humanity, then. It is rather Christ's sharing in shame which provides a remedy for the shame that attaches to the species as a whole.

Furthermore, it is reasonable to conclude that this sharing defeats the shame attaching to the species itself. That is, it is reasonable to think that the honor of having God out of love share human shame as well as human nature is greater than the good lost, namely, the honor that the species lost in virtue of its deplorable history. And, in addition, it is arguable that, on Christian doctrine, God's sharing human nature and human shame would not have occurred without the lamentable post-Fall condition of human beings. There is a tradition, promoted by some medieval philosophers and theologians,[23] that God would have become incarnate even without the Fall; but the majority position for most of the Christian tradition is that Christ's incarnation, passion, and death were a response to the Fall, with its consequent problems, including the problem of shame. So, for example, Aquinas says,

> But suppose that no one had sinned. Would Christ still have come? It seems not, because he came in order to save sinners. Otherwise, there would have been no need for the Incarnation.[24]

On this majority position, because Christ's sharing of human nature and human shame would not have occurred without the Fall, Christ's being joined to human nature and shame does not just outweigh human shame; rather, it does indeed defeat it.

THE LIMITATIONS OF THE REMEDY FOR THE FOURTH KIND OF SHAME

Someone might suppose that this remedy for the shame of the species is actually sufficient to cover all the kinds of shame and not just the fourth kind. If humankind is so honored by God himself that God adds their nature to his and joins in human shame out of love for human beings, why would the resulting honor not be sufficient to defeat all human shame? Why would God's passion and death not be enough to remove the shame of people such as Newton, Malala and Scholl, and Merrick?

The answer is that a remedy for shame is sufficient just in case it defeats the shame. But for something to defeat the shame of Merrick's deformity, for example, it would have to be the case both that the shame caused by the deformity was inextricably interwoven with the good supposed to be the remedy for his shame and that that good was greater than the good Merrick lost in consequence of the shame of the deformity, on some standard of value that Merrick himself accepts and should accept. These conditions are not met by the honor Merrick had from his community later in his life. The force of this point can be appreciated by imagining what Merrick would say if he were asked whether, given the choice, he would accept his disfigurement and the place in society it led him to have, or whether he would choose to lose that place as long as he lost the disfigurement with it. It is easy to imagine that Merrick would refuse the disfigurement even on those conditions. *Mutatis mutandis*, it is not unreasonable to suppose that the same conclusion would be reached if we were to ask Merrick about the honor accruing to the human species from Christ's passion and death. Why think that the honor accruing to humanity is sufficient for Merrick—or for us reflecting on Merrick's case—to defeat Merrick's shame stemming from the disfigurement of his disease?

People who think that the honor to humanity is sufficient as a remedy for shame such as Merrick's tend to suppose that the value of the atonement is so great that it outweighs all the bad things in the world.[25] But the evaluation by which a person feels himself shamed is typically relative to others who are better off than he is. An American child shamed because he has no shoes for school would not be consoled by being informed that virtually no Masai children in Kenya have shoes for school either, for example. A person shamed by the defects of nature or the depredations of other human beings will feel his disadvantages by comparison with other human beings whose lives are not lacking in these ways, at least not by comparison with his own. And that relative disadvantage for the shamed person will remain even if the species as a whole is honored. Since the honor done to humanity by Christ's incarnation, passion, and death affects all human beings equally, that honor will not remedy the shame of those who are singled out by what happens to them or is done to them by comparison with more advantaged others. What elevates all equally is no help for those who feel themselves at a serious disadvantage with respect to others. Newton's past had slave-trading in it, and the past of most other human beings does not. And that shaming difference between Newton and other human beings remains, even if all humankind is honored by the shame Christ willingly suffered out of love for human beings.

So the remedy for the fourth kind of shame is not sufficient to handle the other three kinds of shame. If there is a remedy for shame of those kinds, it must lie elsewhere.

MUTUAL INDWELLING

The remedy for the fourth kind of shame will not help with the other kinds of shame just because it is a remedy for the shame of the whole species. What is needed as regards the other kinds of shame is something personal to each individual who suffers shame. If God's coming into humanity and joining humankind's shame heals the shame of the species, then it seems as if what is wanted as a remedy for the shame of an individual person Jerome is Christ's joining himself to Jerome and Jerome's shame, if one can speak in this way.

In my view, this is in fact what we find in orthodox Christian accounts of life in grace.

When a person Jerome surrenders to God in love, the Holy Spirit comes to dwell in Jerome. In addition, the Holy Spirit infuses into Jerome the dispositions and orientations that are the gifts and fruits of the Holy Spirit. The gifts are infused dispositions that help to integrate Jerome's will and intellect around the good, and the fruits are the orientations that result from those dispositions, including love, joy, peace, patience, and long-suffering. There is love, because Christ who loves Jerome is present to him. There is peace, because in being united with Christ in this way, Jerome somehow has his deepest heart's desire stilled. And there is joy, because Jerome's union with the God who loves him is a joyful thing for him. Patience and long-suffering, the next two orientations on the list, arise in consequence. In the presence of a loving God who is second-personally present to and with Jerome, Jerome can stand under suffering, which is still really suffering, without losing the thread of love, peace, and joy. And, on the doctrine of the Trinity, when Jerome is in this condition, Christ is indwelling in Jerome too; the mind and will of the Holy Spirit are also the mind and will of Christ.

There is also a sense in which Jerome dwells in Christ. Without himself actually becoming guilty of any moral wrongdoing, on the cross Christ bore the sins of all human persons in himself. In his openness to human psyches then and by means of his divine power, Christ received in his human mind all other human psyches. Because Christ opened himself up to human psyches in this way, the indwelling between Christ and a person in grace is mutual. The Holy Spirit indwells in a person in grace Jerome, but then Jerome indwells in Christ as well. Consequently, it is not just that Jerome has joined himself to Christ. Rather, on this view, it is also the case that Christ has joined himself to Jerome. On the cross, Christ opened himself up to what is Jerome's—not only all the sinfulness in Jerome's psyche, but everything else in his psyche as well. In joining himself to Jerome, Christ has shared all that is Jerome's— Jerome's sorrow, his self-alienation, and his shame.

If there is a remedy for the shame of the species in having Christ share the shame of the species, then it seems that there could also be some kind of remedy for each of the three kinds of personal shame that afflict every post-Fall person in having Christ himself come to join that person in mutual indwelling. We can think of the point this way: to be united with Christ in mutual indwelling is to be made one with God, and to be made one with God is to be made like God; and this is what it is to be deified. It is hard to see what could count as a greater honor than being deified.[26]

PERSONAL SHAME, HONOR, AND RELATIVE STANDING: THE CASE OF PETER

A question still remains, however, whether this remedy can defeat a person's shame, because shame is generated by relative standing with respect to something on some scale of value. If Christ is joined to every person in grace in mutual indwelling, then what happens to the shame generated by relative standing?

The difficulty can be appreciated by considering the story of the apostle Peter. On the story in the New Testament, Christ was united to each of the apostles in grace, but only Peter among them betrayed Christ in his hour of need.[27] If all the apostles in grace are honored in the same way because Christ is united to each of them, then why would Peter's shame not remain even so? Furthermore, if Christ is united to every person who is in grace, then it does not seem as if anything about Peter's shame is essential to Peter's union with Christ. It is possible, as the case of the other apostles shows, to be united to Christ without Peter's kind of shame. But if Peter's shame is not intrinsically connected to the union with Christ that brings honor to Peter, then it seems as if Peter's shame is not defeated by his union with Christ either.

But here it is worth reflecting on the fact that shame itself is a kind of suffering. Whatever kind of shame is at issue, it involves either something that diminishes a person's wellbeing or something that impedes his having the desires of his heart (or both); and so in one way or another a person's shame is a suffering for that person. (And this point remains whether a person feels shame without being shamed or is shamed without feeling shamed.) But, on Christian views, the loss of wellbeing or heart's desire can lead to flourishing for the sufferer. The greatest flourishing for a human being on the scale of value at issue for Christian theology is in relationships of love, and the greatest of these is union of love with God. It is possible for the loss of wellbeing or of heart's desire to lead to deepened union of love with God, so that, in an apparently paradoxical way, such loss can lead to flourishing, in which a person has more wellbeing and more fulfillment of heart's desires than he lost in his suffering.

Furthermore, union of love with God admits of degrees, not because God wants to give some people less than others, but because some people are more willing to be open to God's love than other people. On the thought of 2 Corinthians,[28] consolation increases with affliction for every person who is in grace, because suffering can enable a person to be more open to God. In that increased openness, she is more willing to love and trust God; and, in consequence, God can be more present to her. The full openness of Christ's human mind on the cross to her psyche will be increasingly matched by her openness to God in suffering, so that she grows in union with God. For these reasons, through suffering both her wellbeing and her consolation increase;[29] and that is why, however paradoxical it sounds to say so, she flourishes through suffering.

Consequently, insofar as shame is a suffering for a post-Fall person, then it is possible that the degree of the shame is matched by the degree of union with God.

The case of Peter illustrates this point too. Peter betrayed Christ, but Christ also entrusted his church to Peter. Between the shame of Peter's betrayal and Peter's being honored above all the other apostles in grace by his office as head of the church lies the meeting in which Christ and Peter are restored to their mutually loving relationship after Peter's betrayal and Christ's resurrection.

One might have expected the writer of the Gospel to tell the story of their meeting in this way. Christ would have said to Peter something along these lines: "You know that I love you and will always love you; your betrayal of me was your withdrawing from me, but I do not withdraw from you in consequence. On the contrary, my love and forgiveness are and always have been there for you."

But that is not at all the way the writer of the Gospel tells the story. In the Gospel story, Christ does not tell Peter about Christ's love for Peter; in fact, he does not tell Peter about anything. Instead Christ just asks Peter a question: "Do you love me?"

Like all post-Fall human beings, Peter is double-minded and fragmented in will in many things; for Peter, even his relationship to Christ is no exception to this claim. On the one hand, Peter desires Christ and his relationship with Christ; that is, he desires his being on Christ's side, as we might say. Before Christ's arrest, Peter had even assured Christ that he was willing to die with Christ.[30] On the other hand, as the scene in which Peter betrays Christ makes clear, Peter also desires his own safety and comfort, even when they conflict with his relationship with Christ. And so he is divided within himself. With one part of his divided will, he desires Christ more than his own life. But with another part of his divided will—and this is the part on which he acts when he betrays Christ—Peter desires his comfort and safety more than he desires Christ. When Peter betrays Christ, the part of Peter that is his worse self wins. That is why Peter acts on his desire for comfort and safety rather than his desire for Christ.

When Christ asks Peter, "Do you love me?", Christ is asking Peter whether Peter is willing to identify his true self with the side of himself that wants Christ: "Do YOU (the true self that you are) love me?"

And Peter answers 'yes.'

In identifying this side of his divided self as his true self, Peter is then forming a will that is like the will of Christ during Christ's prayer in the Garden of Gethsemane.[31] The elements in Peter's will that are not on Christ's side do not go away when Peter answers 'yes' to Christ's question, "Do you love me?" But the second-order will that Peter's 'yes' expresses indicates that Peter is taking sides in the conflict within himself, and the side that he takes is the side that is his best self, the self that is on Christ's side. In his prayer in the Garden of Gethsemane, Christ sided with God against the side in himself that wanted not to die, and for that reason Christ was willing to will what God willed even though Christ retained a desire not to die. In the same way, in saying 'yes' to Christ's question, Peter is on Christ's side and willing to will what Christ wills. To this extent, Peter is then also being willing to be united to Christ, even against that part of his will that desires his own comfort and safety more than it desires Christ.

This way of thinking about Peter's 'yes' to Christ illuminates the difference between Peter, who is the head of the church, and Judas, who is the chief villain of the Christian story. In the Gospel stories, each of them betrayed Christ. And each of them also repented that betrayal.[32] But seeing the guilt and shame of his betrayal of Christ, Judas hanged himself.

And why did he do so? Surely not because by doing so he hoped to escape punishment for his action. None of the ruling authorities of his society had any interest in punishing Judas for that betrayal; and suicide is no way to escape punishment from an omnipresent God. So the explanation for Judas's suicide cannot lie in any hope on Judas's part to escape some suffering coming to himself as punishment for his betrayal of Christ. On the contrary, Judas is inflicting suffering on himself in committing suicide, both the earthly suffering of losing his life and the other-worldly suffering stemming from dying in despair.

A different and better way to understand Judas's despair and suicide, then, is to see Judas's psychic state as the mirror image of Peter's. Judas identifies his true self with the part of his will that acted to betray Christ. And if that is who Judas is, if that is the true self of Judas, then he is as alienated from Christ as he is from himself when he acts as both the judge and the guilty party in his own case. In committing suicide, Judas is in effect answering 'no' to the question Christ asks Peter: "Do you—the real you, the true self—love me?"

Looking at the story of Peter and Judas in this way helps explain why Christ asks Peter three times "Do you love me?" Christ asks this question one time for each of the three times Peter betrayed Christ. In answering 'yes' each time, Peter heals what was broken in himself through his betrayal of Christ. The result is not just that the distance Peter introduced between himself and Christ is removed, but that new and increased closeness is produced. Peter might have reacted to his own past evil with such deep shame that he, like Judas, tried to throw himself away. And then the distance introduced into his relationship with Christ through Peter's betrayal would have been maximized by Peter. But because Peter was willing to stay faithful to Christ even in the face of his own evil and shame over it, so that Peter was willing to say 'yes' to Christ's question, "Do you love me?", Peter came closer to Christ than he had been before his betrayal. The love and trust Peter had for Christ grew greatly with Peter's 'yes' because of the strength of commitment to Christ produced by Peter in the act of will behind his 'yes.'

In 1 Peter, an Epistle traditionally attributed to Peter, the letter writer comforts those experiencing temptations to sin by explaining that the trial of faith in temptations is a precious thing, because, at the appearing of Christ, it yields great honor to the person who was so tempted.[33] This is a claim that these stories of Peter and Christ illustrate and support. Peter's role as head of the church, with all its honor, rightly comes from Peter's willingness to say 'yes' to Christ's question "Do you love me?", even after Peter's own betrayal of Christ and his shame over it.

In this way, then, Peter's shame over his betrayal is inextricably interwoven into his increased union with Christ and the honor it accords Peter. The shame that is a suffering for Peter makes a greater intimacy for Peter with Christ because it leads Peter to greater integration around the love of Christ when he stays faithful to Christ in the face of his own shame. In his passion and death on the cross, Christ opens himself up to Peter. When Peter opens himself further to Christ in consequence of his shame over his betrayal of Christ, then the mutual indwelling between God and Peter is also increased, in ways that magnify Peter.

And so, for Peter, his shame is an integral part of the honor that redeems it. Peter is honored not in spite of but because of having suffered the shame that unites him more intimately with Christ. Furthermore, Christ shares Peter's shame on the cross insofar as Christ bears the sins of all humanity, including Peter's. And so, in being willing to identify with the side of himself that wants Christ, Peter comes to share not just Christ's righteousness but also Christ's suffering; and so, in this way too, he is more intimately united with Christ.

For these reasons, what was Peter's shame becomes an essential part of his glory in the greatness of the mutual indwelling between Peter and Christ.

PERSONAL SHAME AND TRUE HONOR

Here, then, is a way to think of true honor, on this interpretation of the atonement's remedy for shame. True honor, which is the defeat of shame, results from a person's allying his truest or deepest self with the God who joins himself on the cross to every post-Fall person and shares all that is in that person's psyche, including the shame.

Thinking of true honor in this way helps to make sense of one notable but otherwise odd element in the Hebrew Bible. Consider, for example, Ruth, the Moabite, who became the maternal ancestor of David and so also the maternal ancestor of Christ. The man who was first offered the chance to marry her but who refused to do so for self-regarding reasons having to do with money is never named in the story of Ruth, although he seems to have been a person of some standing and weight in his community at that time.[34] But the men who carried dirt and stones and labored to build the wall of Jerusalem—those men are honored by having their names recorded in the Hebrew Bible, which has made their names known and honored through many centuries.[35]

On this way of thinking about the matter, true honor does not come from relative standing with other human beings on a human scale of value. On the contrary, the loss of such relative standing, which is characteristic of shame, can lead to that true and redemptive honor that defeats shame, through Christ's atonement in Christ's own shaming suffering on the cross when he opens himself up to the psyches of human beings in all their guilt and shame. And so the degree of the honor that comes from union with Christ can have a source in the correlative degree of shame suffered by a human person.

No matter what the standard is with respect to which a person is shamed, then, that standard is trumped by the standard set by loving union in mutual indwelling with Christ. For a person to be in this union is for her to be someone for whom God has a desire.[36] In virtue of being desired by the most powerful and most good being possible, she is desirable by the ultimate of all standards. And since the degree of her shame, whatever it is or whatever its source, can yield a correlative degree of depth of union, her shame can be inextricably interwoven into her union with Christ. By *this* standard, all shame is defeated and falls away.

In Christ's atonement, then, there is also a full remedy, a defeat, for the shame of a post-Fall human person, whatever the source and extent of that shame might be.

THE PROBLEM OF GUILT: INTELLECT AND WILL

We can now turn to the problem of guilt; and we can begin by considering the psyche of the wrongdoer.

In the spiritual regeneration of a wrongdoer Paula, Paula acquires a new global second-order will, a will to will the good; and she also forms the states of intellect that go with that second-order volition. In this condition, Paula is on track to lose the morally wrong states of intellect and will she had before this regeneration. With regard to her morally wrong acts, her occurrent states of intellect and will are or are in the process of becoming those of a morally good person; and if the spiritual regeneration is powerful enough at the start or goes on long enough, Paula's dispositions in will and intellect with regard to that sort of action will also become good.

In consequence of her justification and ongoing sanctification, then, Paula becomes a new person, at least in the sense that she identifies herself with the part of her still-divided self that is on the side of the good she herself wills to will.[37] By this means, the defects of her intellect and will that are the lamentable psychic leftovers of her wrongdoing are healed, at once to some extent and then increasingly over time.

On the interpretation of the doctrine of the atonement argued for in this book, Christ's life, passion, and death play a central role in the initiation of a person's justification and sanctification, because they are the best means available in the circumstances to help her cease resisting God's grace. Without her surrender to God's love, none of the process leading to her sanctification and union with God can so much as get started. When she does cease resisting God's grace, then in consequence of Christ's opening of himself to her in Christ's passion on the cross, a mutual indwelling between her and Christ is established. And when she persists in the process of sanctification, she does so in at least nascent union with God, whose presence within her in the person of the Holy Spirit is a rich help and consolation. Furthermore, in the rite of the

Eucharist, she is recurrently reconnected with Christ's passion and death in ways that are also a powerful aid to her perseverance.

Consequently, on this interpretation of the doctrine, there is an explanation of the connection between Christ's atonement and the remedy for this part of the problem of guilt. Christ's atonement enables a person's justification and also aids her ongoing sanctification in more than one way, and so Christ's atonement is instrumental in removing a wrongdoer's guilt as regards its effects on her intellect and will.

REPENTANCE AND THE RESTORATION
OF RELATIONSHIPS

Because through justification and sanctification, Paula becomes a new person, her old relationships are also altered. Forgiving a wrongdoer requires desiring the good for the wrongdoer and union with the wrongdoer; but what the good for the wrongdoer is depends on the state of the wrongdoer, and the nature of the union appropriately desired does so as well. Insofar as Paula is a new person through the spiritual regeneration of justification and sanctification, it will be possible for those who love her and forgive her to react to her as the new person she is, as they could not do if she were unregenerate. To this extent—and it is a limited extent, as will become clear below—Christ's atonement is instrumental in healing these effects of Paula's guilt as regards Paula's relationships with other human beings.

As for Paula's relationship with God, God is always loving and therefore also always forgiving. There is no human being, no matter how morally monstrous, whom God's love and forgiveness does not embrace; even the German soldier of Wiesenthal's *Sunflower*, even the unrepentant among the wicked, are covered by that forgiveness of God's. God's love and forgiveness not only do not depend on the removal of Paula's guilt, but they are in fact the source of the grace that enables Paula to accept God's love. Furthermore, because God's forgiveness includes a desire for union with the wrongdoer, God's forgiveness includes God's acceptance of reconciliation with the wrong-doer. What is missing for actual reconciliation between God and Paula lies therefore only in Paula. Because Christ's passion and death can melt Paula's resistance to God, Christ's atonement is the means by which Paula herself comes to be willing to be reconciled to God and is consequently opened to the indwelling Holy Spirit of God. And because in his passion Christ received within himself the psyches of all post-Fall persons, Paula's surrender to love, enabled by Christ's atonement, is the last thing required for mutual indwelling between God and Paula. For these reasons, Christ's atonement is also the remedy for the distance Paula had put between herself and God.

As I argued in Chapter 3, although Paula's wrongdoing goes contrary to God's will, the amends Paula owes should be made to the human victims of her wrongdoing. In this connection, one might well consider the story of the Gibeonites in the Hebrew Bible. In the story, when King David asked God why God was afflicting the Israelites with famine, God's response pointed to the aggression against the Gibeonites on the part of the preceding king, King Saul. Saul had warred against the Gibeonites and killed many of them.[38] But years before the period of kings in Israel, in the time of Joshua, the Israelites had sworn an oath to God and to the Gibeonites not to put the Gibeonites to death but to take them as allies.[39] Saul's slaughter of the Gibeonites violated that oath. When David understood that God was angry because of Saul's war against the Gibeonites and its violation of the Israelite oath, David did not ask God what David could do to pay the debt *owed to God* for the morally wrong violation of the oath which was made to God. Rather, David gathered the Gibeonites together and asked *them*, "What can we do to make an atonement to you for Saul's acts?"[40] In the story, God finds David's approach the acceptable way to appease God's anger against the Israelites. What God requires from the Israelites, who have betrayed their vow to God, is their making amends not to God but to the human victims of this wrongdoing. In the story, their making amends to these human victims *is* their making amends to God. What is owed to God is given when the debt owed to the human victims of wrongdoing is paid.

Insofar as he is regenerate, a person in grace Jerome will want to make amends for his wrongdoing to the extent to which he can. He will want to help remedy the damage he did in the world,[41] and he will want to repair the injustice he did to particular people affected by his wrongdoing. Insofar as Jerome can and does make amends to those he has harmed or treated unjustly, his guilt with regard to the damage and injustice he did to other human persons are diminished or removed.

Not only that, but Jerome's new life in union with God, with its second-personal love, joy, and peace, will also find its expression in Jerome's willingness to contribute to good wherever he can, so that his return for the gift of grace he has been given will not be limited to trying to undo the ill effects of his earlier wrongdoing but will ripple out everywhere. When Jerome makes satisfaction for his previous wrongdoing, then, his efforts will not be a matter of trying to avert punishment by making up for his wrongdoing, in an attempt at balancing the moral books of his life. Rather, his satisfaction will be the generous giving of his life in shared outpouring of good with the indwelling Lord who loves Jerome and is present to him. This attitude on Jerome's part will incline him to make amends to the victims of his wrongdoing, but it will also make his life characterized by magnanimity towards all others.

Since Christ's atonement is not only instrumental in Jerome's regeneration but is also essential to the mutual indwelling that is Jerome's union with God, then Christ's atonement is also responsible for Jerome's satisfaction, in which Jerome, in union with the Holy Spirit of Christ, helps to heal the ill effects in the world of his wrongdoing and to give generously of himself in every other way as well.

THE LIMITS OF SATISFACTION

Contrary to what these reflections might lead one to suppose, however, the spiritual regeneration and attempts at satisfaction on the part of a person such as Newton are not sufficient to remedy the whole problem of guilt for Newton. None of these things is sufficient to take away completely the effects on Newton of his past acts in the slave trade. To take just one example of the remaining problems, Newton's repentance and satisfaction do not take away from Newton the memory of his having done those wrong acts—and of his having wanted to do so. The leftovers of evil in his psyche and the relational effects of his past wrongful acts on the world are among the things that constitute the stain on the soul for him; and they are not completely remedied by his repentance and satisfaction. Others will also remember what Newton did; and that memory will color his relationship with them, no matter how repentant he is or how much satisfaction he has made.

And then there is also the problem of the damage and the injustice that Newton did. After his religious conversion, he was a new man; and he spent the rest of his life working for the abolition of the slave trade in which he had previously engaged. This work was Newton's satisfaction. To make satisfaction is to do enough—*satis facere*—by doing what one can. Certainly, Newton did all that he could, and he was admirable in that work of his. But the *enough* of human satisfaction is relative only to the ability of the wrongdoer. It is most definitely not *enough* relative to those whom a wrongdoer has treated unjustly or harmed. How could anything Newton did be enough for those who suffered from his slave-trading? How could his work of satisfaction be enough for those who had died on his slave ships, or those who lived to see their children born into slavery?

So the work of satisfaction engaged in by a wrongdoer such as Newton to make amends for some significant wrongdoing on his part has a useful purpose in the world. But, at least in cases of serious wrongdoing, the *enough* of any human satisfaction a person could make could not possibly be enough relative to the victims of his wrongdoing. For this reason, it also could not be enough for a full remedy of either the stain on the wrongdoer's soul or the removal of his guilt.

Thinking of the victims of serious moral wrongdoing, Jerome Miller says,

The evil done to a person enters her life, her history, her being. In spite of the fact that it's abhorrent to her, and utterly foreign to her original created goodness, she can't separate herself from it...Our therapeutic belief that the victim can eventually 'move past' what was done to her fails to appreciate how being the victim of sin differs from other kinds of trauma. In order to 'move past' it, the victim would have to find some way to integrate it into her life. And to do that would involve accepting what's absolutely abhorrent and repugnant to her.... One can't live *with* it because the goodness of one's being recoils from it. And one can't get back to the life one had before because time isn't reversible. Evil forces the victim into a cul-de-sac—the dead end of history. She can't bear evil, and can't escape it.[42]

There was nothing that the German soldier in Wiesenthal's *Sunflower* could have done that might have been enough to make amends to the victims of his evil.[43] The victims of the worst of his evil were dead; but even for those who survived, nothing that the soldier could have done would have compensated them for their suffering at his hands. That is why many of the respondents in *The Sunflower* felt there were no possible amends that would have removed the guilt of the German soldier or that would have returned him to ordinary moral standing in the human community.

For all these reasons, human efforts at satisfaction, at doing enough, are not enough to remove guilt. A perpetrator of serious wrongdoing will not be able to remove all his guilt through his own satisfaction. And since he cannot, he will remain alienated from others—or, if the wrong is evil enough, even outcast from the human community. And the psychic leftovers of his wrongdoing will also continue to be an affliction to him.

In my view, these reflections highlight what is another of the serious flaws in the Anselmian kind of interpretation of the doctrine of the atonement. On the Anselmian kind of interpretation, all the satisfaction attributed to Christ is given only to God, as if nothing were needed for the human victims of moral wrongdoing.[44] To suppose, as the Anselmian kind of interpretation does, that the justice of God requires that amends for human wrongdoing should be paid to God alone or primarily is to have an inadequate idea of justice.

Thinking of the Anselmian kind of interpretation of the doctrine of the atonement, Miller puts the problem for the Anselmian interpretation this way:

moral theology and soteriology have traditionally focused primarily, if not exclusively, on the impact sin has on the *sinner* and how the sinner is redeemed by Jesus' death. The victims of sin were passed over in silence, as if their salvation were an altogether different issue. In the traditional view, the redemption of the sinner is unrelated to, and can be considered independently of, the salvation of those the sinner has violated.

There's something passing strange and, I'm inclined to say, appalling about this disconnect. After all, the evil from which the sinner needs to be redeemed isn't evil just because of the deleterious moral impact it has on him or her. It's evil because it violates a child of God. When we focus on the sinner's need for salvation, without considering the victim, we're distorting the real effects of evil—and turning its victim into a mere afterthought.... If we judge it wrong to prioritize care for the abusers over care for the abused, we have to do more than rethink our pastoral practices. We have to reexamine our understanding of redemption itself.[45]

Supporters of the Anselmian kind of interpretation sometimes claim that taking evil seriously requires adopting the Anselmian kind of interpretation. But the reflections here show that in fact it is the Anselmian kind of interpretation that does not take seriously enough the real objective evil in human wrongdoing. Because it does not, the Anselmian kind of interpretation overlooks completely one crucial element required to remove guilt for a wrongdoer. In focusing only on what might be owed to the greatness of God, the Anselmian kind of interpretation is blind to what is owed to the suffering which comes to human beings from the evil of others. Without adequate amends for that suffering, the guilt of the wrongdoer who caused that suffering is not removed entirely—or at all, in cases of great evil.

So if the whole of Christ's atonement is a matter of offering satisfaction to God, then Christ's atonement is inefficacious to remove the guilt of wrongdoers, even if God ceases to be offended at wrongdoers because of Christ's atonement. God's ceasing to be offended at Newton is not by itself sufficient to transform Newton from the wretchedness of being a person who had been a slave trader, even when Newton found himself saved by amazing grace.

A BRIEF DIGRESSION

But this is not the end of the story as regards guilt and satisfaction. It is important to see that the atonement of Christ can in fact make vicarious satisfaction which can do what no wrongdoer could do for himself, both as regards making amends and as regards the stain on the soul.

And now we should see that the problem of the removal of guilt and the problem of evil converge at this very point. A perpetrator of serious wrongdoing Jerome cannot altogether (or at all) remove his guilt through repentance and satisfaction because Jerome has nothing to give his victims that can compensate completely (or at all) for their suffering. But the question of what *could* defeat the suffering of unwilling innocents is precisely the central question of the problem of evil.

A theodicy[46] offers a morally sufficient reason for God to allow the suffering of unwilling innocents, and this morally sufficient reason typically consists in some benefit for the sufferer which comes to her through her suffering, outweighs the suffering, and could not be gotten readily or at all without her suffering. In earlier work on the problem of evil,[47] I argued that the role of suffering in the justification and sanctification of a person and in her growth in union with God are a benefit of the sort sought in theodicy. As the previous chapters show, however, this very benefit has its ultimate source and grounding in the atonement of Christ. On the interpretation of Christ's atonement argued for in this book, what Christ offers to every human being, including those who are the victims of the depredations of others, is the best thing possible for human beings, namely, union with God. This union is the greatest flourishing for a human being and also the fulfillment of the deepest heart's desire for any human being.

Here it is worth pausing for just a moment to notice the implications of these claims. At the outset of this project, I listed as one of the desiderata for an acceptable interpretation of the doctrine of the atonement that it connect in some way with theodicy, if there is an acceptable theodicy. What these claims show is not just that there is some connection between an acceptable theodicy and an acceptable interpretation of the doctrine of the atonement but that, in fact, neither can be properly constructed without the other. For this reason, any attempt to find a solution to the problem of suffering that omits serious consideration of the doctrine of the atonement is a bit like trying to find a medical explanation for lung cancer with no connection to explanations about environmental pollutants and air quality. Certainly, some profitable explanation can be found in this way. But complete comprehension requires connecting the two to each other.

Both the problem of suffering and the doctrine of the atonement are therefore threads in the same tapestry that begins with the story of the Fall and continues to the end of the story in everlasting union with God.[48] Contemplating that larger picture is not my project in this book, however. And, for my purposes in this chapter, it is sufficient just to see that the problem of suffering and the doctrine of the atonement are inextricably connected in this whole story.

THE VICARIOUS SATISFACTION OF CHRIST

If we consider the role of Christ's atonement in the moral and spiritual regeneration of every human person, it is apparent that what Christ offers to each human person *is* more than enough to compensate any human suffering. There cannot be anything greater for a person to have or to want. Since a perpetrator of moral evil is responsible for the suffering of unwilling innocents, then the benefit to a sufferer that is central to a theodicy can become the satisfaction of the perpetrator if some way can be found to connect the perpetrator to the benefit highlighted in theodicy, whose source is the atonement of Christ.

One person can make vicarious satisfaction for another if the two are united in love at least with respect to the satisfaction being made.[49] Insofar as a human person such as Newton is united with Christ and allies himself with Christ's passion and death, then what Christ does in love for each human being, including the victims of Newton's slave-trading, can also become something offered to those victims by Christ on behalf of Newton through Newton's being allied in love with Christ's work of satisfaction. In this sense, then, Christ is the *Stellvertreter* for Newton: Christ does for Newton what Newton should do for the victims of his moral wrongdoing but is unable to do himself. What Christ offers to the victims of Newton's slave-trading (as to all human beings) can become for Newton vicarious satisfaction for his evil actions against those people. And, clearly, the same point applies with respect to all the wrongdoing of every human person, insofar as that person, like Newton, is united with Christ. Even for the German soldier in *The Sunflower*, there is that which is enough to restore him to reconciliation with the human family—not in anything the German soldier could possibly do by himself but in Christ's vicarious satisfaction, if the soldier would accept it and would ally himself with it by uniting himself with Christ.

Someone might object at this point that some victims of human evil die in their suffering and so cannot receive any satisfaction.[50] But this objection is mistaken. The satisfaction offered by Christ's atonement is available to all human beings, even to those who die in their suffering. Because, on the Chalcedonian formula, Christ in his divine nature is eternal and so not bound by time, the openness of God to human beings is also not bound by time. For mutual indwelling, then, all that is needed from any human being is the cessation of resistance to God's love, something that Aquinas himself thinks happens in an instant. No dying is so swift that it precludes such an instant.[51] Therefore the good of Christ's satisfaction as offered to human beings is psychologically available to every human person at any time, including at the time of a person's dying. Furthermore, it is possible for a person to know and love Christ without much if any awareness that she does so, and certainly without awareness of much if any theology. It is possible, that is, that there be anonymous Christians, who are related to Christ with faith that is only implicit.[52]

For these reasons, in addition to the other things that Christ does in his passion and death, Christ also makes vicarious satisfaction for all human sin. But that satisfaction is not a present made to God to enable God to pardon sinners, as the Anselmian approach to vicarious satisfaction supposes. It is rather an offer of union in love made to each human sufferer of the depredations of others. For a wrongdoer such as Newton who is united to Christ and who allies himself in his own repentance and satisfaction with the work of

Christ, Christ's passion and death can serve as vicarious satisfaction which makes up what was still lacking in the satisfaction for his evil that Newton himself made.

Someone might suppose that since the offer of union with Christ is made to every human person, some people pay a much greater cost than others for the same thing. On this way of thinking about Christ's vicarious satisfaction, that satisfaction still lacks something of the *enough* needed to make amends to the victims of human wrongdoing. Part of what needs to be made up to the victims of wrongdoing is the injustice of what was inflicted on them. But if the victims of Newton's slave-trading receive the same offer of the same thing as Newton himself received, then it seems that the injustice Newton's victims suffered in consequence of Newton's slave-trading is not after all made up to them. It may be that the greatness of union with God is sufficient to defeat all the damage done to the people Newton kidnapped and enslaved; but injustice is a matter of relative standing, not just of damage. And so it can seem that something is lacking as regards satisfaction if the victims of Newton's slave-trading are offered as satisfaction the good Newton himself received.

But here it is important to remember the connection between suffering and glory. Full union with God is not an all-or-nothing thing, but rather something that admits of degrees. As suffering increases for a person in grace, if that person does not react by returning to a resistance of grace, the suffering deepens that person and connects her more powerfully to Christ in Christ's suffering for her. Because this union with God is the best condition for a human person, then as her union with Christ increases, she also grows in greatness, or in glory, as 2 Corinthians explains the thought.[53]

Consequently, it is not entirely true that what Christ offers to each human person in his vicarious satisfaction is the same thing. It is generically the same: union with God. But the depth of that union varies largely from one person in grace to another, and the suffering of a person in grace is one route to deepening that union. So when a person who has suffered the depredations of others becomes a person in grace, that very suffering then becomes something that can unite her further to Christ, in such a way that her own loveliness in union with God is greater than that of those who are also in grace but have suffered less. That is why in the Christian tradition suffering has been considered something that can be not just instrumental to the good of the sufferer but also something to celebrate. Newton died an honorable man and he is still honored now by many people, including me; but Harriet Tubman's life greatly outshines his.

What Christ offers to every human person, then, is sufficient to justify suffering,[54] and that is why Christ's atonement is also enough as vicarious satisfaction for the victims of human evil, whose glory is commensurate with their suffering if they will receive the love of God. Christ's atonement, and the good that it offers suffering human persons, can make amends for their suffering; and so it can constitute vicarious satisfaction for a perpetrator of serious evil such as Newton, who in his repentance and his own satisfaction allies himself with Christ's gift to those harmed by Newton. For these reasons, because of the vicarious satisfaction of Christ, there is also a remedy for what was disturbed in the relations with others on the part of a wrongdoer such as Newton. Through Christ's satisfaction and his own, a man such as Newton can heal what would otherwise leave his relations with those hurt or horrified by him sadder or smaller than he himself would want.

Furthermore, it is clear that on this interpretation of Christ's vicarious satisfaction, there is no question of Christ's satisfaction counting as a penalty for human sin or as a payment of debt owed to God. Consequently, this interpretation is not subject to the objections I leveled against the Anselmian interpretation earlier, namely, that the penalty for human sin is paid twice for those who are not redeemed, or that God does not forego any part of what is owed him by human beings. On the interpretation of the doctrine of the atonement argued for in this book, in the vicarious satisfaction of Christ there is no punishment due human beings being suffered by Christ or any debt owed to God for human sin being paid by Christ. God simply foregoes everything that is owed to God because of the offense against God incurred by human wrongdoing. And yet the justice of God is nonetheless fulfilled. Justice is a matter of giving each person what is due to him. Any good in a human being is already a gift of God, so that the justice of God is more a matter of what God owes to himself, rather than what God owes to human beings. But what God owes to himself is that God's will should be fulfilled, and the will of a perfectly loving God is to give each human person as much good as she will receive and to unite with her as much as her own state of psyche allows. And this is what God does have through the atonement and the vicarious satisfaction of Christ.

So, Christ's atonement does not *compensate* for human evil, as it does on the Anselmian interpretation. Christ's atonement *defeats* human evil, by weaving it into union in love with God in a way that removes guilt and shame from wrongdoers and satisfies fully for the suffering of their victims if they will receive what Christ offers them. It is in this sense that Christ is the propitiation for the sins of the whole world, as the line in I John puts it (I John 2:2).

Consequently, in the atonement of Christ, there is sufficient satisfaction for the wrongdoing that a person such as Newton did; and when Newton unites himself in love with Christ, Christ's satisfaction becomes vicarious satisfaction for Newton. But, unlike the Anselmian interpretation, this interpretation holds that what Christ offers to God as pleasing to God's justice is satisfaction given *to human sufferers* for the wrongdoings of other human beings. Human sufferers are the primary beneficiaries of Christ's vicarious satisfaction.

It is important to see, though, that there is nonetheless also a gift offered to God through Christ's passion and death, even on this interpretation of the doctrine of the atonement of Christ. On the interpretation of the doctrine of the atonement I have argued for here, Christ's offering to human sufferers something that defeats their suffering *and* their guilt and unites them with God is itself also a gift given to God by Christ's atonement. The best gift for a loving mother is not the mangling of an innocent child of hers (or of herself) as an aid to her pardoning a guilty or alienated child of hers. The best gift for her is to have her guilty child or her broken and suffering child restored to her in love as a good and honorable person whose guilt and shame have been removed. On orthodox theology, God lacks nothing in himself; but still, in love for his people, God does nonetheless have a desire that can go unfulfilled, namely, the desire for union with human beings. And so the spiritual regeneration offered to all post-Fall people in Christ's atonement is a worthy gift, and in fact the only conceivable gift, for a perfect and perfectly loving God.

THE REMAINING STAIN ON THE SOUL

Even with so much said about satisfaction, however, this is still not the end of the story as regards guilt. That is because even all these things taken together— the spiritual regeneration on the part of a person such as Newton, his own efforts at satisfaction, and the vicarious satisfaction of Christ—cannot alter the past; and that past lives on at least in Newton's memories and the memories of others. If, as Newton hoped, remembering his slave-trading would always be the cause of shuddering and humiliation for him,[55] then it is hard to see that the stain of his wrongdoing, which includes its effects on his memory and empathic capacities, is healed for him.[56] On the other hand, it is also hard not to share his view that he ought never to forget the horror of what he did. There would be something terrible about his forgetting the evil of his participation in the slave trade. In fact, it is arguable that there is a duty to remember wrongdoing if the wrongdoing is serious enough.[57]

For that matter, the evil Newton did lives also in God's mind, not in God's memory but—much worse—in God's occurrent vision, on the doctrine of God's eternity. How could the stain on Newton's soul be remedied, how could Newton rejoice in union with God, if his very slave-trading acts in all their horrifying evil are always before God—and always before himself and every other human being among the redeemed in heaven, whose minds are united with the mind of God? How could Newton find peace or have joy if such evil and the heartbreaking suffering it caused are always before his eyes?

It is true that there are biblical texts in which God claims that in the messianic age he will not remember any more the evils his people have done.[58] But consider how such texts have to be interpreted.

In the eternal *now*, the execrable evil Newton did is always present to God (and also to all those in heaven who are fully united with God). So there is no question of any actual forgetting on God's part (or on the part of the redeemed in heaven), since God's cognitive access to what is past for Newton does not come from God's memory. As far as that goes, on the doctrine of eternity, God does not have a memory, since nothing is past for God. How then could God actually forget what Newton did?

Furthermore, even if God were temporal, and even if omnipotent God could will to eliminate a memory God had once laid down, it is hard to figure out how to make a claim that God literally forgets something God once knew consistent with the doctrine that God is omniscient. If there is something about the past of a person such as Newton that Newton knows and God does not, then in what sense is God omniscient?

One might try giving up omniscience as well as eternity. If God is temporal and also is not omniscient, things could be erased or hidden from God's memory. But then one would also have to suppose that Newton's union with God would be furthered by God's not knowing something of such significance to Newton, which Newton knows and knows is hidden from God. Union seems impeded and not fostered by the failure on Newton's part to be fully revealed to God.

Finally, even if we assume that God erases this memory from Newton's mind as well as from God's mind, it is really insupportable to think that union between God and a human person depends on their both being ignorant of a central fact of that human being's life. Union of love is not promoted by hiding and self-deception, even self-deception arranged by God, if one can speak in such a way.

So the biblical texts claiming that in messianic times God will not remember the sins of his people have to be interpreted a different way.

Here it is worth noticing that we do sometimes speak about forgetting past wrongs when real forgetting is not at issue but rather something more nuanced. To see this point, suppose, for example, that Jerome has done Paula some harm that he now bitterly repents (and, for the sake of the example, stipulate that his repentance is genuine, trustworthy, and manifest to Paula); and suppose that in consequence of their sorting out together Jerome's repentance, Paula says to Jerome, "It's all right! You can forget this! We won't talk about it anymore!" In saying this, Paula does not mean that she intends this past event to be erased from Jerome's memory—or hers either. And it is also unlikely that she intends the past event to be a forbidden subject for any future conversation between her and Jerome. Rather, what Paula wants to communicate to Jerome by these words of hers is that this past event, now a subject of pain to both of them because of its evil, will remain in their memories but without its ability to cause either of them pain.

That a memory which was once painful to both Jerome and Paula can stay in their memories but lose its painful character stems from the fact that the harm which Jerome did Paula and now so regrets has become part of their ongoing joint story of mutual love and care. Their relationship is stronger because Jerome has come to Paula in repentance and Paula has accepted him as the repentant person he is. In his repentance and her acceptance of him, their relationship has not been restored to the same condition it had before he harmed her. His repentance cannot return either of them or their relationship to the relative innocence of the period before he hurt her. But his repentance and her willingness to be reconciled to him alter the relationship by making it more deeply rooted in each of them. Through his repentance and her reconciliation with him, the past hurt has been interwoven into a renewed commitment on the part of each of them to the other. This fact—that there is such a deepening of their relationship because of Jerome's hurting Paula but repenting it and Paula's accepting his repenting—does not mean that, retroactively, the very harm that Jerome did Paula is now not harm or that his harm should be welcome to her or that his harm is in some other way not the evil that it was. But this episode in their shared lives, in which Jerome did real and unwelcome harm to Paula, may nonetheless become precious to both of them because of what they have gone through together in it.

Or, if this example is not persuasive enough, then consider a much smaller-scale example: consider the very early years of child-raising. When the parents of a much loved and hoped for first child bring the baby home from the hospital, they expect and imagine a kind of Eden for them all, an Eden in which they give unstintingly to this little human being, and the baby bonds with them in love, so that they are all so happy together. The parents will quickly realize that the path to this imagined Eden is blocked for them by the very baby for whom such happiness was intended. But, as they get past one trial after another, they look back on the bad times—the toddler's tantrums, the negativity of the four-year-old—with laughter and affection, as they remember and retell the stories to anyone who has not heard them too often already. The things that were painful to them in the events, when the events were happening, become woven into a story of shared love that has its roots in those very bad times they now want to remember, and do remember without pain.

This is the sense in which one can forget even great sins too if they are part of the history of human salvation. The acts are remembered, and so is their character as wrongful. But the remembered wrongful acts lose their power to produce pain in virtue of being wrongful, because they have become interwoven into a story of love that is worth prizing. And so there is a sense in which the sinfulness of those acts *is* forgotten.

Think of the difference in kinds of forgetting this way. A person may remember that he was born in Chicago, but his doing so is different from his remembering being born in Chicago—something he clearly cannot do. Remembering being born would be something like viewing in mind a video-tape of one's birth. One cannot remember being born in Chicago, because the infant being born did not lay down in memory a video of his own birth.

It is important to recognize that this as-it-were video in memory can alter its emotional coloring after the fact when the person reviewing the video has himself altered. So, for example, a teenage prank that harmed a disabled person may have seemed funny to the teenaged prankster when he did it; but that teenager, grown to adulthood and seeing that event again in the video of memory, may not feel the funniness that the event originally held for him but may rather experience the memory only with cringing pain at his own past cruelty. The emotional coloring of the memory video is thus an emergent characteristic which the memory video has in interaction with the person reviewing it.

For this reason, it can be the case that Paula remembers some past turn of events in which Jerome harmed her, but it can also be true that Paula no longer feels pain on reviewing the video in memory of those events. That is, she remembers *that* Jerome harmed her, but her remembering his harming her alters. Something about the pain that his actions caused her can be missing for her as she reviews her video in memory of those events. She remembers *that* she was pained, but she does not remember being pained, any more than the adult person who was the teenaged prankster remembers the funniness of his harming a disabled person, even if he does remember that it was funny to him then. And so it could also be the case for Paula that she is not pained in remembering that Jerome pained her.

In this sense it is possible for Paula to forget Jerome's wrongdoing against her.

And this is the sense in which even an omniscient, eternal God can forget a person's wrongdoing. Because the past sins of a person in grace Jerome are part of Jerome's story of shared love in union with God, then those sins are forgotten (in this nuanced sense of 'forgotten') by God. And if they are forgotten in this sense by God, then they will also be forgotten in this sense by Jerome, and a fortiori by all the redeemed in heaven for whom Jerome's wrongdoing is also visible. The famous hymn Newton wrote after his religious conversion begins with the line, "Amazing grace—how sweet the sound!—that saved a wretch like me!" With that line, Newton shows that he remembers *that* he was a wretch, as he surely was and should remember that he was; but the pain of that memory is lost in his joy in the amazing grace of God, with whom he is united in love.

And so this last part of the stain on the soul from past sin, the shadows in memory and their connection to the empathic capacities, is healed also through the atonement of Christ, which brings a wretch like Newton to spiritual regeneration through amazing grace.

Aquinas, who supports a similar conclusion, puts the point this way:

> whoever violates God's decree is subject to a debt of punishment. This violation is retained in the person's memory, which it disturbs and stains; it is retained in God's memory, who is to judge such matters; and in the memory of the demons with regard to those who will be tormented.... And it is Christ who has forgiven all by *blotting out the handwriting, that is, the memory of the transgression....* [the] violation is not forgiven in such a way as to bring it about that there was never any sin. Rather, such sin is not remembered by God as something to be punished; it is not remembered by the demons as something to accuse us of; and we do not remember our sins as reasons for sorrow....[59]

There is a biblical line which says that it is a fearful thing to fall into the hands of the living God.[60] But the living God will be fearful in this sense only to those who themselves refuse the love of God that is always there for them. Even a human person with something so worth shuddering over as the memory of having been a slave trader does not need to fear the wrath of God or his own memories of his past evil, if only he will surrender to the love of God made manifest in Christ's atonement. If he does, then he will be united to God through mutual indwelling. In that union, God will forget even sins such as Newton's, not because they are not worth remembering forever but because they lose their power to hurt the person who committed them when they are remembered in love, and when the vicarious satisfaction of Christ defeats the suffering of all victims of human wrongdoing.

In all these ways, then, through Christ's atonement, the problem of guilt for a post-Fall human person has a full and complete solution.

CONCLUSION

The central problem to which the atonement is meant to be a solution is the problem of the post-Fall human condition, the absence of union between God and human beings, whose source is the human proneness to moral wrong-doing, with its consequent guilt and shame, and the inner fragmentation and willed loneliness characteristic of this condition. The primary work of this chapter has been to consider whether the interpretation of the doctrine of the atonement for which I have argued is able to show why and how the atonement is a solution to this problem. If the atonement as I have interpreted it can defeat both guilt and shame, then it remedies fully the obstacles to union between God and human beings. There are other desiderata for an acceptable interpretation of the doctrine, as I presented those desiderata at the outset of this project, and I will turn to them in the final chapter; but the main desideratum is the success of the interpretation in explaining and defending Christ's atonement as a remedy for guilt and shame.

In this chapter, I have considered shame in its major varieties, the shame of wrongdoing, of suffering the wrongdoing of others, of enduring the defects of nature, and of being a member of the human species. And I showed that each of these kinds of shame has a defeat in the atonement of Christ. Through shame, there is an honor, a true honor, that accrues to the species and to those particular sufferers of shame who come to grace. That true honor, which is vastly greater than the shame suffered, would not have come (or not have come to the same degree) to a person in grace without his suffering the shame he endured. Consequently, for a person in grace, the suffering of shame is also defeated in union with God through the atonement of Christ, on this interpretation of the doctrine.

Then I considered guilt in all its elements, including the brokenness in the psyche of the wrongdoer and the bad effects on the world resulting from his wrongdoing. And I showed that, on the interpretation of the doctrine of the atonement for which I have argued, the atonement can remedy all human guilt, both through the ability of the atonement to regenerate a person into a new life in grace and through its ability to make vicarious satisfaction for the damage and injustice done by the wrongdoer. One result of the atonement, so understood, is that the wrongdoer can accept God's forgiveness of his guilt and cease fearing God's wrath. With God, his sins are forgotten, not because the wrongdoer and God fail to remember what the wrongdoer did, but because the wrongdoer's past is interwoven into a life of love, joy, and peace with God not only for him but also for those who suffered at his hands, if they also will surrender to the love of God offered them in Christ's atonement. Consequently, through the atonement of Christ, a person in grace is freed from guilt and reconciled with God and with other human beings as well, and his guilt is defeated in his flourishing.

On this interpretation of the doctrine, then, one can see the way in which the atonement of Christ makes sense as a solution to the main problem that the atonement was meant to remedy.

What remains for the conclusion of this book is therefore just a final reflection on the remaining desiderata, including the consistency of this interpretation of the doctrine with the major biblical texts describing atonement, especially those that describe the atonement as a sacrifice. I will turn to these remaining desiderata in the next and final chapter.

11

Conclusion

The Remaining Desiderata and Final Reflection

INTRODUCTION

In Chapter 1, I laid out a number of desiderata for any acceptable interpretation of the doctrine of the atonement. In the succeeding chapters, I argued for an interpretation that, in my view, meets all these desiderata better than the traditionally prominent competing interpretations. This interpretation takes God's love to be maximally expressive of God's nature and central to the atonement, and it takes God's forgiveness to be God's love in operation towards human beings suffering from guilt. God's love and forgiveness are always there for any human being. There is no human being, however steeped in evil, with whom God does not desire union, which is the true good for that human being. In a sense, then, all of this book is an explanation of the love of God.

Although I have avoided it till now, in what follows it will finally be necessary to have some brief way to refer to the interpretation of the doctrine of the atonement given in this book. So, for ease of reference, I will here just baptize that interpretation with a name. I will call it 'the Marian interpretation of the doctrine of the atonement', or 'the Marian interpretation', for short. There is no shortage of Marys who might be referred to by the use of this name. There is Mary who is the mother of Christ. There is Mary, the sister of the mother of Christ, who was with her at the crucifixion. There is Mary Magdalene, who is the apostle to the Apostles because the risen Christ appeared first to her, and she announced the resurrection to the apostles. And then there is Mary of Bethany, who anointed Christ's feet and wiped them with her hair.[1] In varying ways, each of these Marys exemplifies the understanding of God's love that is fundamental to the interpretation of the doctrine of the atonement that I have argued for in this book. Each of them is therefore a suitable typological exemplar for this interpretation, and it would be honored by being named after any of them. I leave it to readers to choose which Mary strikes them as the best iconic representation of this interpretation, and I will simply call it 'the Marian interpretation' without further comment in what follows.

The most important desideratum for any interpretation of the doctrine of the atonement has to do with the main problems of the post-Fall human condition, namely, the problems of guilt and shame. In Chapter 10, I evaluated the Marian interpretation by examining the way in which it explains Christ's life, passion, and death as the remedy for those problems. As I argued in that chapter, the Marian interpretation yields a much better explanation of the atonement as healing for guilt and shame than any of its main competitors do. On the Marian interpretation, Christ's life, passion, and death constitute a full and satisfactory remedy for both shame in all its varieties and guilt in all its parts.

Besides this main desideratum, however, there are also other desiderata. They include these:

(1) an acceptable interpretation of the doctrine of the atonement should be able to explain or at least accommodate biblical texts about Christ, including especially the cry of dereliction from the cross, but also other texts, such as those that describe Christ's atonement as a sacrifice;

(2) it should have a role for the Holy Spirit so that the interpretation is Trinitarian in character;

(3) it should be able to explain why the passion and death of Christ are especially significant for the work of atonement while also explaining the significance of the details of Christ's life in that work;

(4) it should be able to accept Christian exclusivism without succumbing to the dismaying implications of that exclusivism;

(5) it should be able to show both that the Eucharist has a role in the process of salvation and yet that all the work of salvation is done fully by Christ in his life, passion, and death;

(6) it should be able to connect into one coherent account the benefits supposed to be brought about by Christ's atonement and the benefits thought to justify God in allowing suffering, on at least one candidate for an acceptable theodicy.

These desiderata are not met well by the major competing interpretations of the doctrine of the atonement, or, worse, are not so much as addressed by them. But attentive readers will have noticed that, in the preceding chapters, virtually all of these desiderata have already been shown to be met satisfactorily by the Marian interpretation.

The cry of dereliction was extensively discussed in Chapter 5, where I argued that the Marian interpretation is the only one of the major competing interpretations that can give a satisfactory account of the cry. In addition, the

Marian interpretation's explanation of the cry has a number of other advantages; for example, it illuminates the story of Christ's anguish in the Garden of Gethsemane, and it suggests a plausible connection between that cry and Christ's death. Most importantly, it gives a deep insight into the nature of the mutual indwelling which is the hallmark of union with God, as witness Christ's own words in the Gospel of John and other biblical texts as well.

The Marian interpretation of the cry of dereliction clarifies one part of that mutual indwelling, namely, the indwelling of human psyches in Christ. On the Marian interpretation, Christ's passion and death are essential to that part of the mutual indwelling. The other part is the indwelling of the Holy Spirit in persons of grace. In Chapter 4, I showed the nature of the Holy Spirit's indwelling; and, in Chapter 7, I explained the effects of the Holy Spirit's indwelling on the psyche and life of a person in grace. As I showed in Chapter 8, on the Marian interpretation, Christ's passion and death (and, to a lesser extent, Christ's life, on the details given about it in the Gospels) are means by which a human person can be brought to surrender to God's love, so that the Holy Spirit can come to indwell in her. For these reasons, the Marian interpretation is thoroughly Trinitarian in character, unlike the competing interpretations. On the Marian interpretation, the atonement is the work of the love of the Father, through the incarnation, passion, and death of the Son, by means of the Holy Spirit.

These chapters make clear that on the Marian interpretation there is a twofold role for Christ's passion and death. On the one hand, Christ's passion and death are essential to the indwelling of human psyches in Christ, so that it is true that no one comes to union with God in mutual indwelling except through Christ's passion and death. On the other hand, Christ's passion and death are not necessary to bring a person to the surrender that enables the indwelling of the Holy Spirit in her, but only the most promising means to this end. Consequently, it is not necessary that any human person have conscious awareness of Christ's passion and death or of stories about them, or that any human person have a particular set of theological beliefs about them, in order to provide the part of the process of salvation that enables the indwelling of the Holy Spirit. Conscious awareness of all or some of these things is the most promising means for bringing a person to the surrender to the love of God which is requisite for the indwelling of the Holy Spirit. But, even for a perfectly good God, the most promising means are not necessary means. What is in general most promising might be not needed, not available, or not promising for some persons in some particular circumstances.

The fact that, on the Marian interpretation, the passion and death of Christ are essential in one spiritual or metaphysical respect but not necessary in some psychological respects gives this interpretation the ability to handle the problem of exclusivism. As Chapter 8 shows, on the Marian interpretation, it is possible both to maintain Christian exclusivism and to reject the hateful implications it has been thought to carry with it.

So, as this brief review makes evident, virtually all of desiderata (1), (2), (3), and (4) have already been addressed. The preceding chapters have shown that, though they are not addressed satisfactorily or at all by major competing interpretations, these desiderata are very well met by the Marian interpretation.

Desiderata (5) and (6) are in effect the subject of Chapter 9. As Chapter 9 shows, even on a minimalist account of the Eucharist, the Marian interpretation can show the way in which the Eucharist is significant for perseverance in the life of grace because of the connection of the Eucharist to Christ's passion and death. On a richer account of the Eucharist, the connection between the rite and Christ's passion is even tighter; and the role of the Eucharist in the process of atonement is correspondingly more powerful. In addition, Chapter 9 argued that suffering also plays a significant role in perseverance in the life in grace. For a person in grace, her sufferings join her more closely to the passion and death of Christ, in ways that can not only strengthen her for perseverance but also greatly console her and intensify her union with Christ. Her suffering and the atonement of Christ can work together to increase her flourishing and her joy. Therefore, on the Marian interpretation, the problem of evil and the doctrine of the atonement are not only connected but in fact inextricably intertwined, so that neither can be properly or fully explained without the other. Unlike the competing interpretations, the Marian interpretation meets desiderata (5) and (6) very well, too.

What remains, then, for this last chapter is what some readers have no doubt been impatiently waiting for, namely, an examination of the way in which the Marian interpretation fits with well-known biblical texts about the atonement of Christ, and especially those texts that seem to privilege the Anselmian kind of interpretation. Perhaps the most notable of such texts are those having to do with sacrifice, but there are other important texts as well. It is not possible in one chapter to consider all the biblical texts relevant to the doctrine of the atonement. So in the interest of bringing this work to completion, I will consider just a few of those that might be thought to be most troublesome for the Marian interpretation. I will start with texts about sacrifice; then I will turn more briefly to some of the endlessly discussed passages in Romans; and, finally, I will end with a short consideration of one of the passages on the suffering servant in Isaiah. After this review of biblical texts, I will end with a last reflection on the project of this book.

SACRIFICE: GENERAL CONSIDERATIONS

The claim that in his passion and death Christ is a sacrifice is based on biblical passages, especially those found in the New Testament book of Hebrews, which maintain that Christ is both priest and sacrifice for human sin. Among contemporary philosophers of religion, Richard Swinburne is representative of an old school of interpretation which takes these biblically based claims to support an Anselmian kind of interpretation of the doctrine of the atonement.[2] The idea behind this approach to sacrifice is that a sacrifice is something offered to a perfectly just and righteously offended deity in order to make amends to the deity or to ameliorate the deity's righteous wrath or to avert the deity's punishing of those who are the just targets of that wrath or something else along these lines.[3] In all its varieties, this idea seems to me unsustainable if we look closely at biblical stories of sacrifice.

The sacrifices that are mandated for offenses in the Hebrew Bible are often animal sacrifices. On the idea represented by Swinburne's interpretation of sacrifice, something about killing an animal makes an offended God more likely to pardon the offending human being, or more likely to forego imposing punishment on the human being who deserves it, or something similar. For reasons I gave in Chapter 3, this idea of sacrifice seems to me very hard to support on any ethical theory that is compatible with the doctrine that God is perfectly good and loving. And so there are ethical and theological reasons for rejecting this interpretation of sacrifice and its use in an interpretation of the doctrine of Christ's atonement.

But what is most telling against this idea of sacrifice are the biblical texts about sacrifice themselves. It is clear that the notion of sacrifice in Hebrews is meant to be set in the context of the Jewish sacrifices described in the Hebrew Bible, not just in the Mosaic Law but in the biblical stories and descriptions of sacrifice more generally. In fact, the stories which Hebrews evokes most as regards sacrifice and the priesthood of Christ come from Genesis and not from Leviticus, the biblical book which prescribes the sacrifices for violations of the law. For example, the stories evoked by Hebrews in connection with Christ's priesthood and sacrifice have to do with Melchizedek, a priest who is described in Genesis and who is definitely not a member of the Levitical priesthood established in the Mosaic Law. In my view, a careful consideration of the relevant biblical stories about sacrifice will not support the understanding of sacrifice adopted by interpreters of the doctrine of the atonement, such as Swinburne, who suppose that biblical mention of sacrifice mandates the Anselmian kind of interpretation of the doctrine of the atonement.

Consider in this connection the first sacrifices described in Genesis, those of Cain and Abel. Cain offers God things he has grown, and Abel offers God animals. There is no suggestion in the story that Abel's offering animals to God has anything to do with sin on Abel's part or with Abel's attempting to placate an offended deity. On the contrary, the story emphasizes that Abel and his offering, unlike Cain and his offering, are already completely acceptable to God. Furthermore, there is no indication in the story that Abel offered these animals to God by killing them. In fact, there is a rabbinic interpretation of the story which says that Abel could not have killed animals in order to offer them to God since killing of animals was not allowed by God at this point in the biblical narrative of antediluvian times. On this rabbinic reading, which strikes me as plausible, whatever it is that makes Abel's offering a sacrifice which God accepts must be understood in some way other than Abel's trying to give God a dead animal as a present to make God more favorable to Abel.

There are also stories of sacrifices that do involve offering God a dead animal, but which still cannot be construed as stories about an attempt to use a dead animal as a present to propitiate an angry or offended deity. Consider, for example, the next sacrifice described in Genesis, that of Noah. According to the story in Genesis, Noah is perfectly righteous. That is why God picks Noah as the new Adam, to make a fresh start for creation. To ensure the renewal of the whole creation, God commands Noah to save a certain number of animals from the destruction of the old world. As the story describes God's command to Noah, Noah is to gather the animals into his boat, feed them for months, and then release them from the boat to be fruitful and multiply on the earth. And yet, in the story, the first thing Noah does after the flood when he is finally able to leave the boat is to sacrifice a large number of the animals on his boat, killing them as a burnt offering to God. I do not see how this sacrifice of Noah's could possibly be understood as an attempt to diminish punishment due for Noah's sin or to placate a God who is offended at Noah.

And there are many other such cases one might mention, where the point of the sacrifice also is not to satisfy an offended God. When Jonah is rescued by God from death by drowning and is filled with gratitude for that rescue, he tells God in prayer that he will offer God the sacrifice of thanksgiving (Jonah 2:9). Here manifestly the sacrifice is supposed to stem from gratitude and not from guilt. Or consider one of the other sacrifices in that same biblical narrative. Jonah was in danger of drowning because, at his urging, the sailors on the boat threw Jonah overboard to avoid shipwreck in the storm that God was bringing about because of Jonah. When the sea calms after Jonah is thrown out of the ship and the sailors realize that God is not angrily pursuing any of them, *then* after this the sailors offer God sacrifices (Jonah 1:16). Here, too, it is hard to see the sacrifice as an attempt to placate an offended deity. The calmness of the sea is the indication to the sailors that God is not angry with *them*, and they offer sacrifices after they see that the sea is calm and understand the implications of that calmness.

As far as that goes, in the New Testament Christ is said to be not just any sacrifice but in fact a Passover sacrifice (I Cor. 5:7). In the story of the Passover, God is delivering the Israelites from their bondage in Egypt. In that story, God is caring for the Israelites and building them into his chosen people; and the point of God's instituting the Passover sacrifice is to protect the Israelites from the angel afflicting the Egyptians. The Passover sacrifice also cannot be understood as an Israelite attempt to do penance for Israelite sin by giving an angry or otherwise offended God dead animals.

So it is true that, on the general constraints governing interpretations of the doctrine of the atonement, something about Christ's passion and death has to be understood as a sacrifice. But sacrifice itself has to be understood in the context of the texts about sacrifice in the Hebrew Bible, which are themselves the context for the New Testament claim that Christ is both priest and sacrifice. And when sacrifice is understood in the light of those texts, then, in my view, the nature of sacrifice and the character of Christ's death as a sacrifice are not compatible with the notion of sacrifice Swinburne and others in this tradition need for the Anselmian kind of interpretation of the doctrine of the atonement.

SACRIFICE AS ALTERING SOMETHING ABOUT GOD

So, in order to understand the New Testament claim that Christ's atonement is a sacrifice, it is necessary to focus on the notion of sacrifice in the Hebrew Bible, which is the context for the New Testament claim. There is, of course, an immense scholarly literature on this subject. It is not possible to engage with this literature briefly in passing in a book that is already long. For my purposes here, however, it is enough to highlight just a few features of sacrifice in the relevant texts in the Hebrew Bible.

To this end, it is helpful to approach the topic of sacrifice in the Hebrew Bible by looking first at one representative sketch of a pagan sacrifice in early Greek culture. So consider sacrifice as Homer presents it. In Homer's *Iliad*, when Chryses, the priest of Apollo, wants Apollo to help him get his daughter back from the Greeks who have kidnapped her, the priest says to Apollo,

> if ever it pleased you that I burned all the rich thigh pieces of bulls, of goats, then bring to pass this wish I pray for: let your arrows make the Danaans pay for my tears shed.[4]

And, in response to this prayer on the part of his priest, Apollo sends a plague on the Greeks that leaves many of them dead. In order to stop this plague, the Greeks return Chryses's daughter; but they also bring the priest a hundred animals to offer in sacrifice to Apollo so that Apollo will stop sending the plague on the Greeks.

Greek culture is the schoolteacher for Western civilization, and Homer is a wellspring of the wisdom that the Greeks bequeathed to the West. Homer's *Iliad* is one of the greatest works of human culture, and I myself was formed by it when I was a student. So I have no wish to belittle it in any way; on the contrary, I honor it. But it remains the case that in this Homeric picture of sacrifice, one can see why Augustine would have thought that the Greek gods were fallen angels.

In the story in the *Iliad*, Apollo's first and final care is for his own honor; and his honor is for hire. The reminder that Chryses has burned many thigh pieces of animals in Apollo's honor is sufficient to get Apollo to kill many Greeks in order to give support to his priest. There is certainly no indication that the justice or injustice of the situation has any weight with Apollo. There is not even any particular interest on Apollo's part in connecting those Greeks killed by the plague with any responsibility for the taking of Chryses's daughter. As far as that goes, when Chryses first comes to ask for his daughter, the ordinary Greek soldiers are in favor of returning her to him. It is their leader Agamemnon who sends the priest away empty-handed and humiliated. But it is the ordinary Greek soldiers who die in droves in the plague; Agamemnon is not in the number of the dead. And when Apollo's plague has its desired effect and his priest gets what he wanted, the return of his daughter, with all that her return implies, it still takes a hundred animals to get Apollo to stop making the Greeks sick, as if Apollo were a kind of killing machine difficult to stop once it has got started.

In Homer's story, Apollo does not care whether those Greeks who die deserve to die at his hands. He has no particular concern for animals either; he shows no interest in whether they are living or dead beyond the connection between dead animals and his own honor. And he does not even care much for his priest. He does nothing to prevent the Greeks from taking Chryses's daughter in the first place, and only the mention of the previous sacrifices to Apollo on Chryses's part prompts Apollo finally to do something to aid the priest in his deepest distress. Moral considerations are not much in evidence here, to say nothing of love or mercy. There is something almost humorous about wondering whether Apollo loves his priest Chryses. On the contrary, there is something fearfully amoral about Apollo. Even when Apollo's purpose in killing the Greeks through a plague is fulfilled, he does not care enough about human beings to stop killing the Greeks until he is bribed to do so by an enormous sacrifice of animals. The honor of having so much animal wealth destroyed just for him finally is enough to persuade him to do what the Greeks (and Chryses) want and to stop the plague.

I call attention to this episode in Homer's *Iliad* to highlight what sacrifice to a perfectly good and loving God cannot be. However sacrifice to such a God is to be construed, it cannot be understood this way.[5] But any way of interpreting the biblical sacrifices which sees the purpose of those sacrifices as getting God to do something that God would otherwise not do is in effect dangerously like this Homeric idea of sacrifice to Apollo.

Attempting to explain one of the rules for animal sacrifice, the Midrash Rabbah on Leviticus repudiates such a Homeric notion of sacrifice and draws out one of its religiously intolerable implications. It says,

> [The rule for sacrifice is formulated as it is] in order that man shall not say of himself, 'I shall go and do things that are unseemly, things that are improper, and I shall bring an ox, on which there is much flesh, and bring it up on the altar, and I shall be in favour with Him, and He will accept me as a penitent.'[6]

This repudiation of what is in effect a pagan notion of sacrifice holds even if what is at issue is placating God with both sacrifice and serious repentance for one's sin. Think of the matter this way. Suppose that two human beings Paula and Jerome have each separately and individually committed the same grave sin, but that Paula is rich whereas Jerome is so poor he can barely feed himself. Then suppose that each of them is equally contrite and repentant for the sin. Finally, suppose that Paula brings a sacrifice to God, but that Jerome, having nothing, brings nothing. So Paula offers God a sacrifice, but Jerome does not. If a biblical sacrifice is something that makes God more benevolent in one way or another, making God more willing to grant pardon, for example, then rich repentant Paula will find more acceptance with God after her sin than equally repentant but poor Jerome will find after his sin. But then, on this interpretation of sacrifice, God's benevolence, like Apollo's honor, is for sale.

It makes this conclusion only worse that the price of the deity's benevolence is supposed to be dead animals. Why would the Creator of animals be made to feel pleased or be made to be more benevolent by having his beasts killed? What is there about the death of a beast that would constitute a present to God? Is God loving only towards some of his creatures, the human ones who can bring sacrifices, and indifferent towards all the others? Or is there something that pleases God about making dead, in God's honor, a beast which was lovely in its living form? In my view, there is a decidedly pagan flavor of the Homeric sort about such a view of biblical sacrifice. And, as I explained above, this view is also difficult to make compatible with some of the biblical stories of sacrifice most notable as the context for the New Testament descriptions of Christ as sacrifice.

SACRIFICE AS ALTERING SOMETHING ABOUT A HUMAN PERSON

Against these background considerations, I want to examine the notion of sacrifice in the biblical stories in a different light. Consider, to begin with, the sacrifice that Gideon brings.

In the book of Judges (Judg. 6:11–21), an angel comes to visit Gideon to announce news that ought to be thrilling for Gideon.[7] Speaking for (and later apparently even as) the Lord, the angel begins this way: *The Lord is with you, you mighty warrior.*[8] But Gideon is not elated by this line, as one might unreflectively suppose he would be. Rather, he is only skeptical and anxious, and even a little oppositional. Basically, what Gideon says to the angel's announcement that God is with Gideon is this: *No, he isn't. Look at us! God has abandoned us into the hands of the Midianites.*

In the face of this discouraging response, the angel persists. *God is sending you, in your strength, to save your people from the Midianites,* the angel tells Gideon. Gideon's response shows that this line on the angel's part has done nothing to mitigate Gideon's original skepticism and anxiety. Gideon's response comes to this: *Me?! My family is poor, and I'm the least important person in my family—how could I save Israel?*

It is as if the Nobel Prize committee called a scientist working at an underprivileged department in a backwater school to announce that she has won a Nobel Prize. Her reaction may well be not one of euphoria, but rather one of disquiet or even apprehension. It is not that she thinks the committee has made a mistake; it is that she thinks the universe must somehow be out of order in a way that could, just possibly, be her fault or lead to something miserable and humiliating for her. When in the Gospel of Luke the angel announces to Mary that the Lord is with her and that she is highly favored by the Lord, her first reaction is fear, not elation. The text says that she was troubled in her mind (Luke 1:29). The angel calms her down by saying, "Don't be afraid!" before giving her the rest of his message.

In the face of Gideon's skepticism and anxiety, the angel returns to his original line, for want of a better idea: *The Lord is with you,* the angel tells Gideon.[9] And then the angel returns to his first attempt at encouraging Gideon: *you will hit the Midianites as if they were just one man,* the angel says. These claims were not successful in allaying Gideon's anxious and untrusting attitude before. It is not easy to see why the angel thinks that repeating them will help.

What is interesting about this story for my purposes is what happens next. Gideon says to the angel: *If I have found favor in your eyes, then give me a sign that it is you who are talking with me. Wait here until I come back with a present for you.*

Here Gideon is proposing his own solution to his distrust and anxiety. As he says, he wants a sign that will help him believe that he has found favor with God. So much is not hard to understand, of course, given what the angel has said to Gideon: God is asking Gideon to lead his people in warfare against an enemy that has so far been completely dominant over them. What is surprising is Gideon's idea of a sign. He is not asking the angel to give him a gift. He is asking the angel to wait for him while he races home to get a gift for the angel.

What sense is there in this part of Gideon's story? Why does Gideon think that his giving the angel a present will allay his own anxiety about whether he really has found favor with God and God is really with him?[10]

Once we reflect on the practice of gift-giving, I think it is not so hard to see the answer to these questions. The rules of gift-giving in any culture are typically Byzantine, tacit, and unpromulgated, but nonetheless generally recognized and widely observed by the people in that culture. If a secretary gives his married boss a gift of underwear on her birthday, she will be concerned (or intrigued, depending on her character). She will not be similarly concerned if her husband gives her a gift of underwear on her birthday. And if she should accept her secretary's gift, her accepting his gift will draw them closer, thereby fulfilling what he hoped for with his gift, just because she accepted it. The point remains largely the same even if the content of the gift is not itself notable. In ordinary circumstances, if the boss gives her secretary an ordinary gift on his birthday, his acceptance of her gift is unremarkable. But if he gives her a birthday gift, even a gift commensurate with their relationship as employee and employer, her glad accepting of his gift will give him a sense of comfort where their relationship is concerned.

In his excellent discussion of sacrifice, Moshe Halbertal has called attention to this feature of the practice of gift-giving. Halbertal asks, "What is it about sacrifice that is so essential to human expression and life?"[11] He begins his own answer to that question by turning to the sacrifices in the story of Cain and Abel. He says,

> the first biblical account of sacrifice has its source in the spontaneous giving from the produce of each of the brothers to God. The story stresses the expectation of the giver that his sacrifice be accepted, and the utter devastation that results from its rejection.... While [the Hebrew word for 'gift'] *matanah* signifies a gift that has been immediately transferred from giver to receiver, the term [used for sacrifice] *minchah* or *korban*... indicates that it is the receiver who will decide whether to take it or not. (The verb "to offer" as distinct from "to give" captures the nuance in English.)[12]

And Halbertal goes on to say,

> An important linguistic phenomenon in the biblical material supplies the key to understanding sacrifice. In biblical language, gifts given between equals or from a superior to an inferior are always designated by the noun *matanah*..., implying that no gap between giving and receiving exists. The gift is an actual transfer to the beneficiary's domain. Only in the gifts offered from an inferior to a superior is the term *minchah* utilized, to stress the fact that the superior has the privilege of rejecting the gift. The giver... is merely presenting something before the future beneficiary. His superior will take the next step, either to refuse or accept what was laid before him.[13]

When the person to whom the gift is offered is God, this feature of sacrifice as offering a gift becomes even more central. Halbertal says,

> The fact that the offering is given within such a hierarchical structure precludes the suspicion that it is a crude form of bribe[14]... by the believer [footnote omitted]. A middle-class person cannot bribe a billionaire... The gift of sacrifice to God, who is in the first place the provider of the good and in no need of it, functions as a token of submission and gratitude, and its reception is not driven by need or interest but rather is an expression of welcoming and goodwill.[15]

Halbertal seems to me insightful in these remarks, and they make sense out of the story about Gideon and the angel as well. Gideon can allay his anxiety by offering God through the angel a gift, as he could not do by receiving a gift from God or the angel.[16] The angel's accepting the gift on God's behalf draws Gideon closer to God, and Gideon feels that it does so. And so Gideon's succeeding in giving a gift to the angel diminishes Gideon's anxiety and distrust about the angel's message that God is with him and will help him to save his people from the Midianites.

One way to think of sacrifice, then, is as a gift from a small creature, a human being, to the Creator God, the effect of which, and the purpose of which, is to allay the post-Fall human tendency to anxiety and distrust before God. By offering a gift to the Creator and having it accepted, a person himself draws closer to God and is in consequence more willing to trust God and to be open to God.

In fact, on Halbertal's view of sacrifice, one function of the biblical laws of sacrifice is to close the gap between offering and gift.[17] If what is offered to God and the way in which it is offered are in accordance with the rules God himself has mandated for gift-giving, then there is an additional help with the purpose of sacrifice. It is easier to believe that God will accept an offering given to him if the offering is made in accordance with God's own rules for giving gifts to God.[18]

At this point, a defender of the Anselmian kind of interpretation of the doctrine of the atonement might complain that the sacrifices in the stories about Cain and Abel or about Gideon are odd in one way or another; and so, the putative objector might suppose, these instances of sacrifice are also unrepresentative. On the objector's view, the really representative sacrifices are those mandated in Leviticus, many of which have to do with offerings for sin. And these sacrifices, the putative objector might claim, are indeed offerings meant to propitiate an offended God.

But in his overview to the volume on Leviticus in the ArtScroll Tanach series, Rabbi Nosson Scherman actually repudiates such an attitude towards the animal sacrifices prescribed in Leviticus. He sums up what he and his community take to be the traditional Jewish attitude towards these animal sacrifices in a way entirely consonant with Halbertal's view of sacrifice. Scherman recognizes the possibility of assimilating the Jewish practice of sacrifice to the kind of sacrifice which I have highlighted in the discussion of the story in Homer's *Iliad*, and he repudiates such a view of sacrifice energetically. He says,

> The word *sacrifice* implies that the person bringing it is required to deprive himself of something in order to satisfy someone else's need or caprice – but God finds no satisfaction in inflicting pain or deprivation upon His children....
> [The word] *offering* implies that the recipient of the gift must be appeased, that

He requires a tribute that will somehow assuage His wrath or make Him receptive
to the entreaties of a supplicant or that He has a need that can only be satisfied by
someone other than Himself. As if God required our gifts! .... What then is the
purpose of the offerings? The root of [the Hebrew word '*korban*'] is ... *to come
near*. The person bringing an offering does so in order to come closer to God, to
elevate his level of spirituality.[19]

Finally, it should be said in this connection that what is at issue in Scherman's
lines and in the discussion of sacrifice in this chapter is the purpose of sacrifice.
There are, of course, many other things that might be discussed in connection
with sacrifice. The ordinary non-religious use of the term 'sacrifice' suggests
something given up, often with some real loss to the giver, for the sake of
something and someone else. In this sense, too, sacrifice can be understood as
gift. The purpose of a gift is not the same as the effect on the giver of giving the
gift. Sometimes the giving of a gift can come with great cost to the giver, as
shown vividly, for example, by O. Henry's famous story *The Gifts of the Magi*;
and yet the purpose of the gift remains focused on the relationship between the
giver of the gift and its recipient.[20]

SACRIFICE: THE STORIES

Consequently, a non-Homeric way to think about the purpose of sacrifice is as
an attempt to allay human anxiety about God by offering God a gift and by
this means to take a step closer towards God in trust. Thought of in this way,
the sacrifices in the early biblical stories are easier to understand.

In the story of the sacrifices of Cain and Abel,[21] at the time of the sacrifice
neither brother has yet committed a notable or recorded sin against God;
neither brother is trying to placate God for having offended him. In fact, the
text vouches for Abel's acceptability with God.[22] On the other hand, it seems
reasonable to suppose that the story assumes both brothers know that they are
subject to death by God's decree.[23] In this condition, it is understandable that
they might feel some anxiety with regard to God and some uncertainty about
their relationship to him.[24]

The story of Noah's sacrifice of the very animals Noah has so painstakingly
cared for in his boat is also easier to explain on this approach to sacrifice. In
the story, Noah understands that God intends him to begin the human race
again, and he also understands that God has saved his life and the lives of his
children from the destruction God has visited on all other human beings for
their evil. If Noah is uneasy in this condition, who could fail to understand it?
It must at least cross Noah's mind that if he or his children or his further
descendants become less than righteous, they too might be subject to similar
destruction. In multiple senses, then, Noah's life is a gift given Noah by God.

In the circumstances of the story, Noah obviously cannot give God his own life as a gift in gratitude to God for saving him and his family from the flood. But he can offer God a substitute for his life by giving God the most valuable lives Noah has, that of the animals he has worked to save. And in offering God with thanksgiving this vicarious sacrifice, these lives in return for the gift of his own life, Noah himself is drawing nearer to God against his own unease. In sacrificing to God the lives of animals, Noah is quieting himself and committing himself to trust in God.

That anxiety of this sort lies behind Noah's offering of the animals is confirmed by God's response to the offering. In the story, in answer to Noah's sacrifice, God makes a covenant with Noah, the first of many covenants in the biblical texts. For his part in this covenant,[25] God promises never to bring a flood again.[26] And God commits himself to putting a rainbow in the sky whenever it rains, so that when the water starts to come from heaven, and Noah feels understandably anxious, Noah can see the rainbow and remember God's promise.

This reading of Noah's sacrifice is also confirmed by the oddity of the notion of God's making a covenant. In the biblical texts, God makes covenants by various means, including by swearing by himself.[27] But suppose that a wife, feeling uneasy about her husband's commitment to her, says to him anxiously, "Do you love me?" What would it help her if he said to her, "I promise you that I do!"—or even if he said something analogous to God's swearing by himself, as, for example, "On my honor, I promise you that I do!" Would it make it any better if he said, "As long as you love me, I promise you that I will never leave you!"? That line is a kind of minimal covenant. But how does it help? Suppose even that the covenant is maximal. Suppose that in response to his wife's asking her husband if he loves her, the husband sets up an elaborate ceremony for reconfirming their original marriage vows. Would elaborate rituals help? The basic problem is her trust in him. And if there is something worth distrusting in him, then his promises, his engaging in ceremonies and rituals, his covenants are still only as much worth trusting as he is. If he is untrustworthy, so are all these things. Nonetheless, as everyone has experienced, even in such circumstances promises and rituals may allay an anxious person's unease. In ways hard to explain but widely known and experienced, rituals and covenants have the ability to allay human anxiety about interpersonal relationships.[28]

Someone might object that in making promises a person incurs an obligation that she did not have before. This point is entirely true. Someone might further suppose that even God can incur new obligations through promises and covenants. Contrary to those who suppose that God cannot have obligations, I think this point is true as well.[29] But the issue is not whether God has obligations. The issue is whether God can be trusted to meet them. The unease that finds comfort in God's covenants is an anxiety about whether God can be trusted to keep his promises. If he cannot, then he might well fail at his obligations, however much he has bound himself through covenants. Making promises or entering into covenants cannot make a person more trustworthy than he was before he made them. But, in ways hard to explain and yet generally felt, what promises, rituals, and covenants can do is to help bring peace to the troubled mind of someone understandably anxious about his standing with another person, or with God.

In the story of Noah and in a number of other stories as well, sacrifice is correlated with a covenant on God's part, so that in fact the Psalms can speak about covenants made by sacrifice (cf. Ps. 50:5). But, as the considerations adduced here make clear, the point of making the sacrifices and entering into covenants with God through sacrifice cannot reasonably be supposed to be the enhancing of God's trustworthiness or the binding of God to more goodness or more love than God would otherwise have had. Rather, as the story of Noah makes clear, what the sacrifices can do is help a human being to trust God more and to open himself more to God's goodness, even in the face of an understandable human anxiety about doing so.

The story of the Passover sacrifice of the lamb is too rich to be dealt with in detail in passing here; but, even so, it is clear that the Passover sacrifice can be understood in this same general way. The story of the Israelite exodus out of Egypt is the story of God's forming the Israelites into his people, through experiences of being cared for by the goodness and power of God, through suffering, but also through miracles, laws, and sacrifice. In the story of the first Passover in Egypt, the blood of the sacrificed lamb substitutes for the blood of the first-born in an Israelite household, a life which is given to the Israelites as gift by God, who is redeeming the Israelites from slavery. In giving God the blood and the life of the animal, the Israelites acknowledge in a most memorable way that their own lives are gifts from God. By remembering this transformative experience in their history, and memorializing it in the ritual sacrifice of the Passover lamb, the Israelites strengthen their own willingness to be close to God as God's chosen people.

This way of thinking about sacrifice also helps to make sense of the passages in the Hebrew Bible in which God says he despises the very sort of sacrifice that God's own ritual laws prescribe. So, for example, in Amos 5:21–2, God angrily tells the Israelites that he hates their feasts and will not accept their sacrifices. It is possible to offer God sacrifices in a spirit similar to that of the Homeric sacrifice, and then the sacrifices move people further away from God, not closer.[30] If the point of ritual fasting or sacrifice is to get God to be more benevolent to the human person engaged in the ritual, if in effect it is to offer God a bribe to do what the human gift-giver wants, then the non-Homeric biblical point of sacrifice and fasting is lost. And that is why the same religious sentiment can both validate animal sacrifice and repudiate it in favor of its spiritual analogue. It is possible to fast or offer animal sacrifices while walling oneself off within oneself, and then the non-Homeric point of the sacrifice has been lost.

The same thing cannot be said about a broken contrite spirit, which, as one line in the Hebrew Bible says, is the true sacrifice that God will never despise (Ps. 51:17). Psalm 40:6–7 contrasts burnt offerings and sin offerings, which God does not want from the Psalm's audience, with delighting to do God's will. This is an odd contrast, of course, since in other biblical texts God mandates these offerings. But it makes sense when one considers the line the Psalm places between the burnt offerings that are then unacceptable and the acceptable delight in God's will: "I come," the Psalmist says. And that is the point, of the animal sacrifices, the broken and contrite heart, and the delight in doing God's will. God's presence to human beings is always assured by God's goodness and love. The distance between God and human beings is put there by human beings, and not by God; and even God cannot unilaterally remove it. Human beings must come to God, at least in the minimal sense that they lay down their resistance to God and surrender to God's love. On this way of understanding sacrifice in the Hebrew Bible, sacrifice is one way in which human beings do so.

In still other texts in the Hebrew Bible, praise is called a sacrifice (see, e.g., Ps. 50:23, Lev. 22:29). To praise God is to be deeply enough affected by God's goodness and love to want to tell God about it, and a heart so moved is open to God. In the sacrifice of praise, what is offered to God is oneself, through the openness of heart that the praise expresses.

There is even an evocative line in a Psalm that speaks of the sacrifices of joy (Ps. 27:6). In what sense could joy possibly be considered a sacrifice? How could the same notion apply both to the ritual slaughter of an animal and to the experience and expression of joy?[31] On the construal of sacrifice I have argued for here, it is not hard to understand what is on the Anselmian approach to sacrifice a most perplexing connection. As I have explained sacrifice, it is a means by which a person draws near to God. When a person finally draws near enough to open herself to the love of God, then she will be close enough to God to know his love and forgiveness of her. The effects of this closeness are love, joy, peace, and the other fruits of the Spirit. And so, insofar as sacrifice is meant to facilitate a movement towards God, the best kind of sacrifice is the expression of the completion of this movement in joy.

The notion of sacrifice as a present given to an offended deity as reparation for sin so that that deity will pardon the sin or accept reconciliation with the sinner has an initial (although mistaken) plausibility when it comes to the sacrifice of animals. It is even possible to argue that contrition or delighting to do God's will somehow fits this notion, though that argument would lack plausibility in my view. On any religiously acceptable construal of the Anselmian approach to sacrifice, sacrifice is supposed to be something given God in addition to repentance. But contrition and commitment to doing what is good are normally taken as parts of repentance, not as something extra added to repentance, so that it is hard to see how contrition could count as a sacrifice, on the Anselmian approach to sacrifice. That approach becomes stretched to breaking when thanksgiving is supposed to be the present offered to God as reparation. If a sinner comes to God to thank God for past favors, in what sense is this thankfulness something that is a penance offered to God for past sin? And, finally, I see no way at all to construe joy as a sacrifice on the Anselmian approach to sacrifice, as a present a person offers to propitiate a deity offended by her sins.

For all these reasons, I think that considerations of sacrifice in the Hebrew Bible not only offer no support to the Anselmian kind of interpretation of the doctrine of the atonement, but in fact count as good evidence against it.

CHRIST'S SACRIFICE: THE ANSELMIAN INTERPRETATION

With these background reflections on sacrifice in the Hebrew Bible, we can turn to the New Testament and the claim that Christ is a sacrifice offered to God.

On the Anselmian interpretation of the doctrine of the atonement, this claim is hard to explicate. On the Anselmian interpretation, human sin offends God, even if it does God no harm. Consequently, although there can be no question of any reparations for damage done to God, some suitable penance for the injustice offered God is nonetheless necessary. This penance is supposed to be provided by Christ's sacrifice, which is a present offered to God that more than makes up for the offense to God of human sin, on the Anselmian approach to sacrifice.[32] God's forgiveness of sinners and God's acceptance of reconciliation with them is dependent on God's receiving this sacrifice. That is, if God were not to receive Christ's sacrifice, God would not (and should not) forgive sinners or accept reconciliation with them.

So, for example, Swinburne, who is in this tradition of interpretation, says,

> God takes something valuable as a gift of reconciliation whose benefits he will often share with worshippers—like, to use a humble modern analogy, the box of chocolates which one gives to one's host, who then offers one in return a choice from the box. The sacrifice of Christ is then Christ giving the most valuable thing he has—his life; both a lived life of obedience to God, and a laid-down life on the Cross—as a present to God, whose benefits will flow to others.[33]

One problem for this Anselmian approach to Christ's sacrifice lies in the supposition that the one offering the sacrifice is the same God as the one receiving the sacrifice. That is, on the Anselmian approach, God gets as penance or present what God gives to himself. But the idea of penance is that the offended party gets something in addition to what is owed him; he has more than he would have had if he had not been given the present that is the penance. In God's case, however, since the present is given by the very God who receives it, it is hard to see in what sense God has been given anything.

Swinburne, however, thinks that through Christ God does receive something God did not have before, namely, a perfect human life. So, for example, Swinburne proposes that human beings should say to God,

> We have made a mess of the life which you gave us, we have made no reparation of our own for our sins, ... But we have been given a perfect life, not owed to you, O God. We offer you this life instead of the life we should have led . . . . Take its perfection instead of our imperfection.[34]

So, Swinburne's variant on the Anselmian kind of interpretation has the advantage that God does receive something through Christ's sacrifice. But this advantage of Swinburne's position comes at a considerable cost. On Swinburne's interpretation of Christ's sacrifice, it is not easy to see why Christ's suffering and death should count as part of the present given to God. On Swinburne's position, Christ's passion and death seem marginalized or incidental, and not central to the present offered to God, as they need to be on traditional Christian views about Christ as sacrifice. Any Anselmian kind of interpretation has to maintain that, in addition to the life of Christ, the suffering of Christ's crucifixion and Christ's death count as a present that is pleasing enough to God or fulfills enough of God's justice that it enables God to forgive sinners and accept reconciliation with them. The biblical texts relevant to atonement emphasize Christ's passion and death as the atonement, much more than Christ's life.

And there is still an additional problem for the Anselmian approach to sacrifice. Even if one can make sense out of the idea that God would not and should not forgive sinners without God's giving himself a present, it remains very hard to understand why the present, the thing that God likes and takes pleasure in, includes centrally the suffering and death of an innocent human being.

It gets even harder to explain the Anselmian approach to sacrifice when one reflects that the person who is tortured to death actually is God. The God who is crucified in his assumed human nature is the God who receives the present of the sacrifice made by Christ's passion and death. What sense can be made of the idea that God likes this process or that it constitutes a present for God or that it makes up to God for the offense of human sin? Why would this anguished present given by God to God be something pleasing to God or something necessary to enable God to pardon human sin?

It only makes things worse if we remember that it is sinners who crucify God incarnate. On the Anselmian interpretation of the doctrine of the atonement, Christ's sacrifice to God is in fact the occasion for the worst sin possible, the worst offense offered to God. Thinking of this problem for the Anselmian kind of interpretation, Jerome Miller says,

> Because sin offends God's perfect holiness, its evil is incalculable. Only the sacrifice of an incalculable good can possibly atone for it. As divine, Jesus was a sacrificial offering of infinite worth; as human, he was able to make atonement on our behalf... Viewed from this perspective, the self-sacrificial death of Jesus was the definitive salvific event.
>
> But this way of understanding atonement doesn't address some important truths about it—the fact that it was a murder, and the fact that Jesus was, in the first place, a victim of sin, not an atonement for it .... It's true that, to understand the full meaning of the Crucifixion, we have to consider how Jesus responded to his murder and murderers. But we can't appreciate this response, or understand its purpose, unless we recognize the Crucifixion itself as an unequivocal evil that no just God could countenance. Insofar as the idea of atonement leads us to think that divine justice in some way required that an innocent man be murdered by way of compensation, it covers up the horror.[35]

So, one insuperable problem for the Anselmian approach to Christ's sacrifice and for the Anselmian kind of interpretation in general is to explain why God's giving to himself a present makes up for the offense done to God's honor or in some other way enables God to pardon sinners. But another, and worse, insuperable problem is to explain why having an innocent person (or God's own incarnate self) suffer torment and death is pleasing enough in God's eyes to count as the needed present. In my view, there is no acceptable resolution of these problems and consequently also no salvaging of the Anselmian approach to Christ's sacrifice.

CHRIST'S SACRIFICE: THE MARIAN INTERPRETATION

Hebrews is the New Testament book that has the most extensive discussion of Christ as sacrifice. What is notable about the description of Christ as sacrifice in Hebrews is that the effects of the sacrifice are described as intrinsic changes in the psyche of human beings saved by Christ. Contrary to what one would expect on the Anselmian approach to sacrifice, the effects are not described as any alteration in God's willingness or ability to accept reconciliation with sinners. So, for example, Hebrews 9:14 says that the blood of Christ will purify the human conscience and turn it from dead works to true service of the living God. Hebrews 10:1 contrasts the sacrifice of Christ with the ritual sacrifices of animals and says that the animal sacrifices were not able to make perfect those who offered them. Explaining why God would do away with the animal sacrifices of the Hebrew Bible and substitute the sacrifice of Christ, Hebrews says,

It is not possible that the blood of bulls and goats should take away sins...God takes away the first [that is, the divine will which commanded animal sacrifice] that he may establish the second [that is, the divine will which provided Christ as a sacrifice], by which will we are sanctified through the offering of the body of Jesus Christ once for all.   (Heb. 10:4, 9–10)

In contrast to the sacrifice of animals, by his one sacrifice of himself, Christ has perfected those who are sanctified (Heb. 10:14).

This way of thinking about the effects of Christ as sacrifice illuminates what in the Gospels Christ says repeatedly. Where one might unreflectively have expected him to give moral lessons or rules for life, he more frequently invites his listeners to draw near to him. To take just one example, in the Gospel of Matthew (Matt. 11:28–9), Christ says, "Come to me, you who are weary and burdened,.... And you will find rest for your souls." There is a resonance here with the line in Isaiah (Isa. 57:21), "There is no peace for the wicked." A person who is psychically fragmented wants and does not want the same thing, or wants to want what he does not want. In one way or another, he does not get what he wants, no matter what he gets; and so peace eludes him as he tries to get what he wants. True peace, true rest, requires internal integration. And, on orthodox Christian doctrine, which eschews Pelagianism, this peace is available only through the processes of justification and sanctification. So when Christ urges those who are weary to come to him to find rest, he is presenting coming to himself as the source of peace and thus also as the means of union with God.

On the Marian interpretation of the doctrine of the atonement, in his passion and death, Christ provides unilaterally one part of what is needed for union between God and human beings, namely, the indwelling of human psyches in God; and he also provides the most promising means for the other part, namely, the surrender to God by human beings alienated from themselves and from God. In offering these things to all human beings, Christ makes satisfaction to human beings for the evil done to them by others; and this satisfaction of Christ's can become vicarious satisfaction for those wrongdoers united to Christ in love. Consequently, by his passion and death, Christ can defeat the suffering of the victims of human evil and remedy the guilt and shame of the perpetrators of it.

On the Marian interpretation, there are no perplexing problems about God's offering a present to God or God's accepting with pleasure the present of his own crucifixion and death. On the Marian interpretation, Christ who is God suffers and dies in his human nature in order to bring human beings into a union of mutual indwelling with God. This return of estranged human persons to God *is* something that God would otherwise not have had; it *is* a gift given to God through Christ. And it is clear why this gift should be something of value for God. It is hard to imagine that there could be a better gift for God than the restoration to God of God's beloved but alienated and self-destructive creatures.

Furthermore, a person such as Abel or Noah who offers God the life of an animal as a gift in return for the gift of his own life makes a ritual and symbolic act of identification between the life of the animal and his own life. But a metaphysically greater unification occurs in the case of the sacrifice that is Christ. Because through his passion and death Christ enables the mutual indwelling between Christ and human persons in grace, there is in Christ a more powerful analogue to the identification between a human giver of sacrifice and the animal sacrifice he brings to God. The identification sought in sacrifice between the gift and the giver is not something analogous or figurative when Christ is the sacrifice offered to the Father. Rather, between human persons in grace and the gift that is Christ, there is metaphysical union. Because a person in grace is united to Christ in love, when Christ offers himself as a sacrifice to the Father, those human persons in grace are also offered with Christ in virtue of being united with what is offered as sacrifice. And so, in Christ's offering himself as gift to God, all those who are united to Christ in love are also offered to God. What was merely ritual and symbolic in the case of animal sacrifice becomes a metaphysical actuality when the sacrifice is Christ.

In addition, since it is Christ who as priest offers this sacrifice of himself, there can be no doubt about its acceptance. The gap between offering a gift and successfully giving a gift that Halbertal calls attention to is closed in this case because the people on whose behalf the gift is offered are united in Christ who is the sacrifice, *and* the sacrifice which is given to God is in fact the very person who is offering the sacrifice as priest, *and* the priest is the God to whom the sacrifice is offered.

Here, then, we have an explanation that helps makes sense of the notion that in the sacrifice of Christ God gives a gift to himself. When Christ, who is God, gives himself to God as a gift, he is not giving God a penance that honors God and so enables God to accept reconciliation with sinners. Rather, on the Marian interpretation, when Christ offers himself as a gift to God, he is giving to God all those human persons united to Christ. This is the ultimate version of what the sacrifices of Abel and Noah were meant to be; it is also the ultimate way of forming human beings into God's people, as the Passover sacrifice did. And, from the point of view of a human person who accepts Christ as sacrifice, in this sacrifice there is the greatest remedy for the understandable post-Fall human anxiety about facing God.

SACRIFICE: THE MORAL OF THE STORIES

Even the animal sacrifices of the Hebrew Bible should not be understood as an attempt to get God to do what the human person offering the sacrifice wants

God to do. Rather, those animal sacrifices are a means by which the person offering the sacrifice can deepen his trust in God and his closeness to God by giving his own life symbolically in giving the life of the sacrificed animal. When in the biblical story Noah sacrificed animals to God after the flood, he was offering the life of the animals as standing in for his own life, which had been given him as gift by God; and, by this means, Noah was allaying his anxiety about God. And so, in effect, he was seeking not God's closeness to him but his own closeness to God.

Through surrender in love, and then through suffering and through the Eucharist, a person in grace is united to Christ in the mutual indwelling enabled by Christ's life, passion, and death. For this reason, Christ's giving of his life to God in his willingness to suffer and die is not just something that stands in for the life of a person in grace, as the lives of the sacrificed animals stood in for the life of Noah. Rather, because Christ's atonement enables a person in grace actually to be united to Christ, Christ's giving of himself includes also the giving of the lives of all those united with Christ. And so, in being united to Christ, a person in grace gives his life to God in love—but he does so not just symbolically, as in animal sacrifice, but rather metaphysically and really, through the mutual indwelling enabled by Christ's atonement.

The Marian interpretation of the doctrine of the atonement thus yields an account of Christ's passion and death as a sacrifice that is as different as one might hope from the Homeric idea of sacrifice as a present designed to promote divine benevolence towards human desires. On the Marian interpretation, the atonement is a sacrifice, certainly, but the point of the sacrifice is not to give God a present to win God's pardon, or to provide a condition for God's forgiveness or any other form of benevolence towards human beings on God's part. Instead, like the sacrifice of Noah or the Passover sacrifice, Christ's giving of himself in sacrifice to God is a matter of helping human beings to come to God. And so, on the Marian interpretation, one can see the way in which Christ's passion and death count as a sacrifice, not in the mode of Homeric sacrifice, but in the mode of sacrifice presented in the best traditions of the Hebrew Bible.

In my view, Augustine summarizes well this view of sacrifice and of its concomitant view of Christ as both priest and sacrifice; and I am glad to let him have the last word here. Augustine says,

> the true sacrifice is every act whose purpose is that we may cling to God in a holy fellowship.... Therefore a man who is consecrated in the name of God and dedicated to God, in so far as he dies to the world that he may live to God, is himself a sacrifice.... It assuredly follows that all this redeemed city, which is today the assembly and fellowship of the saints, is offered to God as a universal sacrifice through the High Priest who in his passion offered even himself for us in the shape of a slave that we might be the body of so great a head.... This is the Christian sacrifice: 'though many, one body in Christ.' And this sacrifice the Church continually celebrates in the rite of the altar well known to the faithful, in which it is made clear to her that in her offering she herself is offered to God.[36]

THE EPISTLE TO THE ROMANS

The Epistle to the Romans attributed to the Apostle Paul is one of the central New Testament texts generally invoked in debates about interpretations of the doctrine of the atonement. There have been thoughtful, sophisticated commentaries on it, or on the most pertinent parts of it, by outstanding theologians over centuries. What is perhaps most clear about this Epistle by now is that the passages in it particularly relevant to the doctrine of the atonement can be read in radically different ways by equally committed and learned commentators. It would take a sizeable book of its own to review this history of commentary, and it would be a monumental task to argue for one interpretation of the Epistle as preferable to all others. This is therefore a task that I will eschew here at the end of this book.

A lesser task, but still a large one, would be to review all the passages in the Epistle relevant to the doctrine of the atonement and try to make a case that the Marian interpretation does in fact fit all of them, contrary to what other commentators with other views might maintain. In my view, this is a task that could be done successfully, but it too would lengthen this chapter and this book very considerably, because there is scarcely anything about the Epistle that has not been the subject of much contention in the past. That contention would have to be addressed in detail in any effort to argue that the Marian interpretation does match all the relevant passages of the Epistle.

In these circumstances, I will content myself with a smaller task that is nonetheless sufficient for my purposes. What I will try to establish is just that it is possible to argue reasonably that the Marian interpretation fits the most relevant texts in the Epistle. Establishing this conclusion falls short of demonstrating that the Epistle supports the Marian interpretation. It shows only that it is not obvious that the Epistle disconfirms the Marian interpretation. Without a book of its own on the Epistle, in my view this is the best that can be done.

It is worth noting at the outset that an interpretation of the doctrine of the atonement can focus its attention on different elements of the doctrine. There are (a) the details of what things exactly are provided by Christ's atonement. There are (b) the explanations of the way in which Christ's passion and death provide those things. And then there are (c) the elucidation of the post-Fall condition of human beings and (d) the description of the condition of human beings in a state of grace. The Epistle itself concentrates on (a), (c), and (d); it has less to say about (b). By contrast, some interpretations of the doctrine of the atonement—the Anselmian kind, for example—typically concentrate on (a) and (b) and say little about (c) and (d).

The Marian interpretation attempts to deal with all four, (a)–(d); but, given the Epistle's own focus, the main question for this chapter is the correspondence between the Marian interpretation and the Epistle's claims about (a), (c), and (d).

There can be little question, in my view, about the fit between the Marian interpretation and the Epistle as regards (c) and (d). On the contrary, some passages in the Epistle seem to be an evocative delineation of the very phenomena the Marian interpretation highlights. So, for example, consider this passage from Romans 7, which describes the psychic state of a post-Fall human person.[37] (In this case, the King James translation is both widely known and lucid, so I am reproducing it here.)

> For that which I do I allow not: for what I would, that do I not; but what I hate, that do I. If then I do that which I would not, I consent unto the law that it is good. Now then it is no more I that do it, but sin that dwelleth in me. For I know that in me (that is, in my flesh,) dwelleth no good thing: for to will is present with me; but how to perform that which is good I find not. For the good that I would I do not: but the evil which I would not, that I do. Now if I do that I would not, it is no more I that do it, but sin that dwelleth in me.   (Rom. 7:15–20)

The Epistle is here vividly depicting the internally fragmented psychic state of post-Fall human persons that is central to the Marian interpretation's exposition of (c).

The Marian interpretation depends on a rejection of Pelagianism and an affirmation of the claim that there is nothing good in a human psyche, not even faith, which is not put there by God. It also makes faith the necessary and sufficient condition for salvation. These elements in the Marian interpretation stem from a theological tradition that is actually grounded in Romans (as well as other epistles of Paul's). So, for example, Romans says,

> But now apart from the Law the righteousness of God has been manifested, being witnessed by the Law and the Prophets, even the righteousness of God through faith in Jesus Christ for all those who believe; for there is no distinction; for all have sinned and fall short of the glory of God, being justified as a gift by His grace through the redemption which is in Christ Jesus; whom God displayed publicly as a propitiation in His blood through faith. This was to demonstrate His righteousness, because in the forbearance of God He passed over the sins previously committed; or the demonstration, of His righteousness at the present time, so that He would be just and the justifier of the one who has faith in Jesus. Where then is boasting? It is excluded. By what kind of law? Of works? No, but by a law of faith. For we maintain that a man is justified by faith apart from works of the Law.
> (Rom. 3:21–8, New American Standard Version)[38]

And the Epistle's explanation of the condition of a person in grace focuses on the indwelling Holy Spirit, which is central to the Marian interpretation's exposition of (d). So, for example, the Epistle says,

Those who are in the flesh cannot please God. You, however, are not in the flesh but in the Spirit, if in fact the Spirit of God dwells in you. Anyone who does not have the Spirit of Christ does not belong to him. But if Christ is in you, although the body is dead because of sin, the Spirit is life because of righteousness. If the Spirit of him who raised Jesus from the dead dwells in you, he who raised Christ Jesus from the dead will also give life to your mortal bodies through his Spirit who dwells in you. (Rom. 8:8–11, English Standard Version)

For these reasons and others as well, it should be clear that the Marian interpretation matches the Epistle well as regards (c) and (d). Since the Epistle itself says little about (b) that is developed in detail, the real issue as regards the Marian interpretation's fidelity to the Epistle has to do with (a), the details of what things exactly are provided by Christ's atonement. This issue therefore will be my focus here.

The difficulty with this issue is that some of the most contentious debate about the proper interpretation of the Epistle has centered precisely on (a). Both Calvin and Aquinas, for example, wrote impressive commentaries on Romans, but in various places they come to significantly different conclusions about what it is that the Epistle is claiming on this score.

And this is actually not the end of the difficulty, because, at least in recent years, there has also been controversy over Calvin's position on (a), with some scholars emphasizing a great difference between Calvin's position and that of Aquinas, and others seeing more similarity between the two.[39] Calvin's commentary on Romans can itself therefore be interpreted in varying ways.

The debate over Calvin's position includes the question whether the justification consequent on faith changes something intrinsic in a person in grace or whether it is merely a change in the status God accords to a person in grace. On this score, Charles Raith explains the difference between the interpretations of Romans by Calvin and Aquinas this way:

[the difference] is due in large part to Aquinas's doctrine of justification as transformation rather than Calvin's extrinsic imputational understanding of justification.... Calvin held together biblical images of a legal and transformational nature. But it is the way Calvin held them together that displays the limits of [a believer's] participation [in Christ] in his account of salvation.... [T]he forensic aspect of justification as the imputation of Christ's justice is linked with [Calvin's] doctrine of union with Christ—believers come to 'possess' Christ and his righteousness. Yet... [for Calvin] 'possessing' Christ leaves the possessor still damnable *in se*, and this in distinction from one's standing *in Christo*.... Calvin declares all our works condemnable *in se* even if pardoned and rewarded *in Christo*....[40]

In these circumstances, it is doubtful that there is any reasonably brief review of the evidence that would settle decisively the debate between Calvin and Aquinas on the correct interpretation of the passages in Romans on justification or the issues as regards Calvin's own interpretation of these passages, which would have to be resolved first. Consequently, because the Marian interpretation accepts Aquinas's account of justification as including a change brought about by God in the person being justified by faith, it is not possible to settle to everyone's satisfaction the question of the fit between the Marian interpretation and Romans as regards (a).

Of course, if it is not easy to argue conclusively that one interpretation of Romans is the best or the only acceptable one, by parity of reasoning it is not easy to argue conclusively that one of the competing interpretations is ruled out as inadequate or unacceptable either. So, what is not difficult to show is that there is *one* theologically sophisticated reading of Romans, namely, that given by Aquinas in his commentary on the Epistle, according to which the Marian interpretation corresponds well with the Epistle.

To see this correspondence, consider just one of the most disputed passages in Romans. (I give it here in the King James Version, since that is a good clear Protestant translation, influenced by Calvinist ideas; and I am going to present an interpretation of the lines that comes from the different world of Aquinas's commentary.)

> But now the righteousness of God without the law is manifested, being witnessed by the law and the prophets, even the righteousness of God which is by faith of Jesus Christ unto all and upon all them that believe; for there is no difference, for all have sinned, and come short of the glory of God, being justified freely by his grace through the redemption that is in Christ Jesus, whom God hath set forth to be a propitiation through faith in his blood, to declare his righteousness for the remission of sins that are past, through the forbearance of God, to declare at this time his righteousness: that he might be just, and the justifier of him which believeth in Jesus.   (Rom. 3:21–6)

Aquinas comments on these lines this way:

> God's justice is said to be through faith in Christ Jesus, not as though by faith we merit being justified, as if faith exists from ourselves and through it we merit God's justice, as the Pelagians have claimed; but because in the very justification, by which we are made just by God, the first motion of the mind toward God is through faith ... Hence this very faith, as the first part of justice, is given to us by God .... But this faith, from which justice comes, is not unformed faith, about which James says, *faith without works is dead* (James 2:26), but it is faith formed by charity ... through which Christ dwells in us. *That Christ may dwell in your hearts through faith* (Eph. 3:17), which does not happen without charity: *he who abides in love abides in God and God in him* (I John 4:16) ....[41]

There is nothing in the lines of the Epistle as Aquinas interprets them that is in conflict with the Marian interpretation. On the contrary, these lines highlight what is of central importance to the Marian interpretation.

Or, to take just one more example, consider this culminating expression of the treatment of the atonement in Romans:

> If God is for us, who can be against us? He who did not spare his own Son but gave him up for us all, how will he not also with him graciously give us all things.
> (Rom. 8:31–2, English Standard Version)

Aquinas says about those lines,

> God the Father gave Christ up to death by appointing him to become incarnate and suffer, and by inspiring Christ's human will with such love that he would willingly undergo the passion. Hence he is said to have given himself over.... Therefore, when Christ was given up for us, all things were given to us. Hence, Paul adds, 'how has he not also with Christ given us all things,' so that all things come together for our good, even the highest things, namely, the divine persons to enjoy, rational spirits to live with, lower things to use, not only prosperity but adversity as well: *all things are yours and you are Christ's and Christ is God's* (I Cor. 3:23).[42]

Aquinas here supposes that, for Paul in Romans, the passion and death of Christ have as their main effect a transformation of human beings, because they enable human persons to come to union with God through being joined to Christ in love; and he reads Paul as holding that a person in grace can consequently find something to celebrate even in adversity because it also contributes to her being transformed into increased union with God.

On Aquinas's understanding of Romans, then, the Marian interpretation is fully in accord with the Epistle. This conclusion does not settle the issue of whether the Epistle supports the Marian interpretation, but it does demonstrate that the Epistle does not obviously disconfirm it. Given the contentious history of interpretation of this biblical text, showing that the Marian interpretation is not ruled out by the Epistle is a successful defense of that interpretation.

ISAIAH AND THE SUFFERING SERVANT

Finally, it is worth reflecting on some of the passages in Isaiah on the suffering servant. Although both historical Jewish sources and modern commentators are divided among themselves as to the identity of the suffering servant in these passages and the meaning of the suffering attributed to the servant, from early Christian times Christians have supposed that these passages predict Christ and describe Christ's passion and death. In what follows, I will accept that Christian reading for the sake of one last evaluation of the Marian interpretation, because some readers might otherwise suppose that the Marian interpretation founders on these passages in Isaiah, read as the Christian tradition has taken them.

One of the most notable of such passages is presented in the box below. I quote it at length to make sure that I am not inadvertently omitting something that others might find crucial to the discussion. There are also other passages in Isaiah that pertain to the suffering servant, but this text is the one which some readers might suppose is the most telling against the Marian interpretation. I am giving it in the translation provided by the Jewish Publication Society Tanakh translation. Every translation of this passage in Isaiah has something that some readers will find tendentious; but my hope is that this Jewish translation might be considered impartial in debates among Christian commentators. On the other hand, the King James Version will be the translation of some lines in this text that are known by many people, including even some people who might otherwise know nothing of the Hebrew Bible, because Handel's *Messiah* has made those lines in the KJV words familiar to them. To avoid causing such readers annoyance, I have added the KJV translation of this text in a parallel column. (The discrepancy among the translations should also inspire some caution in the interpretation of the text.)

The suffering servant

52:13 Indeed, My servant shall prosper, be exalted and raised to great heights.

52:13 Behold, my servant shall deal prudently, he shall be exalted and extolled, and be very high.

14 Just as the many were appalled at him—so marred was his appearance, unlike that of man, his form, beyond human semblance—

14 As many were astonied at thee; his visage was so marred more than any man, and his form more than the sons of men:

15 just so he shall startle many nations. Kings shall be silent because of him, for they shall see what has not been told them, shall behold what they never have heard.

15 So shall he sprinkle many nations; the kings shall shut their mouths at him: for that which had not been told them shall they see; and that which they had not heard shall they consider.

53:1 Who can believe what we have heard? Upon whom has the arm of the Lord been revealed?

53:1 Who hath believed our report? and to whom is the arm of the LORD revealed?

2 For he has grown, by His favor, like a tree crown, like a tree trunk out of arid ground. He had no form or beauty, that we should look at him: no charm, that we should find him pleasing.

2 For he shall grow up before him as a tender plant, and as a root out of a dry ground: he hath no form nor comeliness; and when we shall see him, there is no beauty that we should desire him.

3 He was despised, shunned of men, a man of suffering, familiar with disease. As one who hid his face from us, he was despised, we held him of no account.

3 He is despised and rejected of men; a man of sorrows, and acquainted with grief: and we hid as it were our faces from him; he was despised, and we esteemed him not.

(*continued*)

(Continued)

4 Yet it was our sickness that he was bearing, our suffering that he endured. We accounted him plagued, smitten and afflicted by God;
5 but he was wounded because of our sins, crushed because of our iniquities. He bore the chastisement that made us whole, and by his bruises we were healed.
6 We all went astray like sheep, each going his own way; and the Lord visited on him the guilt of all of us.

7 He was maltreated, yet he was submissive, he did not open his mouth; like a sheep being led to slaughter, like a ewe, dumb before those who shear her, he did not open his mouth.
8 By oppressive judgment he was taken away, who could describe his abode? For he was cut off from the land of the living through the sin of my people, who deserved the punishment.
9 And his grave was set among the wicked, and with the rich, in his death— though he had done no injustice and had spoken no falsehood.
10 But the Lord chose to crush him by disease, that if he made himself an offering for guilt, he might see offspring and have long life. And that through him the Lord's purpose might prosper.

11 Out of his anguish he shall see it; he shall enjoy it to the full through his devotion. My righteous servant makes the many righteous, it is their punishment that he bears;
12 assuredly, I will give him the many as his portion, he shall receive the multitude as his spoil. For he exposed himself to death and was numbered among the sinners, whereas he bore the guilt of the many and made intercession for sinners. (Isa. 52:13–53:12, Jewish Publication Society Tanakh Translation)

4 Surely he hath borne our griefs, and carried our sorrows: yet we did esteem him stricken, smitten of God, and afflicted.
5 But he was wounded for our transgressions, he was bruised for our iniquities: the chastisement of our peace was upon him; and with his stripes we are healed.
6 All we like sheep have gone astray; we have turned every one to his own way; and the LORD hath laid on him the iniquity of us all.

7 He was oppressed, and he was afflicted, yet he opened not his mouth: he is brought as a lamb to the slaughter, and as a sheep before her shearers is dumb, so he openeth not his mouth.
8 He was taken from prison and from judgment: and who shall declare his generation? for he was cut off out of the land of the living: for the transgression of my people was he stricken.
9 And he made his grave with the wicked, and with the rich in his death; because he had done no violence, neither was any deceit in his mouth.
10 Yet it pleased the LORD to bruise him; he hath put him to grief: when thou shalt make his soul an offering for sin, he shall see his seed, he shall prolong his days, and the pleasure of the LORD shall prosper in his hand.
11 He shall see of the travail of his soul, and shall be satisfied: by his knowledge shall my righteous servant justify many; for he shall bear their iniquities.

12 Therefore will I divide him a portion with the great, and he shall divide the spoil with the strong; because he hath poured out his soul unto death: and he was numbered with the transgressors; and he bare the sin of many, and made intercession for the transgressors. (Isa. 52:13–53:12 KJV)

As Christians read it, this text describes Christ. So understood, the text sketches evocatively the suffering of Christ, and it presents Christ's suffering as an atonement for human sin. According to this text, understood in this Christian way, although Christ himself is sinless, he bears the sins of post-Fall human beings; and the chastisement or punishment of those sins falls on Christ, because, by God's design, Christ is an offering for those sins. As a result, many people are made righteous.

Clearly, this text can be read as some confirmation of the Anselmian kind of interpretation of the atonement; in fact, the mention of punishment in the Tanakh translation (Isa. 53:8) can seem to give some support to the penal substitution theory. On an Anselmian reading of the text, the punishment merited by human sin is death or death with torment, and this is the punishment that Christ undergoes on behalf of sinners. That Christ undergoes this punishment constitutes an offering to God; and because God is given this offering, human beings do not have to undergo the punishment their sins deserve. Somehow, in consequence of Christ's being punished in place of human beings, human beings are made righteous.

Although the text can be read in this Anselmian spirit, what I hope all the preceding work of this book has made evident is that the very different Marian interpretation of the atonement also fits these lines beautifully. In fact, to my mind, the Marian interpretation fits them much better than the Anselmian interpretation does.

What is most striking about this text is its description of Christ's suffering. He was crushed, wounded, bruised, and afflicted in bearing human sin. His face was marred more than that of any other human being; in fact, he was so disfigured that he hardly looked human anymore. People who saw him rejected him and turned away from him, appalled at him.

What is it to bear the sins of others? And what is it that disfigures a person? On Christian doctrine, human beings are made in the image of God, and that image makes them beautiful. How could it not do so? The beauty of God is reflected in the beauty of his image. This view gives one explanation for why we can find a human being beautiful even when he has serious impairments of body or mind. But the evil that a person does leaves him inwardly divided against himself and fragmented, broken in pieces, one might say. That evil is what truly disfigures a person. People who knew Joseph Merrick found him a movingly beautiful person, but no one is willing to describe Joseph Goebbels as beautiful. Goebbels suffered from a club foot, but it is not the deformity of his foot that singles Goebbels out as fearfully ugly. He is disfigured by his inward brokenness, by the ugliness of the evil he cleaved to.

If in bearing human sin, Christ was taking human evil within himself by opening himself up on the cross to all human psyches, as the Marian interpretation maintains, then it is understandable that in the inrush of all human

evil into himself Christ would be so badly marred as to seem hardly human
in form. The collective evil of all the members of the species does disfigure
past recognition the beautiful thing that human beings were meant to be and
might still be.

On this way of understanding the disfiguring of Christ, what is it for Christ
to be crushed or wounded or bruised for human sins? What is the chastisement or punishment that Christ endured for human beings? There are
sorrows that come from the depredations people endure at the hands of others
or from nature in the post-Fall world; certainly there are. When Christ is
crucified, he suffers terribly from what other people do to him. But he is
crucified with two other men, so that the suffering of crucifixion does not
single Christ out as suffering specially. The special character of Christ's
affliction, which he alone endures on behalf of all human beings, should
therefore be sought elsewhere than in his physical suffering.

There is an understandable human smallness that thinks of punishment as
something external to a human person heaped on him by others or by God.
But it is important to see that the deepest suffering for a human person comes
not from being beaten by something external to him—by nature, or other
people, or even God; rather, it comes from something internal to him, from
the brokenness of the post-Fall human tendency to evil. That brokenness
would leave a person in anguish even if he were to find himself in Eden.
Milton's Satan discovers this truth when, flying into Eden and seeing its great
peace and beauty, he nonetheless feels hell within himself even while he is in
Eden. Discovering the suffering of his condition, Milton's Satan says with
despairing misery, "Whither I go is Hell. Myself am Hell."[43] Could any
external pain added to a person's condition compete with this inner anguish
as an affliction? The fearsome punishment of Milton's Satan is not confine-
ment to Hell with its pains. The worst of his punishment is intrinsic to his
condition as a person alienated from love and himself. There is no peace to the
wicked, as Isaiah claims, because whatever an evil, self-alienated person gets,
he gets what he does not want; in wretchedness, he rejects the very love he
wants. This frustrated, fearful, lonely condition is itself an agonizing punishment for an evildoer.

For Christ to have within himself the broken human psyches that have no
peace is for Christ to feel what it is like to be an evil person—or, better, what it is
like to be all evil persons at once. The pain of this condition is merited by the sin
that brings it about, and so it is right to describe it as a natural and internal
punishment deserved in consequence of wrongdoing. It counts as punishment,
as hellish punishment if it gets bad enough. When Christ allows himself, in his
human nature, to be open to all human psyches, he bears for human beings
what they would otherwise have to bear themselves forever as punishment.

The Marian interpretation thus gives an explanation of Christ's suffering
and of Christ's bearing human punishment that makes sense. If the

punishment for sin is considered to be God's inflicting everlasting torment on sinners, then it is hard to see how Christ can be said to bear the punishment of sinners. But to think of hell this way is itself a mistake that has its roots in the Anselmian interpretation. It is to suppose that hell is something like a bad place where God inflicts torture on sinners who somehow have not managed to be among the redeemed. But the love and forgiveness of God are always offered to every human being, and only those who resolutely refuse it forever fail to be united to God in heaven. When Milton's Satan says, "Myself am Hell," he is expressing the very condition of hell, on the Marian interpretation of the atonement. And this is the condition Christ experiences in the cry of dereliction, when all human psyches come into Christ, and he endures the simulacrum of the stain on the soul of all human evil.

Finally, the claim that human beings are healed by the affliction that Christ endured is not easy to understand on the Anselmian interpretation, since on that interpretation the sufferings of Christ do not by themselves help human beings to draw nearer to God's love and goodness. But on the Marian interpretation, this claim is clearly right, because it is precisely by means of Christ's passion and death that the mutual indwelling of union with God becomes available for human beings.

For all these reasons, the Marian interpretation fits beautifully this passage from Isaiah on the suffering servant. It is Christ's willingness to endure the extreme disfigurement of human evil that heals a broken post-Fall person. By bearing the anguish of that disfigurement, which is the natural and merited punishment for wrongdoing, Christ offers human beings salvation from being immured in the painful prison of their lonely selves. It is Christ's immersion in human evil and its misery that heals post-Fall human beings.

FINAL REFLECTION

With that review of some of the biblical texts commonly adduced in discussions of the doctrine of the atonement and the support which that review gives the Marian interpretation, the project of this book is complete. What remains by way of conclusion is just one last reflection on the central idea of the book.

The doctrine of simplicity entails that there is no distinction among God's attributes, because there is just one indivisible thing that God is. But, on traditional Christian views, the names of the standard divine attributes are nonetheless not synonymous. That is because finite human minds contemplating the deity must break the one divine nature into separable attributes; limited human minds cannot take in as one whole the greatness of the divine nature. And since human minds, like a prism, break the white light of God's nature into a rainbow of divine attributes, it is clear that individual philosophers and theologians can also highlight one divine attribute as most indicative of God's nature, as most important to human beings.

It makes a great difference to one's philosophical theology which divine attribute is picked out in this way. One can isolate and emphasize God's honor or God's justice, for example, and the resulting theology will be imbued with that emphasis, for better or, as I hope this book has shown, for worse.

The Marian interpretation is centered on God's love, and in this focus it is in accord with the New Testament. The first Epistle of John identifies God with love:

> Beloved, let us love one another, for love is of God, and everyone that loves is born of God and knows God. He who does not love does not know God, for God is love.   (I John 4:7–8)[44]

I do not want those accustomed to thinking of love as something sentimental, lame, weak, or even vapid to become disoriented here. On the Thomistic account of love, which is part of the Marian interpretation, God's love is not a light thing, limply validating anything human beings do as long as they like doing it. On the contrary, on the Marian interpretation, God loves human persons enough to want to be united with them. But to be united with God is to be made like God in order to be in communion with God. God's love can therefore be wild as well as gentle. Hebrews says, "our God is a consuming fire" (Heb. 12:29). As fire sets other things on fire, so God's love enables human spirits to blaze in love too, by consuming in them what is ruined in self-willed loneliness and leaving the loveliness that is left in them to flourish in beauty which is like God's own. On the Marian interpretation, when, for the sake of making wrecked human beings beautiful again in union with God, Christ suffers and dies on the cross, when Christ lets the beauty of his human psyche be disfigured by the invading human evil, the consuming fire of the love of God is manifest.

In biblical texts, water is sometimes used as a symbol of chaos and confusion, of the absence of being, of nothingness. Genesis 1:1 describes the beginning of creation by saying that God's spirit moved on the face of the waters, the unformed void of nothing, when God's word brought forth light. Human evil is also a kind of chaotic, unformed nothing—a nothing in human nature where goodness ought to be, a chaos where peace might be. The whole earth is soaked with the tears of the suffering victims of human evil, who float as flotsam and jetsam in the wreck that human beings have made of themselves and their world. In the power generated by science and technology, human evil begins to dismantle even the order that made the earth a good place for beasts and humans, until it seems that the pandemonium and disorder evocatively described as water threaten to overrun the world.

Watching this looming catastrophe, some scientists have urged that human beings should try to find and colonize another suitable planet. In their view, the earth itself is dreadfully damaged, and so human beings should settle a different planet. But this attitude is reminiscent of the Brave New World slogan, "Ending is better than mending!" There is little love in abandoning what one has spoiled.

The Song of Songs therefore has a better watchword. It says, "Many waters cannot quench love" (Song 8:7). On the Marian interpretation, the atonement of Christ is the unquenchable love of God offered to all the suffering, the self-alienated, and the evil, so that in their own beauty they might be at peace with themselves and with others and at home in the love of God.

Notes

PREFACE

1. Mike Gale's beautifully done book documenting the thirty-year history of the St. Louis Jesuits is *The St. Louis Jesuits: Thirty Years* (Portland, OR: Oregon Catholic Press, 2006).
2. Dan Schutte is a member of the highly acclaimed St. Louis Jesuits, founded by Fr. John Foley, SJ, and he is in his own right a sought-after musician and composer of liturgical music. His website is http://www.danschutte.com/WordPressSite/.

CHAPTER 1

1. This is, of course, a very rough characterization of natural theology. For a more detailed consideration of the character of theology and its relation to reason, see my "Athens and Jerusalem: The Relationship of Philosophy and Theology," *Journal of Analytic Theology* 1.1 (2013): 45–59.
2. For a more detailed discussion of the nature of orthodoxy and its correlative notion of heresy, see my "Orthodoxy and Heresy," *Faith and Philosophy* 16 (1999): 487–503.
3. *Summa theologiae* (ST) I q.32 a.1 For translations of this work, I like and therefore have used the translations of the Fathers of the English Dominican Province. It has become standard, and in most cases I do not think I could improve on it substantially. But I freely emend it in those cases where I think I can do better. So the translations of Aquinas's *Summa theologiae* in this book are largely but not entirely the translations of the Fathers of the English Dominican Province. In what follows, I will cite the *Summa theologiae* by nothing more than the part, question, and article number. But a reference to the translation by the Fathers of the English Dominican Province should be assumed.
4. ST I q.32 a.1.
5. Eusebius Pamphili, *Ecclesiastical History*, translated by Roy J. Deferrari (New York: Fathers of the Church, 1953), 51–3.
6. See ST II–II q.174 a.6, q.176 a.1 ad 1; *In Eph.* I, lec. 3. I am grateful to Thomas Joseph White for these references.
7. John Newman, *An Essay on the Development of Christian Doctrine* (Notre Dame, IN: University of Notre Dame Press, 2017, reproduction of the 1845 edition).
8. For some discussion of the problems with Newman's criteria, see Mark McInroy, "Catholic Theological Receptions," in *The Oxford Handbook of John Henry Newman*, edited by Frederick D. Aquino and Benjamin J. King (Oxford: Clarendon Press, 2018). I am grateful to King for calling my attention to the literature critical of Newman's criteria and to this essay in particular.
9. Linda Radzik, *Making Amends: Atonement in Morality, Law, and Politics* (Oxford: Oxford University Press, 2009), 6.

10. In correspondence with Nicholas Lombardo, from whose excellent book *The Father's Will: Christ's Crucifixion and the Goodness of God* (Oxford: Oxford University Press, 2014) I have learned a lot, Lombardo has expressed to me a strong desire to eliminate the word 'atonement' from the vocabulary of the discussion of this doctrine, because of its connotations. But the word is established in this discussion, and my hope is that adopting this unusual typography will help call attention to the more broad and neutral sense of the word.

11. The point of the disjunction is to avoid adjudicating among complicated theological disputes not relevant to this discussion, at least not relevant to it at the outset. From this point on, to avoid the clumsy disjunction, I will speak only of the passion and death of Christ, but the whole disjunction should be understood. In Chapter 8, I will return to the subject of the details of Christ's life to discuss their place in the *at onement* on the interpretation of the doctrine I argue for in this book. Finally, it should be said that the resurrection of Christ is also part of the story of the *at onement*, and I had originally planned to include consideration of it in this book. But in the end considerations of space required leaving it for another project.

12. By 'salvation' in this context, I mean what Christ does in his life, passion, and death. The rest of this book is an attempt to explain that salvation.

13. See my *Aquinas* (London and New York: Routledge, 2003), ch. 14.

14. For some excellent recent work on the doctrine of the incarnation, see Timothy Pawl, *In Defense of Conciliar Christology: A Philosophical Essay* (Oxford: Oxford University Press, 2016); see also Pawl's "A Solution to the Fundamental Philosophical Problem of Christology," *The Journal of Analytic Theology* 2 (2014): 61–85; "The Freedom of Christ and Explanatory Priority," *Religious Studies* 50 (2014): 157–73; "The Freedom of Christ and the Problem of Deliberation," *International Journal for Philosophy of Religion* 75 (2014): 233–47; "Conciliar Christology and the Problem of Incompatible Predications," *Scientia et Fides* 3 (2015): 85–106; and "Temporary Intrinsics and Christological Predication," in *Oxford Studies in Philosophy of Religion*, vol. 7, edited by Jonathan Kvanvig (Oxford: Oxford University Press, 2016), 157–89.

15. I have discussed the doctrine of eternity extensively in other work. See, for example, my initial article on the subject, with Norman Kretzmann, "Eternity," *Journal of Philosophy* 78 (1981): 429–58; and, more recently, my "The Openness of God: Eternity and Free Will," in *Philosophical Essays Against Open Theism*, edited by Benjamin H. Arbour (New York: Routledge, 2018).

16. See my *The God of the Bible and the God of the Philosophers*, Aquinas Lecture (Marquette, WI: Marquette University Press, 2016); see also my "God's Simplicity," in *The Oxford Handbook of Aquinas*, edited by Brian Davies and Eleonore Stump (Oxford: Oxford University Press, 2012), 135–46.

17. Stump, *Aquinas*.

18. C.S. Lewis, *Mere Christianity* (New York: MacMillan, 1953), 43–4. I owe this reference to Rob MacSwain.

19. Or, as he puts it, incarnation and atonement. As I am using '*at onement*', it implies incarnation.

20. Alvin Plantinga, "Supralapsarianism, or 'O Felix Culpa,'" in *Christian Faith and the Problem of Evil*, edited by Peter van Inwagen (Grand Rapids, MI: Eerdmans, 2004), 10.

21. The defense or theodicy I myself favor I have explained and defended at length elsewhere; see my *Wandering in Darkness: Narrative and the Problem of Suffering* (Oxford: Oxford University Press, 2010). For some critical commentary on the theodicy Plantinga proposes in Plantinga (2004), see Marilyn McCord Adams, "Plantinga on 'Felix Culpa': Analysis and Critique," *Faith and Philosophy* 25 (2008): 123–39. I share some of her concerns about attempts at theodicy based largely or wholly on comparisons of the summed value of worlds.

22. The qualifier 'on Christian doctrine' is necessary, but it is clumsy to keep inserting it; so readers should take it as understood in the remainder of this text.

23. Of course, although this word is relatively new, the thing designated by the word is old. To take just one example, rituals of *at onement* figure prominently in the Hebrew Bible, as, for example, in the prescriptions for the Day of Atonement laid out in Leviticus.

24. I am using 'unity', 'oneness', and 'union' interchangeably in this connection to signify a state in which two things come to be intimately joined together without ceasing to be two things.

25. There were certainly Patristic philosophers and theologians who are outside the tradition I will presuppose in this book, in virtue of taking the absence of unity, the distance, between God and human beings as a function of some metaphysical difference between God and human beings. There is, of course, a great metaphysical difference between God and human beings, between creatures and the Creator. But some Patristic thinkers supposed that the problem for which the *at onement* is a solution is *primarily* or *only* the distance constituted by this metaphysical difference between the Creator and any of his creatures. So, for example, in the history of theological interpretation of the doctrine of the *at onement*, some thinkers focused on the fact that human beings are made out of matter and so are necessarily at a great distance from an immaterial God. Others emphasized the fact that human beings are finite, and their finitude makes them remote from an infinite God. (For some discussion of this history, see, for example, the classic treatment by Jaroslav Pelikan, *The Christian Tradition: A History of the Development of Doctrine*, vol. 1, *The Emergence of Catholic Doctrine (100–600)* (Chicago, IL: University of Chicago Press, 1971), especially the section "Systems of Cosmic Redemption," 81–96.)

    But whatever the variations on this theme, by the time of Augustine, this sort of interpretation of the doctrine had been rejected by the community considered to be the orthodox Christian church, and it was argued against strenuously by some of the influential thinkers who helped to formulate the versions of views that became standard Christian doctrine. There have of course been sophisticated contemporary theological accounts of the *at onement* that reject that emergent Patristic consensus in favor of some other view. For one contemporary example, see Marilyn McCord Adams, *Christ and Horrors* (Cambridge: Cambridge University Press, 2006). She explains the metaphysical distance between God and human beings in terms of the vulnerability to horrors that human beings have in virtue of being embodied in a world of relatively scarce resources, and she explains Christ's *at onement* as a matter of bridging that metaphysical distance. But I will leave to one side consideration of such interpretations of the doctrine. My project in this book is confined to the doctrine of the *at onement* as it came to be interpreted by orthodox philosophers and theologians of the Patristic period and subsequent tradition, on the sensible grounds that it is not possible to do everything in one book; the examination of the doctrine of the *at onement* so understood is enough for one volume.

26. Not all contemporary theologians are committed to this view of the nature of sin. For an alternative contemporary interpretation, see, for example, Marilyn McCord Adams, "Sin as Uncleanness," in *Philosophical Perspectives*, vol. 5, *Philosophy of Religion*, edited by James Tomberlin (Atascadero, CA: Ridgeview, 1991), 1–27. In what follows, I will confine the discussion to the position that has been central in the Christian tradition and is represented by Augustine's position, although I hope that in the discussion of shame in subsequent chapters some of what exercises Adams is addressed. I am grateful to the reading group at York for calling my attention to the need to make this point explicit.

27. Aquinas is not a divine command theorist; and so, for him, the metaphysical grounding of ethics lies in God's nature, not God's will. For him, moral wrong-doing will go contrary to both the nature and the will of God. For discussion of this issue, see my *Aquinas*, ch. 2. Since I am presupposing a Thomistic worldview here, in what follows I will understand sin as moral wrongdoing that goes contrary to God's will and nature.

28. For a discussion of the virtue ethics that is presupposed in this book, see my *Aquinas*, ch. 2, and also my "The Non-Aristotelian Character of Aquinas's Ethics: Aquinas on the Passions," *Faith and Philosophy* 28.1 (2011): 29–43.

29. For some discussion of these claims, see my *Wandering in Darkness*, ch. 13.

30. It is part of the theological story of the Fall that it left human beings with original sin, and that the sacrament of baptism is a remedy for this part of the post-Fall human condition. Without doubt, there is a connection between Christ's *at onement* and original sin and baptism. But it is not possible to consider everything in one book, even one big book, and so this part of the story has to be left to one side. It is sufficient for my purposes here that human beings have a proneness to moral wrongdoing and that, on orthodox Christian doctrine, God is not responsible for this proneness. What the sacrament of baptism contributes to the story of salvation is just outside the scope of this book.

31. In the early Christian period, some thinkers supposed that the defect lies primarily in the human intellect. From the point of view of some writers such as Justin Martyr, for example, human beings sin because they lack appropriate knowledge; but Christ is the true teacher, the complete philosopher. On views such as this, the defect that is the source of the human tendency to sin is fundamentally ignorance; and the faculty in which the defect lies is the intellect. Consequently, the remedy for the defect is correct or complete teaching, especially moral teaching, which provides the knowledge lacking to human beings left to themselves. On this interpretation of the doctrine of the *at onement*, Christ provides the remedy for the human tendency to sin by being in his life and death the ultimate teacher of ethics and the perfect exemplar of moral behavior. Sometimes, on views such as these, the saving knowledge is thought of as hidden and available only to the

initiate. So, for example, some Christian versions of Gnosticism supposed that salvation from the problem afflicting human beings lies primarily in Christ's providing an esoteric, rather than simply ethical, knowledge. Nonetheless, well before the time of Augustine, Gnosticism, or any other form of the view that took the source of sin to be primarily in the intellect, had been rejected by the Christian community. In taking a defect in the will to be the primary source of the human tendency to sin, Augustine represents what had come to be the orthodox view by his time. For a helpful summary of the history at issue here, see, for example, Pelikan, *The Christian Tradition*; for discussion of Justin Martyr, see especially pp. 141–55.

32. For some discussion of the relations between intellect and will, see my *Aquinas*, ch. 9.
33. I do not mean that a person with a disposition to a particular sin is guilty of that sin just in virtue of having the disposition. I mean only that there is something contrary to the moral good, and to God's will and nature, in the character of such a person. A man with a disposition to beat his wife is not guilty of beating her just in virtue of having such a disposition; but his having such a disposition is a feature of his character that is morally lamentable. We can assess character as well as actions; a person's character can also be the subject of positive or negative moral appraisal. It does not follow that a person is invariably morally responsible for having the character he does. He might be, or he might not be. It also does not follow that if his character is subject to a negative moral appraisal, he himself is subject to a negative moral appraisal or is deserving of punishment for his character. He himself might be deserving of compassion, for example, rather than punishment, if circumstances external to him are responsible in part or in whole for his having the character trait in question. But it remains the case that a person's having a sinful disposition is something that is contrary to God's will and nature, and so having a sinful disposition is itself sinful in this respect and to this extent.
34. Aquinas takes a person in such a condition to be exemplifying the vice opposed to wisdom, namely, folly. For a discussion of folly as self-deception, see my *Aquinas*, ch. 11.
35. I hope it goes without saying that this claim is not the same as and does not imply the clearly false and deplorable claim that anxiety and depression are sinful. The psychological results of being in a certain state are not the same as that state. It follows that not everything contrary to the will of God is sinful. This is a position that Aquinas explicitly maintains; see Chapter 6 for further discussion of the issue. I am grateful to Jonathan Rutledge for calling my attention to the need to make this point explicit.
36. For a more detailed argument for this claim, see my *Wandering in Darkness*, ch. 6.
37. The doctrine of the immaculate conception of Mary makes Mary another exception. The doctrine of the immaculate conception was not codified as doctrine until some centuries after Aquinas's time. Since in this book I am taking the philosophical and theological worldview of Aquinas as general background, I am relegating the issue as regards the immaculate conception of Mary to the notes. In everything that follows, readers should understand that for those who accept the doctrine of the immaculate conception of Mary, Mary is another exception to the

claims about the sinfulness of post-Fall human beings. I am grateful to Andrew Pinsent for calling my attention to the need to underline this issue.

38. Some readers will feel that it is inappropriate to speak of God as a person. But on orthodox Christian theology there is one mind and one will in God; and, given our ordinary parlance, this claim is enough for us to consider God a person. Other readers will feel that the doctrine of simplicity makes it inappropriate to speak of God as an entity of any kind. In my view, such readers have misunderstood the implications of the doctrine of simplicity. For an argument to this effect, see, for example, my *The God of the Bible and the God of the Philosophers*.

39. In Chapter 7, I discuss the way in which a person in grace, even with continuing sinful dispositions, can nonetheless have nascent or incipient union with God. Nonetheless, complete union is possible only in the afterlife in heaven, because only then are all sinful dispositions totally removed.

40. Or with the exception of the incarnate Christ and the Virgin Mary. This caveat should be understood throughout in what follows.

41. With this claim, I do not mean to imply that it is not possible for a human being below the age of reason to sin. I mean only to sidestep the issue of whether it is possible for children below the age of reason to sin. For my purposes in this book, it is not necessary to sort this issue out.

42. I will have much more to say about guilt and forgiveness and related concepts in the following chapters. But see also my *Wandering in Darkness*, ch. 5 and my "Personal Relations and Moral Residue," *History of the Human Sciences* 17.2/3 (2004): 33–57.

43. For a different categorization of the basic kinds of interpretation, see Lombardo, *The Father's Will*, 12ff. Lombardo takes as one of his basic kinds of interpretation of the doctrine of the *at onement* that formulated by Abelard. But, in my view, Abelard's account of *at onement* does not have the standing in the history of thought about *at onement* that warrants taking it as one of the basic approaches to the doctrine. For Lombardo's own reasons for rejecting Abelard's account, see pp. 178–9 of his book.

44. There is a large literature on Patristic theories of the *at onement*. For a helpful survey, see, for example, Junius Johnson, *Patristic and Medieval Atonement Theory* (New York: Rowman and Littlefield, 2016) and Lombardo, *The Father's Will*. As Lombardo maintains, the Patristic theories differ from one another in various respects; nonetheless they form a clear family of interpretations with converging characteristics (pp. 186ff.).

45. The point of Lombardo's book is to resurrect the Patristic theories and show their acceptability as one kind of interpretation of the doctrine of the *at onement*. I appreciate Lombardo's arguments on this score, and I share his conviction that the Patristic theories are worth attention; but I am not persuaded that he has succeeded in his project.

46. I am grateful to Ingolf Dalferth for calling my attention to the need to make this point explicit.

47. See Anselm, *Cur Deus homo* (CDH), c.7. I have liked and therefore, unless otherwise indicated, have used the translation in *Anselm of Canterbury: The Major Works*,

translated by Brian Davies and G.R. Evans (Oxford: Oxford University Press, 1998). In CDH, Anselm lays out what he takes to be the argument for this Patristic interpretation of the *at onement* and concludes by confessing himself unable to find anything cogent in the argument for that interpretation.

48. Aquinas himself appears to accept at least some part of the Patristic interpretation (see ST III q.49 a.2). But, in discussing this interpretation in his commentary on Romans 8, Aquinas gives it short shrift, explaining that there are other interpretations that are better; cf. *Commentary on Romans*, c.8, l. For a good translation of this text, see Aquinas, *Commentary on the Letter of St. Paul to the Romans*, translated by F.R. Larcher, edited by J. Mortensen and E. Alarcón (Lander, WY: The Aquinas Institute for the Study of Sacred Doctrine, 2012). The Thomistic Institute has translated all Aquinas's biblical commentaries. I have liked and therefore have used their translations of these commentaries throughout this book, but I have felt free to emend them on those few occasions when I thought I could do better. Where I have also consulted another translation of a biblical commentary, I will indicate that other translation in the notes.

49. See, for example, Lombardo, *The Father's Will*.

50. At least some Anglicans can be found arguing against the first, Anselmian kind of interpretation. So, for example, R.C. Moberly says, "no theories of Atonement which try to explain the whole meaning of it as a transaction completed . . . can state, with any adequacy, that aspect of the truth to which the consciousness of the present day is most keenly . . . alive. It can hardly be denied that a fallacy of this sort is discernible . . . through every line of the elaborate treatise of Anselm, which . . . reduces everything to a strictly mathematical calculation, of the equation kind" (*Atonement and Personality* (London: John Murray, 1924), 218). For accounts of *at onement* that are in the Calvinist tradition but that also seem to include elements of the Thomistic kind of interpretation, see, for example, Alan J. Torrance, "The Theological Grounds for Advocating Forgiveness and Reconciliation in the Socio-political Realm," in *The Politics of Past Evil: Religion, Reconciliation, and the Dilemmas of Transitional Justice*, edited by Daniel Philpott (Notre Dame, IN: University of Notre Dame Press, 2005); and J. McLeod Campbell, *The Nature of Atonement*, with a new introduction by James B. Torrance (Grand Rapids, MI: Eerdmans, 1996).

51. Both Luther and Calvin talk at length about God's grace given for the regeneration and the sanctification of human beings; for that matter, so does Anselm. For Anselm, at least, the subject of God's giving of grace seems not clearly or directly connected to the passion and death of Christ, however. For him, as also for the Reformers, the main or even the whole good for human beings brought about by Christ's passion and death has to do with Christ's paying the debt or the penalty owed to God in justice by sinful human beings. But see the discussion in Chapter 11 of Calvin's commentary on Romans for some idea of the complications here.

52. Anselm, Luther, and Calvin all see the need for some kind of alteration in the nature of the human will or mind, too, and they all suppose it to be effected in part or in whole through divine grace. But in their discussions of the effects of Christ's passion and death, the emphasis is the difference that the *at onement* makes to

God, rather than the effects of Christ's passion and death on human wills or psyches.

53. For that matter, there are some texts where Aquinas seems to be accepting elements of the kind of theory represented by the Reformers' interpretations, too. See, for example, the discussion of Christ's passion as paying the debt of punishment at ST III q.49 a.1. In his commentary on Romans, however, Aquinas gives an explanation of paying the debt of punishment as a matter of altering human sinfulness; the debt of punishment is canceled when the cause for punishment is removed. See Chapter 11 for more discussion of Aquinas's commentary on Romans.

54. This seems to be the version of the Anselmian account that Richard Swinburne favors. See Chapter 3 for further discussion of Swinburne's views.

55. The order of repayment and the acceptance of reconciliation is a logical and not a temporal order. That is, God's acceptance of reconciliation with human beings is logically dependent on Christ's repayment of what is owed to God, but it does not come after that repayment in any temporal sequence. For more discussion of this issue and its importance for evaluating the Anselmian kind of interpretation, see Chapter 3.

56. Anselm, *Basic Writings: Cur Deus Homo*, edited and translated by Thomas Williams (Indianapolis, IN: Hackett Publishing Co., 2007), 278.

57. For ease of diction, I will omit the caveat 'or something else along these lines' from the subsequent discussion, but it should be understood throughout. In the history of this kind of interpretation of the doctrine of the *at onement*, there are subtle variations on the general theme that do not make a difference to the points under consideration here. One particular variant on the Anselmian kind of interpretation is given by Richard Swinburne in his *Responsibility and Atonement* (Oxford: Oxford University Press, 1989). There Swinburne argues that Christ's passion and death serve as a kind of penance that human beings can offer to God in addition to their own repentance and apology to God. In my view, the limitations of the Anselmian kind inhere also in Swinburne's variant. For a detailed discussion of Swinburne's position, see my review of his book in *Faith and Philosophy* 11 (1994): 321–8; and my "Love and Forgiveness: Swinburne on Atonement," in *Reason and Faith: Themes from Richard Swinburne*, edited by Michael Bergmann and Jeffrey E. Brower (New York: Oxford University Press, 2016), 148–70. Parts of that paper are incorporated in Chapter 3 of this book. Michael Rea has also called to my attention a variant sometimes called 'the Mafia theory' of the *at onement*. On this theory, Christ does God the Father a favor by living a life of perfect obedience, so that God the Father owes Christ a reward; and Christ claims as his reward God's remitting the debt human beings owe to God. Even a variant such as this one seems to me to fall still within the Anselmian kind of interpretation.

58. Anselm, *Basic Writings: Cur Deus Homo*, 348.

59. Cf., e.g., Thomas Aquinas, *Super ad Hebraeos*, c.12, 2.

60. See, for example, Aquinas, *Expositio super Job*, ch. 9, sects. 24–30. See also Thomas Aquinas, *The Literal Exposition on Job: A Scriptural Commentary concerning*

Providence, translated by Anthony Damico and Martin Yaffe (Atlanta, GA: Scholars Press, 1989), 179.

61. Both Aquinas's account and his terminology are more complicated than can be presented in the short space here. The presentation of justification and sanctification that follows, and the very terms themselves, are my own abbreviation of Aquinas's own position and terminology. For a fuller exposition of Aquinas's views on this score, see my *Aquinas*, chs. 12 and 13, on faith and grace, and Chapter 7 in this volume.

62. For detailed discussion and defense of these claims, see Chapter 7.

63. ST III q.48 a.1.

64. Even on the so-called 'Mafia theory' (see note 57 above), God receives at least the equivalent of what was owed him in the human debt, so that even on this theory God does not forego what is due him.

65. For discussion of still further problems internal to this interpretation, see my *Aquinas*, ch. 15.

66. The proponent of the Anselmian interpretation may try to counter these objections by altering the interpretation, so that the debt or penalty Christ pays for human beings is only death and suffering. But this rejoinder is inefficacious for two reasons. First, on orthodox Christian doctrine, the debt or punishment for sin is not just suffering and death but damnation, so that this alteration of the interpretation has the infelicitous result that what Christ undergoes is not the debt or penalty owed for human sin. Secondly, even with this alteration, Christ's suffering and death still do not remove the debt or penalty from human beings, since suffering and death come to all human beings anyway. For a discussion of Calvin's interpretation of Christ's suffering, see Chapter 5 of this book. Even on Calvin's version of the Anselmian interpretation, the most Christ suffered is a small time in hell or the equivalent to a small time in hell; and this is definitely not the same as damnation, which is everlasting.

67. Calvin's interpretation of the *at onement* is an exception here, since (at least on one common understanding of Calvin's interpretation) for Calvin Christ's *at onement* is limited, not universal or for all people. In fact, on one understanding of Calvin's position, the *at onement* is limited to providing salvation only for those people predestined to be saved, because God would be inflicting punishment for sins twice if Christ suffered the penalty for the sins of those people who themselves suffered that penalty for their sins in hell. This argument for limited *at onement* seems to me another reason for rejecting the penal substitution variant on the Anselmian kind of interpretation.

68. Unwarranted qua debt or penalty at any rate. It could always be warranted on utilitarian or consequentialist grounds having to do with the welfare of the state.

69. I say '*seeming* to solve' because, in Chapter 10, I will raise issues implying that the Thomistic emphasis on grace for the sinner in fact cannot solve completely the backward-looking problem of guilt either.

70. In saying so much, I am giving a vastly oversimplified description of a process that has to be as complicated as the human psyche is. An example of a more complicated, but still really simple case is Augustine's famous prayer for celibacy, which (in Augustine's view of it) came to this: "Please, God, give me celibacy, but not

yet." If Paula both asks and rejects the strengthening of her will, as Augustine does in this example, then God cannot give her what she is asking for, on pain of violating her will by forcing on it what she herself does not want to have as her will.

71. In helping Paula to integrate her first-order and second-order desires God does not undermine Paula's free will. Instead, he enhances or evokes it. That is because Paula's own will brings it about that she has the first-order volition she does, not in the sense that it is the strength or even the agency of Paula's will that produces the desired first-order volition in her, but rather in the sense that unless Paula had desired that God do so, God would not have acted on her will in this way. So if Paula's second-order will had been different, her first-order volition would have been different also. God operates on Paula's will to enable Paula to have the will she herself wants to have.

72. Someone might suppose that, if this position were right, then, with one act of higher-order will, a human person could achieve, all at once, a full integration of her will around moral goodness, if she would only desire that God unify her will in this way. But this supposition fails to take account of the reality of human psychology. Sanctification is generally a lengthy process just because, typically, a human person's will is recurrently liable to internal division. Furthermore, even a particular higher-order desire for help in willing some one particular good can be wavering.

73. This is a culmination that occurs after death, on Christian doctrine.

74. I will discuss the nature of this second-order will in detail in Chapter 7.

75. For discussion of justification, see Chapter 3, where I will call attention to alternative accounts of justification, and Chapter 7, where I will discuss what is distinctive about Aquinas's account in more detail.

76. The phrase 'moral and spiritual' is my attempt to find some brief way of indicating that the regeneration in question has to do not only with intrinsic qualities of a human person but also with that person's closeness to God and second-personal connection to God.

77. The contention over the right way to understand this doctrine, or even the right way to understand Aquinas's understanding of this doctrine, has prompted not only books but pitched political battles. Elsewhere I have defended a particular interpretation of the doctrine and Aquinas's construal of it; in this context, unfortunately, it is possible to give only the briefest summary of that interpretation. For more detailed discussion, see my *Aquinas*, chs. 12 and 13.

78. Because of Aquinas's commitment to a tight interconnection between the faculties of intellect and will, on his account the will of faith is necessarily accompanied by the beliefs of faith, which include the belief that God will give help if the help is not refused. But I mention the matter of the state of the intellect only to set it to one side. For my purposes in this project, the salient thing is the condition of the will in justification.

79. ST I–II q.113 a.5; cf. also I–II q.113 a.6–7. A person does not have to remember and detest each sin he has ever committed in order to be justified, Aquinas says; rather he has to detest those sins of which he is conscious and be disposed to detest any other sin of his if he should remember it.

80. It has seemed hard to many people, even those who are generally in the Thomist camp, to see how God can be thought to bring about a second-order volition in a

human will by operative grace without taking away the freedom of the will. If the operative grace of God which is introduced into the will is what makes the will inclined to the good, then it seems as if God has determined the human will. On incompatibilist views of freedom, it can appear as if the will's freedom is thereby undermined or destroyed. I myself have addressed this problem and tried to find a solution to it in my *Aquinas*, ch. 13.

81. For a defense of this claim, see my *Aquinas*, ch. 13. It is important to note that the global second-order desire of the faith which justifies a person is compatible with any amount of first-order willing of particular evils, provided that that first-order willing does not destroy the second-order desire of faith. It is possible, in other words, for a person to have a second-order desire for a will that wills the good and also to reject a particular reform that he sees as morally needed but that he finds himself unable to accept at a particular time. This condition is, of course, one way of being divided against oneself.

82. ST III q.46 a.2 ad 3.

83. Elsewhere I have argued that there are two different senses of the self, a metaphysical and a psychological sense. Someone who is one and the same metaphysical self can become a new self in the psychological sense of self. See my *Wandering in Darkness*, ch. 7.

84. I put the point about Speer in this hedged way because there is evidence to suggest that Speer in fact was not repentant but only prudent about building a new life for himself in the postwar world. For discussion of the details of the case, see my *Wandering in Darkness*, 577, n.69.

85. For some discussion of the appropriateness of punishment even for the repentant, see Chapter 3.

86. Insofar as Speer accepted willingly all these elements of his postwar life, they do not constitute punishment for him. However exactly punishment is to be understood, it has to be something that goes against the will of the person being punished. If it is something he himself wills to have in his life, then it loses something of the character of punishment. (On some models of hell, such as Dante's, for example, those in hell in some sense will to have what they get in hell; but this claim does not undermine the claim that punishment is always against the will of the person punished. On Dante's model of hell, those in hell are divided in will, so that they will and also will against the same thing. For that reason, their punishment is both in accordance with their wills and also against their wills. I am grateful to Kimberley Kroll for calling my attention to the need to address this point.)

87. In Chapter 10, I will nuance this conclusion in ways that highlight the need for something more than these elements in Aquinas's account can give.

88. For a more detailed and complicated assessment of the problem of shame and the Thomistic account, see Chapter 2 of this book.

89. ST III q.46 a.2.

90. See my *Wandering in Darkness*, ch. 13 for a defense of the claim that allowing suffering is justified only if the benefit brought about by the suffering goes primarily to the sufferer. But the point in the text holds even if the benefit brought about by the suffering goes primarily to humanity as a whole, provided that the

benefit in question constitutes something that is or is necessary for the ultimate good for human beings.

91. And I myself do not think that he is; for my reasons for rejecting his position, see my *Wandering in Darkness*, ch. 13.
92. Other than that of Christ, of course.
93. See Matt. 27:46 and Mark 15:34.
94. Cf., e.g., ST III q.46 a.8.
95. Cf., e.g., Calvin, *Institutes of the Christian Religion*, Bk. II, c.XVI.
96. See, e.g., ST II–II q.2 a.7 ad 3. C.S. Lewis is responsible for making this idea widely known with the depiction in his Narnia stories of a man who took himself to be a worshipper of the god Tash when in fact it was actually the true God Aslan whom the man worshipped without realizing that he did so.
97. For a strong defense of this position, see Kathryn Tanner, *Christ the Key* (Cambridge: Cambridge University Press, 2010).
98. For a recent discussion of *at onement* in connection with sacrifice, see Sarah Coakley, *Sacrifice: Defunct or Desired?* (Charlottesville, VA: University of Virginia Press, 2018).

CHAPTER 2

1. For explanation and defense of Aquinas's account, see my *Aquinas* (London and New York: Routledge, 2003), chs. 2, 9, and 10, and my *Wandering in Darkness: Narrative and the Problem of Suffering* (Oxford: Oxford University Press, 2010), ch. 13.
2. For a defense of this claim, see my "The Non-Aristotelian Character of Aquinas's Ethics: Aquinas on the Passions," *Faith and Philosophy* 28.1 (2011): 29–43.
3. Since I have done what I could in Chapter 1 to highlight the sense of the word I am assuming in this book by writing the word as '*at onement*', in the subsequent chapters I will return to the ordinary typography for the word.
4. Much, but not all, of what is in this chapter can be found discussed in more detail elsewhere in my earlier work. Here I have tried to pull together elements from different books and articles to make a summary useful for the rest of the book, so that I do not need to rely on readers to be familiar with all that earlier work. For those familiar with the earlier work, the new material in this chapter will be apparent.
5. For a more detailed examination of Aquinas's account of love, see my *Wandering in Darkness*, ch. 5. This section includes parts taken from that chapter.
6. Aquinas uses four words for love; in Latin, they are '*amor*', '*dilectio*', '*amicitia*', and '*caritas*.' (Cf., ST I–II q.26 a.3.) The first of these is love in its most generic sense, which is included in all the other kinds; for Aquinas, even a rock falling from a higher to a lower place can be said to have love for the place to which it falls, in this generic sense of 'love.' (Cf., ST I–II q.26 a.1.) The second, '*dilectio*', emphasizes the element of voluntariness in the love of rational persons; and the third, '*amicitia*', picks out the dispositions of love in friendship. But, for Aquinas, the fourth, '*caritas*', is the word for love in its real or complete sense. Since Aquinas privileges *caritas* in this way, I will focus on *caritas* in explaining his account of love,

although I will understand his views of *caritas* in light of what he says about the more generic *amor*.

7. See, e.g., ST II–II q.25 a.3.

8. See, e.g., ST I–II q.26 a.4, where Aquinas says that to love is to will good to someone. Cf. also ST I–II q.28 a.4, where Aquinas explains the zeal or intensity of love in terms of the strength of a lover's desire for the good of the beloved.

9. See, e.g., ST I–II q.26 a.2 ad 2, and q.28 a.1 sc., where Aquinas quotes approvingly Dionysius's line that love is the unitive force. Cf. also ST I–II q.66 a.6, where Aquinas explains the superiority of charity to the other virtues by saying that every lover is drawn by desire to union with the beloved, and ST I–II q.70 a.3, where Aquinas explains the connection between joy and love by saying that every lover rejoices at being united to the beloved. For an interesting recent attempt to defend a position that has some resemblance to Aquinas's, see Robert Adams, "Pure Love," *Journal of Religious Ethics* 8 (1980): 83–99. Adams says: "It is a striking fact that while benevolence (the desire for another person's well-being) and *Eros*, as a desire for relationship with another person, seem to be quite distinct desires, we use a single name, 'love' or '*Agape*', for an attitude that includes both of them, at least in typical cases" (p. 97).

10. There are many other details of Aquinas's account of love that are important but that cannot be explored in passing here. For a fuller treatment, see my *Wandering in Darkness*, ch. 5.

11. If there is a relationship between persons in which it is not appropriate for one person to desire the good for and union with the other, then the relationship is not a relationship of love. Insofar as it is possible to have a general love of humankind, however, then there is no connection between persons which is not also in effect a relationship for which some species of love is appropriate.

12. See, for example, ST II–II q.26 a.6–12.

13. For a discussion of the offices of love, see my *Wandering in Darkness*, ch. 5.

14. See, for example, David Velleman, "Love as a Moral Emotion," *Ethics* 109 (1999): 338–74 (p. 353).

15. The claim that the good desired for the beloved is an objective good therefore results from Aquinas's analysis of the nature of love together with his meta-ethics. It is not itself implied by Aquinas's analysis of love. I am grateful to Ish Haji for calling my attention to the need to make this point clear.

16. In my view, one important difference between Christianity and ancient Greek worldviews lies in this standard of value. By way of illustration, there is among the sayings on the oracle of Delphi the exhortation "Know thyself." But for a view such as Aquinas's, the enterprise of trying to know yourself is likely to be marked more by self-deception and isolation than by anything that could count as success even at self-knowledge. It is better, and also more likely to be successful for self-knowledge, to try to know others, God most specially, and to be known by others in return. The African proverb that a person is a person through other persons is more nearly like Aquinas's view than is the Delphic saying. (For the proverb, see M.K. Asante and A. Mazama (eds.), *Encyclopedia of African Religions* (Thousand Oaks, CA: Sage Publications, 2009), 143. I am indebted to Monica Green for the proverb and the reference.)

17. In the history of Christian theological and philosophical reflection, the relevant analogue to the word 'person' is an equivocal term. On the doctrine of the Trinity, there are three persons in one God, and a person of the Trinity is a subsistent relation. In addition, on the well-known Boethian formula, a person is an individual substance of a rational nature. Neither of these senses of the word 'person' or its Latin or Greek analogue is what we mean with our ordinary use of the word 'person.' For us, anything that has one mind and one will of sufficient complexity counts as a person. On traditional Christian doctrine, there is just one will and one intellect in God, and they are sufficiently complex for God to count as a person in our sense of 'person.' Consequently, it is true to say that for Aquinas God is a person in our sense of that word.

     Clearly, the technical sense of 'person' as it is used in the doctrine of the Trinity and the Boethian formula for 'person' are both compatible with the claim that God is a person, in our sense of the word 'person.' Nothing about the claim that God has a mind and a will of the requisite complexity rules out there being three persons in God, in the Trinitarian sense of 'person', or invalidates the Boethian formula for a person, applied as Boethius meant to apply it.

     The contemporary sense of the word 'person' makes 'person' a functional term. That is because on this sense the word 'person' does not pick out any particular genus or quiddity that a thing must have in order to be a person. For this reason, considered as persons in our ordinary sense of the word, God and a human being can share no quiddity, can fail to belong to any common genus, however abstract; and it can still be true that God and a human being are both persons, in this sense of the term.

18. The correlation between goodness and being that Aquinas accepts also provides a metaphysical foundation for this view of his. For this part of Aquinas's theory of value, see my *Aquinas*, ch. 2.

19. I do not mean to say that in desiring union with God a person desires deification. One can desire something under multiple descriptions, and one might even desire something under a mistaken description. A person's desires need not be transparent to that person. For further discussion of this point about the nature of desire, see my *Wandering in Darkness*, ch. 5.

20. For a discussion of the notion of deification in the history of Christian thought, see David Meconi and Carl E. Olson (eds.), *Called to be the Children of God: The Catholic Theology of Human Deification* (San Francisco, CA: Ignatius Press, 2016); see especially the excellent essay "No Longer a Christian but Christ: Saint Augustine on Becoming Divine," by Meconi in that volume, pp. 82–100.

21. Because of the connection he accepts between the intellect and the will, Aquinas thinks that there is no major change of heart possible after a person has his first experience of the afterlife and sees whatever of God he can see. For further explanation of Aquinas's moral psychology, see my *Aquinas*, chs. 9 and 11.

22. It is for these reasons that it is a mistake to try to find a boundary line in the continuum of goodness that separates those allowed into heaven from those relegated to hell. (See, for example, Ted Sider, "Hell and Vagueness," *Faith and Philosophy* 19 (2002): 58–68.) Those in heaven are not those whose lives have summed to a certain degree of goodness on the continuum. They are those who at

the time of death have the desires of love for God. This condition is not degreed, as Sider's argument supposes, but all-or-nothing. Finally, someone might wonder where the notions of purgatory and Limbo fit in this picture. But it is not necessary to address either notion in detail here since, as traditionally understood, Limbo is part of hell and purgatory is part of heaven.

23. In my view, it would be possible to retain the basic Thomistic views I sketch in this chapter as well as the interpretation of the atonement that I argue for below and reject the doctrine of hell in favor of some other view regarding those who permanently reject God. But it is not similarly possible to reject the doctrine of heaven. For some discussion of the issues involved in these claims, see my *Wandering in Darkness*, ch. 13.

24. On the doctrine of simplicity, which Aquinas accepts, God is both goodness itself and also a good being. For explanation and some defense of this claim, see my *The God of the Bible and the God of the Philosophers, Aquinas Lecture* (Marquette, WI: Marquette University Press, 2016).

25. I am grateful to John Cottingham and Ish Haji for making me aware of the need for a distinction here, and I am grateful to Robert Audi and John Foley for helping me see how to draw the needed distinction.

26. By 'final good' here, I mean the good for the sake of which all other goods are desirable. I do not mean to imply that this final good is the only good or that all other goods are only apparent goods.

27. Union with God will also join them with all the human persons who, in their own true good, are united with God, so that shared union with God is inclusive.

28. And, of course, in the case of self-love, the lover and the beloved can be the same person.

29. Cf., e.g., ST II–II q.28 a.1.

30. To say that it is obligatory is not to say that anyone has a right to be loved. For more discussion of this claim, see Chapter 3; see also my "God's Obligations," in *Philosophical Perspectives*, vol. 6, *Ethics*, edited by James Tomberlin (Atascadero, CA: Ridgeview, 1992), 475–91.

31. See, for example, ST I q.20 a.2.

32. If Pelagianism is understood as the position that there can be something good in a human person which is *not* a gift of God's, then Aquinas is resolutely, vehemently anti-Pelagian. For further discussion of these elements of Aquinas's philosophical theology, see my *Aquinas*, chs. 12 and 13.

33. As I explained in Chapter 1, I will use 'sin' and 'moral wrongdoing' interchangeably in this book, for the reasons I gave in that chapter.

34. There are currently many excellent studies of the nature of shame and its effects on human life. For one recent and broad-ranging discussion of shame, see Julien Deonna, Raffaele Rodogno, and Fabrice Teroni, *In Defense of Shame: The Faces of an Emotion* (Oxford: Oxford University Press, 2012).

35. In connection with the problem of evil, Marilyn McCord Adams has emphasized the importance of what she calls 'the devaluation' of human beings. Contrasting her own approach to the problem of evil with that of other analytic philosophers, she says that they emphasize human free will and so focus on "what humans *do*," whereas her approach to the problem highlights "a metaphysical devaluation of

humankind in relation to Divinity, and so in what both God and humans *are*." She goes on to identify this devaluation as a kind of defilement, in ways which make clear that at least some kinds of shame are at issue for her. (See Marilyn McCord Adams, *Horrendous Evils and the Goodness of God* (Ithaca, NY: Cornell University Press, 1999), esp. pp. 86 and 124.)

36. See my *Wandering in Darkness*, ch. 7. I am altering that earlier account slightly here.

37. Since for the shamed person the desire of love at risk is the desire on the part of others for *him*, it is easy to see why shame has been understood as a negative reaction to what a person is, rather than to what he does. The objection to this same understanding of shame is consequently also easy to grasp. On the view of shame I am arguing for here, it is not hard to understand why a person could feel shame over what he has done. Jerome may do some action such that Paula turns away from him and repudiates any desire for him. In that case, Jerome is shamed because of an action of his. And yet the shame is focused on his whole self, rather than on the action giving rise to Paula's rejection of him. That is because what Paula loses because of Jerome's action, and what Jerome wants her not to lose, is a desire for *him*. Consequently, there is something right both about the view linking shame and the whole person and about the objection to that view.

38. In a limiting case, a person Jerome might feel guilty when the only real or imagined person angry at Jerome is Jerome himself.

39. Of course, depending on one's theory of punishment, it might be the case that anything which counts as appropriate punishment is actually for the good of the person punished. I will discuss punishment in more detail in Chapter 3.

40. Perhaps the most famous case of someone anxious about rejection by a person he knows not to be among the living is Dante. As Dante writes the reunion between him and Beatrice in his *Purgatorio*, it opens with Beatrice (who was dead long before Dante wrote these lines) excoriating Dante mercilessly for his faults. Even an entirely imaginary character can serve the same role. A person who never knew his father or anything about his father might have imagined a father for himself, and he could come to feel shamed in the eyes of this imaginary father.

41. These claims about what a guilty person or a shamed person Jerome anticipates may seem to imply that people who react as Jerome anticipates that they will react are people who lack love for Jerome, in consequence of failing to have one of the two desires of love for Jerome. But drawing this conclusion from these claims would be an invalid inference. For the reasons why the inference is invalid, see the distinction between the anger and hatred that are opposed to love and the anger and hatred that are part of love in Chapter 3.

42. There has been some discussion about whether aesthetic standards might trump moral standards, at least on some occasions; so, for example, some people are tempted to suppose that a person's betrayal of his family's trust in him might be justified if it conduces to his doing great works of art. But that this supposition is mistaken is highlighted by the general consensus in discussions of the problem of evil that considerations of aesthetics could never justify God in violating ordinary moral considerations in his treatment of human beings.

43. For further discussion of the nature of suffering, see Chapter 6.

44. I am generally in sympathy with the views of shame expressed from a different perspective by Matthew Rukgaber, in his helpful paper, "Philosophical Anthropology, Shame, and Disability," *Res Philosophica* 93 (2016): 743–66.
45. For the details, see my *Aquinas*, especially chs. 8, 9, and 11.
46. For a detailed discussion of Aquinas's account of the human intellect, see my *Aquinas*, ch. 8. Perception, as we currently think of it, is part of intellectual functioning for Aquinas; faculties below the level of intellect are sensory rather than intellective.
47. See, for example, ST I–II q.10 a.1 and I q.82 a.1.
48. See ST I q.5 a.6, where Aquinas distinguishes the good into the virtuous, the useful, and the pleasant. To say that the will is a hunger for goodness therefore does not mean that the will always desires the *moral* good. Rather, it means only that the intellect finds a way to present to the will as a good of some kind or other whatever it is that the will then wills.
49. For this reason, the intellect is said to move the will not as an efficient cause but as a final cause, because its presenting something as good moves the will as an end moves an appetite. See, for example, ST I q.82 a.4.
50. For discussion and defense of this interpretation of Aquinas's views, see my *Aquinas*, chs. 9 and 13.
51. Although faith is divinely infused, according to Aquinas, he also supposes that faith results from such an action of the will on the intellect. See, for example, Aquinas's *Quaestiones disputatae de veritate* (QDV) where Aquinas talks of the will's commanding intellect to produce faith; QDV 14.3 reply, ad 2, and ad 10. For further discussion of this issue, see my *Aquinas*, ch. 12.
52. See ST I–II q.17 a.1 and 6. For further discussion of Aquinas's account of the will's control over the intellect, see my *Aquinas*, ch. 11.
53. If the intellect does present something to the will as good, then, because the will is an appetite for the good, the will wills it—unless the will directs intellect to reconsider, to direct its attention to something else, or to stop considering the matter at hand. The will's doing this is, of course, a result of the intellect's presenting such actions on the part of the will as good, and such an act on the part of the intellect may itself be a result of previous acts on the part of the will directing the attention of the intellect. For this reason, although Aquinas's account of the will assigns a large role to intellect, he is not committed to seeing morally wrong actions simply as instances of mistakes in deliberation, since the intellect's deliberations are also influenced by the will.

    In cases of incontinence, where the intellect seems to be representing something as good which the will isn't willing, Aquinas would say that the intellect, influenced by the will, is in fact being moved by opposed desires to represent the thing in question as both good (under one description) and not good (under a different description), so that the intellect is double-minded. In the last analysis, what the intellect of the incontinent person represents as the best alternative in these circumstances at this time is not that which the agent takes to be the good considered unconditionally or in the abstract. Cf., e.g., ST I–II q.17 a.2 and a.5 ad 1.
54. See, for example, Bettina Stangneth, *Eichmann Before Jerusalem: The Unexamined Life of a Mass Murderer*, translated by Ruth Martin (New York: Knopf, 2014).

55. See, for example, ST I–II q.19 a.3, where Aquinas explains that the will's object is always proposed to it by intellect, so that understood good (as distinct from what is really good) is what the will wants. See also ST I–II q.15 a.3, where Aquinas explains the progression towards action in this way: intellect's apprehension of the end, the desire of the end, counsel about the means, and the desire of the means. See also ST I–II q.74 a.7 ad 1, ad 2, and ad 3, where Aquinas says that consent to sin is an act of the appetitive power in consequence of an act of reason, so that reason's approving as good something which is in fact not good precedes sinful acts. Finally, in ST I–II q.75 a.2 Aquinas explains that the cause of sin is some apparent good, and therefore both intellect and will play a role in sinning.

56. In *Pilgrim's Progress*, Bunyan has a vivid image for this process. As he illustrates it in his allegory, the soul that strays from the right path has to walk every step of the way back; there are no shortcuts.

57. In order to avoid this clumsy locution, from this point on I will use the expression 'shamed person' to mean 'a person who is shamed and/or feels shame.'

58. Reported and quoted in http://www.nytimes.com/2012/06/02/world/asia/afghan-rape-case-is-a-challenge-for-the-government.html.

59. Sylvia Nasar, *A Beautiful Mind* (New York: Simon & Schuster, 1998).

60. The connection may also hold the other way around. If a person Paula rejects another person Jerome, then if Jerome finds Paula's reaction to him appropriate, he will be shamed by it, because he will see his own unworthiness in her rejection of him.

61. For an argument in support of this claim, see my *Wandering in Darkness*, chs. 6 and 7.

62. And there are other psalms with similar lines; see, for example, Psalm 69:6. I am grateful to Robert MacSwain for calling these psalms to my attention in this connection.

63. By 'morally defective state', I mean a state that would not be found in a morally perfect person and that should be a source of moral disapprobation by others, whether or not that state is culpable or punishable. (Not everything worthy of moral disapprobation merits punishment of any kind.)

64. Of course, one can do harm without doing an injustice in cases where doing the harm is not a morally wrong act. If a person knocks another down by falling on him in the course of fainting, he will have done some harm but no injustice. But the issue here has to do with acts of moral wrongdoing. I am grateful to John Perry for calling my attention to the need to clarify this point.

65. Actions of this sort, which harm but do no injustice, are like actions in the category that some philosophers have called 'the subrogatory': those actions that an agent is not obligated to do but that he is blamed for not doing. Those who accept that rights and obligations can come apart would not accept this particular way of describing such actions. On their view, it is possible for an agent Jerome to be obligated to treat another person Paula in a certain way, even though Paula has no right to be treated in this way. Aquinas's discussion of the almsdeeds makes this point clear. The almsdeeds are obligatory from Aquinas's point of view; but Jerome's being obligated to give away some of his money to others does not mean that any of those others has a right to Jerome's money. For some recent

discussion of these and related issues, see, for example, Julia Driver, "Appraisability, Attributability, and Moral Agency," in *The Nature of Moral Responsibility*, edited by Randolph Clarke, Michael McKenna, and Angela Smith (Oxford: Oxford University Press, 2015), 157–74.

66. Anselm, *Why God Became Man*, in *Anselm of Canterbury: The Major Works*, translated and edited by Brian Davies and G.R. Evans (Oxford: Oxford University Press, 1998), 283. I like and therefore have often used their translation. Where I have used a different translation, I will cite it in the notes.

67. Anselm, *Why God Became Man*, 287.

68. See Chapter 1 for this general characterization. As I described the Anselmian kind of interpretation there, all its variants share this feature: they see the main obstacle to union between God and human beings in something about God, which the atonement of Christ addresses.

69. ST I–II q.86 a.1 ad 3.

70. One might think of Harry Frankfurt's "volitional necessities" in this connection. A person who has done a serious evil has lost some of the moral volitional necessities that characterize most ordinary other human beings. See his *Necessity, Volition, and Love* (Cambridge: Cambridge University Press, 1999).

71. Not everything that is morally deplorable is also culpable. That is at least in part because it is possible for a person to be in a morally bad condition without being responsible for being in that condition and therefore worthy of blame for it. A man in an isolated area of Mongolia in the time of the Great Khan might have been completely persuaded that wife-beating in certain circumstances was obligatory for him. When he beat his wife in those circumstances, his psychic state would have been morally deplorable. But most people would hesitate to consider him culpable or worthy of punishment for that act, because we would suppose that he is not responsible for his morally bad psychic condition, and we would think that the morally bad psychic condition is not itself an act for which punishment would be appropriate.

72. Aquinas's terminology here has a certain ambiguity to it. Sometimes he describes the stain as if it were a characteristic stemming from a relation of the agent's, as in the example in the quotation just given, where the stain seems to be a characteristic, namely, darkness, which is in a soul separated from the light of God. But in other places Aquinas seems to take the stain just as the very relation itself, as the separation of the soul from God, for example. For my purposes here, it is not important to sort out this ambiguity, and so for simplicity's sake I will take the stain on the soul to include both intrinsic characteristics and the relation of being separated, from God or from some other person.

73. For an excellent recent discussion of this possibility, see Richard Moran, *Authority and Estrangement: An Essay on Self-Knowledge* (Princeton, NJ: Princeton University Press, 2001).

74. I have argued this claim in my *Wandering in Darkness*, chs. 6 and 7.

75. To be divided in will in this sense, then, is not the same as having desires for incompatible goods. Consider the standard trolley case, in which an agent at the switch has to choose between saving five lives or saving one. The agent might desire to save all the lives; and if he chooses to save the five over the one, he might

well regret greatly being the cause of the death of the one. But his desires in this case are not incompatible in the sense at issue here. There is one desire that the agent wants to make his own, namely, the desire to save five rather than one; and in doing so, he is integrated in willing to this extent, that he is acting on the desire he wants to have. By contrast, the division in the will at issue here is a matter of willing both for and against the same good.

76. For more exposition and defense of this claim, see my *Wandering in Darkness*, chs. 6 and 7.

77. The context here should make clear that what is at issue are those desires and volitions that are ingredients in moral decisions. Presumably, if a person were internally divided only with regard to a desire for something trivial, then the internal division in his will would have little or no effect on his ability to be close to others.

78. For these details of Speer's life, see, for example, Gitta Sereny, *Albert Speer: His Battle with Truth* (New York: Knopf, 1995), 36–7.

79. Sereny, *Albert Speer*, 141.

80. In the case of the others who are separated from him, the separation might be considered in the nature of a loss but not a stain.

81. ST I–II q.86 a.2.

82. See, for example, ST III q.90 a.2 ad 3.

83. Penance as a virtue is to be distinguished from penance as a sacrament administered by a priest acting in his priestly office. See, for example, ST III q.86 a.2. See also ST III q.86 a.6 *sc.*, where Aquinas distinguishes between penance as a sacrament and penance as a virtue as regards the forgiveness of sins. In interpreting Aquinas's thought on these issues, it is important to be clear about whether he is speaking of penance as a sacrament or as a virtue.

84. See, for example, ST III q.90 a.2.

85. See, for example, ST III q.84 a.5.

86. ST III q.84 a.5.

87. I will discuss forgiveness in detail in Chapter 3. For now, it is enough to see that the desires of love are the desires of forgiveness as well.

88. ST III q.85 a5.

89. See, for example, ST III q.86 a.6.

90. ST III q.85 a.3 and q.86 a.2.

91. Since doing so is likely to be something that the wrongdoer would otherwise rather not do, making satisfaction has something of the character of punishment; but it is differentiated from punishment by the fact that the wrongdoer does it voluntarily.

92. For those who find this claim incoherent, consider the punishment of children. A loving parent, who desires only the best for her child, may nonetheless deprive the child of some things that she herself considers a good for the child—playing with friends after school this week, for example—as a means of bringing the child to a better condition after the child has engaged in some wrong behavior. In such a case, the parent desires the good for the child even while she also desires something bad for the child, namely, the temporary deprivation of the good of friends.

93. For those who find this claim highly counter-intuitive, consider that the desires of forgiveness include the desire for the good of the person being forgiven. But it may be that the good of the person being forgiven, the true good that helps that person be the best he can be, requires that he undergo some punishment. Here, too, the punishment of children is a helpful example. A loving parent of a two-year-old who has hit his sister yet again may impose a temporary isolation on the two-year-old, which is a punishment for the two-year-old, even while she fervently desires nothing but the good for her child.

94. For a helpful review of the concept and the biblical passages that inspire or support the concept, see http://www.bibelwissenschaft.de/stichwort/53986/. I owe the reference to Godehard Brüntrup, whose questioning of me on this topic prompted me to think through the issue much more carefully than I had previously done.

95. Gitta Sereny, *The German Trauma: Experiences and Reflections 1938–2001* (New York: Penguin Books, 2001), 291.

96. Sereny, *German Trauma*, 305–6.

97. Sereny, *German Trauma*, 288.

98. Sereny, *German Trauma*, 308.

99. ST I–II q.87 a.8.

100. ST I–II q.87 a.7.

101. ST III q.48 a.2.

CHAPTER 3

1. By 'reconciliation', I mean the union in love of whatever kind of uniting is suitable for persons being united after being apart, where the kind of union suitable is a function of the office of love in which those persons are. At the least, the office of love can be that relation suitable between human persons just insofar as they are members of the human family; and the kind of union in that minimal case is that which is possible for people who have no more relation to each other than generally equal moral standing in the human family. By 'the acceptance of reconciliation', I mean the volition on the part of a person Paula who has been harmed or wronged by a person Jerome for reconciliation with Jerome. And by 'volition', I mean a desire that would be efficacious in being translated into action if nothing outside the will of the willer prevented it. So if Paula accepts reconciliation with Jerome, there will be reconciliation between Paula and Jerome unless something in Jerome or something else external to Paula's will prevents it. These are rough characterizations, not definitions; but, in my view, a rough characterization of this sort is sufficient for this chapter.

2. There are many other issues in Anselm's treatise that are not addressed here because, in my view, they are not relevant to the considerations of this chapter. For some idea of one of these issues, see Joshua Thurow, "Finding Collective Sin and Recompense in Anselm's *Cur Deus Homo*," *American Catholic Philosophical Quarterly* 91.3 (2017): 431–46, and "Communal Substitutionary Atonement," *Journal of Analytic Theology* 3 (2015): 47–69.

3. Anselm, *Basic Writings: Cur Deus Homo*, edited and translated by Thomas Williams (Indianapolis, IN: Hackett Publishing Co., 2007), bk. I, chs. 12–13, 262–5. I have added the Latin in brackets in the first line.

4. There was a medieval Franciscan tradition which held that the second person of the Trinity would have become incarnate even if there had not been a Fall. In my view, this is a minority opinion in the history of the Christian tradition. For some further discussion of it, see Chapter 5.

5. Thomas F. Torrance, *Incarnation: The Person and Life of Christ* (Downers Grove, IL: InterVarsity Press, 2008), 255.

6. J. McLeod Campbell, *The Nature of Atonement*, with a new introduction by James B. Torrance (Grand Rapids, MI: Eerdmans, 1996), 8–9.

7. For a helpful argument that Anselm himself is not a penal substitution theorist, see Thomas Williams, "Anselm on Atonement," unpublished lecture.

8. Richard Swinburne, *Responsibility and Atonement* (Oxford: Oxford University Press, 1989). For a detailed discussion of Swinburne's position, see my "Love and Forgiveness: Swinburne on Atonement," in *Reason and Faith: Themes from Richard Swinburne*, edited by Michael Bergmann and Jeffrey E. Brower (New York: Oxford University Press, 2016), 148–70. Some portions of this chapter are taken from that paper.

9. I will return to the issue of sacrifice in Chapter 11.

10. Steven L. Porter, "Swinburnian Atonement and the Doctrine of Penal Substitution," *Faith and Philosophy* 21 (2004) 228–41; reprinted in *Oxford Readings in Philosophical Theology*, vol. 1, *Trinity, Incarnation, Atonement*, edited by Michael C. Rea (Oxford: Oxford University Press, 2009), 321. In this connection, see also Jada Twedt Strabbing, "The Permissibility of the Atonement as Penal Substitution," in *Oxford Studies in Philosophy of Religion*, edited by Jonathan Kvanvig (Oxford: Oxford University Press, 2016), 239–70.

11. Oliver D. Crisp, *The Word Enfleshed: Exploring the Person and the Work of Christ* (Grand Rapids, MI: Baker Books, 2016), 170. In addition to the works of the major reformers, there is also a flood of contemporary literature defending one or another variant on the Anselmian kind of interpretation. In addition to the other books and articles cited in this chapter, here is a random sample of highly varied twentieth-century works defending some version of the Anselmian kind of interpretation: James Beilby and Paul R. Eddy (eds.), *The Nature of the Atonement: Four Views* (Downers Grove, IL: InterVarsity Press, 2006); Robert Letham, *The Work of Christ* (Downers Grove, IL: InterVarsity Press, 1993); Donald MacLeod, *Christ Crucified: Understanding the Atonement* (Downers Grove, IL: InterVarsity Press, 2014); R.C. Moberly, *Atonement and Personality* (London: John Murray, 1924); David M. Moffat, *Atonement and the Logic of Resurrection in the Epistle to the Hebrews* (Leiden: Brill, 2013); Leon Morris, *The Atonement: Its Meaning and Significance* (Downers Grove, IL: InterVarsity Press, 1983); John Stott, *The Cross of Christ* (Downers Grove, IL: InterVarsity Press, 2006); N.T. Wright, *Justification: God's Plan and Paul's Vision* (Downers Grove, IL: InterVarsity Press, 2009) and *Reconsidering Jesus' Crucifixion: The Day the Revolution Began* (New York: HarperCollins, 2016).

For some attempts to extend the Anselmian kind of interpretation to take account of contemporary work in disciplines adjacent to theology or to address contemporary sensibilities opposed to the Anselmian kind of interpretation, see, for example, Mark D. Baker and Joel B. Green, *Recovering the Scandal of the Cross: Atonement in New Testament and Contemporary Contexts* (Downers Grove,

IL: InterVarsity Press, 2011); Cynthia Crysdale, *Embracing Travail: Retrieving the Cross Today* (New York: Continuum, 1999) and *Transformed Lives: Making Sense of Atonement Today* (New York: Seabury Books, 2016); Colin Gunton, *The Actuality of Atonement: A Study of Metaphor, Rationality and the Christian Tradition* (New York: Continuum, 1988); Kelly M. Kapic, *Sanctification: Explorations in Theology and Practice* (Downers Grove, IL: InterVarsity Press, 2014); J. Denny Weaver, *The Nonviolent Atonement* (Grand Rapids, MI: Eerdmans, 2011).

12. John Bunyan, *Pilgrim's Progress* (Oxford: Oxford University Press, 1984), 31.
13. Fleming Rutledge, *The Crucifixion: Understanding the Death of Jesus Christ* (Grand Rapids, MI: Eerdmans, 2015), 170.
14. For more discussion of the fruits of the Holy Spirit, see Chapter 7.
15. See, for example, Wright, *Justification*, 250–1.
16. Wright, *Justification*, 222–3.
17. John Milton, *Paradise Lost*, Bk. IV, l.75.
18. For an excellent comparison of the views of Calvin and Aquinas on the connection between the work of the Holy Spirit and the atonement of Christ, see Charles Raith II, *Aquinas and Calvin on Romans: God's Justification and Our Participation* (Oxford: Oxford University Press, 2014).
19. Crisp, *The Word Enfleshed*, 166.
20. Proponents of the Anselmian kind of interpretation sometimes speak of the inward work of the Holy Spirit uniting a person to Christ. For a sophisticated and detailed presentation of such an account, see, for example, Thomas F. Torrance, *Atonement: The Person and Work of Christ* (Downers Grove, IL: InterVarsity Press, 2009). In my view, the problem with such accounts is that they do not give any intrinsic connection between the Holy Spirit's inward working to produce union with God and Christ's passion and death. It seems as if there are two separate processes of salvation then, one provided by Christ's passion and death, and a separate one provided by the working of the Holy Spirit.
21. For a helpful review of discussion of the penal substitution account and an attempt to preserve what is best in it, see Mark Murphy, "Not Penal Substitution but Vicarious Punishment," *Faith and Philosophy* 26 (2009): 253–73.
22. Aquinas, *Commentary on 1 Thessalonians*, C.1, L.1, in *Commentary on the Letters of St. Paul to the Philippians, Colossians, Thessalonians, Timothy, Titus, and Philemon*, translated by F.R. Larcher, edited by J. Mortensen and E. Alarcón (Landor, WY: Aquinas Institute for the Study of Sacred Doctrine, 2012), 157. I like and therefore have used the translations of the Aquinas Institute, but I have felt free to emend them on those few occasions on which I thought I could do better.
23. For discussion of some of this literature, see Kathryn Tanner, *Christ the Key* (Cambridge: Cambridge University Press, 2010). For a survey of feminist critique, see Deidre Nicole Green, *Works of Love in a World of Violence* (Tübingen: Mohr Siebeck, 2016). For an attempt to sustain the theological notion of sacrifice in the face of such criticism, see Sarah Coakley, *Sacrifice: Defunct or Desired?* (Charlottesville, VA: University of Virginia Press, 2018).
24. For further discussion of concerns with the Anselmian kind of interpretation, see also my *Aquinas* (London and New York: Routledge, 2003), ch. 15.

25. This is an issue to which I will return below and also in Chapter 10.

26. In fact, Daniel Philpott argues that one way to define forgiveness is as the relinquishing of what one is owed by the wrongdoer, although in the end he himself thinks that something more is needed for true forgiveness. See Daniel Philpott, *Just and Unjust Peace: An Ethic of Political Reconciliation* (Oxford: Oxford University Press, 2012), 259–63.

27. This is a question Anselm himself considers (see, for example, *Cur Deus Homo*, chs. 8–10), but I myself do not find Anselm's response to the question satisfactory.

28. In *The Word Enfleshed*, ch. 7, Oliver Crisp attempts to rebut this objection by arguing that Christ and human beings constitute one four-dimensional object and that in the case of such a corporate or perduring object the sins of some are the sins of the whole object, so that the punishment for the sins is suitably visited on the whole object as well. But this argument seems to me inefficacious to rebut the charge of injustice against a God who would proceed in the way proponents of the penal substitution theory propose. The sins that offend God are not sins of the whole four-dimensional object but of parts of it. As far as that goes, the whole four-dimensional object is capable of action only in a derivative sense, in consequence of the actions of some of its parts. That is because there is no one will which constitutes the will of this four-dimensional object, and any agency requires an act of will. For this same reason, there is no sin that could be committed non-derivatively by a four-dimensional corporate object of this sort, since any sin also requires an act of will. So even if it were true that Christ and human beings constitute one four-dimensional object, it remains the case that when Christ is punished for sins committed by other human beings, those who willed the sin are not punished and someone who did not will a sin is punished. And therefore the charge of injustice is not rebutted.

29. It is sometimes alleged that although Christ did not endure eternal damnation, his suffering was equivalent to it for one reason or another. But if it is morally permissible for God to forego extracting the penalty due the guilty in favor of something else suited to the person suffering, then it seems that after all a perfectly good God does not need to impose the exact penalty due to human sin. And so the objection of inconsistency remains even on this more nuanced version of the penal substitution variant.

30. In fact, Aquinas bases his distinction between punishment and satisfaction on the claim that satisfaction is voluntary but punishment is always involuntary.

31. Herbert Fingarette, "Punishment and Suffering," *Proceedings and Addresses of the American Philosophical Association* 50 (1977), 510.

32. Someone might object that God does no injustice in damning some sinners since no sinner has any right to God's grace. But from the fact that no sinner has a right to God's grace, it does not follow that God does nothing unjust in refusing grace when he could give it.

33. For attempts to maintain Anselm's kind of interpretation but in a transformed way that evades some standard criticisms, in addition to the work by Oliver Crisp cited above, see, for example, David Brown, *God in a Single Vision: Integrating Philosophy and Theology*, edited by Christopher R. Brewer and Robert MacSwain (New York: Routledge, 2016), esp. 124–41; and Richard Cross, "Atonement without Satisfaction,"

in *Oxford Readings in Philosophical Theology*, vol. 1, *Trinity, Incarnation, Atonement*, edited by Michael C. Rea (Oxford: Oxford University Press, 2009), 328–47.

34. For some discussion of the difference between the claim that God is love and the claim that God is loving, and the metaphysics needed to render these two claims compatible, see my "God's Simplicity," in *The Oxford Handbook of Thomas Aquinas*, edited by Brian Davies and Eleonore Stump (Oxford: Oxford University Press, 2011), 135–46.

35. Although it is certainly my intention to be true to Aquinas's views, this is not intended as a book of historical scholarship on Aquinas's thought. For that book, see my *Aquinas*. In that book, I have argued for my interpretations of Aquinas's positions; here I will just use the interpretations I have argued for previously.

36. To take just one example, see ST I q.20 a.2.

37. On Aquinas's views, God gives grace to every person who does not reject grace, but God does not give grace to a person who rejects grace, since doing so would violate that person's will. God's giving of grace to a person is therefore responsive to whether that person rejects grace or not. But it is always open to a human being to reject God's grace or to cease rejecting God's grace. With regard to God's giving of grace, then, alternative possibilities are always available to a human person.

38. By contrast, Daniel Philpott argues that forgiveness always involves reconciliation, although he admits that full reconciliation may not be possible. He says,

> Right relationship is restored in one significant way by a victim's decision to reconstrue her view of a perpetrator and is thus furthered by every act of forgiveness. In some cases, little more will occur. (*Just and Unjust Peace*, 261)

My reasons for rejecting this view will emerge in this chapter.

39. For a different argument to the conclusion that Anselm's kind of interpretation of the doctrine of the atonement has to be ruled out on philosophical grounds, see Nicholas Lombardo, OP, *The Father's Will: Christ's Crucifixion and the Goodness of God* (Oxford: Oxford University Press, 2013), ch. 8.

40. A classic account of differing positions in dialogue is given in Jean Hampton and Jeffrie Murphy, *Forgiveness and Mercy* (Cambridge: Cambridge University Press, 1988). A fairly standard and representative account can be found in Charles Griswold, *Forgiveness: A Philosophical Exploration* (Cambridge: Cambridge University Press, 2007). Excellent thoughtful discussions are given in Martha Nussbaum, *Anger and Forgiveness: Resentment, Generosity, Justice* (Oxford: Oxford University Press, 2016); Linda Radzik, *Making Amends: Atonement in Morality, Law, and Politics* (Oxford: Oxford University Press, 2009); and Margaret Urban Walker, *Moral Repair: Reconstructing Moral Relations After Wrongdoing* (Cambridge: Cambridge University Press, 2006). Representative accounts of forgiveness more in line with the Continental tradition of philosophy can be found in Hent de Vries and Nils F. Schott (eds.), *Love and Forgiveness for a More Just World* (New York: Columbia University Press, 2015).

41. For a representative account of this position, see Swinburne, *Responsibility and Atonement*.

42. Swinburne, *Responsibility and Atonement*, 85.

43. See Radzik, *Making Amends*, for nuanced discussion of the reactive attitudes of victims of wrongdoing.

44. See Nussbaum, *Anger and Forgiveness*, for discussion of this problem with the standard account of forgiveness.

45. See Radzik, *Making Amends*, for a good account of this dissociation between forgiveness and reconciliation.

46. Because it is clumsy continually to insert 'morally appropriate' or 'morally justified' or similar locutions, I will omit them after this; but this qualification should be understood throughout.

47. In fact, on my view, love is necessary and sufficient for forgiveness. But it is not the case that forgiveness is nothing but love or that forgiveness reduces to love, or that the definition of forgiveness is love. Analogously, being risible (having the capacity for laughter in response to rational assessment of a situation or story) is necessary and sufficient for being human—anything that is risible is human and anything that is not risible is not human—but being human is not reducible to being risible. Risibility picks out human beings by an accident which is had by all and only human beings, but the nature of human beings is not nothing but risibility. Analogously, forgiveness does not reduce to love, although love is necessary and sufficient for forgiveness. It is not part of my purposes here to define forgiveness, and so I leave to one side what else might need to be added to love for a definition of forgiveness. Walker argues convincingly that what exactly is involved in forgiveness is a function at least in part of the nature of the wrongdoing being forgiven; for her excellent nuanced discussion of the varieties of forgiveness, see Walker, *Moral Repair*, ch. 5.

48. There is a complication as regards this claim, though, and I will address it below in the section on hatred and anger.

49. If Paula's wrongdoing against Jerome is evil enough, then she may have destroyed whatever office of love she previously had or might reasonably have expected to have with Jerome. But even in such a case, Jerome can have a desire for union with Paula at least to the extent of desiring that they share community in the human family. For more discussion of this point, see the discussion of *The Sunflower* below.

50. This claim implies that love is under voluntary control. Consequently, it also is an implication of this claim that some desires are under voluntary control. Not all desires are, of course. Aquinas distinguishes between desires that stem from the sensory appetite, closely tied to the senses, and desires that stem from the rational appetite, closely tied to reason. The latter desires are under voluntary control in one way or another. To see this distinction, consider the desire to be vegetarian. Clearly, there are two ways to think about this desire. First, there is a desire for vegetarian food that consists in a kind of bodily inclining towards food that is not meat. This is the kind of desire found in a person who really hates eating meat and likes eating vegetables. But this is not the only kind of desire for vegetarian food that there is. There is also the kind of desire for vegetarian food found in a person who loves eating meat and does not care much for eating vegetables but who is determined to be vegetarian out of ethical considerations. The first kind of desire is not under direct voluntary control, but the second kind clearly is. The desires of love are of the latter sort. For more discussion of this point about desire and voluntary control, see my *Aquinas*, ch. 9. I am grateful to Michael McKenna and Michael Rea for calling my attention to the need to make this point explicit.

51. On this view, it can be blameworthy to fail to have a desire. Although this claim sounds counter-intuitive, a little reflection will show that it is right. Consider a slave trader such as John Newton who was not moved by the suffering of the Africans on his ships to any desire to relieve their suffering. The failure on his part to have such a desire is surely morally horrifying and blameworthy. I am grateful to Michael Rea for calling my attention to the need to make this point explicit.

52. For more discussion of this claim, see my "The Non-Aristotelian Character of Aquinas's Ethics: Aquinas on the Passions," *Faith and Philosophy* 28.1 (2011): 29–43.

53. For a helpful discussion of the issue of whether forgiveness is obligatory, see Philpott, *Just and Unjust Peace*, 272–4. Philpott largely accepts this conclusion but with some caveats because he wants to maintain that wrongdoers have no right to forgiveness. If one accepts that rights and obligations are not correlative, then Philpott's caveats are not necessary.

54. This account has the apparently counter-intuitive result that one person Paula can accrue an obligation to a stranger Jerome to love him in virtue of his engaging in wrongdoing against Paula. That is, on this account, if Jerome is a stranger to Paula but succeeds in robbing her of her pension funds, then Paula gains an obligation of love with regard to Jerome of a kind that she did not have before his theft of her funds. I appreciate that this result sounds counter-intuitive, but a little reflection will show that it is sadly true nonetheless. When Jerome drives drunk and in consequence has a collision with Paula's car, injuring Paula seriously, he thereby establishes a relationship with Paula whether she likes it or not, because after his injuring her through drunk driving there is a connection between them that there was not before. His injury of her establishes a relation between them in which some things are possible that were not possible before, most notably that Paula can now forgive or fail to forgive Jerome, something not possible for her before he harmed her. I am grateful to Michael McKenna for calling to my attention the need to make this point explicit. For more discussion and support of this point, see Walker, *Moral Repair*, ch. 5.

55. The sense that rights and obligations are correlative may underlie the claim made by Richard Swinburne and others that forgiveness is not obligatory for God; for a discussion of this issue, see Cross, "Atonement without Satisfaction," 341–5. In this paper, Cross begins by arguing against Swinburne's version of the Anselmian kind of interpretation and then goes on to offer his own version, which he calls 'a merit theory.' On Cross's merit theory, God is conditionally obliged to forgive sinners, given that Christ has merited that God do so.

56. I have argued for this claim at length in "God's Obligations," in *Philosophical Perspectives*, vol. 6, *Ethics*, edited by James Tomberlin (Atascadero, CA: Ridgeview, 1992), 475–91. To see the point here, consider, by way of analogy, that if Paula were a very rich tourist traveling in a very poor country, she would be obligated to give some of her money away for charitable purposes in that country if she were solicited to do so; if she refused all such solicitations, she would be subject to appropriate moral censure. But it would not be the case that any particular recipient of her donations would have a right to her money.

57. This is the sort of objection typically raised against forgiveness that is given without the wrongdoer's having made sufficient amends. For a detailed presentation of this objection, see Murphy's half of Hampton and Murphy, *Forgiveness and Mercy*. See also Swinburne, *Responsibility and Atonement*, 81–5, for an argument that forgiveness requires repentance and penance on the part of the perpetrator of the wrong being forgiven.

58. It might appear that Aquinas's account of love succumbs to the same problems as those that seem to some people to afflict an ethics of care. If the value of loving others or caring for others is the fundamental ethical value, then it is not easy to explain why it is morally acceptable to withhold care for others in the interests of pursuing one's own projects. And yet if there is no morally acceptable way of doing so, caring, or loving, can become deeply destructive, dreadfully unjust, with regard to the one doing the caring or loving. So, for example, Virginia Woolf describes the "angel in the house" who loved others totally, who cared for them completely, in this way:

> she never had a mind or a wish of her own, but preferred to sympathize always with the minds and wishes of others.... I did my best to kill her. My excuse, if I were to be had up in a court of law, would be that I acted in self-defence. Had I not killed her she would have killed me. (From "Professions for Women," quoted in Jean Hampton, "Feminist Contractarianism," in *A Mind of One's Own: Feminist Essays on Reason and Objectivity*, edited by Louise Antony and Charlotte Witt (Boulder, CO: Westview Press, 1993), 231)

    In my view, considerations similar to those showing that Paula is not loving Jerome in enabling him to harm her apply also to this worry about the ethics of care. Paula is not loving others in allowing them to hurt her, even if the harm done to her takes the actions of a whole group to accomplish.

59. Wisd. 11:25 and I John 4:8. Cf. ST I q.20 a.2.

60. Mal. 1:2. Cf. ST I q.23 a.3.

61. There are also passages that seem to imply that God's love and forgiveness are conditional. For example, Christ says that if people do not forgive others, God will not forgive their sins either (see, for example, Matt. 6:15). It is possible to interpret this saying as claiming that God withholds forgiveness from some people. But, so understood, the saying would be at least in serious tension with other texts, such as Christ's telling people to love their enemies so that they will be like God, who sends his good gifts on both the just and the unjust (Matt. 5:45). Furthermore, in the parable in which this saying about forgiveness occurs, the king (who represents God in the parable) is portrayed as forgiving his servant first, before the episode in which the servant fails to forgive his fellow servant (Matt. 18:23–35). So, in my view, a better way to interpret the saying in the Gospel text about God's forgiveness is to take it as a claim about God's forgiveness-plus-actual-reconciliation, and to understand it as claiming that the hard-hearted cannot be united to God because of their resistance to love, not God's resistance to them.

62. Cf., e.g., ST II–II q.34 a.5. In that question, Aquinas explains that there are two kinds of hatred. One kind arises when something is hated insofar as it is incompatible with what is naturally good. The other kind arises when something is hated which is a real good but is taken to be an evil by someone who has become corrupt. This latter kind of hatred is vicious, Aquinas says, but the former kind is not. See

also ST I–II q.29 a.2 ad 2, where Aquinas maintains that love and hatred are contraries if considered in respect of the same thing; but if they are taken in respect of contraries, they are not themselves contrary but rather consequent to one another. As he puts it, it amounts to the same thing that one love a certain thing or that one hate its contrary.

63. It is a consequence of this account that one and the same psychic state can count both as hatred and as love. It counts as hatred insofar as it consists in a rejection of the hated person, but it counts as love insofar as the rejection of that person is encompassed within an overarching desire for ultimate union with that person. I am grateful to Michael Rea for calling my attention to the need to discuss the apparently implausible character of this claim. The subsequent discussion of the two kinds of hatred should help to make the rightness of this claim clear.

64. See Chapter 2 for a presentation of the case of Otto Moll.

65. For fuller discussion of this claim, see my *Wandering in Darkness: Narrative and the Problem of Suffering* (Oxford: Oxford University Press, 2010), chs. 6 and 7.

66. Cf., e.g., ST II–II q.34 a.3. As Aquinas explains here, love is due to one's neighbor on account of the nature and grace he has from God, but not on account of the sin or lack of justice he has from himself. Although one cannot hate the nature and grace in one's neighbor without sin, it is obligatory to hate the sin in one's neighbor. It is part of love for one's neighbor that one hate the lack of good in him since the desire for another's good is equivalent to the hatred of his evil. In the objections in this question, Aquinas considers cases in which God is said to hate some human persons or in which Christ seems to be commanding hatred of others; and in the replies to these objections Aquinas explains these cases as ones in which hatred is in fact a kind of love.

67. Daniel Philpott puts an analogous point this way. He says,

> Renouncing resentment is also a component of forgiveness as articulated here, but it is crucial to understanding constructive forgiveness that we not draw the distinction between resentment and forgiveness too sharply. Not only does constructive forgiveness not condone or necessarily forget evil but it takes evil seriously in the same ways that resentment does. It names, confronts, and draws attention to the evil, asserts that the victim has been the target of evil, and wills that the perpetrator renounce the evil. The difference between constructive forgiveness and resentment is the manner in which they seek this defeat.   (*Just and Unjust Peace*, 263)

68. As Aquinas understands anger, it is a passion, in its most basic sense; and, in this sense, it includes a bodily alteration. In virtue of being immaterial, God can have no passions in this sense. But God can have what Aquinas thinks of as the formal part of a passion without the bodily part. In addition, as anger is ordinarily understood, it carries with it a connotation of sadness over having been unable to prevent an injustice of some sort. This sadness also needs to be omitted in the case of God's anger, since God's power is sufficient to prevent anything God wills to prevent. Nonetheless, Aquinas thinks, what is at the heart of the notion of anger can also be applied to God. See, for example, ST I q.20 a.1 ad 1 and ad 2.

69. The word 'wrath' is also sometimes used to indicate great righteous indignation on God's part. But for the sake of a consistent terminology, I will reserve the term 'wrath' for anger that is not compatible with love, unlike righteous indignation, which is.

70. For a discussion of losing what one very much desires as a real, objective bad thing for the desirer, see my *Wandering in Darkness*, ch. 14.

71. For the first position as regards anger, see Murphy's part of Hampton and Murphy, *Forgiveness and Mercy*, and for the second position as regards anger, see Nussbaum, *Anger and Forgiveness*.

72. There is also a further distinction to be made here, namely, the distinction between being angry at a person and being angry at the action of a person; and something roughly analogous can be said as regards hatred. It is compatible with the account of anger, hatred, and forgiveness given here that, even after a person has not only forgiven but has also been reconciled with a wrongdoer so that she no longer has either anger or hatred *for him*, she nonetheless retains anger or hatred for the wrong actions that the wrongdoer did. Discussing this sort of issue as regards forgiveness, Jeffrey Blustein says,

> Forgiveness...does not necessarily erase the wronged party's memory of having been wronged.
> (*Forgiveness and Remembrance* (Oxford: Oxford University Press, 2014), 74)

On the contrary, Blustein holds,

> The wronged party may continue to have emotional memories of being wronged and be disposed to remember the wrong with negative emotions, even after she has forgiven her wrongdoer. These memories, while they may not impede forgiveness, can nevertheless signify that she continues to disvalue how she was mistreated and by whom.... [T]he norms for how one should feel about past wrongdoing do not proscribe continuing to disvalue it in one's memories after the wrongdoer is forgiven.
> (*Forgiveness and Remembrance*, 87)

In my view, Blustein is right in this view, but considerations of space prohibit pursuing this issue further here.

73. In any actual case, of course, hatred and anger may be messy, and elements of both may be present in a person's reactive attitudes towards someone who has wronged her.

74. Cf., e.g., ST I–II q.46 a.6, where Aquinas compares anger and hatred. In each case, Aquinas explains, whether Paula is angry with Jerome or hates Jerome, she wishes something bad for Jerome. But when she is angry with him, she wishes that bad thing for him under the aspect of vengeance because of some bad act he has done; when she hates him, what she rejects as bad is Jerome. Cf. also ST II–II q.34 a.6, where Aquinas says that anger desires the neighbor's evil as that evil falls under the heading of vengeance; but hatred is a desire of the neighbor's evil absolutely.

75. Cf., e.g., ST I–II q.46 a.2, where Aquinas is also comparing anger and hatred. There Aquinas holds that when a person Paula is angry with a person Jerome, Paula is interested in restoring justice by willing the bad for Jerome; but when Paula hates Jerome, she is simply averse to Jerome as himself evil.

76. On traditional Christian doctrine, it is possible for a human person to persist in such a condition indefinitely; to be in such a condition, after bodily death, is to be in hell. In my view, the interpretation of the doctrine of the atonement that I develop in this book is logically independent of the doctrine of hell. That is, this interpretation of the doctrine of the atonement is compatible both with the acceptance and with the rejection of the traditional doctrine of hell. It is compatible, that is, with the view that those who decisively reject God's love are simply annihilated at death and also with the view that all human beings are ultimately saved. In *Wandering in Darkness*, I argued that although the doctrine of heaven is necessary for any acceptable theodicy, the doctrine of hell is not; and the same point holds, on my view, for acceptable interpretations of the doctrine of the atonement. Any acceptable interpretation of the doctrine of the atonement needs to hold that there is a worst state for human beings, but it does not need to hold that this worst state is hell. For this reason, I will not consider the doctrine of hell in any detail in the remainder of this book.
77. Fingarette, "Punishment and Suffering," 513.
78. Fingarette, "Punishment and Suffering," 510.
79. Cynthia Ozick, "The Symposium," in Simon Wiesenthal, *The Sunflower: On the Possibilities and Limits of Forgiveness* (New York: Schocken Books, 1960), 216.
80. For helpful discussion of some of the issues regarding retribution, in addition to the other works cited in this chapter, see, for example, John Braithwaite, *Crime, Shame and Reintegration* (Cambridge: Cambridge University Press, 1989); R.A. Duff, *Trials and Punishments* (Cambridge: Cambridge University Press, 1986); Jeffrie Murphy, *Punishment and the Moral Emotions: Essays in Law, Morality, and Religion* (Oxford: Oxford University Press, 2012).
81. The concern that forgiveness readily given fails to take wrongdoing seriously enough is at the heart of Murphy's argument for retributive punishment. See Murphy's part in Hampton and Murphy, *Forgiveness and Mercy*.
82. For a well-argued statement of such a case, see, for example, Jeffrie Murphy, *Getting Even: Forgiveness and Its Limits* (Oxford: Oxford University Press, 2003).
83. It is worth noting here that the condition on forgiveness I gave in the introduction to this chapter, that forgiving a sinner includes failing to impose all the punishment due him, is compatible with this account of forgiveness in terms of love. If Paula forgives Jerome when he has done her an injustice, then in virtue of continuing even so to desire his good and his union with her, she is thereby failing to exact all the punishment due him. This point is another way of spelling out the claim that a wrongdoer has no right to forgiveness.
84. In fact, Moll was executed in Germany in May 1946. But the historical fact that he was punished with the death penalty does not invalidate the thought experiment here, since the period between the time that Moll's evil actions ended and the time at which Moll was put to death would have been sufficient for Moll to appropriate the benefits to him of retributive punishment.
85. For the sake of the argument, I am assuming a case in which Moll is completely, genuinely, wholeheartedly repentant. Any actual case of repentance is likely to be messy and less than wholehearted.
86. I put the point in this awkward way to withhold judgment about whether Speer was in fact really repentant. Although many people believe he was, there is strong

evidence to support a claim that his repentance was either insincere or double-minded. See, for example, Dan Van der Vat, *The Good Nazi: The Life and Lies of Albert Speer* (New York: Houghton Mifflin, 1997).

87. Someone might object that this conclusion is false if the penalty is death. In my view, this objection is mistaken; but it is not necessary to argue the case. If the objection is right, then its implication is only that the penalty in question should not be death. The claim that punishment can be a good for the wrongdoer is not affected.

88. For some discussion of the life of such Nazis in Argentina after the war, see Bettina Stangneth, *Eichmann Before Jerusalem: The Unexamined Life of a Mass Murderer*, translated by Ruth Martin (New York: Knopf, 2014).

89. In this connection, see also Jeffrie Murphy's reasons for softening his original stern stand about retributive punishment in "Shame Creeps Through Guilt and Feels Like Retribution," in his *Punishment and the Moral Emotions*, 94–113.

90. For a different sort of argument to the conclusion that forgiving a wrongdoer is compatible with requiring punishment of him, see Daniel Philpott, *Just and Unjust Peace*. Philpott says,

> In forgiving, the victim defeats the perpetrator's injustice by naming and condemning it, asserting her own dignity as a subject and enactor of justice, and inviting the perpetrator also to name, disclaim, and show remorse for it. In willing punishment, the victim claims that the defeat of the perpetrator's injustice also requires the hard treatment of punishment, both as a communication from the community and, should the perpetrator accept it, the perpetrator's own communication of penance.   (*Just and Unjust Peace*, 271)

91. Neither of these states is a good state. Refusing God's grace is obviously not a good state. And simply abstaining from refusing it is not equivalent to accepting it; since it is not yet an acceptance of grace, which is necessary for anything good, it is not a good state either. It is a *better* state than refusing God's grace; but comparatives do not presuppose positives. I am taller than my baby granddaughter, but I am not tall. So it is possible to reject Pelagianism and yet to accept, as Aquinas does, that it is always open to a human person either to refuse grace or to abstain from refusing grace. This issue is discussed in detail in Chapter 7, but it seemed necessary at least to touch on it here.

92. See, for example, ST I q.21 a.2.

93. See, for example, ST I q.21 a.1 ad 3.

94. See, for example, ST I q.21 a.1 ad 4.

95. See, for example, ST I q.21 a.3.

96. For a helpful discussion of the moral obligation to have and retain anger towards a wrongdoer in certain circumstances, see Daniel Philpott, *Just and Unjust Peace*, ch. 12.

97. Wiesenthal, *The Sunflower*.

98. For an opposing view, that forgiveness is or carries with it openness to reconciliation, see Jada Twedt Strabbing, "Divine Forgiveness and Reconciliation," *Faith and Philosophy* 34 (2017): 272–97. The reasons given in this chapter for supposing that forgiveness and reconciliation can come apart are also objections to Strabbing's thesis.

99. These lines are true, but they are not the whole truth. Elsewhere I have argued that it is not possible to be single-minded and wholehearted in doing a morally wrong act. So, when Jerome's intellect and will are on the side of acting unjustly against Paula or injuring her, Jerome is psychically fragmented. Some part of his intellect, however buried beneath conscious awareness, also dissents from his act against Paula; and some part of his divided will, however feeble in its desire, also wants not to treat her in this way. See my *Wandering in Darkness*, ch. 7.

100. This can happen in such a way as to leave relatively untouched the building dispositions or habits in the intellect and will, as often happens when a person repents some particular act of moral wrongdoing without a deeper change of heart. But if the repentance is deep enough and fervent enough, then it may also alter for the better the habits of the intellect and will which were building or already in place inclining the agent to the morally wrong acts in question.

101. And this conclusion can hold even when the wrongdoing is not morally monstrous. Arguing for something like this conclusion, in the context of a thought experiment about an imaginary friend who has wronged him, Jeffrey Blustein says,

> The question is whether, having forgiven the wrongdoer, some sort of reorientation in how I related to him [before he wronged me] may be justified and appropriate. The answer, I believe, is yes. Forgiveness does not necessarily wipe the slate clean, and this means in part that it does not necessarily restore the relationship to its prior state, emotionally or behaviorally... Forgiving another person doesn't mean that the relationship with him or her has been fully repaired or that they have been reconciled.
>
> (*Forgiveness and Remembrance*, 45–6)

102. See Chapter 2 for further discussion of the stain on the soul. For a discussion of the stain on the soul in connection with Thomist and Calvinist accounts of justification and Christ's atonement, see Raith II, *Aquinas and Calvin on Romans*, ch. 4.

103. I am simplifying here, of course. The soldier's repentance remedies his intellect and will to the extent to which the repentance is complete, genuine, and wholehearted. No doubt, all actual human repentance falls somewhat short of this ideal and so also is limited in its remedy for the wrongdoer's intellect and will.

104. See Radzik, *Making Amends*.

105. For an excellent explanation of the role of bystanders or others in the community, both in suffering damage to trust and in responsibility for ensuring that the wrongdoer make amends for that damage, see Walker, *Moral Repair*.

106. For those who might see this conclusion as definitive confirmation of the Anselmian kind of interpretation of the doctrine of the atonement, it is important to notice that the obstacle to full reconciliation between Paula and the person who wronged her lies *not* in Paula but in the wrongdoer Jerome. Nothing is needed for Paula's desires of love in forgiveness of Jerome and her willingness to be fulfilled in reconciliation with him. What is needed for her desires to be fulfilled is that something change in Jerome. In effect, in this case Paula has pardoned Jerome, but her pardon is insufficient to produce in Jerome the kind of state necessary for him to return to company with her.

107. Here and earlier I have qualified these claims with such expressions as 'humanly speaking' because of the issue of the vicarious satisfaction of Christ, which needs

to be considered in this condition. Because the issue of vicarious satisfaction cannot be fully examined until Chapter 10, the complexities of the full consideration of reconciliation are postponed till then.

108. Wiesenthal, *The Sunflower*, 169.
109. Wiesenthal, *The Sunflower*, 266–8.
110. Wiesenthal, *The Sunflower*, 271.
111. Wiesenthal, *The Sunflower*, 172–3.
112. The example of the German soldier and his mother is a matter of injustice between people already in a relationship; but similar things can be said if the wrongdoer is a complete stranger to the person or persons he injures. In that case, there is no question of a return to former habits of companionship, of course; but if the perpetrator of the wrong were completely repentant, he might still want some sort of reconciliation with his victims. Even if a perpetrator of great evil such as the German soldier were completely repentant, however, his victims might find the idea of any kind of personal connection with him intolerable. The soldier's terrible acts alter his relationship not only to his victims but also to all human beings. They make him into something horrible, from which other people shrink. Because this is so, it is possible for his victims to count as loving and forgiving of him while they have for him no greater desire for union, or any kind of reconciliation, than the generic desire appropriate to the general love of humanity.

    Cases in which someone suffers at the hands of a conglomerate such as a corporation or a political group are too complicated to be dealt with adequately in passing, but roughly analogous claims will hold, on the Thomistic account of love and forgiveness. Employing legislative means against Shell Oil, for example, or boycotting the company in return for injustices it has committed will be compatible with forgiveness of those injustices, on the Thomistic account. (As far as that goes, Aquinas is not a pacifist; he thinks that violence is compatible with love in some cases. See, for example, his view of tyrannicide as compatible with love of God; cf., e.g., *Scriptum super Sententiis*, II, d.44, q.2, a.2 ad 5.) On the other hand, it is clearly also possible to be vengeful towards a conglomerate or to desire to exclude a whole group from the civilized society of humankind, as happens in long-standing nationalist battles. But such attitudes are incompatible with love and forgiveness, on Aquinas's account.

113. For more discussion of this issue, see my "Personal Relations and Moral Residue," *History of the Human Sciences* 17.2/3 (2004): 33–57.
114. See, for example, ST III q.85 a.3.
115. ST I–II q.87 a.6. It is important to notice, though, that satisfaction is not intended to substitute for punishment; and, in any given case of wrongdoing, punishment may be required, for example, because the punishment is a legal sanction for wrongdoing that is also a crime. In such a case, the wrongdoer's acceptance of legally meted out punishment will be part of his satisfaction.
116. ST III q.85 a.3 and q.86 a.2.
117. ST III q.84 a.5.
118. Richard Swinburne is one person who holds a different view of the relationship between satisfaction and forgiveness; he sees satisfaction as a prerequisite for forgiveness. Swinburne says,

An agent's guilt is removed when his repentance, reparation, apology, and penance find their response in the victim's forgiveness.

(*Responsibility and Atonement*, 85)

I have argued against Swinburne's position in my review of his book: "Review of Richard Swinburne's *Responsibility and Atonement*," *Faith and Philosophy* 11 (1994): 321–8.

119. ST I–II q.113 a.2.

120. ST III q.90 a.2.

121. See *The Journal of a Slave Trader (John Newton) 1750–1754*, edited by Bernard Martin and Mark Spurrell (London: The Epworth Press, 1962), 98.

122. Even the small-scale penance for small-scale sins is not an exception to this claim here, since accepting small penances as merited for one's past wrongdoing has a certain humility about it that was lacking in the self-will of the wrongdoing.

123. See, for example, *Scriptum super Sententiis*, IV, d.15, q.1, a.2.

124. ST III q.89 a.3. See also ST I q.20 a.4 ad 4, where Aquinas presents two different ways of affirming the claim that a penitent person has more grace and more love of God than an innocent person does.

125. ST III q.89 a.2.

126. That is, insofar as every redeemed person is united to omniscient God, in having access to the mind of God every redeemed person is able to see what God sees. It does not follow, of course, that a redeemed person is omniscient. A limited human mind can appropriate only a small fraction of what is in the mind of God, and no doubt a limited human mind can also attend only to a few things at a time. But, even so, it remains the case that if a redeemed person were to turn her attention to Newton, then in her union with the mind of God she would see Newton's evil and shameful acts in the slave trade, even if she does not see as much of that evil as God does.

127. Theological relativism comes in differing varieties, but they share a common commitment to tying goodness entirely to God's will, so that a thing is good only because God wills it.

128. For a defense of this claim and some survey of the relevant literature, see my *Aquinas*, ch. 2.

129. McLeod Campbell, *The Nature of Atonement*, 4.

130. This claim is about the independence of God's nature, not about the necessity of God's existence. On the doctrine of simplicity, God is God's nature. Because 'God is love' is true, there is nothing on which God's love is dependent, any more than there is anything on which God is dependent for his nature.

131. Luke 23:34.

132. That is, forgiveness in the sense of forgiveness-plus-reconciliation. See, for example, Aquinas, *De Malo* q.3, a.15.

133. Matt. 7:23; cf. Luke 13:27.

134. For some discussion of God's having unfulfilled desires, see the comments on the Thomistic distinction between God's antecedent will and God's consequent will in my *Wandering in Darkness*, ch. 13.

135. One of the implications of these claims, and one which Aquinas accepts explicitly in discussions of the distinction between God's antecedent and consequent will, is that God does not have everything he desires. In particular, God's desire that every human

being come into a union of love with God is not fulfilled. Part of God's love for human persons is that God grants human persons the good of free will. Without free will on the part of human beings, no union in love between God and human persons is possible. There cannot be a union of wills in love unless there are two wills to unite. But since God does give human beings free will, God cannot determine by himself that every human being will respond to God's desire for union with correlative desires of love. Consequently, God's giving human persons free will has the result that God cannot ensure that the desires of God's love are completely fulfilled.

136. For a good introduction to Aquinas's own account of the atonement, see Nicholas M. Healey, "Redemption," in *The Cambridge Companion to the Summa Theologiae*, edited by Philip McCosker and Denys Turner (Cambridge: Cambridge University Press, 2016), 255–68.

CHAPTER 4

1. See Chapter 1 for more discussion of this issue.

2. The notion of defeat here is taken from discussions of the problem of evil. Roughly put, a benefit defeats an instance of suffering if the benefit outweighs the suffering and could not be gotten without the suffering.

3. It should be said here that the nature of union is not exactly the same as the nature of composition. Composition is the making one of things that are many; union is what it is to be one without losing the many that come together into the one.

4. C.S. Lewis, *The Screwtape Letters* (New York: Simon & Schuster, 1961), 70–1.

5. See my *Wandering in Darkness: Narrative and the Problem of Suffering* (Oxford: Oxford University Press, 2010), chs. 6 and 7.

6. As I have tried to show (*Wandering in Darkness*, ch. 6), personal presence and closeness are interconnected in complicated ways. Minimal personal presence, including second-person experience, is required for closeness; and mutual closeness is itself required for rich shared attention, which is in turn required for the most significant personal presence. My formulation of union as a matter of the most significant personal presence and mutual closeness is therefore pleonastic. As I explained closeness and personal presence, the most significant personal presence entails all the rest of the items on the list of things required for union, including mutual closeness. There is nonetheless some heuristic value in the pleonastic formulation. In human interactions, significant personal presence can be momentary or episodic, whereas mutual closeness is a matter of dispositions and considerable shared history as well. The pleonastic formulation keeps us from thinking of union itself as an ephemeral thing.

7. Although this chapter's treatment of God's omnipresence focuses on God's presence to human beings, I do not mean to imply that God's personal presence is limited to human beings. It is customary in philosophical theology to suppose that every created thing participates in being in virtue of being created by a God who is *being*. But if God is also irreducibly personal, an entity with one mind and one will, then every created thing somehow also participates in personhood in virtue of being created by such a God. (For an argument to this effect, see my *The God of the Bible and the God of the Philosophers*, Aquinas Lecture (Milwaukee, WI: Marquette University Press, 2016).)

This claim is not equivalent to some form of panpsychism, however. Panpsychism attempts to find elements of personhood intrinsically in every thing that there is. But what the melding of classical theism and biblical theism yields is a God who is personally engaged, personally present, and interactive with everything that God has made. The traces of personhood left in things in virtue of being created by God, then, need not (or, better, should not) be thought of as intrinsic characteristics in the things themselves. Rather, these traces emerge in interaction with the creator, who is ever present to his creation. On this way of thinking about the traces of personhood in created things, it makes sense for God to say 'you' to the sea (Job 38:11) or to a fig tree (Mark 11:14), but it does not make sense for any human being to do so, as perhaps it might on some contemporary versions of panpsychism. The sea or the fig tree might have traces of personhood only in relation to the mind and will of its creator, and not in its own right. This is a position taken by Jerome in his commentary on Matthew 8:26, where Christ is said to rebuke the winds and the sea. Jerome says,

> From this passage we understand that all created things perceive the Creator. For those to whom the rebuke and the command are given perceive the one giving the command. This accords with the majesty of the Creator, but not with the error of the heretics, who think that all things have souls. Things which are insensible to us are sensible to him. (St. Jerome, *Commentary on Matthew*, translated by Thomas P. Scheck (Washington, DC: The Catholic University of America Press, 2008), 103)

But I mention this element of God's omnipresence only to set it aside, since it is not directly relevant to issues of atonement.

8. God's omnipresence is the subject of an increasing literature in contemporary philosophy. For a representative excellent example, see Hud Hudson, "Omnipresence," in *The Oxford Handbook of Philosophical Theology*, edited by Thomas P. Flint and Michael C. Rea (Oxford: Oxford University Press, 2009), 199–216. My focus in this chapter is on a side of omnipresence not often investigated in the standard treatments of it.

9. Although these elements in God's presence to human beings might seem irrelevant to the nature of divine and human union, in fact they will matter crucially in later chapters, so that it is worth sorting them out here rather than having to return to them in the middle of other issues.

10. For detailed discussion of the doctrine of eternity, see my *Aquinas* (London and New York: Routledge, 2003), ch. 4 and my "The Openness of God: Eternity and Free Will," in *Philosophical Essays Against Open Theism*, edited by Benjamin H. Arbour (New York: Routledge, 2018).

11. See Eleonore Stump and Norman Kretzmann, "Eternity," *Journal of Philosophy* 78 (1981): 429–58. A relationship that can be recognized as a kind of simultaneity will of course be symmetric. But since its relata have relevantly distinct modes of existence, ET-simultaneity will be neither reflexive nor transitive. In particular, each of two temporal events can be ET-simultaneous with one and the same eternal event without being ET-simultaneous with each other.

12. But it does not follow and is not true that all of time is present with respect to anything temporal at any particular temporal location.

13. Aristotle, *Physics* 211b.
14. Eleonore Stump and Norman Kretzmann, "Eternity, Awareness, and Action," *Faith and Philosophy* 9 (1992): 463–82.
15. As a first approximation of a general rule, we might say that an instance of a use of a cognitive faculty aimed at something S_1 in the world is mediated when S_1 is cognized only in virtue of that very cognitive faculty's apprehension of something else S_2. On this way of thinking about direct and unmediated cognition, Paula's seeing Jerome on a video screen counts as mediated *visual* cognition on Paula's part, because Paula *sees* Jerome only in virtue of seeing the image on the video screen. But Paula's knowing Jerome by means of video-conferencing with him is not mediated *second-personal* cognition, because the video screen itself is not an object of cognition for the system subserving knowledge of persons.
16. See my *Wandering in Darkness*, ch. 6.
17. For a classic attempt to give a philosophical explanation of shared attention in connection with sexual desire and sexual union, see Thomas Nagel, "Sexual Perversion," *The Journal of Philosophy* 66 (1969): 5–17. I am grateful to Scott Davison for calling the relevance of this paper to this chapter to my attention.
18. Even the terminology is fluid. What I am calling 'shared attention' or 'joint attention' here is a dyadic relation. Some writers reserve these terms for a triadic relation, between two persons and a third object. In what follows here, by 'shared attention' I mean only the dyadic relation.
19. For more argument to this effect, see my *Wandering in Darkness*, ch. 6.
20. I have discussed the nature of both these conditions for union in detail elsewhere; see my *Wandering in Darkness*, chs. 4 and 6.
21. A caveat is needed here, because (as I will explain below) a person needs to be internally integrated if others are to be close to him. It is possible to think of internal integration as a person's being close to himself, in some extended or analogous sense.
22. In the description of closeness that follows, I am focusing on a relation of friendship between fully functional adult human beings; but this general account can be modified in one way or another to fit closeness between persons when at least one of them is not an adult or is not fully functional or both.
23. For an interesting discussion of mutual vulnerability in love, see Bruce Langtry, *God, the Best, and Evil* (Oxford: Oxford University Press, 2008), 168–70.
24. It is also possible for there to be something analogous as regards the intellect. It is possible for a person to be unclear, uncomprehending, or even mistaken about his own beliefs. A self-deceived person, for example, is someone who has invested considerable psychic energy in hiding from himself some of the beliefs (or the beliefs and desires) he has. He has a stake in not recognizing some of his beliefs (or beliefs and desires) as his own, and he cares about seeing himself as other than he is. Such a person is divided within himself as regards his beliefs (or beliefs and desires). So, a person can be alienated from himself in mind as well as in will. Jerome's internal alienation from himself in either intellect or will puts Paula at some distance from him. For more argument to this effect, see my *Wandering in Darkness*, ch. 6.

25. For a discussion of the relation between divisions in the will and divisions in the intellect, see my *Aquinas*, ch. 12.

26. I am grateful to Marilyn McCord Adams for insightful questions that prompted some of the development of this section.

27. He might also be confused, irrational, self-deceived, or have other impairments of this sort.

28. In his cell during the trial in Nuremberg, Hans Frank discussed with the prison psychologist G.M. Gilbert "the two-sided character" of many of the leading Nazis, himself most certainly included. Gilbert quoted Goethe's line, "Two souls dwell, alas, in my breast," and Frank approvingly finished the quotation for him. See G.M. Gilbert, *Nuremberg Diary* (New York: Da Capo Press, 1995), 44.

29. See, e.g., ST II–II q.45 a.4 and 6.

30. For discussion of the details of this sort of division in the self, see my "Augustine on Free Will," in *The Cambridge Companion to Augustine*, second edition, edited by David Meconi and Eleonore Stump (Cambridge: Cambridge University Press, 2014), 166–86.

31. See Gilbert, *Nuremberg Diary*, 259.

32. This claim will raise some worries in those who hold to the doctrine of simplicity. I have addressed those worries in my *Wandering in Darkness*, ch. 6, and considerations of space keep me from addressing them again here.

33. I note that when in the Gospels Jesus wants to portray those people most given to moral wrongdoing, he describes himself addressing them in second-person terms and saying to them, "I never knew you" (cf., e.g., Matt. 7:23). What is at issue here is not his knowledge of facts about these people; rather, the focus is on the knowledge of persons. For Jesus to say that he does not know these evildoers is to presuppose a connection between internal integration on their part and their ability to be known by another person. Their evildoing prevents Jesus' knowing *them*. The consequence is also clear. One cannot be close to a person one does not know. The point of the claim in that passage, then, seems to be that, in virtue of their lack of integration in goodness, Jesus cannot be close to these people or united with them.

34. For a discussion of the way in which Aquinas understands the compatibility of the God of the Bible with the God of classical theism, who is immutable, eternal, and simple, see my *The God of the Bible and the God of the Philosophers*.

35. In fact, even unfulfilled desires of a certain sort can be attributable to God as traditionally understood. Aquinas interprets the biblical text "God will have all men to be saved" (1 Tim. 2:4) as describing an unfulfilled state of God's will; he explains the text in terms of what he calls 'God's antecedent will' (see, e.g., *De veritate* q.23 a.2). Aquinas thinks of God's antecedent will not as a volition on God's part but as an inclination; it is, as it were, the volition God would have had if everything in creation had been up to him and nothing at all had been up to the will of human beings. For further discussion of the distinction between God's antecedent and consequent wills, see my *Wandering in Darkness*, chs. 13 and 14.

36. I am grateful to John Foley for pointing out to me the need to address explicitly the issues in this section.

37. I have discussed the nature of the second-personal at length in my *Wandering in Darkness*, chs. 4 and 6. For an excellent contemporary attempt to explain the

nature of the second-personal in connection with child development, see Vasudevi Reddy, *How Infants Know Minds* (Cambridge, MA: Harvard University Press, 2008).

38. It is of course possible to have some kind of personal presence without shared attention, as one does when one sits in silence with a close friend through a movie that is riveting to each of the friends; but such a personal presence is limited, as is clear from the fact that after the movie the friends are glad for a chance to discuss the movie together, with each attending to the other's reaction to the movie. The point in this chapter is just that the greatest kind of personal presence, the most significant personal presence, requires shared attention.

39. Some third element, hard to characterize, is also necessary. Suppose, for example, that Paula mind-reads Jerome and has empathy with Jerome at the same time that Jerome mind-reads Paula and has empathy with Paula, *but* that neither of them is aware of what the other is doing. Suppose, for example, that each of them is seeing the other through a one-way mirror. Then there would be mutual mind-reading and mutual empathy among them, but there would not be shared awareness. The need for a third element, in addition to mutual mind-reading and mutual empathy, to capture the notion of shared attention is clear. But what to name this third element and how exactly to characterize it is a subject of discussion and controversy among contemporary philosophers. For an excellent discussion of this issue, see Naomi Eilan, "Joint Attention and the Second Person," unpublished. I will leave this issue to one side in what follows.

40. Among philosophers, there is not one universally accepted understanding of the notion of mind-reading. It is taken ambiguously, in a way analogous to the ambiguity in the notion of perception. The notion of perception can be taken as (i) perception, (ii) perception as, and (iii) perceptual belief. To say that Max has a perception of a cup can be understood to mean:

   (i) the cup is an object of perception for Max,
   (ii) Max perceives the cup as a cup,
   (iii) Max perceives that *that* is a cup.

The notion of mind-reading is ambiguous in the same way. The reason for the ambiguity is that, in ordinary cases in which a cognitive capacity is operating normally, it operates as part of a whole system to give information available to consciousness, connected with other information stored in the system, and formulable in beliefs. For reasons I have given elsewhere, it seems to me better to take perception in sense (ii) than in sense (i) or sense (iii). (See my *Aquinas*, ch. 8, especially the section on perception.) In this book, I will understand mind-reading analogously, in sense (ii), rather than sense (i) or sense (iii).

In this respect, I dissent from Alvin Goldman's use of the term 'mind-reading.' His use of the term is a variant on (iii). He says: "By 'mind-reading' I mean the attribution of a mental state to self or other. In other words, to mind-read is to form a judgment, belief, or representation that a designate person occupies or undergoes (in the past, present, or future) a specified mental state or experience" (Alvin Goldman, "Mirroring, Mindreading, and Simulation," in *Mirror Neuron Systems: The Role of Mirroring Processes in Social Cognition*, edited by Jamie Pineda

(New York: Springer, 2009), 312). On Goldman's usage, it would not be true to say that autistic children are impaired with respect to mind-reading, since it is possible for them to form judgments about the mental states of others.

But in order to explain what is impaired in autism, we need a term like 'mind-reading' in sense (ii). Since 'mind-reading' is the term already employed for this purpose by many philosophers and researchers on autism, it seems to me better to continue to use the term in that way rather than in Goldman's way. Goldman's goal is to interpret mind-reading in such a way as to make the new results in neurobiology compatible with his own attempts to understand mind-reading in terms of simulation theory. For arguments against Goldman's position on this score, see Shaun Gallagher's article in the same volume: "Neural Simulation and Social Cognition," pp. 355–71.

41. Although early work on autism emphasized its impairments, much recent research has called attention not only to the cognitive strengths possible for human beings with autism but also to the way in which, by alternate systems, human beings with autism can flourish in human relationship and human community. It is important to me to make sure that this point is not lost, even if for my purposes here the impairments of autism are to the fore. The impairments of autism help to highlight human cognitive capacities that we might otherwise overlook or be skeptical of; and I raise the issue of autism only for that purpose. But if autism were a main subject for me, then I would be at pains to emphasize that human beings can flourish and be in union with others in a way well worth honoring, no matter what cognitive impairments they work through. For further discussion of this general point, see Chapter 9.

42. Mind-reading or some analogue of it can be found in species other than human beings and also between members of different species, including between human beings and other animals; and so the qualification 'in human beings' is necessary here.

43. The neuroscience presented here is not necessary to my points, which could be made from phenomenology alone. But there is a heuristic value in being aware of this current neuroscience, whether it stands the test of time or not, because it shows at least one way in which the brain could be engineered to subserve the mental states in question. There need not be anything mysterious about mind-reading and empathy. But if all the neuroscience apparently demonstrating the existence and function of a mirror neuron system were to be disproved, the points I am trying to make through discussion of the mirror neuron system would not be disproved in consequence. The neurobiology is only propaedeutic to my purposes.

44. There is a considerable literature on empathy. For a good introduction to some of the issues involved, see Alvin Goldman, "Two Routes to Empathy: Insights from Cognitive Neuroscience," in *Empathy: Philosophical and Psychological Perspectives*, edited by Amy Coplan and Peter Goldie (Oxford: Oxford University Press, 2011), 31–44. It is clear that there are at least two different kinds of empathy or levels of empathy. One is more nearly involuntary and also more coarse-grained. The other is under more voluntary control, more fine-grained, and more dependent on past experience and training. The first is in play when a person winces as he sees someone else get hurt. The second is engaged when someone is deeply involved in

reading a novel. It seems clear that there is no sharp demarcation between these kinds, but rather a kind of continuum. The first kind of empathy, and any kind of empathy closer to that end of the continuum, is what is at issue in this chapter. But, in my view, it would be possible to preserve the general point of this chapter even if it turned out that the cognitive processes at issue required empathy of the second kind.

45. In this example I focus on mind-reading that includes information garnered from the visual system, but other sensory systems can also be used for the same purpose. In fact, it is possible to mind-read through cues that do not employ sensory perception, at least not in their ordinary modes. One can mind-read another person during a texting conversation, for example. For further discussion of the details of such issues, see my *Wandering in Darkness*, chs. 4 and 6.

46. It is not easy to say precisely what it is for a system to run off-line, but the general idea is this. In the case of dreamed motion, the brain's motor programs for actual physical running are off-line in that while these motor programs are firing, they are disconnected from the muscles in the legs and so do not produce running in the legs. In the case of mind-reading, the brain's mirror neuron system runs the programs it would run if one person were doing what the other, observed person is doing; but it runs these programs disconnected from those states of will and intellect the observer would have if she herself were doing those acts. In this way, she shares in the observed person's mental states but without having them as he has them, in virtue of having her own states of intellect and will, not his, even while she feels what she would feel if she were doing what he is doing.

47. And, of course, on this basis she also knows *that* Jerome is in pain. Empathic feeling of his pain is a reliable ground for knowledge that he is in pain.

48. Vittorio Gallese, "'Being Like Me': Self-Other Identity, Mirror Neurons, and Empathy," in *Perspectives on Imitation: From Neuroscience to Social Science*, edited by Susan Hurley and Nick Chater (Cambridge, MA: MIT Press, 2005), 111.

49. Gallese, "'Being Like Me,'" 111 and 114.

50. As many researchers working on these topics testify, it is very hard to capture the phenomenon at issue. But this much has now become clear. Attention, closeness, and presence can be mutual as between Paula and Jerome and yet not yield union because they are not shared. For example, Paula can be mind-reading Jerome without Jerome's being aware that she is doing so while Jerome is mind-reading Paula without Paula's being aware that Jerome is doing so. So mutuality does not imply sharedness. But sharedness is what is crucial for union.

51. Some people will object that this is not a position compatible with Catholicism because Catholicism takes God's presence to be mediated through the Scriptures, through the agency of a priest, and through the sacraments. In my view, this is a mistaken objection that rests on a confusion about the notion of mediation. If I see the coffee cup in front of me, is my cognition direct and unmediated? Most of us would say 'yes', even though we know the story about the neurobiological processing necessary for vision. What makes the cognition of the cup direct and unmediated is that I do not cognize the cup by means of *visually cognizing* something else, even if there is considerable processing of visual data in the

brain in order for me to see the cup. In the same way, on the Catholic doctrine of the Eucharist, for example, although the real presence of Christ in the Eucharist is mediated by a priest, Christ is directly present to those participating appropriately in the sacrament. That is because Christ is not present to those participating only in virtue of the priest's being present to them, even if on Catholic doctrine the agency of the priest is a means by which the bread and wine become the real body and blood of Christ. Something similar applies also to the other cases, where there is a means which enables the presence of God to a person without its being the case that that means makes the presence of God mediated to such a person. Just as my seeing by means of my contact lenses does not imply that I see other things in virtue of first seeing my contact lenses, so also the agency of priests, the sacraments, and the Scriptures are means by which one may have direct and unmediated presence of God. That Aquinas holds such a position is made overwhelmingly clear in his biblical commentaries (among many other places) and in his explanation of the gifts and fruits of the Holy Spirit, in my view; but this is not a subject that can be canvassed in detail in passing here. For further discussion of this issue with respect to the Eucharist, see Chapter 9. I am grateful to Paul Weithman for calling to my attention the need to address this issue.

52. The phenomenon of the dark night of the soul, as it is called in Christian tradition, is an exception to this claim. This phenomenon is traditionally supposed to be reserved for the spiritually advanced and is designed to draw such persons even closer to God. It is too complicated a topic to be dealt with in passing here, and so it can just be taken as an exception to the general claim I make here.

53. The doctrine of simplicity complicates any attribution to God, so that God's knowledge of truths may need to be explained in a way only analogical to human propositional knowledge.

54. It does not follow that if this claim is right, then God would not be omniscient. An omniscient God lacks perceptual knowledge in virtue of not having eyes, for example, but his omniscience is not thereby impugned. An omniscient God must know everything, in some suitably nuanced form of this general claim; but the mode of God's knowledge depends on God's nature.

55. For a different conclusion, see Linda Zagzebski, *Omnisubjectivity: A Defense of a Divine Attribute* (Milwaukee, WI: Marquette University Press, 2013). My reasons for not sharing Zagzebski's view are in effect given in this chapter. For a good presentation of problems with Zagzebski's account, see also Adam Green, "Omnisubjectivity and Incarnation," *Topoi* 36.4 (2017) 693–701. I am largely in sympathy with Green's own account of the phenomenon, given in the same paper.

56. For a discussion of this claim, see my "The Non-Aristotelian Character of Aquinas's Ethics: Aquinas on the Passions," *Faith and Philosophy* 28.1 (2011): 29–43. The character of an emotion and its relations to the character of a feeling has been the subject of extensive discussion, which I cannot canvass in passing here. But it is clear that there is a distinction, and that distinction matters in this context. At any rate, not every emotion is accompanied by feelings; and it is possible to have a feeling which does not rise to the level of an emotion, as when one discovers that one has been feeling hunger because of the smell of baking bread; the feeling which had gone unnoticed till that discovery is not an emotion.

57. It is also true that there never is a *when* in the life of eternal God that the suffering of Christ on the cross is not with him. For some discussion of the apparent counter-intuitive implications of this claim, see Chapter 10. It should be noted in this connection that on any view of God's mode of duration Christ in heaven retains the marks of his crucifixion in his human body, so that even if God is temporal, something of Christ's passion is always with Christ.

58. To say this is, of course, not the same as saying that God's becoming incarnate is necessary to him. For Aquinas, for example, God's eternity and immutability are compatible with God's ability to do otherwise than God does.

59. On orthodox theological doctrine, the second person of the Trinity is God, and so it is true to say that God has an assumed human nature. Since this is so, in the assumed human nature that God never lacks (on the doctrine of eternity), God can experience passivity in his own person. Those who use the doctrine of simplicity to emphasize the absence of all passivity in God in effect resurrect the Eunomian heresy which supposed that the Son, incarnate in Christ, was not the same as God. But since on orthodox theology the person in the incarnate Christ is God, then those things true of Christ in his human nature are also attributable to God, in the human nature God took on as God's own.

60. In Chapter 5, I will argue that, to do so, Christ has to be willing to open himself up simultaneously to every human psyche. The idea that Christ opens himself at once to this kind of spectacular mind-reading is one way of understanding the traditional, scripturally based claim that on the cross Christ bore the sins of all humankind. As I will explain in detail in the next chapter, on this way of interpreting that scriptural claim, the power of God gives the human mind of Christ the more than human power of feeling within himself at one and the same time the minds of all human persons.

61. For a detailed discussion of the nature of faith and its relations both to grace and to free will, see my *Aquinas*, chs. 12 and 13.

62. There are two minds in the incarnate Christ, but only one mind in God. The explanation of this claim, which might strike someone as puzzling, is that what is in God is only God's nature. The incarnate Christ has *two* natures, one fully human and one fully divine. There is only one mind in God, because in God there is only the divine nature. There are two minds in Christ because each of the natures of Christ has its own mind.

63. There is a separate issue of the degree to which Paula, in this condition, is aware of the presence of the Holy Spirit as the Holy Spirit. To have a person present to one is not the same thing as knowing that person under every appropriate description of that person. For further discussion of this complicated issue, see the section on exclusivism in Chapter 8.

64. For a helpful discussion seeking to explain the effects of the indwelling Holy Spirit, see Aquinas's *Summa contra Gentiles* (SCG) IV.21–2.

65. I am grateful to John Foley, who suggested to me this way of explaining the point and its usefulness for understanding the nature of God's indwelling in a person of faith.

66. As recent work in metaphysics highlights, there are also criteria for determining that a person's mind is his own, that it belongs to him, in ways hard to specify with

precision, but crucial for issues of moral responsibility and freedom of will. For a discussion of some of the issues, see, for example, my "Persons: Identification and Freedom," *Philosophical Topics* 24 (1996): 183–214.

67. When something goes wrong with these latter brain systems, dysfunctional mental conditions involving delusions can result. For example, in consequence of an injury, a patient can suffer the delusion that some part of his body is not his own. For a vivid and popular description of such a case, see Oliver Sacks, *A Leg to Stand On* (New York: Harper and Row, 1984). In the view of some researchers, the psychological delusion of thought intrusion is also a result of the malfunctioning of these brain systems. In Fregoli's syndrome, a patient has the intractable delusion that he knows familiar people when he looks at the faces of strangers. In Capgras syndrome, a patient has the intractable delusion that he does not know the people he is looking at when he looks at the faces of persons who are in fact familiar to him. For discussion of such syndromes, see, for example, Sandra Blakeslee and Vilayandur Ramachandran, *Phantoms in the Brain* (London: Harper Perennial, 2005), ch. 8.

Both Fregoli's syndrome and Capgras syndrome are a kind of loss, after neurological damage, of the capacity to know something *as* the thing it is. Although these syndromes have been described largely as they affect the knowledge of persons, there are also reported cases in which the lost capacity extends to the knowledge of familiar things other than persons. So, for example, some researchers describe "a patient who claimed his actual home was not his 'real' home, although he recognized that the facsimile home has the same ornaments and bedside items as the original" (Todd Feinberg, John Deluca, Joseph T. Giacino, David M. Roane, and Mark Solms, "Right-Hemisphere Pathology and the Self: Delusional Misidentification and Reduplication," in *The Lost Self: Pathologies of the Brain and Identity*, edited by Todd Feinberg and Julian Paul Keenan (Oxford: Oxford University Press, 2005), 103. See also pp. 105–6 and 114–25).

68. It is a common conceit of science fiction that the alien mind and the human mind can interact within the mind of the human person, without either mind losing its identity. In the science fiction literature depicting a human being in such a condition, the indwelling mind is typically that of an alien. The alien is generally portrayed as smarter and more powerful than the human being his mind indwells. But in addition the alien mind is depicted as invading the human mind, entering it without the consent of the human being in question; and the alien's purpose is typically either indifferent to the welfare of the human being or actively malevolent towards him. Robert Heinlein's *The Puppetmasters* is an example.

69. If one Googles 'schizophrenia and demon possession', one will find that this sort of belief is still prevalent in some communities today.

70. For more explanation of the nature of this mutual mind-reading between a human person and God, see my "Faith, Wisdom, and the Transmission of Knowledge through Testimony," in *Religious Faith and Intellectual Virtue*, edited by Laura Frances Callahan and Timothy O'Connor (Oxford: Oxford University Press, 2014), 204–30.

71. For different understandings of this union, see Chapter 6.

72. For an excellent discussion of this subject in connection with Aquinas's ethics, see Andrew Pinsent, *The Second-Person Perspective in Aquinas's Ethics: Virtues and Gifts* (London and New York: Routledge, 2012), especially ch. 4, in which Pinsent likens the fruition of second-person relatedness, an 'abiding in' the other, to a state of resonance.

73. See Chapter 7 for more discussion of the fruits of the Holy Spirit.

74. It may be that there are also cases in the New Testament in which the Holy Spirit comes on human persons, in a phenomenon distinct from the indwelling of the Holy Spirit. Consider, for example, the story of the coming of the Holy Spirit on the apostles at Pentecost, when the apostles spoke in languages other than their native speech. It may be that the kind of phenomenon reported in that story is distinct from the indwelling of the Holy Spirit and more like some of the cases in the Hebrew Bible. I make no claims about such cases, however. My point is only to distinguish *one* New Testament phenomenon, the indwelling of the Holy Spirit, from apparently analogous phenomena in the Hebrew Bible.

75. For a defense of the ahistorical approach I take toward biblical texts in this section, see Chapter 1, where I explain the reasons for my doing so. My purpose in this book is not historical insight into biblical texts or any other contribution to contemporary biblical studies; it is rather an exercise in philosophical theology.

76. In the case in Exodus, the Hebrew word translated 'spirit' is '*ruach*'; but there are other Hebrew words also sometimes translated 'spirit.' There is a complicated and wonderful Jewish tradition regarding the *shekinah*, the dwelling or presence of God with human beings, which has its origin in biblical texts about the tabernacle of God, literally and figuratively understood. The idea of the *shekinah* has at its heart God's dwelling not with an individual human person but with God's people. In this respect, although it has manifest connections to the notion of the spirit of God in or on a person, it is still different enough in character that it cannot be brought easily into the discussion here. Furthermore, sometimes the Hebrew word for 'presence' is '*panayim*', which in its most concrete meaning signifies the face. For example, Moses says to God that if God's presence, God's *panayim*, does not go with Moses and the people as they make their way to the promised land, Moses does not want to lead the people (Exod. 33:14). I would be glad if there were space to examine all these evocative stories in connection with a consideration of the indwelling spirit of God, but it is not possible to do everything in one book.

77. Since God is eternal and thus not bound by time, it is in principle possible for there to be a person in grace who has the indwelling Holy Spirit at a time before the passion and death of Christ, where the coming of the Holy Spirit to that person is nonetheless enabled by the passion and death of Christ. On contemporary Roman Catholic doctrine, Mary was such a person. It remains clear, however, that a case of this sort is still to be distinguished from the kind of case manifested by the spirit's coming on Samson for victory in battle. For further discussions of this complication, see Chapter 8, on the discussion of exclusivism.

78. Aquinas calls this human attuning to the divine mind a human person's 'connaturality' or 'sympathy' with God, and he says "sympathy or connaturality for divine things is the result of love, which unites us to God..." ST II–II q.45 a.2.

79. In addition to those listed in the acknowledgements section of the Preface, I am grateful to the students in Scott Davison's Philosophy of Love and Sex class at Morehead State University for helpful comments on this chapter.

CHAPTER 5

1. I recognize that the nature of the organization of parts into a whole is a controversial subject and that some philosophers suppose that there is very little that counts as an organized whole. (See, for example, Peter van Inwagen, *Material Beings* (Ithaca, NY: Cornell University Press, 1990).) It is no aim of this project to construct or defend a particular account of the nature of wholes and parts or the nature of their organizing principles. But, for some attempt to sketch the rudiments of an Aristotelian and Thomistic account of composition, see my "Emergence, Causal Powers, and Aristotelianism in Metaphysics," in *Powers and Capacities in Philosophy: The New Aristotelianism*, edited by Ruth Groff and John Greco (New York and London: Routledge, 2012), 48–68. On that Aristotelian and Thomistic account, one can reverse engineer, as it were, from causal power to organized whole. Where there is a causal power had by something that is not had by any isolated bit of the thing, then the thing is an organized whole in the sense at issue here. On this way of thinking about organized wholes, an infant and its primary care-giver bonded in the shared attention way are an organized whole for the time that they share attention. The power for learning language resides in the dynamic system of that whole, for example. The care-giver cannot teach language or the infant learn it outside that system.

2. In his book, *Strange Tools: Art and Human Nature* (New York: Hill and Wang, 2015), Alva Noë puts an analogous point about organization composing more than one person into a larger whole this way:

   Living beings are organisms—organized wholes. . . . To be alive is to be organized, and insofar as we are not only organisms but are also persons, we find ourselves organized, or integrated, in a still larger range of ways that tie us to the environment, each other, and our social worlds. People find themselves organized by such shared activities as breast-feeding . . . [or] conversation. At one level, at the level of consciousness . . . when two people talk, they express ideas and pay attention to each other. But it is a remarkable fact that conversation puts together, integrates, and organizes what we do at a much more basic level as well. Two people talking tend to take up the same posture, they adjust their volumes to an appropriate level, they look at each other and at objects in their immediate environment in highly controlled ways, and, of course, in doing so they participate in a complicated activity of listening, thinking, paying attention, doing and undergoing. . . . [For conversation as for breast-feeding,] the same basic organizing structure is in place, however modulated, amplified, and so altered by different skills, interests and situations. (6–7)

3. For more discussion of the mind-reading at issue in the case of the indwelling Holy Spirit, see my "Faith, Wisdom, and the Transmission of Knowledge through Testimony," in *Religious Faith and Intellectual Virtue*, edited by Laura Frances Callahan and Timothy O'Connor (Oxford: Oxford University Press, 2014), 204–30.

4. For a recent discussion of indwelling as Trinitarian, see Gilles Emery, "L'inhabitation de Dieu Trinité dans les justes," *Nova et Vetera* 88 (2013): 155–84.
5. Matt. 27:46; Mark 15:34.
6. John Calvin, *The Institutes of the Christian Religion*, vol. 1, translated by Henry Beveridge (Grand Rapids, MI: Eerdmans, 1970), bk. II, ch. xvi, p. 445. Calvin is speaking of Christ's suffering in the Garden before his passion, but the point applies as well to Christ's suffering on the cross.
7. There are states that are not what one would expect to find in a morally perfect person but that are not morally blameworthy and that do not merit punishment. A steady temptation to racism in a person who steadfastly always resists that temptation in every way is an example.
8. For an excellent contemporary discussion of the cry, see Thomas Joseph White, *The Incarnate Lord: A Thomistic Study in Christology* (Washington, DC: The Catholic University of America Press, 2017), ch. 7. White reaches conclusions different from my own, but I found his reflections on the issues helpful. My reasons for preferring my interpretation to his are given in this chapter.
9. Thomas H. McCall, *Forsaken: The Trinity and the Cross, and Why It Matters* (Downers Grove, IL: InterVarsity Press, 2012), 38.
10. McCall, *Forsaken*, 41.
11. I understand that not all readers will share this judgment. Those who are inclined to accept that in uttering the cry of dereliction Christ meant to express the entire Psalm including its optimistic ending might nonetheless be willing to grant that this one line has something desolate about it, and they can then consider this chapter as focused on the desolation expressed by the utterance of that one line in the Psalm.
12. For detailed discussion of the nature of this prayer, see Chapter 6 of this book. For more discussion of Christ's experience in the Garden of Gethsemane, see Chapter 8.
13. These issues are discussed in detail in my *Wandering in Darkness: Narrative and the Problem of Suffering* (Oxford: Oxford University Press, 2010), ch. 6.
14. For example, one set of instructions to labor coaches says,

   > Stay right by her side, your face near hers... Tell her to open her eyes and look at you. Say it loudly enough for her to hear you—but calmly and kindly. (Penny Simkin, "Labor Coping Tips From a Trained Professional," *She Knows Pregnancy and Baby*, 19 April 2016, http://www.pregnancyandbaby.com/pregnancy/articles/936891/the-take-charge-routine-tips-for-the-labor-coach)

   And another one says,

   > Moms often need firm direction as to what to do during a contraction at this [advanced] stage. Give commands firmly but lovingly.... If she panics or loses control momentarily, get close to her face, look in her eyes, and speak gently but firmly. (Penny Simkin, *The Birth Partner* (Boston, MA: Harvard Common Press, 1989), 167))

15. In this respect, closeness differs from shared attention, where something external to the intellect and will of the persons in the relationship can break or obviate shared attention, as I will discuss below.

16. This point holds even for those in hell. God desires union with them even while he is separated from them. For further discussion of this claim, see Chapters 2 and 3 in this volume on the nature of love and forgiveness. In addition, someone might suppose that this claim is false on the penal substitution kind of interpretation. But, even on penal substitution interpretations, God still wants to be united with Christ; God only wants Christ to experience God as absent in order to pay the penalty for sinful human beings. I consider this kind of explanation of the cry of dereliction below, in connection with Calvin's account of the cry.

17. This conclusion needs some nuancing, however. A wife whose husband is unfaithful may move out of their home, in the hope that her absence will cause him to reconsider his behavior. Similarly, when human persons turn away from God, it is possible for God to withdraw from them as a means to prompt them to be willing to return to him. In such a case, although God is absent, his absence is prompted by the lack of the desires of love for him on the part of human persons; it does not stem from God's own lack of a desire for union with the human persons in question. A case of this sort is at issue in this line from Isaiah: "your evildoings have separated you from your God, and your sins have hidden his face from you" (59:2). In this sort of case, God withdraws from human persons for a brief period; but, even while he does so, it remains true that God has the desires of love for the persons from whom he withdraws. His withdrawal is a manifestation of his love and forgiveness for them. It is a response to their withdrawal from him and is an extreme attempt on God's part to prompt those human persons to turn again to God. Consequently, even God's withdrawal from them is encompassed within his desire for union with them. Since this nuancing in fact attributes ultimate responsibility for the distance between God and human persons to the human persons, then, it can safely be assimilated to POSSIBILITY (2).

18. Calvin, *Institutes*, bk. II, ch. xvi, pp. 443–4.

19. Calvin says, "If anyone now ask, Did Christ descend to hell at the time when he deprecated death? I answer, that this was the commencement, and that from it we may infer how dire and dreadful were the tortures which he endured when he felt himself standing at the bar of God as a criminal in our stead" (Calvin, *Institutes*, bk. II, ch. xvi, p. 446).

20. Calvin, *Institutes*, bk. II, ch. xvi, p. 444.

21. Richard Overy (ed.), *Interrogations: The Nazi Elite in Allied Hands, 1945* (New York: Viking Penguin, 2001), 419.

22. Overy, *Interrogations*, 401.

23. For one example of a story in which this description of Christ seems to apply, see the episode of the woman at the well (John 4:5–29).

24. Someone might worry that in this case Christ foreknows future human free actions in a way that raises the problem of foreknowledge and free will. But in my view this worry is misguided. The human mind of Christ at t_1 has access to the mind of God in the eternal now, and the eternal now is ET-simultaneous with every moment in time as that time is present. So when at t_1 Christ mind-reads a person born at t_n, after the death of Christ, Christ can do so because at t_1, which is ET-simultaneous with the eternal *now*, Christ knows the mind of God, and God's

mind is ET-simultaneous with t_n. But ET-simultaneity is not transitive. Consequently, what is future at t_n is not already present at t_1, as it needs to be in order to raise the problem of foreknowledge and free will. For detailed discussion of this issue, see my "The Openness of God: Eternity and Free Will," in *Philosophical Essays Against Open Theism*, edited by Benjamin H. Arbour (New York: Routledge, 2018). Finally, there are biblical texts apparently claiming or implying that on the cross Christ bore the sins of all human people, and most theologians in the Christian tradition accept this claim. But this claim alone raises the same problem. So a solution to the problem raised by claims about the relation of Christ on the cross to human beings future in time with respect to his crucifixion is required by traditional Christian interpretation of these biblical texts.

25. That is, as I have explained Christ's experience of human psyches within his own, it takes the power of Christ's divine nature and its eternality to enable Christ's human nature to be in such a relation. And in Chapter 4, I explored the way in which the divine attributes of God make possible God's indwelling in every human person in grace. So the mutual indwelling at issue here is made possible by the fact that one of the relata is God.

26. For a different and more favorable exposition of Abelard's own position, see Philip Quinn, "Abelard on Atonement: 'Nothing Unintelligible, Arbitrary, Illogical, or Immoral About It,'" reprinted in *Oxford Readings in Philosophical Theology*, vol. 1, *Trinity, Incarnation, Atonement*, edited by Michael C. Rea (Oxford: Oxford University Press, 2009), 348–64.

27. I am grateful to John Foley, whose patience and persistence in discussion of these issues helped me to see that these points needed to be stressed in explicit formulation.

28. In case it helps to see the point here, think of a light governed by a rheostat. There is an all-or-nothing state of the light's being on; but, once it is on, the light admits of greater or lesser degrees, as governed by the rheostat.

29. For more discussion of the notion that union comes in degrees, see my *Wandering in Darkness*, ch. 6.

30. McCall, *Forsaken*, 111.

31. Calvin, *Institutes*, bk. II, ch. xvi, p. 441. Calvin's own interpretation of Christ's descent into hell is complicated. In addition to this discussion in *The Institutes*, see also John Calvin, *A Harmony of the Gospels, Matthew, Mark, and Luke*, vol. III, translated by A.W. Morrison, edited by David W. Torrance and Thomas F. Torrance (Grand Rapids, MI: Eerdmans, 1972), 207–8, where Calvin seems to say that in uttering the cry of dereliction Christ was experiencing hell. There, in explaining the cry, Calvin says,

> for Christ to make satisfaction for us He had to stand trial at God's tribunal.... Those who reckon that Christ took on the office of Mediator on condition of bearing our guilt in soul as in body will not wonder at the struggle He had with the pangs of death; as though under the wrath of God, He were cast into the labyrinth of evil. (207–8)

See also John Calvin, *The Epistle of Paul the Apostle to the Hebrews and the First and Second Epistles of St. Peter*, translated by William B. Johnston, edited by David W. Torrance and Thomas F. Torrance (Grand Rapids, MI: Eerdmans, 1980),

292–5, where Calvin seems to deny that Christ's soul actually descended into hell but that instead Christ's spirit was manifested to the dead in some more extended or analogical sense.

32. The Nicene Creed specifies that Christ was buried, and what was buried was the human body of Christ; but, unless Christ, the second person of the Trinity, continued to be united to the body, it would not be true that Christ was buried. For Aquinas's discussion of this issue, see, for example, ST III q.50, esp. a.2. This creedal claim does seem to give one more reason why Christ should have been resurrected in his human nature.

33. In this respect, *being united with* is different from *being identical with*. If A is identical with B, and A is identical with C, then B is identical with C. But if A is united with B and A is united with C, it may still not be the case that B is united with C. Anyone who has loving relations with each of two persons who are in the process of getting a divorce understands this point as regards union between persons. The point is obviously more complicated when parts of persons are among the relata. But even here there are relative ordinary cases that seem to illustrate the point. If Max's hand is being reattached after an accident that severed it, then while the surgeons are preparing the hand for the surgery, both the hand and the body are Max's. They are in some sense therefore in union with Max. But they are not united to each other until the surgeons' work is done. The case of Christ is sui generis, of course, as orthodox theological tradition has explicitly maintained. And so these more ordinary cases are prompts to intuition, rather than strict analogues.

34. For more discussion of the Aristotelian hylomorphism at issue here, see my *Aquinas* (London and New York: Routledge, 2003), ch. 1.

35. For some discussion of this dispute, see, for example, Nicholas Lombardo, *The Father's Will: Christ's Crucifixion and the Goodness of God* (Oxford: Oxford University Press, 2013), 4ff.

36. For a contemporary defense of such a position, see Oliver D. Crisp, *The Word Enfleshed: Exploring the Person and the Work of Christ* (Grand Rapids, MI: Baker Books, 2016), esp. 159.

37. The process of sanctification is discussed in detail in Chapter 7.

38. Someone might suppose that the doctrine of eternity gives aid to the penal substitution interpretation at least in this respect. On the penal substitution interpretation, Christ bears the penalty for human sin; but that penalty is everlasting damnation. Since Christ's suffering on the cross is permanent, in virtue of Christ's eternality, then, someone might suppose, the penal substitution interpretation is right in supposing that Christ took on the penalty for human sin. But this supposition is mistaken, in my view. The penalty for human sin is separation from God that never ends. For the incarnate Christ suffering on the cross, the separation from God is short-lived, even if that short period remains a permanent part of the present life of an eternal God. In addition, it is good to remember here that Christ bears the sins of humankind in his human mind, but not in his divine mind. For this reason, the suffering of his bearing human sin is God's suffering, but it is God's suffering in the human mind God assumed through the incarnation. This suffering and the mind-reading of sinful human beings is not in the

divine mind of God. For that reason, it is not shared by either the Father or the Spirit on the doctrine of the Trinity.

39. On the view that Christ bears the sins of all humanity on the cross, the psyches of all human beings are in Christ while Christ is on the cross; but since some human beings are in hell after death, not all the human beings who indwell Christ on the cross finish their lives in union of love with Christ. For some human beings, then, their indwelling Christ on the cross brings with it their permanent refusal of love, which is something that Christ also mind-reads. Nonetheless, with respect to those human beings indwelling Christ who continue their lives in hell, Christ has the consolation of the whole story of creation, with its outpouring of love in creation and in the recreation of the atonement. That story encompasses the suffering of the cross for Christ. For discussion of the way in which encompassing love transforms experiences of pain, see Chapter 9.

CHAPTER 6

1. In this context, as I explained in Chapter 2, I am using the word 'person' not in its theologically technical sense according to which a person of the Trinity is a subsistent relation, but in its current ordinary sense in which anything with sufficient intellect and will counts as a person. (I am not claiming that only things which actually, currently, have sufficient intellect and will count as persons, and I am deliberately leaving vague how much intellect and how much control over will is sufficient for personhood.) On this ordinary sense of the word, it is appropriate and accurate to call God a person in virtue of the fact that there is in God only one intellect and will, and they are of more than sufficient degree to merit the designation 'person.'

2. Some scholars suppose that mystics take union with God to involve or consist in the loss of the self, but it should be clear from Chapters 4 and 5 that the sense of union at issue in this book takes union even with God to constitute a union in which a human person does not lose his personhood in consequence of union. This prayer of Christ's seems to me to confirm this view of union. Even in the one God, the persons of the Trinity remain three. A fortiori, in union with God, a human person does not lose his personhood.

3. I am here summarizing views explained in earlier work; see my *Wandering in Darkness: Narrative and the Problem of Suffering* (Oxford: Oxford University Press, 2010), chs. 1 and 13. Brief reprise of this sort is the only appropriate alternative to supposing or requiring that the readers of this book have read this earlier material.

4. On the Thomistic account of the will I sketched in Chapter 2, the will wills only what the intellect presents to the will as the good in the circumstances, where the good in question ranges over the pleasurable and the efficient as well as the moral. But this claim is compatible with the will's willing what is not good, since an erring intellect can present as good what is in fact not good.

5. Augustine, *Confessions*, VIII.9. I like and have therefore used (with slight modifications) the translation by William Watts (Cambridge, MA: Harvard University Press, 1968).

6. For a detailed account of the basics of Aquinas's moral psychology, see my *Aquinas* (London and New York: Routledge, 2003), ch. 9.

7. She might also be confused, irrational, self-deceived, or have other impairments of this sort.

8. For more discussion of these claims about internal integration, moral goodness, and mutual closeness, see Chapter 4.

9. For the import of the qualifier 'fully', see my *Wandering in Darkness*, ch. 7. For presence, closeness, and union, as also for freedom, there are ordinary versions common among human beings; and then there is the real thing, the strenuous version, which is full and which is what most people want, even if they settle for the ordinary version.

10. There are some contemporary philosophers who maintain that an agent can be fully internally integrated around what is objectively morally evil. On their view, it is possible for a person to be wholehearted in evil. But this view is implausible, and good accounts of moral psychology are against it. For further discussion, see my *Wandering in Darkness*, ch. 7.

11. There is no Pelagianism in this claim that God's love and forgiveness are responsive to something in a human being. Any good in a human being is put there by God if the human being in question does not refuse God's grace. But then that human being does in fact have the grace in question, and God can respond to that person as a person in grace.

12. Some theologically literate readers who care about the doctrine of simplicity will balk at the idea of God's being responsive to things in the human will. For a detailed argument to show that divine simplicity does not rule out such responsiveness, see my *The God of the Bible and the God of the Philosophers, Aquinas Lecture* (Milwaukee, WI: Marquette University Press, 2016).

13. Or Christ's life, passion, and death. I will omit this qualifier in what follows, but it should be taken as understood.

14. This claim will strike some readers as outrageous or callous, and it is not possible to deal adequately with such reactions in a note. I have, however, dealt with them at length in *Wandering in Darkness*, ch. 13. In Chapter 9 of this book, I develop the account in that earlier work.

15. Aquinas, *Commentary on the Letter of St. Paul to the Hebrews*, translated by F. R. Larcher, edited by J. Mortensen and E. Alarcón (Lander, WY: The Aquinas Institute for the Study of Sacred Doctrine, 2012), L.2. Although I have generally used the translations of commentaries on biblical texts from this Institute's texts, in this case I have used my own.

16. Aquinas, *Expositio super Job*, ch. 1, sects. 20–1; *Thomas Aquinas, the Literal Exposition on Job: A Scriptural Commentary concerning Providence*, translated by Anthony Damico and Martin Yaffe, The American Academy of Religion Classics in Religious Studies (Atlanta, GA: Scholars Press, 1989), 89.

17. For more discussion and defense of this claim about suffering, see my *Wandering in Darkness*, ch. 1.

18. In *Horrendous Evils and the Goodness of God* (Ithaca, NY: Cornell University Press, 1999), Marilyn McCord Adams makes a distinction which is at least related to the distinction I am after here. She says, "the value of a person's life may be assessed from the inside (in relation to that person's own goals, ideals, and

choices) and from the outside (in relation to the aims, tastes, values, and preferences of others) . . . My notion is that for a person's life to be a great good to him/her on the whole, the external point of view (even if it is God's) is not sufficient" (145).

19. The expression 'the desire of the heart' is ambiguous. It can mean either a particular kind of desire or else the thing which is desired in that way. When we say, "the desire of his heart was to be a great musician," the expression refers to a desire; when we say, "in losing her, he lost the desire of his heart," the expression refers to the thing desired. I will not try to sort out this ambiguity here; I will simply trust to the context to disambiguate the expression.

20. It is important to emphasize that what is at issue here is God's *consequent* will. For the distinction between God's antecedent and God's consequent will, see, for example, *Wandering in Darkness*, ch. 12. I explain the distinction further below as well.

21. See my *Wandering in Darkness*, ch. 14.

22. Those scholars who are convinced that the position I am ascribing to Eckhart is not actually the view that Eckhart held can take what follows as an argument against an Eckhart-like position. It is not material to my point in this chapter that the position being rejected was actually held by the historical Eckhart.

23. Teresa of Avila, *The Interior Castle*, translated by Kieran Kavanaugh and Otilio Rodriguez, The Classics of Western Spirituality (Mahwah, NJ: Paulist Press, 1979), 98, 99, 100.

24. Augustine, *Confessions*, IX.12.

25. Quoted in R.W. Southern, *Saint Anselm: A Portrait in a Landscape* (Cambridge: Cambridge University Press, 1995), 165.

26. Cited in Ann Astell, *The Song of Songs in the Middle Ages* (Ithaca, NY: Cornell University Press, 1990), 126.

27. Cited in Astell, *Song of Songs*, 130.

28. Cited in Astell, *Song of Songs*, 133.

29. Quoted in Southern, *Saint Anselm*, 155–6.

30. *Meister Eckhart: The Essential Sermons: Commentaries, Treatises, and Defense*, translated by Edmund Colledge and Bernard McGinn (Mahwah, NJ: Paulist Press, 1981), "The Book of Divine Consolation," 211.

31. *Meister Eckhart: The Essential Sermons*, 215–16.

32. *Meister Eckhart: Mystic and Philosopher*, translated with commentary by Reiner Schuermann (Bloomington, IN: Indiana University Press, 1978), Sermon "See What Love," 135–6.

33. *Meister Eckhart: Selected Writings*, translated by Oliver Davies (London: Penguin Books, 1994), "The Talks of Instruction," 41–2.

34. Aquinas, *Commentary on the Gospel of John*, translated by F.R. Larcher, edited by The Aquinas Institute (Lander, WY: The Aquinas Institute for the Study of Sacred Doctrine, 2013), John 14:28, C.14 L.8. Although I like and generally use the translations of the Aquinas Institute, in this case the translation is mine.

35. And, of course, in other moods, when she is not self-consciously evaluating her own spiritual progress, Teresa herself sounds more like Bernard and Aquinas than like the stern-minded. For more discussion of this issue and more defense of the claim about Aquinas's position, see my *Wandering in Darkness*, ch. 14.

36. It is easy to become confused here because the phrase 'the good' can be used either attributively or referentially. ('The commander of the armed forces' is used referentially when it refers to the particular person who is the President; it is used attributively when it refers to anyone who holds the office of commander without reference to a particular person who in fact currently holds the office.) That is, either 'the good of the beloved' can be used to refer to particular things that are conducive to the beloved's wellbeing; or it can be used opaquely, in an attribution of anything whatever under the description *the good of the beloved*. A mother who is baffled by the quarrels among her adult children and clueless about how to bring about a just peace for them may say, despairingly, "I just want the good for everybody." She is then using 'the good' attributively, with no idea of how to use it referentially.

37. For Aquinas's beautifully argued and carefully nuanced explanation of this point, see ST I–II q.19 a.10.

38. It is important to put the point in terms of what *happens* to her father, rather than in terms of any action on her father's part, since there are certainly things her father might do that would cause Teresa a grief she would approve of having.

39. Cited in Astell, *Song of Songs*, 133.

40. Cited in Astell, *Song of Songs*, 130.

41. Roughly put, God's *antecedent* will is what God would have willed if things in the world had been up to God alone. God's *consequent* will is what God in fact wills, given what God's creatures will. God's consequent will is his will for the greatest good available in the circumstances, where at least some of the circumstances are generated through creaturely free will. See, for example, ST I q.19 a.6 ad 1, which finishes this way: "whatever God wills simpliciter [i.e., in God's consequent will] comes to be, even if what God wills antecedently does not come to be." See also, for example, Aquinas, *Commentary on 1 Timothy*, C.2, L.1, where Aquinas gives a detailed explanation of the distinction. See also Chapter 4, note 35 in this volume.

42. Aquinas makes this point explicitly in connection with the biblical line that God wills all human beings to be saved, even though (on the theological doctrine Aquinas accepts) not all human beings are saved. See, for example, ST I q.19 a.6.

43. Or, one can *try* to desire—a condition illustrated by Teresa's own description of herself.

44. ST I–II q.19 a.9.

45. ST I–II q.19 a.10 obj.1.

46. ST I–II q.19 a.10 ad 1.

47. ST I–II q.19 a.10.

48. ST I–II q.19 a.10 obj.3.

49. ST I–II q.19 a.10.

50. For this reason, one can also be in harmony with God's will when one is protesting what one takes to be God's actions. That is why when God comes to adjudicate the dispute between Job and his Comforters, he proclaims that Job has said the thing that is right (Job 42:7).

51. See, for example, Luke 9:23.

52. Eckhart, *Mystic and Philosopher*, Sermon "Blessed are the Poor," 215.

53. Someone might suppose that in trying not to have a self, a person in Eckhart's camp would be actually trying to have a true self, a self that is in harmony with God because it is willing what God wills. For a discussion of the notion of the true self and different understandings of the true self, see my "Persons: Identification and Freedom," *Philosophical Topics* 24 (1996): 183–214. For the reasons given in that paper, I do not think that this objection on behalf of Eckhart's position is successful. The putative objector might respond that cases of conversion, in which a person alters something in his psychology drastically, puts pressure on the notion of the true self I argued for in that paper; but even in cases of conversion a person preserves control over his will, at least in this sense, that if he would want not to undergo conversion, he would not do so. (For further discussion of this last claim, see Chapter 8.)

54. *Eckhart: Selected Writings*, 16. The German word translated 'selfhood' is 'eigenschaft.'

55. See, for example, ST III q.21 a.3 and 4, where Aquinas explains the different ways in which the prayer in the Garden of Gethsemane instructed human beings and gave them a model to follow.

56. What is at issue in this discussion is, of course, the human mind and the human will of Christ. This assumption governs the discussion that follows of Christ's prayer in Gethsemane. In addition here, by 'crucifixion' I mean not just a particular way of bringing about death; rather I use 'crucifixion' as a shorthand way of referring to the entire suffering endured by Christ in the process of dying on the cross.

57. ST III q.18 a.5.

58. The cry of dereliction is not evidence against this claim, since even during the cry of dereliction Christ does not express a desire not to be crucified. The cry is an expression of desolation, not an expression of a desire not to be crucified. A woman who cries out in pain in labor is not expressing a desire not to have the child.

59. ST III q.21 a.2.

60. C.S. Lewis, *The Problem of Pain* (New York: Macmillan, 1962), 113.

61. Putting the point this way is necessary because, presumably, even an adherent to the no-self position would be distressed at finding sin in himself (and maybe even at finding sin in others), since sin cannot be considered in accordance with God's will.

62. For a good philosophical explanation of the way in which Christ's will was opposed to God's will but without culpability, see Aquinas's discussion of the issue in ST III q.18 a.5.

63. Or, at any rate, he tries to have no first-order desire for any particular thing. Having no first-order desires for particular things may be a state of will that human beings are unable to achieve completely or to maintain for long if they do achieve it. And, of course, it is necessary to have first-order acts of will of some sort in order even to move. One's limbs would not move if one did not want them to do so.

64. For a discussion of the difference between these two justifications for suffering, see my *Wandering in Darkness*, ch. 13.

65. I am grateful to John Greco for calling this point to my attention.

CHAPTER 7

1. It should be noticed in this connection that those thinkers who would have to be included in any historical survey of discussions of the doctrine did not themselves produce their work on the doctrine by engaging in historical surveys of their predecessors. Although Luther and Calvin, for example, have Catholic thought (including that of Aquinas) in mind, and Aquinas has Anselm in mind, and Anselm has the Patristics in mind, none of these thinkers builds his own theory of the atonement by writing the history of his predecessors' thought on the doctrine.

2. In particular, in my *Aquinas* (London and New York: Routledge, 2003).

3. For detailed discussion and defense of these claims, see my *Wandering in Darkness: Narrative and the Problem of Suffering* (Oxford: Oxford University Press, 2010), chs. 6–8.

4. Because of the close connection Aquinas accepts between the intellect and the will, any defect in the will has a correlate of some sort in the intellect as well. But because the defect in question is primarily in the will, I will leave to one side any consideration of the concomitant state of the intellect. For further discussion of these issues, see my *Aquinas*, ch. 9.

5. It is a universal condition only for post-Fall human people; because Aquinas accepts the doctrine of original sin, he also supposes that in its original condition humankind was free of this propensity. It is clumsy to keep adding the qualifier 'post-Fall', and so I will omit it hereafter; but it should be understood throughout in the discussion that follows. Aquinas thought that the doctrine of original sin adds something to our understanding of the moral record of human history and psychology. What the doctrine contributes, on his view, is a story designed to explain why the moral condition of human beings is not God's fault. Those who are philosophically willing to do so can add the doctrine of original sin into the description of the Thomistic worldview taken as background in this book. But the doctrine of original sin is not essential to the project of this book. It can be omitted, and those readers who want to do so should feel free to omit it. Readers who accept the existence of a perfectly good God but reject the doctrine of original sin and readers who reject the existence of God can substitute for the doctrine of original sin their own explanation of the human propensity to evil. Clearly, whatever explanation either of these groups gives for the human propensity to moral wrongdoing, it will not assign responsibility for this propensity to God.

6. See, for example, Aquinas, *Commentary on the Letter of St. Paul to the Hebrews*, translated by F.R. Larcher, edited by J. Mortensen and E. Alarcón (Lander, WY: The Aquinas Institute for the Study of Sacred Doctrine, 2012), C.12, L.2.

7. For detailed discussion and defense of this claim, and for a connected distinction between ordinary and strenuous versions of closeness and union, see my *Wandering in Darkness*, chs. 6 and 7.

8. Harry Frankfurt is one example. Although Frankfurt accepts objective standards of value, including moral value, he does not think that these standards constrain the ways in which agents can be identified with their own desires and volitions. It is possible, on his views, for an agent to be integrated around his second-order desires when those desires are for a will that wills something that is objectively morally wrong. Such an agent would be wholehearted in evil. For a summary of his

views on the subject, see Harry Frankfurt, *The Reasons of Love* (Princeton, NJ: Princeton University Press, 2004). For insightful criticism of Frankfurt's position, see Richard Moran, "Review Essay on *The Reasons of Love*," *Philosophy and Phenomenological Research* 74 (2007): 463–75.

9. See my *Wandering in Darkness*, ch. 7 for further discussion and defense of this claim.

10. It is also necessary for other things significant in this connection, including, for example, true freedom; for further discussion, see my *Wandering in Darkness*, ch. 7.

11. By 'guilt' in this connection, I do not mean the *feeling* of guilt but the condition of having done what is morally wrong or the disposition to do what is morally wrong.

12. For documentation of this view in Aquinas's work, see my *The God of the Bible and the God of the Philosophers* (Milwaukee, WI: Marquette University Press, 2016).

13. Both Aquinas's account and his terminology are more complicated than can be presented in the short space here. For a fuller exposition of Aquinas's views on this score, see my *Aquinas*, ch. 13.

14. Though the fact goes largely unnoticed, these same processes are also an antidote to shame. The healing of the will that mends the psychic fragmentation springing from moral wrongdoing also repairs the inner alienation stemming from shame. As I will argue in Chapter 10, when the processes of sanctification and justification are properly understood, it emerges that justification and sanctification are a solution for the internal divisions arising from shame, too.

15. In focusing here on justification and sanctification, I am giving an accurate portrayal of Aquinas's views, but I am omitting the story about Christ that is part of those views. The connection between justification and sanctification, on the one hand, and Christ's life, passion, and death, on the other hand, will be the subject of Part III.

16. Aquinas discusses the nature of grace at length, but the exact metaphysical character of grace is not something that I can discuss in passing in this book. For present purposes, it is sufficient to think of the grace at issue in this chapter as a kind of quality or configuration added directly to the will by God, where God's adding is a matter of formal causation and *not* efficient causation, as I explain below. This kind of grace is to be distinguished from grace more broadly understood as anything good that God does in a human life, including the provision of health or friends or anything else along these lines that does not involve adding a quality directly to the will.

17. The qualification 'cooperative' is not meant to distinguish this grace from its correlate, which is operative grace, by means of some distinction within kinds of grace. Rather, the qualification is meant just to pick out what grace is and does when it is received by a person in a state able to cooperate with grace.

18. I have adapted slightly Harry Frankfurt's use of the terms 'desire' and 'volition', for reasons explained in my "Sanctification, Hardening of the Heart, and Frankfurt's Concept of Free Will," *Journal of Philosophy* 85 (1988): 395–420. As I am using the terms, a volition is a desire that is effective enough in its strength to produce action if nothing outside the will impedes it.

19. See my *Aquinas*, chs. 9 and 13 for further discussion of these issues. Cf. also, e.g., SCG III.148 and ST I–II. a.111 q.2 ad 1, in which Aquinas says that grace operates on the will in the manner of a formal cause, rather than in the manner of an

efficient cause. For more discussion, see the section "God's Action on the Will" later in this chapter.

20. Cf. my "Augustine on Free Will," in *The Cambridge Companion to Augustine*, edited by Eleonore Stump and Norman Kretzmann (Cambridge: Cambridge University Press, 2001), 124–47; revised and reprinted in expanded edition of *The Cambridge Companion to Augustine* (2014), 166–88, which gives a detailed argument for a similar position held by Augustine.

21. For detailed defense and discussion of this claim, see my *Aquinas*, chs. 9 and 13.

22. In the strenuous mode. The distinction between the ordinary and the strenuous modes of free will is roughly the distinction between the sense of free will at issue in findings of moral praise or blame and the sense of free will in Harry Frankfurt's sense in which free will requires harmony between first-order and second-order volition. See my *Wandering in Darkness*, ch. 7.

23. The sudden conversion of the apostle Paul in consequence of a religious vision on the road to Damascus is generally taken to be an example.

24. There may also be a kind of kindling effect. Being effective in her higher-order desire to become a vegetarian will change Paula's life as well as her will, and she will grow and develop in consequence. What began as a worry over the ethical treatment of animals may grow into a broader ethical ecological concern or may branch out into other concerns with social justice. Such development on Paula's part will typically be accompanied by new higher-order desires as well.

25. By the same token, people become moral monsters slowly; see my *Aquinas*, ch. 11.

26. In this section, as I explained at the outset, I am relying on Aquinas's account, as I understand it. For a helpful comparison of Aquinas's account of justification with Calvin's account and their differing interpretations of Romans, see Charles Raith II, *Aquinas and Calvin on Romans: God's Justification and Our Participation* (Oxford: Oxford University Press, 2014). For further comparison of their views on justification and on the relevant texts in Romans, see Chapter 11. For a detailed discussion of the difference between Aquinas's account and that of the early Franciscans, see Marilyn Adams, "Genuine Agency, Somehow Shared? The Holy Spirit and Other Gifts," in *Oxford Studies in Medieval Philosophy*, edited by Robert Pasnau (Oxford: Oxford University Press, 2013), 23–60. My own interpretation of Aquinas's theory differs in some details from Adams's, and my conclusion therefore also differs from hers. She supposes that Aquinas has great difficulty with the problem of genuine agency for human beings on the supposition that the virtues are infused. As this chapter shows, I think that Aquinas's account has no such problem. Finally, there are also other theological understandings of justification in the tradition of the Anselmian kind of interpretation of the doctrine of the atonement. For some comment on them, see Chapter 3.

27. The phrase 'moral and spiritual' is my attempt to find some brief way of indicating that the regeneration in question has to do not only with intrinsic qualities of a human person but also with that person's closeness to God and second-personal connection to God.

28. Norman S. Care, *Living with One's Past: Personal Fates and Moral Pain* (New York: Rowman and Littlefield, 1996), 28.

29. Care, *Living with One's Past*, 28–9.

30. Care, *Living with One's Past*, 23–4.

31. As distinct from metaphysical identity. For an explanation of the difference between these two kinds of identity, see my "Persons: Identification and Freedom," *Philosophical Topics* 24 (1996): 183–214.

32. To ward off possible misunderstanding, it should be emphasized that the faith in question includes a hatred of one's own sin and a longing for God's goodness, as the subsequent text makes clear. There is a use of 'faith' that emphasizes just a set of beliefs, but the set of beliefs in question is typically one which devils might also accept; that set of beliefs does not count as the faith that justifies precisely because it does not include the state of will central to faith on Aquinas's account of faith. I am grateful to Andrew Pinsent for helping me see the need to ward off potential misunderstanding on this score.

33. For a detailed discussion of this claim, see my *Aquinas*, ch. 12.

34. ST I–II q.113 a.5; cf. also ST I–II q.113 a.6–7. A person does not have to remember and hate each sin he has ever committed in order to be justified, Aquinas says; rather, he has to hate those sins of which he is conscious and be disposed to hate any other sin of his if he should remember it.

35. I put the point in this clumsy way, "the goodness that is God's," because on the doctrine of simplicity God is his own nature, which is goodness itself, insofar as being and goodness are correlative.

36. For Aquinas, any act of will is preceded by an act of intellect; but the will can also act on the intellect with efficient causation. In the case of faith, although the will of faith is preceded by an act of intellect, in fact that act of intellect is itself a product of the will. For more discussion of this complicated issue, see my *Aquinas*, ch. 13. In addition, there are complicated issues having to do with the intellect's ability to recognize the good and discern its difference from evil. For some discussion of these issues, see my *Aquinas*, ch. 11. See also the brief discussion of the gifts of the Holy Spirit in sections "Aquinas's Ethics" and "Two Problems and a Solution" later in this chapter. Wisdom, understanding, counsel, and knowledge are gifts given to every person in grace through the indwelling Holy Spirit; and all of these are intellective dispositions.

37. To ward off gratuitous confusion, however, it should be pointed out that as regards the intellectual component of faith, for Aquinas, there is implicit faith as well as explicit faith. That is because Aquinas believes it is possible to be rightly related to the object of faith without knowing some of the theological truths about that object. That is, he thinks it is possible to know God, with a knowledge of persons, without knowing all or even very many truths about God. (See, e.g., ST II–II q.2 a.5–7.) According to Aquinas, some of those who lived before the advent of Christ or who live in places where Christianity is not known might nonetheless count among those saved by faith because of their right relation to God, the object of faith, even if they do not explicitly hold the articles of faith. So, for example, Aquinas thinks that pagans before the time of Christ might have had implicit faith in virtue of believing in the providence of God. For Aquinas, such faith is justifying, too. (See, e.g., ST II–II q.2 a.7 ad 3.) For more discussion of this issue, see the section "The Problem of Exclusivism" in Chapter 8.

38. On traditional Christian doctrine, in heaven all desires for things that are not good and not in accord with the will of God are gone.

39. For more discussion and defense of this claim, see my *Wandering in Darkness*, ch. 8.

40. See, for example, my *Aquinas*, ch. 3, and my *The God of the Bible and the God of the Philosophers*.

41. For a discussion and defense of this claim, see my *The God of the Bible and the God of the Philosophers* and my *Aquinas*, ch. 2.

42. Aquinas, *Commentary on the Letter of St. Paul to the Romans*, translated by F. R. Larcher, edited by J. Mortensen and E. Alarcón (Lander, WY: The Aquinas Institute for the Study of Sacred Doctrine, 2012), C.4, L.1.

43. In *Wandering in Darkness*, ch. 11, I explored in detail the narrative of Abraham's binding of Isaac; and I explained that, in the tradition Aquinas accepts, Abraham becomes the father of faith in consequence of his willingness to offer Isaac to God. In that chapter, I focused on the way in which Abraham comes to understand the goodness of God and to trust in it, and I took that trust and that understanding to be Abraham's exemplary faith. The story of Abraham's faith therefore illuminates the details of the intellectual and volitional attitude towards God's goodness necessary for faith. On that narrative illustration of the nature of faith, faith is irreducibly second-personal in character. In this chapter, the account of faith is necessarily abbreviated.

44. At least with minimal personal presence, that is, with presence that may be limited in degree. For the difference in kinds of personal presence, see my *Wandering in Darkness*, ch. 6. For some discussion of the degree of transparency of this presence of God's to particular human persons and for some discussion of the worries related to the apparent hiddenness of God to some people, see the section "The Problem of Exclusivism" in Chapter 8.

45. There is probably more contention over how to understand this position of Aquinas's than over any other part of his work. In my *Aquinas*, chs. 12–13, I tried to produce textual evidence to show that Aquinas cannot be classed as a theological compatibilist but has to be taken as a libertarian of a certain sort. And I argued that Aquinas's philosophical psychology contains the resources for explaining the compatibility of his claims that the will of faith is produced in a human person by God and yet that it is a free act on the part of the human willer, in the libertarian sense of 'free.'

46. There are different kinds of quiescence, but the quiescence of this option is only one kind. The issues are too complicated to review in passing, but there is a discussion of them in my *Aquinas*, ch. 13. Roughly put, the quiescence in the will at issue here is the state of will correlated with a condition of double-mindedness in an intellect so divided against itself that it does not allow for any one act in the will, so that the will refrains from willing in consequence.

47. See, for example, ST I–II q.9. a.1.

48. I say "in theory" because on theological doctrine accepted since Augustine's time, the will of a post-Fall human being is actually blocked by its inner fragmentation from one of these moves, namely, that from rejecting to accepting grace. For a discussion of Augustine's position and its historical influence, see my "Augustine on Free Will," 124–47, revised and reprinted in expanded edition of Stump and Kretzmann, *The Cambridge Companion to Augustine*, 166–88.

49. To say so is not to imply that a person is blameworthy for this refusal or that it occurs in consequence of something blameworthy or that there is any other reason for moral disapproval of a person because of this refusal. For further discussion of this issue, see the section "The Problem of Exclusivism" in Chapter 8.

50. Clearly, this account of becoming a person in grace does not apply to infants or children below the age of reason, whatever age that might be. On Christian tradition, however, even such persons may be saved through the atonement of Christ. For some discussion of the way in which Christ's atonement is applied to such persons, see the section "The Problem of Exclusivism" in Chapter 8. Baptism is also part of this story, but I have omitted consideration of baptism in this work on the sensible grounds that it is not possible to do everything in one book.

51. The detailed metaphysics of the nature of infused grace is beyond the scope of this book; but, roughly put, this kind of grace can be thought of as a quality or configuration that God adds to the will with formal, rather than efficient, causation. For more on this distinction among kinds of causation and the importance of the distinction to the issues at hand here, see the section "God's Action on the Will" later in this chapter.

52. Even on accounts that see justification as largely or entirely forensic, something additional is needed in order to apply justification to a particular individual; and that something additional is typically taken to be something in the person justified. For discussion of this issue, see, for example, Raith II, *Aquinas and Calvin on Romans*, esp. ch. 1.

53. Someone might suppose that attributing responsiveness to God in this way contravenes the doctrine of simplicity, but this supposition would be mistaken. For a discussion of this issue, see my *The God of the Bible and the God of the Philosophers*.

54. See my "Augustine on Free Will," 124–47, revised and reprinted in expanded edition of Stump and Kretzmann, *The Cambridge Companion to Augustine*, 166–88.

55. She has alternative possibilities because she can reject grace or she can be quiescent with respect to grace. For an argument that neither option is Pelagian, see my *Aquinas*, ch. 13.

56. For the distinction between desiring a person and desiring that something-or-other be done or be the case, see my *Wandering in Darkness*, ch. 3.

57. Aquinas thinks that in his initial prayer in the Garden of Gethsemane Christ is an example of someone who desires union with God (and is in fact in such union) but whose desires are (non-culpably) discordant from God's. In that prayer—"Father, let this cup pass from me"—Christ desires what in fact God does not desire and he desires that God should desire what Christ desires. And yet in making this prayer Christ is not in rebellion from God but in union with him. (See, for example, ST III q.18 a.5.) For further discussion of this issue, see Chapter 6.

58. There are of course biblical passages exhorting submission of one sort or another, but in my view in such contexts the term is used to indicate obedience done out of love and not submission as I have described here.

59. ST II–II q.19 a.4.

60. For a review of the disputes over the connection between Aristotle and Aquinas in the history of Thomism, see, for example, Mark Jordan, "The Alleged Aristotelianism of

Thomas Aquinas," in *The Gilson Lectures on Thomas Aquinas*, edited by James Reilly (Toronto: Pontifical Institute of Mediaeval Studies, 2008), 73–106.

61. ST I–II q.55 a.4.
62. ST I–II q.55 a.4.
63. ST I–II q.63 a.4 *sc.*; cf. also, for example, *Quaestiones disputatae de virtutibus in communi* q.un aa.9–10 and ST I–II q.55 a.4.
64. ST I–II q.65 a.1.
65. For a discussion of the anti-Pelagian cast of Aquinas's thought, see my *Aquinas*, ch. 12.
66. Care, *Living with One's Past*, 31–4.
67. Care, *Living with One's Past*, 76. Care cites this essay of Frankfurt's: "Rationality and the Unthinkable," in *The Importance of What We Care About*, edited by Harry Frankfurt (Cambridge: Cambridge University Press, 1988), 177–91. I do not think Care is right in assimilating the constraints on the will at issue for him to Frankfurt's necessities of the will, but I point out the connection Care makes to such necessities of the will to help underline the power of the constraints on the will to which Care rightly wants to call attention. On the other hand, it is worth reflecting on the relation between the inability of a post-Fall person to will the good, on anti-Pelagian views, and Frankfurt's necessities of the will, because on the anti-Pelagian view something that is within the will itself makes a certain kind of willing impossible, in the sense of the modality at issue for Frankfurt. But I raise this issue only to leave it to one side, on the grounds that one cannot do everything in one book.
68. Care, *Living with One's Past*, 86.
69. Care, *Living with One's Past*, 135–6.
70. Care, *Living with One's Past*, 136.
71. Care, *Living with One's Past*, 139.
72. Care, *Living with One's Past*, 138–40.
73. Care, *Living with One's Past*, 136–7.
74. Care, *Living with One's Past*, 151.
75. Care, *Living with One's Past*, 151–2.
76. ST I–II q.65 a.3.
77. To say that the spiritual life is perfected by the virtues is to say only that the infusing of the virtues contributes to the process of being perfected in righteousness, not that the process ends with the infusion of the virtues. All the virtues are infused in the first instant of faith, but they can exist in a person with contrary dispositions as well, as the remainder of this chapter will make clear.
78. ST I–II q.65 a.2 *sc.*
79. *Quaestiones disputatae de veritate* (QDV) 28.9 reply. (The translation is mine.)
80. In the *Summa contra Gentiles* (SCG), Aquinas makes clear that, in his view, God himself, the whole Trinity, indwells a person of faith when that person has the indwelling Holy Spirit:

> Since the love by which we love God is in us by the Holy Spirit, the Holy Spirit himself must also be in us . . . Therefore, since we are made lovers of God by the Holy Spirit, and every beloved is in the lover . . . by the Holy Spirit necessarily the Father and the Son dwell in us also.   (SCG IV.21)

Here and elsewhere I like and therefore have used the translation of Anton Charles Pegis (reprinted 1991), though I have felt free to modify it where I thought I could do better.

81. ST I q.38 a.1 *sc.*
82. ST I q.38 a.1 corpus.
83. Aquinas, *Commentary on the Letter of St. Paul to the Romans*, C.3, L.5. I like and therefore have used throughout the translations of this series from the Aquinas Institute, but I have felt free to modify it if I thought I could do better.
84. Aquinas, *Commentary on the Letter of St. Paul to the Romans*, C.5, L.1.
85. Aquinas, *Commentary on the Gospel of St. John*, translated by F.R. Larcher, edited by The Aquinas Institute (Lander, WY: The Aquinas Institute for the Study of Sacred Doctrine, 2013), C.14, L.4, pp. 249ff.
86. Aquinas, *Commentary on the Letter of St. Paul to the Ephesians*, translated by F. R. Larcher and M.L. Lamb, edited by J. Mortensen and E. Alarcón (Lander, WY: The Aquinas Institute for the Study of Sacred Doctrine, 2012), C.1, L.5.
87. For a detailed defense of these claims, see my "The Non-Aristotelian Character of Aquinas's Ethics: Aquinas on the Passions," *Faith and Philosophy* 28.1 (2011): 29–43.
88. ST I–II q.68 a.1.
89. ST I–II q.68 a.2.
90. As Aquinas explains the first five fruits of the Holy Spirit, they are in fact all consequences of shared love between a human person and God. The remaining seven have to do, one way or another, with the love of one's neighbor understood as beloved of God or with suitable love of oneself and one's body. See, for example, ST I–II q.70 a.3.
91. ST I–II q.70 a.3 corpus.
92. For an excellent discussion of this subject in connection with Aquinas's ethics, see Andrew Pinsent, *The Second-Person Perspective in Aquinas's Ethics: Virtues and Gifts* (London and New York: Routledge, 2012), especially ch. 4, in which Pinsent likens the fruition of second-person relatedness, an 'abiding in' the other, to a state of resonance.
93. For more discussion of the nature of the second-personal, see my *Wandering in Darkness*, ch. 6.
94. ST I q.43 a.3.
95. See, for example, *Commentary on the Letter of St. Paul to the Romans*, C.5, L.1.
96. It is perhaps worth highlighting here that the biblical text implies a mutual indwelling between God and a person in grace, and Aquinas understands the biblical text in this way.
97. Aquinas, *Commentary on the Letter of St. Paul to the Galatians*, translated by F. R. Larcher and M.L. Lamb, edited by J. Mortensen and E. Alarcón (Lander, WY: The Aquinas Institute for the Study of Sacred Doctrine, 2012), C.5, L.6.
98. Aquinas, *Commentary on the Letter of St. Paul to the Philippians*, translated by F. R. Larcher, edited by J. Mortensen and E. Alarcón (Lander, WY: The Aquinas Institute for the Study of Sacred Doctrine, 2012), C.4, L.1.
99. At the risk of overdoing it, I want to highlight here as well Aquinas's supposition that there is mutual indwelling between God and a person in grace.
100. SCG IV.23.

101. See, in this connection, ST I–II q.27 a.3 and q.28 a.1.
102. For more discussion of this notion, see my "Faith, Wisdom, and the Transmission of Knowledge through Testimony," in *Religious Faith and Intellectual Virtue*, edited by Laura Frances Callahan and Timothy O'Connor (Oxford: Oxford University Press, 2014), 204–30.
103. Just as the will can be divided against itself as regards desires, so it can also be divided against itself as regards dispositions. The infused disposition for temperance in general can co-exist in the will with a long-established habit of gluttony, for example.
104. ST I–II q.65 a.3 ad 2.
105. ST I–II q.65 a.3 ad 3.
106. This view is one more non-Aristotelian element of Aquinas's ethics.
107. Clearly, there are many more problems that arise in connection with Aquinas's account, perhaps most obviously the question whether a position which implies that only Christians are moral people is itself morally intolerable. What helps in this connection is the recognition that for Aquinas, as for Karl Rahner, there are people who are rightly related to God in this second-personal way even if they have never heard of Christianity or even if they have heard of it and reject it entirely. It is the right relationship to God, implicit or tacit, that makes a person moral, not membership in a religious club. (In this connection, see also note 37 above.) For further discussion of this and related issues, see my *Aquinas*, chs. 12 and 13, and *Wandering in Darkness*, ch. 8. I will also return to this issue in the section "The Problem of Exclusivism" in Chapter 8.
108. ST I. q.82 a.1.
109. SCG III.88.
110. ST I–II q.113 a.3.
111. SCG III.148.
112. QDV 22.8.
113. What Aquinas has in mind with this description of the first way in which God changes the will is the subject of some discussion, which I cannot canvass in passing here. But my own view is that the best clue to his meaning is given by the lines in the remainder of the paragraph, namely, that in giving the will a nature God puts a particular will (the will to happiness, as Aquinas holds in other texts) into the will. Whatever is at issue in this first way, however, is not the way in which Aquinas thinks God changes the will when God infuses grace into the will, and so I will leave consideration of this part of Aquinas's account to one side in what follows.
114. By 'wayfarers' Aquinas means people in grace in this life.
115. QDV 22.8 reply.
116. QDV 22.8 ad 9.
117. QDV 27.1 ad 3.
118. QDV 28.7 ad 5.
119. QDV 28.9 reply.
120. See my "Persons: Identification and Freedom."
121. As I argued in *Wandering in Darkness*, chs. 6 and 7, in the discussion of closeness and of shame, there can be a desire for a person or a rejection of a person; and so there can also be resistance to a person.

CHAPTER 8

1. For discussion of the ordering of heart's desires and for defense of the claim that union with God is required to fulfill the deepest heart's desire, see my *Wandering in Darkness: Narrative and the Problem of Suffering* (Oxford: Oxford University Press, 2010), ch. 14.

2. Abelard's name is associated with an interpretation of the doctrine of the atonement according to which Christ's passion and death mediate human salvation only by serving as an exemplar of right conduct. Whether Abelard actually held such an interpretation is a matter of dispute.

3. *Wandering in Darkness*, ch. 4. (I will discuss the issue of the role of narrative in more detail in Chapter 9.)

4. For more discussion of this issue, see my "Theology and the Knowledge of Persons," in *New Models of Religious Understanding*, edited by Fiona Ellis (Oxford: Oxford University Press, 2018), 172–90.

5. Because my purpose is not to do biblical scholarship on particular biblical texts but rather to do philosophical theology with respect to the doctrine of the atonement, I will approach the biblical texts with the theological data included in that doctrine presupposed. For this purpose, authorial intent and beliefs of those who produced the biblical stories and their historical milieu is not relevant. For further discussion of this issue, see Chapter 1. Furthermore, since what is at issue for me in this chapter is the biblical stories as stories, and not as history, historical investigation of the texts is also not relevant. Finally, there is of course an important question of whether these stories present historical truth or theologically creative fiction. But for this question historical scholarship is also not relevant; only theological inquiry is. Historical investigation, for example, is manifestly not relevant to the question whether the person who was Jesus of Nazareth was the incarnate Christ. No investigation of the history of the life of this person could yield evidence relevant to such a claim. So, for example, since, on the Chalcedonian formula for the incarnate Christ, Christ has a fully human nature, any lack of those attributes essential to Deity that historical investigation could discover in Jesus of Nazareth could be assigned to the human nature of Christ; they therefore would not count as evidence against the claim that Jesus of Nazareth also had a second divine nature. For all these reasons, I will not be approaching the biblical texts at issue in this chapter with the methods of historical biblical scholarship.

6. See Matt. 4 and Luke 4. The relative ordering of the second and third temptations is not the same in these two Gospels. There are different explanations for the varying order in the history of the Christian tradition. One standard explanation is that neither Gospel is giving a temporal ordering. Rather, the ordering reflects a spiritual or moral order. On that way of understanding the ordering, which order a Gospel gives is a function of the spiritual or moral insight it has and wants to share concerning the temptations of Christ. In his harmony of the Gospels, Augustine offers still other clever explanations for the difference in ordering. But I will leave discussion of the explanations for the different ordering to one side on the sensible grounds that one cannot do everything in one examination of a complicated narrative.

7. Others have suggested to me that there is some resonance between the interpretation of the temptations I argue for in this chapter and the Grand Inquisitor scene in Dostoyevsky's *The Brothers Karamazov*; but the resemblance seems limited to me.

8. In the subsequent examination of the narratives, I approach the text as a story in which Satan is one of the main characters. For my purposes in this chapter, it does not matter if the story is metaphysically or historically accurate; that question is logically irrelevant to my central points about the doctrine of the atonement. That is, my central points are compatible with there being no such entity as Satan or no historical interaction between Christ and an entity such as Satan. Of course, by parity of reasoning, my central points are also compatible with the literal truth of the narrative.

9. For an understanding of an approach to biblical texts that admits without anxiety of multiple readings of the same text, or even multiple versions of the same text, see my explanation of medieval biblical exegesis in "Revelation and Biblical Exegesis: Augustine, Aquinas, and Swinburne," in *Reason and the Christian Religion: Essays in Honor of Richard Swinburne*, edited by Alan G. Padgett (Oxford: Clarendon Press, 1994), 161–97.

10. This feature of the story is either less evident or missing entirely, depending on one's interpretation, in the version in Matthew.

11. The phrase 'but by every word of God's' does not appear in some modern editions of Luke. But it is important to remember here the methodology of this project. I am not attempting to do contemporary biblical exegesis. I am attempting to interpret a doctrine central to orthodox Christian theology, as it developed in the course of Christian tradition.

    The biblical phrase at issue here is accepted by notable Christian theologians in their commentaries on the Gospel, including, for example, Ambrose, Augustine, Aquinas, and Calvin. It also appears in the Vulgate and in Martin Luther's German translation. Since the phrase is part of the tradition of interpretation of these texts, I have included it here. Furthermore, the phrase is the second part of the line in Deut. 8:3 which is being quoted by Christ in the Gospel story. It is hard to imagine that Christ would have had the first part of the line in memory but not the immediately next few words, which are crucial to the meaning of the line.

12. Deut. 8:3.

13. In older versions of the texts, the same phrase is included in Luke 4:8.

14. Some interpreters point out that Satan is not quoting the text accurately but is omitting a detail that makes a difference to the meaning of the lines; on this view, Satan is omitting the phrase 'in all your ways' from the first line. It is not clear, however, that the story intends its audience to understand that this detail is missing, and it is also not clear what difference the omitted words make to Satan's line if they are intentionally omitted in the story. And so I will leave this issue to one side here.

15. Milton, *Paradise Regained*, Bk. IV, ll.581–95.

16. This is a claim about Christ in his human nature; it should go without saying that in his divine nature God is unable to sin, given that God's goodness is essential to God.

17. Milton, *Paradise Lost*, Bk. I, ll.159–67.
18. Milton, *Paradise Lost*, Bk. II, ll.358–73.
19. There is a philosophical explanation that reconciles this text with the orthodox doctrine that God's will is always efficacious. For some discussion of this explanation, see my *Wandering in Darkness*, ch. 13.
20. This interpretation presupposes not only that Satan is smart but also that Satan knows something about the nature of the expected Messiah and the work of the Messiah. But this presupposition requires only that the story's Satan has as least as much knowledge of these things as the ordinary people among the Israelites, who clearly were expecting the Messiah and the salvation brought about by the Messiah at this time, as numerous stories in the New Testament attest. This interpretation also presupposes that Satan knows something about God's plan to save his people from their sins through the suffering of the Messiah; but since the story's Satan is familiar with the Hebrew Bible, he must also know the passages in the prophets, especially Isaiah and Ezekiel, which highlight this plan.
21. This claim presupposes that Satan's temptations are addressed to the human nature of Christ. But this is a safe presupposition. It makes no sense to suppose that Satan's temptations would be addressed to the divine nature of Christ.
22. Thomas Nagel, *The Last Word* (Oxford: Oxford University Press, 1997), 130.
23. See, for example, my "Libertarian Freedom and the Principle of Alternative Possibilities," in *Faith, Freedom, and Rationality: Philosophy of Religion Today*, edited by Daniel Howard-Snyder and Jeff Jordan (Lanham, MD: Rowman and Littlefield, 1996), 73–88; "Alternative Possibilities and Moral Responsibility: The Flicker of Freedom," *The Journal of Ethics* 3 (1999): 299–324; and "Moral Responsibility without Alternative Possibilities," in *Moral Responsibility and Alternative Possibilities: Essays on the Importance of Alternative Possibilities*, edited by Michael McKenna and David Widerker (Aldershot: Ashgate Press, 2003), 139–58.
24. There are miracles in which Christ provides for the needs of people by miraculously producing food for them; but in those cases he is multiplying bread and fish without altering their natures. The one miracle in which he seems to do what Satan is suggesting to him here, altering the nature of a created thing in order to supply human need, is a case in which the need is purely social, and not biological or necessary for life. That is when he turns water into wine at a wedding, where the host has run out of wine. In that case, his mother suggests that he do something of this sort, and he seems to rebuke her before in fact doing the miracle. The details of that miracle and the connection between it and the first temptation would be wonderful to expound on; but I will withstand that temptation myself in the interests of brevity.
25. I say that it is central to Christianity because it is the Christian doctrine of atonement that is the subject of this book; but, of course, this same claim is central to other worldviews as well, including, of course, Judaism. For discussion of the role of love of God in human flourishing, see Jon Levenson, *The Love of God* (Princeton, NJ: Princeton University Press, 2016).
26. For the reasons given in this chapter and the preceding one, on my view this divine promise in Ezekiel should not be read as a promise on God's part to unilaterally produce a completely righteous will in post-Fall human beings. On the contrary, in

my view, what is being promised in this text can be exemplified by the whole process of atonement that is the subject of this book.

27. Levenson, *The Love of God*, 36.

28. For explanation and defense of this claim, see Chapter 7.

29. See Chapters 4 and 5 for more discussion of this claim.

30. Milton, *Paradise Regained*, Bk. I, l.347.

31. The point here is that there is a real good lost when a person Paula suffers, but that in her suffering she also gains a good which is a real advantage for her, and enough of an advantage that if she understood her situation and were in a position to choose, she might well choose to keep the suffering even with all its disadvantages for the sake of the good that comes to her through the suffering. This is a topic I have addressed in detail in *Wandering in Darkness*, and I am here only gesturing to that discussion. For further discussion of this issue in this book, see Chapter 9.

32. The Greek term translated 'word' in the story of the temptation in Luke is not the same Greek word as that used in the identification of Christ as the Word in the prologue to the Gospel of John. But it is not necessary for the same Greek word to be in both places for the association between the ideas signified by the Greek terms to be made. When the term refers to Christ, I will capitalize it as 'Word.'

33. It is also available to all those readers of the story who remember Christ's speeches about himself as bread. I understand that Christ's speech about himself as the true bread from heaven comes after the temptations, but the fact that the speech comes afterwards does not mean that the thought expressed by the speech comes afterwards. The speech that comes afterwards may reflect a thought that came to Christ before, maybe even during the temptations, in the course of Christ's finding the right response to Satan's first temptation.

34. Milton, *Paradise Regained*, Bk. 2, ll.410–31.

35. Milton, *Paradise Regained*, Bk. 3, ll.9–42.

36. Milton, *Paradise Regained*, Bk. 3, ll.152–80.

37. The Wikipedia entry on Sophie Scholl says, "Since the 1970s, Scholl has been celebrated as one of the great German heroes who actively opposed the Third Reich during the Second World War...The White Rose's legacy has, for many commentators, an intangible quality. Playwright Lillian Garrett-Groag stated in *Newsday* on February 22, 1993, that 'It is possibly the most spectacular moment of resistance that I can think of in the 20th century...The fact that five little kids, in the mouth of the wolf, where it really counted, had the tremendous courage to do what they did, is spectacular to me. I know that the world is better for them having been there, but I do not know why.' In the same issue of *Newsday*, Holocaust historian Jud Newborn noted that 'You cannot really measure the effect of this kind of resistance in whether or not X number of bridges were blown up or a regime fell...The White Rose really has a more symbolic value, but that's a very important value.' Posthumously, Sophie Scholl has been given many honors, and the recent movie of her life, *The Final Days*, has been widely acclaimed" ("Sophie Scholl," *Wikipedia: The Free Encyclopedia*, https://en.wikipedia.org/wiki/Sophie_Scholl, accessed January 21, 2016).

38. I am quoting from the 1917 JPS Tanakh translation of the Psalm.

39. Or the anti-Christian belief—some scholars argue that Docetism is not strictly speaking a Christian heresy because it arose from outside Christianity. Its association

with Gnosticism and Manicheanism is also a reason for supposing that it should not be classified as a heretical part of Christianity but rather as simply one more anti-Christian view of the early Church period.

40. Some varieties of Docetism supposed that some other person was substituted for Christ at the last moment but that those observing the crucifixion were misled into supposing that the suffering dying person was Christ.

41. The Nicene Creed is dated to 325 AD, but earlier documents attest to a widespread Christian rejection of Docetism. The letters of Ignatius of Antioch, a first-century Christian figure, are regularly cited in this connection.

42. Rachel Moran, *Paid For: My Journey through Prostitution* (Dublin: Gill and Macmillan, 2013), 143–5.

43. Moran, *Paid For*, 273.

44. Nagel, *The Last Word*, 130.

45. John Stuart Mill, *An Examination of Sir William Hamilton's Philosophy and of The Principal Philosophical Questions Discussed in His Writings* (London: Longman, Green, Longman, Roberts & Green, 1865), ch. 7, p. 103.

46. Milton, *Paradise Lost*, Bk. I, l.263.

47. Just in case it is not overwhelmingly obvious, the Landlord represents God.

48. C. S. Lewis, *The Pilgrim's Regress* (Grand Rapids, MI: Eerdmans, 1933), 63.

49. Moran, *Paid For*, 272.

50. For some discussion of the notion of God's suffering, on the Chalcedonian formula for the incarnate Christ, see Chapter 1.

51. *Wandering in Darkness*, chs. 4 and 6.

52. I am grateful to Sarah Coakley for calling my attention to this line in the Psalm in this connection. See her "On the Fearfulness of Forgiveness: Psalm 130:4 and its Theological Implications," in *Meditations of the Heart: The Psalms in Early Christian Thought and Practice*, edited by Andreas Andreopoulos, Augustine Casiday, and Carol Harrison (Turnhout: Brepols, 2011), 33–51.

53. *Wandering in Darkness*, ch. 12.

54. There are also other references to the episode at Massah which are worth considering in this context; see, e.g., Ps. 95:8 and Heb. 3:7–11. The density of the biblical stories is such that each line has myriad references and allusions, but considerations of space make it sadly necessary to leave most of them unexplored here.

55. Two episodes are being summarized in this line, one at Massah and one at Meribah. Both are interesting, but the one at Meribah raises a number of issues not relevant for my purposes; and so I am concentrating here just on the episode at Massah.

56. See the detailed discussion in Chapter 5 for exposition and defense of this claim.

57. Some scholars suppose that Hans Urs von Balthasar held such views. See, for example, Karen Kilby, *Balthasar: A (Very) Critical Introduction* (Grand Rapids, MI: Eerdmans, 2012).

58. Analogously, as I argued in *Wandering in Darkness*, ch. 9, it is a most appropriate end to the story of the sufferings of Job that he returns to being what he himself wanted to be, namely, a prosperous *paterfamilias*.

59. Calvin, *The Institutes of the Christian Religion*, vol. 1, translated by Henry Beveridge (Grand Rapids, MI: Eerdmans, 1970), bk. II, ch. xvi, p. 445. Calvin is speaking

of Christ's suffering in the Garden before his passion, but the point applies as well to Christ's suffering on the cross.

60. In just a few words, Augustine hints at a similar idea. See his *Enarrationes in Psalmos*, translated as *Augustine on the Psalms*, vol. II, translated by Dame Scholastica Hebgin and Dame Felicitas Corrigan (New York: Newman Press, 1961), Second Discourse on Psalm 30, pp. 11–12.

61. John Newman, *Favorite Newman Sermons*, selected by Daniel M. O'Connell, SJ (Milwaukee, WI: The Bruce Publishing Company, 1932), Discourse 16: "Mental Sufferings of Our Lord in His Passion." Online at http://www.newmanreader.org/controversies/guides/favorites.html.

62. Newman, *Favorite Newman Sermons*, Discourse 16.

63. For one contemporary commentator holding this view, see Thomas H. McCall, *Forsaken: The Trinity and the Cross, and Why It Matters* (Downers Grove, IL: InterVarsity Press, 2012), 38.

64. Newman, *Favorite Newman Sermons*, Discourse 16.

65. Newman, *Favorite Newman Sermons*, Discourse 16.

66. With caution, I would like to suggest one more implication of the view that I have been arguing for as regards the suffering of Christ. Although there is now considerable skepticism about the authorship of the Apocalypse, it has been thought in the past that the apostle John is its author. Suppose for just the length of time it takes for a thought experiment that this attribution is correct. I am *not* here endorsing this attribution (although in fact I find the arguments against it very unpersuasive); I intend only to use this supposition to show one more possible implication of the interpretation of Christ's suffering I have argued for in this chapter and in Chapter 5.

In the Gospels of Matthew (20:20–3) and Mark (10:35–40), James and John (and their mother) ask Christ to let James and John sit on Christ's right hand and on his left hand in his glory. Although this request is frequently interpreted as if the two apostles were asking vaingloriously for the best seats in heaven, Christ interprets the request as if it had to do with being crucified next to him. He responds with a question to the two apostles which is expressive of some disbelief: "Can you drink of my cup?" In the Garden of Gethsemane, Christ uses the metaphor of drinking a cup to refer to his passion; and in this story about James and John, it seems that the two apostles understand this metaphor in the same way. They respond to Christ's question with a short and determined "We can!"

In response to this commitment on their part, Christ denies their request to be on his right and on his left, on the ground that these places have been prepared for others—as the story of Christ's passion develops, the places have been reserved for two ordinary human beings who are being put to death for stealing. But Christ prefaces this denial with an affirmation of their commitment to him and their determination to drink his cup. He says to them, "You will indeed drink it!"

Given this promise on Christ's part, one would then expect martyrdom on the part of both these apostles. And, in fact, James is one of the first to be martyred after Christ's own death (cf. Acts 12:2). But the early tradition, which largely accepts the attribution of the Apocalypse to the apostle John, is unanimous in supposing that John was not martyred but in fact lived into old age. It can seem, then, that Christ's promise to these two apostles was fulfilled in the case of James but not of John.

If, however, the interpretation of Christ's suffering that I have argued for here and in Chapter 5 is right, then Christ's cup has to be understood not only as physical suffering leading to death but also as the anguish of experiencing vividly and empathically the great evil of others. The events which the prophet records as seen by him in the experiences he records in the Apocalypse are terrible and frightening outworkings of human evil. And so, if Christ's suffering can be understood as I have argued, then (on the hypothesis about John which is the assumption of the thought experiment here), it is possible to suppose that Christ's promise to James and John was fulfilled also for John. Christ's cup consists not just of physical pain but also of the mental anguish underlying the anguish in the Garden of Gethsemane and the cry of dereliction. It is then possible that one can drink of Christ's cup not only by martyrdom but also by standing instead of falling apart under deep psychic distress of this sort.

Finally, this line of thought suggests a helpful and plausible interpretation of the story of Christ's transfiguration. In that story, Christ takes just Peter, James, and John with him to witness him in a transformed condition that shows him both lovely and powerful, a winner rather than a loser, glorious rather than humiliated, shamed, and suffering. Why would the story of Christ include such an episode? Why in the story would Christ want to show himself in this condition to his followers? One might suppose that the purpose is the same as the reason for his resurrection: his followers need to understand that the suffering is not the ultimate conclusion of the story of Christ's life or of the Christian life in general. But then one would have thought that all the apostles would witness Christ's transfigur- ation, as they all witness Christ's resurrection. But in the story only Peter, James, and John witness the transfiguration. Why only these three? The same Christian traditions which report that James was martyred and John was not report that Peter also died in martyrdom, in fact by crucifixion, like Christ. If the hypothesis I have suggested in this note is right, that John also participated in the cup of Christ but by psychic anguish rather than death by martyrdom, then an interpret- ation of the story of the transfiguration suggests itself. Since James, John, and Peter will drink of Christ's cup, even if in differing ways, then they will be strengthened for their ordeal by a vivid and powerful experience showing them that at the end of their ordeal there is transfiguration, theirs as well as Christ's. On this way of interpreting the story, it makes sense that before his own death Christ would do what he could to equip these three apostles in particular for their own drinking of his cup by showing them that the end of the anguish is worth the anguish.

I want to finish by reiterating that I am not endorsing these interpretations of the story of the apostle John and of the transfiguration. (I am not rejecting them either, of course; a failure to endorse them is not a rejection of them.) But I wanted to call attention to them as one possible implication of the interpretation of Christ's suffering that I have endorsed and argued for in this chapter and in Chapter 5.

67. The most notable episode involving angels that I am omitting is the annunciation to Mary. One cannot do everything even in one very large chapter.

68. Those readers who suppose that baptism is the solution in such cases can restrict the group to unbaptized small children who die before the age of reason. Although the sacrament of baptism is also part of the story of salvation, I have left it out of this book entirely on the sensible grounds that one cannot do everything in one book.

69. Or, die unbaptized.

70. See, e.g., ST II–II q.2 a.7 ad 3.

71. Quoted in Levenson, *The Love of God*, 74.

72. These points obviously have relevance for the discussion of the question of God's hiddenness. For an excellent treatment of this question, see Michael C. Rea, *"Though the Darkness Hide Thee": Seeking the Face of the Invisible God* (Oxford: Oxford University Press, 2018). For a recent collection of essays on this subject, see *Hidden Divinity and Religious Belief: New Perspectives*, edited by Eleonore Stump and Adam Green (Cambridge: Cambridge University Press, 2015). Furthermore, it is possible to know a person even without being aware that one is doing so. Suppose that a person Paula who has been socially isolated for most of her life is finally rescued and meets her mother for the first time; but suppose also that the villain who isolated her contrives somehow to convince her that she is hallucinating. Then in fact Paula will have knowledge of her mother without believing that her mother exists, and so also without knowledge that her mother exists. (It is noteworthy that in such a case there is nothing culpable about Paula's lack of knowledge; and there is nothing to suggest that she is resistant to such knowledge either.)

    And here it is also important to see the implications of the doctrine of simplicity. On that doctrine, it is true to say that God is being, as well as true to say that God is a being with a mind and a will. (For a defense of this claim, see my *The God of the Bible and the God of the Philosophers*, Aquinas Lecture (Milwaukee, WI: Marquette University Press, 2016).) Being is correlative with goodness; and therefore, on the doctrine of simplicity, it is also true to say that God is goodness. Furthermore, beauty is goodness under a particular description, or goodness perceptible to the senses (where intellectual vision counts as a kind of sight, too). So in knowing goodness or in sensing beauty, a person is also knowing God, to one degree or another. (For more detailed discussion of this claim, see my "Beauty as a Road to God," *Sacred Music* 134.4 (Winter 2007): 11–24.)

    So from a person's sincere self-report that he does not believe in an omniscient, omnipotent, perfectly good God, it does not follow that he does not know God in any way or to any degree. And, clearly, knowing God is not a transparent matter. A person can know God, through sensing of beauty or through second-personal connection of however limited or dreamy a means, without being aware that he has this knowledge of God. A fortiori, it is not clear how others would determine whether or not a person had knowledge of God. As far as that goes, it is in theory possible, and compatible with the data that many people report themselves to be atheists, that all persons have some knowledge of God. I am not claiming that it is true that all persons have some knowledge of God; I am claiming only that it takes more than self-reports of atheism to show that it is false.

73. Just as God can count as perfectly good without its being the case that God creates the best possible world, so God can be perfectly good without using the most promising means to achieve his ends. It might be, to take just one example from the voluminous literature on this topic, that there are very many means to the same end that are close enough in value to the means that God chooses that it makes no significant difference to goodness which of these very promising means God chooses. In picking this example, I am not endorsing it, only pointing out one way in which to validate the claim that the most promising means need not be a necessary means for God.

74. For those inclined to worry about the consistency of the modal claims, they come to this. It was not necessary that God choose Christ's atonement as the means to salvation for human beings; but since God did, on that supposition, Christ's passion and death (or, more accurately, Christ's life, passion, and death) are necessary (that is, conditionally necessary) to human salvation. But, even so, what is (conditionally) necessary in this sense is Christ's passion and death. Explicit theological beliefs about Christ's passion and death are not necessary in any sense. A person's explicit understanding of Christ's passion and death is the most promising way for her to come to a surrender to God's love, but it is not the only way.

75. Dante, *Inferno*, Canto 27, ll.119–20.

CHAPTER 9

1. That is, being in this condition is necessary and sufficient for salvation, but it is not necessary that a person be in this condition; she stays in this condition only if she does not choose to leave it.

2. This line is not meant to imply that alternative possibilities are necessary for free will. (I have argued against this view in my "Libertarian Freedom and the Principle of Alternative Possibilities," in *Faith, Freedom, and Rationality: Philosophy of Religion Today*, edited by Daniel Howard-Snyder and Jeff Jordan (Lanham, MD: Rowman and Littlefield, 1996), 73–88; "Alternative Possibilities and Moral Responsibility: The Flicker of Freedom," *The Journal of Ethics* 3 (1999): 299–324; and "Moral Responsibility without Alternative Possibilities," in *Moral Responsibility and Alternative Possibilities: Essays on the Importance of Alternative Possibilities*, edited by Michael McKenna and David Widerker (Aldershot: Ashgate Press, 2003), 139–58.)

    Rather, I point out that a person Paula has alternative possibilities for the sake of those readers who are on the other side of the controversy and suppose that there is no free will without alternative possibilities.

3. And it is compatible with surrender in love that Jerome wants Paula to want what he wants. That is, Jerome's wanting to want what Paula wants may come with a desire on his part that Paula's will accommodate to Jerome's will, rather than the other way around.

4. For explanation and discussion of this claim, see Chapter 7.

5. See Chapter 6 for explanation and discussion of Aquinas's position.

6. C.S. Lewis, *The Great Divorce* (New York and San Francisco: Harper San Francisco, 1946, reprinted 1973), 61.

7. For some discussion of this experience of one's own distance from others as a kind of abandonment by those others, see Chapter 5.

8. For discussion of wisdom and folly and a defense of this characterization of the interaction of will and intellect producing folly, see my *Aquinas* (New York: Routledge, 2003), ch. 11.

9. Some Christians suppose that if Paula rejects God and dies in that rejection, then it never was true of Paula that she was justified, even if it seemed as if she was. Other Christians suppose that Paula could reject God entirely even after having received justification. But this difference of view makes no difference to my point here. What everyone agrees on is that it is possible for a person who seems to be a devout Christian to reject God and die in that state of rejection. And that point is all I need for my purposes here.

10. Norman S. Care, *Living with One's Past: Personal Fates and Moral Pain* (New York: Rowman and Littlefield, 1996), 143.

11. Aquinas describes this process in a more fine-grained way, in terms of five effects of God's grace on a human soul: (1) healing of the soul, (2) desire of the good, (3) carrying out the good desired, (4) perseverance in good, and (5) attainment of eternal life. It is noteworthy that perseverance is on the list just before the last element, eternal life. See ST I–II q.111 a.3.

12. For the marriage to last as a good marriage, of course, there also has to be a deepening in the relationship of love between the married persons. That this is so helps to illuminate the difference between sanctification and perseverance. Sanctification is a matter of increasing integration around the good and so also deepening in relationship with God. Perseverance is a matter of not giving up on the entire process, of marriage or of sanctification.

13. See, for example, his treatise *De dono perseverantiae*.

14. Augustine, *On the Gift of Perseverance*, in *Saint Augustine: Four Anti-Pelagian Writings*, translated by John A. Mourant and William J. Collinge (Washington, DC: The Catholic University of America Press, 1992), 310.

15. *Saint Augustine: Four Anti-Pelagian Writings*, 316.

16. *Saint Augustine: Four Anti-Pelagian Writings*, 324.

17. For some discussion of such power of beauty with regard to music, see my "Beauty as a Road to God," *Sacred Music* 134.4 (2007): 11–24. It should be clear that helps of this sort also make a difference to bringing a person to the initial surrender to God; but I have left them to one side in Chapter 7 in the interest of addressing the direct action of grace on the will, which is the help that raises the most philosophical difficulty.

18. Or grape juice. This disjunction should be understood throughout. My purposes in this chapter do not require my taking a stand on whether it is essential to the ritual that the juice of the grapes be turned into wine. For ease of exposition in what follows, I will simply talk of wine.

19. For one good recent account of Aquinas's own view of the sacraments, see Olivier-Thomas Venard, "Sacraments," in *The Cambridge Companion to the Summa*

Theologiae, edited by Philip McCosker and Denys Turner (Cambridge: Cambridge University Press, 2016), 269–87.

20. ST III q.62 a.5.

21. For discussion of many of these issues in the scholastic period, see Marilyn McCord Adams, *Some Later Medieval Theories of the Eucharist: Thomas Aquinas, Giles of Rome, Duns Scotus, and William Ockham* (Oxford: Oxford University Press, 2010).

22. Because it is clumsy to add the qualifier 'in grace', in what follows I will omit it; but readers should understand that by 'participants' in this connection I mean persons in grace. It is obviously possible to participate in the rite without being a person in grace, either because one is a religious believer but not one in grace or else because one is not a believer in the theology enacted or presupposed in the rite. What is at issue for me in this chapter is the perseverance of persons in grace in the original surrender to the love of God; and in this section I am exploring the role of the Eucharist in such perseverance. So only persons in grace are relevant to my discussion here.

23. Not all participants in the rite in all Christian groups receive the cup, and so the claim in this sentence needs some qualification to apply also to those participants. Readers should take this qualification as well as the qualification about the nature of the liquid in the cup as understood throughout. See note 18 above.

24. Because philosophers take knowledge to be a matter of knowledge *that*, a more common philosophical formulation of mutual knowledge would be in terms of knowing *that*: Paula knows that Jerome knows that Paula knows that Jerome knows, and so on. In the case of infants, of course, shared attention cannot be a matter of knowing *that* in this way. For an interesting study of mutual knowledge in connection with joint attention, see Christopher Peacocke, "Joint Attention: Its Nature, Reflexivity, and Relation to Common Knowledge," in *Joint Attention: Communication and Other Minds*, edited by Naomi Eilan, Christoph Hoerl, Teresa McCormack, and Johannes Roessler (Oxford: Clarendon Press, 2005), 298–324.

25. See Chapter 4 for more discussion of the nature of the metaphysically greater union based on indwelling.

26. For more discussion of these claims about union, see Chapters 4 and 5.

27. I do not mean to say that a story can itself yield a second-person experience between a character in the story and the audience for the story; I mean only that some of the knowledge gained through second-person experience can be transmitted to one extent or another through a story. The question whether a person can have a second-person experience of a character in a story is vexed, and I am leaving it to one side here; but I am assuming that one can gain some knowledge of persons even with respect to an imaginary character in a story through the re-presentation of imagined second-person experiences described through the story.

28. In this respect, a second-person experience differs from a first-person experience of the sort we have in perception. There is no way for me to convey to someone who has never seen colors what I know when I know what it is like to see red.

29. I am not here implying that the only function, or even the main function, of narratives (in one medium or another) is to convey real or imagined second-person

experiences. My claim is just that much less is lost of a second-person experience in a narrative account than in a third-person account, *ceteris paribus*.

30. I do not mean to say that the storyteller or artist does not contribute something of her own in the narrative presentation. On the contrary, part of the importance of narrative is that its artistry enables us to see what we might well have missed without the help of the narrative, even if we had been present as bystanders in the events recounted in the narrative. It is for this reason that the quality of the artistry in a narrative makes a difference to what there is to know on the basis of it.

31. The Apostle Paul is said to have been connected with Christ directly through some individual revelation or mystical experience. It may be that cases of this sort constitute another way of coming to Christ without a story, although in such a case one might well suppose that a story about Christ's passion and death is still either part of the mystical experience or (as in Paul's case) part of the background knowledge of the person having the experience. I will leave further consideration of the role of mystical experience in this connection to one side in what follows.

32. I frame this claim in this way in order not to rule out the possibility that a person can surrender to God's love without explicit awareness of Christ's passion and death. For further discussion of this issue, see the section "The Problem of Exclusivism" in Chapter 8.

33. It should perhaps be emphasized that neither the story nor the knowledge of persons Paula gains from it act on her will with efficient causation. They can nonetheless prompt in her the yielding of resistance needed to begin the process of salvation for her because of the way in which stories can mediate the knowledge of persons.

34. It should go without saying that nothing about a person Paula's appropriating knowledge of persons from a story constitutes a proof that that story is historical or that the story's claims about what happened are true. It is possible to gain knowledge of persons from stories which are completely fictional. That is, someone well versed in Tolkien's *Lord of the Rings* will have some knowledge of persons of Frodo, say, but, of course, Frodo is only a character in the story and not a historical person.

On the other hand, the central thesis of Aquinas's meta-ethics is that the terms 'being' and 'goodness' are the same in reference but different in sense. (See, for example, ST I q.5 a.1; QDV 21.1–2.) On the doctrine of simplicity, God is being itself. (For an explanation of the way in which this claim is compatible with the many other claims about God made in more ordinary religious discourse, see my *The God of the Bible and the God of the Philosophers* (Marquette, WI: Marquette University Press, 2016).) Given the correlation between being and goodness, God is also goodness itself. Since 'goodness' and 'being' are the same in reference, where there is being there is also goodness, at least goodness in some respect and to some degree. But the relationship between being and goodness also holds the other way around. The presence of goodness also entails the presence of being. And where there is perfect goodness, there is perfect being, which is God.

So if what the will hungers for is goodness that is perfect and unlimited, and if, largely because of that hunger on the part of the will, the intellect is moved to assent to the proposition that what is hungered for exists, the resulting belief will not be unjustified; an intellect that assents to the proposition that God exists on the basis of the will's hungering for God's perfect goodness *will* be reliably right, because of the connection between goodness and being.

Nonetheless, as William Alston showed, a person *S* might be justified in believing *p* without *S*'s being justified in believing that he is justified in believing *p*. (See, e.g., William P. Alston, "Level Confusions in Epistemology," in *Midwest Studies in Philosophy*, vol. 5, edited by Peter A. French, Theodore E. Uehling, Jr., and Howard K. Wettstein (Minneapolis, MN: University of Minnesota Press, 1980), 135–50; reprinted in Alston's *Epistemic Justification: Essays in the Theory of Knowledge* (Ithaca, NY: Cornell University Press, 1989), 153–71.) The explanation of the justification for belief in the existence of God derived from the will's hunger for goodness that is provided by Aquinas's account of being and goodness gives reasons for thinking that a believer is justified in believing that God exists, but not for thinking that a believer is justified in believing that he is so justified.

Aquinas's views explain only what it is about reality and the will's relation to it that accounts for the justification of a belief in God's existence acquired in consequence of the will's being drawn to the perfect goodness of God. In ordinary cases, as in the kinds of cases good experimental design is intended to prevent in science, beliefs stemming primarily from the will's moving the intellect to assent to something because of the will's hungering for some good would not have much (if any) justification. Because goodness and being are correlative on Aquinas's account of the metaphysics of goodness, limited goods have limited being, so that they may or may not actually exist. But if the will moves the intellect to assent to the existence of God on the basis of the will's hungering for what is perfect goodness, then in that case, on Aquinas's account of the correlation of being and goodness and the doctrine of God's simplicity, the resulting belief will have a great deal of justification.

But to say this is not to say that in consequence a person is justified in believing that he is justified in believing that God exists.

35. There is a large literature on the nature of liturgy and the nature of knowledge mediated by liturgy, but for the sake of brevity I will have to leave to one side the myriad issues raised by those specially concerned with the nature of liturgy. For some idea of what is at issue here, see Michael C. Rea, "Narrative, Liturgy, and the Hiddenness of God," in *Metaphysics and God: Essays in Honor of Eleonore Stump*, edited by Kevin Timpe (New York: Routledge, 2009), 76–96; Nicholas Wolterstorff, *Acting Liturgically: Philosophical Reflections on Religious Practice* (Oxford: Oxford University Press, 2018); and Terence Cuneo (ed.), *Ritualized Faith: Essays on the Philosophy of Liturgy* (Oxford: Oxford University Press, 2016), as well as his "Ritual Knowledge," *Faith and Philosophy* 31 (2014): 365–85 and "Liturgical Immersion," *Journal of Analytic Theology* 2 (2014): 117–39. For an excellent engagement with the topic by a well-known composer of liturgical music, see John Foley, *Creativity and the Roots of Liturgy* (Washington, DC: The Pastoral Press, 1994).

36. For detailed discussion of the nature of faith on Aquinas's view, see my *Aquinas*, ch. 12.

37. ST III q.62 a.5 ad 2.

38. QDV 27.4.; see also QDV 27.7.

39. See, e.g., ST III q.73 a.3.

40. ST III q.73 a.3 ad 3.
41. Cf. ST III q.49 a.3.
42. Since, as I showed in Chapter 7, Aquinas holds a unity of the virtues thesis, it is not possible for a person to have faith without also having love of God. Furthermore, as the New Testament itself explains, there is a kind of belief that even fallen angels have; but it does not conduce to salvation because it lacks love of God. See Jas. 2:19: "the devils also believe and tremble."
43. ST III q.49 a.1.
44. Cf., e.g., *In Sent* III.19.1.1.2. Cf. also ST III q.1 a.2, where Aquinas is discussing the benefits of the incarnation and points especially to charity in human beings, which (he says) "is stimulated to the highest degree by this."
45. John 3:16. Since nothing turns on the choice of translation here, I helped myself to the King James translation, which I typically find better as regards translation than its main competitors, which can be historically scrupulous but literarily tone-deaf and thereby unfaithful to the original.
46. ST III q.49 a.1.
47. Aquinas says that the bread and wine of the Eucharist are nourishment for the psyche (SCG IV.61) and that they provide growth in virtue because of the way in which the Eucharist connects a person of faith to the passion and death of Christ (ST III q.79 a.1).
48. See Matt. 26:26, Mark 12:22, Luke 22:19; see also I Cor. 11:23.
49. See Matt. 26:26–8, Mark 14:22–4, and Luke 22:19–20.
50. For an excellent discussion of Aquinas's account, see Adams, *Some Later Medieval Theories of the Eucharist*.
51. See Chapter 4 for further discussion of the doctrine of eternity in connection with divine omnipresence. See also my *The God of the Bible and the God of the Philosophers*, ch. 4.
52. This clumsy locution is necessary since one cannot frame the claim in terms of time. Since there is no time in the life of eternal God, one cannot make the point by saying that there is no *time* at which God is not incarnate.
53. By parity of reasoning, on the doctrine of eternity, Christ in his passion is present to Paula always, as I explained in Chapter 4. But, on any account of the Eucharist, Paula is not always as open to Christ as she is during her participation in the rite of the Eucharist, when she is focused on Christ in his passion; and the point is only stronger on the metaphysically richer account of the Eucharist. Finally, even on the metaphysically richer account, participation in the Eucharist remains a lesser union with Christ than is possible in the final and full union with Christ in heaven, which is unmediated by the intermediaries of eating bread and drinking wine.
54. It is *also* a matter of representation, of course, because, as Aquinas explains a long-standing tradition, any sacrament is a kind of sign, whatever else it may be. See, for example, ST III q.60 a.1.
55. ST III q.79 a.1 ad 2.
56. That is, as a person in grace.
57. See, for example, ST III q.74 a.1 and q.79 a.1.
58. See, for example, ST III q.80 a.2.

59. Aquinas, *Commentary on the Letter of St. Paul to the Galatians*, translated by F.R. Larcher and M.L. Lamb, edited by J. Mortensen and E. Alarcón (Lander, WY: The Aquinas Institute for the Study of Sacred Doctrine, 2012), C.5, L.6.

60. For detailed discussion of the way in which this same process contributes to a person's growth in cooperative grace and to a person's incorporation into the mystical body of Christ, see my *Aquinas*, ch. 15.

61. I am grateful to Claire Crisp and Kevin Timpe for helpful comments on this section, which is much better than it would have been otherwise because of their generous help. For Crisp's moving memoir of dealing with a child with a disability, see her *Waking Mathilda* (Palace Gate Press, 2017). For Timpe's own excellent work on disability, see his "Executive Function, Disability, and Agency," *Res Philosophica* 93 (2016): 767–96, and his more general account of disability and agency in "Agency and Disability," in *The Routledge Handbook of Agency*, edited by Luca Ferrero (New York: Routledge, 2018).

62. Elizabeth Barnes, *The Minority Body: A Theory of Disability* (Oxford: Oxford University Press, 2016), ch. 6; the excerpt from the quotation is found on p. 185.

63. Although I have preferred to use my own translation, there are two translations currently readily available: (1) St. Gregory the Great, *Moralia in Job* (Ex Fontibus Company, 2012); and (2) Gregory the Great, *Moral Reflections on the Book of Job*, translated by Brian Kerns (Athens, OH: Cistercian Publications, 2014). The quotation is from bk. 5, introduction.

64. John Chrysostom, *Commentary on Saint John the Apostle and Evangelist: Homilies 48–88*, in *The Fathers of the Church*, vol. 41, translated by Sister Thomas Aquinas Goggin (Washington, DC: The Catholic University of America Press, 1960), 165.

65. I say '*can* intensify' because a sufferer is not compelled to accept the consolation that loving presence is able to provide. She can reject it if she chooses to, just as she can reject any offer of love she does not want.

66. See, for example, Graham Oppy, "Problems of Evil," in *The Problem of Evil: Eight Views*, edited by N.N. Trakakis (Oxford: Oxford University Press, 2018), and my response, "The Problem of Evil and Grand Unified Theories of Everything: Comments on Graham Oppy," in the same volume.

67. See, for example, Julia Driver, "The Subrogatory," *Australasian Journal of Philosophy* 70 (1992): 286–95.

68. I am grateful to Kevin Timpe for calling my attention to the need to address this issue.

69. Aquinas, *Commentary on the Letter of St. Paul to the Romans*, translated by F.R. Larcher, edited by J. Mortensen and E. Alarcón (Lander, WY: The Aquinas Institute for the Study of Sacred Doctrine, 2012), C.8, L.6.

70. Those who find it counter-intuitive to think of being a sinful person as a suffering for that person should consider that, on the view of suffering at issue here, a diminishment in wellbeing counts as a suffering for a person who has it whether or not that person recognizes it as such a diminishment. And, on the orthodox Christian theology that is the subject of this book, sinning, which moves a person further from God, will always count as a diminishment of wellbeing. For further discussion of the scale of value at issue in these judgments, see my *Wandering in Darkness*, ch. 13.

71. For detailed discussion of this notion, see my *Wandering in Darkness*, ch. 14.

72. It is inhuman not to have any heart's desire, and so (in an apparently paradoxical but nonetheless consistent way) a person's objective flourishing as a human being includes having highly subjective heart's desires, which are a function of what that particular person happens to care about independently of her flourishing. I have discussed these issues and the apparently paradoxical character of the relation between subjective and objective flourishing in *Wandering in Darkness*, chs. 1 and 14.

73. The terminology in the contemporary discussion of happiness, wellbeing, thriving, and flourishing is fluid; but, in this chapter, for the sake of clarity, I will reserve 'wellbeing' for the objective side of what human beings care about, and I will use 'flourishing' as a more general term to cover both the objective and the subjective side. In making this distinction in terminology for purposes of clarity in this chapter, I am departing from some current conventions of terminology and from my own previous usage in *Wandering in Darkness*, where the usefulness of this distinction was not so apparent.

74. In this connection, there is an apparent paradox that affects all attempts at theodicy (or defense), because a person's suffering arises when she is deprived of something that she cares about, so that suffering has its source in the deprivation of her wellbeing or her heart's desires. In order for her suffering to be defeated, it has to be the case that her suffering contributes to her having what she cares about more than she cares about what she has lost in the suffering. But it is hard to know what a person would care about more than her wellbeing or her heart's desires. And so it seems that in order for suffering to be defeated, the diminishment in objective wellbeing or the loss of heart's desires has to be the best or most promising way for the sufferer to achieve wellbeing or heart's desires. Her deprivation of flourishing has to be defeated by her flourishing.

   In *Wandering in Darkness*, I showed the way in which Aquinas's theodicy resolves this paradox with regard to objective human wellbeing. It is orthodox theological doctrine, which Aquinas accepts, that the life of a human person can be divided into two unequal portions: one very small this-worldly portion and one everlasting other-worldly portion. On Aquinas's theodicy, the suffering of a person Paula in the this-worldly portion of her life can be defeated in virtue of its contributing to her wellbeing in the everlasting other-worldly portion of her life since it is reasonable for her to care more about everlasting wellbeing than about wellbeing in the transient and evanescent portion of her life. I also argued that the suffering of the loss of heart's desires can be defeated in an analogous way, by refolding of a heart's desire and its fulfillment at the deepest level of heart's desires. For this part of the defense explained and argued for, see *Wandering in Darkness*, ch. 14.

75. See *Wandering in Darkness*.

76. To hold, as Aquinas does, that warding off a greater harm for a person or providing a greater good for her justifies God in allowing suffering is not to say that God designed the world in such a way as to produce that suffering for that person. It is important to remember in this connection the distinction between God's antecedent and God's consequent will. Aquinas's theodicy rests on a claim about what justifies God in

willing what God wills in his consequent will. But that is not equivalent to a claim about God's antecedent will, about what God would have willed if human beings had themselves willed something other than they actually did.

77. Actually, in his commentary on the book of Job, Gregory the Great, who is the schoolteacher of the later Middle Ages in this as in many other things, lists four reasons for God to allow *any* suffering. On Gregory's view, God allows suffering if it constitutes (1) punishment that does not eventuate in correction, (2) punishment that does eventuate in correction, (3) the shaping of a psyche in a way which wards off future sin, or (4) the shaping of a psyche in a way which leads to greater love of God and greater union with God. It is clear that not all of these are mutually exclusive. Furthermore, at least sometimes, which of them is the result that justifies a particular instance of suffering will be a function not of something the sufferer has already done but rather of the response of the sufferer to that suffering. Of Gregory's four cases, the first is outside the scope of the discussion, which is confined to the suffering of unwilling innocents. But the remaining three can be mapped onto the two reasons I attribute to Aquinas, insofar as the benefit Gregory assigns to suffering contributes either to redemption or to glory. See Gregory, *Moralia in Job*, V.12.

78. Since, on Aquinas's scale of value, permanent absence of union with God is the worst thing that can happen to a person, the negative value of the permanent absence of union with God outweighs the negative value of suffering of any other kind. Avoiding that outcome is, therefore, of more value for a person than avoiding any other kind of suffering. Analogously, since union with God is the intrinsic upper limit to human flourishing, attaining this union is of greater value for a person than avoiding suffering.

79. It should be added that this is a theodicy or a defense that gives only general reasons justifying God in allowing suffering in general; it does not explain why any particular person has just the suffering she does in these particular circumstances. In this respect, the traditional Christian theodicy is like contemporary medicine, which explains, for example, that smoking is a cause of cancer, without explaining why any particular smoker got or failed to get a particular cancer.

80. It is important to note this qualification. Given the nature of the processes of justification and sanctification, nothing can guarantee that these processes will occur or will be successful.

81. Care, *Living With One's Past*, 140.

82. Of course, the same person at one time might not be a person of faith and at another time might be a person of faith (or vice versa). So the benefit defeating suffering has to be relativized not only to a person but also to the condition of that person at a particular time.

83. This attitude toward Job's suffering and this understanding of the benefits defeating suffering, argued for in a very different way, can be found in medieval Jewish thought also. So, for example, Saadia Gaon says: "the tribulations [of a person such as Job] are not on account of some past sin on the servant's part. They are spontaneously initiated by God. Their purpose, therefore, lies in the future" (Saadia Gaon, *The Book of Theodicy: Translation and Commentary on the Book of Job*, translated by Len Goodman (New Haven: Yale University Press, 1988),

127). I have discussed Saadia's theodicy in "Saadia Gaon and the Problem of Evil," *Faith and Philosophy* 14 (1997): 523–49.

84. Two patients whose cancers are identical and identically advanced may get very different treatments from the same doctors, depending on the doctors' estimation of the effects of those treatments on the patients. The bone-marrow transplant that may cure the young woman of her multiple myeloma might kill the old man who has the same disease at the same state of development, because his system is no longer able to respond well to the treatments as her system is. And so the doctors will be justified in giving her the medical treatments they deny him based on their estimation of the future states of the patients. Although the doctors consider the current state of each patient, it is their estimate of the future state of each patient that justifies their decision to treat or not to treat the patient.

85. It is hard to give a complete and accurate description of a heart's desire, but, roughly considered, it is a desire for something that has the value it does for the desirer because she has set her heart on it—and there is very little limit to what a human person can set her heart on.

86. *Wandering in Darkness*, chs. 13 and 15.

87. In this chapter I am trying to use terminology that does not in effect associate me in a misleading way with one or another side in the disputes over disabilities. In my view, the best current philosophical discussion of disability can be found in Elizabeth Barnes's book, *The Minority Body*; and her general view of disability as what she calls 'mere difference' rather than 'bad difference' seems to me entirely right. Her own care to disambiguate her position from other similar-sounding views in the near neighborhood has persuaded me to try expressing my position here with terminology not in regular use in the disability literature as she engages with it. In addition, I am using the terminology of 'flourishing' and 'wellbeing' in ways that are somewhat out of line with their use in the contemporary literature on wellbeing and happiness. Because I want terms that correlate with the account of suffering I have given and the connection between suffering and union with God at issue for my interpretation of the doctrine of the atonement, I will use the relevant terms in the way explained here, even if they have somewhat different uses in other areas of philosophy.

88. When the proper functioning of some organ or activity within a system is diminished or prevented by something else within that system, then there is an impediment to the organ or activity in question. When the proper functioning is diminished or prevented by something internal to the organ or activity, then there is an impairment. I mean 'impediment' and 'impairment' to be generic enough to cover all the varieties of loss or lack of typical structure and/or function in any part of a person, whether that part has to do with an organ or an activity. For more narrowly defined terms and careful distinction among them, see Sheena L. Carter, "Impairment, Disability and Handicap," Emory School of Medicine, http://www.pediatrics.emory.edu/divisions/neonatology/dpc/Impairment%20MX.html, accessed May 5, 2017. I am grateful to Kevin Timpe for calling my attention to this useful site.

89. In this chapter, it is not my intention to participate in the burgeoning and insightful literature on disability; but there is some overlap between that literature and the issues central for me here. I have learned and benefited from Elizabeth

Barnes's work on disability, but my focus in this chapter is not on disability per se. In addition to her book cited above, see also her "Valuing Disability, Causing Disability," *Ethics* 125 (2014): 88–113; "Disability and Adaptive Preference," *Philosophical Perspectives* 23 (2009): 1–22; and "Disability, Minority and Difference," *Journal of Applied Philosophy* 26 (2009): 337–55.

90. Barnes, *The Minority Body*, 45.

91. Because it is awkward to write 'impediments or impairments' repeatedly, in what follows I will simply write 'impediments' as shorthand for the longer phrase.

92. For a good discussion of these kinds of health and their connection to human flourishing, see, for example, Richard Kraut, *What is Good and Why: The Ethics of Well-Being* (Cambridge, MA: Harvard University Press, 2007), and especially the discussion beginning on p. 133. Nonetheless, it should be said that this distinction between kinds of health is coarse-grained and imprecise. It is imprecise because human beings are embodied minds and so what affects the body affects the mind and vice versa, if one can even speak this way. To distinguish between health of body and health of mind is therefore only a rough approximation to the correct distinction. And this rough distinction is also coarse-grained because it is based on only a large-scale distinction among parts of human beings. Those parts have parts too, and impairments in the varying smaller-scale parts make correspondingly different impairments for a person suffering from them. Some of these impairments will make life harder for the sufferer than others. For an excellent discussion of even the most philosophically complicated of such issues, namely, the connection between disability and executive function, for example, see Timpe, "Executive Function, Disability, and Agency." Even with the caveats in this note, however, the imprecise and coarse-grained distinction between health of body and health of mind is useful for showing the theological claim at issue in this section of this chapter, and so I will adopt it in what follows.

93. I am grateful to Claire Crisp for calling my attention to the need to make this point explicit.

94. Harriet McBryde Johnson, "Unspeakable Conversations," *New York Times Magazine*, February 16, 2003, http://www.nytimes.com/2003/02/16/magazine/unspeakable-conversations.html.

95. In arguing for the rationality of those people who say that their disability is not a disadvantage to them, Barnes excepts those who are severely mentally ill. For example, she says,

> Ceteris paribus, for any person x, x is a good source of evidence about x's own wellbeing. This is a fairly weak principle, and one that most people would readily agree to ... And the claim is ceteris paribus—[people] are not a good source of evidence if they are crazy.... ("Disability and Adaptive Preference," 9)

As the next part of this chapter shows, I disagree with Barnes in the last claim in this quotation. I think that even a person Jerome who is seriously mentally ill can have personal flourishing; and so in that case Jerome's testimony that he is flourishing will be a good source of evidence that he is flourishing, even with mental illness or other mental impairments.

96. At some point, of course, the two modes of diminishment will converge, insofar as the mind is correlated (in some way or other, depending on one's theory of mind) with the brain. But, clearly, at least in many cases, it is possible to have impediments to bodily thriving without having any impediments to thriving of mind.

97. Kevin Timpe and Aaron Cobb, "Disability and the Theodicy of Defeat," *Journal of Analytic Theology* 5 (2017): 100–20.

98. See, for example, Jean Vanier, *Becoming Human* (Mahwah, NJ: Paulist Press, 1998).

99. Eva Kittay, "Deadly Medicine: Project T4, Mental Disability, and Racism," *Res Philosophica* 93 (2016): 734.

100. For an excellent discussion of some of the challenges posed to those with mental disabilities by the communities in which they live, see Josh Dohmen, "'A Little of Her Language': Epistemic Injustice and Mental Disability," *Res Philosophica* 93 (2016): 669–92.

101. See, for example, Vasudevi Reddy, *How Infants Know Minds* (Cambridge, MA: Harvard University Press, 2008).

102. Quoted in William Alston, *Perceiving God* (Ithaca, NY: Cornell University Press, 1991), 18–19.

103. It is an open question, which I cannot deal with in passing here, whether flourishing in loving personal relationships is compatible with every kind of impediment to thriving of mind. Nonetheless, as Kevin Timpe has called to my attention, Jean Vanier's work with persons suffering from severe impediments to thriving of mind is suggestive in this regard. For a detailed description of a particular case, see Henri Nouwen, *Adam: God's Beloved* (Maryknoll, NY: Orbis Books, 2000), 3rd printing. For Jean Vanier's own views on the subject, see his *Becoming Human*. For a brief discussion of some of Vanier's work in connection with the problem of suffering, see my *Wandering in Darkness*, ch. 14.

104. In a helpful paper commenting on the controversy generated by the claim that disability is a not a bad difference, Ian Stoner argues for a distinction in kinds of wellbeing and in ways of being worse off. The distinction he makes has at least a family resemblance to the one I make here, although without the metaphysics I depend on here. See Ian Stoner, "Ways to be Worse Off," *Res Philosophica* 93 (2016): 921–50.

105. For two differing biographies of Harriet Tubman, from which I am taking these details of her life, see Sarah Hopkins Bradford, *Harriet the Moses of Her People* (Lexington, KY: The Perfect Library, 2016 [orig. pub. 1886]); and Catherine Clinton, *Harriet Tubman: The Road to Freedom* (New York: Back Bay Books, 2004).

106. Quoted in Bradford, *Harriet Tubman*, 65.

107. "What is Williams Syndrome?", Williams Syndrome Association, https://williams-syndrome.org/what-is-williams-syndrome, accessed May 5, 2017.

108. Teri Sforza (with Howard Lenhoff), *The Strangest Song: One Father's Quest to Help His Daughter Find Her Voice* (New York: Prometheus Books, 2006), 197.

109. Sforza, *The Strangest Song*, 251.

110. Quoted in Sforza, *The Strangest Song*, 184.

111. See Chapters 6 and 7 for further discussion of this claim. See also in this connection Kevin Timpe, "Cooperative Grace, Cooperative Agency," *European Journal for Philosophy of Religion* 7 (2015): 225–47.

112. See Chapter 7 for detailed discussion of this view.

113. In this connection, see the section "The Problem of Exclusivism" in Chapter 8. By parity of reasoning with the arguments in that chapter, on this Christian view of thriving, personal thriving is not limited to those who identify as Christian.

114. Underlying these claims is a rejection of a certain kind of reductionism; on these claims, the whole is not just the sum of its parts. That is why there can be thriving of the whole even when the parts of the whole have some impediments to thriving. For further discussion of the metaphysical position at issue here, see my "Emergence, Causal Powers, and Aristotelianism in Metaphysics," in *Powers and Capacities in Philosophy: The New Aristotelianism*, edited by Ruth Groff and John Greco (New York and London: Routledge, 2012).

115. For more discussion of the position summarized in these lines, see my *Wandering in Darkness*, ch. 14.

116. For detailed defense of this claim, see my *Wandering in Darkness*, ch. 13.

117. There might, of course, be flourishing of some different sort if the impediments to thriving of body and of mind were removed. The point is only that for the flourishing under discussion, the impediments to thriving are woven into the fabric of the flourishing which a person actually has and are not related to that flourishing in any merely accidental or instrumental way. Furthermore, nothing about the removing of one kind of impediment to thriving, as, for example, the miraculous removal of blindness when Jesus restores the sight of a man born blind, prevents there from being other impediments to thriving of mind or of body in the same person which lead to flourishing of a different sort. Short of perfection in heaven, human beings in this life will not be entirely without some impediments to thriving in mind or body.

118. I do not mean to say that suffering is sufficient for personal thriving or that everyone who suffers has personal thriving in virtue of suffering. For some people, suffering is destructive rather than productive of thriving. For further discussion of this point, see my *Wandering in Darkness*, ch. 13.

119. For some attempt to describe the evidence and argue for the claim, see my *Wandering in Darkness*, chs. 13–15.

120. *Wandering in Darkness*, chs. 5–7.

121. For more discussion of this claim, see Chapter 6.

122. Even those suffering only involuntarily *secundum quid*.

123. See the discussion of Eckhart's views in Chapter 6 for a defense of this claim.

124. For a discussion of this case, see my *Wandering in Darkness*, ch. 9.

125. It is certainly true, as some readers will be quick to point out, that suffering can also cement a person into angry or despairing isolation. Insofar as a person's surrender to love, or even just to the compassion and care of others, is always in the control of that person, nothing can guarantee that a person will incline to such surrender.

126. Some people suppose that there are special cases in which a person suffers from a trauma associated with a religious context, so that the one thing such a person is unlikely to do is turn to God in suffering. (For discussion of such cases, see Michael C. Rea, *"Though the Darkness Hide Thee": Seeking the Face of the Invisible*

God (Oxford: Oxford University Press, 2018).) If in fact there are such cases, then I will omit them from the claims made here.

127. Henry Louis Gates, Jr. (ed.), *The Classic Slave Narratives* (New York: Mentor Library, 1987), 326.
128. Clinton, *Harriet Tubman*, 83.
129. Quoted in Bradford, *Harriet Tubman*, 54–5. Different versions of this story are given in other sources, but the version quoted in Bradford's biography seems to me to give correctly the general flavor of Harriet's daring, determination, and selfless care for others, whether or not it has all its details historically accurate.
130. See Chapter 2 for more explanation of this claim.
131. It would be a mistake to suppose that her suffering increased simultaneously and correlatively. Nothing about the role of suffering in flourishing implies that the suffering and the flourishing are simultaneous.
132. Clinton, *Harriet Tubman*, 91.
133. For discussion and defense of this claim, see my *Wandering in Darkness*, ch. 13. From the fact that an impediment of one part of a person can exist together with great thriving of the whole person, it does not follow that any such impediment itself is a good thing. It means only that an impediment with regard to one part of a human person can be completely eclipsed or defeated by the thriving of the whole person.

    In a related point regarding disability, Elizabeth Barnes has argued in various works that this claim:

    (1) disability by itself does not make a life worse than it otherwise would be,

    does not entail this claim:

    (2) it is morally permissible to cause disability or to fail to remedy disability. (See, for example, her "Disability, Minority and Difference," p. 339.)

Her position seems to me entirely correct. One can think of the point this way. An impediment to the flourishing of a part of a person Paula is something bad for that part; and insofar as it is bad for that part, it ought to be prevented or remedied if it can be so *ceteris paribus*. But it is also possible for Paula to thrive as a person in virtue of the impediment of one of her parts. In that case, Paula's personal thriving defeats the badness of the impediment to the flourishing of a part of Paula. When the badness of the impediment is defeated by the thriving of the whole person, then it may well be the case that the conditions in the *ceteris paribus* clause are not met. Consequently, in a case of that sort, Paula might well prefer to keep the impediment and to be glad of it (as, in an analogous case, the disability rights movement argues with respect to disability). But in cases where the prevention or the remedy of some impediment to the flourishing of a part of Paula would not diminish or destroy Paula's personal thriving, then the prevention or remedy of the impediment ought to be sought. Since the impediment itself is some defect in a part of Paula, and since human beings are rarely in a position to know whether keeping or causing such a defect will enhance the personal thriving of a person who has that defect, then if a person Jerome caused or kept such a defect in Paula when he could readily prevent or repair it, Jerome's actions are not rendered morally permissible by any good effects that might follow for Paula.

134. For further explication and defense of this claim, see my *Wandering in Darkness*, ch. 1.
135. For that matter, nothing about the claims here explains or justifies Christ's suffering either. That explanation can be found in the arguments of Chapters 5 and 8 of this book.
136. See, for example, Rom. 12:5, 1 Cor. 12:27, Col. 1:18 and 1:24.
137. This biblical line obviously also has significant implications for connection among suffering human beings, too; but considerations of space prevent me from exploring further these implications.
138. To say that they converge is not to say that they become identical. Theodicy is the project of finding and defending a general morally sufficient reason for God to allow the suffering of unwilling innocent people. The interpretation of the doctrine of the atonement argued for here helps to explain the way in which that morally sufficient reason is part of the general story of God's salvation of post-Fall human beings.

CHAPTER 10

1. Or, more accurately, Christ's life, passion, and death. I will not use the full phrase in what follows because it is clumsy to do so, but it should be understood.
2. See also, for further examples, Isa. 61:7 and Zeph. 3:19.
3. I am making no claims about what Abelard himself may have defended; what is at issue here is only an interpretation commonly associated with Abelard.
4. For more detail as regards the nature of shame and its sources, see Chapter 2.
5. With apologies to those who will find the practice objectionable, I will from this point onwards refer to Malala Yousufzai by her first name alone. She herself has tended to do so; the title of the movie telling her story does so; and, in consequence, to me at any rate, referring to her just by her last name (which is the common practice for names in academic works) seems inappropriate or even disrespectful.
6. For a critical discussion of retributive punishment as a means for righting the unjust relative standing between a wrongdoer and his victim, see Martha Nussbaum, *Anger and Forgiveness: Resentment, Generosity, Justice* (Oxford: Oxford University Press, 2016).
7. For one good statement of the case for retributive punishment as including good for the victims of injustice, see Jeffrie Murphy, *Getting Even: Forgiveness and Its Limits* (Oxford: Oxford University Press, 2003).
8. A limitation of nature is something we have in mind when we say something of this sort to a person suffering from shame: "You did your best!", "You're only human!", "It could have happened to anyone!" A defect of nature is a particular diminishment not typical of all human beings. In what follows, I will focus on defects of nature; but, in my view, analogous things can be said about limitations of nature. I am grateful to Michael Rea for calling this distinction to my attention.
9. I am here leaving to one side the more complicated issue of communal agency, where the things for which one feels shamed are a result of a condition or action that is a result of the whole group's activity or history. Communal guilt and shame are outside the scope of this book, on the grounds that one cannot do everything in one book. What is at issue for me here is just an individual's sense of his own

shame in consequence of something about his family or social group. A human being born to a Nazi parent near the end of World War II may be shamed by what his parent did; but this shame has to be distinguished from the shame of his parent, who was actually in the Nazi party during that war, even when his parent somehow bore no personal responsibility for any particular act of horrendous evil.

10. For further discussion of this kind of case, see Chapter 2. See also the insightful study by Gitta Sereny in her book *The Healing Wound* (New York: W.W. Norton, 2001).

11. Mark Twain is famous for black-spirited remarks indicating such a view. He is reported to have said, "God made man at the end of the week's work, when God was tired"; "if you were to cross a man with a cat, you would improve the man and deteriorate the cat"; "it often seems a pity that Noah didn't miss the boat"; "man is the only animal that blushes or needs to do so."

12. I am not claiming that these are the only kinds of shame, only that they are major ones and that they are connected to human wrongdoing, directly or indirectly. No doubt, there are trivial sources of minor shame and superficial instances of very small shame, not long remembered by the sufferer of the shame. I see no reason to suppose that such things need defeat by the atonement. What is at issue here are the major kinds of memorable and painful shame.

13. For a detailed exposition and defense of this view, see Marilyn Adams, *Horrendous Evils and the Goodness of God* (Ithaca, NY: Cornell University Press, 1999).

14. What is at issue here is the distinction between compensation for suffering and defeat of the suffering. It is difficult to spell out this distinction in a fully determinate way, but the following thought experiment highlights it. Suppose that an extremely rich person Jerome offers to pay a very poor person Paula to let him harvest one of her kidneys; and suppose that the price he offers is outrageously lavish. By any ordinary economic scale of value, the amount of money offered is enormously greater than the economic value of Paula's kidney. In this case, the evil of losing a kidney would be outweighed by the compensation of the money. But Paula might reject Jerome's offer indignantly, because, on a different scale of value, which is the one of significance to her, the value of the money is much less than the value of the kidney. Paula might think, for example, that the very offer is humiliating to her, and she might feel with anger that money could not compensate for the degradation of accepting the offer. In addition, it should be noted, it is certainly possible for Jerome to give Paula money even if she does not give him her kidney. Paula's losing a kidney to Jerome has no intrinsic or essential connection to his giving her money.

By contrast, suppose that Paula has a child Julia dying of kidney failure and suppose (what is biologically implausible but philosophically propaedeutic) that Paula is the only person whose tissue type is close enough to Julia's so that the donated kidney can be safely transplanted into Julia. Suppose also that, by Paula's own scale of value, the life of her child is of much greater value than the good of not losing her kidney; Paula greatly prefers saving Julia's life over keeping both her kidneys. Furthermore, as I have constructed the example, Paula could not save Julia's life without losing her kidney, so that the evil of losing her kidney is essential in these circumstances to the good that outweighs it. In these circumstances, if

Paula donates a kidney to save Julia's life, the evil of losing her kidney is defeated for Paula.

15. As different strands in Western thought make clear, honor can be thought of in two different ways. So, for example, in Homer's *Iliad* (Book IX), Achilles differentiates between honor from men and honor from Zeus; and, in the Gospel of John (John 5:44) Jesus distinguishes between honor from men and honor from God. For the sake of clarity of discourse, we can think of one of these kinds of honor as 'glitter honor' and the other as 'gold honor.' In each kind of honor, a person Jerome has honor because of the laudatory reaction on the part of some others. But, when it comes to glitter honor, honor is something that remains entirely in those others; it confers nothing on the person who receives the honor. If Jerome receives glitter honor from others one day, he may lose it the next; and there will be no change in him either when he gains it or loses it. Minor-league, untalented movie stars who achieve a flare-up of fame which dies down equally quickly and who are then entirely forgotten have glitter honor in their short period of fame. Glitter honor can be seen to be a small good from the fact that it diminishes when it is distributed. By contrast, if Jerome receives gold honor from others, it will be more stable; and receiving it will constitute a change in Jerome.

In my view, there is an example of gold honor in the fairy tale of Cinderella and the Prince. When the Prince, who is an unusually admirable and good man in the story, asks Cinderella to marry him, then Cinderella gains in gold honor. She receives this honor from the Prince; but she herself is altered by receiving it. She grows in receiving the love of the Prince, one might say. If the Prince were to die shortly after having asked Cinderella to marry him, this growth in her would not vanish and her gold honor would not diminish. (No doubt, there is also glitter honor for Cinderella in being asked to marry the Prince in virtue of her growth in social rank accruing from her joining the royal family. But that is the kind of honor that would be lost if the Prince were to die shortly after making his marriage proposal.) The gold honor Cinderella gains when the Prince loves her is therefore stable. And it does not diminish by being shared. If the Prince loves the children he comes to have once he has married Cinderella, they also will have gold honor in virtue of being loved by him; but their having this honor does not diminish the gold honor of their mother.

The fact that honor comes in these two varieties helps to explain why magnanimity could be a virtue for both Greeks and Christians. As Aristotle explains magnanimity, it seems to be a matter of a proud, rich man's willingness to spend money on public works for the sake of fame in his community. As Aquinas explains magnanimity, it is a matter of being willing to spend oneself unstintingly for others in joyful response to being loved by God. The honor being sought in the first case is glitter honor given by humans; in the second case, it is gold honor given by God.

By 'honor' in what follows, I mean gold honor, not glitter honor. That is why when a person gains this honor (gold honor), it is also true (as I claim in the text) that others have a *warranted* desire for him. There is a great deal more that needs to be said to delineate and explain the difference in the two kinds of honor; but, for my purposes here, this much is sufficient. As the subsequent text makes clear, the honor in question is correlated with real value on a deep and significant scale of value in the person being honored; and that point alone wards off the worry that glitter honor is in question here.

16. Quoted in Ashley Montagu, *The Elephant Man: A Study in Human Dignity* (Lafayette, LA: Acadian House, 2001), 46.

17. There is, of course, considerable complexity in the details being glossed over here. How much of something worthy of honor is needed before the whole group gains in honor? How much gaining in honor is needed before the shame of the group is overturned? And so on. It is not possible in passing to try to sort out all such details, but the general point is sufficient for my purposes in this book.

18. All the examples discussed in this section involve exceptional people, and so someone might worry that the sample is unrepresentative. But it is worth noting that these people were not exceptional in their families or social standing or wealth; they did not begin their lives as exceptional. Rather it was their very response to their shaming that made them worthy of honor and consequently exceptional.

19. See Chapter 9 for further defense of this claim.

20. For a discussion of this issue, see Adams, *Horrendous Evils and the Goodness of God*.

21. Someone might suppose that if a person is honored by others, there is distance between him and those others too. But *that* distance is one which others wish to cross, insofar as people desire to join themselves to the honored. So the distance from others inherent in being honored is not a distance of the kind concerned in shame.

22. I owe this objection to Evan Fales.

23. For a discussion of this position, see Marilyn Adams, *Christ and Horrors: The Coherence of Christology* (Cambridge: Cambridge University Press, 2006).

24. Aquinas, *Commentary on 1 Timothy*, C.1, L.4, in *St. Thomas Aquinas, Commentary on the Letters of St. Paul to the Philippians, Colossians, Thessalonians, Timothy, Titus, and Philemon*, translated by F.R. Larcher, edited by J. Mortensen and E. Alarcón (Lander, WY: The Aquinas Institute for the Study of Sacred Doctrine, 2012), 256. I like and therefore have used this translation, but I have felt free to modify it slightly in those few cases where I liked my idea for translation better than theirs.

25. For an example of this kind of view, see Alvin Plantinga, "Supralapsarianism, or 'O Felix Culpa,'" in *Christian Faith and the Problem of Evil*, edited by Peter van Inwagen (Grand Rapids, MI: Eerdmans, 2004), 1–25.

26. For a helpful discussion of the notion of deification in early Christian thought, see David Meconi, *The One Christ: St. Augustine's Theology of Deification* (Washington, DC: The Catholic University of America Press, 2013).

27. Of course, Judas also betrayed Christ; but Judas is not included among persons in grace, because Judas despaired after his betrayal of Christ.

28. See Chapter 9 for detailed discussion of the relevant portions of this biblical text.

29. Someone might suppose that if this point is true, then suffering should be sought. But seeking suffering runs the risk of trying to turn what is only an instrumental good into an apparently intrinsic good; and it also runs the risk of eviscerating suffering of one of its medicinal characteristics, namely, its involuntary character. For further discussion of the nature of suffering, see Chapter 6.

30. See Luke 22:33, for example.
31. For a discussion of Christ's prayer in Gethsemane, see Chapters 6 and 8.
32. See Matt. 27:3 for textual support for the claim that Judas repented.
33. I Pet. 1:6–7.
34. See Ruth 4:1–9.
35. See Neh. 3:1–32.
36. Cf. in this connection Job 14:15, where Job attributes to God a desire for Job.
37. For a discussion of the notion of identification at issue here, see my "Persons: Identification and Freedom," *Philosophical Topics* 24 (1996): 183–214.
38. 2 Sam. 21:1.
39. Josh. 9:3ff.
40. 2 Sam. 21:3. The Hebrew word translated with 'atonement' is an inflected version of the verb '*kippur*.' Etymologies of words in ancient languages are often speculative, but one proposed etymology for this Hebrew word is *washing off*. The range of meanings for the word in the Hebrew Bible include propitiation, ransom, covering over, and atonement.
41. For more discussion of making amends or making satisfaction, see Chapters 2 and 3.
42. Jerome Miller, "The Cry of Abel's Blood: Christ's Wounds and Ours," *Commonweal* 144.7, April 14, 2017, 18. I am grateful to Sarah Legett for calling this article to my attention. Miller's article finishes by calling for a new interpretation of the doctrine of the atonement, one which focuses on Christ's offering satisfaction to the victims of human evil, and he suggests focusing on empathy as an element of such an interpretation.
43. For more discussion of this case, see Chapter 3.
44. Joshua Thurow uses a very similar point to argue that one of the purposes of purgatory is to atone for the harm and injustice done to other human beings; see his "Atoning in Purgatory," *Religious Studies* 53 (2017): 217–37.
45. Miller, "The Cry of Abel's Blood," 16.
46. Strictly speaking, one should say here 'a theodicy or a defense', but I am leaving this distinction to one side here in order not to burden an already demanding discussion with any more detail than is necessary. For the distinction and its importance in this connection, see my *Wandering in Darkness*, ch. 1.
47. *Wandering in Darkness.*
48. No doubt, this is the point at which insight into Patristic interpretations of the doctrine of the atonement would help to complete the picture. Those interpretations are typically supposed to include a focus on the fallen angels and their part in the human drama of fall and redemption. The whole cosmic story is evidently incomplete without that inclusion.
49. See the discussion of vicarious satisfaction in Chapter 2 for elucidation of this claim.
50. This issue arises because, on traditional Christian doctrine, human beings do not change their basic spiritual condition after death. If this supposition is not accepted, then this objection is obviated.
51. In one of his stories, C.S. Lewis depicts the process of dying as a matter of going through a doorway and passing Christ in doing so, so that no one dies without seeing the face of Christ and either loving or hating it. As far as I can see, nothing in Christian theology precludes this speculative metaphor on Lewis's part. And so,

if for no other reason, even swift dying does not preclude a momentary opportunity for redemption.

52. See the section "The Problem of Exclusivism" in Chapter 8 for discussion of these claims.

53. See Chapter 9 for discussion of these claims and this biblical text.

54. For more discussion of this claim, see Chapter 9. Insofar as this claim is connected to the problem of evil, see my *Wandering in Darkness*.

55. See Chapter 3 for discussion of this line of Newton's in his pamphlet *Reflections on the Slave Trade*.

56. In focusing on memory here, I mean to call attention to the lingering stain on the soul; I am not implying that amnesia would help heal Newton's guilt. (For a brief discussion of amnesia and guilt, see Chapter 2.) In any event, on traditional Christian views of heaven, amnesia is not possible for the redeemed in heaven, so that it is not available as a remedy for the stain on the soul even if it were a morally acceptable solution, as it is not, in my view.

57. See, for example, Jeffrey M. Blustein, *Forgiveness and Remembrance* (Oxford: Oxford University Press, 2014). Blustein's position is discussed in more detail in Chapter 3.

58. See, for example, Isa. 43:25 and Heb. 8:12.

59. Aquinas, *Commentary on Colossians*, C.2, L.3.

60. Heb. 10:31.

CHAPTER 11

1. For discussion of the biblical stories about Mary of Bethany, see my *Wandering in Darkness: Narrative and the Problem of Suffering* (Oxford: Oxford University Press, 2010), ch. 12. In that chapter, I also briefly comment on the view held by Augustine and others that Mary Magdalene is Mary of Bethany.

2. Richard Swinburne, *Responsibility and Atonement* (Oxford: Oxford University Press, 1989).

3. For a helpful review of contemporary interpretations of sacrifice as presented in the biblical book of Hebrews, together with a detailed argument for an alternative interpretation, see David Moffitt, *Atonement and the Logic of Resurrection in the Epistle to the Hebrews* (Leiden: Brill, 2013). I am not persuaded by Moffitt's argument for reasons given throughout this book.

4. Homer, *Iliad*, translated by Richmond Lattimore (Chicago, IL: University of Chicago Press, 1951), Bk. I, ll.40–2.

5. This is, of course, a general point that others have also called attention to. So, for example, Thomas McCall says, "certainly we should resist all conceptions of propitiation that echo pagan notions of God. It is not as though we somehow change God—as if God were the one who needed to be changed" (McCall, *Forsaken: The Trinity and the Cross, and Why It Matters* (Downers Grove, IL: InterVarsity Press, 2012), 110). On the other hand, it is hard to resist the suspicion that some thinkers who share McCall's attitude have nonetheless fallen into interpreting the doctrine of the atonement in this way anyway. For a helpful historical and theological survey of the notion of sacrifice and its connection to atonement, see Stephen

Whitfield Sykes (ed.), *Sacrifice and Redemption* (Cambridge: Cambridge University Press, 1991).

6. J. Israelstam and Judah Slotki (eds.), *Midrash Rabbah. Leviticus* (London: Soncino Press, 1983), 32–3.

7. Like all biblical stories, this one has neutron-star density, so that a proper consideration of it would take considerable space. In trying to deal with the story in passing, and by picking out only one detail from it, I am not attempting an exegesis of it, but only trying to highlight one thing to be learned from it. There are two complications to this story that might be thought to undermine the feature of it which will be salient for my purposes. One is the varying identification of the speaker who is talking to Gideon. As in some other well-known cases in the Hebrew Bible, a message is delivered by an angel who appears as a human being or as a more supernatural being and who sometimes speaks for the Lord or who sometimes seems to be the channel through which the Lord speaks to the human who is visited by the angel. In this story about Gideon, in fact, the Lord continues to speak to Gideon somehow after the angel has disappeared (Judg. 6:23). So there can be some dispute about Gideon's attitude towards the messenger. Some commentators suppose that Gideon did not know that the messenger was an angel, a supposition that has textual support in Gideon's reaction of dismay after the angel does a miracle. But against this supposition is Gideon's reverential address towards the angel from the beginning of the angel's appearance to him. Secondly, there is the angel's doing of a miracle. Some commentators suppose that in the story Gideon is trying to test the messenger to see if he really is an angel and can do miracles. But against this is the character of Gideon's anxiety from the beginning of his conversation with the angel. He does not express uncertainty about who it is who is talking with him. He expresses skepticism about whether God is on the side of the Israelites or not. So, although there are myriad details in this story that complicate any attempt to deal with it expeditiously, in the end these details seem to me not to militate against the reading of the story I give here. I am grateful to Yehuda Gellman for helping me see that this footnote is necessary.

8. I am using italics to indicate that I am conveying the content of what was said, as distinct from translating what is written in the Hebrew. Translating Hebrew is an art requiring considerable linguistic expertise not only in Hebrew but also in English, so that the resonance and flavor of the original language is not lost in translation. I have neither the expertise nor the patience for such a task in the last chapter of this book. While I have been careful to check the Hebrew throughout this book at any point where I have discussed a passage from the Hebrew Bible, my own experience translating texts from ancient languages makes me sure that I do not want to be responsible for good translation if all that is needed for my purposes is the communication of the content of the lines in the Hebrew text. In the case of Gideon's lines, I have also departed from the literal content of the Hebrew in order to convey better what I take to be the emotional tone of the lines.

9. Actually, the text presents this line as delivered by the Lord through the angel, so that the text reads "The Lord said, 'Surely, I will be with you'" (Judg. 6:16).

10. I have not forgotten the fact that in the story the angel eventually does a miracle with the present that Gideon brings the angel. Someone might suppose that the angel's doing a miracle is itself evidence that Gideon brings the present just in

order to test the identity of the being talking to him; he brings the present to see if that being will do a miracle with the present and so confirm his identity as an angel. But, in the preceding part of the story, the object of Gideon's doubt has not been whether or not the being speaking with him is an angel or is God's messenger. The object of Gideon's doubt has been whether God is really on the side of the Israelites and will really be on Gideon's side if Gideon undertakes to do the mission he is being handed by the angel. Nothing in the preceding conversation suggests that Gideon can't decide whether the being speaking to him is an angel or is really just another human being acting as a prophet. But if the point of Gideon's bringing the angel a gift were to see if the angel would do a miracle, then this is the only doubt the gift would address.

Furthermore, it is worth asking what it is that the angel's miracle serves to show. Without doubt, it demonstrates God's power over nature. And while it is true that such a demonstration confirms the identity of the angel, its more vivid effect, in my view, is its reassurance that God's power will be on Gideon's side. It should not be forgotten that the angel has asked Gideon to lead the Israelites in battle against the Midianites, to whom they have so far been subordinated. So the question of interest for my purposes, then, is just the question I raise here: Why does Gideon suppose that his bringing the angel a present will help him feel less anxious about the angel's message to him? I am grateful to Yehuda Gellman and Jon Levenson for calling my attention to the need for this note.

11. Moshe Halbertal, *On Sacrifice* (Princeton, NJ: Princeton University Press, 2012), 7.
12. Halbertal, *On Sacrifice*, 8.
13. Halbertal, *On Sacrifice*, 10–11.
14. For those who might worry that Homer's story undercuts this claim on Halbertal's part, it is helpful to notice that what Apollo cares about in Homer's story is not the thing offered to him, the killed beasts, for which Apollo has no use himself, but rather the fact that humans are willing to honor him by giving up so much of their wealth for the sake of being on his side. Even in this case, then, Halbertal is right: the killed beasts offered to Apollo are not a bribe given him. On Halbertal's reading of sacrifice, the difference between the sacrifice given to Apollo and that given to the God of the Hebrew Bible lies in the purpose of the giving, as these lines from Halbertal indicate. The purpose of the sacrifice to Apollo is to get Apollo to act as an agent carrying out the will of those bringing the sacrifice. The purpose of the sacrifice at issue in the Hebrew Bible, on Halbertal's explanation, is to strengthen the relationship between those offering the sacrifice and God.
15. Halbertal, *On Sacrifice*, 13. In this connection, for excellent discussion of the same general idea, see Jon Levenson, *The Love of God* (Princeton, NJ: Princeton University Press, 2016).
16. I have not forgotten that elsewhere in the story of Gideon, when Gideon wants a sign, he wants God to do something for Gideon. But in that case the issue is Gideon's discernment of the wisdom of a particular course of action. In effect, in those parts of Gideon's story, Gideon is asking God to help him see what exactly to do next. So nothing about the later episodes of Gideon's getting a sign invalidates the explanation of this first part of Gideon's story, in which he brings an offering to God through the angel.

17. For insightful discussion of the connection between keeping the Mosaic Law and the love of God, see Levenson, *The Love of God*.

18. Ingolf Dalferth summarizes this sort of attitude towards sacrifice, which is at the heart of the Christian notion of sacrifice on his view, in this way:

> Sacrifices presuppose consecration, that is, the making of something into a symbol ... Thus the thing sacrificed, in blood sacrifices usually another living creature and most often a domestic animal, is made to stand for or to symbolize something else, namely 'the person or persons who are making the sacrifice ...' [footnote omitted]; and in the sacrificial act man is symbolically giving (part of) himself by killing the consecrated animal and offering its life to God as a vicarious sacrifice of himself. But this essentially vicarious function of sacrifice depends wholly on the consecration; and consecration involves and presupposes a whole system of religious rules and ritual conventions. ... In brief, sacrifice presupposes a regulated relationship between God and man, a cultic framework ... that assigns certain roles and functions to the participants ... Only in a context like this the idea of a sacrificial, vicarious death begins to make sense.

(Ingolf Dalferth, "Christ Died for Us: Reflections on the Sacrificial Language of Salvation," in *Sacrifice and Redemption*, edited by Stephen Whitfield Sykes (Cambridge: Cambridge University Press, 1991), 307–8)

19. *Leviticus: A New Translation with a Commentary Anthologized from Talmudic, Midrashic and Rabbinic Sources*, translated and edited by Rabbis Nosson Scherman, Hersh Goldwurm, and Yehezkel Danziger (New York: Mesorah Publications, 2003), 21. In quoting this text, I am not validating every claim it makes or implies. I am pointing out only that one authority in this religious tradition which is often taken by Christians to support the Anselmian approach to sacrifice in fact repudiates that approach.

20. I am grateful to Andrew Pinsent for calling my attention to the need to make this point clear.

21. Someone might wonder whether it is appropriate to consider the offering of Cain and Abel as a sacrifice, especially if one accepts the rabbinic suggestion that in bringing animals to God, Abel did not kill them. In Heb. 11:4, however, the word used to describe what Abel brought is a Greek term regularly translated 'sacrifice' when it occurs elsewhere in the New Testament texts.

22. God accepts Abel's offering but not Cain's; and when God talks with Cain about having rejected Cain's offering, God tells Cain that Cain will be accepted if he does well. This line implies that Abel did do well and that is why his offering was accepted.

23. For those inclined to doubt this line, consider that at this time in the story Adam and Eve are still living, Cain attacks his brother to kill him, Cain shows no surprise when his attack results in Abel's death, and Cain does not excuse himself to God by claiming that he had no idea that Abel was subject to death.

24. The story never explains why God did not accept Cain's offering. Instead, the story leaves the reader in Cain's position. God asks Cain a pointed question: if you do well, will you not be accepted? In other words, from the fact that God did not accept Cain's offering, Cain has to conclude either that there is something not good about his offering or that there is something not good about God. Because

the story never resolves the issue for Cain, it does not resolve the issue for readers either. The story of Cain and Abel is the story of the first great evil after the Fall, and it sets the stage for the post-Fall world coming. In that world, with its evil and suffering, a post-Fall person will have to find some explanation for the evil in the world, and that explanation will have to be grounded either in something defective about human beings or in something defective on God's side. The story of Cain and Abel therefore invites readers to take a stand that will govern their subsequent response to the world after the Fall, but the story does not answer for readers the question that God asks Cain. I am grateful to Andrew Pinsent for helping me see the need for this note.

25. There is a part of the covenant that is enjoined on Noah and his descendants too; but since it is not central to my purposes here, I leave that part of the covenant unexamined. For an excellent recent discussion of the human part of God's covenants in the Hebrew Bible, see Levenson, *The Love of God*.

26. I understand that, for some readers, these lines may raise the jaundiced question why God brought the flood and wrought so much destruction even once. This question is part of the larger issue of the problem of evil, which cannot be suitably addressed in a note. But readers for whom this issue is a stumbling block here might consider that in the story God's bringing the flood but saving righteous Noah to restart the human race is the divine analogue to an autologous bone marrow transplant. In order to prevent the destruction of the whole person (or the whole human species), one can take out some small part of the whole that is healthy, reproduce it, and reintroduce it to reinvigorate the whole. This way of looking at the story does not give a morally sufficient reason for God's action in bringing the flood, but it does at least focus attention on God's action as aimed at healing the species rather than punishing the people killed in the flood. For detailed discussion of the problem of evil, see my *Wandering in Darkness*.

27. See, for example, Gen. 22:16. I am grateful to Jon Levenson for reminding me of this odd case of making a covenant.

28. For an excellent philosophical examination of the function and power of liturgy, see Nicholas Wolterstorff, *Acting Liturgically: Philosophical Reflections on Religious Practice* (Oxford: Oxford University Press, 2018).

29. For a discussion of this issue and support for my claim here, see my "God's Obligations," in *Philosophical Perspectives*, vol. 6, *Ethics*, edited by James Tomberlin (Atascadero, CA: Ridgeview Publishing, 1992), 475–91.

30. And there are similar passages elsewhere; see, for example, Isa. 1:11. In another text, God rejects the fasting of the Israelite people by telling them, "Is this the fasting that I have chosen?" (Isa. 58:5). On one reading of that line, what is wrong with their fasting, God tells them, is that they fast to make God on their side.

31. The word translated 'sacrifice' in Ps. 50:23 and Ps. 27:6 is the same Hebrew word used for the sacrifice of animals in other parts of the Hebrew Bible, such as Exod. 13:15 and I Sam. 2:13.

32. To say so much is not to rule out the penal substitution variant on the Anselmian kind of interpretation. It is possible to argue that Christ both suffers the human punishment for sin and also offers God a suitable sacrifice in doing so.

33. Swinburne, *Responsibility and Atonement*, 152.

34. Swinburne, *Responsibility and Atonement*, 154–5.

35. Jerome Miller, "The Cry of Abel's Blood: Christ's Wounds and Ours," *Commonweal* 144.7, April 14, 2017, 17.

36. Augustine, *City of God*, translated by David S. Wiesen (Cambridge, MA: Harvard University Press, 1968), Loeb Classical Library, 275–7. I owe this reference to Jonathan Nebel.

37. There is debate about whether the Apostle is speaking of a person in grace or not in this passage; but both Aquinas and Calvin suppose that he is, and that is the supposition I am therefore also adopting.

38. For translations of the New Testament, I have for the most part picked relatively randomly among the widely used translations, in the hope of showing some impartiality among them. I have checked the Greek for these passages myself, but I have not altered any of the translations I cite.

39. For a helpful and detailed discussion of the contentious points, see Charles Raith II, *Aquinas and Calvin on Romans: God's Justification and Our Participation* (Oxford: Oxford University Press, 2014). For a detailed examination of Calvin's position, see J. Todd Billings, *Calvin, Participation, and the Gift* (Oxford: Oxford University Press, 2007).

40. Raith II, *Aquinas and Calvin on Romans*, 5.

41. Aquinas, *Commentary on the Letter of St. Paul to the Romans*, translated by F.R. Larcher, edited by J. Mortensen and E. Alarcón (Lander, WY: The Aquinas Institute for the Study of Sacred Doctrine, 2012), C.3 L.3, 301. I am grateful for the translations of this group and so have used them, though (as in this case) I have felt free to emend them on those few occasions on which I thought I could do better. Later in his commentary on this part of Romans, Aquinas explicates the notion of the debt of punishment for sin and Christ's work of satisfaction as paying that debt. This part of his commentary might lead an unwary reader to suppose that Aquinas here is espousing an Anselmian kind of interpretation of the doctrine of the atonement. But in multiple places Aquinas explains that the debt of punishment is correlated with the cause of the debt, namely, sin, so that the debt is removed when the cause is removed. On Aquinas's view, Christ cancels the debt of punishment for sin by bringing about the removal of sin in persons in grace. For the correlation of the debt of punishment with sin, see, for example, ST I–II q.87 a.3; on Christ as removing the debt of sin by removing sin, see, for example, Aquinas, *Commentary on the Letter of St. Paul to the Colossians*, translated by F.R. Larcher, edited by J. Mortensen and E. Alarcón (Lander, WY: The Aquinas Institute for the Study of Sacred Doctrine, 2012), C.1, L.3, 28.

42. Aquinas, *Commentary on the Letter of St. Paul to the Romans*, translated by F.R. Larcher, edited by J. Mortensen and E. Alarcón (Lander, WY: The Aquinas Institute for the Study of Sacred Doctrine, 2012), C.8, L.6, 713–4.

43. John Milton, *Paradise Lost*, Bk. IV, l.75.

44. The Greek is so simple that I translated it myself, but it has to be admitted that the KJV version of this line is widely known, and my translation deviates from it very little. *Mutatis mutandis*, the same point applies to the Hebrew of the lines in the quotation from the Song of Songs below.

Select Bibliography

This bibliography does not include references to the works of Aquinas. A full bibliography of the works of Aquinas can be found in my *Aquinas* (listed below); where I have used translations of his works, references to those translations can be found in the notes.

Adams, Marilyn McCord. "Sin as Uncleanness." *Philosophy of Religion*, vol. 5, *Philosophical Perspectives* (1991): 1–27.

Adams, Marilyn McCord. *Horrendous Evils and the Goodness of God* (Ithaca, NY: Cornell University Press, 1999).

Adams, Marilyn McCord. *Christ and Horrors: The Coherence of Christology* (Cambridge: Cambridge University Press, 2006).

Adams, Marilyn McCord. "Plantinga on 'Felix Culpa': Analysis and Critique." *Faith and Philosophy* 25 (2008): 123–39.

Adams, Marilyn McCord. *Some Later Medieval Theories of the Eucharist: Thomas Aquinas, Giles of Rome, Duns Scotus, and William Ockham* (Oxford: Oxford University Press, 2010).

Adams, Marilyn McCord. "Genuine Agency, Somehow Shared? The Holy Spirit and Other Gifts," in *Oxford Studies in Medieval Philosophy*, edited by Robert Pasnau (Oxford: Oxford University Press, 2013), 23–60.

Adams, Robert. "Pure Love." *Journal of Religious Ethics* 8 (1980): 83–99.

Alston, William P. "Level Confusions in Epistemology," in *Midwest Studies in Philosophy*, vol. 5, edited by Peter A. French, Theodore E. Uehling, Jr., and Howard K. Wettstein (Minneapolis, MN: University of Minnesota Press, 1980), 135–50.

Alston, William P. *Perceiving God* (Ithaca, NY: Cornell University Press, 1991).

Alston, William P. *Epistemic Justification: Essays in the Theory of Knowledge* (Ithaca, NY: Cornell University Press, 1989).

Alter, Robert. *The Art of Biblical Narrative* (New York: Basic Books, 1991).

Anselm. *Anselm of Canterbury: The Major Works*, translated by Brian Davies and G.R. Evans (Oxford: Oxford University Press, 1998).

Anselm. *Basic Writings, Cur Deus Homo*, edited and translated by Thomas Williams (Indianapolis: Hackett Publishing Co., 2007).

Asante, M.K. and A. Mazama (eds.). *Encyclopedia of African Religions* (Thousand Oaks, CA: Sage Publications, 2009).

Astell, Ann. *The Song of Songs in the Middle Ages* (Ithaca, NY: Cornell University Press, 1990).

Auerbach, Eric. *Mimesis: The Representation of Reality in Western Literature* (Princeton, NJ: Princeton University Press, 2003).

Augustine. *Augustine on the Psalms*, vol. II, translated by Dame Scholastica Hebgin and Dame Felicitas Corrigan (New York: Newman Press, 1961).

Augustine. *Confessions*, translated by William Watts (Cambridge, MA: Harvard University Press, 1968).

Augustine. *Saint Augustine: Four Anti-Pelagian Writings*, translated by John A. Mourant and William J. Collinge (Washington, DC: The Catholic University of America Press, 1992).

Baker, Mark D. and Joel B. Green. *Recovering the Scandal of the Cross: Atonement in New Testament and Contemporary Contexts* (Downers Grove, IL: InterVarsity Press, 2011).

Barnes, Elizabeth. "Disability and Adaptive Preference." *Philosophical Perspectives* 23 (2009): 1–22.

Barnes, Elizabeth. "Disability, Minority and Difference." *Journal of Applied Philosophy* 26 (2009): 337–55.

Barnes, Elizabeth. "Valuing Disability, Causing Disability." *Ethics* 125 (2014): 88–113.

Barnes, Elizabeth. "Reply to Guy Kahane and Julian Savulescu." *Res Philosophica* 93.1 (2016): 295–309.

Barnes, Elizabeth. *The Minority Body: A Theory of Disability* (Oxford: Oxford University Press, 2016).

Beilby, James and Paul R. Eddy (eds.). *The Nature of the Atonement: Four Views* (Downers Grove, IL: InterVarsity Press, 2006).

Billings, J. Todd. *Calvin, Participation, and the Gift* (Oxford: Oxford University Press, 2007).

Blakeslee, Sandra and Vilayandur Ramachandran. *Phantoms in the Brain* (London: Harper Perennial, 2005).

Blustein, Jeffrey. *Forgiveness and Remembrance* (Oxford: Oxford University Press, 2014).

Bradford, Sarah Hopkins. *Harriet the Moses of Her People* (Lexington, KY: The Perfect Library, 2016)].

Braithwaite, John. *Crime, Shame and Reintegration* (Cambridge: Cambridge University Press, 1989).

Brown, David. *God in a Single Vision: Integrating Philosophy and Theology*, edited by Christopher R. Brewer and Robert MacSwain (New York: Routledge, 2016).

Bunyan, John. *Pilgrim's Progress* (Oxford: Oxford University Press, 1984).

Calvin, John. *The Institutes of the Christian Religion*, vol. 1, translated by Henry Beveridge (Grand Rapids, MI: Eerdmans, 1970).

Calvin, John. *A Harmony of the Gospels: Matthew, Mark, and Luke*, translated by A.W. Morrison, edited by David W. Torrance and Thomas F. Torrance (Grand Rapids, MI: Eerdmans, 1972).

Campbell, J. McLeod. *The Nature of Atonement* (Grand Rapids, MI: Eerdmans, 1996).

Campbell, J. McLeod. *The Nature of the Atonement*, with a new introduction by James B. Torrance (Grand Rapids, MI: Eerdmans, 1996).

Care, Norman S. *Living with One's Past: Personal Fates and Moral Pain* (New York: Rowman and Littlefield, 1996).

Cesarani, David. *Becoming Eichmann* (Cambridge, MA: Da Capo Press, 2004).

Chrysostom, John. *Commentary on Saint John the Apostle and Evangelist: Homilies 48–88*, in *The Fathers of the Church*, vol. 41, translated by Sister Thomas Aquinas Goggin (Washington, DC: The Catholic University of America Press, 1960).

Clinton, Catherine. *Harriet Tubman: The Road to Freedom* (New York: Little, Brown and Company, 2004).

Coakley, Sarah. "On the Fearfulness of Forgiveness: Psalm 130:4 and its Theological Implications," in *Meditations of the Heart: The Psalms in Early Christian Thought and Practice*, edited by Andreas Andreopoulos, Augustine Casiday, and Carol Harrison (Turnhout: Brepols, 2011), 33–51.

Coakley, Sarah. *Sacrifice: Defunct or Desired?* (Charlottesville, VA: University of Virginia Press, 2018).

Crisp, Claire. *Waking Mathilda: A Memoir of Childhood Narcolepsy* (Palace Gate Press, 2017).

Crisp, Oliver. *The Word Enfleshed: Exploring the Person and the Work of Christ* (Grand Rapids, MI: Baker Books, 2016).

Cross, Richard. "Atonement without Satisfaction," in *Oxford Readings in Philosophical Theology*, vol. 1, *Trinity, Incarnation, Atonement* (Oxford: Oxford University Press, 2009), 328–47.

Crysdale, Cynthia. *Embracing Travail: Retrieving the Cross Today* (New York: Continuum, 1999).

Crysdale, Cynthia. *Transformed Lives: Making Sense of Atonement Today* (New York: Seabury Books, 2016).

Cuneo, Terence. "Liturgical Immersion." *Journal of Analytic Theology* 2 (2014): 117–39.

Cuneo, Terence. "Ritual Knowledge." *Faith and Philosophy* 31 (2014): 365–85.

Cuneo, Terence. *Ritualized Faith: Essays on the Philosophy of Liturgy* (Oxford: Oxford University Press, 2016).

Dalferth, Ingolf. "Christ Died for Us: Reflections on the Sacrificial Language of Salvation," in *Sacrifice and Redemption*, edited by Stephen Whitfield Sykes (Cambridge: Cambridge University Press, 1991), 299–325.

Davies, Martin and Tony Stone (eds.). *Mental Simulation* (Oxford: Blackwell, 1995).

DeMaria, Robert, Jr. *The Life of Samuel Johnson: A Critical Biography* (Oxford: Blackwell, 1993).

Deonna, Julie, Raffaele Rodogn, and Fabrice Teroni. *In Defense of Shame: The Faces of an Emotion* (Oxford: Oxford University Press, 2012).

Dohmen, Josh. "'A Little of Her Language': Epistemic Injustice and Mental Disability." *Res Philosophica* 93 (2016): 669–92.

Driver, Julia. "The Subrogatory." *Australasian Journal of Philosophy* 70 (1992): 286–95.

Driver, Julia. "Appraisability, Attributability, and Moral Agency," in *The Nature of Moral Responsibility*, edited by Randolph Clarke, Michael McKenna, and Angela Smith (New York: Oxford University Press, 2015), 157–74.

Duff, R.A. *Trials and Punishments* (Cambridge: Cambridge University Press, 1986).

Eckhart, Meister. *Meister Eckhart: Mystic and Philosopher*, translated with commentary by Reiner Schürmann (Bloomington, IN: Indiana University Press, 1978).

Eckhart, Meister. *Meister Eckhart: The Essential Sermons, Commentaries, Treatises, and Defense*, translated by Edmund Colledge and Bernard McGinn (Mahwah, NJ: Paulist Press, 1981).

Eckhart, Meister. *Meister Eckhart: Selected Writings*, translated by Oliver Davies (London: Penguin Books, 1994).

Eilan, Naomi, Christoph Hoerl, Teresa McCormack, and Johannes Roessler (eds.). *Joint Attention: Communication and Other Minds: Issues in Philosophy and Psychology* (Oxford: Oxford University Press, 2005).

Emery, Gille. "L'inhabitation de Dieu Trinité dans les justes." *Nova et Vetera* 88 (2013): 155–84.

Feinberg, Todd, John Deluca, Joseph T. Giacino, David M. Roane, and Mark Solms. "Right-Hemisphere Pathology and the Self: Delusional Misidentification and Reduplication," in *The Lost Self: Pathologies of the Brain and Identity*, edited by Todd Feinberg and Julian Paul Keenan (Oxford: Oxford University Press, 2005), 100–30.

Fingarette, Herbert. "Punishment and Suffering." *Proceedings and Addresses of the American Philosophical Association* 50 (1977): 499–525.

Foley, John. *Creativity and the Roots of Liturgy* (Washington, DC: The Pastoral Press, 1994).

Frankfurt, Harry. "Rationality and the Unthinkable," in *The Importance of What We Care About*, edited by Harry Frankfurt (Cambridge: Cambridge University Press, 1988), 177–91.

Frankfurt, Harry. *Necessity, Volition, and Love* (Cambridge: Cambridge University Press, 1999).

Frankfurt, Harry. *The Reasons of Love* (Princeton, NJ: Princeton University Press, 2004).

Gallagher, Shaun. "Neural Simulation and Social Cognition," in *Mirror Neuron Systems: The Role of Mirroring Processes in Social Cognition*, edited by Jamie Pineda (New York: Springer, 2009), 355–71.

Gallese, Vittorio. "'Being Like Me': Self-Other Identity, Mirror Neurons, and Empathy," in *Perspectives on Imitation: From Neuroscience to Social Science*, vol. 1, edited by Susan Hurley and Nick Chater (Cambridge, MA: MIT Press, 2005), 101–18.

Gaon, Saadia. *The Book of Theodicy: Translation and Commentary on the Book of Job*, translated by Len Goodman (New Haven, CT: Yale University Press, 1988).

Gates, Henry Louis, Jr. (ed.). *The Classic Slave Narratives* (New York: Mentor Library, 1987).

Gilbert, G.M. *Nuremberg Diary* (New York: Da Capo Press, 1995).

Goldman, Alvin. "Mirroring, Mindreading, and Simulation," in *Mirror Neuron Systems: The Role of Mirroring Processes in Social Cognition*, edited by Jamie Pineda (New York: Springer, 2009), 311–30.

Goldman, Alvin. "Two Routes to Empathy: Insights from Cognitive Neuroscience," in *Empathy: Philosophical and Psychological Perspectives*, edited by Amy Coplan and Peter Goldie (Oxford: Oxford University Press, 2011), 31–44.

Green, Adam and Eleonore Stump (eds.). *Hidden Divinity and Religious Belief: New Perspectives* (Cambridge: Cambridge University Press, 2015).

Green, Deidre Nicole. *Works of Love in a World of Violence* (Tübingen: Mohr Siebeck, 2016).

Griswold, Charles. *Forgiveness: A Philosophical Exploration* (Cambridge: Cambridge University Press, 2007).

Gunton, Colin. *The Actuality of Atonement: A Study of Metaphor, Rationality and the Christian Tradition* (New York: Continuum, 1988).

Halbertal, Moshe. *On Sacrifice* (Princeton, NJ: Princeton University Press, 2012).

Hampton, Jean. "Feminist Contractarianism," in *A Mind of One's Own: Feminist Essays on Reason and Objectivity*, edited by Louise Antony and Charlotte Witt (Boulder, CO: Westview Press, 1993), 227–56.

Hampton, Jean and Jeffrie Murphy. *Forgiveness and Mercy* (Cambridge: Cambridge University Press, 1988).

Healey, Nicholas M. "Redemption," in *The Cambridge Companion to the Summa Theologiae*, edited by Philip McCosker and Denys Turner (Cambridge: Cambridge University Press, 2016), 255–68.

Hoehne, Heinz. *The Order of the Death's Head* (New York: Penguin, 2001).

Homer. *Iliad*, translated by Richmond Lattimore (Chicago: University of Chicago Press, 1951).

Hudson, Hud. "Omnipresence," in *The Oxford Handbook of Philosophical Theology*, edited by Thomas P. Flint and Michael C. Rea (Oxford: Oxford University Press, 2009), 199–216.

Israelstam, J. and Judah Slotki (eds.). *Midrash Rabbah: Leviticus* (London: Soncino Press, 1983).

Jerome. *Commentary on Matthew*, translated by Thomas P. Scheck (Washington, DC: The Catholic University of America Press, 2008).

Johnson, Junius. *Patristic and Medieval Atonement Theory: A Guide to Research* (New York: Rowman and Littlefield, 2016).

Jordan, Mark. "The Alleged Aristotelianism of Thomas Aquinas," in *The Gilson Lectures on Thomas Aquinas*, edited by James Reilly (Toronto: Pontifical Institute of Mediaeval Studies, 2008), 73–106.

Kapic, Kelly M. *Sanctification: Explorations in Theology and Practice* (Downers Grove, IL: InterVarsity Press, 2014).

Kilby, Karen. *Balthasar: A (Very) Critical Introduction* (Grand Rapids, MI: Eerdmans, 2012).

Kittay, Eva. "Deadly Medicine: Project T4, Mental Disability, and Racism." *Res Philosophica* 93 (2016): 715–41.

Kraut, Richard. *What is Good and Why: The Ethics of Well-Being* (Cambridge, MA: Harvard University Press, 2007).

Langtry, Bruce. *God, the Best, and Evil* (Oxford: Oxford University Press, 2008).

Letham, Robert. *The Work of Christ* (Downers Grove, IL: InterVarsity Press, 1993).

Levenson, Jon. *The Love of God* (Princeton, NJ: Princeton University Press, 2016).

Lewis, C.S. *The Pilgrim's Regress* (Grand Rapids, MI: Eerdmans, 1933).

Lewis, C.S. *Mere Christianity* (New York: Macmillan, 1953).

Lewis, C.S. *The Screwtape Letters* (New York: Simon & Schuster, 1961).

Lewis, C.S. *The Problem of Pain* (New York: Macmillan, 1962).

Lewis, C.S. *The Great Divorce* (New York and San Francisco: HarperCollins, [orig. pub. 1946] 1973).

Lombardo, Nicholas E. *The Father's Will: Christ's Crucifixion and the Goodness of God* (Oxford: Oxford University Press, 2013).

Ludlow, Peter, Yukin Nagasawa, and Daniel Stoljar (eds.). *There's Something About Mary: Essays on Phenomenal Consciousness and Frank Jackson's Knowledge Argument* (Cambridge, MA: MIT Press, Bradford Book, 2004).

McBryde-Johnson, Harriet. "Unspeakable Conversations." *The New York Times Magazine*, February 16, 2003.

McCall, Thomas H. *Forsaken: The Trinity and the Cross, and Why It Matters* (Downers Grove, IL: InterVarsity Press, 2012).

MacLeod, Donald. *Christ Crucified: Understanding the Atonement* (Downers Grove, IL: InterVarsity Press, 2014).

Meconi, David. *The One Christ: St. Augustine's Theology of Deification* (Washington, DC: The Catholic University of America Press, 2013).

Meconi, David and Carl E. Olson (eds.). *Called to be the Children of God: The Catholic Theology of Human Deification* (San Francisco, CA: Ignatius Press, 2016).

Mill, John Stuart. *An Examination of Sir William Hamilton's Philosophy and of The Principal Philosophical Questions Discussed in His Writings* (London: Longman, Green, Longman, Roberts & Green, 1865).

Miller, Jerome. "The Cry of Abel's Blood: Christ's Wounds and Ours." *Commonweal* 144.7 (April 14, 2017).

Moberly, R.C. *Atonement and Personality* (London: John Murray, 1924).

Moffitt, David M. *Atonement and the Logic of Resurrection in the Epistle to the Hebrews* (Leiden: Brill, 2013).

Montagu, Ashley. *The Elephant Man: A Study in Human Dignity* (Lafayette, LA: Acadian House, 2001).

Moore, Derek, Peter Hobson, and Anthony Lee. "Components of Person Perception: An Investigation with Autistic, Non-Autistic Retarded and Typically Developing Children and Adolescents." *British Journal of Developmental Psychology* 15 (1997): 401–23.

Moran, Rachel. *Paid For: My Journey through Prostitution* (Dublin: Gill and Macmillan, 2013).

Moran, Richard. *Authority and Estrangement: An Essay on Self-Knowledge* (Princeton, NJ: Princeton University Press, 2001).

Moran, Richard. "Review Essay on *The Reasons of Love* by Harry Frankfurt." *Philosophy and Phenomenological Research* 74 (2007): 463–75.

Morris, Leon. *The Atonement: Its Meaning and Significance* (Downers Grove, IL: InterVarsity Press, 1983).

Murphy, Jeffrie. *Getting Even: Forgiveness and Its Limits* (Oxford: Oxford University Press, 2003).

Murphy, Jeffrie. *Punishment and the Moral Emotions: Essays in Law, Morality, and Religion* (Oxford: Oxford University Press, 2012).

Murphy, Jeffrie. "Shame Creeps Through Guilt and Feels Like Retribution," in *Punishment and the Moral Emotions* (Oxford: Oxford University Press, 2012), 94–113.

Murphy, Mark. "Not Penal Substitution but Vicarious Punishment." *Faith and Philosophy* 26 (2009): 253–73.

Nagel, Thomas. "Sexual Perversion." *The Journal of Philosophy* 66 (1969): 5–17.

Nagel, Thomas. *The Last Word* (Oxford: Oxford University Press, 1997).

Nasar, Sylvia. *A Beautiful Mind* (New York: Simon & Schuster, 1998).

Newman, John Henry. *An Essay on the Development of Christian Doctrine*, 6th edition (Notre Dame, IN: University of Notre Dame Press, 2017).

Newman, John Henry. *Favorite Newman Sermons*, selected by Daniel M. O'Connell, SJ, (1932), Discourse 16, "Mental Sufferings of Our Lord in His Passion" (Whitefish, MT: Kessinger Publishing, 2007).

Newton, John. *Thoughts Upon the African Slave Trade* (London: Printed for J. Buckland, in Pater-Noster Row; and J. Johnson, in St. Paul's Church-yard, 1788).

Newton, John. *The Journal of a Slave Trader (John Newton) 1750–1754*, edited by Bernard Martin and Mark Spurrell (London: The Epworth Press, 1962).

Noë, Alva. *Strange Tools: Art and Human Nature* (New York: Hill and Wang, 2015).

Nouwen, Henri. *Adam: God's Beloved* (Maryknoll, NY: Orbis Books, 2000), 3rd printing.

Nussbaum, Martha. *Anger and Forgiveness: Resentment, Generosity, Justice* (Oxford: Oxford University Press, 2016).

Oppy, Graham. "Problems of Evil," in *The Problem of Evil: Eight Views*, edited by N.N. Trakakis (Oxford: Oxford University Press, 2018).

Overy, Richard (ed.). *Interrogations: The Nazi Elite in Allied Hands, 1945* (New York: Viking Penguin, 2001).

Ozick, Cynthia. "The Symposium," in *The Sunflower: On the Possibilities and Limits of Forgiveness* by Simon Wiesenthal (New York: Schocken Books, 1960), 213–20.

Pamphili, Eusebius. *Ecclesiastical History*, translated by Roy J. Deferrari (New York: Fathers of the Church, 1953), 51–3.

Pawl, Timothy. "The Freedom of Christ and Explanatory Priority." *Religious Studies* 50 (2014): 157–73.

Pawl, Timothy. "The Freedom of Christ and the Problem of Deliberation." *International Journal for Philosophy of Religion* 75 (2014): 233–47.

Pawl, Timothy. "A Solution to the Fundamental Philosophical Problem of Christology." *The Journal of Analytic Theology* 2 (2014): 61–85.

Pawl, Timothy. "Conciliar Christology and the Problem of Incompatible Predications." *Scientia et Fides* 3 (2015): 85–106.

Pawl, Timothy. *In Defense of Conciliar Christology: A Philosophical Essay* (Oxford: Oxford University Press, 2016).

Pawl, Timothy. "Temporary Intrinsics and Christological Predication," in *Oxford Studies in Philosophy of Religion*, vol. 7, edited by Jonathan Kvanvig (Oxford: Oxford University Press, 2016), 157–89.

Peacocke, Christopher. "Joint Attention: Its Nature, Reflexivity, and Relation to Common Knowledge," in *Joint Attention: Communication and Other Minds*, edited by Naomi Eilan, Christoph Hoerl, Teresa McCormack, and Johannes Roessler (Oxford: Clarendon Press, 2005), 298–324.

Pelikan, Jaroslav. *The Christian Tradition: A History of the Development of Doctrine*, vol. 1, *The Emergence of Catholic Doctrine (100–600)* (Chicago: University of Chicago Press, 1971).

Philpott, Daniel. *Just and Unjust Peace: An Ethic of Political Reconciliation* (Oxford: Oxford University Press, 2012).

Pinsent, Andrew. *The Second Person Perspective in Aquinas's Ethics: Virtues and Gifts* (London and New York: Routledge, 2012).

Plantinga, Alvin. "Supralapsarianism, or 'O Felix Culpa,'" in *Christian Faith and the Problem of Evil*, edited by Peter van Inwagen (Grand Rapids, MI: Eerdmans, 2004), 1–25.

Porter, Steven L. "Swinburnian Atonement and the Doctrine of Penal Substitution." *Faith and Philosophy* 21 (2004): 228–4; reprinted in Michael C. Rea (ed.), *Oxford*

Readings in Philosophical Theology, vol. 1, *Trinity, Incarnation, Atonement* (Oxford: Oxford University Press, 2009), 314–27.

Quinn, Philip. "Abelard on Atonement: 'Nothing Unintelligible, Arbitrary, Illogical, or Immoral About It,'" reprinted in Michael C. Rea (ed.), *Oxford Readings in Philosophical Theology*, vol. 1, *Trinity, Incarnation, Atonement* (Oxford: Oxford University Press, 2009), 348–64.

Radzik, Linda. *Making Amends: Atonement in Morality, Law, and Politics* (Oxford: Oxford University Press, 2009).

Raith II, Charles. *Aquinas and Calvin on Romans: God's Justification and Our Participation* (Oxford: Oxford University Press, 2014).

Rea, Michael C. "Narrative, Liturgy, and the Hiddenness of God," in *Metaphysics and God: Essays in Honor of Eleonore Stump*, edited by Kevin Timpe (New York: Routledge, 2009), 76–96.

Rea, Michael C. *"Though the Darkness Hide Thee": Seeking the Face of the Invisible God* (Oxford: Oxford University Press, 2018).

Reddy, Vasudevi. *How Infants Know Minds* (Cambridge, MA: Harvard University Press, 2008).

Ruckgaber, Matthew. "Philosophical Anthropology, Shame, and Disability." *Res Philosophica* 93 (2016): 743–66.

Rutledge, Fleming. *The Crucifixion: Understanding the Death of Jesus Christ* (Grand Rapids, MI: Eerdmans, 2015).

Sacks, Oliver. *A Leg to Stand On* (New York: Harper and Row, 1984).

Sacks, Oliver. *The Man Who Mistook His Wife for a Hat* (New York: Harper Perennial, 1985).

Schellenberg, John. *Divine Hiddenness and Human Reason* (Ithaca, NY: Cornell University Press, 1993).

Scherman, Nosson, Hersh Goldwurm, and Yehezkel Danziger (eds. and trans.). *Leviticus: A New Translation with a Commentary Anthologized from Talmudic, Midrashic and Rabbinic Sources* (New York: Mesorah Publications, 2003).

Sereny, Gitta. *Albert Speer: His Battle with Truth* (New York: Knopf, 1995).

Sereny, Gitta. *The Healing Wound* (New York: W.W. Norton, 2001).

Sereny, Gitta. *The German Trauma: Experiences and Reflections 1938–2001* (New York: Penguin Books, 2001).

Sforza, Teri, with Howard Lenhoff. *The Strangest Song: One Father's Quest to Help His Daughter Find Her Voice* (New York: Prometheus Books, 2006).

Sider, Ted. "Hell and Vagueness." *Faith and Philosophy* 19 (2002): 58–68.

Southern, R.W. *Saint Anselm: A Portrait in a Landscape* (Cambridge: Cambridge University Press, 1995).

Stangneth, Bettina. *Eichmann Before Jerusalem: The Unexamined Life of a Mass Murderer*. Translated by Ruth Martin (New York: Knopf, 2014).

Stoner, Ian. "Ways to be Worse Off." *Res Philosophica* 93 (2016): 921–50.

Stott, John. *The Cross of Christ* (Downers Grove, IL: InterVarsity Press, 2006).

Strabbing, Jada Twedt. "The Permissibility of the Atonement as Penal Substitution," in *Oxford Studies in Philosophy of Religion*, vol. 7, edited by Jonathan Kvanvig (Oxford: Oxford University Press, 2016), 239–70.

Strabbing, Jada Twedt. "Divine Forgiveness and Reconciliation." *Faith and Philosophy* 34 (2017): 272–97.

Stump, Eleonore. "Dante's Hell, Aquinas's Moral Theory, and the Love of God." *The Canadian Journal of Philosophy* 16 (1986): 181–98.

Stump, Eleonore. "Sanctification, Hardening of the Heart, and Frankfurt's Concept of Free Will." *Journal of Philosophy* 85 (1988): 395–420. Reprinted in *Perspectives on Moral Responsibility*, edited by John Martin Fischer and Mark Ravizza (Ithaca, NY: Cornell University Press, 1993), 211–34.

Stump, Eleonore. "God's Obligations," in *Philosophical Perspectives*, vol. 6, *Ethics*, edited by James Tomberlin (Atascadero, CA: Ridgeview Publishing, 1992), 475–91.

Stump, Eleonore. "Revelation and Biblical Exegesis: Augustine, Aquinas, and Swinburne," in *Reason and the Christian Religion: Essays in Honor of Richard Swinburne*, edited by Alan G. Padgett (Oxford: Clarendon Press, 1994), 161–97.

Stump, Eleonore. "Review of Richard Swinburne's *Responsibility and Atonement*." *Faith and Philosophy* 11 (1994): 321–8.

Stump, Eleonore. "Libertarian Freedom and the Principle of Alternative Possibilities," in *Faith, Freedom, and Rationality: Philosophy of Religion Today*, edited by Daniel Howard-Snyder and Jeff Jordan (Lanham, MD: Rowman and Littlefield, 1996), 73–88.

Stump, Eleonore. "Persons: Identification and Freedom." *Philosophical Topics* 24 (1996): 183–214.

Stump, Eleonore. "Saadia Gaon on the Problem of Evil." *Faith and Philosophy* 14 (1997): 523–49.

Stump, Eleonore. "The Flicker of Freedom." *The Journal of Ethics* 3 (1999): 299–324.

Stump, Eleonore. "Orthodoxy and Heresy." *Faith and Philosophy* 16 (1999): 487–503.

Stump, Eleonore. "Augustine on Free Will," in *The Cambridge Companion to Augustine*, edited by Norman Kretzmann and Eleonore Stump (Cambridge: Cambridge University Press, 2001), 124–47 rev. ed. Meconi and Stump 2014, 166–88.

Stump, Eleonore. *Aquinas* (New York and London: Routledge, 2003).

Stump, Eleonore. "Moral Responsibility without Alternative Possibilities," in *Moral Responsibility and Alternative Possibilities: Essays on the Importance of Alternative Possibilities*, edited by Michael McKenna and David Widerker (Aldershot: Ashgate Press, 2003), 139–58.

Stump, Eleonore. "Personal Relations and Moral Residue." *History of the Human Sciences* 17.2 (2004): *Theorizing from the Holocaust: What is to be Learned?*, edited by Paul Roth and Mark S. Peacock, 33–57.

Stump, Eleonore. "Love, By All Accounts." *Proceedings and Addresses of The American Philosophical Association* 80.2 (2006): 25–43.

Stump, Eleonore. "Beauty as a Road to God." *Sacred Music* 134.4 (2007): 11–24.

Stump, Eleonore. *Wandering in Darkness: Narrative and the Problem of Suffering* (Oxford: Oxford University Press, 2010).

Stump, Eleonore. "Eternity, Simplicity, and Presence," in *The Science of Being as Being: Metaphysical Investigations*, edited by Gregory T. Doolan (Washington, DC: The Catholic University of America Press, 2011), 243–63.

Stump, Eleonore. "The Non-Aristotelian Character of Aquinas's Ethics: Aquinas on the Passions." *Faith and Philosophy* 28 (2011): 29–43.

Stump, Eleonore. "Atonement and the Cry of Dereliction from the Cross." *European Journal for Philosophy of Religion* 4.1 (2012): 1–17.

Stump, Eleonore. "Emergence, Causal Powers, and Aristotelianism in Metaphysics," in *Powers and Capacities in Philosophy: The New Aristotelianism*, edited by Ruth Groff and John Greco (New York and London: Routledge, 2012), 48–68.

Stump, Eleonore. "God's Simplicity," in *The Oxford Handbook of Aquinas*, edited by Brian Davies and Eleonore Stump (Oxford: Oxford University Press, 2012), 135–46.

Stump, Eleonore. "The Nature of the Atonement," in *Reason, Metaphysics, and Mind: New Essays on the Philosophy of Alvin Plantinga*, edited by Kelly Clark and Michael C. Rea (Oxford: Oxford University Press, 2012), 128–44.

Stump, Eleonore. "Athens and Jerusalem: The Relationship of Philosophy and Theology." *Journal of Analytic Theology* 1.1 (2013): 45–59.

Stump, Eleonore. "Conversion, Atonement, and Love." In *Conversion*, edited by Ingolf Dalferth and Michael Rodgers (Tübingen: Mohr Siebeck, 2013), 115–33.

Stump, Eleonore. "The Nature of a Simple God." *Proceedings of the American Catholic Philosophical Association* 87 (2013): 33–42.

Stump, Eleonore. "Omnipresence, Indwelling, and the Second-Personal." *European Journal for Philosophy of Religion* 5.4 (2013): 63–87.

Stump, Eleonore. "Faith, Wisdom, and the Transmission of Knowledge through Testimony," in *Religious Faith and Intellectual Virtue*, edited by Laura Frances Callahan and Timothy O'Connor (Oxford: Oxford University Press, 2014), 204–30.

Stump, Eleonore. "Simplicity and Aquinas's Quantum Metaphysics," in *Die Metaphysik des Aristoteles im Mittelalter – Rezeption und Transformation*, edited by Gerhard Krieger (Berlin: De Gruyter, 2014), 191–210.

Stump, Eleonore. "The Atonement and the Problem of Shame," in *Selected Papers in Honor of William P. Alston*, special supplement to *Journal of Philosophical Research* 41 (2016), edited by Thomas Senor and Michael DePaul, 111–29.

Stump, Eleonore. *The God of the Bible and the God of the Philosophers*, Aquinas Lecture (Milwaukee, WI: Marquette University Press, 2016).

Stump, Eleonore. "Love and Forgiveness: Swinburne on Atonement," in *Reason and Faith: Themes from Richard Swinburne*, edited by Michael Bergmann and Jeffrey E. Brower (New York: Oxford University Press, 2016), 148–70.

Stump, Eleonore. "The Problem of Evil and Atonement," in *Being, Freedom, and Method: Themes from the Philosophy of Peter van Inwagen*, edited by John A. Keller (Oxford: Oxford University Press, 2017), 186–208.

Stump, Eleonore. "The Openness of God: Eternity and Free Will," in *Philosophical Essays Against Open Theism*, edited by Benjamin H. Arbour (New York: Routledge, 2018).

Stump, Eleonore. "Response to Graham Oppy's 'Problems of Evil,'" in *The Problem of Evil: Eight Views*, edited by N.N. Trakakis (Oxford: Oxford University Press, 2018), 80–2.

Stump, Eleonore. "Theology and the Knowledge of Persons," in *New Models of Religious Understanding*, edited by Fiona Ellis (Oxford: Oxford University Press, 2018), 172–90.

Stump, Eleonore and Norman Kretzmann. "Eternity." *Journal of Philosophy* 78 (1981): 429–58.

Stump, Eleonore and Norman Kretzmann. "Eternity, Awareness, and Action." *Faith and Philosophy* 9 (1992): 463–82.

Swinburne, Richard. *Responsibility and Atonement* (Oxford: Oxford University Press, 1989).

Sykes, Stephen Whitfield (ed.). *Sacrifice and Redemption* (Cambridge: Cambridge University Press, 1991).

Tanner, Kathryn. *Christ the Key* (Cambridge: Cambridge University Press, 2010).

Teresa of Avila. *The Interior Castle* (Mahwah, NJ: Paulist Press, 1979).

Thurow, Joshua. "Finding Collective Sin and Recompense in Anselm's *Cur Deus Homo*," *American Catholic Philosophical Quarterly* 91 (2017): 431–46.

Timpe, Kevin. "Cooperative Grace, Cooperative Agency." *European Journal for Philosophy of Religion* 7 (2015): 225–47.

Timpe, Kevin. "Executive Function, Disability, and Agency." *Res Philosophica* 93 (2016): 767–96.

Timpe, Kevin. "Agency and Disability," in *The Routledge Handbook of Agency*, edited by Luca Ferrero (New York: Routledge, 2018).

Timpe, Kevin and Aaron Cobb. "Disability and the Theodicy of Defeat." *Journal of Analytic Theology* 5 (2017): 100–20.

Torrance, Alan J. "The Theological Grounds for Advocating Forgiveness and Reconciliation in the Sociopolitical Realm," in *The Politics of Past Evil: Religion, Reconciliation, and the Dilemmas of Transitional Justice*, edited by Daniel Philpott (Notre Dame, IN: University of Notre Dame Press, 2006), 45–85.

Torrance, Thomas F. *Incarnation: The Person and Life of Christ* (Downers Grove, IL: InterVarsity Press, 2008).

Torrance, Thomas F. *Atonement: The Person and Work of Christ* (Downers Grove, IL: InterVarsity Press, 2009).

Turnbull, Colin. *The Forest People* (New York: Simon & Schuster, 1961, repr. 1968).

Van der Vat, Dan. *The Good Nazi: The Life and Lies of Albert Speer* (New York: Houghton Mifflin, 1997).

Van Inwagen, Peter. "The Magnitude, Duration, and Distribution of Evil: A Theodicy." *Philosophical Topics* 16.2 (1988): 161–87.

Van Inwagen, Peter. "The Place of Chance in a World Sustained by God," in *Divine and Human Action: Essays in the Metaphysics of Theism*, edited by Thomas V. Morris (Ithaca, NY: Cornell University Press, 1988), 211–35.

Van Inwagen, Peter. *Material Beings* (Ithaca, NY: Cornell University Press, 1990).

Van Inwagen, Peter. "The Problem of Evil, the Problem of Air, and the Problem of Silence." *Philosophical Perspectives* 5: *Philosophy of Religion* (1991): 135–65.

Van Inwagen, Peter. "Reflections on the Essays of Draper, Gale, and Russell," in *The Evidential Argument from Evil*, edited by Daniel Howard-Snyder (Bloomington, IN: Indiana University Press, 1996), 219–43.

Van Inwagen, Peter. "Probability and Evil," in *The Possibility of Resurrection and Other Essays in Christian Apologetics*, edited by Peter van Inwagen (Boulder, CO: Westview Press, 1997), 69–87.

Van Inwagen, Peter. "The Argument from Particular Horrendous Evils." *Proceedings of the American Catholic Philosophical Association* 74 (2000): 65–80.

Van Inwagen, Peter. "The Argument from Evil," in *Christian Faith and the Problem of Evil* (Grand Rapids, MI: Eerdmans, 2004), 69–87.

Van Inwagen, Peter. "The Problem of Evil," in *The Oxford Handbook of Philosophy of Religion*, edited by William Wainwright (Oxford: Oxford University Press, 2005), 188–219.

Van Inwagen, Peter. *The Problem of Evil* (Oxford: Oxford University Press, 2006).

Vanier, Jean. *Becoming Human* (New York: Paulist Press, 1998).

Velleman, David. "Love as a Moral Emotion." *Ethics* 109.2 (1999): 338–74.

Venard, Olivier-Thomas. "Sacraments," in *The Cambridge Companion to the Summa Theologiae*, edited by Philip McCosker and Denys Turner (Cambridge: Cambridge University Press, 2016), 269–87.

Vries, Hent de and Nils F. Schott (eds.). *Love and Forgiveness for a More Just World* (New York: Columbia University Press, 2015).

Walker, Margaret Urban. *Moral Repair: Reconstructing Moral Relations After Wrongdoing* (Cambridge: Cambridge University Press, 2006).

Weaver, J. Denny. *The Nonviolent Atonement* (Grand Rapids, MI: Eerdmans, 2011).

White, Thomas Joseph, OP. *The Incarnate Lord: A Thomistic Study in Christology* (Washington, DC: The Catholic University of America Press, 2016).

Wiesenthal, Simon. *The Sunflower* (New York: Random House, 1998).

Wolterstorff, Nicholas. *Acting Liturgically: Philosophical Reflections on Religious Practice* (Oxford: Oxford University Press, 2018).

Wright, N.T. *Justification: God's Plan and Paul's Vision* (Downers Grove, IL: InterVarsity Press, 2009).

Wright, N.T. *Reconsidering Jesus' Crucifixion: The Day the Revolution Began* (New York: HarperCollins, 2016).

Zagzebski, Linda. *Omnisubjectivity: A Defense of a Divine Attribute* (Milwaukee, WI: Marquette University Press, 2013).

General Index

0

Index of Biblical Books Cited